MW00580847

LEAVING THE BUILDING

THE LUCRATIVE AFTERLIFE OF MUSIC ESTATES

EAMONN FORDE

OMNIBUS PRESS

Copyright © 2021 Omnibus Press
(A division of the Wise Music Group
14–15 Berners Street, London, W1T 3LJ)

Cover designed by Rehan Abdul

ISBN 978-1-913172-10-7

A catalogue record for this book is available from the British Library.

Printed in the Czech Republic

www.omnibuspress.com

To Sonja van Praag – for bringing me life

Contents

Prologue

There is an oft-quoted line about death from Gore Vidal when asked to comment on the passing of Truman Capote in 1984.

"A wise career move," sneered Vidal about the man with whom he had been locked into a bitter and very public feud for almost a decade.

In popular music, death might not be the wisest career move, but it can see an artist elevated, celebrated and validated in ways they never were in life. It also becomes the catalyst for a renewed interest in them and their art. First there is the public mourning and then the business of legacy management, both culturally and economically, begins in earnest.

This book pulls back the curtains on the business of music estates, considering how they operate, how they have changed and where they must go next.

The book title is, of course, a reference to Elvis Presley and his is a recurring presence throughout. He was not the first major artist to die. Nor was he the first major artist to have posthumous hits. (Otis Redding did that almost a decade earlier when '(Sittin' on) The Dock of the Bay' went to number one mere weeks after he died and Buddy Holly had similar success in death almost a decade before that.) However, the origins and many of the tropes of the modern estates business stem from the death of Elvis in 1977. The proof lies in how his name, his image and even his home (and, yes, his music) became the motors of the business of what music writer Greil Marcus termed "Dead Elvis".

Each year since 2001, *Forbes* has compiled a list of the biggest dead celebrity earners. Elvis was, barring one year, number one for the first eight years of that *Forbes* list and has never fallen out of the top five in its entire history. This is, it is worth remembering, someone who died more than four decades ago and whose recording career while still alive did not even last a quarter of a century. He has now been posthumously famous for longer than he was ever alive.

The Dead Elvis business is a phenomenon for a reason. His estate, through Elvis Presley Enterprises, had to – out of necessity as much as out of duty – become a carefully run machine from the off. A large chunk of Elvis Presley Enterprises has been sold twice over this century and each time the new owners have looked to vivify the "brand". It is an ongoing project. As this book was being completed, a release date of 2022 was being set for a major new biopic about Elvis, directed by Baz Luhrmann, and Netflix was developing Agent King, described by *Variety* as an "adult animated action comedy series". The wheels must never stop turning.

Even Graceland, his Memphis home for two decades, was kept operational during the global pandemic in 2020 and 2021 by charging $100 for a two-hour virtual tour of where he lived and died.

Elvis is just one of hundreds of music estates covered in this book, but the shadow his estate casts over all that have followed is inescapable. The things it has done well are widely copied (and often improved on) and the missteps it has made are studied closely so as to be avoided by others.

An estate like that of Elvis Presley does not remain a blockbuster 44 years on by resting on its laurels. It keeps evolving and keeps trying to find ways to introduce new generations of fans – ones born decades after he died – and get them interested in him, his music and his mythology. It has birthed what we can consider to be the industrialisation of estate management and many others have taken what it has achieved and run with it.

Different parts of the estates business are dissected in depth in the book, with the separate components intended to collectively illuminate the whole.

Everything that happens in an estate hinges on the will being clear from the off, but, despite so many disastrous examples, the same mistakes keep on being made: a will does not exist or is, frankly, a mess.

Even with a solid will in place, heirs can and do fight among themselves over the direction the estate is taking, all of which the media (and social media) eagerly lap up. Plus the whole enterprise can collapse in on itself if new and disturbing information comes to light about an act that could see them, in modern parlance, cancelled.

These are the eruption points – a contested will, a family at war, a posthumous scandal – that define much of the public understanding of an estate and what it does; but there is so much more to it than the scurrilous.

It is also not just about ensuring that the famous in life remain famous in death – with the estates of acts like Nick Drake and Eva Cassidy making them significantly more celebrated after they died.

To feed the estates machine, archives of recordings get plundered to keep fans interested (something that streaming has accelerated to a furious degree) and personal items line both the walls of exhibitions and pack the lots of auctions.

Estates have to walk a fine line between appeasing existing fans (and rewarding their loyalty without them feeling they are being milked for every penny they have) while also inducting new generations of fans. The means of doing that are many and varied – from signing off on their music being used in ads to stamping their faces on all manner of merchandise items and even resurrecting them as holograms to send them back on the road. This is "grave to the cradle" marketing.

The book traces the rich and complex history – and points to the future – of estate management, noting how the twin goals of an estate (to keep the artist relevant in the public eye and to keep them making money) have not fundamentally changed since those early days in August 1977 when the Dead Elvis business came to life; it is only the ways in which these goals are achieved that have changed, adapting to new technologies, different cultural theologies and shifting market ideologies.

Death is not exactly the dream career move as suggested by Gore Vidal; but, if handled carefully and presciently by an estate, death can elevate and sanctify the already famous while also rewarding the obscure with the éclat they never lived to see.

CHAPTER 1

The Cornerstones of the Modern Estates Business

"We Need the Money, Son"

The unfiltered opportunism and bracing ambition that enabled Colonel Tom Parker to turn Elvis into not just the biggest pop star in the world but also an icon of semi-religious proportions did not evaporate on 16 August 1977 when his sole management charge died. If anything, it simply and intuitively moved everything up a gear.

It was a summer defined by a new type of scale. Opening in US cinemas in May that year, *Star Wars* was to dramatically change Hollywood, turning films into events and finding ways to create a bewildering number of spin-off products that kept the fans doing two things: talking about the film; and spending money around the film. The film became, in many ways, ancillary to the *idea* of *Star Wars* and how it really made its money – through licensing and merchandise, taking the tricks of pop music and applying them to cinema. It had a shaky start and initial industry feedback was that this film would tank spectacularly. Then the public saw it and it took on a life of its own, becoming the template for blockbuster cinema ever since. That year, in the US alone, it grossed just over $460 million, more than the next three biggest films *combined*.[1] [2] Here was a modern phenomenon without precedent.

The same is true of Elvis, except it all happened slightly slower. His estate was in bad shape and ill-prepared for his passing, but within a few years it had become a blockbuster enterprise by selling not just Elvis but also a *new idea* of Elvis.

"I can't waste time mourning," Parker was reported to have said on hearing of the death of Elvis. "There's plenty of people ready to come in and cut the ground from under your feet."[3]

He immediately swung into action, knowing that wasting time was wasting money. Money of which, as per his highly advantageous contract with Elvis, he was set to take upwards of 50 per cent. He put pressure on

RCA, Presley's record label, to ensure the racks in record shops were stuffed to the gills with Elvis albums and that new "hits" albums – a process of slicing and dicing his catalogue that eventually reduced it to a constantly re-marketed 50 or so songs – just kept coming. In his lifetime, Elvis released 24 studio albums and 17 soundtrack albums across a 23-year career. Since he passed away, over 100 posthumous compilations have been released.

In 2020, Elvis was the fifth-highest-earning dead celebrity (and second-highest-earning dead musician) according to numbers compiled by *Forbes*, with his estate turning over $23 million that year.[4] This, the first major pop estate, remains a blockbuster, and, much like the musical blueprint that the singer created in those exhilarating years in the 1950s, the business and cultural template that other musical estates all follow. Elvis did not invent rock'n'roll and he did not invent the music estate, but he sent both supernova.

* * *

Elvis was the Big Bang for music estates, but a number of artists before him were to plant markers for the estates business, showing how death does not have to mean the end for a musician.

In one significant case it began not by amplifying and keeping alive existing fame, but rather by building a legacy for an artist who was relatively unknown in his lifetime.

Blues legend Robert Johnson released 11 78 rpm records while still alive on Vocalion Records but he was unknown outside of a small circle of folk and blues connoisseurs. Indeed, even his family – according to his stepsister – only knew about the release of 'Terraplane Blues' during his lifetime and only learned about the others long after this death.[5] Only two photos of him were thought to exist for many years. A third was eventually unearthed in 2020.[6] He died in 1938 but it was not until the release of the 16-track *King of the Delta Blues Singers* by Columbia in 1961 that his legacy really began to grow, being cited as a huge influence on the British blues scene of the early 1960s that led to the formation of The Rolling Stones, The Yardbirds and more.

Annye Anderson is Johnson's stepsister and knew him while he was alive. In 2020, she published the book *Brother Robert: Growing Up with Robert Johnson*, having inherited half of his estate from Carrie Thompson (Johnson's half-sister) when she passed away in 1983. Anderson said it was not until reading about British musicians citing Johnson as an influence in, of all places*, Ladies' Home Journal* in the late 1960s that she was made aware his music had travelled.[7]

The family of Johnson claimed they were hornswoggled out of his estate by producer Steve LaVere, a process which began with him persuading Johnson's half-sister, Carrie Thompson, to give him a photo of the blues musician to go along with the release of previously unheard music in 1973.[8] The following year, LaVere persuaded Carrie to transfer all of Johnson's copyrights to him under the guise of helping her track down unpaid publishing royalties and reclaiming the recording rights. LaVere would take 50 per cent as a kind of finder's fee and also took his songwriting rights into his publishing company. It was possibly "the greatest example of a white man stealing a black man's soul", according to Annye Anderson.[9]

A lengthy legal battle led by Thompson and Anderson followed that ran into the 1980s. However, the subsequent death of Carrie weakened Anderson's claim on the estate as she was not a blood relative, even though she was the administrator of Carrie's estate.

Anderson says LaVere wrote to her in October 1990 to offer her a share of the 50 per cent that he would make from the Robert Johnson estate. "I never responded," she said. "If I got the estate, I wasn't about to split it with LaVere. I think he knew that."[10] She stated that in 1991 LaVere secured himself 50 per cent of the composer royalties related to sales of the 41-track *The Complete Recordings* album released the previous year. "The other half went into an escrow account for the estate," said Anderson, "but I never saw a penny."[11]

A late claim was made on the estate by 61-year-old Claud Johnson, who said he was Johnson's son. The courts ruled in 1998 that Claud was the legitimate heir. Other relatives of Johnson sued Claud in 2000, but the Supreme Court ruled that the lawsuit had been filed too late.[12] Claud inherited everything as the sole heir.[13] Anderson blamed LaVere for sidelining her and Carrie from the off, saying he was "a crook from his heart".[14] This was, sadly, to be a situation repeated again and again in the years since across various estates.

While Johnson was to step into the spotlight almost a quarter of a century after his death and be feted as a pioneer, he was never to attain superstar status. If one is to judge the start of music estates as a business defined by chart and commercial success, that did not happen until later in the 1960s.

*   *   *

On his second attempt at recording '(Sittin' on) The Dock of the Bay' on 7 December 1967 at Stax Studios in Memphis, a song he had co-written with guitarist Steve Cropper, soul singer Otis Redding knew he was closing in on something special. "This is my first No. 1 record," he said of the song that was nearing completion. "It's the biggest song I ever had."[15]

Three days later, he and his band the Bar-Kays boarded a twin-engine Beechcraft private plane in Cleveland that was to take them to Madison, Wisconsin, where they were due to play the Factory nightclub. It was four miles from its destination when it crashed into Lake Monona. Only Ben Cauley, trumpet player in the band, survived. Redding's body was recovered the following day when the lake was dragged. He was 26.

The famous whistle on the song's outro was actually an ad-lib as he had forgotten the words. Cropper went back to finish the recording, adding seagull noises and the sound of waves crashing as Redding had intended. The whistle was retained.

"I got this call on a Monday, and of course Otis's plane went down on a Sunday morning," Cropper told NPR in 2000. "And they said, 'Get that thing finished and get it to us.' So, I went to work on it. And probably the music is the only thing that kept me going."[16] Redding's label, Stax/Volt, was not keen on wasting time as the music world mourned the singer's passing. "The grim reality was that tragedy sold in the record business," wrote Jonathan Gould in his 2017 biography of the soul star.[17] Cooper sent his completed version of the track to the label within a week.

"Jerry Wexler up in New York at Atlantic, the overlords of Stax, said, 'No, we can't release this. His vocal is too recessed. It needs to be remixed,'" claimed Redding biographer Mark Ribowsky. "Cropper said, 'OK, I'll change it: I'll overdub it, I'll do this, I'll do that' – [and] didn't change it whatsoever. Sent it back to Wexler, who said, 'Oh yeah, this sounds a lot better now.'"[18] Gould disputes this, saying Cropper "made some adjustments" as per Wexler's requests.[19]

"Otis's death inspired an outpouring of publicity that far exceeded the sum of what was written about him during his life," writes Gould.[20]

The single was released on 8 January 1968, just over four weeks after Redding's death, and became the first posthumous single to top the US charts (getting there in March 1968 for a four-week run).[21] It sold over a million copies in that time and was number one on both the pop and R&B charts.[22] A "hastily assembled"[23] album, *The Dock of the Bay*, quickly followed, made of up previous singles 'Tramp', 'The Glory of Love' and 'I Love You More Than Words Can Say', along with an outtake of ballad 'Open the Door' as well as 'Ole Man Trouble', which had previously opened the *Otis Blue* album from 1965.

That summer, Atlantic scooped up 11 tracks from Redding's final sessions and released them under the title of *The Immortal Otis Redding*. That album went Top 10 and stayed in the charts for six months. This all foreshadowed the sometimes desperate archive-scraping activities of record labels that was to become a staple of posthumous releases, where supply often struggles to meet demand.

And '(Sittin' on) The Dock of the Bay' has endured, with BMI naming it the sixth most-performed song of the 20th century, with over six million plays on US radio.[24]

*　*　*

Redding was the first star of the modern pop era to have a posthumous number one in the immediate aftermath of his death, but tinkering with a late star's unfinished (and finished) recordings stretches back slightly further. 'Down the Line' was originally released by Buddy Holly in January 1965, but was reissued soon after his death in 1959 where "some of the guitar work was over-dubbed".[25]

7

This was a trick that Holly's producer Norman Petty was to perfect in the years following the singer's death. Some tracks that had been previously released were embellished by Petty in the studio, but demos cut by Holly in his New York home in December 1958 – known as *The Apartment Tapes* – also got a full release after his death. These tracks were "never intended for release" and were taped by Holly "for his own amusement", but they "offer an insight into Petty's ambition for Holly as a solo artist".[26]

There were some missteps here, however, when Petty brought in The Fireballs, a group he had under contract, to add instrumental backing to Holly's home recordings. Whereas the "sparseness and simplicity" was the calling card of Petty's work on Holly's hits in his lifetime, the gilding of the lily with the addition of The Fireballs made for "a grandiose sound engulfing Holly's voice rather than highlighting it", according to Dave Laing's book, meaning that "the posthumously issued tracks do not add anything to Buddy Holly's musical achievement".[27] Fans in the UK wrote to the music papers questioning if the "unquenchably alive and effervescent voice" on some of these records even belonged to Holly.[28]

The crash on 3 February 1959 that killed Holly as well as Ritchie Valens and The Big Bopper is forever referred to as "The Day the Music Died", following the release of 'American Pie' by Don McLean in 1971. It also reveals where posthumous reputations can ebb and flow and how estate management can intentionally elevate or accidentally erase an act and their legacy.

In his 1971 book on Buddy Holly, music writer and one of the founders of the academic study of popular music in the UK Dave Laing notes that news reports of the crash in the US led with Valens (helped by the fact his single 'Donna' was at number four in the charts at the time), but Holly dominated the headlines in the UK where he was a much bigger deal.[29] Despite the spike in interest in Valens following the *La Bamba* biopic in 1987, in the long term, Holly is considerably more famous in death.

"The sense of Buddy being deeply and sincerely mourned was palpable," wrote Philip Norman in his 1996 biography of the singer, stating that the public nature of the grief was, in itself, an event. "In schools throughout America and Britain, whole classes turned up for lessons wearing black armbands."[30]

According to Norman, the fans might have been acutely aware of what this all meant, but the music business was not totally awake to its macro implications. "The most hardened music industry opportunist did not dream at that point how Buddy's death would be the means of lifting his fame – and sales – into the stratosphere," he wrote. "It had never happened before."[31]

Norman argues that Buddy Holly's death marked a sea change in the record business. The death of a popular musician before that point had marked a boom in the mythology around them but a bust in their commercial power. He cites jazz cornettist Bix Beiderbecke, Robert Johnson, Billie Holiday and Hank Williams as all seeing their legend elevated in death, but it was also to apply the brakes to the industry's view of their posthumous sales potential. "All [...] had ceased to be regarded as commercial proportions from the moment they were lowered into the earth. Until Buddy, the accepted wisdom among record companies was that 'stiffs don't sell'."[32]

Holly's last single before his death, 'It Doesn't Matter Anymore', took on a whole new bleak symbolism and what was previously a flop rocketed into the charts, rising as high as a poignant number 13 in the US.

Such industry naivety and tardiness to jump on what can be morbidly referred to as the opportunities of death would be short-lived.

THE MUSIC ESTATE FOLLOWS THE LEAD OF THE ART ESTATE

Dave Laing has fascinating insights into the posthumous fame machine, bearing in mind that he was writing six years before the passing of Elvis, after which point it became truly industrialised.

"The death in mid-career of a singer, a sportsman or a film actor always has a more dramatic effect than that of a writer, painter or director; because they are performers, people with an immediate physical presence for their audience," he writes. "This fact gives their records or films, and especially those released for the first time after their death, a new significance. What before had seemed to be only the first stage in a career (Valens) or the first peak (Holly), now has to be seen in a new perspective, as the whole of that career, something completed. The work of the performer has consequently to be revalued, and it attains a new scarcity value."[33]

It is somewhat fitting that Laing mentions painters as there are important parallels here in terms of how a new type of hyper-mediated celebrity came about in the 1950s, due to the rise of television, and how both musicians and artists became famous (and enormously rich) while still alive. This started with the likes of Pablo Picasso and Salvador Dalí and went through Jackson Pollock, Roy Lichtenstein, Jean-Michel Basquiat and Louise Bourgeois. From that, the role of the estate – in both cultural and economic terms – became as important for Andy Warhol and Mark Rothko as it was for Jimi Hendrix and Janis Joplin.

Of course, these are artists, whose work is based on the finite – a set number of paintings or sculptures they created in their lifetime – rather than musicians, whose recordings can be endlessly mechanically reproduced for low cost and sold widely. Even so, the two posthumous industries around art and music have moved in a curious lockstep since the second half of the 20th century.

"The sculptor Henry Moore was the first British artist to reckon with his legacy on an institutional scale," claimed Harriet Fitch Little in a feature for the *Financial Times* in 2016.[34] To that end, he set up the Henry Moore Foundation in 1977, although he did not die until 1986. "In a way, what you're doing is turning yourself into an institution while you're still alive," explained Mary Moore, his only child and custodian of his legacy.[35]

There is a beguiling parallel between the world of sculpting and the world of pressing records, however, that has huge resonance here. LPs (or CDs and cassettes) can be physically reproduced at scale and one copy is identical to the millions of others produced. Success is measured in terms of just how many of these identical items can be sold in the marketplace. For a sculptor like Moore, his works can also be – theoretically – reproduced multiple times from the same mould. The difference is that success here, artistically and commercially in terms of the prices they can command, is measured in scarcity rather than ubiquity. To that end, Moore wanted to set physical limits to his work.

"He thought about sculptors like Rodin and Maillol who didn't limit the editions of their sculptures, or various estates where the widows went on to create posthumous casts," said Mary. "He was thinking about these things all the time."[36]

Musicians were eventually to start thinking and operating with the long view in mind, just as Henry Moore did; but it was to be decades later that they could be said to think about their estates and legacies with such attention to detail.

Seeing the mismanagement of other estates spurred Moore into action, but for Andy Warhol it was the brutal impact of Aids in the 1980s that made him start to plan for his own death and how his estate should be run. Patrick Moore, general manager of the Andy Warhol Museum in Pittsburgh, said it was seeing friends from the art world dying that shook Warhol into estate planning. These artists were sometimes estranged from their families and, on their death, their work was simply dumped into skips and lost for ever. "Over and over again, their entire lives' work was being discarded," said Moore of Warhol's jolt into action around his own estate and legacy planning. As Warhol himself is reported to have said, "Death means a lot of money, honey. Death can really make you look like a star."[37]

The dawn of the Dead Elvis business

For Andy Warhol, Elvis Presley was a towering symbol of American ambition and the blank allure of fame long before his passing. Drawing on a 1960 publicity still for Western movie *Flaming Star* featuring Elvis as a cowboy drawing to shoot, Warhol replicated the image to form a triptych of the singer. Created in 1963, one version of *Triple Elvis* (Warhol made 22 in total) was eventually sold at auction in 2014 for just under $82 million.[38]

Even though Elvis was to become a symbol for the estates business and offered a financial template for others to follow and attempt to replicate it, in the spirit of Warhol's screen prints, it was far from a given that it would turn into such a posthumous powerhouse when the music business learned of his death in August 1977.

Priscilla Beaulieu married Elvis in 1967. Their only child, Lisa Marie, was born in 1968, but the couple were eventually to divorce in 1973. Despite the tumultuous nature of their marriage and tensions around co-parenting of Lisa Marie, it was Priscilla who was to seize the reins of power from Colonel Tom Parker after Elvis died and turn what was a career on the slide into an enormously profitable operation. Much of this was born out of necessity as his finances were in a parlous state.

While she was to manoeuvre Parker out of the picture eventually, she learned a great deal about turning a plump profit from the music business by observing the former carnival huckster up close. She recalls Parker's management philosophy in the book *Elvis and Me.* "If you want to see Elvis Presley," she wrote, "you buy a ticket."[39] He was opposed to handing out freebies as freebies meant lost earnings. "He stuck to that policy to the day Elvis died," she wrote.[40] In many ways, this same philosophy has steered the Elvis estate ever since.

The far from egalitarian contract Elvis had with the Colonel was to prove a Gordian knot for the estate, primarily because Elvis had transferred almost all financial responsibility to his manager. "He and the Colonel had an unwritten agreement," explained Priscilla. "Elvis would handle the artistic end and the Colonel would take care of the business matters."[41]

Despite Parker's 50 per cent cut at the top end, Elvis still made vast sums of money. The problem was that, while he was alive, he "continued spending money as if it were going out of style" according to Priscilla.[42]

Most alarmingly, Elvis took financial guidance from his own father, Vernon, a man wholly unsuited to the job of keeping America's most famous high-roller in check. "Vernon operated on pure instinct, refusing any suggestion of tax breaks, which he found too complicated to consider," recalled Priscilla. "He let the IRS figure Elvis's taxes and had done so ever since Elvis had been audited while in the Army and assessed eighty thousand dollars in back taxes. 'Let's just pay the taxes, Daddy,' Elvis said. 'I make enough money. I'll make a million dollars and I'll give them half.'"[43]

Vernon would also regularly talk Elvis into appearing in more and more of the schlocky movies he increasingly grew to loathe – all to try and cauterise the profligacy of Elvis and the people around him. "We need the money, son," he would tell Elvis.[44] And Elvis would obey his father.

This unnervingly cavalier approach to finances was to put the estate in a deep hole and it struggled to find a way out. But when it did clamber out of the hole, it would operate with a keen and constant awareness of the financial recklessness of Elvis's past.

At the heart of this was a massive chasm between what people presumed Elvis was worth and what he was actually worth. It fell to the estate to try and recalibrate it. The probate court of Shelby Country in Tennessee heard the reading of Elvis's last will and testament on 24 August 1977 – just over a week after his passing. It was only 13 pages long. Everything was left to Lisa Marie, but it would be held in trust until she turned 25. Vernon was appointed executor.

The probate session was done and dusted in 20 minutes but there was no official value placed on the estate. Doing an inventory to arrive at a final figure would take 60 days. Joseph Evans, the probate judge, suggested it would be the largest estate ever recorded in Tennessee. He pinned a tentative value of $150 million on it.[45] He had, it turned out, massively overvalued it – by roughly $143 million.[46]

On the day of Elvis's funeral, Parker attended dressed in slacks, Hawaiian shirt and a baseball cap. He had, as he always had where Elvis was concerned, business on his mind. He made a beeline for Vernon, a man who had only just buried his son, and asked him to sign a contract that would extend Parker's tenure as Elvis's manager. It was to be a simple continuation of the contract that Elvis and Parker had signed on 22 January 1976.[47] "If you show signs of weakness at this moment, everything will fall apart," he told Elvis's grieving father.[48]

"He was already planning ways to keep Elvis's name before the public," recalls Priscilla. "He acted quickly, fearful that with Elvis gone, Vernon would be too distraught to handle correctly the many proposals and propositions that would be in the offing. Vernon signed."[49]

In a letter to Parker dated 23 August 1977, Vernon outlined that things would carry on as they were, carrying on an agreement he had last signed with Elvis on 22 January 1976, allowing the Colonel to remain in the driving seat.[50]

That Vernon would sign a renewal of the contract was, for the Colonel at least, never in doubt as he "had always been something of a pushover".[51] Parker also felt it was more than a mere formality to take over running his interests – it was his right. "I owned 50 per cent of Elvis when he was alive," he reportedly crowed, "and I own 50 per cent of him now that he's dead."[52]

He might have carried Elvis in his life and carried the estate in its earliest years, but Parker, as inappropriately dressed as he was, refused to carry Elvis's coffin. He also took immense pride in the fact that he did not shed a single tear at the funeral. "No, sir," he said. "If anybody had seen my eyes mist up for a second they must have had their hands in my pockets."[53]

To his credit, Parker hit the ground running. He had already stitched up Elvis's merchandise rights when he was alive, creating a company called Boxcar Enterprises with Elvis in 1974 and channelling everything though it. "At the time, it was a relatively small gear in the Elvis money machine," noted Sean O'Neal.[54] It was to become a significant cog in the machine for decades to come.

Parker could not help himself and was finding whole new ways to go beyond the 50 per cent per cent of Elvis's earnings he was already taking. By 1977, Parker had grown his share of Boxcar to 56 per cent, with only 22 per cent of its profits going to the Elvis estate and the remaining 22 per cent going to Tom Diskin, Parker's long-term assistant.[55] [56]

Within two days of Elvis dying, Parker – via Boxcar – signed a deal with merchandise company Factors Inc to give it the exclusive licence to exploit the name and likeness of the star. Parker was rewarded handsomely for that Factors deal. "Factors paid Boxcar, and thus the Colonel, $100,000 upfront and guaranteed him an annual income of $150,000."[57] The "boy" (as Parker would call Elvis) was to be a cash cow for many years for all those who swooped in to keep his name in the public eye by keeping the cash registers ringing.

The most famous quote attributed to Parker about the death of Elvis deserves repeating in full here. "Elvis didn't die," he is reported to have said. "The body did. It don't mean a damned thing. It's just like when he was away in the army [...] This changes nothing."[58] This quote is a solid synopsis of what Parker was to set up for Elvis and what every major music estate since has looked to refine. Elvis might physically be gone, but the *idea* of Elvis can be kept going. And if it can be kept going, it can make money. Almost half a century on, the *idea* of Elvis is still alive. And it is still making money. A lot of it. And this is all down to the fact that Parker wasted no time in putting the estate to work.

The first loosening of Parker's white-knuckle grip on the estate, however, was to occur on 26 June 1979 when Vernon Presley died. He was 63.

Vernon was appointed executor of the estate in Elvis's will and Lisa Marie named as the sole heir. Priscilla managed to persuade an initially resistant Vernon to make her the new executor of the Elvis estate, arguing it would be to the benefit of Lisa Marie to have her mother look after the business of her dead father. He agreed, but on the condition that Joe Hanks (Elvis's accountant) and the National Bank of Commerce in Memphis were signed on as co-executors. Hanks and Priscilla were responsible for overseeing the estate until Lisa Marie turned 25 on 1 February 1993.[59]

The estate was, frankly, not in the best shape after Vernon passed away. Running costs for Graceland were nudging close to half a million dollars a year, but the estate itself was barely generating $1 million a year in income.

Besides his other interests in Elvis, in March 1973 Parker had struck a deal with RCA where Elvis would waive the right to future sound recording royalties on his entire catalogue of, at the time, 700 songs. This deal was done for the relatively paltry sum of $5.4 million, meaning that Elvis, and his estate, would be locked out of future earnings from his record sales. Of that sum, following Parker's cut as well as tax, Elvis got $1.35 million for washing his hands of "arguably the most valuable body of work ever recorded".[60] RCA pays the estate royalties on recordings made after 1973, but the bulk of Elvis's hits pre-date that and so the estate does not earn from the biggest jewels in his catalogue. Sean O'Neal derided it as possibly "the single most financially damaging contract in the history of the music industry".[61]

A new stratum of professionalism, arising out of cold-blooded fear about the future of the Elvis legacy, came into the estate with the ascension of Priscilla and she was to eventually push Parker from the centre of the Dead

Elvis business to its periphery. Even so, he was to continue on the same management deal into the 1980s.

D. Beecher Smith II, a Memphis attorney for the Elvis estate, sent up a red flag after the co-executors filed to approve Parker's compensation agreement and commission (which, depending on the deal, varied between 25 per cent and 50 per cent). "We weren't aware of the extent of Parker's commissions until Vernon died," he said. "Vernon had been relatively secretive about it. We filed a petition with the probate court to rule on the propriety of the commissions."[62]

Judge Joseph Evans at Shelby County probate court in Tennessee was astonished by the size of the cut Parker continued to receive from the Elvis business. Attorney Blanchard E. Tual was ordered to undertake what was to become a four-month investigation and a 300-page report into Parker's financial arrangements with the estate in order to protect Lisa Marie's interests in it.

Tual concluded that the January 1976 contract Parker had signed with Elvis should not have been continually extended as "all agreements with Elvis Presley terminated on his death", calling Parker's 50 per cent commission "excessive, imprudent, unfair to the estate, and beyond all reasonable bounds of industry standards".[63] All money due to the estate, concluded Tual, should be paid to the executors and bypass Parker completely. All commissions that were pending to Parker should also be frozen until the investigation was complete.

The most egregious part of it all, according to Tual, was the Boxcar agreement where Parker had 56 per cent control of the company on top of the 50 per cent deal commission package he was on. This was, Tual argued, "self-dealing and overreaching" and Parker had "violated his duty both to Elvis [...] and to the estate".[64]

Parker's reaction was one of apoplexy. He believed that he had made Elvis the biggest star in the world and therefore deserved to be paid a commensurate amount for that. Parker was asked back in 1968 if it was true that he took 50 per cent of Elvis's earnings when the typical management deals of the time gave the manager 15–20 per cent. "No," replied Parker after a pause. "That's not true at all. He takes 50 per cent of everything I earn."[65]

Tual's report thought differently and the findings were utterly damning. "Agreements were unethical, fraudulently obtained and against industry standard," he continued. "Those actions against the most popular American folk hero of the century are outrageous."[66]

The judge came down hard on the Colonel and ruled on 14 August 1981 that all further payments from the estate to Parker should be halted and that the executors should file a suit against Parker for alleged fraudulence regarding business dealings with Elvis.

Jaw-dropping details of Parker's financial management of Elvis were to eventually emerge. Under instruction from an utterly out-of-his-depth Vernon, Parker had let the IRS calculate Elvis's annual tax liability during his lifetime. Without proper financial advice, Elvis was typically in the 75 per cent tax bracket at the height of his earning power. Even more incredibly, Parker saw this as something to brag about, putting in a press release that Elvis was the highest individual tax-payer in the US. Author Sean O'Neal claimed this calamitous approach to taxation "probably cost Elvis around $100 million".[67]

The estate at the stage of the investigation into Parker's financial mishandling had just $5 million in cash and was at risk of slipping into bankruptcy, especially with the IRS demanding $14.6 million in additional taxes. A lengthy legal battle could have sunk it. Parker maintained he was still owed $1.6 million from an advance he gave Elvis shortly before his death and went to a Nevada court to try and have the estate liquidated.

To prove how unbalanced his management deal with Elvis was, the estate gathered together paperwork from March 1973 that showed Parker had been paid $6.2 million in a seven-year period. In contrast, Elvis had been paid $4.6 million. The case had also cost the estate $2m.[68] At this stage there was precious little money coming in. "By 1981 the estate was running at an annual deficit of $160,000," claims Elvis author Ted Harrison.[69] Something had to give. And quick.

Tual and the executors eventually reached an out-of-court settlement with both Parker and RCA in November 1982. Parker had to sever ties not just with the estate but also with RCA. On top of this, he had to pay the estate back $1.1 million in recorded music royalties earned since 1973.[70] Parker was excluded from future estate earnings and prohibited from commercially exploiting Elvis's name for five years.

The final documents expunging Parker from the estate were signed in 1983, by which stage Priscilla and her board of directors were gearing up to take the Elvis estate to a whole new level and turn Graceland into one of the biggest tourist attractions in the US. By its 30th anniversary of opening to the public, Graceland had drawn close to 18 million visitors.[71]

Parker died on 21 January 1997, not quite 20 years after Elvis passed away. Alanna Nash estimated that Parker made $100 million from Elvis but died leaving only $913,000, split across savings bonds, securities and memorabilia. By that stage, with Priscilla firmly in charge, Elvis was the sine qua non of the music estates business. Priscilla built a highly successful team around her when the estate needed it most and this equation of hyper-professionalism plus direct family involvement has been the guiding principle for numerous estates that have followed in Elvis's wake.

Joe Hanks was the first key part of the team and a feature by Robert Hilburn in the *Los Angeles Times* in June 1989, a decade after Vernon's death and Priscilla's appointment as the estate's figurehead, detailed the other key names Priscilla brought together. These included at the time: Jack Soden (executive director of Graceland), C. Barry Ward (attorney), Joseph F. Rascoff (business manager) and Jerry Schilling (creative affairs director).

Hilburn described the seven-strong estate team as its "life-support system". It is a bleak metaphor but it is a neat summation of what estates are tasked to do. They have to keep the artist alive – both culturally and economically – by keeping the public's interest in them alive.

Soden was keen to stress that Priscilla was far from a mere benign figurehead. "I've met a lot of Harvard MBAs that I'd be far less inclined to want to be in a partnership with than Priscilla," he said. "I'd take her common sense every time when it applies to business."[72]

Priscilla talked of her initial reluctance to opening up Graceland to make it into a shrine-cum-tourist-attraction. "Graceland was the only thing Elvis and I had that wasn't [on public view]," Priscilla said. "To open up your home was like being robbed."[73] It was really only raised as a possibility after the death of Vernon, but for two years the estate leaned on merchandising to bring in the cash. It did – but not enough. And the more the estate made, ironically, the more precarious its position became.

Ted Harrison, in his book *The Death and Resurrection of Elvis Presley*, argued that it was desperation for cash, rather than a compulsion to create a machine to maintain his legendary status, that turned the Elvis estate into what it eventually became. It all stems from not just Colonel Tom Parker over-generously slicing the pie in his favour but also from Elvis's own unstoppable profligacy, burning through cash at a frightening rate.

"The Elvis story might have been very different if his family had been left the fortune they might have expected when he died," Harrison proposes. "The family would have had no incentive to set up the Elvis business if the singer's finances had not been at such a low ebb at the time of his death."[74]

Left with no other option, the estate opened the doors of Graceland to the paying public on 7 June 1982.[75] Not all the house was open to visitors initially. More rooms and sections would be made accessible over the years, but initially it was a partial opening, with the entire upper floor sealed off to visitors. There was the added fact that Elvis's aunt Delta Presley Briggs (along with Edmond, her dog) still lived upstairs until she herself died in 1993.[76] That fact informed the decision to keep parts of the house out of bounds for many years.

Priscilla claimed a visit to Hearst Castle (the ostentatious California home of press baron William Randolph Hearst that inspired Xanadu in *Citizen Kane*) provided the template for Graceland as a public attraction. "[T]here was nothing [commercial] on the grounds," she said. "It was kept exactly the same as when people had lived there. That's what I wanted, too."[77]

Elvis Presley Enterprises was set up to keep direct control of Graceland. Jack Soden, a former investment banker and stockbroker, was brought in to manage the house ahead of its public opening. Soden was reportedly not even a casual fan of Elvis and this appealed to Priscilla, as it meant he would be focused on the business of Graceland, not the celebrity of Elvis. "In

Soden, Priscilla found someone whose only concern would be the maximisation of profits."[78] He was hired on an annual salary of $60,000 along with a bonus package.

Joel Weinshanker, a former music manager, in partnership with Authentic Brands Group, who bought 85 per cent of Elvis Presley Enterprises,[79] took over management of Graceland operations in 2013[80] through his Graceland Holdings company, although Lisa Marie still owns Graceland and her father's possessions on display there, while Priscilla is a consultant.[81] Soden, meanwhile, remains president and CEO of Elvis Presley Enterprises.

To get the house ready for the public, it needed investment of $560,000. The estate only had around half a million in liquid assets at the time and was unable to borrow money due to its looming tax bill. It used advance sales of tickets to make up the remainder. Soden termed the gamble "one shot, for all the marbles" and it reportedly earned back the investment of $560,000 in just 38 days.[82]

As visitor numbers (and earning potential) grew, so more doors in the house were unlocked to the public. "The kitchen was not added to the Graceland tour until 1993," says the official Graceland website. "Today, fans can see the living room, dining room, Elvis's parents' bedroom, the kitchen, pool room, TV room and Jungle Room [Elvis's den and studio]."[83]

On the opening day of Graceland, a total of 3,024 people paid $5 each to tour the residence. Now it draws in over half a million visitors a year (with peak season in July seeing 4,000 visitors a day). The estate estimates that the total economic impact of Graceland on the city of Memphis is $150 million a year.

This tension in the business between what to make public and what to keep private is something other estates, although rarely on the same scale, have had to try and resolve ever since.

Bootleggers were a huge concern for the newly opened Graceland, with a mushrooming of souvenir shops opening up on the streets around the house. Mark Roesler is now chairman and CEO of CMG Worldwide, but he was inducted into the team based at Graceland in the early 1980s to bring what he calls "an element of quality licensing to the Elvis Presley estate". Part of that was cleaning up around Boxcar Enterprises, which had been making the merchandise. "We turned it into a licensing operation where we went out and got quality companies, from the [likes of] Hallmark to the different collectible companies that did various collectible merchandise."

He says things were in stasis for the estate, and that was holding it back from competing directly with the bootleggers by offering items that were not only official but also of superior quality. "Graceland wasn't open," he recalls of that limbo period. "There was no licensing being done. There was the litigation with Colonel Parker. Jack Soden had been brought in to get it in order. There were all these little shops set up across the street from Graceland to exploit the goodwill associated with Elvis."

Roesler led the licensing activities of the estate and began to work with what he termed "quality companies" to make official products. "That was our job – to up the image of Elvis and to perpetuate the legacy," he says. "We licensed a whole host of different products. We had a very successful doll programme, we had collectible guitars, we had high-end figurines, we had collector plates, prints, calendar, posters – things like that."

With dark humour, Soden would refer to Elvis Presley Boulevard, peppered with unlicensed retail outlets, as "the DMZ".[84] To tackle this, he got a series of trusted investors to buy up properties around Graceland (where the unlicensed souvenir shops were) without mentioning any connection to the Elvis estate in case the sale price rocketed. They paid $2.5 million for 7.3 acres and waited until the rental leases expired (the last one expired in 1988) and then redeveloped the area to add a ticket booth and official souvenir shops.[85]

Speaking to *Time* magazine in 1997, Soden described the war on bootleggers thus: "[A]ll we want […] is to run our own business and not have every little schlocky guy around ripping off Elvis and putting his face on edible underwear and all kinds of things that demean the long-term value of what we've got."[86] He added that what he was doing was "clearing the swamp".

* * *

There is a complex and powerful symbiosis between Graceland, as a very public manifestation of the estate (existing as both a shrine and a cash register), and the rest of the Elvis enterprises. Soden told the Elvis Australia fan club in 2004 how they all support and fuel each other. "For instance, even if Graceland just broke even, it would remain critically important as a support for music, licensing, publishing and other things," he said.[87]

The Elvis estate has been the cartographer, drawing the business map (often on the fly) for other estate businesses to follow. Mistakes were made, of course; dead ends were run down; opportunities were missed or squandered; money was wasted on white elephants; some decisions were made in desperation. Despite all that, the influence of the Elvis estate – as both a business entity and a philosophy – on every other artist estate is as undeniable as it is profound.

When 'Heartbreak Hotel' went to number one in the US in early 1956 (his first of eight number ones that year alone), Elvis arguably created not just the template (for good and ill) for the modern pop icon, and also laid the foundations of the modern music business. What is certain is that Elvis also created the modern music estates business.

Elvis may have left the building, but he merely stepped into the estate.

The *Forbes* Posthumous Rich Lists

Every year since 2001 *Forbes* has compiled a list of the highest-earning dead celebrities.

Because their work straddles so many different income streams (recorded music, music publishing, licensing, endorsements, branding and so on), musicians tend to dominate the lists – simply because there are more ways that their estates can make money. Actors, authors, cartoonists, sports personalities, doctors, scientists and business people also appear, but historically the lists have been heavily dominated by those from the music world (both performers and songwriters).

Only twice have non-musicians topped the *Forbes* chart. Fashion designer Yves Saint Laurent did in 2009, the year following his death, with earnings of $350 million. That was in a large part down to the sale of his art collection and other items, including his house in Morocco. He has never appeared in a subsequent list.

The only other estate from outside music to out-earn everyone else in a given year was the Elizabeth Taylor estate in 2010, when it made $210 million. The lion's share of that came from an auction of her items at Christie's in New York where her jewellery collection alone brought in just shy of $116 million.[88] She has, unlike Yves Saint Laurent, been a regular in the *Forbes* list, appearing seven times since 2011.

Elvis's posthumous earnings have been so consistently strong that he has never dropped outside the top five for the entire history of the *Forbes* list. Indeed, he topped the first five lists and a subsequent two. He was overtaken by Michael Jackson, who has consistently been the biggest earner every year since 2010, with the exception of 2012.

There is a lot of ripe symbolism here. Elvis was called "The King" while Jackson anointed himself "The King of Pop"; plus Elvis was technically Jackson's father-in-law, albeit from beyond the grave, after Lisa Marie was briefly married to the singer from 1994 to 1996.

Most years, Jackson's estate turned over in excess of $100 million a year, reaching a staggering $825 million in 2016 (most of it from the sale of his stake in Sony/ATV Music Publishing). No other estate is likely to come close to making that much money in a single year. It was unquestionably the peak year for celebrity estates.

The details for each year are available from www.forbes.com.

2001

1	Elvis Presley	$35 million
2	Charles Schulz	$20 million plus
3	John Lennon	$20 million
4	Theodor "Dr. Seuss" Geisel	$17 million
5	Jimi Hendrix	$10 million plus
6	Bob Marley	$10 million
7	Andy Warhol	$8 million
8	J. R. R. Tolkien	$7 million
9	Frank Sinatra	$6 million
10	Jerry Garcia	$5 million
11	Keith Haring	$4 million plus
12	Marilyn Monroe	$4 million
13	James Dean	$3 million

2002

1	Elvis Presley	$37 million
2	Charles Schulz	$28 million
3	John Lennon	$20 million
4	Dale Earnhardt	$20 million
5	Theodor "Dr. Seuss" Geisel	$19 million
6	George Harrison	$17 million
7	J. R. R. Tolkien	$12 million
8	Bob Marley	$10 million
9	Jimi Hendrix	$8 million
10	Tupac Shakur	$7 million
11	Marilyn Monroe	$7 million
12	Jerry Garcia	$5 million
13	Robert Ludlum	$5 million

2003

1	Elvis Presley	$40 million
2	Charles Schulz	$32 million
3	J. R. R. Tolkien	$22 million
4	John Lennon	$19 million
5	George Harrison	$16 million
6	Theodor "Dr. Seuss" Geisel	$16 million
7	Dale Earnhardt	$15 million
8	Tupac Shakur	$12 million
9	Bob Marley	$9 million
10	Marilyn Monroe	$8 million
11	Frank Sinatra	$7 million
12	Richard Rodgers	$7 million
13	Oscar Hammerstein	$7 million
14	Jimi Hendrix	$7 million
15	Cole Porter	$6 million
16	Irving Berlin	$6 million
17	Robert Atkins	$6 million
18	James Dean	$5 million
19	Jerry Garcia	$5 million

2004

1	Elvis Presley	$40 million
2	Charles Schulz	$35 million
3	J. R. R. Tolkien	$23 million
4	John Lennon	$21 million
5	Theodor "Dr. Seuss" Geisel	$18 million
6	Marilyn Monroe	$8 million
7	George Harrison	$7 million
8	Irving Berlin	$7 million
9	Bob Marley	$7 million
10	Richard Rodgers	$6.5 million
11	George Gershwin and Ira Gershwin	$6 million
12	Jimi Hendrix	$6 million
13	Alan Lerner and Frederick Loewe	$6 million
14	Cole Porter	$6 million
15	James Dean	$5 million

16	Dale Earnhardt Sr	$5 million
17	Jerry Garcia	$5 million
18	Freddie Mercury	$5 million
19	Tupac Shakur	$5 million
20	Frank Sinatra	$5 million

2005

1	Elvis Presley	$45 million
2	Charles Schulz	$35 million
3	John Lennon	$22 million
4	Andy Warhol	$16 million
5	Theodor "Dr. Seuss" Geisel	$10 million
6	Marlon Brando	$9 million
7	Marilyn Monroe	$8 million
8	J. R. R. Tolkien	$8 million
9	George Harrison	$7 million
10	Johnny Cash	$7 million
11	Irving Berlin	$7 million
12	Bob Marley	$6 million
13	Ray Charles	$6 million

2006

1	Kurt Cobain	$50 million
2	Elvis Presley	$42 million
3	Charles Schulz	$35 million
4	John Lennon	$24 million
5	Albert Einstein	$20 million
6	Andy Warhol	$19 million
7	Theodor "Dr. Seuss" Geisel	$10 million
8	Ray Charles	$10 million
9	Marilyn Monroe	$8 million
10	Johnny Cash	$8 million
11	J. R. R. Tolkien	$7 million
12	George Harrison	$7 million
13	Bob Marley	$7 million

2007

1	Elvis Presley	$49 million
2	John Lennon	$44 million
3	Charles Schulz	$35 million
4	George Harrison	$22 million
5	Albert Einstein	$18 million
6	Andy Warhol	$15 million
7	Theodor "Dr. Seuss" Geisel	$13 million
8	Tupac Shakur	$9 million
9	Marilyn Monroe	$7 million
10	Steve McQueen	$6 million
11	James Brown	$5 million
12	Bob Marley	$4 million
13	James Dean	$3.5 million

2008

1	Elvis Presley	$52 million
2	Charles Schulz	$33 million
3	Heath Ledger	$20 million
4	Albert Einstein	$18 million
5	Aaron Spelling	$15 million
6	Theodor "Dr. Seuss" Geisel	$12 million
7	John Lennon	$9 million
8	Andy Warhol	$9 million
9	Marilyn Monroe	$6.5 million
10	Steve McQueen	$6 million
11	Paul Newman	$5 million
12	James Dean	$5 million
13	Marvin Gaye	$3.5 Million

2009

1	Yves Saint Laurent	$350 million
2	Rodgers & Hammerstein	$235 million
3	Michael Jackson	$90 million
4	Elvis Presley	$55 million
5	J. R. R. Tolkien	$50 million
6	Charles Schulz	$35 million
7	John Lennon	$15 million
8	Theodor "Dr. Seuss" Geisel	$15 million
9	Albert Einstein	$10 million
10	Michael Crichton	$9 million
11	Aaron Spelling	$8 million
12	Jimi Hendrix	$8 million
13	Andy Warhol	$6 million

2010

1	Michael Jackson	$275 million
2	Elvis Presley	$60 million
3	J. R. R. Tolkien	$50 million
4	Charles Schulz	$33 million
5	John Lennon	$17 million
6	Stieg Larsson	$15 million
7	Theodor "Dr. Seuss" Geisel	$11 million
8	Albert Einstein	$10 million
9	George Steinbrenner	$8 million
10	Richard Rodgers	$7 million
11 (tie)	Jimi Hendrix	$6 million
11 (tie)	Steve McQueen	$6 million
13	Aaron Spelling	$5 million

2011

1	Michael Jackson	$170 million
2	Elvis Presley	$55 million
3	Marilyn Monroe	$27 million
4	Charles Schulz	$25 million
5	John Lennon	$12 million
6	Elizabeth Taylor	$12 million
7	Albert Einstein	$10 million
8	Theodor "Dr. Seuss" Geisel	$9 million
9	Jimi Hendrix	$7 million
10	Stieg Larsson	$7 million
11	Steve McQueen	$7 million
12	Richard Rodgers	$7 million
13 (tie)	George Harrison	$6 million
13 (tie)	Bettie Page	$6 million
13 (tie)	Andy Warhol	$6 million

2012

1	Elizabeth Taylor	$210 million
2	Michael Jackson	$145 million
3	Elvis Presley	$55 million
4	Charles Schulz	$37 million
5	Bob Marley	$17 million
6	John Lennon	$12 million
7	Marilyn Monroe	$10 million
8	Albert Einstein	$10 million
9	Theodor "Dr. Seuss" Geisel	$9 million
10	Steve McQueen	$8 million
11	Bettie Page	$8 million
12	Richard Rodgers	$6 million
13	George Harrison	$5.5 million

2013

1	Michael Jackson	$160 million
2	Elvis Presley	$55 million
3	Charles Schulz	$37 million
4	Elizabeth Taylor	$25 million
5	Bob Marley	$18 million
6	Marilyn Monroe	$15 million
7	John Lennon	$12 million
8 (tie)	Albert Einstein	$10 million
8 (tie)	Bettie Page	$10 million
9 (tie)	Theodor "Dr. Seuss" Geisel	$9 million
9 (tie)	Steve McQueen	$9 million
12 (tie)	Bruce Lee	$7 million
12 (tie)	Jenni Rivera	$7 million

2014

1	Michael Jackson	$140 million
2	Elvis Presley	$55 million
3	Charles Schulz	$40 million
4	Elizabeth Taylor	$25 million
5	Bob Marley	$20 million
6	Marilyn Monroe	$17 million
7	John Lennon	$12 million
8	Albert Einstein	$11 million
9 (tie)	Theodor "Dr. Seuss" Geisel	$9 million
9 (tie)	Bruce Lee	$9 million
9 (tie)	Steve McQueen	$9 million
9 (tie)	Bettie Page	$9 million
13	James Dean	$7 million

2015

1	Michael Jackson	$115 million
2	Elvis Presley	$55 million
3	Charles Schulz	$40 million
4	Bob Marley	$21 million
5	Elizabeth Taylor	$20 million
6	Marilyn Monroe	$17 million
7	John Lennon	$12 million
8	Albert Einstein	$11 million
9	Paul Walker	$10.5 million
10	Bettie Page	$10 million
11	Theodor "Dr. Seuss" Geisel	$9.5 million
12	Steve McQueen	$9 million
13	James Dean	$8.5 million

2016

1	Michael Jackson	$825 million
2	Charles Schulz	$48 million
3	Arnold Palmer	$40 million
4	Elvis Presley	$27 million
5	Prince	$25 million
6	Bob Marley	$21 million
7	Theodor "Dr. Seuss" Geisel	$20 million
8	John Lennon	$12 million
9	Albert Einstein	$11.5 million
10	Bettie Page	$11 million
11	David Bowie	$10.5 million
12	Steve McQueen	$9 million
13	Elizabeth Taylor	$8 million

2017

1	Michael Jackson	$75 million
2	Arnold Palmer	$40 million
3	Charles Schulz	$38 million
4	Elvis Presley	$35 million
5	Bob Marley	$23 million
6	Tom Petty	$20 million
7	Prince	$18 million
8	Theodor "Dr. Seuss" Geisel	$16 million
9	John Lennon	$12 million
10	Albert Einstein	$10 million
11	David Bowie	$9.5 million
12	Elizabeth Taylor	$8 million
13	Bettie Page	$7.5 million

2018

1	Michael Jackson	$400 million
2	Elvis Presley	$40 million
3	Arnold Palmer	$35 million
4	Charles Schulz	$34 million
5	Bob Marley	$23 million
6	Theodor "Dr. Seuss" Geisel	$16 million
7	Hugh Hefner	$15 million
8	Marilyn Monroe	$14 million
9	Prince	$13 million
10	John Lennon	$12 million
11	XXXTentacion	$11 million
12	Muhammad Ali	$8 million
13	Bettie Page	$7 million

2019

1	Michael Jackson	$60 million
2	Elvis Presley	$39 million
3	Charles Schulz	$38 million
4	Arnold Palmer	$30 million
5	Bob Marley	$20 million
6	Theodor "Dr. Seuss" Geisel	$19 million
7	John Lennon	$14 million
8	Marilyn Monroe	$13 million
9	Prince	$12 million
10	Nipsey Hussle	$11 million
11	XXXTentacion	$10 million
12	Whitney Houston	$9.5 million
13	George Harrison	$9 million

2020

1	Michael Jackson	$48 million
2	Theodor "Dr. Seuss" Geisel	$33 million
3	Charles Schulz	$32.5 million
4	Arnold Palmer	$25 million
5	Elvis Presley	$23 million
6	Kobe Bryant	$20 million
7	Juice WRLD	$15 million
8	Bob Marley	$14 million
9	John Lennon	$13 million
10	Prince	$10 million
11	Freddie Mercury	$9 million
12	George Harrison	$8.5 million
13	Marilyn Monroe	$8 million

CHAPTER 2

The Inescapable Importance of the Will

"Don't You Guys Get It? It's Private"

On 8 April 1973 at his sprawling 35-room villa and studio, set in a 17-acre estate in Villa Notre-Dame-de-Vie at Mougins in the south of France, Pablo Picasso died from pulmonary oedema and heart failure.[1] He was 91. In the days before his passing, he was preparing for an exhibition at Avignon Arts Festival, pulling together 201 of his paintings for display there, furiously productive to the end despite rarely leaving the house.

On 21 April 2016, in an elevator in the 65,000-square-foot complex that comprised his home, a recording studio and rehearsal space, where he lived in great privacy since 1987, Prince died after overdosing on fentanyl, an opioid he had been taking to deal with severe hip pains.[2] He was 57. Exactly a week before, he had played the last date of a 12-show run on his *Piano & a Microphone Tour* and was typically spending long hours in his studio, furiously productive to the end.

Here were two towering and singular artists of the modern era who showed entirely new ways to create. Their work was *extraordinary* on every level. Both were phenomenally prolific throughout their lives. They became deeply associated, to a profoundly symbiotic level, with a particular colour (blue for one, purple for the other) where it is almost impossible to see one without thinking of the other. They were known by one name – the surname for one, the first name for another – and even shared the same initial.

They also had another crucial, complex and controversial thing in common – neither of them left a will. As such, their estates were compromised and constrained from the off. If the origins of the modern music estate business has its roots in the art world, it also shares some of the same mistakes. Key to this, and the absolute bedrock of the estates business, is the will.

Picasso did not leave a will because he carried throughout his life a deep and unfounded phobia of them. To write one, he believed, was to accept his own mortality and, in doing so, he would lose the power to create. "There is no will," Armand Antebi, his friend and lawyer, said on announcing Picasso's death. "He never made one because of superstition. A way of avoiding death, one might say."[3] The painter was reported to have even banned any discussion of death in his presence.

Why Prince did not leave a will is less clear. There has been speculation that he too was superstitious about writing one and having to confront the idea of his art existing in a world without him. More benignly, possibly he did not see it as a pressing issue. He was in his fifties, a phenomenally energetic performer, he had no children and was not married (he had married Mayte Garcia in 1996 but they divorced in 2000). It is entirely plausible that he believed there was plenty of time to think about that later.

Ken Abdo, a partner at the Minneapolis offices of legal firm Fox Rothschild, became involved in the Prince estate dispute, representing three of the then-presumptive heirs who were eventually to be adjudicated as recognised heirs as the courts attempted to figure out who should share in his estate.

"It was absolutely unprecedented, very messy and it remains as such," he says, speaking in early 2020. "It's probably the textbook case of why artists need to have wills and trusts. There are many ironies in that particular estate, but probably the biggest irony is that, in as much as Prince did not really have loyalty to lawyers and didn't like to pay them, in the wake of his death the lawyers have been required to be involved in it and paid *a lot*."

The lack of a will is, particularly among musicians and other celebrities, all too common a problem. Musicians who have died without leaving a formal or complete will include Kurt Cobain, Amy Winehouse, Jimi Hendrix, Tupac Shakur, Bob Marley, Billie Holiday, John Denver and Sam Cooke.[4] These tend to be the examples industry professionals fixate on to stress the importance of writing and regularly updating a will.

"Most artists just don't run their affairs properly," is the blunt summation of a senior partner at a major law firm which represents many of the leading names in entertainment, including A-list musicians. "They have old agreements or they just don't think about having a will. Or even if they do have a will they don't record the changes." They add, with a sigh so loud that it echoes back years of corrosive experience of trying to tidy things up legally after an artist has died, "Artists don't think of their own mortality. That's the big problem."

Los Angeles-based music lawyer Erin M. Jacobson says it can be a Sisyphean struggle to get artists – who can sometimes be more focused on their own creativity rather than the business underpinning it all –not just to think about their estate planning but also to treat it with the seriousness it deserves.

She says, "I have to sit down with them [her music clients] and say, 'How would you want your music to be used? Who do you want to own your music? Who do you want to benefit from the income of your music?' A lot of times, initially, they look at me with blank stares and go, 'Well I don't know, I've never thought about that. Hmm.' It takes a little work there to get them comfortable with the idea that, at some point, these issues are going to become a reality and it's better for them to get to decide now. It's a process, I guess!" She laughs.

Wills are either never drafted or never updated, via a codicil, as life circumstances change. Occasionally, conflicting wills are unearthed after a star's death and huge fights erupt over who is to receive what, and also what the artist did or did not want done with their intellectual property after they have gone. Some even draft handwritten wills (referred to as "holographic wills"), which are, in many jurisdictions, legal – but they lack the authority of one drafted by an expert and signed by witnesses. Even wills that some consider to be airtight can crack badly when kicked through the courts.

Wills and trusts – their more robust and precise counterparts – are the vehicles of an estate. Without one, everything is on hold and any attempt at estate planning is at risk of swerving off the road as too many hands scramble for the steering wheel. Or, very simply, they can run out of fuel and grind to a halt, the estate left immobile on the hard shoulder and starting to rust away to nothing.

* * *

"The form in which an artist's estate will be administered is determined by the artist, whether he or she wants to or not, by leaving behind a last will and testament – or through not doing so," notes Loretta Würtenberger in her book for artists on how to prepare their estate. "With a will, artists have the ideal opportunity for self-stylization and personal mythmaking."[5]

There are a plethora of horror stories around poorly written or utterly absent wills – with many of them relating to celebrities in general and musicians in particular. Music lawyers Andrew Mayoras and Danielle Mayoras have even turned this into something of a specialism via their Probate Lawyer blog and tie-in book.[6] [7]

A 2020 study by senior care company Caring.com claims that only 32 per cent of Americans have a will or living trust (which is down from 42 per cent in 2017) and so it should not be so surprising that famous and successful musicians also fail to leave a will.[8] In the early days of rock and pop, just as it was becoming truly globalised, this was not uncommon, with acts like Jimi Hendrix passing away at an early age with no will in place.

This issue continues to dog estates, with the courts having to get involved and sometimes reaching decisions that trigger years of internecine fighting and protracted legal battles. These can not only freeze estates but can also drain them of much, or even all, of their value as legal fees rapidly mount up.

While a will can help to clarify things, a trust – especially when there are hugely important assets like recording and publishing rights as well as those relating to name, image and likeness at stake – is regarded as a better way to proceed. Even so, they can only go so far and cover so much. "From my perspective, as an attorney who is often tasked with helping my clients by shooting holes in a will or trust document, I can report that 'bulletproof' estates are a rarity, if not an impossibility," argue the Mayorases. They both, however, look for "certainty over uncertainty" in what they do, writes US lawyer Michael Hackard.[9]

THE MUSICIAN'S WILL IN MOTION

John Branca had been Michael Jackson's attorney during the 1980s and 1990s and was brought back into the fold shortly before the singer's death in 2009. Jackson's will named Branca and John McClain as co-executors and co-trustees of his estate.

"There are different roles here," Branca explains of his obligations. "The co-executor oversees the assets of the estate and is then instructed by the person whose will it is, Mr Jackson, how to distribute the assets and monies over time. The role of most executors is not to actively manage a business. For example, Sumner Redstone owns the controlling shares of Viacom, but there are CEOs and people in place to actually operate the business. So the parallel with a celebrity estate like Michael Jackson's means, as executors, you would be the legal owner of the assets; but, if you have an ongoing business, you would have to have somebody manage that business. In our case, the probate court judge then appointed John McClain and I to manage the Michael Jackson business as personal managers."

He says that Jackson's three children are not involved in the running of the estate but they (along with Jackson's mother) are the named beneficiaries. "When you have an estate and a trust, it is the co-executors of the estate and the trustees of the trust who are charged and empowered to make the decisions – business, legal and otherwise – for the benefit of the beneficiaries," he explains. "But the beneficiaries are not the legal persons who are charged with making those decisions."

Darryl Porter runs the Miles Davis estate (among others) and says that, despite many examples of superstars dying without wills and trusts in place regularly hitting the headlines, the same mistakes get made over and over again, but it is something he tries to impress on living clients.

"Miles Davis had a great trust," he says. "But then you juxtapose that with Prince who died way too soon and had no trust. He had no estate planning. Then you look at one that's even more tragic where Aretha Franklin knew that she had pancreatic cancer and she knew it was terminal. And she still died [without a formal will]."

Individuals can draft their own wills – as Aretha Franklin did, for example – but this is never recommended as they tend towards the vague rather than the specific. And with large estates where music rights and celebrity are involved, vagueness is often the quickest route to a quagmire of complications.

* * *

33

Different musicians in their idiosyncratic ways expose the importance of the will and what happens – or does not happen – to their estate when they die. The following series of case studies show the different approaches, or lack of approaches, to making wills and trusts. Each case here reveals an important aspect of will drafting and estate planning.

AN UNEQUAL SPLIT BETWEEN HEIRS: FRANK ZAPPA (DIED 4 DECEMBER 1993)

When Zappa died, his estate transferred in totality to his widow, Gail Zappa. She, however, passed away on 7 October 2015 and divided the estate unequally between her four children with Frank. Moon and Dweezil each received a 20 per cent stake in the estate, but Ahmet and Diva each got 30 per cent. Moon referred to the lopsided estate split as "unconscionable" while Dweezil compared himself and Moon to "shareholders who have no say in anything".[10]

An uneasy armistice was reached in 2018 but it was not made clear if all the siblings' shares in the estate were recalibrated to a more egalitarian 25 per cent each. Ahmet, however, suggested that the brothers and sisters served distinct functions for the estate – some on a cultural level and others on an economic level.

"What everyone needs to understand is that this is not a black and white situation," he said in a statement. "But it is certainly solvable. I have an emotional responsibility because he [Dweezil] is my brother and I care about him – despite what he continues to say publicly about me. But I also have a legal and fiduciary responsibility to do the right thing as a co-trustee of the Zappa Family Trust (along with our sister Diva), a position we never asked for but were given by our mother."[11]

Speaking a year later on the *Bob Lefsetz Podcast*, Ahmet said the will caused a huge strain between the siblings. He added that – because they are governed by an irrevocable trust – "that means I can't go against it and they [Moon and Dweezil] can't go against it". He added, "And so it doesn't make me an asshole. By law, I have to follow the rules."[12]

A MULTITUDE OF CONFLICTING WILLS: ARETHA FRANKLIN (DIED 16 AUGUST 2018)

The problem with Aretha Franklin's will is not that she did not leave one. She did. The problem is that she left three.

Initially, the family believed there was no will (and this situation was reported as fact by *TMZ* mere days after her passing away).[13] Therefore, as per Michigan law, her estate would be divided equally between her four sons. Working on the straightforward presumption that her estate would transfer automatically to them, they approved the appointment of their cousin, Sabrina Owen, as the estate's executor.

Eventually, three different handwritten wills emerged – two from 2010 (from June and October that year) that were found in a locked cabinet and one from March 2014 that was unearthed beneath cushions in her home – and a protracted process began to determine which one stood as the final, and definitive, will. The June 2010 will was found to revoke one that Franklin had made in Michigan in 1970 as well as a later one that was written in New York.[14] A handwriting expert subsequently confirmed that the 2014 will found under the cushions was in Franklin's handwriting.[15]

It was reported in May 2019, as the convoluted situation was starting to come into some sort of focus, that the will from June 2010 was being regarded as "the most extensive" as it was made up of "11 cramped pages" of instructions where she detailed the weekly and monthly allowances that should go to her four sons on her death. She also, according to reports from the Michigan probate court, signed every page.[16] The March 2014 will, in contrast, ran to a mere four pages.

A year after her death, her son Ted White Jr was pushing for all three wills to collectively represent the singer's full and final wishes.[17]

The problem, of course, was that the wills "contradicted each other".[18] An inventory of her possessions, undertaken as the will dispute unspooled, laid bare her temerarious approach to her personal finances, making the lack of a formal and professionally drafted will appear a sad inevitability. A number of uncashed cheques from a variety of music publishers, collecting societies and film companies were found in her home and they totalled $988,656.17.[19]

Her long-term lawyer Don Wilson states that he had been advising the singer, for several years before her passing, not only to make a formal will but also to set up a trust. This situation was exacerbated when she began cancelling shows but the full extent of her illness was still unknown.

"She did tell me she was undergoing treatments and different things so I had an idea what the illness was and that it was cancer – even before it was made known to the public," he says. "So I was trying to get her to do a will and a trust. I basically told her, like I tell other clients, two things: one, you're able to have control from beyond the grave as to who gets what and how it gets distributed; and two, you can keep it private, so the public doesn't have to know all your business."

The singer assured him that things were being taken care of. "She never really fought me on the issue," he says. "She just went, 'Oh yeah, you're right, I'll get to it, I'll do it, I'll do it.' But she never did in a formal sense."

He says that holographic wills are valid in a number of jurisdictions in the US – including Michigan where Franklin lived – but they are inherently partial as the creator will not be thinking through every eventuality or potential complication.

"When you go to a professional, they are in a position to guide and direct you, ask you the questions, give you the issues to think about, to make it a more thorough and complete will," he argues. "When you're sitting there in your living room just handwriting it yourself, you're not likely to think of everything, you're not likely to think of things in as much detail as you would normally do – or should do." Such a will cannot account for the incredible complexity associated with music rights and also who should be in charge of them on behalf of the estate.

"When you have multiple heirs and you have master recordings and musical composition, you can't just say – or you shouldn't say – 'I'm just going to leave it to all of them equally,'" says Wilson. "It's not something you can clearly divide and parcel well. Sure you can divide up the copyrights and give them each, if there's four [heirs], 25 per cent copyright interest. But it really needs proper administration and handling."

Despite the fact that Franklin did not listen to his advice, Wilson insists that setting up trusts are the best approach here. A trust serves as another entity into which an individual can place their assets and possessions. "In essence you're giving up ownership, because now those assets are owned by the trust," Wilson explains. "But you, as the trustor and the trustee, during your lifetime administer the trust and then the trust has [named] beneficiaries."

The key difference between a will and a trust is that the latter does not have to be probated. "That really gives you an opportunity for confidentiality because […] whoever the trustee is after you pass, they're the ones who will just follow your instructions and even maintain the assets and give periodic distribution or distribute it all at once," he says. It means that the creator of the trust can decide to pay dependants – and this is particularly applicable to children who may not be old enough or who are simply deemed incapable of managing a significant inheritance – on a regular basis rather than giving them a lump sum.

"The mindset is different for the creators than the heirs because the creators have a tendency to look at these things as their creation – their babies, so to speak," explains Wilson. "A trust gives them the opportunity – if it's well crafted and structured – to control their assets from beyond the grave."

Except, in yet another shock development in a story that has had more twists than Lombard Street in San Francisco, Franklin may actually have started to plan a trust before her death.

Incredibly, in March 2021 a possible fourth will was discovered. This eight-page will, reportedly from 2018, came with another 23-page document that was said to have outlined plans for her trust. Neither the will nor the trust were signed, however, and both were marked as "draft". It was also revealed that Franklin had been corresponding with Henry M. Grix, a Detroit lawyer, since late 2017 to assist with her estate planning.[20]

The *New York Times* spoke to lawyer David P. Lucas, who was also chair of the probate and estate planning section of the State Bar of Michigan, and he argued the will could be accepted as a valid will despite the absence of a signature. "If the person who wants this to be Aretha Franklin's will can prove in court by clear and convincing evidence that Ms. Franklin wanted this to be her will," he said, "then yes, the court may decide that this is her will."[21]

(The case had not been resolved before this book went to press.)

THE PERFECTLY PLANNED WILL: DAVID BOWIE (DIED 10 JANUARY 2016)

Estates and wills going wrong or threatening to collapse in on themselves can make for invigoratingly scurrilous reading. Yet the adroitly executed will is what every estate should be aiming for. In the research for this book, one name was mentioned more than others in terms of having the most impeccable estate planning, all stemming from a carefully structured will: David Bowie.

In death, as in life, Bowie was a trailblazer, but the orderliness of his will was not without precedent and may have been influenced by the estate of an artist he had collaborated with in the early 1980s – Freddie Mercury. One senior music industry source, who did not wish to be named but who has insight into both estates, says the Freddie Mercury estate was held up during the 1990s and 2000s as a shining example of how to do things properly.

"Queen's manager Jim Beach is the executor of the Freddie Mercury estate," they explain. "He had been their manager from *A Night at the Opera* [the album released in 1975] and had been their lawyer at Harbottle & Lewis from before that. He was a lawyer so he had all the skills – all the longevity and continuity of thinking – and the closeness to Freddie that was needed in order to construct a situation which would mean that things would be done right."

Bowie's first will was dated 25 August 2004 and was updated with a codicil on 4 May 2007. In it, he left 50 per cent in a marriage trust for Iman (his second wife) and 25 per cent (in a trust) for Alexandria Zahra Jones (known as Lexi), their only child together. The remaining 25 per cent went outright to Duncan Jones, his son from his first marriage to Angie Barnett.[22]

According to the will, on the death of Iman, 50 per cent of her half share of the estate transfers to Duncan (if her survives her) and 50 per cent to Lexi (ditto). Until she turns 21, the trustees of the estate can make discretionary payments to Lexi, after which point she receives all income from the trust. When she turns 25, the trust structure is phased out and she receives all the assets in the trust outright.[23]

"Because Iman had a child from a previous marriage, had Bowie left Iman's share to her outright, she could have left the property to her own two children and excluded Duncan," note the authors of a feature on estate planning for the American Bar Association. "The creation of a marital trust in Bowie's will protected Duncan and his issue from the risk of being disinherited by Iman from her share of the estate."[24]

The 20-page will for the estate, rumoured to be worth $100 million, was filed at the Surrogate's Court in Manhattan on 29 January 2016, just over two weeks after Bowie's death. "The will named two executors, Mr. Bowie's business manager, William (Bill) Zysblat, and a lawyer in London, Paddy Grafton Green," reported the *New York Times*. "But documents filed with the will indicated that Mr. Green had stepped aside, leaving Mr. Zysblat as the sole executor."[25]

Being so well organised here makes Bowie – fittingly – something of an outlier. "I think it is extremely hard, as it has been in my entire career, to get an artist to focus on what's going to happen after they're gone," says Bill Zysblat, who is speaking here about wills and estate planning in general rather than the specifics of the Bowie estate, something he said he would not comment on publicly. "They certainly care about who's going to inherit their estate because they care about their families. And they certainly care about their place in history from that point of view. But to get an artist to sit down and actually do some legitimate planning for their future and their estate is difficult at best."

He adds, "I think there's always a reluctance to make a will. It's not just artists – it's people in general. It's not that hard to do when you sit them down and say, 'Look, if you die without a will, here's what's going to happen to your money by law.' And very often, that's a wake-up call."

A source with knowledge of the inner workings of the Bowie estate (and speaking on condition of anonymity) reveals just how carefully structured things were long before Bowie's death so as to avoid any problems further down the line. "David's financial situation was very, very rosy indeed," they say of his wealth management towards the end of his life.

The appointment of Zysblat to run everything is, the source says, absolutely essential to the long-term success of the estate. "If you ever want anybody in your corner in a situation like that, it's Bill Zysblat," they say. "It's essentially Bill who makes a lot of the creative decisions. The family don't really get involved unless it's really, really big."

PARENTS ARE CUT OUT AND BACK IN AGAIN: JIM MORRISON (DIED 3 JULY 1971)

As lead singer of The Doors, Jim Morrison quickly became a poster boy for the pernicious "live fast, die young" mythology that has dogged rock music for half a century. He did have a will in place before his death, but because he was estranged from his parents, the will named Pamela Courson, his girlfriend at the time of his passing, as his sole heir – with the condition that she must outlive him by at least 90 days before she inherited anything. If she died within this time period, everything would go to Morrison's brother and sister.[26]

The will, drafted two years before his death, was described as "badly worded" and it had not been updated since it was first written.[27] A number of women stepped forward after Morrison's death, claiming he was the father of their children. Until the courts could test the veracity of the claims (they were all eventually dismissed), the estate was on hold, but Courson was paid an allowance from it until it could all be resolved. In the eyes of the courts, Courson was deemed to be his common-law wife anyway and eventually inherited everything. An added twist came when Patricia Kennealy put in a claim for the estate, stating she had secretly married Morrison in a pagan ceremony. This claim was dismissed.

Things became much more complex, however, when Courson herself passed away on 25 April 1974, because she did so without leaving a will. According to intestate succession laws in California, everything (including the Jim Morrison estate) passed to Courson's parents, Corky and Penny. Morrison's own parents, Steve and Clara, contested this (as well as Courson's status as his common-law wife). Eventually Penny Courson agreed to split the estate with Morrison's parents and, as Doors drummer John Densmore put it, "share equally in The Doors interests that she owned".[28] [29] The Coursons, however, took control of the rights to manage his image and music.[30]

"Jim's parents, shunning public life and the media, leave it to the Coursons to manage artistic rights for the estate and to defend their son's reputation," claimed a 1980 feature in *People*.[31]

THE NO-CONTEST CLAUSE: FRANK SINATRA (DIED 14 MAY 1998)

Sinatra's fourth wife, Barbara, inherited the bulk of his property portfolio as well as his name and image rights and a share in his early recordings. On top of this, she got 25 per cent royalties from Sheffield Enterprises, the company Sinatra had established to handle licensing of his name and likeness.[32]

His three children – Frank Jr, Nancy and Tina – each received $200,000 in cash, some stock and interest in an office building he owned in Beverly Hills. The will also transferred $1 million to a trust fund that had been set up in his lifetime for his two grandchildren. There had been a separate trust – known as a living trust – where the bulk of his estate had been placed. Through that trust, his children had rights to a substantial portion of his back catalogue. Frank Jr also got the rights to his father's sheet music. "There are very substantial assets in the trust," said Harvey Silbert, Sinatra's attorney.[33]

It was suggested that the bulk of his net worth – estimated at anywhere between $200 million and $600 million – was put into a living trust before he died. "It is known that each child had a trust," wrote Sinatra biographer, J. Randy Taraborrelli, "but what is not known is how much was in it."[34]

The critical part of the will was that it contained a "no contest" clause (also known as a "terror clause") and in Sinatra's case it contained 13 separate actions that could trigger a disinheritance should any heir raise objections to what they were left. "[These included] challenging the validity of the will, claiming entitlement to any asset through an agreement or promise, filing a claim (valid or invalid) for money against the estate, or even seeking (unsuccessfully) to remove an estate administrator."[35]

Within days of Sinatra's death, however, the media was reporting that the family was battling over control of the estate, with the three children squaring up against his widow. The heart of that tussle was less over the money, intellectual property and possessions being inherited and more over how his image and name were to be used.

Tina had taken over as chief executive of Sheffield Enterprises the year before his death and referred to herself as the "keeper of the Sinatra flame" (even going so far as to say a number of times, "I am Frank Sinatra").[36] Barbara Sinatra had been opposed to what she saw as Tina's heavy-handed marketing of her father, which included branching into neck ties, pasta sauce and "singing" porcelain plates.[37]

Given the enormous stakes for all involved, the will went uncontested. What happened to his name, image and likeness, however, was under less rigid control.

A COMPLEX SERIES OF COMPANIES AND TRUSTS: MICHAEL HUTCHENCE (DIED 22 NOVEMBER 1997)

In the case of INXS frontman Michael Hutchence, the complications arose not from his will but rather in the way his assets when he was still alive had been placed into a series of convoluted companies and sub-companies. What this meant, ultimately, was that his daughter Heavenly Hiraani Tiger Lily (known as Tiger Lily), his siblings (half-sister Tina and brother Rhett) and his parents were unable to access the bulk of them.

Estimates put Hutchence's estate worth at between AU$10 million and AU$20 million. After a protracted process lasting eight years, the executor of his will, however, informed the family that he had passed away leaving almost nothing.[38]

A protracted legal battle in the Australian courts between Hutchence's family and Colin Diamond, Hutchence's business manager (see Chapter 3), tried to bring clarity to the head-spinningly labyrinthine series of off-shore trusts and tax havens that had been set up to handle the singer's fortune.

Diamond rarely does interviews but he spoke to music magazine *axs* in 1998. When asked where Hutchence's money was, Diamond tersely replied, "None of your business. That's the point; it's private. Don't you guys get it? It's private."[39]

Rhett Hutchence, brother of Michael, discussed the complexity of the issues here with regard to Chardonnay Investments, a company about which very little is known of its structure and inner workings but which handled many of the star's rights.

"Chardonnay, to my understanding, is Michael Hutchence's discretionary trust which was made in 1992," he claimed. "It's supposed to be a carrier for

Michael's royalties. The copy of the trust that I have shows my father being a beneficiary."[40]

Tina Hutchence, Michael's half-sister, in her 2000 book *Just a Man: The Real Michael Hutchence* (which she co-wrote with their mother) outlines what was involved in the complex business structures that surrounded him when he first became wealthy.

"Like many wealthy people, Michael was now making considerable efforts to lighten his tax burden," she wrote. "Houses, cars, properties, even businesses can be placed under trusts with company names. These companies are often set up in the British Virgin Islands, Cayman Islands or Liberia where the tax burden is low. Michael's name would still not be on them of course unless in a beneficiary capacity. Royalty cheques could also be paid into such a trust, by one means or another."[41]

She adds that the villa Hutchence bought in the early 1990s in Roquefort-les-Pins in the south of France was purchased under the company name Leagueworks Pty Ltd, which had an address in Monaco. This was, she said, usual for major purchases such as this.[42]

In 1991, the singer also bought some land – sight unseen – in Southport on Australia's Gold Coast for AU$1.3 million which was placed in a trust company named Nextcircle.[43]

Then in 1994, he bought the Paradise Lanes Bowling Alley in Labrador (also on the Gold Coast) for AU$2.25 million. "Michael was exhilarated at the prospect of investing for the future," said his mother.[44] Another Gold Coast purchase included an AU$1 million house on the Isle of Capri.

Tina Hutchence, in her second book about Michael (published in 2018), claimed everything around her half-brother's business interests was intentionally confusing.[45]

A November 2017 investigation by *Four Corners* on ABC in Australia used the leaking of what were termed the Paradise Papers (covering 13.4 million confidential documents from offshore legal services company Appleby) to attempt to untangle the inordinate complexities here. It raised as many new questions about Hutchence's financial affairs as it delivered answers to old ones.

The *Four Corners* programme was far from the final word on the matter. A major documentary followed two years later. It was primarily about Hutchence's life and career but it also dug into his business arrangements in general and the terms of his will in particular.

Richard Lowenstein, maker of the *Mystify: Michael Hutchence* documentary, said in a 2019 interview in the *Sydney Morning Herald* that Tiger Lily had told him that a meeting with Diamond took place, but no resolution relating to the estate was arrived at.[46]

"The estate paid for Tiger's school, nanny and upkeep until she turned 18, but the big payments she was supposed to receive at different stages of her life, when she turned 18 and 21, never arrived," claimed Tina Hutchence in a 2019 interview with the *Mail on Sunday*. "My response to that is, 'How dare they?'"[47]

Hutchence had updated his will on 3 October 1996, a year before he died, which replaced one he had written in 1992. The executors in what was to be his final will were Andrew Paul (Hutchence's Hong Kong-based accountant) and Colin Diamond. It was witnessed by Stephen Diamond, Colin's brother.

In her 2000 book, Patricia Glassop claimed there were a number of mistakes regarding the spelling of beneficaries' names in the will, leading her to believe it was signed in haste.[48]

His mother and half-sister were eventually to drop their case around reclaiming his assets from the series of companies and discretionary trusts that housed them. In 2001, they reached an out-of-court agreement. It was reported they received AU$293,000 as a final settlement.[49]

NO WILL FOR RELIGIOUS REASONS: BOB MARLEY (DIED 11 MAY 1981)

Unlike Picasso, Bob Marley's refusal to create a will was not down to superstition; rather it was down to his religious beliefs.

"For Marley, dealing with his estate probably signified a surrender to the forces of Babylon, the metaphorical site of oppression and Western materialism that Rastas hope to escape," wrote Hua Hsu in a 2017 feature for the *New Yorker*. "When he died, in Miami, his final words to his son Stephen were, 'Money can't buy life.'"[50] Even so, he was reportedly worth $30 million when he passed away.[51]

"He never made out a will and part of that was his desire that the devils unmask themselves after he passed," said reggae archivist Roger Steffens.[52] Just who he felt those "devils" were, was unclear, but many were to be accused of underhand tactics and greed in the decades it took to get the estate onto something approaching an even keel.

Under Jamaican law, where Marley was domiciled, 10 per cent of his assets would transfer to his widow, Rita Marley, and she would be able to use a further 45 per cent in her own lifetime. The rest of the assets would be carved up between his 11 recognised children at the time of his death (although the precise number of children he fathered has been disputed for many years).[53]

David Steinberg, Rita Marley's US attorney, and Marvin Zolt, her accountant, wanted to put together a posthumous estate plan but, to do so, they had to persuade her to forge her dead husband's signature on a series of documents and date them to before his death.[54] "This was done to transfer control of the large majority of Marley's corporate holdings, along with much of his royalty rights and money, to herself."[55]

The ruse was exposed by one of Marley's former managers and it snowballed into a court case where the accountant and attorney were found guilty of conspiracy, falling under the Racketeer Influenced and Corrupt

Organizations Act (RICO). Rita Marley admitted her involvement, although she said she was simply following the advice of her attorney. She was not charged with a crime but the net result was her removal as a co-administrator of the estate. It also triggered a lawsuit that claimed she "fraudulently diverted" up to $14 million in assets when she was in charge of the estate between 1981 and 1986.[56]

Rita was not charged with a crime but she was removed as one of the executors of her late husband's will. She remained unabashed about the fraud charges, telling *Newsweek* in 1991 that she was only acting on the advice of her legal team, and besides, she was the primary heir anyway and so no harm was being done. "How," she asked, "can I steal from myself?"[57]

The year 1984 was a crucial one for the estate as it saw the release of the *Legend* compilation album – which remains a major seller to this day. Marley's annual royalties went from $200,000 to over $1 million after its release.[58]

In the early 1990s, the estate was being administered by Mutual Security Merchant Bank, the largest bank in Jamaica, "with courts intervening when necessary – which is often". The costs racked up over a five-year period by administrators and lawyers – split between Miami, New York and Kingston – ran to $4 million.[59] The tussles over control of the estate were to last many years.

Speaking in 1991, Cedella Booker, mother of Bob Marley, dismissed the argument that, given his highly valuable assets including his records and music publishing, he should have made a will and therefore avoided the turmoil and pain that followed. "This will business is a big insult," she said. "To make a will is to make [a man] small. God never limit nobody! Jah never make no will!"[60] Under Jamaican law, however, she was not entitled to any of her son's money or assets.[61]

TWO WILLS AND SIGNIFICANT DEBT: LUCIANO PAVAROTTI (DIED 6 SEPTEMBER 2007)

Before Italian tenor Luciano Pavarotti died, his fortune was estimated at £200 million. Roughly half a year later, it emerged that this figure was way off the mark. He had died with debts of £7m.[62]

Rumours of the opera star being in chronic debt began circulating within a month of his death, with Italian newspaper *La Repubblica* claiming his Monte dei Paschi di Siena (MPS) bank account had run up a £7 million overdraft and he owed £5 million in mortgage payments across three properties he owned in New York, Monte Carlo and Modena. His other bank accounts, however, held £14 million in cash and stocks.[63]

Giorgio Bernini, the lawyer for Nicoletta Mantovani, his widow, said, "It is no secret that the maestro had debts. In the final years of his life he cut back on his performances and he also had very expensive hospital bills to pay."[64]

By March the following year, a final tally of his finances had been arrived at. The overdraft at MPS bank was larger than initially reported, standing at €11 million (£8 million). Pavarotti's account at the Monaco branch of the same bank had just $0.49 in it.[65]

The final estimate across the 100-page document covering his worth was that he had debts of £7 million. There was no value placed on his properties, which included an apartment and three villas in Italy, and an apartment in Monaco.

In the weeks after Pavarotti's death, Bernini confirmed that two wills had been written in the final months of the singer's life. The earlier will, dated 13 June 2007, stated that half of his assets were to be given to Nicoletta and the other half was to be split equally between his three daughters from his first marriage and his daughter with Nicoletta. The later will, dated 29 July 2007, built on the first one and bequeathed his US holdings to his widow.[66]

As it transpired, his estate was split in compliance with Italian law. Half was shared equally between all four of his daughters and the rest went to Nicoletta.

A fight between the three daughters from his first marriage and his widow over how his assets were to be split was avoided, however, with all sides coming to an agreement by July 2008. Key to this was Nicoletta renouncing ownership of Pavarotti's holiday villa in Pesaro on the north-east coast of Italy, meaning his eldest three daughters would take possession of it.

Anna Maria Bernini, the lawyer for Nicoletta Mantovani, told regional newspaper *Il Resto del Carlino*, "The assets have been divided equitably and in keeping with legal parameters."[67] She would not, however, give any further details of the settlement between the two sides.

CHARITABLE TRUSTS AND THE CHILDREN: RAY CHARLES (DIED 10 JUNE 2004)

Just over 18 months before he died, Ray Charles gathered his 12 children from multiple relationships for a summit at a hotel close to Los Angeles International Airport. He told them he was ill – that he was dying – and outlined what they could all expect to receive in his will.

Much of his estate would go into the Ray Charles Foundation, a charitable body designed to offer "support to educational institutions and non-profit education programs" to aid young people affected by hearing disorders.[68] Each of his dozen children would receive $500,000 in the shape of an irrevocable trust that would be paid out over the following five years.[69] Accepting the money would mean them waiving any future claims against the estate.

Some of the children claim Charles had hinted there was more to come. Another presumption was that they would inherit his name and likeness rights for licensing and merchandising purposes. They were badly mistaken. Everything would go into the foundation.

The children would eventually take action against Joe Adams, Charles's manager since 1962 and the person he had put in charge of the Ray Charles Foundation. They accused him of mismanaging the foundation and also looked to claim termination notices of highly valuable composition copyrights created by Charles. Both these cases will be looked at in more detail in later chapters of this book.

"After Charles' death, Adams ended up with virtually unchallenged power over the estate," wrote the *Los Angeles Times* in 2008 as the war between Adams and Charles's children escalated. "He was head of Ray Charles Enterprises, director of the foundation and trustee of the children's trusts."[70] The children also claimed they were unable to get proper and complete accounting from the estate with regard to how much revenue it was generating and where it was going.

His son, Ray Charles Jr, detailed the issues relating to the foundation and the trusts in his book about family life and business life with his father. He claimed his mother was eventually pushed out of Ray Charles's business operations by Adams.

Ray Jr said, on receiving the invite to the December 2002 meeting with the rest of his siblings, that he knew "something important was in the air because he had never called us all together before" but that he also felt "an uncomfortable feeling in the pit of my stomach that something was wrong".[71]

He recalled that Ray Snr "looked uncomfortable as the children began to assemble in the room" but that, as soon as he had outlined what was happening with the trusts and the foundation, he "seemed relieved, as though a burden had been lifted off him".[72]

According to Ray Jr, Adams spoke after Ray Snr had sat down, saying that he felt a distribution of funds to the children over a four-year period was preferable to them receiving it all in one lump sum.

"Mr. Adams would serve as trustee for all our trust funds," wrote Ray Jr. "As I listened to him, it was clear Mr. Adams would be in control of my father's estate and our individual trusts. After this uncomfortable announcement, we all gathered around my father to take family photos. These would become the first and only pictures of almost all of my father's offspring together with him."[73]

Ray Jr claimed, immediately following his father's death, that Adams locked him out of the offices of Ray Charles Enterprises and was initially barring the family from entering the private viewing room at the funeral home where the body of Ray Charles was laid out. Adams eventually relented and they were allowed in.

"Mr. Adams stood there, watching us," wrote Ray Jr. "We were intensely aware of his eyes on us. Even in death, we were not allowed to be alone with my father. We struggled with a mixture of grief and anger."[74]

This was all a prelude to a long and bitter battle over control of the estate and its revenues between Joe Adams and the children of Ray Charles. Adams himself passed away on 3 July 2018 at the age of 94.[75]

CHAPTER 3

Controlling Interests

Fights Over Ownership of Estates

Outside the music industry trade press, music estates tend to be covered in the media only when things go spectacularly wrong. There are often issues with the will (see Chapter 2), especially if the artist involved has died intestate. Addressing the absence of a will can be a convoluted and protracted legal process, but typically some sort of resolution is eventually reached.

The topics that the wider media tend to latch on to, however, come after this point, when those running the estates start to fall out with each other. This is frequently over money, but it can also be over the direction in which the artist's legacy is moving (or not moving). Or it can be when the family claims to have been sidelined or hoodwinked out of the business by nefarious, duplicitous and shadowy business figures, such as a former accountant or manager.

These are the stories packed with salacious details, intrigue and years of bubbling animosity that can explode in the most dramatic – and the most public – manner imaginable. Some erupt suddenly in controversy and then all involved might seek to find a resolution. Others are hauled through the courts for years, even decades, and the longer this takes, the more obstinate each side becomes and the less able (even defiantly unwilling) they are to find a compromise, often with mounting legal bills destroying the estate through financial exsanguination.

Inter-family fighting is, simply, an unfortunate reality for many estates, especially when a star has been married multiple times or has children from multiple relationships. Historic animosities and politics can shape what happens to the estate, mainly over not only who controls it but also what share of the resulting revenues they receive.

"There is the estate where you sometimes have the kids from the first marriage, the kids from the second marriage and the wife who was from the third marriage who is still alive and who hates the kids from the first marriage and the second marriage and they hate her and now they're all bound together," says Bob Donnelly, a transactional attorney at legal firm Fox Rothschild. "Sometimes, unfortunately, without the benefit of a document which guides exactly who's in control. That can really get to be a food fight."

Another lawyer at a major international legal firm working with A-list artist sighs when asked about this. "Artists are colourful and creative people and they often lead lives that are not so typical; as a result, they sometimes have complex family or personal relationships," they say, alluding to years of professional strain that comes with having to try and navigate festering issues between competing and conflicting heirs. They choose not to mention any by name but they pull enough faces at key points in the conversation to make it clear that sitting in the middle of unaligned heirs is arduous in the extreme.

TRYING TO MAKE THE DYSFUNCTIONAL FUNCTIONAL

Jeff Liebenson, a New York-based music lawyer and founder of Liebenson Law, reiterates this and points out that problems regularly occur in estates simply because the heirs are stepping into a business world – one that is complex, esoteric and often confusing to outsiders – of which they only have passing knowledge and have to become experts in very quickly.

"Often the beneficiaries – the family, the survivors – are not as good at business or they don't get it," he says. "When representing estates, it's not just a matter of identifying the IP [intellectual property] issues and finding the opportunities. Sometimes it's about dealing with challenging people who might be descendants and who have unrealistic expectations. Or maybe, for instance, there are three children that have to agree but they never agreed about anything – but now they're in charge of this business enterprise. It's just not well run because they can't agree."

He continues, "When there's a team of people, you almost wish they would just say, 'Look, we're not going to get into something that's going to cause everything to ground to a halt. Why don't we all agree just once that there should be a structure and we all agree to employ someone from outside to make all the decisions? That way things can run in a straight line, with a single vision, whether we agree with it or not, and we'll share equally in the proceeds. That way we'll have something instead of having nothing.' Otherwise, it can be a challenge with all these conflicting personalities."

Jim Griffin is a consultant for a number of estates and says that they are often very delicate structures anyway, and that any long-standing problems among heirs become amplified all too easily, meaning the most minor of disagreements can escalate quickly. Estates, he feels, are often dangerously dysfunctional enterprises and always have to be approached as such.

"On a psychological level, these are very precarious affairs," he says. "That is unfortunate, but inherent. That's the first thing that becomes super clear as you go down this road. What becomes very important is that heirs need to work things out amongst themselves in many cases – but maybe never will."

THE NEXT GENERATION: WHERE THINGS START TO COME UNDONE

A recurring theme that came up in interviews for this book was that, even if estates are clearly and cleanly set up by the artist before they die and even if all the heirs are in harmony, things can and will shift when the estate moves down a generation, where a form of meta-estate crisis, uncertainty or recklessness can kick in.

Some of that is for emotional reasons – where the next generation of heirs may not have known the original artist and have no emotional investment in their decisions. And some of that can be for financial reasons – where the artist's work is naturally ageing and the estate is seeing declining revenues, and so sometimes desperate measures can be taken to try and revive it, or at least to squeeze as much money out of it as possible before it dissolves completely.

This is all something that Costa Pilavachi, with his years of experience in the classic record-label world dealing with long-established estates, feels is an inevitability of the estates business. Control of an estate dropping down a generation can mark a dramatic gear shift for it as a business. "A good estate is one that lifts the whole thing, that finds new ways to exploit the artist in a good way, to generate money for everybody, to promulgate the reputation of the artist to a new generation of people," he says. "It's the next wave of people [running estates, rather than immediate family] who are less concerned [about running things]."

Owen J. Sloane, a partner at US legal firm Eisner Law, concurs with this. "A lot of these people were not in the entertainment business," he says of heirs of music estates. "Some [heirs] are more interested in the artistic integrity and others are more interested in making money [...] Some people are interested in cashing out, walking away and just having a nice lump sum payment; and others are really into running the business and being active. That creates a good deal of tension among multiple survivors."

One label catalogue executive says one of the worst situations an estate – or, more precisely, the people who have to deal with an estate – can find itself in is when heirs take over but they only had the most tenuous relationship with the artist whose estate they find themselves running. If the artist had no children or was never married and they also died intestate, their estate could go to estranged family members or half-siblings who had no real relationship with the artist. They are parachuted into a highly lucrative business and they quickly find they are ill-suited to the job at hand.

"They now think they are rich people in the music industry, even though they are not," says the executive about these individuals who luck into an estate in this way. "They are really, really pushing for money. Therefore the advances that they are looking for are stretching reality. For example, I put in what I thought was a generous sum with one estate [of a superstar act] for a particular project. They came back with a much, much higher number. It was a ridiculous number. It was not going to work. I could not persuade my company to do that."

On the positive side, a senior record company executive with decades of experience here argues that, from the label's perspective at least, an estate passing down a generation can make it more in tune with business and technological changes, and more willing to experiment and not cling to the old ways of doing business.

Never has that been more critical than since the late 1990s, when digital started to change the way the business had to operate. "When the torch passes to the next generation, they start looking at more interesting potential uses," says the executive, mentioning the children of a number of major global stars who are now old enough to work for the estate and have begun spearheading digital initiatives that would have been rejected outright a few years earlier by their surviving parents.

The head of catalogue at a label says they also have experienced this generational shift, making estates more open to ideas, more eclectic in what they do and generally being more progressive. From the label's perspective, this sometimes has to become a waiting game, as pushback from the initial heirs can give way to a more accommodating next generation.

Celeste Bell is the only child of Poly Styrene of X-Ray Spex, so inheritance of her mother's estate and her running of it has proven to be straightforward and devoid of drama. She says she is thankful that it was not a giant estate with lots of interested parties competing for control as she is able to do things independently and in a more measured way. "The more money there is in an estate," she says, "the more drama there is."

Specific cases show just how problematic things can get. So what happens to an estate, both commercially and culturally, in the middle of a power struggle?

THE "SECOND MARRIAGE TINDERBOX": JOHNNY HALLYDAY, TOM PETTY, CONWAY TWITTY AND LUCIANO PAVAROTTI

The wicked stepmother is a recurring character in fairy tales, often shot through with a hefty dose of misogyny. It is also a narrative that is recycled again and again in media coverage of the world of music estates, where the children of a deceased pop star (and it is almost always a male pop star) are being pushed out of an estate as the new wife takes full control.

Of course, this is so very rarely the reality. Families are made up of complex relationships and politics, but when an estate worth millions is being fought over it becomes catnip for the tabloids who like to reduce it all to simple – and often misleading – tales of cruel stepmothers cheating the children of a dead pop star out of their inheritance and their birthright. That is not to say that this does not happen, but the stories that tend to make the press are the pressure-cooker ones or those that have already exploded in the most horrific manner imaginable.

*   *   *

Country singer Conway Twitty (real name Harold Lloyd Jenkins) died on 5 June 1993, leaving behind an estate worth an estimated $15 million. His will had not been updated since 1984 and so did not include his third, and final, wife, Dolores Virginia Henry Jenkins (known commonly as Dee). He had four children – Michael from his first marriage and Joni, Kathy and Jimmy from his second marriage. They were left everything in his will with the exception of $50,000 that Twitty had left to his own mother, Velma Jenkins.[1] Tennessee law, the state where Twitty resided, stated that the last surviving spouse was also entitled to a share of the estate, even if they were not named in the will.

The situation was made more fraught because Dee was a friend of his daughter Joni when they were teenagers and before she entered into a relationship with Twitty in the 1970s (they married in 1987) and started working on his business operations. "I didn't want to hate Dee," said Joni in an *Investigation Discovery* documentary about the Twitty estate in 2011. "I didn't. I didn't want to get to this place with her; but she drew the line, and we had to go to battle to protect our father."[2]

The children were, however, split on the issue of Dee's inheritance and how much they believed she was due.[3]

A concurrent fight between the four children and the two executors of the estate (Hugh Carden, who had been Twitty's business manager since 1967, and Don Garris, a certified public accountant who had worked with Twitty since 1972) also broke out. Dee had been left an $1.8 million home and $900,000 in life insurance benefits – a sum the children believed was more than enough.

The children lived in (and paid rent on) condominiums on the grounds of Twitty City[4] which was described as "a cross between a family compound and a business venture" as it also housed a museum and music venue.[5] However, Twitty City was sold a year after Twitty died and the children had to move out. Dee received a third of the proceeds and the four children were given the rest. Kathy and Joni appealed against the decision but it remained in place.[6]

In April 1996, the executors proposed a compromise whereby the four children would inherit Twitty's songwriter and artist royalties (valued at $3.4 million) while Dee would take control of his name and likeness (valued at $380,000). The children turned the offer down and a private auction between the two sides was set up. The children collectively bid $4.2 million to acquire his music rights. In June 1999, an appellate court ruling gave the children full control over his intellectual property rights. "It was Father's

Day so Joni and I took the final judgment out to dad and we laid it at his grave," said Kathy Twitty. "We took him justice."[7]

The years of fighting over control, however, was seen as causing enormous damage to the estate's worth and potential. "I think the unfortunate thing of the estate battle is that it has, in a sense, prevented carrying his legacy forward," said Robert K. Oermann, a music writer and friend of Twitty.[8]

The Twitty dispute is certainly more public than other inter-family tussles where the battles may go to court but are rarely spread across the pages of *People* magazine or become the focus of salacious documentaries.

*   *   *

The estate of Luciano Pavarotti was mired in controversy in its early years because he had significant debts and had left two wills with uncertainty over how his assets should be split between his widow, Nicoletta Mantovani, and the three daughters from his first marriage (see Chapter 2).

Mantovani was quick to downplay any sense of a rift between her (and her child with Pavarotti) and the opera star's older daughters.[9] It did take, however, until July 2008 for Mantovani and the three daughters to reach a settlement over how the estate was to be divided up, sending out a media message that they were all "now firm friends" and in full agreement about everything.[10] The fact that things were resolved within a year of his death suggests that any differences between the two sides were swiftly – and silently – settled.

*   *   *

The situation with the Tom Petty estate erupted publicly – and in an extremely ugly manner – in the summer of 2019 but was fixed by Christmas that same year.

Petty passed away on 2 October 2017 and his will had been split equally between his two daughters from his first marriage, Adria Petty and Annakim Violette, and his second wife, Dana York Petty. In April 2019, however, Dana filed a petition in probate court relating to control of the estate and trust.

"According to her filing, Dana York Petty is the sole trustee of her late husband's trust," reported *Variety*. "The trust directs her to establish an entity to control Petty's catalog, with equal participation from his daughters. Adria and Annakim have interpreted 'equal participation' to mean they should get control of the entity by a two-thirds majority vote. Dana York Petty has argued that a professional manager should run the operation with consent from all parties."[11]

This was swiftly followed by Adria filing her own probate petition that would give her control over her father's catalogue.

In mid-May 2019, both of Petty's daughters filed a suit in Los Angeles County court against his widow and a number of other defendants[12] who worked with her, relating to a competing LLC, Tom Petty Legacy, that had been set up.

At the end of May 2019, things moved up another gear when Dana filed a new appeal against the two daughters. She was seeking to use Petty's assets to fund Tom Petty Legacy, but the daughters objected.

A settlement was eventually reached on 18 December 2019. The compromise was to set up a new entity (Tom Petty Legacy LLC) to handle the estate's affairs with each family member having an equal share.[13] Also as part of the settlement, Petty's manager Dimitriades was replaced by Will Botwin and Coran Capshaw at Red Light Management, who would "guide, advise and execute on behalf of the estate".[14]

* * *

For the estate of French superstar Johnny Hallyday (real name Jean-Philippe Smet), the dispute was over not just an issue of disinheritance but also which jurisdiction would decide what happened with his estate.

Hallyday died on 5 December 2017. He had been married five times to four different women (he married Adeline Blondieau twice). Hallyday had a son (David Hallyday) from his first marriage to singer Sylvie Vartan and a daughter (Laura Smet) from his four-year relationship with actor Nathalie Baye. His final marriage, to Laeticia Hallyday (née Boudou), lasted from 1996 until his death and the couple had adopted two daughters.

When he died, Hallyday's fortune was estimated at €100 million, but in his will he had left everything to Laeticia (who was also executor of his estate), having disinherited his two eldest children. Hallyday, reportedly, had said he had made adequate provisions for them in his lifetime. His will had been written in July 2014, in English, when he lived in Los Angeles.[15]

In March 2018, his eldest son and daughter went to court in France to stake their claim. They were also seeking to have direct involvement in posthumous releases of his music. His final album, *Mon pays c'est l'amour*, was released in October 2018 and broke first-week sales records in France, selling 780,177 copies in its opening seven days, with 97.2 per cent of those sales being on CD.[16] It stayed at number one in France for 12 consecutive weeks and had sold 1.5 million copies by the end of 2018.[17]

The central issue for the estate was that, under French law, it is impossible to disinherit one's children. That would have meant Laeticia got 25 per cent and each of his four children would have got 18.75 per cent. Lawyers acting for his widow argued that Hallyday's will was drawn up under US law, where he lived with Laeticia and their adopted daughters, and allowed him to distribute it as he saw fit.[18]

In April 2018, Hallyday's eldest children, David and Laura, were able to impose a temporary freeze on a number of Hallyday's real-estate assets as well as his music royalties in France.[19] Before the ruling and with animosities running at their highest, Laeticia spoke to weekly magazine *Le Point* about how their relationship was turning toxic.[20]

In an incredibly modern twist, in May 2019, his two eldest children offered the locations of Hallyday's Instagram posts between 2012 and 2017 as evidence, claiming he spent at least 151 days in France in 2015 and 168 days in 2016. He also spent eight consecutive months, due to his illness with lung cancer, in France in 2017. The French court accepted their argument and decided that it had, as the *New York Times* put it, "competence to decide on Mr. Hallyday's estate".[21]

At the end of May 2019, the French court ruled that Hallyday was a French resident and therefore the country's inheritance laws should apply. As such, Hallyday's estate must be shared between his widow and four children, overruling the fact it was drafted in the US.[22] By August 2020, it was all over and all sides were putting on a unified face, although details of the settlement were not made public. The *Daily Mail*, unsurprisingly, chose in its coverage to refer to Laeticia as the "'wicked' widow of French Elvis Johnny Hallyday", playing on the fairy-tale cliché.[23] It claimed to be merely repeating claims made in French magazines, but the fact that it referred to her as such in its headline in a 2020 feature on the case speaks volumes.

While many of the estate battles are explained in terms of how much money is at stake, for family members the most important part – and the most emotional part – is about the legacy of the artist and how the estate is run in a way that builds and protects it. Money makes the headlines, but directing what the estate actually does is often at the heart of these battles.

CUTTING A PARENT OUT OF AN ESTATE: MICHAEL JACKSON

Joe Jackson made Michael Jackson the star he became, with his relentless drive to make his sons world-famous in the Jackson 5. He also broke Michael Jackson. He pushed and pushed and pushed…

"He was a great trainer, and he spent a lot of money and time working with us," remembered Michael Jackson of his earliest days going to talent shows and auditions as a young child along with his brothers. "Talent is something God gives to a person, but our father taught us to cultivate it."[24]

There was a much darker side, however. He was a cruel and violent disciplinarian who regarded his sons as his way to make a fortune and also lived vicariously through them, making up for the fact that his own musical career never progressed beyond Gary, Indiana.

"Joseph believed in the value and impact of brute force as a disciplinary tool," wrote J. Randy Taraborrelli in his biography of Michael Jackson. "'Either you're a winner in this life, or a loser,' he liked to say. 'And none of my kids are gonna be losers.'"[25] Regular physical punishments were the manifestation of this toxic parenting, beating his children and even holding Michael upside down by one leg to thrash him. He once locked him in a closet for hours as a punishment.[26]

For decades, Joe treated Michael as a cash cow, verbally and emotionally abusing him, but never letting him have his full independence. In his 2002 will, Jackson served his revenge. All his assets were moved into a holding entity called the Michael Jackson Family Trust. Joe Jackson's name was nowhere to be seen on the will. All his assets were split between his mother, Katherine, his children and assorted children's charities.[27]

In November 2009, mere months after Jackson's death, Brian Oxman (acting for Joe Jackson) was arguing to get his client a stake in the estate. Superior Court Judge Mitchell Beckloff made it official. "Joe Jackson takes none of this estate," he said. "This is a decision his son made."[28]

The judge did, however, say that Joe was allowed to pursue a motion to get an allowance from the estate because he claimed his son had been financially supporting him before his death. In January 2010, however, the Jackson estate filed papers stating it should not have to pay Joe Jackson's monthly allowance of $15,000.[29] In June 2010, Joe Jackson admitted defeat and dropped his claim for a stipend.

A *New York Post* story in August 2014 tracked Joe Jackson down to his $500,000 condo in Las Vegas. "[T]the man who ruled his brood with an iron fist and icy demeanor is frail and alone," it said. In its bleak portrait of a fallen man, it quoted an unnamed insider who said Joe Jackson was "no longer part of the family".[30]

It heaped misery upon misery by saying that Joe had "scrounged for cash" to make ends meet and was even reduced to selling bottles of perfume, with Michael Jackson's image on them, in a Vegas strip mall. That olfactory enterprise was a short-lived one as the mall demanded Joe show proof that he had the rights to sell products bearing his son's image. He could not and his retail operation ceased.[31]

He was, according to the *Post*, trying to carve out a career charging $50,000 appearance fees. There were, said the report, "few takers". It ended with an insider hammering home just how bleak Joe's pariah status had become. "The phone never rings," they said. "The doorbell is always quiet."[32]

Joe Jackson died on 27 June 2018 aged 89. His death came just two days after the ninth anniversary of the passing of Michael Jackson.[33]

THE DNA TESTS: JOHN LENNON AND JOHNNIE TAYLOR

People stepping forward after a pop star dies claiming to be their long-lost child is an occupational hazard for the modern estate. This was something the Prince estate had to contend with, sifting out the opportunists and fantasists from those who had a legitimate claim, with over 30 claimants being ruled out before six more had to submit to genetic testing.[34] Other major estates face this and the claims are usually processed – and almost always rejected – swiftly and quietly.

In November 2011, Canadian dentist Michael Zuk bought one of John Lennon's molars for £19,500.[35] Two years later, Zuk was suggesting he could clone Lennon from DNA in the tooth, prompting inevitable outrage at the very idea.[36] It all moved up another gear in 2018 when he said the tooth would be the deciding factor in any paternity suits and claims on the Lennon estate.

"I am looking for people who believe they are John Lennon's child and have a claim to his estate and hopefully I can legitimise their claim," Zuk told the *Sun*. "John was a very popular guy who was having sex with lots of women and I doubt birth control was on his mind."[37]

He then outlined what – for want of a better term – his business model would be. "I would ask anyone who is participating to sign a commission agreement which would mean if they were related they would pay my company a percentage of their inheritance," he said. "Like a finder's fee."[38] To date, no formal dental DNA-powered claim on the late Beatle's estate has been made.

*　*　*

The case of R&B and soul singer Johnnie Taylor, who died on 31 May 2000, took the issue of DNA testing to whole new levels. He had died intestate and left behind an estate worth an estimated $1.3 million which is, in the wider world of estates, small beer. It was mostly made up of property and was set to be divided equally between his six acknowledged children. In the August following his death, a petition was filed in the Dallas probate court from Fonda Bryant, who claimed to be Taylor's daughter. She had been kept secret from the rest of Taylor's family and news of her appearance caused enormous uproar among the other children.

"He only claimed us," said Floyd Taylor, one of his sons. "So when it came out of the woodwork that he had more children, it was like, 'Whoa! OK.'"[39] The six acknowledged children joined against Bryant. At a hearing in autumn 2000, there was another twist and Tyrone "TJ" Hooker showed up to the courtroom also claiming to be Taylor's child.

Hooker had no attorney of his own so he joined with Bryant and had her lawyer, Mark McCraw, represent them both. As if those weren't enough twists, a third person, Schiffon Brown, came forward claiming to be yet another of Taylor's unacknowledged children. Bryant, Hooker and Brown joined forces as the other six children circled their wagons.

Making this the estate version of Monty Python's Spanish Inquisition sketch, things took yet another dramatic turn. Taylor had married his second wife, Gerlean, in 1970 but they split in 1996 and divorced in the spring of 2000, just a month before Taylor died. In the divorce documents, it was decreed that Gerlean (who was mother to the youngest two of Taylor's acknowledged children) would get half of his estate. In order for her to get her 50 per cent, Taylor's $1.2 million house would have to be sold – and that could only happen when all the estate issues were resolved. The most pressing need was to confirm or dismiss the three paternity claims that had come forward since his death.

To settle the three paternity claims, McCraw suggested that, rather than draw on Taylor's DNA, a sibling study be conducted (taking DNA from the acknowledged children to compare against the DNA of the three claimants). As a back-up plan, McCraw suggested exhuming Taylor and taking DNA from his corpse. Faced with this upsetting possibility, Sabrina Taylor agreed to give a sample of her DNA so this sibling study could be carried out. Four months later, in January 2001, it was found there was a problem with the tests. The lab conducting the tests found there was what they called "a mutation in the DNA" of one of the samples but would not say whose sample it was. Fresh samples from Sabrina and the three claimants had to be taken. It took until October 2002 for an heirship judgment to be issued and it was ruled that all three claimants were indeed Taylor's children. Floyd Taylor, one of the original six acknowledged heirs, was far from happy with the result. "For the courts to give us two more sisters and another brother, I thought was very crummy," he said.[40]

With all nine heirs confirmed, the sale of the $1.2 million house could go ahead. Gerlean bought out the other half owned by the children. They then divided up – minus all their legal fees and taxes – what was left. It was, frankly, very little. "When we got finished we got a check for, like, 2,000-something dollars from the sale of the house and everything," said Fonda. "That was it."[41]

Hooker was more sanguine. "We did not receive a lot of money from the estate and we were kind of bamboozled out of a whole lot of our inheritance, to be honest with you," he said. "It's time for us to come together, put all the hatred to the side and be a family and celebrate this man, his music and his legacy the way it should be – as a family."[42]

THE ESTATE THAT "DISAPPEARED": MARC BOLAN

To say that the Marc Bolan estate was a mess is a towering underestimation. This is almost certainly the most chaotic, the most incomprehensible and the most *unknowable* estate of any major star. Trying to figure out exactly what happened is like trying to catch a shadow in a glass.

Marc Bolan (real name Mark Feld) was killed in a car crash on 16 September 1977. His death occurred exactly a month after the passing of Elvis Presley and on the exact same day as Maria Callas.

Bolan was one of the biggest stars in Britain in the early 1970s and at the peak of his fame with T. Rex between late 1970 and late 1973 he had four number one singles and a further seven Top 10 hits. He had three number one albums in the same time period.[43]

The problems of the estate all go back to Bolan trying to hold on to as much of his fortune as international tax laws would allow. In September 2003, a British TV documentary – *Who Got Marc Bolan's Millions?* – tried to get to the bottom of it all. It claimed that Bolan "appeared to have made millions" but was only worth £10,000 when he died. Bolan's brother, Harry Feld, said, "None of my family have got anything from it. So it's just lying dormant. What we used to call the Bermuda Triangle. It's all missing. It's still there, but you can't get it."[44]

In the first wave of his success in the early 1970s, Marc set up two different music rights companies, Wizard Artists and Warrior Music Projects Ltd (previously T. Rex Ltd). The latter was 60 per cent owned by Bolan with the other 40 per cent owned by June Child, his wife at the time.[45] [46] Bolan was in control of his masters (the official original recordings) after he set up the T. Rex Wax Co label in 1971. This was described as "little more than a vanity affair" that "had no use for anything other than Marc's own releases". It struck a tape-lease deal with EMI towards the end of that year which gave him control over what was released under the T. Rex name.[47]

In her biography of Bolan, Lesley-Ann Jones tries to map out the complex business timeline here as a variety of companies covering his rights were set up in 1973 and 1974. "Lawyers and accountants set up offshore companies/ accounts to handle Marc's financial affairs: 19 July [1973], Wizard (Bahamas); early August 1973, Wizard (Jersey) and Wizard (Delaware); 11 February 1974, Wizard Publishing," she wrote.[48]

Mark Paytress, another Bolan biographer, also attempted to cut through the business obfuscation here. He added that Wizard Artists, which had been originally been set up in 1972, had its share capital transferred to Wizard's operations in the Bahamas in July 1973.[49]

"It was all a clever tax-avoidance scheme," said the *Who Got Marc Bolan's Millions?* documentary. "The idea was that half of T. Rex's songs were owned by Warrior Music with record sales taxed in Britain. The other half was owned by Wizard Artists and claimed as written or recorded abroad – and so declared as foreign earnings to avoid tax. The stakes were high. In 1972, Bolan's songs earned more than £2 million."[50]

Musicians in particular were being hit by high tax rates in Britain in the late 1960s and 1970s, with some like The Rolling Stones, David Bowie and Rod Stewart all choosing to live abroad for periods of time to reduce what they paid in tax in the UK.[51]

Paytress argued that this complex business and rights structure, all designed to "alleviate the burden of the British tax system", was a doomed enterprise. "[W]hat may have looked extremely beneficial back in 1973 acquired a more sinister aspect after 1977," he wrote. "That's because the Marc Bolan Estate – a faceless edifice that hid behind a wall of solicitors – continued to reap the benefits of the Bolan legacy while Marc's dependants were left in the dark and unrewarded."[52]

Things started to unravel when Bolan and June Child separated. The assets of Warrior Music Projects Ltd were transferred to Wizard Jersey and Wizard Publishing (based in Delaware) at some point around 26 July 1973 to prevent her from making money from it (despite her 40 per cent stake).[53] "When someone sets up a foreign trust, it is quite common for that trust to be set up in a way which means that it is not in the control of the person who generates the income that goes into the trust," was the gnomic take of James

Ware, Bolan's lawyer in the final year of his life.[54] The end result was that neither the tax office nor Child could claim this money, but also Bolan himself ceded control of it.

In Bolan's will, made just days after he and Child separated, he named both Child and Gloria Jones, the singer he left Child for, as recipients. Lesley-Ann Jones dates the writing of this will to some point in October or November 1973.[55] Named beneficiaries included Bolan's parents (to get £20,000), the parents of Child (£5,000), Tony Howard (his manager, £10,000), Mickey Finn (his fellow band member in T. Rex, £10,000), Tony Visconti (his producer, £5,000), Teresa Whipman (his former girlfriend, £5,000) and a number of charities getting the remainder (described as "a huge, incalculable sum").[56]

Archive footage of Bolan in 1975 being interviewed on the *Pop Quest* TV show reveals that he – and this was, after all, a man unafraid to declare his own genius at every turn – knew himself that pecuniary matters were not his forte. "I'm not a businessman, you know," he said. "I'm still a little kid. I just do what I want to do and hope it works out [...] I cheat a lot as well."[57]

Bad investments and a fully hedonistic lifestyle – plus the slow desiccation of his pop career – saw his fortune dwindle. In a panic, he dropped his legal team and brought in a new accountant and a new lawyer in 1977 to try and help him straighten things out.

Bolan was planning to marry Gloria Jones and was in the limbo period between decree nisi and decree absolute when the car he was in, which Jones was driving, hit a tree and he was killed. Jones, as she was not married to him at the time of his death, got nothing. "We, the family, lost everything," she said.[58]

Rumours abounded that Bolan had written a second will just after the birth of Rolan on 26 September 1975 to include his son but it was never found. Lesley-Ann Jones claimed this replacement will included "details of a Jersey trust fund for the child" but that "this version is 'lost' – believed destroyed by someone close to Marc." Piling on the intrigue, she said the death of Marc's manager Tony Howard (in 2001) "puts paid to further investigation into the widely-held view that Howard was more responsible for the fate of Marc's fortune than was previously thought".[59]

Paytress said the sheer existence of this Jersey-based trust fund for Rolan supported claims that Bolan had indeed made a second will that included his son. "We will never discover the whole truth now that Tony Howard is dead," said one Bolan acquaintance speaking anonymously, "but I am certain that he knew more than he let on."[60]

James Ware, his last lawyer, refused to confirm either way if this second will existed. "I discussed with Marc in great detail many things about his personal life," he said. "But my discussions with Marc about what he might or might not have put in a will are between me and a client, although that client is dead. That is not something that I wish to discuss on television."[61]

It all got even more disastrous. Unnamed representatives of Bolan's offshore trust sent June Child a cheque, described as an act of charity, but in cashing it she sent up a red flag to the tax office, which was able to link her to Bolan's offshore companies.

"Bolan had set up his offshore empire to avoid the crippling taxes at the time. After his death, the taxman discovered that he had never paid any tax at all […] To get the unpaid tax from Marc's offshore companies, the taxman could now use the unlikely target of his widow, June. On paper she was still a director of Warrior Music, which meant June could be held responsible for unpaid tax from the very company she'd been cut out of years before."[62]

The initial tax assessment was for £170,000 and Child, still listed as a director of Warrior Music, could have been liable for it. She had to take legal action against Warrior to recover her share. Across all of Bolan's companies, the Inland Revenue said there was £2,811,116 in unpaid taxes. Between them, the Inland Revenue, Bolan's offshore companies, Warrior and Child struck a deal, the details of which were not made public.

Who, ultimately, got Bolan's publishing income after his death was shrouded in mystery and secrecy, all of it protected by trust laws. Brian Dunham of Wizard Publishing teased out some information, but only about where the money goes, not who receives it. "The money from all of Marc's creations goes into an account in the Caribbean," he said. "It used to be in the Bahamas; it's now moved to the Caymans." He shrugged. "Offshore accounts."[63]

Then, as if invoking the code of omertà, he said, "I have no idea where the money goes. On a need-to-know basis, I do my job to the best of my ability and that's as far as I take it [pulls face]. I don't know how you feel about that answer, but it's the best you're going to get!"[64] He laughed.

Paytress argued that Tony Howard, as Bolan's business manager, "should have foreseen the potential pitfalls" while noting that others blame "the faceless legal eagles who set up the operation" back in 1973 and 1974. As a result of all this confusion, Bolan's masters "have been sold on and split up on several occasions to the highest bidder", the upshot being that "Bolan's music and reputation has been devalued […] with shoddy product and bad vibes tarnishing a rich heritage". There is, according to Paytress, a grim irony here as Bolan had tried to ensure he controlled his masters and publishing in his lifetime, but the chaos that followed his death has meant his "posthumous career has endured a precarious, prestige-threatening existence".[65]

Tony Visconti, who produced many of T. Rex's biggest records, helped break the impasse when he pursued Wizard over producer royalties for almost a quarter of a century, finally reaching an out-of-court settlement in 2001.[66] "The Estate of Marc Bolan stopped Rolan getting any regular payments," he said of the case in 2007. "They were also holding up my own royalties as producer. I successfully sued and it opened the gates for Rolan, because I got through. The Bolan fortune was quite a huge sum."[67]

Speaking to author Lesley-Ann Jones for her biography of Marc (published in 2012), Rolan explained the complexity of his father's business dealings and the scale of the copyrights mess he left behind. "The Wizard [Bahamas] company no longer exists," he said. "It was acquired by the Spirit Music Group in New York, with whom I am working now. But 'rights' are still all over the place. I'm still looking for questions to be answered. There are still many things that we need to sort out [...] The people who took the money know what they did with it."[68]

After a long legal process, the Bolan trust eventually agreed to buy Rolan a house in Los Angeles as well as give him a "controlled" annual allowance to be paid out of the trust fund.[69]

In July 2013, Rolan filed a $2 million legal action in Los Angeles against Westminster Music Limited (formerly Essex Music International Limited), claiming he was the sole owner of his father's catalogue in the US. His argument was that Westminster did not renew the one-year contract it signed with Bolan in 1968 and, as such, everything should revert back to him as Bolan's only child.[70] In October 2014, a settlement was reached and Rolan was able to obtain 144 Bolan copyrights in the US.[71] While not the full estate, it was at least a start. Rolan Feld began aggressively policing his assets and in August 2017 he sued Sony Pictures, Media Rights Capital, Bambino Films and others for the use of the Bolan song 'Deborah' in the movie *Baby Driver*. He claimed the rights had not been cleared for use in the film.[72] The case was eventually settled in February 2018.[73]

THE WAR WITH THE FOUNDATION: RAY CHARLES

As mentioned in Chapter 2, the children of Ray Charles were told before he died that each of them would receive a lump sum payment but that the rest of his fortune and all future income would go into the Ray Charles Foundation. It would be run by Joe Adams, Charles's manager since 1961, and the money it gathered would be given to education and non-profit organisations helping children with hearing disorders. Adams was also in charge of running Ray Charles Enterprises and was trustee of the children's trust funds. Ray Charles Jr bleakly referred to this as an "uncomfortable announcement".[74]

After Charles's death in 2004, his children and Adams were almost immediately at loggerheads over both the very existence of the foundation and how it was run. Several of his children took legal action against Adams, claiming their father's legacy was being maladministered by his former manager and that his reputation was being badly tarnished as a result. They were seeking to take back control of his name and image. Adams, via a spokesperson, called the claims of the children "old, baseless allegations".[75]

"After Charles' death, Adams ended up with virtually unchallenged power over the estate," noted the *Los Angeles Times*.[76] The children claimed that Adams had been paid almost $1.2 million between 2005 and 2006, something that was described as "improper compensation" in the claim. It was also alleged Adams had sold some of Charles's master recordings.[77]

In April 2012, the foundation sued the adult children of Ray Charles for sending copyright termination notices for a number of Charles's compositions (see Chapter 10). The foundation argued that it owned the rights and depended on the resulting income "to continue the wishes of Ray Charles".[78]

By January 2018, the courts ruled in favour of the children, allowing them to move on reclaiming 60 of Charles's songs. The Ray Charles Foundation immediately responded by saying it planned to appeal against the decision. "The children who filed these termination notices violated the sacred promise they made," said Valerie Ervin, president of the Ray Charles Foundation, in a statement. "They took their father's money and now come back for more. The law is very unsettled in these matters and we intend to seek resolution through the courts."[79]

Joe Adams passed away in July 2018.[80] The foundation remains with Valerie Ervin at the helm. "The Ray Charles Foundation continues its ever-evolving mission as a major philanthropic force assessing needs of communities and organizations where merit is clear but funds unavailable," says its website.[81]

WHEN A BANK RUNS THE ESTATE

When Prince died on 21 April 2016, no one was quite sure just how much chaos and uncertainty the fact he did not leave a will was going to cause. It was presumed that, as with other estates in a similar position, heirs would be appointed and the estate could get on with the business of what estates do.

Not wishing to lapse into hyperbole, things have at times been a shambles. The irony of someone so in control of their art leaving behind so much chaos with regard to the business of their art is certainly not lost here. Early reports focused around his vault and what, if any, music could be released from it or if this would be a betrayal of his artistic ambitions. Estates experts also raised the possibility of a significant tax bill broadsiding the estate.[82]

After weeding out a variety of unproven claims on the estate, a Minnesota judge ruled that Prince's sister Tyka Nelson and five half-siblings (Sharon Nelson, Norrine Nelson, John Nelson, Omarr Baker and Alfred Jackson) were the heirs to the estate.[83] At this stage, the estate was being valued at $200 million although it was expected that federal and state estate taxes would swallow half of that.[84] In early January 2017, the judge overseeing the case around the Prince estate appointed Comerica Bank & Trust to take over the running of the estate, replacing Bremer Trust, which had previously been appointed as temporary special administrator.[85]

The overall situation did not land especially well with three of the heirs. By October 2017 Sharon Nelson, Norrine Nelson and John Nelson were filing a petition to remove Comerica as personal representative to the estate. "No bank or individual alone should control Prince's creative legacy," ran their statement. "Comerica and its advisor has inadequate experience for this Estate."[86]

The bank responded, "Comerica stands behind its team and their administration of the estate and will respond appropriately to the Court. Comerica looks forward to the continued successful administration of the Prince Estate."[87] Comerica's appointment in April 2017 of Troy Carter as its entertainment adviser with regard to the Prince estate was designed to send out a message of stability and that the business was fully operational.[88] Multiple sources involved with the Prince estate all confirmed to this author that Carter was a force for good and for growth in the estate at this crucial stage in its evolution.

In April 2018, two years after Prince died, his estate was still in such an uncertain position that no heirs had received any money from it. However the executors and lawyers had reportedly collected $5.9 million in fees and expenses, with requests for a further $2.9 million in fees and expenses pending.

By 2019, it was being reported that, as the case dragged on, huge sums were being swallowed up by legal fees and probate-related expenses.[89]

The estate argued that, until its IRS and Minnesota state tax liabilities were resolved, "neither the court nor Comerica can close the Estate or make a distribution of assets to the Heirs".[90] The IRS bill alone, it was reported, ran to $31 million.[91]

In April 2019, Sharon Nelson spoke to *Billboard* and made the following prediction. "Before the end of the year," she said, "Prince's estate will be bankrupt." To add extra emotional punch to her list of criticisms, she said, "Prince is not resting in peace while this is going on."[92]

Nelson opened the lid on the numerous problems the heirs were having with the estate. They had, she said, only been given $100,000 each from the estate – and that was only because it was a contractual obligation relating to a 2016 Prince tribute concert. In sharp contrast, Comerica was, she said, paid $125,000 a month to administer the estate. Worse still, in her mind, were the legal fees that were growing by the week. "One day I went to a court hearing and there were 40 attorneys trying to figure out what Prince did," she said.[93]

Sharon expressed concerns about the commercial longevity of the estate. "You will wake up one day and Paisley Park won't be there," she claimed.[94]

In documents filed to the District Court in Minnesota in summer 2019, Angela Aycock (a trust and estate officer at Comerica) outlined the Sisyphean nature of dealing with the heirs and the broader issues of the estate. She said:

Throughout February, March, April and May 2019, Comerica continued to be responsible for engaging with and being responsive to not only the six Heirs, but to the often-changing counsel of those heirs, family members of the heirs, various advisors and assistants to the heirs, lenders to some of the heirs, one or two Court designated Heirs' representatives and a Mediator/Moderator. Moreover, in many cases these relationships led to clandestine activities the purpose of which Comerica could only guess at and do our best to contain, while handling the legitimate activities of the Estate. This represents a complex milieu of different perspectives, competing interests, murky agendas and hidden relationships to manage. Navigating this complicated landscape requires considerable time and attention. Comerica is regularly engaged in communications, meetings, administrative matters, and entertainment-related requests well into the evening and on weekends.[95]

She confirmed that Comerica was paid a flat fee of $125,000 a month (plus expenses), but that it had proposed to reduce this to $110,000 a month (plus expenses) from February 2019. She also outlined some of the monthly expenses, saying $24,300.21 had been claimed for (covering February, March, April and May 2019) "in travel and other expenses incurred on behalf of the Estate" as well as $116 in international wire-transfer fees. She concluded that "Comerica's compensation and expenses are proportionate, reasonable, and should be approved by the Court."[96]

The heirs started buckling under the financial strain, as matters were being stretched out and the distribution of assets was still on hold. As Tyka Nelson's legal debts mounted, *The Blast* reported on her woes, stating she had sold part of her share of the estate in December 2019 to Primary Wave, both to help her out of the financial hole she found herself in and also to have an involvement in the running of the estate.[97] But Comerica swiftly filed its objection to adding Primary Wave to an already crowded table of heirs. "Primary Wave is not an Heir of Prince Rogers Nelson and should not be recognized or treated as such," it said.[98]

Tyka was not the only heir who racked up debts as the case rolled on. Alfred Jackson died in August 2019,[99] but in February 2020 the estate was hit with a bill for $903,640.25 from attorney Justin Bruntjen for legal services provided to Alfred while he was still alive.[100]

Alfred Jackson's death added even more complications to how the estate should be shared between the remaining heirs, and things started to take on the tone of a pulp novel. Mere hours before he died, Alfred had sold 90 per cent of his stake in the Prince estate to Primary Wave (the same company Tyka had sold her stake to). Alfred had written a will but in it he had left all his assets to the extraordinarily named Raffles Van Exel.[101]

Probate court documents for the year ending 31 January 2019 revealed Comerica had been paid $1.5 million in fees, Troy Carter had received $2 million and Fredrikson & Byron (a law firm working for Comerica) had been paid $3.8 million. In the same financial year, the estate had paid $343,000 in attorney bills for the heirs, based on legal fees that the courts had deemed as being helpful to the estate.[102] To complicate things even further, Primary Wave's agreement with Alfred Jackson was being challenged by his family.[103]

In April 2020, *The Blast* reported that Comerica was "asking the court to deny Prince's heirs' petition for compensation", arguing that "if they were forced to pay out money to the heirs, they would have to sell off an asset of the estate". It added, "Comerica is asking the court to shut down Prince's heirs and allow them to deal with the estate issues."[104]

Speaking in January 2021, John Branca compared the Prince estate to Michael Jackson's, which he is in charge of. The disparity between the two could not be greater, he suggested, and this was primarily down to how Jackson carefully planned for his estate while Prince, unfortunately, did not.

"Artists need to pay attention to their legacy," he said. "They need to give some thought in their estate planning, as to who they appoint to represent their estates and carry on their legacy, and be very specific about it. You can really see the difference, for example, in the Michael Jackson Estate versus the Prince Estate. And yes, some of it is about management, but really it was Michael appointing people who he thought could handle his legacy, whereas Prince left it to the courts and a bank."[105]

During their peak in the 1980s, Prince and Michael Jackson were nose and nose as both commercial and artistic rivals. In death, however, the gulf between them is enormous.

THE PRODUCER TAKES THE ESTATE AWAY FROM THE FAMILY: JIMI HENDRIX

Jimi Hendrix died in September 1970. As covered in more detail in Chapter 5, music producer Alan Douglas got hold of the Hendrix archive in the early 1970s. He was introduced to the Hendrix family by lawyer Leo Branton.

It took until April 1993 for Al Hendrix, father of Jimi, to file a multi-million-dollar lawsuit in Seattle against Branton. He had been Al's attorney before that point but was fired in February 1993.

Branton was originally brought in by Al in 1971 after a run of bad investments and legal battles that almost tipped the Hendrix estate into bankruptcy.[106] It was claimed that Mike Jeffery, co-manager of Hendrix and a man the *Independent* referred to as "very shady", informed Al Hendrix there was only $20,000 left in Hendrix's account, but Jimi had left behind a mountain of unpaid bills relating to the construction of the Electric Ladyland studios in New York and there were back taxes pending. Something, Jeffery said, needed to be done – and done quickly – to turn the estate around. This was Branton's entry point into the Hendrix estate.[107]

"Branton restructured the assets, settled all pending litigation and quickly re-established control over most of Hendrix's original master tapes," claimed the *Los Angeles Times*. He also brought in Alan Douglas to oversee posthumous record releases. In 1974, Panamanian corporation Presentaciones Musicales SA was brought in to handle Hendrix's unmastered tapes and his publishing.[108] The posthumous success of Hendrix saw Branton in 1983 extend the stipend Al Hendrix' was paid to $50,000 a year for the rest of his life.[109]

There were, however, questions about the transferral of these rights.[110] "Mr. Hendrix signed away all of his rights to the so-called Hendrix legacy 20 years ago for a very valuable consideration," said a defiant Branton. "He signed the papers himself and he understood them."[111]

Legal action around these matters arose in the wake of MCA Music Entertainment Group's $30 million bid to buy the Hendrix catalogue for recordings and publishing. A legal letter from Al Hendrix to MCA had put the deal on hold until the Branton case was resolved. "I am so angry about this [sale]," Al Hendrix told the *Los Angeles Times*. "Nobody ever informed me that the rights to my son's music were up for sale."

Hendrix claimed he sold the rights to distribute his son's music in 1974 but argued he did not sell the rights to the actual music copyrights.[112]

It was estimated that royalties from Hendrix album and video sales at the time were worth $3 million a year and there was a further $1 million a year being generated by licensed merchandise (which Winterland Productions, an MCA-owned company, had owned since 1985). Al Hendrix claimed that in the past 20 years he had been paid less than $2 million from the posthumous earnings of his son.[113]

There is no doubt that Al Hendrix had signed papers that transferred the Hendrix business to Presentaciones Musicales SA, a Panamanian company that Branton represented. "Under this agreement, Al's lifetime income was further secured and even increased," wrote the *Independent*.[114] Later that same year, Branton then negotiated deals with two offshore investment corporations (Bureau Voor Muziekrechten Elber BV (known as Elber) in the Netherlands and Interlit in the British Virgin Islands) and they had controlled the Hendrix catalogue since then.[115] Elber licensed Hendrix's catalogue to Warner in the US while Interlit licensed it to PolyGram for the rest of the world.[116]

Branton had argued that he was the architect of the success of the Hendrix estate and Al Hendrix was now looking to swoop in and take everything from him. "When I came onto this case, the Jimi Hendrix estate was completely worthless," he claimed. "The main reason for Hendrix's current success is the tremendous amount of money that [the foreign corporations] and its successors pumped into the various projects."[117]

In August 1995, almost exactly a quarter of a century after Hendrix's death, Al Hendrix was able to take back the rights to all of his son's recordings (both released and unreleased), his publishing, his films and videos as well as the rights to exploit his name and image.[118] Branton and his co-defendants, running up enormous legal bills and having to wake up to the fact they were probably going to lose, accepted a late-hour mediated settlement. The terms of the settlement were not made public but Lewis, the lawyer for Al Hendrix, said the settlement payment was "quite modest relative to the value of the legacy".[119] *Rolling Stone*, however, suggested the final sum was between $5 million and $10 million.[120]

Al Hendrix also received immediate payments exceeding $1 million pertaining to the estate, an estate which was estimated to be worth $80 million at the time. He said, however, it was his son's legacy, not his commercial worth, that drove his case against Branton. "I was going for the legacy, and all that's back with the family now, and we will work with it as we see fit," he said. "That's where Jimi would want it."[121]

Janie Hendrix, Al's adopted daughter, explains what happened next. "After about a two-and-a-half-year lawsuit – and thanks to Paul Allen[122] who loaned us the money to fight Leo and his offshore company people – in 1995 we regained the rights and my dad appointed me the CEO and president, which I have always been, of Experience and Authentic Hendrix," she says. "My cousin, Bob Hendrix, who has now passed away, was our VP. He came from Costco and he was the VP there. He selected a few other family members to assist in running the company."

*   *   *

That was not, however, the end of it. A struggle between family members was brewing for many years and went to court in Seattle in March 2004. Al Hendrix died in April 2002[123] but the estate was being run by Janie through Experience Hendrix, the company they had set up to handle the estate's business. Leon Hendrix, Jimi's brother, was seeking to overturn the most recent will and have the preceding one reinstated because in that version he would have roughly a quarter share of the Jimi Hendrix estate. "This is my legacy and heritage and my children's legacy and heritage," he said, "and it's just not right that an adopted daughter can have that."[124] A total of 13 other relatives, including six of Leon's children, were also taking legal action against Janie.

In September 2004, Judge Jeffrey M. Ramsdell of King County Superior Court ruled that Leon was not entitled to a share of Al's will (and hence a share of the Hendrix estate) but was entitled to a gold disc his father had left him when he died.

The feuding and bitterness dragged on for years. Leon publicly expressed his disapproval of the estate being run by someone who was not a blood relative, and who had only met Hendrix a small number of times, when she was a child; Jimi was living abroad or touring a lot while Janie was growing up.[125] He also claimed Al was going to leave him $25 million in a trust fund but that was scuppered when he was cut out of the will. In June 2007, the Washington State Supreme Court declined to review the King County Superior Court ruling on the will in 2004. "What this means is it's done," said John Wilson, attorney for Janie Hendrix.[126]

There was a further legal tussle over Hendrix's name and likeness. In 2004, a District Court judge ruled that Janie and her companies had no ownership of the publicity rights to Jimi Hendrix's name or his likeness. "The judge found that because the will was probated in New York State at a time when publicity rights could not be passed down, those rights were not inherited by Janie," reported the *Seattle Times*.[127] (For more on inheritance of these rights, see Chapter 6.)

Soon after the 2007 Washington State Supreme Court ruling, Leon Hendrix and his business partner Andrew Pitsicalis set up Hendrix Licensing to sell Hendrix-related merchandise, but Janie Hendrix filed a $1.7 million lawsuit against them. An injunction in May 2015 barred Hendrix Licensing from using registered Jimi Hendrix trademarks. In July that year, a jury trial was set to decide how much Hendrix Licensing owed the Hendrix estate in damages, but the two sides settled out of court for an undisclosed amount.[128]

Speaking to the *Guardian* in 2016, Leon tried to put a brave face on it all. "It's their problem," he said of the estate. "They've made their billions, but I'm happy. I *am* my brother's brother. So who's the richest?"[129]

While clarifying that she "loves him and [wishes] him well", Janie says that bridges have been badly burned between them all and she cannot foresee a time when they can work together.

THE LIVING ESTATE: BRITNEY SPEARS

The bulk of this book is concerned with the estates of artists who have passed away. But estate law and estate management can also apply to the living, as the regrettable case of Britney Spears lays out in upsetting detail.

After a very public and painful breakdown in 2008, a legal intervention was made whereby her father, Jamie Spears, was named as co-conservator of her estate alongside entertainment attorney Andrew Wallet. Jamie Spears was being paid $130,000 a year from his daughter's estate for his role.[130] The appositely named Wallet was being paid considerably more. Britney's estate was valued at $47 million at the time.[131]

Jamie Spears was given control of his daughter's financial assets, her credit cards and even her home in Los Angeles. This was initially described as a "temporary conservatorship" and was put in place the day after she was admitted to a UCLA medical centre to undergo a three-day psychiatric evaluation. It had been claimed she had gone five days without sleep before being admitted to the centre. "The order is granted by a court when a person is deemed unable to look after themselves or manage their own affairs," explained the *Guardian*.[132]

Speculation grew about the terms of the conservatorship and the impact this might be having on both Britney's well-being and her civil liberties. This quickly morphed into the fan-driven #FreeBritney movement on social media, spearheaded by the freebritney.net website. "Her conservators decide whether or not she works, as she cannot enter into contracts for herself because she is legally not her own person," says the site. "Britney Spears needs permission from her conservators to leave her house or spend any of her own money."[133] The conservatorship was extended on a rolling basis following regular check-ins with all sides.

Throughout all this time, however, Britney was still making records and touring. She released three new studio albums: *Femme Fatale* in 2011, *Britney Jean* in 2013 and *Glory* in 2016. She also undertook a number of major tours, notably the 97-date *The Circus* world tour in 2009, the 79-date *Femme Fatale* world tour in 2011 and the 31-date *Piece of Me* tour of North America in 2018. She was also confirmed as a judge on TV talent show *The X Factor USA* in 2012[134], although she quit after just one season.[135]

In March 2019, Andrew Wallet resigned from his position as co-conservator. He had, in the months before he quit, negotiated to increase his payment to $426,000 a year but had argued he brought "stability and leadership" to Britney's estate and had helped grow its value by $20 million.[136] He was also awarded $100,000 as a "golden parachute" payment as part of his resignation agreement.[137]

In May 2019, Jamie Spears filed a notice of intent to extend the conservatorship outside the state of California (where Britney was resident) to also include her home state of Louisiana as well as Hawaii and Florida, both places she liked to go on holiday.[138]

The Britney Spears conservatorship is a bifurcated one: one part covers her estate and her financial affairs; the other part covers her as an individual.[139] Jamie Spears had originally controlled both parts, but stood down as her personal conservator in 2019 (citing health reasons) with Jodi Montgomery stepping into that role on a temporary basis.[140]

Montgomery had been Britney's "care manager" for the previous year and also ran a private fiduciary firm with her husband, giving her a wealth of conservator experience.[141] Coinciding with the stepping down of Jamie Spears, the *Los Angeles Times* ran a lengthy investigative piece exploring multiple aspects of Jodi's conservatorship and the wider reaction to it.

Quoted in the feature, Stanton Stein, Britney's attorney, poured cold water on the accusations of the #FreeBritney movement that suggested she has lost all autonomy in her career and her private life. "She's always involved in every career and business decision," he said. "Period."[142]

On 21 August 2020, the courts ruled that Jodi's conservatorship should be extended until at least 1 February 2021. Samuel Ingham, Britney's lawyer, was concurrently pushing for Jodi Montgomery's appointment as interim conservator to be made permanent.[143]

Mere days later, on 25 August, things took another turn. Jamie Lynn Spears, Britney's younger sister, revealed that she had been made a trustee of her sibling's estate two years earlier and was now making a move to have more control over it.

Britney had set up the SJB Revocable Trust in 2004 for her children and in 2018 it was amended to hand over control to Jamie Lynn in the event of Britney's death, in which case Jamie Lynn would administer the assets for Britney's children. Jamie Lynn was proposing that the SJB Revocable Trust be moved into one or more accounts with Fidelity Brokerage Services, where she would act as custodian. "If approved, the move would put Britney Spears' financial assets into those accounts and require a judge's approval to remove them," wrote the *Los Angeles Times*.[144]

In a court filing by Ingham on behalf of Britney, obtained by *Los Angeles Times*, it was described as a "voluntary conservatorship" and that the singer, as conservatee, "wishes to exercise her right to nominate a conservator of the estate".[145] In the same filing, it was revealed that the singer wished to have the Bessemer Trust put in charge of her estate. The Bessemer Trust is a family office that handles investment and wealth management for rich families. "Founded as a family office in 1907, Bessemer Trust brings you more than a century of private wealth management experience," says its website. "In fact, managing private wealth is and always has been our one and only business."[146] The BBC reported that court documents revealed her estate to be worth $57.4 million, of which $2.7 million was available in cash.[147]

Andrew Wallet resurfaced in October 2020, having lobbied to be reinstated as a conservator of the estate. Britney's lawyers had originally argued he was "uniquely unsuitable" to the role but had withdrawn the petition against his reappointment.[148] Speaking to the *Daily Mail*, he attacked those arguing that the singer was being stripped of control over her life. "Britney is in a conservatorship for good reason but a lot of the Free Britney people have no experience with the law," he said. "Their perception is so wrong but you can't go and tell them why because a lot of it is confidential."

Posting a 13-second video online on 3 November 2020, Britney addressed the conservatorship indirectly. She used the posting to reassure fans that she was healthy and happy as well as to counter the claims of the #FreeBritney campaign. "I just want to let you guys know that I am fine," she said. "I'm the happiest I've ever been in my life."[149]

That happiness did not last long. On 11 November 2020, Los Angeles Superior Court Judge Brenda Penny declined to suspend Jamie Spears from his conservator role. Samuel Ingham, acting for Britney, said this was a deeply unwelcome outcome. "My client has informed me that she is afraid of her father," he told the judge. "She will not perform again if her father is in charge of her career."[150]

The judge did, however, say that she would consider future appeals to dismiss or even remove Jamie Spears from his position. As per Britney's earlier request, the judge appointed the Bessemer Trust as a co-conservator.[151]

Despite all this, the business of Britney rolled on. A new single, 'Swimming in the Stars', was released at the start of December 2020 to mark her 39th birthday. It was not, however, a brand-new track but rather one that had been held over from the recording of her *Glory* album in 2016.[152]

Later that same month, Jamie Spears responded to criticisms of his role as conservator of his daughter. He claimed the two were on "good terms" and had been in contact with each other up until August 2020, but they had not spoken since then. "I love my daughter and I miss her very much," he told CNN. "When a family member needs special care and protection, families need to step up, as I have done for the last 12-plus years, to safeguard, protect and continue to love Britney unconditionally."[153]

A whole new light was cast on her conservatorship with the release of the *Framing Britney Spears* documentary (on FX and Hulu in the US initially) in January 2021. "The meteoric rise and disturbing fall of Britney Spears has devolved into a Kafkaesque court battle that has reawakened her fandom and raised pressing questions about mental health and an individual's rights," is how Red Arrow Studios, the parent company of documentary co-producers Left/Right, described it ahead of broadcast.[154]

It became a widely discussed and debated issue as soon as the documentary aired, hinging on the appropriateness (or not) of a 12-year (and counting) conservatorship in her particular case.[155] [156] Coinciding with its broadcast was a ratcheting up of the legal activities around her conservatorship. In early February 2021, Ingham said in court documents, subsequently accessed by *Entertainment Tonight*, that "it would be highly detrimental to Britney's interest" to give Jamie Spears more control over her estate. Jamie had argued some of his powers had been depleted when the Bessemer Trust became a co-conservator and he was motioning to block it from becoming sole conservator. "It is difficult to imagine a better recipe for conflict between the co-conservators and confusion with both Britney and third parties," argued Ingham. "Ultimately, the appointment of Bessemer Trust would be rendered meaningless."[157]

On 11 February, as part of a 30-minute status hearing in Los Angeles, judge Brenda J. Perry denied Jamie's request to retain some of his rights over his daughter's estate. She ruled that the Bessemer Trust should remain as co-conservators with equal authority. Vivian L. Thoreen, attorney for Jamie, stated, "My client looks forward to working with Bessemer to continue an investment strategy in the best interests of his daughter."[158]

At the same hearing, Ingham reiterated that Britney did not want her father in a position of such power over her life and career. "It is no secret that my client does not want her father as her conservator," he said.[159]

The documentary was intended to open a debate about the very nature of conservatorships. "Through Britney's story, we can put a spotlight on the conservatorship system… and really poke at it and see whether maybe there's conflicts of interest or things that should change now that we treat mental health differently," Samantha Stark, director and producer of *Framing Britney Spears*, told *Billboard*.[160]

It gave new impetus to the #FreeBritney movement and saw a groundswell of public support to try and end the conservatorship. "In California, anyone can petition the court to end a conservatorship, including the conservatee, the conservator, a relative or friend of the conservatee or another interested person," wrote the *Los Angeles Times*. "The court may ask the court investigator to evaluate the case and the conservatee's condition to see if the conservatorship should be ended. But the success rate is not high, according to Jamie Spears' lawyer Thoreen."[161]

In the immediate aftermath of the airing of the *Framing Britney Spears* documentary, Thoreen – speaking on behalf of Jamie Spears – said that it was his desire that his daughter's conservatorship came to an end. "[Jamie] would love nothing more than to see Britney not need a conservatorship," Thoreen told CNN. "Whether or not there is an end to the conservatorship really depends on Britney. If she wants to end her conservatorship, she can file a petition to end it."[162]

Around the same time, and as both the media and public reactions to the documentary were intensifying, congressmen Matt Gaetz and Jim Jordan called for House Judiciary Chairman Jerry Nadler to hold hearings into the ethics of such conservatorships. "[It is] incumbent upon our Committee to convene a hearing to examine whether Americans are trapped unjustly in conservatorships," they argued in a joint statement. Gaetz added, "If the conservatorship process can rip the agency from a woman who was in the prime of her life and one of the most powerful pop stars in the world, imagine what it can do to people who are less powerful and have less of a voice."[163]

On 24 March, Ingham used a hearing on the conservatorship to reiterate that Britney wished for Montgomery to be installed permanently in order to handle her personal affairs.[164] Ingham filed court documents requesting that Jamie Spears resign from his role as conservator.[165]

At the very end of March, Britney made a rare public statement on the documentary – or rather the impact of the documentary on her emotionally and psychologically. "I didn't watch the documentary but from what I did see of it I was embarrassed by the light they put me in," she wrote on her Instagram account alongside a 41-second video clip of her lip-syncing and dancing to 'Crazy' by Aerosmith. "I cried for two weeks and well…. I still cry sometimes !!!! I do what I can in my own spirituality with myself to try and keep my own joy… love… and happiness !!!! Every day dancing brings me joy !!! I'm not here to be perfect… perfect is boring… I'm here to pass on kindness !!!!"[166]

There were further developments in the case in late April 2021. The judge in the case agreed that Britney could personally address the Los Angeles court dealing with the conservatorship dispute.

"My client has requested a hearing at which she can address the court directly," said Ingham. "My client has asked that it be done on an expedited basis."[167]

A hearing for the case was set for 23 June 2021.

(The case was still ongoing when this book was going to press.)

THE FAMILY FIGHT TO TAKE THE ESTATE BACK FROM THE BUSINESS MANAGER: MICHAEL HUTCHENCE

The bedlam resulting from the will left behind by INXS frontman Michael Hutchence was discussed in Chapter 2. In August 2005, the executor's report into his estate concluded that he had AU$506 in cash at the time of his death in 1997. His advisers had claimed he had set up his finances in the way he did in order to stop "thieving relatives" and "girlfriends" from carving up his fortune.[168]

In November 1998, the Hutchence family began legal action against Colin Diamond, Tony Alford (a Gold Coast accountant once referred to by a judge in the Queensland Supreme Court as "a witness of little credit"[169]), Andrew Paul (a Hong Kong-based accountant as well as executor of Hutchence's will) and others. Hutchence's half-sister Tina and their mother, Patricia Glassop, were taking action against Paul, then the sole executor of the Hutchence estate.[170]

It was reported that half the estate, should the family win it back, was earmarked for Heavenly Hiraani Tiger Lily, Hutchence's daughter with Paula Yates, and she would receive 50 per cent on her 25th birthday (22 July 2021) with the rest coming in instalments over the next five years. It was also revealed that the first two recipients of the estate, should the legal action be resolved, would be Greenpeace and Amnesty International who, as per Hutchence's will, were bequeathed £300,000 between them. What was left would, in theory, be divided between the family.[171] In 2017, the *Guardian* noted that the bequests to Amnesty International and Greenpeace had never been received.[172]

In February 1999, documents were filed in the Australian court by Belinda Brewin, godmother of Tiger Lily, on behalf of the child, who was then aged two. In the documents, she was seeking to claim money from the estate to cover maintenance, her education and "advancement in life".[173] Amnesty International joined the case as a plaintiff but neither side won and it went to mediation.[174] The case was eventually settled out of court in 1999. While no details of the settlement were made public, the *Sydney Morning Herald* suggested the family received less than the AU$500,000 the case had run up in court costs.[175]

In a rare interview in 2017, Colin Diamond spoke in only the vaguest terms about the legal action taken against him and others by the Hutchence family. "The estate was sued, the trust was sued, I was sued," he said. "There were, you know, 13 or 14 counsels involved for three or four years."[176] He was then asked about Tiger Lily and only had this to say: "She's been well educated and she's very grounded and she's got a great future – which would make both Paula and Michael extremely happy."[177]

In March 2001, Judge Richard Chesterman of the Brisbane Supreme Court ruled that Tiger Lily was the only beneficiary of the Hutchence estate. "Chesterman rejected all other claims on his estate, including those made by members of his own family," reported *Rolling Stone*. It added that the Hutchence estate was valued at $25 million at the time of his death but legal fees had chopped that figure in half.[178] [179]

Talking to the *Mail on Sunday* in 2019, Tina Hutchence said the estate did pay for Tiger's schooling and general upkeep until she was 18 but that was it. "My brother worked with INXS for 20 years and he wanted to leave money for his daughter and family but none of us have seen a penny," she said.[180] The death of Patricia Glassop in 2010, however, created more divisions between the family. She left behind an estimated $2.6 million. Rhett Hutchence, Michael's younger brother, contested the will which gave him 20 per cent.

Rhett and his mother had a turbulent relationship. Glassop reportedly wrote in her will, "Rhett Hutchence must not take any benefit from my estate. The reason for this is that I have already provided for Rhett during his lifetime. I have provided for Rhett's children in this, my will." She also reportedly told a lawyer before she died that Rhett did "not do much other than sunbaking" and was "wealthy in his own right" after he inherited money from Michael as well as their father, Kel.[181] The *Courier Mail* reported that the case was resolved in 2013 but details were not made public. It was another ugly and sad twist in the family's strained history of will complications. "Michael wanted his money to go to his family," said Tina. "He would be appalled if he knew how his family has been treated."[182]

THE ESTATE BY PROXY: SYD BARRETT

Syd Barrett, founding member and original frontman of Pink Floyd as well as a solo artist, died on 7 July 2006, but from the middle of the 1970s his was essentially an estate by proxy.

Due to a series of complex psychological problems and personal issues, he effectively stopped making records in 1970, with the release of the *Barrett* album coming that November. Sessions recorded for John Peel as well as Bob Harris in 1970 and 1971 were eventually released years later and the *Opel* album, gathering together unreleased material and alternative takes, came out in 1988. A box set, *Crazy Diamond*, followed in 1993 that contained further alternative versions of songs, but that was effectively it in terms of record releases. He performed live only sporadically, with fanzine *Terrapin* publishing the last review of him in concert in February 1972.[183]

By the time Barrett had moved back to his home city of Cambridge in the late 1970s, he had long withdrawn from public life. He gave what turned out to be his final interview in 1971, thereafter shunning all media requests.[184] Little was known about his life, although a feature in 1973 by Nick Kent suggested Barrett was "working as a part-time gardener" in Cambridge.[185]

When he was doorstepped at his home in the 1980s by DJ Nicky Horne, his response was reportedly, "Syd can't talk to you now."[186]

David Gilmour, his friend and the person who effectively replaced him in Pink Floyd, ensured that royalties from records he made and songs he wrote for the band were regularly accounted for. "I made sure the money got to him," he said.[187]

Steve Davis was director of catalogue at EMI from 2000 to 2009 and explains how the record label would deal with Syd's brother, Alan Barrett, when it had any issues relating to the catalogue to deal with. "His brother had a big say in what happened," he says. "The family's priority was protecting Syd when he was alive as he was fairly vulnerable. They were also protecting the integrity of the music and the estate."

As it was an estate in all but name, it adhered to the general dynamics of estate management and so little in terms of the business conversations and activities actually shifted when Syd died. "There was a slight change when he did pass away but it was really dealing with most of the same people for the same things," Davis says, adding that it was probably a year after his death that the label would have started to speak to the family about the types of projects they could work on.

During his time at EMI, Davis dealt with the Barrett family on a number of projects while Syd was still alive, including remasters of his two solo albums, *The Madcap Laughs* and *Barrett*, as well as the *Opel* compilation. "Everything went through Syd's brother," he says. "He was polite and helpful but, as I say, protective. At one point, we asked if there would be any chance of Syd saying something, even if not a full-on interview. Maybe we could just record him on audio or video? Unsurprisingly it came back as, 'No. We wouldn't want to do that.' Arguably, unless he could remember something about those times, those tracks and that music, we wouldn't have used it. We totally respected [the family's wishes]. But you can't blame us for asking."

When he died, the net value of Syd Barrett's estate was estimated at £1,250,455.[188] He left his brother Alan £425,000 while his other siblings, Rosemary Breen, Ruth Brown and Donald Barrett were each left £275,000.[189]

Speaking to me for the 2016 *Guardian* feature that was the starting point for this book, Davis explained how the record label dealt with an artist who was still alive but who was both unwilling and unable to deal with business matters pertaining to his solo work as well as his work with Pink Floyd. He said that the label, because it was keenly aware of the complexities and sensitivities around the Barrett catalogue, waited until October 2010 – over four years after he died – to release the album *An Introduction to Syd Barrett*, which compiled tracks from his time with Pink Floyd as well as from his solo career.

"That ambulance-chasing is unseemly," he said of cash-in albums coming out immediately after a pop star dies. "If you are dealing with a family, you don't want to be seen as [crassly] making money out of their tragedy."[190]

WHEN A WIFE IS NOT A WIFE AND A TRUST IS NOT A TRUST: JAMES BROWN

The dispute over James Brown's will is as convoluted as it is ugly. Two major factors shaped how things progressed here: his marital status when he died; and what money was due to a charitable trust he had set up in his name.

Brown passed away on Christmas Day 2006 and after that all hell broke loose when his fourth wife, Tomi Rae Hynie, and the rest of the Brown family were almost immediately plunged into a legal tussle over how his assets should be divided. In a reading of his will on 11 January 2007, the trustees of his estate were confirmed and his six adult children were named as heirs, but Hynie and James Brown II (her son with Brown) were not. Later that same month, the six adult children filed to have the trustees removed from the estate and for a full inventory to be done. In February, Hynie filed her own petition, arguing she was his wife and entitled to half the estate.[191]

Brown had drafted his will in August 2000 and set up an irrevocable trust into which his music rights as well as his $3.5 million mansion (sitting on 60 acres in Beech Island, South Carolina) were placed. He reportedly spent $20,000 on legal fees to have "an airtight will and estate" drawn up.[192]

His son James Brown II was born 10 months later but the will was not updated to include him. In December 2001, he and Hynie married, but no prenuptial agreement had been signed.[193] Brown's marriage to Tomi Rae Hynie – or, rather, questions over the validity of the marriage – had significant repercussions for the Brown heirs and their moves with regard to copyright termination. This, as well as the legal disputes over ownership of these rights, is all covered in detail in Chapter 10.

Brown's fortune at the time of his death was to be valued later at $86 million,[194] although later estimates put it at $100 million with debts of $15 million.[195] "The Godfather's will was perfectly clear," claimed *Atlanta* magazine. "Each of the six named heirs would get a share of his personal property, the inventory of which included thirty-six keys to cities, seventy-one sets of pajamas, an autographed James Brown singing doll, a white fox cape, a black seal coat, and a watch with twenty-eight circular-cut diamonds." The bulk of the estate would, as per his will, go into trusts to educate his own grandchildren as well as to assist needy students in Georgia and South Carolina.[196] The trust fund, named the I Feel Good Trust, had originally been set up in the late 1990s.[197]

David Cannon, a former manager of Brown, was named by the singer as co-executor of the will but he eventually resigned this role in October 2007.[198] In October 2011, Cannon was sentenced to three years of home confinement after entering an Alford plea[199] to two counts of breach of trust. Buddy Dallas also resigned as a trustee in 2007.[200]

David Cannon, Albert Dallas and Alfred Bradley had been trustees of the James Brown estate until late 2007, when they were removed by a South Carolina state judge, replacing them with Pope and Buchanan.[201]

South Carolina Attorney General Henry McMaster brokered a settlement in May 2009 that ruled that half of Brown's estate should go to charity and the rest be carved up among his family. The judge also recognised Hynie as his "surviving spouse" and her son with the singer, James Brown II, as a legitimate heir. A DNA test was ordered to prove his paternity, with suggestions that Brown could not be his father as he had had a vasectomy decades earlier. In the end, James Brown II went through two positive DNA tests.[202] Hynie and her son would get a quarter of the estate, Brown's six adult children would get 25 per cent between them and 50 per cent would go to charity.[203] This settlement effectively scrapped Brown's 2000 will and McMaster set up a new legacy trust.[204]

Pope and Buchanan had objected to the settlement, giving "nearly 400 reasons why they believed it was wrong". It was claimed by them that Brown's education trust had been seriously damaged by the long-running disputes and would find itself "slashed by taxes and payouts from $80 million to about $19 million".[205] They were replaced by Russell Bauknight, a public accountant, who was appointed by the court as the estate trustee.[206]

A lengthy feature in *GQ* in January 2013 tried to make sense of the legal story to date. It had to hold its hands up early and say that things here were impossibly convoluted and confusing. "The suits, countersuits, probate rulings, appeals and subpoenas in the case of the estate of James Brown are of a volume and complexity that it would be perfectly possible to write a PhD thesis on the subject," it said.[207] After following the snaking story, *GQ* concluded glumly, "Whoever you believe should have inherited James Brown's estate, there can be very few cases in which an artist's posthumous fate has deviated so horribly from his apparent intentions."[208]

Mere weeks after the *GQ* feature came out, events took another dramatic turn, piling more confusion and uncertainty on a story that felt like it should be mapped in 3D. In February 2013, the South Carolina Supreme Court overturned McMaster's 2009 settlement, saying he did not follow Brown's wishes with regard to charitable donations (as outlined in his will) in brokering it. At this stage, confusion reigned over what the value of the estate even was, with unhelpfully vague estimates ranging from $5 million to $100 million.[209] At the same time, Bauknight's appointment as trustee was voided but the chance of a reappointment was left open.[210]

As all this was being dragged through the courts, the I Feel Good Trust was sitting in harrowing limbo. A *New York Times* report in December 2014 claimed that, eight years after Brown's death, the trust "has not distributed a penny to its intended recipients".[211] It said that ongoing disputes had seen the South Carolina government seize control of the estate. "Today nothing is settled," it said. "The estate remains mired in lawsuits, two sets of executors have been replaced, and a lower court has yet to follow some of the court's instructions. Millions of dollars have been paid in recent years to creditors, law firms and various vendors, but not to schoolchildren or other beneficiaries."[212]

Brown's marriage to Hynie added whole new complications to the story. They met in the late 1990s when Brown saw her performing a Janis Joplin tribute show in Las Vegas. She was recruited as his principal backing singer as well as support act. They were, by this stage, also lovers.[213] Details emerged that Brown had filed for an annulment in 2004 after learning Hynie was married to another man. A judge, however, had ruled that the marriage to Javed Ahmed, which was done in 1997 to enable him to remain in the US, was invalid as he already had at least three other wives in Pakistan. Hynie claimed she had already annulled her marriage to Ahmed.[214] As such, she was free to marry Brown in 2001.[215]

In early 2018, nine of Brown's children and grandchildren filed a fresh lawsuit against Hynie and the administrators of the estate. Then in June 2020, the South Carolina Supreme Court ruled unanimously that Hynie was in fact not legally married to Brown (as she had not annulled her marriage to Ahmed) and therefore had no claim on his estate.

The court delivered a 20-page decision[216] and said of the protracted legal battles that had defined his estate, "The ongoing litigation since Brown's passing has thwarted his expressed wish that his estate be used for educational purposes [...] a point we find both extraordinary and lamentable."[217]

McBride was damning about how things played out with the estate. "Untold millions have been frittered away by lawyers and politicians who have been loosed on one another by various factions of his destroyed family," he wrote. "It's a sad end to an extraordinary yet tragic life, though you figure with thousands of poor kids in South Carolina and Georgia needing a good education, somebody would have the integrity to figure the whole thing out."[218]

McBride said in its first nine years the estate was embroiled in 47 lawsuits, covering 4,000 pages of litigation, involving an estimated 90 lawyers ("most of whom never knew James Brown").[219]

Brown had, according to former manager Charles Bobbit, predicted an almighty fight over money would happen after he died. "He told me, 'It's gonna be a big mess when I die, Mr. Bobbit,'" he recounted to McBride. "'A big mess. Stay out of it.'"[220]

Frank Copsidas (commonly known as SuperFrank) was the final manager of James Brown. He is adamant the many and complex (as well as public) court cases have held the estate back from doing what it should have been doing since 2006 – keeping Brown's name and his musical legacy alive. He feels this has all been enormously detrimental to Brown's cultural reach, where the estate business has been in limbo for so long that he has started to fade from the public consciousness and has not been introduced to younger music fans in any meaningful way. He may be somewhat over-dramatic in his claims, but it is hard not to see the argument that the estate and Brown's name should be much higher-profile than they currently are.

Speaking to me in early 2020, SuperFrank says, "Well, if you look at it, nobody's remembering him any more. He's gone. It's 14 years since he died. It's an entire generation that has no idea who he is."

GETTING AN ESTATE REOPENED: MUDDY WATERS

Blues guitarist Muddy Waters died on 30 April 1983 and a lengthy legal fight between Waters' heirs and his manager, Scott Cameron, played out over decades. Cameron had managed Waters in the 1970s and early 1980s and was named as executor of his will.

Waters' children argued that his estate had not been properly closed after his death and, as such, there were unsettled assets. They filed a petition in early 2015 against Cameron, "asking the courts to turn over Waters' assets, primarily the rights to music, that were still in Cameron's possession".[221] With macabre timing, Cameron died mere weeks later in March 2015, aged 76.[222]

In April 2015, the judge in the case agreed with Waters' heirs that the estate had not been properly closed and appointed Mercy Morganfield, one of Waters' daughters, to act as administrator of the estate.

Under the terms of the will that Waters had written, Cameron was left to administer the publishing company the two had set up and to distribute due royalties twice a year to Waters' widow, four of his children and a great-granddaughter. They, however, argued that Cameron was not being financially transparent and accused him of failing to properly manage Waters' legacy on a commercial level.[223] They admitted they had received regular payments but that Cameron had missed one in December 2014.[224]

Cameron was no stranger to litigation from estates. He also managed blues musician Willie Dixon (who died in 1992) and Dixon's family took him to court in 1994 in a dispute over payments Cameron claimed he was owed. The jury in a Los Angeles County Superior Court originally sided with Dixon's widow, who had argued her husband had signed an agreement with Cameron that he did not fully understand. A judge overturned that but Cameron and Dixon's family eventually settled out of court.[225]

John Simson, a music lawyer at Fox Rothschild, took on the case for the heirs of Waters. "Mercy, who is Muddy's only college-educated heir, started to get a little concerned as they never got accounts from this guy [Cameron]," he says. "So she sent him a letter at my behest saying, 'Scott, we really need to get an accounting [of the estate's finances]. We've never had one in as long as I can remember.' And he refused. I hired a firm in Chicago, a probate firm that does these kinds of lawsuits, and we sued. The suit was basically saying, 'You're running this estate and you never send accounts.' He would send money to the heirs, but they had no way of knowing [what they were due]. Was he sending them 20 per cent? Was he sending them 80 per cent? Was he sending them 100 per cent?" Simson claims that, as the litigation progressed, he discovered that Cameron was paying the heirs less than half of what he was collecting from Waters' copyrights. "He was clearly just stealing from them," he says.

Mercy Morganfield, in her legal action, was asking that the Waters estate be reopened so that the remaining assets, including his copyrights, could be distributed properly.[226] Simson claims Cameron had been attempting to bully or bamboozle the heirs into backing down by claiming that a clause in the will stated that if they ever contested it then they would forfeit everything (this no-contest clause or "terror clause" is covered in Chapter 2). This, it turns out, was hokum. "I tried to explain to the heirs, 'Look, you're not disputing your share. You're disputing the way the estate is being administered by an executor. You have a right to do that independent of [the will's terms] and you won't lose your share,'" says Simson. "We ended up getting all the rights back and his daughter Mercy took over the administration of the estate."

Elizabeth Cameron, the widow of Scott Cameron, was carrying on the legal fight on behalf of her late husband's company, the Cameron Organization, and in April 2018 she filed new court documents that disputed moves by the heirs of Waters to recover $2 million in royalty payments they claimed had been diverted away from them. Elizabeth Cameron argued that, under the terms of Waters' will, they were not legally permitted to manage his estate.[227]

Reviewing the case, Simson says, "We had got all the rights back, but trying to find all the paper trails has been really, really difficult [...] That's a cautionary tale for estates."

ESTATE APPARATUS: OTHER NOTABLE DISPUTES

Many other major estates have not been without their battles for control. Below are some of the key ones, outlining what the fights were over and, where resolved, what happened.

Aretha Franklin

Tied to her leaving multiple and conflicting wills (see Chapter 2), there were struggles over who should run the estate. A document from 2014 claimed she wanted Kecalf Franklin, her son, to be in charge, but Sabrina Garrett-Owens, her niece, was initially put in control.[228] Speaking in court in August 2019, David J. Bennett, the lead lawyer for the estate, opposed the appointment of

Kecalf.[229] She claimed that she only took on the role as executor under two conditions: that "no fractured relationship develop within the family"; and "we did not end up in court disputes over disagreements with the estate". Both, she said, had happened.[230] In March 2020, a probate judge assigned Reginald M Turner, president-elect nominee of the American Bar Association, as temporary caretaker of the Franklin estate until the issue of distribution of assets was resolved.[231]

Glen Campbell

Campbell had been diagnosed with Alzheimer's disease in early 2011 and passed away on 8 August 2017. His widow, Kimberly, was named executor of his estate but three of his eight children (William, Kelli and Wesley Campbell) had been excluded from receiving any inheritance. Almost a year later, a Tennessee judge ruled that the three could contest the validity of two wills, written in 2001 and 2006, that Campbell had left behind. The children were arguing their father had been subject to undue influence when drafting the details of his estate plan.[232] In March 2019, one of his daughters filed to request a full accounting of a bank account owned by Kimberly but which had previously been a joint account with Glen. His royalty payments had, it was revealed, been paid into that account. In May 2019, Kimberly moved to invoke a Tennessee state law that guaranteed a widow a percentage of their husband's estate should they die without a valid will. She was seeking a 40 per cent share as well as a year's support allowance.[233] In December 2019, William, Kelli and Wesley dropped their contesting of the will.

The Campbell estate was initially estimated at $50 million but court documents in April 2019 suggested it was worth just $410,221.[234] A filing in Davidson Probate Court in December 2019 by interim administrator Stanley B. Schneider, however, valued the estate at $1.2 million based on revised future royalties. As a side note, it was also claimed at the time that the estimated future value of Campbell's likeness and image was just $10,000.[235] In May 2020, the judge at Davidson Probate Court approved a request to excuse Kimberly, as executor of the estate, from filing detailed annual accounting for the estate. This means financial details of the estate, including a precise valuation, will almost certainly remain private.[236]

Kurt Cobain

Courtney Love, Kurt Cobain's widow, sold half of his publishing to Primary Wave in 2006. As Cobain had been Nirvana's primary songwriter, it covered 98 per cent of the band's publishing.[237] Love, however, had a difficult relationship with Frances Bean Cobain, her daughter with Kurt, and that has impacted on his estate. In 2009, Love lost guardianship of Frances Bean (aged 17 at the time) and she was being cared for by Wendy O'Connor

(Kurt's mother) and Kimberly Dawn Cobain (his sister).[238] Love had previously lost custody of her daughter in 2003 (following her arrest on drug charges) but had regained custody in 2005.[239] In August 2010, Frances Bean turned 18 and took ownership of the bulk of her trust fund.[240] Since then, while Frances Bean has taken a greater position of power with regard to the Cobain estate, mother and daughter have had a publicly fractious relationship.

Chris Cornell

The Soundgarden and Audioslave frontman took his own life on 18 May 2017. In the following years, a bitter dispute broke out between his widow, Vicky Cornell, and his former bandmates in Soundgarden. Vicky filed a complaint in the US District Court in December 2019 in a dispute over royalties and the use of archive recordings[241]

The band countersued, though dropped their case in July 2020.[242]

A new legal fight between the surviving band members and Vicky Cornell, however, erupted in February 2021 over a proposed buyout of the band's master recordings, and how much each party would be paid from the investor's offer. Vicky demanded a judicial review of her husband's interests in Soundgarden, including merchandise as well as a future touring revenue, but her attempts to buy out the remaining band members was not successful.

A statement from the Soundgarden members countered, "This dispute has never been about money for the band. This is their life's work and their legacy."[243]

(The case had not been resolved before this book went to press.)

Jerry Garcia

The frontman of The Grateful Dead died on 9 August 1995. He had been married three times. His widow, Deborah Koons Garcia, was sued by Garcia's second wife, Carolyn Adams Garcia (known as Mountain Girl), for cutting off payments due under the terms of her divorce in 1993. The payments were stopped soon after Garcia's death. A Marin County judge ruled in January 1997 that Carolyn Adams Garcia was due all of the $5 million Jerry Garcia had promised her before their divorce. Deborah Koons Garcia pleaded poverty on behalf of her and the estate, of which she was co-executor. "Jerry died broke," she claimed. "We only have a few hundred thousand dollars in the bank. We don't have $4.5 million more to pay Carolyn." (Garcia had paid out $400,000 of the promised $5 million to Carolyn Adams Garcia before his death.)[244]

In documents filed by a probate referee in March 1997, it was revealed the Garcia estate was worth $9,936,492, somewhat above the $6 million Deborah Koons Garcia had suggested it was worth. The *SF Gate* reported that $38 million in claims had been filed against the estate "by an assortment of acquaintances, former lovers and business partners", of which the Carolyn Adams Garcia claim was the single largest. At this stage, some claims had been settled out of court while others were pending.[245]

George Gershwin

One of the strangest claims on an estate, never resolved, came from a man born in 1926 who tried to prove he was the secret lovechild of Broadway composer George Gershwin, who died on 11 July 1937. Alan Gershwin (born Alan Schneider) first stepped forward in the late 1950s and spent the remaining years of his life – he passed away in March 2018 – insisting he was the composer's long-lost son, the result of an affair with a dancer called Mollie Charleston, whose stage name was Margaret Manners. The story was teased in a piece by gossip columnist Walter Winchell that ran on 17 June 1957. "July 11th will mark the 20th ann'y [*sic*] of Gershwin's passing," Winchell wrote. "The date when a lawsuit will break alleging he was the father of an interpretative dancer's son. The chap seeks control of Gershwin's 15 million $ estate."[246] In a feature in American magazine *Confidential*, under the headline "I am George Gershwin's illegitimate son" and with photos of the two men in profile asking readers to try and identify which was the father and which was the son, Alan finally went public.[247] In its obituary of Alan Gershwin, the *New York Times* asked if "this affable but monomaniacal man was one of the greatest victims in American musical history, or a grifter running a long-term con, or someone suffering decades of delusion".[248] "His claims did gain some acceptance and there were newspaper profiles that swallowed his story," noted *The Times* in its obituary. "He was invited to the Cannes Film Festival and once, he said, came down a spiral staircase on French television to the strains of *Rhapsody in Blue*."[249]

The more Alan courted media attention, the more the Gershwin family closed ranks on him, but they did not see him as an existential threat to their fortune. Rather they viewed him as "a crank and an annoyance".[250] Even so, Ira Gershwin (George's brother and musical collaborator) hired a private detective to look into it and opened what he referred to as "the impostor file" on Alan.[251] It was later claimed that Alan had undergone plastic surgery to look more like George.[252] "He never pushed for royalties from the Gershwin estate despite some headlines over the years to the contrary," claims *Syncopated Times*.[253] A blood test cast suspicion on his paternity and a mouth swab in 1999, which Alan reluctantly agreed to, cast even more doubt on his claims. Right up until his death, Alan kept up his assertion that he was George Gershwin's son.

Lemmy

Motörhead frontman Lemmy (real name Ian Kilmister) died on 28 December 2015. The following day it was already being reported there was an "acrimonious legal contest" brewing over his estate which, at the time, was being valued at £6.75 million.[254] His son, Paul Inder, was expected to inherit the estate but Lemmy also had another son, who was adopted, and it was speculated that his "entitlement is likely to have been lost in adoption".[255] In March 2017, however, valuation of the estate was significantly reduced as a London probate office estimated his estate was worth just £528,806 at the time of his death.[256] As this book was going to press, no other information about the value of the estate or the recipients had been made public.

John Lennon

In the late 1990s, the Lennon estate was estimated to be worth £220 million. It was being reported that Sean, his son with Yoko Ono, would inherit the bulk of it. Julian, Lennon's son from his first marriage to Cynthia Powell, was only expected to get a fraction of the fortune. Ono had been resistant to cutting him in before as she "thought her step-son too immature to deal with such a fortune".[257] When John divorced Cynthia in 1968, Julian was to receive £2,400 a year in maintenance and, when he turned 25, a trust fund of £50,000.[258] He did, however, take legal action against the estate and reached a settlement in 1996.[259] It was reported he could not discuss the value of the settlement, but the *Irish Times* claimed in 1998 that it was worth £20 million, a figure repeated in 2011 by the *Daily Mail.*[260] [261] Speaking to the *Daily Telegraph* in 2015 about the settlement, Julian said, "I don't think it was necessarily fair, but I'm OK. The last thing I wanted was a court battle because there's much more money on the estate side than my side. A court case could have gone on for five years. The slanderous remarks would have been horrific. There would not have been a private life for either Sean or me. I just wanted to resolve it, to get the hell out of there; a chapter in my life finished, over with."[262]

Glenn Miller

The big-band star was on a plane that disappeared over the English Channel on 15 December 1944 but the news was not made public until Christmas Eve. He was not declared dead until 1945. His estate went to his wife, Helen, and their two adopted children. Following Helen's death in 1966, lawyer David MacKay – who had been a long-term friend of the Millers – became successor executor of the estate as per Glenn Miller's will. MacKay had agreed a deal with Helen that gave him a third of her husband's royalties. A court case in September 1979, however, saw him ordered to return $800,000 to Miller's two children. The judge in the case ruled that MacKay's deal with

Helen Miller was "fair and reasonable" as she was business-savvy and was not pressurised into signing it. As such, MacKay was allowed to keep the $535,000 he earned during Helen's lifetime. However, imposing a similar contract on the two children after their mother's death was deemed to be improper as they lacked the requisite business background to make sense of it. "[The judge] said one of the children, Jonnie Soper, was shy and tended to allow people to dominate her, while the other, Steve Miller, was considered naive and incompetent in business matters," reported the *New York Times*.[263] MacKay was ordered to repay $593,000 in royalties and commissions that he had earned from the estate between 1966 and 1977 alongside $207,000 in interest.[264]

Elvis Presley

The bulk of the Elvis estate has been sold a number of times (see Chapter 8), but Lisa Marie Presley, his only child, retained a 15 per cent stake in the Elvis business as well as the deeds to Graceland. She did, however, have a series of issues with her former business manager, who she sued in February 2018 over how her business interests were run.[265] He responded with a countersuit.

Barry Siegel had been behind the sale of 85 per cent of Elvis Presley Enterprises in late 2004 to CKX. This deal, he claimed, had "cleared up over $20m in debts Lisa had incurred and netted her over $40m cash and a multi-million dollar income stream". Lisa Marie argued that a subsequent investment in Core Entertainment (CKX's new name from 2012) went up in smoke when it went bankrupt in 2016. She was reported to be $16 million in debt, information that came out from her divorce from her fourth husband, a process that was happening concurrently with the action against Siegel.[266] As the case rumbled on, in September 2018 the judge sided with Lisa Marie by allowing her to shut down subpoenas sent by Siegel to Deutsche Bank pertaining to her bank records. It meant she would only have to hand over bank details prior to 26 February 2016.[267]

Bob Marley

The Bob Marley estate was cast into chaos when he died on 11 May 1981 because he did not leave a will. As we saw in Chapter 2, that meant the heirs (of whom there were many) had to navigate the Jamaican legal system, a process that took years. This was all thrown into even greater disarray amid a scandal involving forged signatures and offshore companies. There were also a multitude of paternity claims. In the 1990s, Mutual Security Merchant Bank and Trust Company were acting as administrators for the estate but the family was trying to take control of it. Settlement, however, was proving impossible to achieve as there was enormous infighting between the mothers of his numerous children as well as claims from former band members. In

1987, the courts ruled that the estate should be sold and proceeds split between beneficiaries.[268]

Chris Blackwell, founder of Island Records and the executive who helped turn Marley into a global star, mounted a bid in 1988 to buy the estate for $8.2 million (including music assets and real estate, notably the Tuff Gong recording studio). This bid was stopped by the UK Privy Council, which had the final say over Jamaican matters, after a number of heirs argued the assets had not been advertised sufficiently in advance.[269] Reggae star Eddy Grant was also putting together a bid, but withdrew. In the summer of 1990, the Privy Council heard the case and sent it back to the courts in Jamaica "with an option that the courts should consider soliciting new bids and reappraising the estate".[270] A larger (and slightly revised) bid was put forward in 1991 from Blackwell, Rita Marley (the singer's widow) and six of his adult children, to try and prevent the estate going into the hands of record company MCA Inc.[271] The sale was contingent on the children Marley had with women other than Rita getting lump-sum payments. Blackwell was opposed to MCA (or any corporation) buying the estate as "they're not involved in the emotional aspects of this" and would "buy an asset which they can exercise as they see fit", which could involve using "Bob Marley's name to sell [...] all kinds of things".[272]

When the courts stated they were looking for potential heirs – aside from Marley's acknowledged family – "hundreds of would-be Marleys appeared from all over the world" but this army of potential claimants was, with the help of Rita, narrowed down to seven. They were mainly from poor backgrounds and each was told their share of the estate would amount to around $210 paid every three months. Five of them were given cash settlements of $70,000 (with more to come when the estate was sold) and it was claimed the estate had paid out $100,000 to the heirs in 1990. Ziggy Marley, the singer's son and a musician in his own right, filed a statement with Dade County Court in Florida suggesting he wanted to extricate himself from the whole mess. "Let them have it," he said of all the competing claims. "Me can go out and make me own money."[273]

On 9 December 1991, the Supreme Court of Jamaica, after a week-long hearing, ruled that the Island Logic consortium made up of Chris Blackwell and 6 of Marley's adult children (out of 11 recognised children in total) were allowed to buy his estate. Island Logic had bid $11.5 million while MCA had tabled a conditional bid of up to $15.2 million. Justice Clarence Walker went with the lower bid as it was considered more "certain" than MCA's.[274] In the bidding, both sides were offering heirs shares in the estate (MCA offered them 4 per cent each while Island Logic was offering something similar to the infant beneficiaries that could be exercised when they came of age). As per the revised Island Logic bid, *Billboard* reported that the adult beneficiaries would "waive their right to immediate financial benefit so that the sale proceeds can be divided equally among the five infant beneficiaries", with each child getting $1,174,000.[275] Island Logic, via the

Bob Marley Foundation, would manage the estate on behalf of its adult beneficiaries, with an initial 10-year management term being put in place (and an option to renew after that).[276]

"Eventually, it was worked out and the estate recognised 11 children as Bob's heirs," said Roger Steffens, author and reggae archivist. "It was only in the 2000s [...] where they could start to build a business where everybody can have a fair share of it."[277] In total, the court actions over the estate had run for a decade, the last five years of which saw $8 million being spent on legal and administrative fees.[278] For the two years leading up to the December 1991 ruling on the sale, the Marley estate was locked in semi-stasis. "We can really get behind it now," said Blackwell. "I'm looking forward to getting on with the job of running the future."[279]

Elliott Smith

The death of American indie-folk artist Elliott Smith on 21 October 2003 was unquestionably shocking. The cause of death was recorded as two stab wounds to the chest, one of which perforated his heart. An apparent suicide note was left behind but detectives in the case concluded that "this death is possibly suspicious, however, circumstances are unclear at this time".[280] In January 2004, a leaked copy of the coroner's report claimed "the possibility of homicide" was not being ruled out.[281] Jennifer Chiba, Smith's girlfriend who was in their Los Angeles home with him at the time of his death, spoke to the media soon after and claimed Smith's family "knew the truth" that his death was by suicide. Relations between Chiba and Smith's family deteriorated further. She was seeking a 15 per cent share of his earnings, estimated at $1 million, but was informed in October 2007 that she would receive nothing from the estate. She was arguing that she was acting as his manager and agent at the time of his death, saying that he had made a verbal promise that she would be taken care of after his death. A Californian appellate court, however, ruled that she was acting as an unlicensed agent and, as such, was not entitled to a share of his estate. As she had a "co-habitative agreement" with Smith that was insufficient to grant her payments related to her management claims. The judge in the case said that she could make a claim based on cohabitation but only if she dropped her management-related claims, but it appears no further action was taken.[282]

Ike Turner

Ike Turner passed away on 12 December 2007 but within a matter of months a struggle over his estate had begun, with a number of ex-wives staking a claim. Jeanette Bazzell Turner had married Ike in 1995 but they separated in 2000. In April 2008, she asked the probate court if she could have a share of the estate but, her lawyer Joseph Rego argued, as a creditor rather than an heir. She claimed the divorce was "riddled with problems" and said she was not given a due share of their property. "She has a claim," said Rego. "If she is entitled to anything under the law, I want to make sure she gets it. I'm not trying to find a loophole here."[283]

The estate was already being fought over by his six children (three sons and three daughters) and his last wife, Audrey Madison Turner, whom he had married in October 2006. They filed for divorce two months later, although they reportedly reconciled before his death. His estate was described as "modest", with a valuation of just $200,000 including $80,000 in a number of bank accounts. The value of his copyrights in some 4,000 songs had, however, not been determined at this stage.[284] James Clayton, Turner's former attorney, had been appointed the estate's administrator and had requested the court allow him to hire a specialist lawyer to resolve his copyright issues, but Turner's children argued the cost of doing this – pegged at $50,000 – would effectively wipe out the value of the estate. Things were compounded by uncertainty surrounding the validity of a one-page handwritten will written in the final months of his life that Audrey produced a week after his death. In it he allegedly left his entire estate to his "x [sic] wife Audrey Madison Turner" including "power of attorney over my health and finances". A subsequent note from Ike Turner appeared to revoke "any and all powers of attorneys, wills, estate plans or other similar documents given to me by Audrey Madison".[285] To add even more confusion, Clayton had also produced a handwritten will from 2001 which he claimed left everything to him. Shortly after his death, one of Turner's sons, Ronald "Ronnie" Turner (Ike's only child with Tina Turner), approached music lawyer Don Wilson for representation in the case around the estate. "He called me and said, 'Dad has passed away. There's all kinds of craziness going on. I need you to come in and represent me,'" says Wilson. "I came in after Ike had passed away to represent four of his children in their battle with ex-wives and his former lawyer." In October 2009, a tentative ruling from Superior Court Judge Richard Cline stated that the 2001 will Clayton was brandishing had been invalidated by the 2007 will Audrey had produced. He added that his revoking of the 2007 will did not reinstate the 2001 will. The upshot of the tentative ruling was that Ike Turner had left no valid will and therefore his adult children were the only heirs of his estate.[286] "Each one ended up in a court decision by the judge," says Wilson of the final decisions on the estate. "So for each case, we won all five. Well, one we settled with an ex-wife and we just gave her some money. It was less than what it would have cost to litigate and so we saved the estate some money. But none of the other people would settle so we had to go all the way through trial and, fortunately in each of those four instances, the court decided in our favour."

J Dilla

Rapper and producer J Dilla (real name James Yancey) died on 10 February 2006 of complications from lupus. He had been ill for a long while and on 8

September 2005, fearing he might not make it through the night, he made out his will, naming his two daughters, his brother and his mother as his heirs. He appointed Artie Erck, his accountant, as the executor. He had left behind a significant IRS bill that was, according to *Fact*, "accrued in part due to his illness and lack of medical insurance". He also left behind a number of business and legacy problems. "Yancey's business dealings had never been simple in life, and that bad luck dogged him in death," added *Fact*.[287] He also, according to *Vibe*, left behind "unresolved legal issues surrounding the use of his beats".[288] Before he died, he had raced to complete the *Donuts* album from his hospital bed and it was released just three days before he died. His mother, Maureen Yancey, was shut out from his estate and so moved to set up the non-profit music education programme the J Dilla Foundation. She added that relations between her and Artie Erck deteriorated so badly that all communication between them had ceased. Erck, however, argued that payments from the estate were delayed due to Dilla's outstanding tax bill, which ran to a "healthy six figures".[289]

Dilla's lawyer Micheline Levine was also involved in the estate and in early 2007 appointed Eothen Alapatt, the rapper's former manager, as its creative director. Part of the estate's plan was to finish and release a "lost" album, the master tapes of which had come via his mother. A legal battle resulted but in February 2009 Alapatt and the heirs emerged victorious. Erck was replaced by Alex Borden, an independent executor who was appointed by the state of California.[290] In 2009, it was reported that Dilla's youngest daughter had started to receive money from the estate and that the eldest would start to receive money in early 2009.[291] The delay in releasing his posthumous album was in part down to the fact that Dilla had made a habit of making CDs of his beats and handing them out to friends and peers, with some of them subsequently being released on albums (such as *Dilla-gence* by Busta Rhymes) without permission. The estate had fired out cease-and-desist letters as well as placing an ad in *Billboard* urging people to stop using his material without authorisation.[292] "People started digging into their archives and thinking about ways that it could be repackaged in light of his death, and the celebrity he became," said Alapatt.[293] The lost album, entitled *The Diary*, was eventually released in April 2016 – a decade after Dilla's death – with Alapatt saying it was "85, 90 per cent" how Dilla had originally envisaged it.[294]

Selena

Selena Quintanilla (known by her first name) was an American singer and was termed the "Queen of Tejano" in reference to her Hispanic upbringing in Texas. She was murdered on 31 March 1995 by the president of her fan club, Yolanda Saldívar. She was just 23. In 1997, the biopic *Selena* was released with Jennifer Lopez in the title role. It generated $11.6 million at the US box office on its opening weekend and has grossed $35.3 million globally to date.[295] In May 2015, a royalties dispute with UMG Recordings was resolved, but details of the settlement were not made public.[296]

Her estate, however, has been at the centre of a long-running fight between her widower, Chris Pérez, and her father, Abraham Quintanilla Jr, over who controls her rights and her legacy. In 2016, Quintanilla Jr moved to block Pérez from making a TV series about the singer based on his 2012 book, *To Selena, with Love*. In December 2018, the judge in the case rejected Pérez's appeal to have the lawsuit filed by Quintanilla Jr dismissed.[297]

Since Selena's death, Quintanilla Jr has ploughed his efforts into the estate, filing a range of trademarks, creating a Selena doll with ARM Enterprise in 1996 and licensing her name and image to Visa for a prepaid debit card in 2012.[298] [299] A quarter of a century on, the disagreement between Pérez and Quintanilla Jr was front and centre in a dispute over a nine-part biopic series on Netflix about Selena (starting in December 2020) which her family both approved and executive-produced. In late 2020, the trial between Pérez and Quintanilla Jr was being scheduled to begin in February 2021.[300]

(The case had not been resolved before this book went to press.)

Billie Holiday

The success of *The United States Vs. Billie Holiday* biopic in 2021 and the revival of her recording of 'Strange Fruit' – because of its resonance with the Black Lives Matter movement – combined to bring new attention to the life and legacy of the great jazz singer who died on 17 July 1959 at the age of 44.

In the final years of her life she lived in relative penury. Legend has it that she had her entire life savings – a mere $750 in used notes – strapped to her leg when she died. Her funeral was paid for by Michael Grace, an affluent jazz fan and in May 1960, jazz magazine *DownBeat* even started a collection to pay for a tombstone for her.[301]

Holiday had died without leaving a will and her estate ended up being inherited by Louis McKay, her third husband, who she was estranged from.[302] McKay was a man of dubious character and credentials (he was tied to the Mafia as an enforcer) but he was relatively protective of her legacy and earning potential. Most significantly, the biopic *Lady Sings the Blues* was released in 1972 with Diana Ross playing the role of Holiday. It was nominated for five Academy Awards the following year.

When Louis McKay died on 10 March 1981, the Holiday estate transferred to his widow, Bernice McKay.[303]

In May 2008, the new heirs filed a lawsuit against Black Hawk Record in a dispute over royalties relating to the release of a recording of Holiday's performance at the Monterey Jazz Festival in 1958, the year before her death.[304]

Bernice McKay held on to the Holiday estate for three decades but sold it to independent publishers Bicycle Music in February 2012.[305] Three years later, Bicycle merged with Concord Music Group to create Concord Bicycle Music.[306]

Because Holiday was primarily a performer, rather than a songwriter, and did not own her master recordings, *Billboard* noted that "most of the value of her estate lies in the name and likeness rights that movie producers usually need to make a film".[307] Alongside *Lady Sings the Blues* and *The United States Vs. Billie Holiday*, she has also been the subject of a musical (*Lady Day at Emerson's Bar and Grill*) which opened on Broadway in 2014 and a children's book (*Mister and Lady Day: Billie Holiday and the Dog Who Loved Her*) which was published in 2017.

Scott Weiland

The frontman of Stone Temple Pilots and Velvet Revolver died of an accidental drug overdose on 3 December 2015. According to leaked documents in November 2017, his interest in Stone Temple Pilots was valued at $446,000 and memorabilia he left behind were estimated to be worth $559,349.83.[308] His will named Mary Forsberg, his ex-wife, as executor of his will – not Jamie Weiland, who he had married in 2013 and was his wife at the time of his death. The will had been written in April 2007 before Weiland and Forsberg divorced.[309] In June 2019, *The Blast* claimed to have seen leaked documents that showed Weiland had not paid federal income tax between 2012 and 2014; as such, he (or rather his estate) owed $818,569.62 to the IRS. The year before, the estate was hit with a lien by the California State Tax Franchise Board for close to $250,000.[310] The following month, Forsberg filed court documents revealing that the estate was now valued at $1,979,261.56 and had brought in $1,054,385.70 in gross royalties since Weiland's death. She stated that she was working to settle state and federal tax liens. It also emerged that the estate faced a lawsuit from a tour bus company seeking $150,000 to pay for damage caused to a vehicle the singer had hired in 2013. The estate was able to negotiate a settlement of $25,000. Lawyers who represented Weiland in a lawsuit were seeking $52,626 plus interest to settle a payment but agreed to accept $32,000.

The biggest concern, however, was a $20 million lawsuit that Vice Inc had filed against Weiland before he died relating to the rock supergroup that it had put together, Art of Anarchy. Despite being a member of the group, Weiland had slated them and refused to promote the band. Yahoo reported, "Vice sued Weiland to recover the $230,000 they paid him upfront and asked for an additional $20 million in damages for ruining any chance the album would be successful and for lost revenue for the planned tour and merchandise sales."[311]

The Blast reported in August 2019 that a creditor's claim, originally filed in March 2016, by Jamie Weiland for $64,406 against the estate had been denied. "Jamie Weiland claimed that her pre-nup with Scott Weiland called for him to put $2,000 in an account every month while they were married," said *The Blast*. "The payments would continue until one of them filed for divorce, and then she would collect the money. She also claimed that agreement called for a 7 per cent increase in the payments every year." Jamie Weiland claims he only made the agreed deposits for the first two months of their marriage.[312] She had, however, been successful in July 2018 in getting the estate to pay her $4,000 per month in child support to help bring up the two children she had with the singer, which would be paid until each child turns 18.[313] Jamie had also been seeking a monthly allowance of $64,000 that stemmed from her pre-nuptial agreement with Scott but Forsberg, who controlled the estate, claimed in 2018 that the paperwork had been filed incorrectly and it had now lapsed.[314]

XXXTentacion

XXXTentacion (real name Jahseh Onfroy) died on 18 June 2018 from multiple gunshot wounds. He was aged 20. Bitter in-fighting between the family members has somewhat tainted the early stages of the estate. Corey Pack, the rapper's half-brother, filed a lawsuit against Cleopatra Bernard, the rapper's mother, in June 2020, over stake in – and control over – the estate.[315]

The *Miami New Times* reported in June 2018 that court documents filed in Broward County showed that XXXTentacion had written his will on 7 November 2017. He did not sign it but Bernard added a note beside her signature saying she had power of attorney over her son. The will made no mention of his then-unborn child with Jenesis Sanchez as it was written before she became pregnant and not updated. She was only a few months pregnant when XXXTentacion was killed.[316]

(The case had not been resolved before this book went to press.)

Amy Winehouse

The singer died on 23 July 2011 but did not leave a will. Her estate, valued at £2.94 million, passed to her parents who soon after set up the Amy Winehouse Foundation to help individuals dealing with drug and alcohol problems. She had married Blake Fielder-Civil in 2007 but they divorced in 2009.[317] He resurfaced after her death and, in July 2019, made a legal bid to secure a £1 million stake in her estate. The media were damning. Winehouse had given him £250,000 when they divorced but there was some uncertainty over the wording of the settlement that could give him grounds to make a claim on the estate. "If there wasn't a 'clean break' there is a case that could be pursued," Frank Arndt, senior partner at Paradigm Family Law, told the *Sun*. "His team will possibly say he needs the money […] and that there is money in the estate."[318] Blake Fielder-Civil was seeking a lump-sum payment as well as an allowance from the estate. "Her friends and family are furious that any successful claim by Fielder-Civil could take money from the charity [set up in her name]" reported the *Sun*. "Latest accounts for the foundation show it spent £757,577 on good causes in a year. That included £454,102 for the Amy Winehouse Resilience programme which aids 11–18-year-olds with drug and alcohol problems."[319]

Ritchie Valens

Ritchie Valens was only 17 when he died on 3 February 1959 in the plane crash that also claimed the lives of Buddy Holly and The Big Bopper. He had only just started making hits[320] when his life was cut short, but the recording contract he had signed in 1958 with Bob Keane at Del-Fi Records was to prove a major conundrum for his family for decades after his death. The family were initially favourably disposed towards Keane, who also served as his producer, but slowly they started to realise things were not necessarily in a good position for them. Speaking in a 2012 documentary, author Larry Lehmer said, "Ritchie's family questioned whether Bob Keane paid all the royalties that were due to him – or due to the family after Ritchie's death. And I think Bob Keane acknowledged that he paid them something like $13,000 during Ritchie's lifetime."[321] Bob Morales, one of Ritchie's brothers, tried to get to the bottom of who owned what and arranged a meeting with him, his mother and Keane in Los Angeles. "It was at Bob's restaurant in North Hollywood at high noon in the lobby," said Morales. "He said there to my mom, 'I own Ritchie's music for eternity.' I said, 'I don't know who elected you God, but I don't think so.'"[322] Keane, it turned out, owned all of Valens's recordings outright and it was alleged he had secured co-writing credits on many of his songs. The family claimed that Keane had no input in their writing.

Concepcion Valenzuela, mother of Valens, spoke to the *Los Angeles Times* in 1987 about what she saw as Keane's hijacking of her son's legacy and money. "You know Bob Keane has controlled Ritchie's music for all these years," she said. "Oh, I get a bit of money now and then. BMI sends me a statement. But do you know that Keane presented me with a bill of $4,000 for Ritchie's funeral? And that '57 black and silver-chromed Thunderbird that Keane gave Ritchie? Well, he kept it in his garage after I lost Ritchie."[323] These accusations were "ridiculous", countered Keane. "She was in worse financial condition than I was," he claimed. "I put up over $7,000 so they'd ship the kid's body back and put him in a decent coffin. I still have the check somewhere."[324] The family could not claim back the master recordings from Keane, but under copyright termination laws in the US they were able to reclaim his publishing rights (see Chapter 10).[325]

Tammy Wynette

Country star Tammy Wynette died on 6 April 1998. She had been married five times, marrying her final husband, songwriter and producer George Richey, in 1978. She had four daughters by previous partners and told them, as well as Richey, that she had taken out two $1 million life insurance policies: one was for Richey; the other was to be split between all four children. Georgette Jones (Wynette's daughter with country musician George Jones) said that they were told that all her personal possessions would go to Richey, were she to die first, and then when he passed away, everything would be split equally between her four children as well as Richey's two children.

When Wynette died, Richey and his brother were made trustees of the will and the estate. The four daughters were not pleased and believed one of them should have been made a co-executor, but a no-contest clause in the will favoured Richey and worked against the daughters. "It forced the children to accept a will that they didn't think was fair to them," said estate-planning attorney Jeff Mobley.[326] Richey asked the daughters to sign a form saying they agreed with the will. Three did – Tina abstained – and they each got $5,000 on signing, believing it to be an advance on their quarter-share of the $1 million life insurance policy.

Richey had been left all Wynette's personal possessions in the will but all her other assets (including royalties and copyrights) also went to him in the form of trusts. Georgette claimed that a yellow legal pad her mother used to outline which items were to go to each daughter was being withheld by Richey. "Richey's explanation to no list being found was that, 'Oh, honey, you know I don't know where that list is and your mom changed it all the time,'" she said. "So there was no list filed with the will, so therefore we never received any items at all. Not our baby books, not anything that my grandmother left to our mom for us. Essentially everything that my mom had – clothes, personal items of all kinds, including things of ours, my sisters and I – none of those things were given to us."[327] After Wynette's death, Richey married Sheila Slaughter (a TV producer and a former cheerleader for the Dallas Cowboys). Slaughter-Richey, as she was now known, was dragged into the dispute. "They weren't just Tammy Wynette's riches," she said of the disputed possessions. "They were George Richey and Tammy Wynette's riches."[328]

When an heir cannot be found

There are occasions, notably with small estates, when it is unclear who revenues should be diverted to when an artist dies. Tom Ferguson works at PPL in the UK, the organisation that collects performance royalties for record labels and musicians (from, for example, TV and radio plays). His role is to track down the rightful heirs and recipients of this income.

"When a performer dies, the rights drop into the estate," he says of the monies PPL collects. "They can't transfer these performer rights. The right to receive equitable remuneration from exploitation of sound recordings is a personal right while they are alive." That means whoever inherits their estate will inherit those rights and the income that results from them. "After death, it's transferable by testamentary disposition or by other legal transfer," explains Ferguson. "What we have to do is find out who's inherited the rights after the performer has died." The potential heirs will have to supply a copy of the will, probate documentation or their own ID for PPL to start the process of transferral.

Occasionally, however, the performer will have left no inheritor details to an organisation like PPL, so Ferguson will have to do detective work to track down the rightful heirs. "Overall, we rely on the families and beneficiaries coming to us and telling us that their mum or dad has died or their husband or wife has died," he says. "In most cases that's how it works – it's fairly straightforward. The beneficiary, the surviving spouse or whoever, will be led through the process. I'm always getting told about people dying and whatever – often guys that are not particularly well known. We keep an eye out for all that stuff."

When the unclaimed money in an account for a performer builds up to a certain level, PPL can make moves to track down potential heirs. A change or closure of a bank account can often be the main way payments are stopped and how they start to accrue on the performer's PPL account. That will trigger a notification that the money is not being paid through and hence the hunt for the rightful recipients can begin.

PPL primarily covers the UK but can also collect money from overseas performances of recordings if the performing artist has mandated them to do so. Ferguson cannot talk specifics but says the unclaimed money can be considerable in some cases, mentioning examples where the payment to heirs was far from insignificant.

There is, however, a time limit on back claims. "By statute, PPL holds six years' worth of money," says Ferguson. "So every seventh year, any held money that would have been payable in that year, or would have been collected in that year, gets washed across every performer who had a payment in that year." It goes into a collective pot that other performers share.

CHAPTER 4

Creating Posthumous Fame

"You Wait Till You Hear This, Matey"

At their private wedding ceremony in Malibu on 29 July 2000, one of the songs Hollywood A-listers Brad Pitt and Jennifer Aniston danced to was by Nick Drake, the diffident English folk singer who died on 25 November 1974. As a moment in a slow-burning career revival, it was a curious one. But it was to become more curious still.

Drake rarely played live, apparently because he could not handle the rough and tumble or the baiting from the audience that defined the London folk circuit at the time. He left behind three mesmerising and beautiful studio albums, released between 1969 and 1972, that contained a mere 31 songs with a combined running time of just 108 minutes. Those albums barely sold at the time but his label, Island Records, always kept them in print. Drake was, for decades, the connoisseur's choice, whispered about in reverential terms by musicians, like a secret they did not want the flame of publicity to hit, ignite and quickly turn to ash.

No known video footage of Drake as a performer exists and he did not do many interviews in his lifetime.[1] He spent his final years in near-seclusion in his parents' house in Tanworth-in-Arden, Warwickshire, where he died from acute amitriptyline poisoning, having overdosed on antidepressants. The mystery around him blossomed slowly through the 1970s and 1980s, but by the late 1990s, things were primed to take his music to whole new audiences. This was music he wanted everyone to hear, but he struggled with the promotional and touring requirements that such a goal necessitated. This was a posthumous fame that happened in no small part because of the determination of his family – his parents Rodney and Molly alongside his older sister, the actor Gabrielle – that his music should be heard.

Normally music estates are concerned with keeping a certain level of fame and success in the air after the artist has died. These people were successful and celebrated in their lifetime and the estate's role is to ensure that legacy does not shrink over time. But they have the advantage – and all the responsibilities that come with that – of the person already being a known entity.

Taking someone who was barely known in their lifetime and elevating them to a whole new tier of fame is both more complex and far less immediate. When achieved, however, it can give their art a thrumming new relevance. The world may not have known about them during their lifetime but their family, as custodians of the estate, are determined to right this terrible wrong.

THE ANTECEDENTS OF POSTHUMOUS FAME

The worlds of art and literature are thronged with the names of people who only achieved fame and success posthumously – individuals whose influence and importance we now take as read. Franz Kafka, Emily Dickinson and Vincent van Gogh were all prolific in their lifetime, but it was not until their death that their legend and their fame really grew. The public then had a wealth of material to retroactively work through and use as prisms through which to understand their art.

In music, the opposite tends to be the case. Like Nick Drake, these artists typically created such a small body of work that what is there starts to take on the luminescence of holy scriptures and a convoluted mythology – that of the pure and the prefect creator – starts to build up around them.

Perhaps the best parallel here outside of music is John Kennedy Toole, who took his own life on 26 March 1969, but whose astonishing picaresque romp of a novel *A Confederacy of Dunces* was eventually published in 1980 and went on to win the Pulitzer Prize for Fiction the following year. It was entirely down to the indefatigability of his mother, Thelma Ducoing Toole, that the book was eventually published, became a hit and finally understood as a pivotal piece of writing. She unearthed the typed manuscript (described as a "badly smeared, scarcely readable carbon") for *A Confederacy of Dunces* five years after his death.[2] This novel, she was certain, had to be published.

At least eight publishers turned it down during the five years she worked solo to get a book deal for it.[3] Eventually she tracked down and lobbied novelist Walker Percy, who was teaching at Loyola University in New Orleans at the time, to help her get it published. He was blown away. "It was the most extraordinary novel I've ever read in manuscript form," he was to tell the *New Orleans Times-Picayune* when the book was eventually published by Louisiana State University.[4] An earlier unpublished book by Toole, *The Neon Bible*, also received its posthumous release in 1989.

These two books comprise the entirety of John Kennedy Toole's published output. As it stands, significantly more books have been written *about* John Kennedy Toole than he himself actually wrote.[5]

DOWN TO THE CROSSROADS: ROBERT JOHNSON AND POSTHUMOUS MUSICAL MYTHOLOGY

In the modern music business, as with the post-war musical styles that it was built on, the origins of the posthumous reappraisal can be traced back to the blues. As we saw in Chapter 1, it was the 1961 release of *King of the Delta Blues Singers*, collecting together 16 recordings by Robert Johnson, that marked the beginning of the estates business and it was fitting that it was based around the work of an artist who died in relative obscurity in 1938.

A test pressing of his track 'Preachin' Blues' had appeared on the 1959 compilation album *The Country Blues* issued by Folkways, which sat alongside recordings by other key names in the blues such as Blind Willie McTell, Big Bill Broonzy and Blind Lemon Jefferson.[6] But this 1961 compilation was to take things to a whole other level.

King of the Delta Blues Singers was compiled by John Hammond, the legendary producer and executive at Columbia Records, and has been described as "arguably the single most important blues reissue album in history".[7] Hammond had originally attempted to track down Johnson in 1938 to perform at the Spirituals to Swing concert at Carnegie Hall in New York, but Johnson had just passed away.[8]

The album's eventual release in 1961 had a profound impact on a whole new generation of musicians, particularly in the UK among the blues-obsessed likes of Keith Richards, Jeff Beck, Eric Clapton and Jimmy Page.[9] In lockstep with the music, the mythology grew, especially around the notion of the crossroads (a recurring motif in the blues) and the dark influence of the devil on the music (symbolised by references to hellhounds in Johnson's songs).[10]

In 2011, marking the 100th anniversary of his birth, Steve Berkowitz, producer at Sony Legacy (who own Johnson's recordings), spoke to NPR about the power of the mythology around him and how that could be explicitly mined. "That was always the heart and soul of the marketing plan," he said. "We always knew the music was great. But a guy sells his soul to the devil at midnight down at the crossroads, comes back and plays the hell out of the guitar, and then he dies. I mean, it's a spectacular story."[11]

Some have tried to push back against this supposed backstory – partly because it devalues Johnson's own talent but partly because it has a worryingly racist subtext – but the mythology remains fixed. As Bruce Conforth, professor of American culture at the University of Michigan, put it in 2015 in an interview with the *Guardian*, "When Robert Johnson died he stopped being a person and he started being a myth."[12]

The transubstantiation of a dead person into a myth underpins a great deal of the work of estates. Here are, runs the logic of estates, superhuman people who deserve to be recognised and praised for eternity. They may have died, but conversely the folklore around them should only grow with every passing year. The paradoxical compulsion at the very core of music estates is that they must keep the dead alive. At their very best, they defy science; at their very worst, they are *Weekend at Bernie's*.

THE ELEGANT RENAISSANCE OF NICK DRAKE

"He didn't want to be a niche, hip star"

The cruel, but true, mathematics of the record business are that only a fraction of artists will ever be deemed good enough – or potentially commercial enough – to be given a record deal. Of those who get signed, a commonly quoted figure in the industry holds that 90 per cent of them will lose money, often a staggering amount that was futilely spent to get the record sounding right, and then even more on the buckshot of marketing to try and salvage at least some of the initial investment.

The reality of the record business is that it is not for the faint-hearted. Nick Drake could be said to be the very definition of faint-hearted but he had, in Chris Blackwell – founder of Island Records – someone who always totally believed in him and who refused to let his music fall into total obscurity.

Drake's first two albums – 1969's *Five Leaves Left* and 1971's *Bryter Layter* – sold minuscule amounts on release. No precise sales figures for their original release exist, but neither of them came anywhere close to entering the UK album chart.[13] But Island – or, more specifically, Blackwell – remained loyal. They even made his failure to sell records on any level a weirdly proud angle in the marketing for what was to be his final album.

"His first two albums haven't sold a shit," ran the press release that was sent out to announce the release of *Pink Moon* in 1972. "But if we carry on releasing them, then perhaps someone authoratative [sic] will stop, listen properly and agree with us."[14]

Drake soon retreated to Tanworth-in-Arden and it seemed like he would remain a beautiful secret. Nick Kent, however, wrote a lengthy obituary in the *NME* that was not actually published until 1975, the year after his death. This was to be the first step in a total – if glacially slow – re-evaluation of his career and his music. "Nick Drake's music should be heard by more people," wrote Kent. "Its own tastefulness speaks for itself."[15]

Island moved slowly in building his legacy, as Drake himself had done in his own career. In 1978, it assembled *The Complete Collected Works* featuring his three studio albums and four previously unreleased tracks. It sold for £9.50 – "a huge sum in those inflation-ridden days" notes Trevor Dann in his Nick Drake biography.[16] This was followed by the *Fruit Tree* box set in 1979, which Dann claims "did little to popularise Nick's music".[17]

Patrick Humphries, however, in his biography of the singer, regards *Fruit Tree* as the real starting point for the Drake estate. "If you want to mark the beginning of the cult which has sprung up around Nick Drake, 9 March 1979 is as good a date as any," he writes. "On that day Island Records released the box set *Fruit Tree*."[18] He argues that Island "fought shy of marketing Nick in the first few years after he died" so *Fruit Tree* marked a step change, not just for the Drake estate, but for catalogue marketing in general.[19]

"What became *Fruit Tree* was one of the first-ever box sets devoted to the work of a single artist, in an attempt to put that artist's work into some sort of perspective, as well as allowing the release of previously unheard material," proposes Humphries. "There had been records in boxes before – George Harrison's *All Things Must Pass* and *The Concert for Bangladesh* – but *Fruit Tree* was the first to try to gain an overview of a life and work, and could be seen as a template for what followed."[20]

Dann argues the "real turning point in Nick's profile" came in the 1980s.[21] Robert Smith of The Cure said the band's name came from the line "a troubled cure for a troubled mind" in Drake's song 'Time Has Told Me'. Other acts like REM and The Dream Academy also cited him as an influence, with the latter writing their 1985 hit single 'Life in a Northern Town' as an elegy to him. The 1985 compilation *Heaven in a Wild Flower* sold a respectable 20,000 copies in the UK which, according to Dann, was "twice as many as the total sales of the first three albums and the boxed set put together".[22] *Time of No Reply*, which added in outtakes and alternative versions of songs, followed in 1987.

It was, however, not until the 1990s that things would really start to gather pace.

Cally Callomon, who now runs the Nick Drake estate along with Gabrielle Drake, was working at Island Records in the 1990s as creative director (having previously worked at Warner in A&R).[23] "I suggested to Chris Blackwell that we do some compilation CDs of the lesser-selling artists – which he didn't like the idea of," Callomon says. "But when I suggested doing it as a library across five different artists, five titles as a set, he liked that idea. So we did John Martyn, Sandy Denny, John Cale, Julian Cope and Nick Drake. These were all artists whose music I liked and thought were criminally undersold."

Before that, however, Callomon says that getting major record shops to stock Nick Drake's music – particularly because Island would not agree to their demands for a significant discount so they could be sold at a budget rate – was an uphill struggle. "We were always up against it when it came to back catalogue at Island," he says. "In general the big retailers like HMV saw these titles as 'rack fodder' – their term – and stocked and filed them all badly. HMV was no place for a music fan unless all you wanted was the new George Michael album at a 'discount price' or a computer game. Even when we joined in with an HMV catalogue campaign, we had to pay for the press advertising and pay HMV for them to rack the CDs out – and we landed a pittance in royalties for these campaigns. They even offered us TV advertising, which Island had to pay for. The current arguments with streaming income come to mind here. Their trade-off was to 'really go for it' on the new Stereo MCs album. The catalogue titles became bribes."

Coming out of this renewed push of Drake's slim, but important, catalogue came 1994's *Way to Blue: An Introduction to Nick Drake* compilation that was compiled by Joe Boyd, Drake's producer. While working on this album, Callomon met Gabrielle Drake for the first time. He had been managing artists alongside his work at Island and, in 1998, Gabrielle asked him to take over the running of her brother's estate. "Both Rodney and Molly had died," he says. "They had died leaving Gabrielle Nick's music and she didn't know what to do. She was acting on TV and on stage all the time. She felt a little bit guilty that she wasn't going to be able to devote the time or expertise needed. I had met her whilst I was working on the *Way to Blue* compilation and we just got on. So it seemed like a logical thing to happen, that I would then pursue the Nick Drake legacy with her always there alongside me."

Having previously been run akin to a cottage industry, the Nick Drake estate was now adding a new layer of both professionalism and proactivity. This was to result in a flurry of activity and elevate the singer far beyond the small but highly dedicated cult following that had grown slowly but steadily since his death.

"I was managing living artists at the time," says Callomon of the new approach he took towards the Nick Drake estate. "I got quite interested in the idea that most people didn't know that Nick was dead: most people didn't know about Nick Drake at all. I liked the idea of manifesting a dead artist as if he was a living entity. Not playing games and not trying to tell people that he's not dead, but selling Nick as though he was a living artist. Gabrielle got it immediately – the idea of not celebrating or commemorating the death of an artist but really starting from a complete rebirth of an artist."

Perhaps *the* defining moment for the Nick Drake estate came in late 1999 when the title track of *Pink Moon* was used in a US TV advert for Volkswagen's Cabrio convertible. The ad, featuring four friends driving through the moonlight-flooded countryside to a bar but then immediately leaving as it is too noisy, is just over a minute long and shot at night with a blue wash, making it appear dreamlike.

The Boston-based Arnold Advertising executives who made the ad had originally intended to use 'Under the Milky Way', a 1988 hit by Australian act The Church. The ad itself had the working title of 'Milky Way' and had already been shot – but without the musical accompaniment. 'Lament' by The Cure and 'You, the Night and the Music' by Tones on Tail were also considered, but The Church were the frontrunner.[24]

The ad was aimed at a very particular demographic – young professionals who still saw themselves as alternative – and Nick Drake very much fitted the bill. "The people who drove Volkswagens, they thought of themselves as being more underground – a little bit cooler and younger – and they were," said Lance Jensen, a copywriter and group creative director at Arnold Advertising when the ad was made.[25]

Callomon says that off the back of this they had what he termed "open season" on sync use in advertising and in films of Drake's music. It snowballed quickly. 'Fly' was on the soundtrack of 2001's *The Royal Tenenbaums* while 'One of These Things First' appeared on the soundtrack of 2004's *Garden State*. "I found that a lot of the people that were in charge of making those decisions were of the same era as I was and they too were people who knew about Nick from their youth," says Callomon. "It was almost like a crusade of revenge – people saying they wanted 'Time Has Told Me' in this film and so on. But every time anyone used any of Nick's songs, obviously they got tremendous feedback from the public and from everyone else."

While there is some mysticism around Drake – his music was so pure and rarefied that it has taken the public decades to finally catch up – that is to wilfully ignore the machine, admittedly a genteel and cautious one, that powers the estate. In his biography of folk blues singer and guitarist John Martyn, Graeme Thomson notes there is a curious contradiction between how Nick Drake's fans see him and what the commercial reality of his renaissance actually involved.[26] "Posthumously, Drake has been almost deified, artfully moulded into the platonic ideal of a tortured artist, a beautiful young man too sensitive for the cut and thrust of the music industry or, indeed, the modern world in general," he writes. "Some of that is true, and some of it is a feat of retrospective branding which has little romanticism about it. The resurrection of Drake in the 1990s as the quintessential cult artist was driven by a hard-headed marketing decision by PolyGram. Having bought Island Records [in 1989], the company were keen to recoup losses on artists who had never sold any records."[27]

This tension between the harsh reality of the music business and the romantic ideal of a precious artistic legacy runs through the very heart of this book, but nowhere is it more exposed than in the case of Nick Drake. He was reborn in the 1990s – and the legacy continues to grow – *precisely because* his estate worked hard to achieve that. But the estate has set very strict parameters on what it will and will not do. There is a delicate balancing act here and finding ways to bring his music to a huge audience – such as in a major TV ad campaign or a Hollywood film – can also risk pushing out fans who, for whatever reason, feel a sense of ownership of an artist who for many years was as far from the spotlight's glare as it is possible to be.

"[Nick] didn't want to be a niche, hip star," said Callomon when speaking to *Quartz* in 2015. "He wanted to be able to have an international voice and for people to appreciate him for what he is. And little by little, on our own terms, I think that's what we've given him."[28]

The estate has, so far, said no to many of the things that other estates would jump at – most notably a biopic, despite multiple approaches, "once a month", from directors and producers over the years. "To make a film, however lucrative that would be both as a film and as a way of selling back catalogue, would kill something that would be unforgivable in my book," says Callomon. "That is one of the classic things where the answer is always no."

Trevor Dann claims that, when he was head of BBC Music Entertainment in the 1990s, the total absence of any archival footage of Drake was not a barrier to pitches coming in trying to find new ways to tell the story of his life and his music. "One UK production company pitched a cartoon treatment of Nick's life," he writes. "Another came up with a plan to use an animatronic Nick intercut with live action."[29] Thankfully the latter idea never progressed beyond that point. Kraftwerk? Maybe. Nick Drake? Never.

Documentaries were also made about Drake, notably *A Skin Too Few*, which premiered in cinemas in 2002 and was subsequently broadcast on BBC Four on 22 May 2004 – the same day as a significant radio documentary on Radio 2. It was created by Dutch filmmaker Jeroen Berkvens and he told *Rolling Stone* how he worked around the absence of footage of Drake as a musician, using it as a feature rather than treating it as a bug. "[Nick] was invisible and hard to grasp," he said, "so that was the basis on which I started the script."[30]

Callomon says this is the only documentary on Drake that the estate has been impressed by, paralleling it with another that was being made for the BBC around the same time that he felt was severely wanting. "Gabrielle and I were taken by the guys from Holland because they said it was going to be a film about the music and less about Nick as a person," he says. "That film was *A Skin Too Few*. I still think it's a really good film. It allows the music to play almost in its entirety. It has a strong emotional quality to it. The BBC one was shockingly bad. We made sure that that would never be seen again. It was just slapdash and the usual limp-wristed affair."

The estate has also turned down potentially lucrative ads – not out of fear of overexposure and damaging the catalogue but more around not being granted the type of creative input and control they would like. In the 2015 *Quartz* interview, Callomon told the story of turning down an initial approach from a major fast food chain that serves to illustrate just how things can work here. "McDonalds approached us recently and started off by saying that they figured we probably wouldn't want to let them use a song in one of their adverts," he said. "I told them that we don't say no to anything but that we have to see the use first. That was the end of the conversation. We never saw it."[31]

The tight control and need for approval on uses is down, for the most part, to Drake's sister having a very clear idea of what is and is not right for the estate. "Gabrielle is a very rare creature," explains Callomon. "She understands the power of saying no. When we get ludicrous offers to use music here or there or a new format or a Best Of, we have tended to say no to most things, waiting for the thing that, when you say yes, it does make sense."

An estate, then, should be invisible, and new audiences finding out about an artist like Nick Drake should be oblivious to the machinations behind their discovery lest it taint their joy. "People still feel that they have discovered Nick for themselves – that it hasn't been thrust on them," is how Callomon puts it. "We have been cautious with social media as we find the fans' word of mouth far more sociable and far more potent," he says. "It's easy to get lost in the clicks. However, we may start to take a limited foray into this soon, if only to improve the direct line that can exist between the songs and the listener."

Drake, however, has some incredibly famous fans and they have played their part in taking him to a much bigger audience. They danced to his music at their wedding, but Brad Pitt and Jennifer Aniston were also heavily involved in the 2004 Radio 2 documentary for the BBC.

A Nick Drake documentary had already been made and broadcast in the 1990s, narrated by Pentangle star Danny Thompson, the folk and jazz musician who had played on *Five Leaves Left*, Drake's debut album.[32] It was revised and expanded upon in the early 2000s and Callomon, having heard about these two Hollywood stars dancing to Nick Drake's music at their wedding, felt the new host had just revealed herself. "It was that that made me want Jennifer Aniston to narrate the radio documentary for the BBC," he says. "Jennifer Aniston being American and being a woman would have a very different feel to it."

By the time *Lost Boy – In Search of Nick Drake* was broadcast on Radio 2 on 22 May 2004, it was Brad Pitt who was the narrator.[33] The documentary, given the Hollywood draw it now had, was also the first time a newly discovered Nick Drake song, 'Tow the Line', was played.

Interviewed in the *Daily Telegraph* just after the Pitt-fronted documentary aired, Gabrielle joked that, coming up to 30 years after his death, she was still having to live in his shadow. "Wretched boy!" she said, feigning indignation. "Here I am, still doing his publicity."[34] She was later to refer – with keen self-effacement – to this canonisation of her brother as "Nickery".[35]

The slow renaissance of Nick Drake is a powerful example of an estate with a clear mission and a zeal around how it intends to see it through to fruition. At the beating heart of it is a desire to secure the recognition they feel his music deserved in his lifetime. Drake, after all, wanted a huge audience for his music but, for a variety of cruel and painful reasons, he was not able to make that happen. His estate has finally made visible that which should never have been invisible.

As Gabrielle herself put it about her brother's growing posthumous fame, "He was a funny combination of not wanting to compromise his work and go commercial, yet wanting his work to be well known. I can't help but be pleased that it now is [...] After all, that is what happens to a lot of young poets: they don't flourish till after their death."[36]

EVA CASSIDY: FROM OBSCURITY TO POSTHUMOUS CHART-TOPPER

"It's basically a home video of a dead girl singing a song that wasn't a hit"

In the late 1990s, Terry Wogan's breakfast show was the biggest show on Radio 2 at a time when radio was the primary anointer of hits. In 1998, Wogan was to launch the career of an obscure US singer who had passed away from melanoma two years earlier.

The story wends its way back to Blix Street Records, a small independent label based in Gig Harbor, Washington. In the 1990s, Blix was having some success with Irish folk singer Mary Black and US folk and Celtic singer Grace Griffith – and it was the latter who was to introduce Blix Street founder Bill Straw to a relatively unknown singer called Eva Cassidy. "I got a call from Grace towards the end of September 1996," says Straw. "She said, 'We have this wonderful nightingale and I'm afraid we're going to lose her. Can I send you a tape?'"

That tape was a copy of the *Live at Blues Alley* album that had been recorded at the Georgetown, Washington. Blues Alley was a tiny 125-seater venue that was opened in 1965 and had hosted performances by legendary names like Ella Fitzgerald, Charles Mingus and Dizzy Gillespie over the years.

Eva Cassidy recorded *Live at Blues Alley* over two nights, 2–3 January 1996, self-funding it. She stated it cost her $4,000, with $1,000 being donated to her by her aunt Isabel.[37] The first night's recording was deemed unusable due to a buzzing, caused by the stage lights, on the tape, so the second night had to be used.[38] She collected a run of a thousand copies of the album from a pressing plant in the Virginia countryside that May but fretted that she might struggle to sell them all.[39] It was not her first release – she had released an album of standards with Chuck Brown in 1992 called *The Other Side* on Liaison Records[40] – but *Live at Blues Alley* was to be the catalyst for everything that followed. This small-run album, via Liaison, was released locally on 20 May 1996. Less than half a year later, at the age of 33 Eva Cassidy passed away.

Straw played the cassette copy of the album that Grace Griffith had given him, which had been cued up to her cover of Sting's 'Fields of Gold'. "I immediately knew it was extraordinary," he says. "By the time I had heard the whole album, I realised it was one of the best pop singers ever." He knew Cassidy was terminally ill and he was, he says, conflicted. He wanted to give the album a wider release beyond the DC area but knew the story was going to have a painful ending. "I knew immediately where she stood in the hierarchy of singers," he recalls. "Music is not an athletic achievement; it isn't who runs the fastest. I thought it was obvious that she was going to be famous. But it was also obvious she wasn't going to be around to enjoy it."

He talked himself out of meeting her, feeling it was inappropriate or even ghoulish to discuss record deals with someone who was nearing the end of their life. "Going back to meet somebody before they die, it sounded kind of weird to me," he says. "I made a mistake. I should have done it. Weirdness be damned!"

Griffith kept him abreast of news about Eva and eventually informed him of her death. He called her parents and spoke to them about Eva and her music, eventually meeting them in Maryland in April 1997. He also met with Chris Biondo, Eva's producer, who played him more of Eva's recordings. Straw discussed a possible deal with the family but they were also talking to other labels. One of those labels was Blue Note, which had shown interest in her several years before, but it all came to nothing as it struggled with how she could be positioned and marketed.[41]

Bill Straw picks up the story.

> The head of Blue Note knew how good she was but he didn't know how to market her. His young marketing staff, like most majors, [tried] to force artists into a one-size-fits-all [model] – make them a jazz singer or make them a blues singer. Make them something identifiable, put them in that box and market it. The majors had yet to learn about the power of public radio. Our label had been dealing in public radio since the early 1990s, because we had signed Mary Black out of Ireland and had had a lot of success with her on public radio and a new format they call NAC – New Adult Contemporary.

Straw eventually signed a deal with Eva's parents in late 1997 – almost exactly a year after she died. Her parents had inherited all her past recordings as the deal with Liaison was a one-off. Straw says the plan was to compile tracks from her previous releases and recordings and present them as the *Songbird* album. It was released on 19 May 1998 and was followed swiftly by a re-release of *Live at Blues Alley* as well as *Eva by Heart* (which had originally come out in 1997).

Straw was slowly working the album in the US, hiring a radio promotions expert in the New Adult Contemporary (NAC) format. A jazz booker in Boston received a promotional copy and passed it on to a friend, Robin Young, who was the breakfast DJ at Boston radio station WBOS-FM. She repeatedly played tracks from *Songbird* on her show.[42] Straw claims that the album sold 10,000 copies in two weeks in the Boston area as a result. "She may have lost her job over that," he says of Young. "She never was clear on that. But she certainly got a lot of heat for playing something [not on the station's playlist] without asking."

Meanwhile in Britain, things were gathering pace. Hot Records was a licensing partner for Blix Street, putting out its releases in the UK and Australia. The UK office of Hot, based in Brighton, was headed up by Martin Jennings, who persuaded plugger Tony Bramwell to come out of semi-retirement to work the album.[43] Bramwell sent a copy of the album to his friend Paul Walters, the producer of the *Wake Up to Wogan* show on Radio 2. "Dear Paul, I know you are a busy man, but you should really pay attention to this particular record," he wrote.[44] Paul Walters played it and its impact was immediate. "[I]t absolutely stopped me in my tracks," he said. "I went in to work the next morning and said to Terry, 'You wait till you hear this, matey.'"[45] Walters put Eva's cover of 'Over the Rainbow' on the show's playlist the following day, starting a phenomenal chain of events.

Both Walters and Wogan claim they were initially unaware that Cassidy was dead and Wogan only twigged when he read the notes that came with the album. This cemented their belief in the need to play it on the show. "This is one Paul brought this morning by a lady called Eva Cassidy – hope you like it," said Wogan. As the track ended, he said, "That was Eva Cassidy, who it seems is tragically no longer with us."[46]

The impact was immediate and enormous. Walters said "the emails lit up like a Christmas tree" and they received over 100 within 10 minutes of the song being played.[47] It is claimed that *Songbird* sold over 100,000 copies in the weeks following the first play on Wogan's show. He was to play her repeatedly on his show, as did other Radio 2 DJs riding the wave.

Songbird went to number one in the UK for two weeks and was in the UK album charts for over 150 weeks.[48] Subsequent albums – 2002's *Imagine* and 2003's *American Tune* – also went to number one in the UK. In total, nine of her albums have gone Top 40 in the UK, with five of them going Top 10.[49] By early 2021, she had sold over 4 million albums in the UK and over 10 million globally.[50]

While the Wogan effect was significant, it was far from an outlier. Straw says there were a "series of explosions all along" as the album's success snowballed in multiple markets. The tipping point, however, was when *Songbird* first topped the charts in the UK. "The story was 'unknown American deceased singer' goes to number one in England," says Straw. "That's a typical feel-good soft news story. All of the networks came to the party on that."

This prompted *Nightline* on ABC in the US to broadcast a short documentary on Eva Cassidy in May 2001. "[T]he response was so strong that it was repeated six weeks later," wrote the *New York Times*.[51] From that, the story was picked up by both music trade titles, music consumer titles and broader entertainment titles in the US such as *Billboard*, *Rolling Stone*, *Entertainment Weekly* and *People*.

A five-minute video of her on guitar performing 'Over the Rainbow' at the second night of her two shows at Blues Alley also helped extend her story beyond radio. It was shot on camcorder by Cassidy's friend Bryan McCulley and was filmed from the audience (the back of one audience member's head obscures her picking hand for the mid-shots). It is what most TV producers would deem un-broadcastable – black and white, one shot, obstacles obscuring the view, an oscillation between mid-shots and head-shots, dim lighting – but it took on its own power and provenance as *Songbird*'s sales grew. "It was never shot to be shown as a music video, but hey, it's all we've got," said McCulley. "It is pretty decent footage though."[52]

Bramwell sent it to Mark Hagen, executive producer of BBC show *Top of the Pops 2*. Despite initial resistance to its lo-fi quality, Hagen agreed to put it at the end of the show that was broadcast on 13 December 2000. "We put it at the very end of the show, so that it wouldn't be a complete disaster if all the viewers left," said Hagen. When it was shown again on *Top of the Pops 2* on 24 January 2001, it became "the most requested video in the history of the programme".[53]

That opened the floodgates in terms of wider media interest in the story. Bramwell claimed that it was the low-budget nature of the video ("basically a home video of a dead girl singing a song that wasn't a hit"[54]) that amplified its emotional impact. "If we'd done the big record company thing and spent loads of money tarting it up, we'd have ruined it."[55] Within weeks of the *Top of the Pops 2* broadcast, her estate claimed the album had sold 900,000 copies in the UK and Cassidy was outselling every other act in the charts with the exception of Dido.[56]

While traditional media – radio and TV alongside magazines – were doing most of the heavy lifting here in terms of bringing Cassidy to new audiences, her cousin Laura Bligh (who runs the evacassidy.org site[57]) says the serendipity of mass internet adoption at the turn of the millennium also played a significant part in the singer's posthumous rise. "[The internet] came along at the right time for Eva Cassidy's music, because people who heard her recordings and wanted to buy her CDs didn't have to rely on local stores, which would not be likely to carry such obscure albums," Bligh told the *Guardian* in 2002.[58] Bligh is keen to stress her site is simply a personal endeavour. "I don't consider it an official website because Eva isn't here to say, 'This is my official website,'" she tells me. It was set up in 1999 ("when the internet was fairly new and exotic and online shopping was fairly new and exotic") simply as a repository for stories about Eva Cassidy, linking to any publication that wrote about her. "People wanted to know more about her but there wasn't the wealth of information that there is now," she says. "There were a few articles in the *Washington Post* and some other minor things. So I made a page of links to those to help people who were just discovering her music to learn more about her. It grew from that in the first year or two. I was thrilled silly if someone just mentioned her in passing and now most passing mentions of Eva I just ignore – unless it's a famous person!"

Bligh made a conscious choice not to have a discussion board on the site. "When I set up the website and the guest book, the interactive communities were only in their infancy," she says. "I decided it was just too difficult to monitor those because I can't stand it if anyone says anything mean about Eva; so I decided that I could not burden myself with that."

This nascent site and the early stirrings of social networking also helped give new fans a sense of ownership of Cassidy and her music – feeling it was something they had discovered themselves without the cattle-prod of market-ing campaigns driving them there. This is a slight delusion, of course, but the lo-fi aesthetic of evacassidy.org (it retains its incredibly rudimentary layout and page design two decades on) arguably helped make fans believe there was not a machine behind her posthumous success.

Without the budgets or resources of a major label, Blix Street capitalised on the success of *Songbird* in a slightly more sedentary fashion. "A lot of the strategy was a lack of strategy," says Straw. "The majors came around and tried to make a deal where they would put everything out right now. And I really wasn't interested in that. I wanted to move it up at a deliberate pace so that we felt good about everything that we did." *Time After Time* followed in June 2000, but the momentum of *Songbird* was such that Straw felt it unnecessary to rush things and flood the market. "I was probably dragging my feet as much as anybody because that's just the way I operate," he says. "We weren't in a hurry."

Songbird was to define Eva Cassidy's posthumous fame and success, but there was opposition from Chris Biondo, her producer, about it coming out originally. Straw claims that Biondo initially opposed the packaging of her music in this way. "He really hated the idea of *Songbird*," says Straw. "His line was, 'How can you put out a Best Of if she's never had a hit?' I said, 'Well, it's not a Best Of – it's an anthology.' So instead of being a negative, it's a real positive. How many artists, when they get ready to put out their first album, can have that much powerful material that no one's ever heard?"

This subtle semantic distinction was key to *Songbird*'s success. The subtext was: here is an artist you have never heard of but who has a catalogue of material that is so deep that the only sensible entry point for a new listener is via a carefully curated selection of tracks.

This ultimately helped to define the narrative around Cassidy and set things up for a long series of releases from the vaults. How Blix Street came up with new album ideas and ways to work the catalogue will be explored in Chapter 5, which looks at archive management, but everything that has followed since was done entirely in the slipstream of *Songbird*.

THE OBSCURE, THE UNKNOWN, THE FADING AND THE DISAPPEARED

Estate management is not always confined to the icon and legend business. Making an unknown artist famous after they have died is an arduous process – like attempting to scale Everest on a unicycle. It is often, first and foremost, a passion project for those involved – people like, on the label side, Chris Blackwell at Island or Bill Straw at Blix Street, or, like, on the family side, Gabrielle Drake. They do not know if anyone will ever hear what they hear, but they have a compulsion to create opportunities where they can, acting like missionaries.

Jeff Jampol is the founder and president of Jampol Artist Management (known as JAM Inc). The company's website is the incredibly telling wemanagelegends.com – and Jampol makes no bones of the fact that he only wants to work with legendary artists. His company's list of clients bears that out, including as it does The Doors, the Ramones, Janis Joplin, Charlie Parker and John Lee Hooker. He also works with the estate of Michael Jackson.

"It's very expensive and time-consuming to move these legacies forward," he says when asked if he could use his expertise to build an unknown artist from the ground up after they had died. "I don't think that we would take a legacy that's unknown and then try and make it known. But if something sparks like an Eva Cassidy or a Nick Drake or a Rodriguez, then we could certainly fan that spark into flames. Would we? It depends. It depends on how I felt about the artist and whether I thought we could do the best job and whether we were passionate about it and whether the estate wanted us to do that. Each case is different; but to me it's about moving it from where they are to some place greater than where they are."

The Spellbound Group is an LA-based company that was founded by Alicia Yaffe, who is also a manager at JAM Inc. The company works with JAM Inc's roster of estates and describes its role as providing "strategic digital marketing and content production services to pop culture icons".[59] Yaffe echoes what Jampol says when asked if her company could use social media and events-based marketing to turn an obscure act into a posthumously famous one. "We really specialise in people that have achieved a certain level of cultural relevance and then build on and augment that [...] We wouldn't take somebody who doesn't really have any cultural cachet now and then try and build it posthumously."

Larry Mestel, founder and CEO of Primary Wave, which bought a 50 per cent stake in the Whitney Houston estate in 2019, is even more blunt about his company's disregard for the unknown.[60] "No," he says firmly when asked if Primary Wave would want to work with the estate of an unknown act. "We are in the icon and legend business."

Record companies, however, have a commercial imperative to turn around the fortunes of the unprofitably obscure acts at the far end of their catalogue's long tail. In the pre-digital era, this was an incredibly expensive and high-risk undertaking. It involved manufacturing physical product and paying heavy marketing costs to try and persuade the public that an act they were utterly unaware of was worth buying. Occasionally a synchronisation deal (e.g. a music placement in a film, TV show, videogame or advert) might shine a light on an unknown artist, but responding to this required lightning reflexes, and by the time physical product could be put in record shops, the momentum could have gone.

Streaming and real-time consumption data now means that much of the risk is inherently mitigated as decisions are being based on existing consumer interest, often driven by a track appearing on a key playlist or being scooped up in a recommendation algorithm on Spotify, Apple Music or Amazon Music.

One record company catalogue executive says that the data insight tools from streaming services that are open to major catalogue owners, as well as their own audience insights, research and analysis, are opening up more opportunities and possibilities that were utterly unthinkable before the 2010s. They say, "Streaming is obviously quite useful in highlighting tracks way deeper in the catalogue [...] Then we quite often apply the same approach we would bring to [marketing] a major estate to that artist. We'll look at who their audience is, what their audience is interested in, what we feel are the opportunities to attract their attention."

The streaming uptick can be considerable in the days following the death of a major musician. For example, US rapper DMX (real name: Earl Simmons) died on 9 April 2021 at the age of 50 and MRC Data reported that his tracks were streamed 75.7 million times in the US on 9 and 10 April. This was a 928 per cent increase on the 7.36 million streams of his catalogue on 7 and 8 April.[61]

The ability to respond to any blip in interest in an act is now immediate – but the moment of opportunity is blink-and-you'll-miss-it brief. "You get a very short window with a fan to see whether they're interested or if they're going to bail," the label executive argues. "You have to get their attention; and then you need to be able to keep their attention."

As with comedy, the secret to estate marketing is timing. But while time can be harnessed as a powerful ally, it can also be the silent enemy. Estates that were once successful can, like a painting left in the full glare of the sun, find themselves bleached into irrelevance and insignificance. An estate can keep a dead artist "alive"; but what happens if the estate itself becomes moribund?

BMG is one of those companies regarding estates as a huge investment opportunity, most notably in 2015 buying up the bulk of Buddy Holly's US music publishing, his global sound-recording royalties and all of the rights to his name, image and likeness.[62] Before this, the Holly estate had been run by María Elena Holly, his widow, since 1959.

David Hirshland is EVP (executive vice-president) at BMG and explains why this was a strategic investment by his company to reintroduce Holly as a pivotal figure in American popular music. "We felt that Buddy was the least recognisable of the big early rock stars and that the way to reintroduce him to the culture was not just through the music – which was an obvious way to do it – but also through getting his image out there," he says. Key to this was the development of a hologram of the singer that could tour, as well as the establishment of a scholarship programme in the music department of North Texas University.

Estates of acts who found fame in the pre-rock'n'roll era have discovered the route back to relevance, once lost, to be an arduous one. Music lawyer Erin M. Jacobson works with a range of estates and, for the older ones, understands this issue all too well. "While there are your evergreen [hits] or certain artists that just will always be relevant and will always be earning a lot of money, there are others in which they were a hit during a certain era, but because it has aged out, they don't have the activity that they did," she says. As a result, labels and publishers who own their rights will see licensing and other revenue sources dry up over time and the catalogues can start to fall into disrepair. As revenues wilt, the estate can atrophy. "Just because someone was once a famous artist or songwriter or just because someone has inherited some copyrights of songs that were a hit at one point, it doesn't mean that they've just totally hit the jackpot," says Jacobson. "It means that they've inherited an asset that is not producing the income that it once was – and that asset then needs to be worked in a specific way in order to make it start producing the income that it should be producing."

What, though, of the case where the individual might have been successful in their lifetime and their work is well known but they themselves are far from household names? This is the particular challenge facing the estates of songwriters who were not performers – those who, by accident or by design, lived outside the spotlight of fame. Their estates are confronted with obscurity and they have to work in a very different way from the estates of recording artists and performers.

Anthony Newley found some fame as a performer, but his most lucrative work came from songwriting. He co-wrote 'Feeling Good' (an enduring hit for Nina Simone) as well as co-writing the theme for *Goldfinger* with John Barry and co-writing the score for the 1971 film version of *Willy Wonka and the Chocolate Factory*. His work is certainly more famous than he is.

In 2017, Downtown Music Publishing[63] signed a global administration deal with the Newley estate.[64] Bruce Lampcov, head of West Coast business development at Downtown, explains the unique challenges of working a writer catalogue. "With Anthony, it's been more of him as a songwriter and [finding] ways for us to create opportunities for his songs," he says. A key licensing deal was using 'Pure Imagination', from *Willy Wonka and the Chocolate Factory*, in an ad for Adobe than ran on US TV in early 2020.[65] "Do people know it's Anthony Newley?" asks Lampcov. "Probably not, but it certainly brought in a significant amount of money for the estate. For Newley, it's a lot more about us trying to create revenue streams on the sync side. Less so again about brand building."

Abby North, founder of music rights management company North Music Group, represents a wide range of songwriters and is, conversely, heavily focused on brand-building around them. Her father-in-law is Alex North, who co-wrote 'Unchained Melody', which appeared in minor 1955 film *Unchained* but became a global hit a decade later when performed by The Righteous Brothers. He also scored movies including *Spartacus* (1951), *Cleopatra* (1963), *A Streetcar Named Desire* (1951) and *Death of a Salesman* (1951).

"One of the things that we do leverage or note [with Alex North] is that not many people recognise or are aware of the fact that the guy who composed the score for *Spartacus* is the same guy who wrote 'Unchained

Melody' – that's the first thing," she says. "But further is the story of 'Unchained Melody'. Alex was hired in 1954 to score a movie that was based on a book written by a prison warden about an honour prison [i.e. a minimum security prison]. This was a pretty forgettable movie, but the theme, obviously, is not. So with Alex, we have stories. It's not so difficult to brand him."

The estate of Harold Arlen brings both of these challenges together: a catalogue ageing out and the writer not being known to the public and therefore not providing a marketing hook. Arlen was a phenomenally prolific composer and his work included multiple Broadway shows as well as evergreens like 'Get Happy', 'That Old Black Magic', 'One for My Baby (And One More for the Road)' and 'I've Got the World on a String'. His most successful and enduring work, however, was writing the songs and music (alongside Herbert Stothart) for *The Wizard of Oz* in 1939, the most famous song from that film being, of course, 'Over the Rainbow', the song that made Eva Cassidy a star after her death.

The Harold Arlen estate is run by his son, Sam Arlen, who is himself both a musician and a music publisher. He argues that his father – because he worked with multiple lyricists throughout his career on many different projects – was not able to create a songwriter partnership brand in the way that, for example, Rodgers & Hammerstein did. The fact that he also worked across multiple genres made him more difficult to box up for the public in an easy-to-understand way.

"You do have to go out there and make people aware of who he [was]," says Sam Arlen of pushing his father's music. "[That's] because they don't know the name as well as people that are writing teams that have been consistently together for years and years where, if you hear one, you hear the other."

Ultimately, the biggest challenge for the Harold Arlen estate is that, for younger generations of both performers and listeners, music from the era when Arlen was in his prime is increasingly viewed as archaic. "There are many artists out there that could do wonderful covers of the American Songbook," Sam says. "They could take different songs and they could really do a good job. What would happen sometimes is that [they say], 'If I do the song now, at the height of my career or on the upswing of my career, and I'm a young person, is this going to age me or age the music that I do?' That's one of the things that has come up and I've heard that from time to time over the years."

He adds that contacts at advertising agencies and film companies – the people who he would have pitched synchronisation ideas to, as they knew the breadth of his father's work – are leaving or retiring. "There are, as always, people that are very open to having that business relationship, to know you're there and talk once in a while; and you have other people that are more standoffish and they really aren't interested," he says. "They're more interested when they have to do a project. 'We'll call you when we need you.'"

There is a natural generation turnover in these ancillary businesses and writers like Harold Arlen risk falling through the cracks. This is a danger for all estates. Even though they might be doing remarkable business now, over time they can be replaced. The struggles of the Harold Arlen estate foreshadow what many other estates will find themselves going through two, three or more generations down the line.

There is a strange symmetry that Eva Cassidy achieved posthumous fame through a cover of 'Over the Rainbow', but the estate of the person who wrote the music to it faces an uphill challenge in having him celebrated in the same way. This, in many ways, lays bare the lifecycle of an estate. As the wheel turns and one spoke rises, so another must fall.

CHAPTER 5

Annals Mirabilis

Controlling the Archive

In the early hours of the first Sunday in June 2008, the backlot of Universal Studios Hollywood in Los Angeles erupted into flames. The fire itself was widely reported by the media at the time. "The fast-moving, early morning blaze destroyed several movie sets and the *King Kong* exhibit," wrote CNN.[1]

Ron Meyer, the COO of Universal Studios, was swift to downplay the damage. "Fortunately, nothing irreplaceable was lost," he said. "The video library was affected and damaged, but our main vault of our motion picture negatives was not."[2] It was all going to be business as usual. Nothing to see here.

Except there was a lot to see here, but it was not going to become public for another 11 years. When it did, chaos ensued.

Under the headline "The Day the Music Burned", Jody Rosen wrote a lengthy investigative piece on the fire that was published in the *New York Times* on 11 June 2019.[3] His focus was on the archives of Universal Music Group (UMG), comfortably the biggest record company in the world. Rosen was unflinching in the details he provided in his exhaustive piece on the fire, its aftermath and the repercussions of it all. He listed the legendary record companies – which, through multiple acquisitions over the decades, had become part of UMG – whose master tapes[4] had been damaged or lost in the fire. These included Decca, Chess, Impulse, A&M, Geffen and Interscope – labels whose signings had directed the shape of popular music for decades. It was as if the record business was seeing its life flash before its eyes.

"Nearly all of these masters – in some cases, the complete discographies of entire record labels – were wiped out in the fire," he wrote. These include "nearly everything" recorded for Chess Records as well as "[v]irtually all of Buddy Holly's masters".[5]

This is hugely important. These masters are the sources for all remasters of records – something that has become a major part of the record business as audio technology incrementally improves and allows for clearer recordings to be reintroduced to the market. In the analogue era, often they are the only high-quality copies of historically and culturally important recordings that exist. "Simply put," argued Rosen, "the master of a recording is that recording; it is the thing itself."[6]

The *New York Times* piece dug deep into the story, drawing on legal and company documents as well as "thousands of pages and internal UMG files" to which Rosen had gained access. A UMG internal document dated March 2009 that he unearthed – marked "CONFIDENTIAL" – set the number of "assets destroyed" at 118,230. He suggested this was a desperately (even deliberately) low number and quoted Randy Aronson, who worked on the Universal lot for a quarter of a century and who was formerly VP of archives and mastering studios, as saying it was more likely "in the 175,000" range. Aronson also claimed that UMG was internally pricing the cost of the loss at $150 million.[7] In December 2009, UMG had filed a lawsuit against NBCUniversal, the former landlords of the vault, seeking compensation for its losses, claiming NBCUniversal had "breached their duty of care".

The fire was bad enough, but the problem was compounded, Rosen wrote, because a comprehensive inventory for what sat in the vaults simply did not exist. Thinking of the losses in the abstract somehow made them even worse as no one would ever fully know what, precisely, had gone up in flames. He says that UMG had started a digitisation of its archives (known as Preservation Project) in 2004 but, by the time of the fire, only 12,000 tapes (analogue multitracks that were most at risk of deterioration) had been exported to digital formats. The thrust of Rosen's piece was that here was a devastating act of cultural vandalism, the scale of which UMG had moved to cover up.

In the October after the fire, UMG swung into what was appositely named Project Phoenix to hunt down duplicates of recordings whose masters had been lost in the fire. It was a global search and lasted two years. Estimates say it found a fifth of what it was after. "The recordings were transferred to Linear Tape-Open, or LTO, a tape format used for archiving digital data," writes Rosen. "Copies were placed in storage holds on both [US] coasts: at an underground vault in Boyers, Pa., and a high-rise facility in Hollywood."[8] The company in charge of both facilities is Iron Mountain, whose tagline is "Protecting What You Value Most".[9] It also holds masters for the other two major labels – Warner Music Group and Sony Music Entertainment – meaning one company now has the responsibility for hosting and indexing the majority of all recorded music in history, with the number of recordings running into the millions.

Exactly a week after the *New York Times* ran its piece in 2019, Lucian Grainge, the CEO of UMG,[10] sent a memo to all staff about the fire. This memo was subsequently leaked to *Billboard* and other music trade publications. "[W]e owe our artists transparency," he wrote. "We owe them answers. I will ensure that the senior management of this company, starting with me, owns this."[11]

By 21 June 2019, ten days after the original article ran, lawsuits against UMG had started to be filed by living acts such as Steve Earle and Hole as well as the estate of Tupac Shakur. The former wife of Tom Petty, but not his estate, was also involved in the suit. "The suit accuses Universal [...] of breaching its contracts with artists by failing to properly protect the tapes," stated the *New York Times*. "It also argues that Universal had a duty to share any income received as settlements from the fire."[12]

The suit said, "UMG concealed its massive recovery from plaintiffs, apparently hoping it would keep it all to itself by burying the truth in sealed court filings and a confidential settlement agreement."[13] It sought damages of over $100 million.

On 26 June, UMG had Pat Kraus, its senior vice-president (SVP) of recording studios and archive management, issue a company-wide memo outlining what he and his team were doing in response to the exposé around the fire. It was leaked to *Variety*, among other titles. In the memo, Kraus said he had set up a worldwide team of over 30 people to deal with this, backed up by a further 40 professionals from Iron Mountain.

In mid-July 2019, an internal UMG memo from Kraus was leaked to the *Los Angeles Times*. The paper said the memo contained claims that only minimal assets were lost in the 2008 fire, heavily downplaying the impact of the entire incident. "Over the past several weeks, our team has been working around the clock, fielding requests from approximately 275 artists and representatives," ran the memo. "To date we've reviewed 26,663 individual assets covering 30 artists. Of those assets, we believe we've identified 424 that could be missing or lost due to the fire, with audio assets accounting for 349 of them."

It continued, "Our data suggests that 22 of those could be 'original masters' which are associated with five artists. For each of those lost masters, we have located high-quality alternate sources in the form of safety copies or duplicate masters. As we complete new work and we fill in gaps of work we've already done, these tallies will continue to evolve by the hour."[14]

Randy Aronson was subsequently quoted in *Billboard* serving up lashings of scepticism. "'Twenty-two losses', to me, is as insulting as 'we really didn't lose anything'," he said.[15]

By July 2019, UMG was seeking to dismiss the $100 million class action against it for being devoid of "any valid legal theory". Despite the "heart-breaking loss" of assets, the music giant argued it was not obliged to share the settlement it received for the fire with any of the acts leading the legal charge against it.[16]

In February 2020, UMG confirmed that masters for 19 different acts – among them Nirvana, Elton John, REM, Beck, Sheryl Crow, Y&T, Slayer, Bryan Adams, Suzanne Vega and Sonic Youth – had been damaged or destroyed in the fire. It added that in the cases of Nirvana, Bryan Adams, Y&T and Beck safety copies of the affected tapes existed.[17]

Things had escalated by November 2019, with Scott Edelman of legal firm Gibson Dunn, acting on behalf of UMG, telling the judge in the case that UMG owned the masters outright and that it was only obliged to pay artists royalties (as per their individual contracts) but not share in the spoils of insurance claims with them. "Artists have specified rights to royalties," said Edelman. "Everything else doesn't belong to them. Artists don't have an interest in the masters. Period. Full stop."[18]

Slowly artists such as Steve Earle started to drop out of the legal action.[19] The former wife of Tom Petty was the last standing plaintiff in March, but the judge issued a 28-page ruling to dismiss her claims, which had, over the course of the legal battle, fallen to six in total. Judge John Kronstadt ruled Jane Petty had failed to bring sufficient evidence to the case.[20] (A revised lawsuit by Jane Petty against Universal was dismissed in late March 2021 and she was barred from refiling the case.[21])

It was also reported in March 2020 that the estate of Tupac Shakur and members of Soundgarden had dropped out of the case.[22] "Though," reported *Variety*, "they did reserve the right to later rejoin as class members."

Speaking in May 2020 to this author, Howard E. King of legal firm King, Holmes, Paterno & Soriano (who represent the Tupac estate) said this dispute was far from over. "It has not been settled," he says. "We are still in litigation." He continues, "We're still in the process of determining what was actually lost and whether what Universal calls 'replacements' really are true replacements," he says. "We're assembling information and we've hired expert engineers and stuff to go in and see what Universal has. And as part of that, [to get an] explanation of how Universal could claim in their lawsuit – to their landlord and insurer – [that there were] 118,000 lost masters and now publicly say that it's just a fraction of that right. Something doesn't add up. I don't have the answer to that yet."

He explains why this case is so important for the Tupac estate – an estate that, it should be noted, has overseen the release of six posthumous albums by the dead rapper as well as an assortment of live and remix albums. "There was outcry really for two reasons," King says. "One reason is the lack of care of these precious assets; and the other was more mundane, which is if Universal collected the tens of millions of dollars or more that the *New York Times* alluded to by suing their landlord and their insurance company, they should have shared that with the artists." This is, King says, an incredibly convoluted case and will take a long time to reach resolution. "It's a legal morass right now on a couple of issues. The big issue is the record companies take the position that the master recordings belong to them, so they don't have any responsibility to care for them. So that's going to be a multi-year dispute. Although the record companies own the masters, the question is this: what, if any, obligations do their ownership of those masters impose upon them? Because if the masters are lost, the artists are deprived of a couple of things. Most importantly, they're deprived of the opportunity to do full-quality remixes, remasters and related-product release."

On a macro level, King says there is an ever bigger issue for the Tupac estate pertaining to copyright termination (see Chapter 10) and hinging on the safety of the master recordings. "At the end of the copyright termination period, the artists have the right – well, some artists have the right – to get their copyright in the sound recording back [from the record company]," he explains. "Those copyrights that they're getting back are adversely impacted on if they don't get the master recordings along with those. That's going to be a big legal issue over the next couple of years. That is where the litigation is right now."

Record companies want to present an image that they are the noble custodians of our shared cultural history and do everything to protect the assets they own – from recordings through to artwork and other artefacts. Indeed, the EMI Archive Trust in Hayes, Middlesex, was set up specifically to protect everything of importance that it owned.[23]

At the upper level, this is undoubtedly true and the EMI Archive Trust is rightly regarded as a pioneer here, setting a high standard that other music archives aspire to. Yet that memo does not always make its way down to staff. In researching my 2019 book, *The Final Days of EMI: Selling the Pig*, on the company's ignoble end, I was told by several sources that, when staff were moved out of the company's Brook Green offices in west London, drawers full of artefacts were simply tipped into the bin or, if the person in charge was feeling environmentally conscious, the recycling. This included photo negatives from press shoots. (Admittedly they mainly related to minor-tier acts, but that does not excuse what happened.)

One senior executive working in catalogue at another major label claims this carefree jettisoning of assets was still happening there in the early 2000s. "I remember there was a time at [the label when we] were moving buildings," they say. "The stuff that was being chucked out! It was ridiculous. It was just skips of photos. And [...] they told an office junior to, for all the acts who had been dropped, just throw away everything. They might have been obscure artists, but all the photos were just going straight in the bin. I was thinking all this needed to be sent to our archive."

Journalist Bill Holland has written at length about the historical reckless-ness of record companies with regard to their archives. In a piece written originally for *Billboard* in 1997 and now republished on his website, Holland noted that labels were improving their archiving, but in many cases this was too little too late. He talks of "untold numbers of recordings, old and not so old, that have been thrown away, mislaid, left behind in warehouses, and even sold for scrap".[24]

"I was in the studio supervisor's office – this was 1980 – and there were a pile of tapes, so I started looking through them," one source tells Holland. "They all had a big S on them, including boxes clearly labelled 'Louis Armstrong – Unreleased Concert.' I said, 'What is this?' The guy said, 'All that's old stuff getting thrown out to make room in the vault.' The S was for Scrap."[25]

Holland goes on to detail stories of band saws being applied to tape reels to save the metal reels for scrap and of tapes being mislabelled. "That's how RCA found an alternate take for 'That's All Right, Mama', Elvis's first single for Sun Records. Lost for, what, 33 years?" a source told him. "They finally figured to check the (matrix) numbers on tapes close to those of the released recordings, and started searching. Believe me, none of the boxes had 'Elvis' written on them, just numbers. Finally they found it."[26]

Holland also shows that the 2008 Universal fire was not an outlier and had a shocking precedent three decades earlier with the fire at Atlantic Records' New Jersey storage facility in February 1978. "The warehouse fire destroyed virtually all of Atlantic's unreleased masters, alternate takes and sessions tapes by artists who had recorded for the label and its offshoots throughout its classic 1948–1969 first golden era," writes Holland.

Even earlier was the "most spectacular case of wholesale vault trashing" in the early 1960s in RCA's warehouse, also in New Jersey. RCA was able to send staff into the building and "withdraw whatever material they could carry". Astonishingly it was then blown up with dynamite and the wreckage bulldozed into the Delaware River. A new pier was eventually built on top of the rubble.

It was only with the dawning of the CD era in the mid-1980s and the reissue boom that came with it, argues Holland, that labels finally woke up to the importance and value of their archive.

The ability to reissue from the archives and pad out original albums with material that, for whatever reason, was deemed unfit for release at the time changed the record business entirely, contributing to its most profitable period. The move into, first, downloading and then streaming was another gear change as it allowed catalogue marketing to happen without the overheads of physical manufacturing and the challenge of persuading record shops to stock your product. The long tail as defined by Chris Anderson[27] could start to come into play, not just for old releases but also for music that was never released (or even releasable) at the time, adding a whole new marketing angle to it.

Items that previously cost vast sums of money to store properly but that were often economically inert could now make the labels millions. As this dollar-shaped lightbulb illuminated itself above their heads, the record labels started to treat the archives with a great deal more respect. What was previously deemed chaff started, in the minds of profit-obsessed labels, to take on the lustre of gold.

UNFINISHED SYMPATHIES: THE CONUNDRUM OF COMPLETING WORK WHEN THE ARTIST IS DEAD

Singles by The Beatles regularly returned to the UK charts in the 1970s and 1980s after the band split, starting with the re-entry of 'Yesterday' in 1976, which rose as high as number eight. For the most part, however, they rarely got inside the Top 20. Then, in December 1995, a full quarter-century after they had disbanded, The Beatles were in the British charts at number two, with a "brand-new" song.[28] It was a remarkable achievement given that it had been a full 15 years, almost to the day, since John Lennon was murdered.

The track had sat in the Lennon archives since 1977 when he recorded it as a home demo for a planned musical, *The Ballad of John and Yoko*, with just a mic on top of his piano, meaning the musical accompaniment and vocals were on the same audio track and could not be separated.[29]

It was subsequently handed to the three surviving Beatles by Yoko Ono, Lennon's widow, to "turn into" a Beatles song. Jeff Lynne was brought in as producer as long-term Beatles producer George Martin declined to work on it. "I kind of told them I wasn't too happy with putting them together with the dead John," Martin told *Rock Cellar* in 2013. "I've got nothing wrong with dead John but the idea of having dead John with live Paul and Ringo and George to form a group, it didn't appeal to me too much."[30]

The release of 'Free as a Bird' is a pivotal moment in not just estate marketing but also catalogue marketing in general. It might have been later described as "the Beatles' worst song" by the *Washington Post*,[31] but its success opened the floodgates for a whole new level of archive mining and the willingness of estates (in this case John Lennon's) to approve en masse the release of material that had arguably been kept in the vaults for a reason.

Indeed, EMI released the four-disc *John Lennon Anthology* in November 1998, made up of demos, alternative takes and other unreleased recordings that Lennon had made between 1969 and 1980. This was, according to Beatles expert Ian MacDonald, drawn from "a reputed eight hundred hours of reel-to-reel tapes" that Lennon had stockpiled and of which Ono subsequently acted as custodian.[32]

Other tracks had been dug out and embellished with studio trickery to have the dead harmonise with the living. Natalie Cole had already had a major international hit with a beyond-the-grave duet with her father, Nat King Cole, on 'Unforgettable' in 1991 – but 'Free as a Bird' was merely the aperitif ahead of a stomach-bursting banquet. It was quickly followed by 'Real Love' in March 1996 (getting to number four in the UK charts), although that song had already been released as a demo (from 1979) on the *Imagine: John Lennon* soundtrack album before a slightly different demo version of the song got Beatles-ised in the 1990s.

A glut of posthumous duets have since appeared over the years. These include Lisa Marie Presley duetting with her father on 'Don't Cry Daddy' in 1997, Rod Stewart singing with Ella Fitzgerald on 'What Are You Doing New Year's Eve?' in 2012 and Faith Evans doing a whole album with Notorious BIG, her late husband, in 2017 (*The King and I*).[33] That was after Barry Manilow had taken it to a new spectral realm with 2014's *My Dream Duets* where he sang only with dead people (including Mama Cass, Maria Callas, Whitney Houston, Louis Armstrong, Dusty Springfield and Judy Garland).

As we saw in Chapter 1, the release of Otis Redding's '(Sittin' on) The Dock of the Bay' in early 1968 was the first major hit to be completed after the main artist had passed away. In truth, that track was almost finished before he died and was worked on by co-writer Steve Cropper, coming out mere weeks after Redding's death. Equally, 'Real Love' and 'Free as a Bird' were singles and there has not, as yet, been a whole Beatles album of unheard music where the surviving members commune with the deceased members via the studio mixing desk.[34]

This all comes with huge ethical issues as one can be left with a queasy feeling that what is done to the artist's music after they have gone might not be what they envisioned for it.

Taking half-completed albums and finishing them is not a modern idea. It was happening in the early 1970s when unfinished tracks from the Jimi Hendrix vault were embellished and lashed together as "new" albums. Alan Douglas, a music producer who started working with Hendrix in 1969, acquired a number of unreleased recordings from the Hendrix archive. Janie Hendrix, who now runs the Hendrix estate and is CEO of Experience Hendrix, is firm in her belief that Douglas hoodwinked Al Hendrix, Jimi's father, out of a number of these tapes.[35] "Alan Douglas had come to the house after the funeral [in September 1970]," she says. "He had attended the funeral and he was telling my dad that he was Jimi's engineer. And my dad said, 'Well, I know Eddie Kramer and I've heard of Eddie, but I've never heard of you.' I guess maybe one should have followed those instincts."

She says Douglas, who passed away in 2014, slowly wormed his way into the family via his connection with lawyer Leo Branton and used this for nefarious ends. Al Hendrix sued Branton in 1993, accusing him of selling the rights to his son's catalogue in 1974 without his consent – see Chapter 3.[36] [37]

"A lot of the [unreleased] masters actually were in our home from 1970 to 1974," Janie says. "At about the end of 1974 [or early] 1975, Alan Douglas started coming out to the house and taking some of the tapes. Over probably about a three-year period of time, all the tapes had left our house."

This was obviously upsetting to the family, but what Douglas was to do with some of those tapes was to stain the Hendrix legacy for many years. It was estimated that Douglas got his hands on over 1,000 hours of Hendrix music.[38] Under his guidance, a number of posthumous releases were put into the market – most controversially the *Crash Landing* (1975), *Midnight Lighting* (1976) and *Nine to the Universe* (1980) albums, as well as the *Voodoo Soup* compilation (1995). On these releases he would bring in new musicians to play on the tracks or even retrospectively oust some of the original players. "When the rhythm tracks aren't working, you replace them," he said. "That's what Jimi would have done." Talking about *Crash Landing*, he brazenly and unapologetically said, "I did what I had to do and it sold 2 million copies."[39]

A music-industry lawyer who was involved in negotiations with the Hendrix estate in the 1990s says that Douglas, ultimately, helped grow the cultural and commercial value of Jimi Hendrix with his overall reissue programme. "Hendrix only made three official studio albums in his entire life. And yet you go into a record store and there's 50 albums of live stuff, there's the Woodstock stuff, the unreleased tapes and all that kind of stuff. He [Douglas] did a very good job of curating that catalogue and really maximising it."

Others felt that he was guilty of "inappropriate tampering during his stewardship of Hendrix's music"[40] and what he did with the recordings by adding new musicians and subtracting others was "sacrilegious".[41]

The effect of Douglas's studio embellishments was, at times, akin to the galumphing brushwork of Cecilia Giménez, who took it upon herself in 2012 to touch up a century-old painting of Jesus by Elías García Martínez that was on the wall of a church in Borja in north-eastern Spain. The original painting was badly flaking so Giménez set to work. The end result of the unsolicited repair job was so spectacularly and hilariously awful that it became known as both Monkey Christ and Potato Jesus, quickly turning into a meme on social media.[42]

When the Hendrix studio archives were eventually returned to Experience Hendrix, all four controversial albums – *Crash Landing*, *Midnight Lighting*, *Nine to the Universe* and *Voodoo Soup* – were deleted from the catalogue.[43] When I asked Janie Hendrix what the reissue strategy was for the estate, she specifically mentioned one of these Alan Douglas albums as the antithesis of what she was doing. "There was not going to be a *Voodoo Soup* where you erase [Hendrix drummer] Mitch Mitchell's tracks and put Bruce Gary on," she says firmly. "There was going to be none of that."

She also claims that Douglas was not working from the original masters so that the audio quality of what was eventually released was seriously compromised. "What Alan did is, he would take a copy of a copy of a copy," she says. When the family took back control of the estate, they had to track down the original masters. From those, they did reissues of the original studio albums that they felt had finally been mixed properly. "If you want a pure sound and you want it the way Jimi wanted it to be or intended it to be, then you really have to go from the very beginning," she says. "So that was our mission – to re-acquire the original masters." Record labels, she says, had copies but not the originals as they had been scattered to the winds following Douglas's "shady deals" around them.

"A lot of times he [Douglas] would record something in a studio and he wouldn't pay the bill so he would just leave the tapes," she claims.

> We had to really go around to various studios and [...] we were able to acquire all the missing tapes. Definitely all the masters. There was a vault that held some of the masters, but a lot of copies. It was not in a secure environment. In fact, the day that we went to pick up the tapes, people were throwing a football in the warehouse and playing Frisbee. It wasn't temperature-controlled. So that was another thing that was on the top of our list: to gather the tapes, put them in a secure vault that was temperature-controlled and where people couldn't just walk around and kick boxes or take something [away].

The Hendrix/Douglas example arguably soured the very idea of completing unfinished recordings after the death of an artist for many years; but what followed was the relatively modern phenomenon of the family being directly involved. This can send out a very public message that care and sensitivity will be going into the work. An endorsement from the family elevates it all from the grubby to something much more laudable.

HAVING TRUSTED COLLABORATORS COMPLETE AN ALBUM

Swedish DJ Avicii (real name Tim Bergling) took his own life on 20 April 2018. He was working on what was to be his third album at the time of his death. His parents eventually took the decision that the album should be completed and released. That album, *TIM*, was eventually released in June 2019, finished by a raft of collaborators including Vincent Pontare, Salem Al Fakir and Joe Janiak. It was six months after his death before they felt emotionally ready to work on the recordings Bergling left behind.

The project was overseen by his parents as well as Universal Music Sweden, his record label. "We assembled a team of people who had worked with Avicii and his music for many years with the brief of creating something for the community based on transparency and honesty as well as creating a way to experience the new music beyond just sound," Eddie Persson, head of Creative Labs at Universal Music Sweden, told me in 2019.[44] "We had to be 100 per cent open about which songs had been completely finished, which songs needed to be finished or mixed and so on," said Persson. "We had to put all our cards on the table for everyone to see. Each song we released came with a mini documentary. Sometimes it is with the vocalist, but often it is with the producers. They talk about how long they had worked with Tim and the memories they cherish of that time. They talk about the specifics of the songs and what Tim was aiming for. They also talk about the process of finishing the songs. This was an important part of the project as it answered a lot of questions we knew people would have."

Speaking in summer 2020 about the *TIM* project, Per Sundin, who was MD of Universal Music Sweden at the time, says, "I think we did a very good job being transparent with the *TIM* album, explaining everything. We didn't hide anything. We were very, very honest with the process we went through. We recorded interviews with everyone, including myself and Klaus [Tim's father], about the project, what happened, how we did it and why felt obliged to do it. I think, knock on wood, we had a very positive response on all that and it didn't feel like the family or the record company was squeezing out music. It was more to give the audience what he actually loved."

FINISHING SCHOOL: COMPLETING RECORDS POSTHUMOUSLY

Jeff Buckley and Tupac Shakur had very little in common in terms of the music they made, but the number of posthumous releases of both artists runs into double figures. Considerably more music has been released by these acts after they passed away than they ever managed in their lifetimes.

Buckley had released two live EPs (*Live at Sin-é* in 1993 and *Live from the Bataclan* in 1995) plus one complete studio album (*Grace* in 1994) before he died in 1997. Since his death, eight live albums and multiple compilation albums have been released, spanning music recorded while he was signed to Sony and also before he had a record deal.

The most contentious is *Sketches for My Sweetheart the Drunk*, which was released a year after his death. Buckley had already scrapped a batch of recordings produced by Tom Verlaine in late 1996 and early 1997 and was preparing to record afresh in Memphis, the place where he drowned in the Mississippi.

Buckley left no will but his estate transferred automatically to his mother, Mary Guibert. While still mourning the loss of her son, she was informed that Sony was going to press ahead with the release of the Verlaine tapes under the title of *My Sweetheart the Drunk* (Buckley's working title for what was going to be his second album) only a matter of months after his death. She had not, she claims, been consulted on this release.

"We found Jeff's body and we had the two memorial ceremonies in July and August," she says. "I went home and then I started to get calls from the band members saying, 'Why are you going ahead with the album? Jeff never wanted those things! He wanted the [Tom] Verlaine tapes burned and blah, blah, blah.' And I'm going, 'Whoa, wait, nobody's doing anything!' I picked up the phone and I called the label. 'Oh yeah, Steve Berkowitz [the Sony executive who signed Buckley] and Andy [Wallace, producer of *Grace*] are in the studio mixing and mastering.' What? What the fuck is that? Well, that turned out to be the first CD. Oh yeah, that was ready. It was going to go into production."

She instructed Conrad Rippy, her lawyer, to contact Sony to halt the release of the Tom Verlaine recordings. "They had put that album on the release schedule for fall 1997," says Rippy of Sony's plans. "Jeff and the band – and therefore Mary – were quite clear that the band was flying into Memphis to record the album that would then replace that album [the Verlaine recordings]. So for Sony just to slap it on the release schedule... I understand it as a business decision, you know, to capitalise [on it]. Literally the first thing I did was dictate a cease-and-desist letter to Sony. Which always gets their attention!"

Guibert says she and Rippy went to meet the senior executives at Sony to work out what, if anything, should be done with Buckley's unreleased recordings. *Grace* was significantly unrecouped, and Sony was keen to get new product in the market; Guibert was less keen. The meeting included Don

Ienner, chairman of the Sony Music Group, and he spoke privately with Guibert about what they should do. "I said, 'I want one thing,'" she recalls of that conversation. "'I want one thing. Just give me control and we'll do it all together. You'll be able to use everything you've got – that's *worth using*.'" She puts extra emphasis on the words "worth using". This led to a standoff with Berkowitz. Guibert accused him of working on the unreleased recordings "behind my back" as he "thought he was going to be the new producer of Jeff's work". A compromise was reached where it became a double-disc release with the Verlaine recordings on one disc and the more recent demos on the other.

Guibert says that she was adamant that Sony could not polish up the four-track demos and they should be released as they were on the double album. "I said, 'No! Listen! I know what you want to do. This is what you would do with his remains – put him in an Armani suit and some shiny shoes and comb his hair and put lipstick on him or something. That's not who he is. These are his true remains – just as they are. Just treat them as if they were his true remains. If this was his body here and we were preparing it for his funeral, we would not put him in a suit. We would put him in a flower shirt and some black jeans and his Doc Martens and leave his hair all mussed up. And maybe a little mustard on his chin. We would not screw this stuff up by putting something out he would not approve of. So I won that argument."

Relations with Berkowitz were so strained as to be deemed unsalvageable by Guibert. She felt betrayed by him (claiming he referred to her as "the bitch") and was also offended that he was trying to be the one who defined her son's legacy. To appease Guibert, Berkowitz was taken off all Jeff Buckley projects at Sony and replaced by Don DeVito, the producer and executive who worked with Bob Dylan, luring him back to Sony/Columbia in 1975 after his brief defection to Asylum and producing his 1976 album *Desire* as well as being the A&R contact for major names like Bruce Springsteen, Carole King and Billy Joel.

"Sony needed to move someone else who had no agenda in releasing [*Sketches for*] *My Sweetheart the Drunk* in fall 1997," says Rippy. "So they moved Don in quite quickly to help smooth the waters. Don ran the Buckley project with Mary for probably the next 10 years. Don and Mary developed a real collaborative partnership. That, especially in the earlier days of the releases, was essential to making sure that everything that came out suited the legacy appropriately."

He says there is a hard lesson to be learned here for label executives trying to overrule heads of estates, especially if they are family members. "Don came in because we wouldn't deal with Steve after that," says Rippy. "I have, in the 23 years I have dealt with Jeff's legacy with Mary, maybe had one conversation with Steve Berkowitz at the very beginning. You don't get very far with Mary by dismissing her."

I approached Sony Music to respond to what both Guibert and Rippy said about the company's behaviour around the album release. A spokesperson for the company declined to comment.

Having a family member – especially one who has previously collaborated creatively with the artist in question – involved to take unfinished recordings to completion is possibly the best route. It's the least likely to face down accusations of, at best, desecration and, at worst, necrophilia.

Leonard Cohen released his album *You Want It Darker* in October 2016 and the following month he passed away. He had been working on new material after *You Want It Darker*, knowing that he was close to death and that he might never complete it. "I don't think I'll be able to finish those songs," he told the *New Yorker* in what was to be his final interview.[45] Cohen had requested that his son, Adam, finish the tracks he was recording in his final months, should he run out of time. Those tracks were eventually released on *Thanks for the Dance* in November 2019. Adam Cohen had also produced six of the nine tracks on *You Want It Darker* so he was intimately familiar with his father's approach to recording.

"Most records you struggle to make, but this was not hard," Adam Cohen told the *Guardian* when promoting the album's release. "It was, as the Arabs say, *maktoob* – already written. I was just a steward, a guardian of the project."[46]

In an interview with the *Irish Times*, Cohen was asked if his father had left specific musical instructions to guide his completion of the album, a process that took seven months to bring to fruition. "Well, there's two ways I can answer that," he said. "The first is more metaphysical. The advantage that a little guy like me has over all of these wonderful, more experienced and seasoned producers like Rick Rubin or Daniel Lanois or Don Was is that I've had a lifetime of conversation with my father. I got to hear and witness all of the choices he was continuously making; I had familiarity with this man's tastes."

He stressed that his father had explicitly instructed him to finish the album and was fully cognisant that it was going to be released after he died. Cohen defined the work he did on it as his duty rather than a crass cash-in. "These are not B-sides and out-takes," he said, "these are works that had simply not been completed yet."[47]

He spoke eloquently about the responsibility he felt in taking these songs to completion and how it was a continuation of the spirit that propelled the previous album. "I was under the command of some larger fate," is how he described it.[48]

In the *Guardian* interview mentioned above, Adam Cohen also claimed "there is no more material" – that these were his father's final recordings. But I attended a launch event in Spiritland in London on 11 November 2019 where Adam Cohen said that a final track was kept off *Thanks for the Dance* because he was unable to get the sound right. This, he intimated, could eventually get a release, but he said after that there were no other recordings to come out.

Having close collaborators involved in completing an unfinished album is not without its problems, but this is increasingly forming part of the story before its release as a means to head off possible fan vitriol. It will be OK, runs the subtext; these people worked with the artist, the artist trusted them, they will do the right thing.

Rob Schnapf and Joanna Bolme were brought in to oversee and finish work on the album that Elliott Smith was working on before he died, *Songs from a Basement on a Hill*. Schnapf co-produced two of Smith's albums (*XO* and *Figure 8*) while Bolme had been the singer's girlfriend. The message being beamed out was this: here were two people intimately involved emotionally and creatively with the artist; they will treat his music with the respect it requires.

The *Los Angeles Times* said that Smith's posthumous albums were "being awaited by his cult of fans like a lost sacred text".[49] This is certainly how certain acts' most ardent fans feel about unheard material. Estates and record companies ignore this at their peril. "This is the last living body of work," Schnapf told the *Los Angeles Times*. "If anything happens after that, then it's just collected, it's not a concept that he had."[50]

(As a side note, it is not always unfinished recordings that an estate can seek to complete. Prince, for example, began working on his autobiography in January 2016 in collaboration with writer Dan Piepenbring. The singer managed to complete 30 handwritten pages for the book's opening chapters before his death in April that same year. Piepenbring was subsequently able to access Prince's personal archives at Paisley Park in order to finish the book, *The Beautiful Ones*, which was published in October 2019.[51] Similarly, metal singer Ronnie James Dio had been working on his memoirs, *Rainbow in the Dark*, before his death in May 2010. Music journalist Mick Wall was brought in by the Dio estate to complete the book and it was set for publication in July 2021, featuring a preface by Wendy Dio, the singer's widow.[52])

A remix of a track from the vaults is, in its own way, a tinkering with the artist's music. However, this not as intrusive and nowhere near as potentially disastrous as sending in teams of musicians and producers to take the skeleton of a song, then to add flesh to it, dress it in gaudy clothing and top it off with a hat.

The June 2019 release of Whitney Houston's cover of Stevie Winwood's 'Higher Love' is an example of this approach. The track was originally recorded by Houston in 1990 and did get a formal release – but only as a bonus track on the Japanese edition of her third studio album, *I'm Your Baby Tonight*.[53] It had reportedly been shelved at the time as a possible single as her label did not want to have her pigeonholed as an artist who did covers of other people's songs.[54] (This is somewhat ironic given she was to go on to have one of her biggest hits in 1992 with a cover of Dolly Parton's 'I Will

Always Love You' from the soundtrack to *The Bodyguard*, which Houston also starred in.)

In May 2019, Primary Wave Music Publishing bought a 50 per cent stake in the Whitney Houston estate, covering all royalties from music and films, merchandise and name and likeness rights.[55] The deal was estimated at $7 million.[56]

Larry Mestel, founder and CEO of Primary Wave, had previously worked at Arista, the label within Sony that had signed and broken Houston. While there he had dealt with her team, including Pat Houston, her manager, sister-in-law and now executor of the Whitney Houston estate. After the deal to buy into the estate had been signed, they met to discuss possible projects. Pat Houston says 'Higher Love' was one of a number of possible archive tracks that she took to Primary Wave – but this was the one they decided on.

"We just discussed what should be done with it and we talked about trying to make it current," she says. "We went to [electronic producer] Kygo and we went to RCA. Clive [Davis, the executive who signed Houston and who still works on assorted projects around her music] loved the idea and we all just worked together."

Mestel says this was the kind of project they needed to give Primary Wave's investment in the Houston estate proof of concept and to set up all the projects that were to follow. "We hit out of the park within the first couple of months when we found 'Higher Love'," he says, brimming with confidence. "Kygo crushed it. We had a number one record in a bunch of countries and a very high charting record in America. It's been, I think, Whitney's second most popular streamed song of all time."

By February 2020, the remix of 'Higher Love' was Houston's longest-running single in the UK Top 100, racking up over 34 weeks on the chart.[57] It was to stay in the charts for 49 weeks altogether.[58] It significantly outpaced 'I Will Always Love You', which spent 32 weeks in the UK charts (ten of which were at number one[59]), showing how a posthumous release can significantly elevate an artist's chart success.

Another relatively modern phenomenon that is not quite a remix and certainly not the elaborate embellishment of unfinished music is the orchestral rework album.

If I Can Dream was a project developed by Sony Music UK in 2015. It took archival recordings of Elvis Presley's voice from 14 of his classic songs and added new orchestral arrangements played by the Royal Philharmonic Orchestra. It was a number one in the British charts on release and, with sales of 1.1 million, was that year's second-biggest album in the UK. Seizing the moment, Sony quickly created a follow-up, 2016's *The Wonder of You*, deploying the same orchestral overdub approach.

The marketing team at Sony for these releases said this creation of a brand-new album category helped to end the ossification of his catalogue. "For the last 40 years, Elvis product has tended to be the same 30 or so greatest hits," said Phil Savill, MD of the Commercial Music Group at Sony

Music UK. "This concept has allowed the producers to go into the deeper catalogue, explore songs and get them in front of an audience outside of the core fans."[60]

The same trick was subsequently pulled out of the bag a number of times for other estates, notably *A Love So Beautiful: Roy Orbison and the Royal Philharmonic Orchestra* (2017) and *Unchained Melodies: Roy Orbison and the Royal Philharmonic Orchestra* (2018), both on Sony, as well as *True Love Ways: Buddy Holly and the Royal Philharmonic Orchestra* (2018) on Decca (part of Universal Music Group). The Bing Crosby estate also gave this a seasonal twist in 2019 with the *Bing at Christmas* album featuring orchestral accompaniment from the London Symphony Orchestra.

These albums have been significant sellers, but one catalogue expert was sniffy about them and saw them as a short-lived gimmick. "You can potentially take older songs and add new instrumentation and take it to the 21st century," they say. "But do you know if you're going to hit a market? Or are you just pissing in the wind?"

How the estates of a number of rappers – all of whom have died young in recent years – handle posthumous releases from these acts is marking something of a sea change in the business. Much of it plays out in real time in the full glare of social media and there is an emphasis on transparency around what is happening to ease any concerns the fans might have.

US rapper Pop Smoke was murdered on 19 February 2020, but his debut[61] album, *Shoot for the Stars, Aim for the Moon*, was eventually released on 3 July 2020 after 50 Cent executive-produced it and brought it to completion. In doing so, he removed some of the original collaborators who had worked with Pop Smoke on it before his death. "[T]his isn't the record he would have presented [if he were still around]," 50 Cent told *Billboard* after it had gone to number one in the US. "You got some of the guys that were on records that got swapped off, and they're upset. I understand it, but they were not a part of what would have made the best records."[62]

Surprisingly the biggest controversy around the album was not that 50 Cent had completed it and removed some of the original collaborators. The biggest controversy among fans was around the planned artwork.

Steven Victor, head of Pop Smoke's label Victor Victor Worldwide, shared the proposed artwork on Instagram on 29 June 2020.[63] The sleeve had been created by Louis Vuitton designer Virgil Abloh, but the fan backlash on social media was immediate. "Almost instantly, Pop Smoke fans weighed in on the design, which many felt seemed rushed, or even worse, just plain bad," noted *Vulture*.[64] Victor responded swiftly to quell the situation. "BRB. MAKING A CHANGE," he posted in block caps. "POP WOULD LISTEN TO HIS FANS!"

A new version of the sleeve was posted online by Victor ahead of the album release, but it also landed badly with fans who again criticised it on social media.[65] It was revised again ahead of release.

Shoot for the Stars, Aim for the Moon was a huge success on its release in July 2020, debuting at number one on the Billboard 200 chart in the US in its first week,[66] and by March 2021 it had spent 20 weeks at number one on *Billboard*'s Top Rap Albums charts, the longest run at the top of this chart since it began in 2004.[67]

It was also the first posthumous album by a solo act to go to number one in the UK.[68] The unfortunate honour of being the first act to have a posthumous number one in the UK, however, was Viola Beach in August 2016. The band, along with their manager, all died when their car plunged off a bridge into a canal in Sweden on 13 February 2016. Their self-titled album was assembled by their families from a mix of live sessions and studio recordings.[69]

The Pop Smoke album marked an interesting shift in the way posthumous albums come out. Before that, such releases were created and signed off behind closed doors. Now ensuring that fans are behind it is an important part of the advance marketing. There is consumer demand for posthumous releases, but the fans now expect – if not outright demand – some of the ownership of the release. Examples like Pop Smoke will have a significant bearing on how posthumous releases in the future are developed.

Juice WRLD died on 8 December 2019 from a seizure caused by acute oxycodone and codeine intoxication. His third album, *Legends Never Die*, was released on 10 July 2020 and ahead of its release the team at his label, Grade A Productions, spoke to *XXL* about completing the album. Key to this was reassuring fans that the music that would eventually be released would be in keeping with the rapper's original plans.[70]

Meanwhile for the posthumous releases from Lil Peep, who died of an accidental overdose on 15 November 2017, the message was that his uncompleted music would be released in its raw form as much as possible, just as the rapper had left it. Fish Narc, Lil Peep's co-producer and collaborator, said, "We basically mastered the original demos and put them out as is."[71]

The politics of posthumous releases, especially where unfinished music is amended and added to, are an ethical minefield. Is it right that this work should even be touched, let alone released? Does it stop being the work of the deceased artist when committees of producers and engineers are set to work on it? Is it just a form of ghoulish greed to keep the artist in the marketplace and the machine generating a profit? Is it what the fans even want? Will it blemish the artist's legacy by having inferior work – work they never signed off on – added to their discography? Or is this the ultimate tribute to their art by giving it the public reception it deserves?

The surest way around this is to have the family involved in the decision about what is and is not released.

Portia Sabin was formerly president of independent label Kill Rock Stars and she recalls the ethical dilemma facing them over the reissue of Elliott Smith's *Either/Or* album in 2017, which was expanded with previously unheard material. "You really want to honour the person's legacy and not put out stuff that's substandard," she says. "You also have to [understand that] the artist made the choice not to release these tracks. There was probably a reason."

Going back further to the release of *New Moon* in 2007, this was an even more fraught and delicate project. All 24 tracks on this album, which was released four years after Smith's death, had never been released before. "That was an amazing album because that was really the best stuff that he had left unreleased," says Sabin. "Gary, his father, sat with us in the room, and listened to the music and made the selections, which was very emotional [...] We picked the stuff that we felt Elliott would have been OK with us releasing, his family was good with us releasing and that the fans wanted to hear." There was other material that the label and Smith's family made an explicit decision not to release as it "didn't represent the legacy that we want to be upholding", adding there is a complex "curation aspect with artists who are deceased" for labels and families to navigate, even if they have left a great deal of material behind that could be released.

Even if the original audio quality of a lost recording is poor, it does not follow that it will not be released. As mastering technology comes on in leaps and bounds, inferior recordings can be brought up to a releasable standard (the processes involved are considered later in this chapter), but a scratchy and murky recording has not stopped labels putting it out.

"In the past, there have been some projects where we've included material from a demo cassette – but it's clearly labelled as such," says one major label executive. "We will say that the audio quality might not be great but it's important in terms of the story it tells." Such releases, it seems, tend to be the exception rather than the rule and it is becoming less of an issue as new mastering technology and software can salvage what might have been dismissed in the past as an unlistenable mess.

"Hopefully, these projects might offer everyday listeners the genuine pleasure that only new music can bring," said Rob Garratt in *The National*, using the posthumous Avicii album as his hook. "But at the same time, it shouldn't be forgotten that this is almost certainly material the artists never wanted to be heard in the first place – and the bottom line is, it's always someone else who stands to benefit from its release."[72]

Martin Aston, in a 2016 piece for *The Vinyl Factory* on the Jeff Buckley archive, argues that the more the archive is mined, the more Buckley's power diminishes. "Sony/Legacy: no more," he says. "Let him lie."[73]

There is a line of argument here that echoes the points in 'Paint a Vulgar Picture', a song on the final Smiths album, *Strangeways, Here We Come*, from 1987. In that song, Morrissey imagines a record company meeting where news of the death of a star on their roster is cause for celebration rather than mourning as the staff cook up increasingly ruthless ways to milk their legacy and sell as many records as they can before the public inevitably gets bored and moves on. Albums are reissued and repackaged but the dead-eyed record company executives will never truly understand the beautiful essence of the deceased artist as Morrissey does, presenting himself as the purest and truest of fans, in sharp contrast to the company's tasteless obsession with sales charts and market share. Trying to argue the case that record companies are some kind of moral superiors is never going to get you far; but regarding them solely as grasping opportunists who see death as something only to be exploited is equally absurd and reductive.

What all these examples have in common is that the debate around them was whether or not such works in progress should be finished and commercially released. No one ever publicly questioned if the artist actually made them. That, however, was the case with *Michael* in 2010, the first posthumous album from Michael Jackson.

Vera Serova, a Jackson fan, filed a lawsuit against both Sony Music and the Jackson estate, claiming that they were deceiving the public with the release as it contained three songs that were based on the vocals of an impersonator. Serova even went as far as hiring a forensic audiologist to analyse the vocals in order to help support her case.[74] It took until 2018 for the case to be resolved, with three appeal court judges ruling in the favour of the estate and Sony.

There remained some doubt, however. *Variety* quoted court documents that said, "Because [Sony Music, MJJ Productions and the Jackson estate] lacked actual knowledge of the identity of the lead singer on ['Breaking News', 'Monster' and 'Keep Your Head Up'], they could only draw a conclusion about that issue from their own research and the available evidence. Under these circumstances, [Sony Music, MJJ Productions and the Jackson estate's] representations about the identity of the singer amounted to a statement of opinion rather than fact."[75]

Howard Weitzman, the lawyer for the Jackson estate, released a statement in which he cited the names of engineers, studio musicians, industry executives and musicologists who all affirmed that the vocals were performed by Jackson. This is a rare example, but with artificial intelligence software able to recreate speech patterns that could dupe many, this could be a foreshadowing of what is to come in the world of posthumous releases (see Chapter 12).

Unquestionably the most decisive act regarding unheard and unfinished material was what Universal Music did with the music Amy Winehouse left behind at her death on 23 July 2011. She had only released two albums in her lifetime – *Frank* in 2003 and *Back to Black* in 2006 – but the release of *Lioness: Hidden Treasures* in late 2011, made up of a dozen unreleased songs and demos, would appear to be the only album of unheard music that will ever be officially released.

Speaking to *Billboard* in 2015, David Joseph, the chairman and CEO of Universal Music UK, said that no more music from the Amy Winehouse vault would ever get a release for one very simple reason – he had had it all destroyed. "It was a moral thing," he said. "Taking a stem or a vocal is not something that would ever happen on my watch. It now can't happen on anyone else's."[76]

Just as releasing music after an artist has died throws those involved into a complex moral maze, so too does destroying it. This is an act of total finality. To make this even more ethically complex, a senior catalogue executive at a major label recounts a tale of this exact thing happening – an artist demanding some of their demo recordings be destroyed – and how they responded. "I handed the demo tapes back to them," they say. "However, I did ensure that there was a copy because I felt it was too important. I made sure they're locked away. I made sure there's a note on them. But I made sure we kept a copy because they were too important to be destroyed. They were paid for by [the record label]. There are two sides to this. One, there was a duty to hand the tapes back for various reasons; but, on the other hand, there was a duty for me to make sure that the company retained a copy as they were historically very important."

The philosophical question at the heart of all this is: who knows best? Is it the artist? Or is it their record company or estate? Making the decision to destroy tapes without any backup copies has a striking finality and has to come from a place of total moral confidence. Losing tapes in a fire is one thing; having the conviction and the certitude to toss them on the flames is another thing entirely.

VAULTING AMBITION: QUALITY OVER QUANTITY

It sometimes feels like there is an arms race happening where the more unreleased material an estate puts out on an album or box set, the more other estates have to not only match it but exceed it, creating a quality nosedive for everyone involved. It did not always happen this way; the packing of albums with a bounty of offcuts is a relatively recent development.

Tim Chacksfield is a label catalogue expert and recalls working on early reissues in the 1980s when such projects were in their nascent stage. He was involved in an Eddie Cochran box set project – one that happened without any of the singer's family or estate being involved. The idea for the box set did not even come from the label – it came from the fans, who felt Cochran was at risk of being forgotten. Today catalogue divisions are hugely important parts of a record company, particularly a major label, but in the early days of the CD, the focus was still on frontline releases and not the archives.

That was soon to change, but Chacksfield offers a snapshot of those more innocent and simpler times. "It was one of the first things we did," he says of the Cochran box set. "This is pre- any kind of internet. You really had to rely on people who had books and knowledge to put these things together. We came up with a listing of material, I travelled to Los Angeles and went to the vault. With the librarian there we found the tapes and they were copied and brought back here [to the UK] to put the set together. That was how it worked."

While there was an emerging market for box sets as the CD started to grow in popularity in the second half of the 1980s, there was no identifiable demand for extras in the shape of outtakes and unheard recordings. Even though CDs could hold almost twice as much music as an LP, it was inconceivable then that this free space had to be filled with whatever was at hand.

"Single CDs were not covered by having loads of bonus tracks – they were usually just straight reissues and people would be spending quite a lot of money on them," says Chacksfield. "Box sets were coming along. For a major set, four CDs was probably the most because the four CDs fitted in a 12×12 box. People still had bits of vinyl and so it worked nicely on that size. You also had plenty of room for graphics and information."

Tony Wadsworth, who was eventually to become chairman and CEO of EMI Music UK & Ireland, said in his first days at the company in the early 1980s there was no catalogue division at all. These were assets that were utterly overlooked. "This catalogue, that we all know now, was unmined; it was just extraordinary," he said. He took the initiative to start to reissue albums from the label's archive. "This was the lowest-hanging-fruit job that you could ever wish for in your life [...] Over the next two or three years, I got to a point where I was releasing 40 albums a month. A month!"[77]

Like Chacksfield, he also turned to the fans to help steer which recordings were reissued. "I'd get people from the Frank Sinatra fan club inviting me down to their social evenings and then wondering who this 27-year-old guy was turning up," he recalled. "Everybody thought that you were a massive fan of what they were a massive fan of. I found all of these huge enthusiasts that would help me do these compilations. So it had authority – the stuff that I was putting out as well."[78]

Today, when a new posthumous album by a major artist is released, like clockwork a comment piece will appear in the press setting up a number of counter-arguments against its release: it is not benefiting the artist's legacy; it is diminishing the artist's legacy; it is tawdry; it is cheap; it is scraping the barrel. On rare occasions (such as Leonard Cohen's *Thanks for the Dance*) it will be applauded as a creative triumph and stand as the exception to the rule that all posthumous albums are, by their very nature, inferior products. The artist did not approve them in their lifetime so why should the public see them as anything more than what they are – a shameless cash-in that puts commerce far above art?

A feature in the *Independent* in November 2019 is typical. Tupac and Jeff Buckley were referred to as "ghoulish lab-rat[s] for posthumous careers in music" as they released more records in death than they ever did in life.[79]

It is ludicrous, of course, to argue that all posthumous releases add beautiful new colours to the tapestry of a creative individual's life. If there is no care or concern applied, they can slowly unpick the delicate needlework of their creations.

The 2003 release of Miles Davis's *The Complete Jack Johnson Sessions* – drawn from sessions recorded in 1970s for the 1971 soundtrack album *Jack Johnson* – was regarded by some as a step too far. The original album was made up of two tracks, "Right Off" and "Yesternow", each running to over 25 minutes, and produced by Teo Macero. "I hate it," Macero, who was not involved in the box set, told the *Guardian*. "I think it's a bunch of shit, and you can quote me on that. And I hope you do. It has destroyed Miles and made him sound like an idiot. It's a terrible thing to do to an artist when he's dead."[80]

Erin Davis, son of Miles, spoke in 2015 about the tensions here between respecting a legacy and also needing to release a steady flow of new and unheard material that keeps fans interested. "We are trying to give people music they haven't heard before, which is hard to do when someone isn't around any more," he said.[81]

While it is invariably the record company that takes the brunt of the criticism for such releases, they can occasionally be the ones that stop the estate making what they regard as a mistake by vetoing certain archive projects.

Costa Pilavachi was president of Philips Classics, based in the Netherlands in the early 1990s, and he recounts the story of having to deal with the estate of Maria Callas. At the time, it was run by Jackie Callas, the opera star's sister, and Jackie's husband at the time. The label was sitting on an unreleased album Callas made a few years before her death (on 16 September 1977). These were among her final recordings. "It was never completed," he says. "Whatever payments had to be made to various artists were never made." It was, Pilavachi claims, "embarrassing" and was never released. "She was in terrible voice," he says. "And her tenor, Giuseppe Di Stefano, wasn't in great voice either. I was not involved yet – this was in the 1970s. I was very close to the producer, who told me the whole story and begged me not to release it. I listened to it and I was horrified at how bad it was."

He claims Jackie's husband was putting pressure on the label to release it. "He was really upset and was begging me to release it – because they needed the money," recalls Pilavachi. "He even put me on the phone to Jackie Callas, the sister, who confirmed that the family wanted this to come out. But they had no idea what they were talking about, because they had nothing to do with music. They weren't at all sensitive [to the issues]."

Pilavachi consulted John Ardoin, Callas's biographer, to get a second opinion. "He said, 'Costa, you cannot release this album. Please, I beg you.' I said, 'Listen, there's no problem. We're not going to release it. There's no way.' That's an example of the record company actually protecting the artist – and our own reputation as a record company – by basically saying no to exploitative members of the family after the artist's death."

There are some artists and their families who foresee this as a problem when the artist is alive, and so take measures to ensure that situations like this do not occur and sub-standard material is not put into public circulation.

Allan Steckler runs the estate of classical pianist and composer Vladimir Horowitz. He passed away in 1989 and his entire estate transferred to his widow, Wanda Toscanini Horowitz. She died in 1998, but before she died she put measures in place to protect her husband's legacy. "She had in her will that, upon her death, if any material is to be considered for release, it has to go by three people who she named," says Steckler.

Jeff Liebenson, a New York-based lawyer who works for the beneficiaries of the Horowitz estate, says this was an extension of stipulations that the composer had in his own will. "Horowitz arranged that previously unreleased recordings could only be released after his death if they were approved by a group of individuals that he hand-selected," says Liebenson. "These are some of the most respected people in the world of music – like Ronald Wilford, the chairman of Columbia Artists Management, Jack Pfeffier, the legendary producer at RCA who produced much of Horowitz's output, and Byron Janis, one of the top classical pianists in the world as well as being Horowitz's first student. He left it to them to review and approve any unreleased material. They have been a great asset to us to make sure that everything is done in the right way. They each really took their role very seriously."

The way it worked is that if just one of these named individuals felt a recording that was being considered for release was deemed to be inferior – in terms of audio quality, performance quality or both – then it would be permanently shelved. "Horowitz was mindful of these matters during his lifetime," says Liebenson. "He was very discerning about what recordings he would allow to be released or not."

Mickey Leigh is the brother of Joey Ramone and runs his estate as well as holding 50 per cent of Ramone Productions, which covers everything related to the band.

He feels that there are only so many times albums can be re-released or padded out with unheard material. In the case of the Ramones, there is now precious little in the vaults that has not already been released on remastered or expanded anniversary editions of the band's classic albums. "With the Ramones there really wasn't any of that," he says of unheard material that could be deemed worthy of release. "There were really no songs that were not put out already. [There are demos and outtakes] but how much of it can you put out? After a while, the fans get a little weary. 'What? Another one? Another version of 'Blitzkrieg Bop'? Another demo of it?' You have got to be very selective and not try and burn people out on it. Maybe by doing that, it's almost like reverse marketing somehow."

One label catalogue executive cautions that quality thresholds still need to be adhered to with raids on the vaults. "Whilst there may be a commercial win or there may be commercial opportunity in that material, if it's not very good or isn't maybe true to what the artist was originally about, it doesn't benefit anyone," they say. "If it's not going to be to the benefit of the overall output of the artist, why would you? But also you've got to think about the people parting with their money or spending their time listening to it. Is it going to work for them as well?"

Asked if arguments about the historical importance of an unreleased track trump concerns about its musical or audio merits, the same executive put it like this. "You wouldn't necessarily record them whistling in the bath," they say, "and then put it out and claim it was a great lost recording."

An important point to remember here is that the bigger the living artist, the more sway they have in their lifetime over what can be taken from the vaults and commercially released. Paul McCartney, for example, controls the rights to all his post-Beatles recordings and his company, MPL, employs two full-time archivists to look after all of his assets, including recordings, artwork and personal affects. He is in a unique position in terms of the power he has over his own legacy. Few acts are as powerful – or as organised – as Paul McCartney with regard to their catalogue and their legacy. Even so, he stands as a utopian model here.

For Eva Cassidy, given how little of her material was released in her lifetime (and even then it was only available in small runs on CDs and cassettes), her posthumous career has almost entirely been based around archival studio and live recordings.

She only released one album – *The Other Side*, a collaboration with Chuck Brown in 1992 – while alive and since her death 12 more albums, not including anniversary reissues, have been released. They are a mixture of studio albums (five in total), live albums (three) and compilations (four, including one of acoustic recordings).

Bill Straw of Blix Street Records suggests there are a significant number of recordings still to come out. Speaking on Lakeshore Public Radio in December 2015, he was asked if there was more material in the vaults that could be released. "The short answer is yes," he said. "We're not going to release anything that we don't think is up to snuff – because it's not fair to Eva. But she didn't do bad work. Anything that is deficient is generally for technical reasons or reasons other than her. We've released several tracks from the Maryland Inn [in Annapolis], which was another live venue she played; it kind of served as a rehearsal for the Blues Alley [site of her most famous live recordings]. So we have more of those left. She did a lot of solo work at a club in Annapolis [Maryland] called Pearls. So there's quite a bit of that stuff left."[82]

Most of her studio work was captured by her collaborator Chris Biondo. Straw says that "he took every opportunity to get her on tape" and there is a treasure trove of demo recordings stretching over a number of years that Biondo has gathered together. "So those things surfaced," he says. "The next thing you know there's over 100 recordings that are much better than you realise they are."

He says that the *Nightbird* album from 2015 scooped up a range of recordings, including some that had already been released on the 1996 album *Live at Blues Alley*; this was expanded with a further 12 tracks that had previously been unreleased. It was felt there was fan demand for more material to be released but Straw believed that it was better to release it in small batches over a long period of time rather than all in one go. This is partly to avoid listener fatigue but also to have a release plan that can run several years into the future.

TAKING STOCK: FIGURING OUT WHAT IS IN THE ARCHIVE

One of the biggest challenges estates face in their early days is that of audio stocktaking – going into the recorded archives of the deceased artist and trying to figure out what is there and, from that, what can even be considered for release.

Daniel Gallagher is the nephew of Irish blues guitarist Rory Gallagher, who died in 1995, and is intimately involved in the numerous releases that have come out in recent years. The estate signed a catalogue deal with Universal Music Group for his solo work in 2017 and that involved developing projects around unreleased material from 2018 onwards.[83] "One of the things we did was move all of Rory's tape archive to their secure locations," says Daniel. "There were over 1,000 tapes we had to catalogue. Many of them are from album sessions. Some are from different tours and live concerts [or come from] Rory's own seven-inch reels from his home reel-to-reel tape machine with demos from the 1970s he'd been working on. There were hundreds of cassette tapes of demos he had. It was a big archive of recordings of his music."

He explains how this cataloguing process – protracted and arduous as it was – eventually turned up the most unexpected items. Gallagher had played with Albert King in 1975 in Montreux and he appeared on two songs – 'Jam in A Flat' and 'As the Years Go Passing By' – that were eventually released on the *Albert Live* album in 1977. In sifting through recordings for a planned album in 2019 called *Blues*, Daniel came across four seven-inch reels that Albert King's team had sent to Rory Gallagher so he could approve them for inclusion on *Albert Live*. The tapes were simply marked "A", "B", "C" and "D" with no details of what was on them.

"There was an extra track ['You Upset Me'] on there that ended up not being on the Albert King album," says Daniel. "So we were able to put out a Rory and Albert King track that no one had ever heard before. With tape, thankfully you can re-work it and get a high-res audio out of it. That's the great thing about having such a tape archive – that ability to make it sound amazing again, even if it was recorded in 1975."

Also buried in the Rory Gallagher archives was an acoustic performance (and interview) for a Cleveland radio station in 1972 that had never been bootlegged before as well as a 1974 session for a French radio station found on an unmarked tape. "It's always worth digging and testing things out," says Daniel. "You can find gold on these tapes."

Artistic collaborators can unearth forgotten recordings for estates too. Dónal Gallagher, Rory's brother and manager, says this happened with folk artist Bert Jansch, who gave Dónal an unheard track as a thank you for helping him deal with some problems he was facing with his own catalogue. He recounts the story of how this lost recording got released. "Bert called me and said, 'By the way, did you ever hear the track Rory and I did together?' I said, 'Rory mentioned to me that you guys were meeting up in the pub. But I thought it was for other reasons!' He said, 'We never quite completed it but I'll finish it for you and send it on to you.' It was 'Ann Cran Ull', Gaelic for 'The Apple Tree', mixed with another piece of music ['She Moved Thro' the Fair']." It was eventually released on the 2003 *Wheels Within Wheels* album.

Rare recordings can also resurface in places where perhaps no one would have thought to look for them as they were within the archives of another late artist. That is precisely what happened in late 2019 when a tape containing 12 unreleased songs and fragments of a thirteenth made by Lou Reed in 1975 was found in the Andy Warhol Museum. Reed, of course, had a long-running connection with Warhol dating back to The Velvet Underground. They played Warhol's *Exploding Plastic Inevitable* events in 1967, and he "produced"[84] the band's debut album in 1967 and also designed the iconic banana cover.

Judith Peraino, a professor of music at Cornell University, found them when conducting archival research at the Warhol Museum in Pittsburgh, sifting through some 3,500 cassettes in the collection. "It sounds like he recorded them in his apartment with an open-air microphone, just voice and acoustic guitar," she told *Variety*.[85] On the other side of the cassette were soundboard recordings of Reed's solo shows in 1975. It has, as yet, never been released.

Occasionally an archive jackpot will reveal itself and the sheer scale of what is contained in it will take everyone by surprise. This was certainly the case in September 2020 which independent label Cherry Red Records announced it had acquired the Joe Meek[86] Tea Chest Tapes (so called because the circa 1,800 quarter-inch reels belonging to the producer, who died in 1967, had originally been sold in 67 tea chests). The label described it as "a near mythical collection", containing early recordings by Ray Davies, Gene Vincent, Rod Stewart, Steve Marriott, Tom Jones, Billy Fury and The Konrads (David Bowie's first band). There were also suggestions of an early recording by Mark Feld (later to change his name to Marc Bolan) in the collection.[87]

Eventually, of course, archives start to dry up and these serendipitous finds simply tail off. These are finite resources and after several decades of releasing unheard material, eventually there is nothing unheard left.

Speaking on the *Opus* podcast by *Consequence of Sound* 2019, Mary Guibert revealed that, "with the exception of maybe a few more full concerts that we have the soundboard recordings of", there was nothing left in the live archive for Jeff Buckley.[88] There may be some radio broadcasts that could get a release but she and the estate did not have the rights or access to them.

She did, however, reveal that that there is "a whole box of tapes that no one's listened to" that was in his apartment.

"I have no idea what's on the tapes," she tells me. "It could be old voicemails, it could be things that he said to himself, personal journals, audio journals. There are some things that a mother shouldn't know! There's some things a mother shouldn't dabble into. Frankly, if I'm not going to use it, I'm not going to leave it behind for someone else to use it. My attorney will take care of that."

When asked if there is much more unreleased Miles Davis music to come out, Darryl Porter, who heads up his estate, is bluntly honest, suggesting a 2019 archive release might be one of the last the estate will put out.

"No, there isn't," he says. "Miles passed in 1991 so we have been releasing much of the unreleased [music] over the years. We released a project called *Rubberband* on Warner Music Group [in 2019]. That was an unfinished session [in 1985] that Miles recorded when he first left Sony and moved over to Warner Brothers. Before he could finish the project, Tommy LiPuma [head of jazz at Warner] grabbed him and took him over to start working with Marcus Miller. And, of course, Miles never looked back, so he didn't go back and finish that project. We got Vince Wilburn, his nephew, Randy Hall and Zane Giles, who were the original producers on the project, to come in and finish it. It has done very, very well for us."

David Hirshland, EVP at BMG, argues that any mining of the vaults has to handled in a "very careful manner"; but for artists who left little unheard music behind, if it is to be released it has to be musically strong and both culturally and historically interesting. BMG acquired the Buddy Holly catalogue and his name and image rights in 2015 but Hirshland says there is "precious little" lost material to come out. "There are a couple of things that we're working on," he says with regard to the Buddy Holly archives. "He recorded what were famously known as *The Apartment Tapes* just before he went on the fateful tour [in 1959]. Those were done in his apartment in New York. He wrote, recorded and produced them. They're actually amazingly complete for what would be called demo recordings. They've been kind of released as part of a box set by Universal, but never really given the attention that they deserve."

Of all the artists who stockpiled incredible amounts of material, no one comes close to Prince. Yet while there are vast amounts of music in his legendary vault, making the decision to release it comes with complex politics. His official release schedule in his lifetime was staggering, but there are still uncomfortable questions – would he ever have been happy with anything he had locked away getting released?

Speaking at the Ignition 2018 conference on 4 December 2018, Troy Carter, entertainment adviser to the Prince estate, recounted his first trip to

Paisley Park when working for the estate. "I remember going and sitting with the team, and one of his creative directors, who we work with, [talked about] this famous vault that I couldn't wait to see," he said. "He had all of these other rooms, just floor to ceiling, and his creative director said that Prince hadn't been in that vault in years. I said, 'What? Did he just want to move past the past and get into the future?' He said, 'No, he forgot the combination to the vault!' [Laughs] But when we got in there, it was amazing. Just 40 years – all of these years' worth of gems and finding music that's never been heard before. Just some beautiful, beautiful work."[89]

In the same interview, Carter added that Prince may have died intestate but he was working on reissue ideas and had left written instructions about what he wanted to happen with them. "He left an incredible blueprint because he was very specific about how he wanted things to roll out," said Carter. "He wanted *Purple Rain* remastered and [it was in] his personal notes about how he wanted it remastered and what he wanted to come next [...] he left behind his legacy and how he wanted his legacy to play out."[90]

This was taken as a green light to start a major reissue programme that has included *Piano & a Microphone 1983* in 2018 and *Originals* in 2019, as well as multi-disc deluxe reissues of *Purple Rain*, *1999* and *Sign O' the Times*, all of which are stuffed to the gills with previously unheard material.

An individual who works with the Prince estate, speaking anonymously, outlined the scale of the task ahead of Michael Howe, the official Prince archivist who had previously been an A&R at Warner Music and who began dealing with Prince towards the end of the star's life. "His job is just literally going through the vaults and finding out what the hell is in there," the source says. "There is so much stuff. Some of it is unlabelled, some of it is in the wrong boxes, some of it has songs that appear at the end of tapes that aren't mentioned on the boxes. It's a ginormous task and it's his job to pull it all together." The same source confirms Carter's claims that Prince was preparing for significant album reissue campaigns before he passed away. "The remastering of *Purple Rain* was done whilst he was alive and he had approved it," the source says. "Things were moving, but they were moving quite slowly."

A *Rolling Stone* feature in 2018 also offered some insight into what was happening here. It said everything in the vault – which included music as well as video footage, handwritten notes and letters – was shipped from Paisley Park in Minneapolis to Iron Mountain, the secure temperature-controlled storage facility in Los Angeles. One box shipped to Iron Mountain reportedly contained 8,000 cassettes. It estimates that up to 30 per cent of the music "was unlabelled or mislabelled", adding there might be upwards of 1,000 studio recordings (not to mention numerous concert recordings) that could be released.[91]

Tyka Nelson, Prince's sister, told *Rolling Stone* that the plan was to release a new collection of unheard music every year in chronological order, starting with 1983. "He had so much, and he wanted his music to be heard," she said.

"If it was up to me, we'd see something every year for the next hundred or thousand years."[92]

Carter also spoke to *Rolling Stone* about the scale of the task in front of them. "It was overwhelming in terms of making sense of it all," he said. "You had multiple versions of songs. We had to figure out what was released, what was unreleased, what songs were finished. Are there songs Prince just wouldn't want anyone to hear there because they weren't quite there yet?"[93]

It turns out Prince was already running quality control of his own archive, with engineer Susan Rogers being told by the singer to mark boxes as "W" (standing for "weak") for performances he was unhappy with and stars assigned to tracks he was pleased with. It all started when Prince was preparing for the *Purple Rain* album, which was released in 1984. "I realised it would be smart for me to get his tapes together in one place," she said. "I was aware there were a lot of pieces missing. It became an obsession. I wanted us to have everything he'd ever recorded [...] When I left in '87, it was nearly full. Row after row of everything we'd done."[94]

Howe told *Super Deluxe Edition* in 2019 that only completed recordings will ever be released and that unfinished works will never be made public. "That all gets to stay with the family," he told *Vulture* in 2018. "There are some things that'll never emerge."[95]

In early April 2021 it was announced that *Welcome 2 America*, a previously unheard album recorded by Prince in 2010, would get a full release in July that year via Sony Music's Legacy Recordings arm.[96]

Coinciding with this, and marking the fifth anniversary of his death, CBS News broadcast a *60 Minutes* special on the Prince vault and the estate's plans to release more music. It estimated that some 8,000 songs had been stockpiled by Prince before his death and none of it had been heard outside of Paisley Park. CBS spoke to Shelby J, a member of New Power Generation since 2006 and a singer who had worked with Prince on several albums, about the wealth of material in the vault and his prolific nature. "Well, music, you know, it ain't milk," she said. "It don't expire."[97]

Troy Carter was also interviewed for the programme and talked about his duty of care to both the material in the vault and Prince's legacy as well as how he exerts quality control over what does and does not get released. "I wanna make sure that Prince isn't somewhere in heaven giving me the side-eye," he said. "You know, that – that famous Prince side-eye [...] You know, the fans think they've heard everything. So whenever we can find things that the fans haven't heard is like a victory."[98]

An estate the size of Prince's has the resources to bring in experts to properly archive and label recordings, but labels themselves have not always been rigorous in their own archiving (perhaps not thinking the material was worthy of being logged properly) and this can cause immense headaches for catalogue departments years down the line. It is, through either negligence or apathy, like leaving an uncrackable puzzle in a time capsule that will not be opened for decades.

"Often just going through tapes you find – particularly on multi-track reels – that all the takes aren't listed properly," says one senior catalogue executive at a major label. "Suddenly you find a tape or you find a track that you just didn't know existed. Engineers are brilliant at not writing down things. Their spelling tends to be appalling. They often don't spell the artist name right, let alone listing all the artists and all the songs. Songs then get marked up incorrectly. You'll find that modern systems tend to have had a batch input by staff that have been brought in from wherever and their interpretation of what's on those tape boxes would be potentially very different from mine."

Tim Chacksfield says that there was a massive disparity between how EMI logged recording sessions and how other labels did – and this had significant bearing on the early years of CD catalogue marketing which still causes issues today. "It was run a bit like the BBC so everything is logged," he says of EMI's system. "If you look at a log sheet, the sheet will have the tape, it will have who produced it and so on. This is available information on the boxes. Some engineers were crap at writing up the boxes. Where people were diligent, you got the date of the recording, all the tapes listed, false starts, breakdowns, the whole bloody lot. The tape box would have what type of tape it is, which had a relevance later on for baking.[99] The whole track listing, timings, everything. For other companies, there is nothing but a title and the number." He adds, "I found things on this artist I was working on recently. I was looking for two Spanish-language recordings he made and they hadn't got them. But when I pulled up other tapes of the period, there they were – but they just hadn't been listed on the system as no one bothered. It was a shit show." This "shit show" makes some archival projects a fearsomely forensic and agonisingly archaeological undertaking.

There is a very real risk that the longer an estate runs, the more reductive the music becomes. A multitude of greatest hits albums over the years can boil a recorded music legacy down to a handful of tracks. Acts start to only exist on Best Of collections or multi-artist compilations and all the rest of their work starts to fade into the background. This was the issue Phil Savill at Sony said the Elvis catalogue was facing until the orchestral albums enabled them to dig deeper into his lesser-known recordings.

For some estates, the discovery and release of a "lost" album can help redress this imbalance. It can reassert the act as an "album artist" rather than a "compilation artist".

Michele Monro runs the estate of her father, Matt Monro, and says there was a process of horse trading with EMI in 2006 in order to allow an album of obscurities, *The Rare Monro*, to be released. She says that she initially faced resistance from the catalogue team because this album did not contain 'Born Free', Monro's biggest hit. "I said, 'For God's sake – how many times can they [the fans] have a copy of 'Born Free'?'" she recalls. "We made a deal where if *The Ultimate* [compilation] sold a certain amount they'd give me the OK for *The Rare Monro*. We did it and it was huge. Huge. Six years later, I did *Matt Uncovered: The Rarer Monro*. I did one with Nelson Riddle.

I did live ones. There were so many we did and they were really good. We remastered them, we put them in stereo. EMI would say they'd release something and they'd end up putting mono tracks on it. It was lazy. This was in the old days. We stopped all that. So literally the entire catalogue is now all remastered and all in stereo."

After EMI was carved up, the Monro catalogue ended up being split between Warner Music and Universal's catalogue department. Michele Monro claims that the former has not been proactive in exploiting it. "Warner bought it and they don't want to do anything," she says. "I don't know why they bought the catalogue. The catalogue in any record company is really their most valuable asset."

Working with Universal, however, led to the release in March 2020 of *Stranger in Paradise: The Lost New York Sessions* based on shelved recordings made with an orchestra in 1966.[100] As with EMI, however, the initial emphasis was going to be on Monro's best-known recordings.

"Originally they wanted to bring out a Best Of and have the *New York Sessions* in as a bonus," says Michele. "I said, 'Absolutely not. The *New York Sessions* is a [stressing each word] *brand-new album*. Nobody has heard Daddy sing like this with only a five-piece orchestra or band. They are only used to hearing him with big orchestras.'"

Even then, the album ran into problems. Universal sent her their proposed artwork for the album. She went, she says, "ballistic". As with the refusal to do another Best Of, she stood her ground. "The album is called *Lost in New York*, and I said, 'It looks like he's bloody lost! He's staring into nothing' – it was awful," she says. "We had a whole photo session from that particular time when he was there in New York. We actually had a photo session from it. And I said, 'You have all these other choices.' I sent them [Universal] two pictures and said, 'You should have used one of these. Don't bother to email me back. I'm not interested.' Yes, I did lose my temper, but don't come to me and say something's been done and then ask me what I think. We hadn't had a new product in six years so it was even more important. It has to be absolutely perfect."

The album eventually came out with the artwork she wanted. It was a Top 10 hit in the UK.

PUTTING TOGETHER ARCHIVE PACKAGES AND IDEAS

The streaming era has given labels new and (most importantly) real-time insights into how catalogues are being listened to, allowing them to capitalise on growing consumer interest in an artist or one of their releases. This is really just an acceleration of what existed in the CD age where audience research guided decision-making. What was most telling about the physical format age, where acts were not being promoted constantly on social media and other digital platforms, was how deceased artists could fall in and out of fashion.

In the 1980s and 1990s, because of the manufacturing and marketing costs involved, only a tiny handful of dead artists were heavily promoted by the catalogue arms of record labels. It was a self-selecting process in a way – they were mega-stars in life and could be promoted to newer generations as mega-stars in death. Plus sales forecasts had to be significant enough to justify the initial investment in shining a spotlight on their releases.

Tony Wadsworth was head of EMI's Parlophone label in the 1990s and enjoying huge frontline success with acts like Blur and Radiohead. He explains how the relevance of certain acts in the label's catalogue ebbed and flowed depending on what was happening in music and popular culture at the time. Rather than labels forcing sales of deceased artists entirely by throwing huge TV advertising budgets at them around an anniversary or the run-up to Christmas, they were increasingly able to spot opportunities in the zeitgeist and capitalise on them.

"The John Lennon [compilation] that I initiated while at Parlophone was called *Lennon Legend: The Very Best of John Lennon* in October 1997," he says. "That image of him on the cover was chosen because he looked like a member of Oasis – because they were huge at the time. We had rolling research going on annually from Omnibus Research on our major artists to get a feel as to how their stock was rising and falling. When Oasis hit, with all of their references and talking about their influences, the stock in The Beatles rose sharply. We always think of The Beatles as being this always-massive catalogue which stays at a certain level but it ebbed and flowed."

Omnibus would base its data on phone calls to a pool of respondents and this would be fed through to the label. "You could factor historic sales data in," says Wadsworth, "but it was also asking people: if there was a new Beatles *Greatest Hits* tomorrow, how likely would you be to buy it? It would be questions like that, that we would ask every year. You'd be amazed how it changed with the weather. *Lennon Legend* and its success was very much shaped by that new slant on The Beatles which Britpop and Oasis had introduced."

The stock of The Beatles was already sky-high in 1997 after the *Anthology* documentary and series of outtakes albums released in 1995 and 1996, but this compilation was capitalising specifically on John Lennon, who had become a totemic figure for a new generation of rock bands at the time, arguably more so than any other Beatle. The Lennon album helped to reinvigorate and recontextualise the Lennon legacy. It went to number four in the UK album chart after release and spent 74 weeks in the chart. Lennon as a solo artist had not had a Top 40 album in the UK since the early 1980s[101] and much of that was down to the emotional aftershock of his assassination in December 1980.

This is a keen reminder that even toweringly important names like John Lennon were not always in huge demand from the public and that deftly timed compilations play a significant role in changing where in the cultural hierarchy the public places them. Oasis, as well as being huge Beatles fans, became a prism through which to introduce Lennon's music in the mid-1990s to teenagers and young adults, for whom John Lennon was simply someone their parents liked.

Underpinning this is the need for estates to introduce the music of late artists to new generations and not just to super-serve existing fan bases. The specifics are dissected in Chapter 9. This includes sampling and remixing, but also creating whole new vehicles such as biopics and podcasts to put the artist and their music in front of entirely new demographics who may not have grown up with their music.

THE PROFESSIONAL ARCHIVIST

Generally, the record label will own the master tapes and have them stored away, but as several catalogue heads confirmed, the further back in time you go, the less likely they are to be properly labelled and tagged. Plus, of course, they may have been turned into landfill or taped over as either a space-saving or a cost-saving exercise. Or they have gone up in flames like those lost in the 2008 Universal fire.

This does not account for the recordings in an artist's possession – covering things like home demos, recordings of rehearsals or even feeds from the sound desk at shows. Then, of course, there are all the other items and artefacts produced as part of their life or creative process – journals, lyric books and sketch books being the most significant.

Some artists have had the foresight to organise their archives in their lifetime. This may be because they want to turn it into an exhibition, such as the *David Bowie Is*[102] exhibition at the Victoria & Albert Museum in London in 2013, which then toured the world; The Jam's *About the Young Idea*[103] at Somerset House in London in 2015; The Rolling Stones' *Exhibitionism*[104] at the Saatchi Gallery in London in 2016; and Pink Floyd's *Their Mortal Remains*[105] at the Victoria & Albert Museum in 2017. Another reason may be because they wish to auction off items to raise money for charity, as Elton John has done several times, notably putting 2,000 items up for auction in 1988.[106]

Others have been fortunate to have someone in their team or family who took on that responsibility for them. Martha Glaser was the manager of jazz pianist and composer Erroll Garner (who died in 1977) and she is a pivotal figure for the music industry and estates business for how she organised and controlled his archives. This included many hours of recordings that had never been heard before, and she kept tight control over if or how they should ever be released.

"If I had been entrusted with the last but un-viewed works of someone such as Picasso, I would be very careful about which museum or gallery they would be shown in," she told the *New York Times* in 1985. "With Erroll's recordings, I'm extremely concerned about sound. Even the Dolby system subtly changes the characteristics of his work, as if we had changed intensities and hues. It even changes the sense of swing in his playing."[107]

Garner is a key figure in the complex history of artistic control with regard to sound recordings – and this all had huge bearing on how his own archive was organised by Glaser. Traditionally artists signed a record deal and, in exchange for an advance and a set royalty rate, signed over ownership of their masters to the label in perpetuity. This was deemed by many acts to be unfair, but was begrudgingly accepted as the way business was done. In 1960, Garner was due to renegotiate his contract with Columbia, which he had originally signed in 1956, but during negotiations the label had started to release material from his archive without his consent, notably the *Swinging Solos* album.

Garner sent a letter to Columbia executive John Hammond about the matter. He wrote:

> I must demand that you immediately withdraw "Swinging Solos" record album which your Columbia Records subsidiary released [...] this took place despite my written notice to your record people [...] the material was not approved and was unworthy of public sale. As a matter of ethics I am amazed that release took place precisely at the time my manager was meeting with [you] at [your] request and while [you] were assuring her that the album would not be released. Is it you feel you can sandbag me because I am a Negro artist? Must demand that sale and distribution of album stop immediately and that it be recalled from press, radio people and record dealers who have previously received it [...] because it not only violates my artistic integrity but that of every artist on your label.[108]

Garner and Glaser sued Columbia and the label responded with a counter-suit. In the middle of this legal maelstrom, Columbia issued two more of Garner's recordings.

Garner was eventually victorious in court. He was given a cash settlement, Columbia had to recall and destroy the albums released without his consent and, most significantly, he got ownership of his masters. He set up his own independent label to handle his releases after that. He was the first artist to win a lawsuit against a major label and Glaser diligently stored all his tapes in her New York office.[109]

This marked an important shift in the power balance between artists and record companies and it also set a precedent for how artists should start to think about how they ran and, ideally, controlled their archives to ensure that only music they wanted to be heard would ever be made public. Glaser as the custodian of his recordings is arguably the architect of modern archiving.

Martha Glaser was professionally tied to Erroll Garner and took on the formal archivist role after he died; but for other artists the archivist can come through less formal channels.

The Jimi Hendrix estate has its own catalogue manager, John McDermott, who oversees releases from the studio and live archives. Speaking on

Corus Radio in 2010, Janie Hendrix described him as "the all-knowing, all-telling historian of Jimi" who has built up knowledge and expertise over the years.[110]

In a May 2013 documentary on CBS show *60 Minutes*, Karen Langford, archivist for the Michael Jackson estate, was interviewed about her role and talked about what was included in the archive. She had known Jackson since 1981 and worked with him until his death. The footage shows her giving Lara Logan, the *60 Minutes* journalist, a tour of the 20,000 sq. ft warehouse where his possessions were stored. This included the sign for Neverland, Jackson's ranch in Santa Barbara County, California, a number of his Grammys, antiques (he was an inveterate shopper), video games, his entire collection of cars and his famous sequinned glove.[111] There was an element of rubbernecking in the programme, but it also indicated just how much a major artist can accumulate in their lifetime beyond their recordings and what the consequences of storing this are for their estate.

Having someone in such a formal role, however, is really only something a handful of major estates – such as those of Jimi Hendrix and Michael Jackson – can afford.

Mark Stielper was, as he puts it, "an historian by education and by inclination" and also grew up as a fan of Johnny Cash. He met the singer in the 1980s and a friendship developed, as well as a recognition from Cash that he had found someone who could help him start to make sense of his vast catalogue and numerous music-related possessions. "As [Johnny] put it," says Stielper, "I knew more about him than he knew about him!" Cash nicknamed him The Vault and he was brought in to work on numerous projects, most significantly the triple-disc thematic compilation *Love, God, Murder* in 2000.

Johnny Cash died on 12 September 2003 (mere months after the death of his second wife, the singer and author June Carter Cash) and his estate approached Stielper to help it understand just what was left and its significance. "When it was time to clean out his desk and his office, I got called to help identify things," he says. "When they sold so much of his memorabilia at the Sotheby's auction in 2004, I was the one that identified and wrote the captions and pictures."

He refers to himself as "an archaeologist" because "I love to dig and I love to look for obscure references". He also feels he is the litmus test with regard to how others were to present Cash after his death – a sounding board that can separate fact from fiction. "You find that a lot of the Johnny Cash story is myth," he says. "And I am disappointed in that because the real stories are even more fascinating."

Stielper says that, in his lifetime, Cash could be reckless with his own archive and that has meant there are huge gaps in what could have been a substantial collection. Cash had opened the House of Cash in Hendersonville, Tennessee, in his lifetime to store many of his items, but that did not mean things were properly protected. "Things didn't get taken care of properly or they would have a flood at the House of Cash and destroy 15 years' worth of records – things like that that were just heartbreaking," Stielper says. "There was no formal – and I would say probably not even an informal – effort to preserve and protect [his possessions and artefacts], if you will, no. It's a shame."

On top of this, the 107-acre ranch that Cash bought and lived in from 1972 was sold for $895,000. It had been left to fall into disrepair after he died. The new purchasers found all manner of Cash artefacts that had been left there. "[This included] several guitars and a VHS tape with a recording of a performance at a nearby convenience store where Cash regularly played low-key and free shows."[112] The house has subsequently been turned into the Storytellers Museum.

Record labels and recording studios have their own archivists, but estates are increasingly appointing their own audio archivists so they have much tighter control over what gets released. These archivists are doing all the forensic work on what is stored on tapes and hard drives that may not be labelled or dated correctly.

"THE BANALITY OF THE FAMILIAR": KNOWING WHAT IS AND ISN'T VALUABLE

Jessica Thompson is a mastering and restoration engineer as well as an audio preservationist. She has worked on a vast number of releases, including *The Complete Concert by the Sea* by Erroll Garner and Ata Kak's *Obaa Sima*. Her work has been Grammy nominated. Part of her job is to take recordings that are deemed to be of inferior quality and make them worthy of release. She also works with estates and archives to make sense of what they have stored away and what, if anything, can be done with it.

She says that artists, no matter how well known they are, need to be planning their archives from the off – but she accepts that this is often quixotic thinking. She calls the boxes of tapes piling up in a studio or under someone's bed "the banality of the familiar" as the artist might not deem them important enough in that moment to log properly.

She also understands the emotional resistance to acts archiving their work when they are still alive. "It can be very emotionally overwhelming sometimes for artists to face their legacy," she says. "That is a big emotional hurdle. Then sometimes it is just straight-up labour; it is getting dirty, it is putting on gloves and dusting off the mouse poop – literally – and spider webs and pulling out these tapes and trying to figure out what they are. So, not everyone is super into that labour side of things."

If an artist is not archiving as they go, the job invariably falls to their family. Thompson says that, with each generation that passes, the less likely it is to be archived properly. "Sometimes the heirs are really invested in preserving that legacy and then sometimes they're just like, 'Ugh! I don't know what to do with this,'" she says. Her expertise is in helping estates who are finding themselves in this position – where there is a stockpile of recordings and they simply do not know where to start to make sense of them – and giving them a strategy for it. "I'm frequently the person who goes to the house, looks at the boxes and says, 'All right, here's what we can do with this. We're going to catalogue this, we're going to make an inventory, here's my plan.' I wind up doing a lot of consulting around preservation planning, budgets, grant writing – soup to nuts from the dusty boxes to a beautifully preserved archive that gets delivered to a university."

Thompson describes her role as that of steward but adds that all estates need to ensure there is a contextual narrative around archive recordings when they are eventually released. "The story is as important as the recording," she says. "If you just drop the recording out there, it's just sound amongst sound." This need for proper contextualisation is accelerated because a glut of lost recordings are now making their way into the marketplace. "There's so many of them out there and many will be forgotten or will wind up in the landfill," she says. "For the ones that are not, you need someone to tell you why they're relevant."

MAKING SENSE OF THE AUDIO ARCHIVES

"You can start seeing a pattern and you see where things fit"

Larry Crane founded Jackpot! Recording Studio in Portland, Oregon, in 1997 and worked closely with Elliott Smith, who used the studio many times. He fell into archiving Smith's recordings by accident.

"Right away, I noticed that he was not the most organised person," he says of Smith's somewhat scruffy working practices. "He wasn't writing track sheets and saying what was on each song when he recorded it or any notes of any sort. He would just get the ideas down and then run away. So I started making backups. Every time we'd track something, I would make a recording or a mix of it right then to a DAT."

He felt that someone needed to start to bring order to the chaos as, at some point, someone would recall a session but be unable to find it. Even so, the tapes were not always under lock and key. "When we opened the studio, in the shelves up front, we had his reels for [Smith's] *Either/Or* and his self-titled album and other stuff," Crane says. "They were all just sitting on the shelf in the front room where the door was open to the street half the time. It's something I would highly advise anyone not to do! We still are missing at least one reel from the self-titled album."

After Smith's death in 2003, Crane became a critical resource for the singer's family as well as the different record companies he had recorded for over the years. Crane says that at a wake for Smith, assorted recordings (ones that Crane himself was not involved with) started coming out of the woodwork, with friends and colleagues of Smith handing him CD-Rs they had acquired and kept of demos and live shows.

Crane was not involved with completing the *From a Basement on the Hill* album in 2004, but soon after this point Gary Smith, Elliott's father, contacted him to work on what was to become 2007's *New Moon* album, gathering up unheard recordings made between 1994 and 1997. This album came together, however, before Smith's studio archives had been fully catalogued. "I really regret that we didn't just pause that project, do the archiving and then do *New Moon*," says Crane. "I feel like I found more stuff, more music and I had a much better sense of the chronology."

He was subsequently able to sort out the sprawling archives, including going through all the tapes held in Iron Mountain, and had the ones of significance shipped back to Portland so he could begin putting them in order. "It was terrifying," he recalls. "I should have really just rented a truck and driven them back up and then just made the estate pay for that."

He started working through what was on the tapes and doing initial rough mixes. "Maggie [Vali from the Kill Rock Stars label] and I would listen to them and try to decide what made sense – what we were looking for versus what we were finding. That's when I found things that I didn't know existed – like the demo for 'Miss Misery'[113] and a few other songs."

Crane says that the work on *New Moon* was psychologically draining and reveals the emotional toll on those who have a personal (as well as professional) relationship with an artist and now have to be the custodian of their work. "It was hard mixing *New Moon*," he says. "I remember emailing Gary and saying that I wished I could just call Elliott and say, 'What about this thing? How do you want this mixed?' That was hard because you want someone to bounce off. I consider myself very much a collaborator and not a dictator. I really miss having that."

Smith's family, however, has final approval over what music from the archives can be released. Everything also goes through a small and trusted circle of people to get feedback on ideas for projects as well as mixes of recordings. "We would pass this by Portia [Sabin at Kill Rock Stars] and Gary and Bunny [Smith's mother]," explains Crane. "Bunny might pass it by Ashley [Welch], Elliott's half-sister, and whatever other people want to have a little input."

Recording and mastering technology has improved so significantly in recent years that tracks deemed unworthy of release can now be brought up to a releasable quality. "It's remarkable what we can accomplish in the world of audio restoration with the tools we have today – speed correction, dealing with major anomalies like a drop out of music or when you're working from vinyl, the clicks and pops and surface noise," says Jessica Thompson.

Michael Howe, when talking to *Super Deluxe Edition* about the Prince archive in 2019, said that low-quality audio recordings of his unheard material that are circulated on bootlegs are a concern for the star's estate as they are "sub-standard" and "not a very satisfying experience". Ironically, some of these bootlegs may have been accidentally put into circulation by Prince himself. Howe claimed, "I think Prince certainly gave cassettes away to people and maybe didn't ask for them back." He also alluded to "some unscrupulous person" who stole certain recordings.[114]

With the "painful listen" of bootlegs in mind, Howe stated the policy at Paisley Park is that any low-fidelity recordings Prince may have made or stored in the vault are never considered for release. "[A]anything that exists on a format with some integrity, like a half-inch reel or, you know, a DAT or anything else, we will release as a master as Prince, theoretically, would have contemplated doing," he says.[115]

In an interview with *Vulture* in 2018, Howe explained the justification for what he and the estate deemed worthy of release from the Prince vault. "He had pretty strong ideas about what was suitable for release and what wasn't, but there were times, and I'm paraphrasing, that he said, 'All these recordings in the vault at some point would see the light of day after I'm gone.' [...] When we are thinking about what might be appropriate for release, the first question is: Is this of the caliber that Prince would've deemed suitable for a theoretical release? Are we doing his legacy justice by putting this out there? Without exception, that's the most important thing and we have to use our best judgement."[116]

Beyond the audio, the other challenge facing an archivist is how the original recordings are logged and labelled – even if they are labelled at all. This can involve looking into when certain tape brands were released and using that to help refine the chronology of recordings. But that only goes so far.

Crane says that a tape that eventually resurfaced of Stranger Than Fiction, Elliot Smith's band at high school, was critical in pinning down certain songs and recordings that were proving impossible to date. "The biggest killer is making incorrect assumptions and then carrying them further and further," says Crane. "You take that branch right there and you just don't get it. I found a couple times where I did that with the old high school band stuff. That was really confusing until I figured that out. You can start seeing a pattern and you see where things fit. That's the most important thing. When you have the context properly aligned, then everything makes a lot more sense. If you just started grabbing at everything and then trying to look at it as one big huge bunch, you're going to be overwhelmed and you're not going to be able to contextualise it."

Thompson cautions against ruthlessly mining the archives simply to make money, arguing that few archival releases make much money anyway and that the role is primarily cultural – keeping the artist in the public consciousness or offering a whole new perspective on their art. "You're lucky if you recoup expenses on a beautiful box set because there's so much work that goes into the curation and the whole production process," she says. "Sometimes you are churning out releases because you have got to pay the bills and pay the lawyers. You just need to generate some income. But that's not always the motivating factor in curating something from the archives."

Howe talked about the rise of what he termed "Prince fatigue" where too much material from the archives floods the market and can cause damage to a legacy. This sometimes rubs up against the more explicitly commercial demands of labels to have a steady flow of "new" material to release.

"I would say, generally speaking, record companies kind of err on the side of 'more is more'," he said. "[B]ut we, the keepers of the Prince legacy, are much more interested in quality over quantity. You know… presenting a finished body of work or shining a light on a particular creative period with respect and integrity [and] not just sort of dumping things into the market-place because somebody's asking for it."[117]

ARCHIVES BEYOND THE MUSIC

"I am motivated by a sense of greater purpose"

Musicians' legacies and careers tend to be established through the records they make in their lifetime, but for estates, dealing as they are with finite resources here, the audio vaults need to be augmented with other things. Name and image rights as well as trademarks can be highly lucrative (see Chapter 6), but the archive is not just confined to what was captured on tape. These items all fall into the general archive of an artist, but choosing to make them public and finding ways to commercialise them can come with an even bigger ethical conundrum than compiling previously unheard music and releasing it.

Journalist David Browne first dealt with the Jeff Buckley estate when working on his 2000 book *Dream Brother: The Lives and Music of Jeff and Tim Buckley*. Browne had been a long-term fan, having seen Jeff play at Sin-é, the tiny coffee house and music venue in New York where he first made his name and where his first EP, 1993's *Live at Sin-é*, was recorded. He had also been one of the first music writers to interview Buckley.

As part of his research, Mary Guibert granted him access to a number of her son's journals. This provided the germ of the idea for what was to eventually become *Jeff Buckley: His Own Voice* in 2019. Browne was approached by an editor at Hachette who was intrigued by the journal entries quoted in *Dream Brother* and asked if this could be expanded into a standalone book. He said it would have to be given the green light by Guibert but, in theory, he was interested in working on it. Guibert was approached and said she would only work on if it Browne was involved. She sent him scans of all Jeff's notebooks and diaries to see what approach could be taken to turn them into a book.

"We did it in a very slow, deliberate and sensitive way," says Browne. "I realised [if we] rearranged things […] and put them in a chronological order, it could almost be a posthumous memoir of sorts, which really intrigued me as a journalist." That idea met with approval from Guibert and he started work on the structure. In the process, sections had to be redacted as they were deemed "a little too personal" in Browne's words and he did not want to be "too invasive" in what was considered for publication.

Guibert says that Jeff's possessions were not in any coherent order when she was given them after he died. "It arrived in three boxes – three huge boxes!" she laughs. "Tapes and personal belongings and papers and flotsam and jetsam and water-damaged books and diaries. It was just a big mess." She was to find out, however, that items had been stolen from his New York apartment.

Conrad Rippy, the lawyer for the estate, says that trying to recover items belonging to Buckley was a recurring issue in the early days of the estate. "There were a number of people who had items of Jeff's that belonged to Jeff and, therefore after his passing, belonged to Mary," he says. "Another one of the roles I played was trying to get people to disgorge personal items and professional items. It was everything from guitars to journals to DATs – anything like that. That's always tricky because if somebody's passed away, people want to hang on to their personal effects. When it has to do with Jeff's music, that's something valuable which belongs either to Mary or to Sony Music. So Sony was helpful in getting some of this material back as well. Ultimately, neither Mary nor I had any real idea if we got everything back. I think you and I can probably surmise that we probably didn't get everything back – people being people."

Even with a wide range of items being removed or simply never returned to the estate, the book project went ahead.

I asked Browne if he felt that Buckley was actually, through these diaries, acting as the archivist of his own history. "I think in a way he was," he says. "I think the fact that he kept these journals, you almost sense that he was writing them for history in some way or another, the way that he was chronicling certain aspects." Browne feels it gives a series of new insights into Buckley, not just as a creative artist – including, as it does, reworked and edited lyrics – but also as someone navigating the music business and starting to experience success and the pressures that come with it.

"You'll see him meticulously writing out his finances – 'OK, here's how much money I have now. I've got to pay the rent,'" he says. "You see the math. Then you'll see another page with his schedule for when he wants to accomplish this and that. 'Get up at 10am and practice scales. 12 o'clock do this, 1 o'clock do that.' And it gave me a new appreciation of and understanding of how driven he was. Jeff always had, publicly, a bit of an endearingly spacey, flaky aspect to him that he put out there."

The whole process took four years from Browne being approached to the book coming out. "I don't feel like the book is exploitative or intrusive," says Brown. "If it had been rushed out a couple of years after he died, maybe you could have made those accusations. But it was 22 years after he passed that we did it. It felt like the book arrived at a point where it felt like a good time to hear from Jeff in his own words about certain parts of his life, given that there have been other books and articles written about him."

In the case of *Jeff Buckley: His Own Voice*, it offered a beguiling snapshot of the creative process in full flow; but another intention behind its publication was to redress some of the mythology and erroneous stories his mother feels have come out about him after his death. It was, in a way, a posthumous right to reply.

The bulk of the non-music assets in an archive tend to be kept behind closed doors, or selected elements are compiled in book form for public consumption. For mega-acts, they can also end up in museum exhibitions or be donated to libraries or foundations (see Chapter 7). Books drawing on an artist's archive can also help expand the story around them.

Celeste Bell is the daughter of musician and artist Poly Styrene (who passed away in 2010). Together with music writer Zoë Howe she published *Dayglo: The Poly Styrene Story* in 2019. It is made up of multiple interviews with those who worked with and knew her and it is augmented with her artwork and sketches.

The book and related exhibition sprang from Bell having to put her mother's archive in order after she died. "There was a ton of lyrics – most of them were typed and many of them weren't published," says Bell. "There was a lot of artwork and she did all the artwork for the band. So there is a treasure trove there."

Going through it all was a protracted and at times painful experience. "It took a while – also because I just kept it in boxes and didn't really deal with it," says Bell. "I had so many other things to do. When my mum passed away, I wasn't really in the headspace to start that process. You know it's a mammoth task so you just put it off. And I put it off for many years."

The book and exhibition serve, for Bell, as an important bulwark against her mother being reduced to "the singer from British punk band X-Ray Spex" and can actually illustrate what a polymath she was. "When I talk about legacy and wanting her importance to be more recognised, the artwork side of things is really huge because there weren't any other musicians who were doing what she was doing at that time," says Bell. "I would say my mum was a multi-disciplinary artist rather than frontwoman of X-Ray Spex. What my mum was doing was important. It wasn't just entertainment. It had a lot of social relevance in the lyrics, in the artwork and who she was as a person […] it's not just something I'm doing because it's a business. I am motivated by a sense of greater purpose."

Like Celeste Bell, Jemima Dury – daughter of Ian Dury and the person who manages his estate on a day-to-day basis – had to make sense of an archive that went far beyond music. It was also in a chaotic state. "It is paintings, manuscripts, books – there's a ton of it," she says. "That is one of the things that can be really difficult about ending up with an estate: what the hell do you do with all the stuff?"

She was 31 when her father died (on 27 March 2000) and assumed most of the responsibility for the handling of the estate. Her brother Baxter is a professional musician and their two half-siblings from another relationship were too young at the time to get involved. She says most of his possessions were put in storage before he died but they did not look to see what was there until 2006 when initial plans for the *Sex & Drugs & Rock & Roll* biopic (which came out in 2010) were being discussed. "Nobody knew what was in there," she says. "And that was a complete revelation. I didn't realise that he had so many paintings and drawings. I didn't realise there were boxes and boxes and boxes of thousands of manuscripts. I've archived about 3,000 to 4,000 bits of paper." Working through it was painstaking as it was "all folded up and squashed in boxes". It took her 18 months, with the estate agreeing to pay her for her work, to get it all in a reasonably coherent order.

Dury was a fanatical hoarder in his lifetime and it appears he rarely threw anything away. Some of this could be used immediately, such as artwork and lyrics, but other parts serve a more subtle function in helping plot out an entire chronology of his career. It may also, in the future, find a way to be published.

"The most interesting and beautiful stuff he kept is a complete audit of [his first band] Kilburn and the High Roads," says Jemima. "To me, that's the most special bit of the archive, apart from the manuscripts, obviously. At some point I think I will do a Kilburn and the High Roads book because it's such a beautiful collection. This is how a pub rock band actually functioned and worked. I have petrol receipts from Teddington to Leeds. You can tell the journey up the M1. It's that detailed and thorough. It was in the days before an accountant and the days before a record company or manager. He just put it all in a series of plastic bags. I've had to slowly sort of work out what it all is. It's a jigsaw. It's amazing. It's handwritten letters to the bank asking for another £10 to go on tour. Things like insurance documents and PRS and Musicians' Union [forms]. It's a complete overview of the situation for about three years."

Jemima gathered together his paintings and tracked down, via friends and associates of her father, other pieces of his art that the family had never seen before. They were exhibited at the Royal College of Art in London in summer 2013. She also oversaw the publication in 2012 of *Hallo Sausages*, a collection of Ian Dury's lyrics alongside a potted history of his career as well as photos, illustrations and manuscripts. (The title of the book came from "the first and only words written for his autobiography".[118]) "It was everything published and some extras that he had probably put back in the drawer and wasn't sure about – but I just dug them out," she says. "It's just good to see some unpublished stuff as well."

The book was done, in part, to stand as the definitive source of his lyrics because assorted sources online were getting them badly wrong. "So many of the lyrics get misinterpreted, especially Ian's tricksy Cockney wordplay," she says. "I thought I had got to do this because I'm so fed up with reading 'Clevor Trever' written out incorrectly. It was just bugging me so much that it was very much an emotional thing. This is for my dad. It was a personal thing. It's really annoying me that the lyrics were wrong. All of those things together drove me on."

The book, especially the sumptuous coffee-table book, is increasingly something estates of erudite and literary musical artists are turning to in order to bring a new gravitas to their work and lives. Adam Cohen published *The Flame* in 2018, a collection of his father Leonard's poetry and sketches.[119] Gabrielle Drake and Cally Callomon published *Remembered for a While*, which included excerpts from Nick Drake's diary as well as fragments and ideas for songs he never got to record.[120] And in 2020, the Janis Joplin estate published a limited run of the *Janis Joplin Scrapbook: 1966–68* which reproduced the singer's own scrapbooks alongside posters for shows and news clippings she collected as her career was taking off.[121] The Joplin book was limited to 2,000 copies, all hand-numbered, and came with a 7-inch single containing two rare tracks recorded by the singer in 1964.

Such publications are seen as adding to the story of an act and imbuing them with a particular from of profundity and artistic respectability. However, not every estate can shoulder something like this.

Apportioning out the estate's non-musical assets in book form is something that estate managers have to plan carefully. *Remembered for a While* was published in 2014 and ran to 450 pages. For an artist like Drake who had such a brief career, one would have presumed this book covered everything that could be made public. When I spoke to Callomon, however, towards the end of 2020, he revealed that a second volume is being planned because there is a cornucopia of material and artefacts in the archive.

This is enhanced further by the fact that the work of Callomon at the Nick Drake estate has expanded to include the music and artefacts of Molly Drake, the singer's mother, who was also a musician, songwriter and poet. In 2013, the 19-track Molly Drake album, made up of her home recordings from the 1950s, was released. An expanded version, running to 26 tracks and packaged up with 79 of her poems in a 196-page hardback book, was released in 2017 under the title *The Tide's Magnificence: Songs and Poems of Molly Drake*.[122]

"Fortunately for us the Drakes never threw anything away – ever," says Callomon. "They always lived in a big enough house. The accoutrements are fascinating and intact. We don't want to water our book down into a paperback abridged version. And we do want to do a second edition because, since we did that book, so much extra stuff has come to light. We'll probably do a second edition in the same sort of format – hardback, full-colour throughout – in maybe three or four years' time."

LIVING ARTISTS PREPARING FOR THEIR ESTATES AND ARCHIVES

Just as horror stories about artists dying intestate are making more living artists ensure that their wills, trusts and estate plans are regularly updated, so too are tales of dysfunctional archives, spurring them into action to put things in order here.

Bob Dylan has been a trailblazer here in terms of putting his vast studio and live archive in order. This began in 1991 with the release of *The Bootleg Series* Volumes 1–3, a collection of outtakes, alternative takes, demos for publishers, live performances and home recordings stretching back over 30 years. This was in part to counteract the many Dylan bootlegs flooding the market (the title of the official releases was a very knowing – a ripely Dylanesque – nod to that). This was all especially poignant given that *The Great White Wonder*, issued in 1969 and including unheard Dylan tracks that eventually got an official release on *The Basement Tapes* in 1975, is regarded as the first rock bootleg of note.[123]

It was also a way for Dylan, in his lifetime, to publicly curate his own legacy. Since then, the *Bootleg Series* has reached Vol. 15, with each subsequent release zooming in on a particular album or period in his long career. This included 2015's *The Bootleg Series* Vol. 12: *The Cutting Edge 1965–1966*, the collector's edition of which ran to 18 discs and included everything Dylan recorded in studios and even hotel rooms in 1965 and 1966 during what was unquestionably his most fertile and innovative period.[124] Related to this was the release in 2016 of *Bob Dylan 1966: The Live Recordings* which, across 36 discs, brought together "every single known recording" from his legendary "electric" tour in the US, the UK, Europe and Australia.[125]

Dylan sold his meticulously collated personal archive in 2016 to the George Kaiser Family Foundation and the University of Tulsa for a fee estimated at between $15 million and $20 million. It is made up of 6,000 pieces – "including lyrics, correspondence, recordings, films and photographs"[126] – and is intended as a resource for academic research. *Rolling Stone* suggested, however, that the collection would eventually be opened to the public.[127]

"There are hundreds of original tape reels, unseen concert films and business contracts going back to the very beginning of Mr. Dylan's career," wrote the *New York Times*.[128]

For an artist as prolific as Dylan and with a career stretching back six decades, a great many artefacts had gone outside his ownership, so the collection the University of Tulsa acquired was only a portion of it. In November 2020, for example, it was reported that a collection of Dylan's letters and unpublished song lyrics were sold at auction for $495,000. They had been privately held by late blues artist Tony Glover, a friend of Dylan's, but he passed away in 2019 and so the collection was auctioned off in a series of individual lots.[129]

This is a recurring issue for an artist (or their estate) trying to make sense of their archives – many items will have been given away by the artist in their lifetime to colleagues and peers and there is no real paper trail. It is only when they are auctioned, often when the person who originally acquired them dies, that the sheer fact of their existence even comes to light.

The ultimate problem, of course, is that when Dylan eventually passes away, much of his rich archive will already have been made available. The reason that he did this, of course, was to ensure that what came out did so under his total guidance and with his approval.

Neil Young has ploughed a similar archival furrow to Dylan, working on expansive archive releases like 2009's *The Archives* Vol. 1: *1963–1972* and 2020's *The Archives* Vol. 2: *1972–1976*. Three more volumes covering, respectively, the 1980s, 1990s and 2000s are planned in the series. Also in 2000, Young released *Homegrown*, an album that was originally recorded between 1974 and 1975 but shelved. He also created the subscription-based Neil Young Archives website, which adds new material from his archives on a rolling basis.[130]

Online is slowly becoming an option for estates as well as living artists (as the examples below about Radiohead and Def Leppard show) to display at least some of the assets in an archive.

In 2019, the John R. Cash Trust and Sony Music launched an archival website that listed all of Johnny Cash's shows from his debut performance in 1954 onwards, as well as all his lyrics and photos from his professional and private life.[131] Josh Matas of Sandbox Entertainment Group, which runs the Cash estate, explains the impetus behind the site. "One of the things that I think is critical to alpha fans is the ability to have a one-stop place to go in and worship at the altar of your star; in short, fans need a Mecca or something like this to go home to," he says. "We wanted to have an all-encompassing place where people could get all the information they could hope for about Johnny Cash in a one-stop shop." He adds: "I was very much inspired by the Neil Young website."

It is not just Boomer-friendly sixties heroes who have taken a hugely proactive leap here to put their archives in order while they still have time. In January 2020, Radiohead launched the Radiohead Public Library, a free and evolving online archive covering their entire career, themed around particular albums and tours, including period-specific merchandise being available to print on demand.[132] It was originally intended to bring some order to the chaotic sprawl of content around the band online and on platforms such as YouTube when searching for anything related to them.

"What came back was a soup of remarkably disconnected content that was reverse chronological, algorithmically picked by popularity, or just wildly inaccurate," is how designer Max Kolombos explained the impetus behind the initiative to *Wired*. "This bothered me, but as I tried to find all the missing material, I ended up crafting some extremely byzantine search queries and frequently coming up empty-handed. It all felt very wrong."[133]

The whole project took two years to organise and assemble but now offers a model for other acts to follow with their own archival work and also explains why, just because something exists online, it does not follow that it is easy to find or organise. "This has opened my eyes to digital archiving and preservation," said Kolombos. "[T]ime can bury things on the internet with frightening ease."[134]

Following suit, British rock band Def Leppard launched The Def Leppard Vault online in January 2021, describing it as a "constantly curated museum" that was made up of "the band's artifacts and related stories".[135]

"I've been a collector—some would say 'hoarder,'" lead singer Joe Elliott told *American Songwriter* on the reason for setting it up and making sense of the band's long history. "I've been a collector since day one because you're eighteen years old and you're in this band and you played a few [local] gigs, and then you start getting a few reviews and you cut them out of the paper and you stick them in a book. You just never stop once that gets going because you never know how long it's going to last."[136]

Swiftly following this, Australian indie-rock star Courtney Barnett launched the Courtney Barnett Online Live Music Experience & Archive in March 2021.[137] *Billboard* described it as "a trove of concerts dating back to 2007, unearthed mixes from the desk, live television performances, gig posters and more".[138]

Even before the likes of Bob Dylan and Paul McCartney were starting to think about their archives, two artists who came to prominence in the first half of the 20th century were already doing it and what they achieved, given that archiving was not industrialised then as it is today, is remarkable.

Holly Foster Wells, granddaughter of Peggy Lee and the head of her estate, says her grandmother was sharply aware of both her legacy and the assets the family needed to preserve after her death. Top of the list were her copyrights, which she set up a company to handle. "She never sold it – no matter how many desperate times she went through," says Foster Wells. "There were hard times when rock'n'roll came in and her music went out and things were lean. She would sell diamonds before she would sell a song. She told me about [the importance of] publishing. 'You will hit hard times, you will think about it, but don't sell! This is going to be the thing that takes care of the family.' She told my family numerous times, 'I just want to leave you a legacy.' And that's what she did."

Lee also saved everything throughout her career, including stage clothes as well as sheet music from her songs, news clippings and photos, all of which she kept in a series of scrapbooks. This has proved to be an invaluable resource to the estate. "Through that scrapbook, we were able to recreate a timeline of her entire career," says Foster Wells.

Most incredibly – and long before Andy Warhol did it – Lee had a recorder running at all the key moments in her career. "Part of what she left behind – which was unbelievable – were her recordings of business meetings and rehearsals and performances," says her granddaughter. "She had a reel-to-reel tape player and she would bring it into parties and even record [those] parties and business meetings and rehearsals. So I have an audio archive of her talking about things and it's really unbelievable. I just came across a rehearsal with Ray Charles and Quincy Jones where they're having a piano session together and a rehearsal with Paul McCartney for 'Let's Love'. She recorded everything." Foster Wells calls Lee "a researcher of her own life" and this prescience bequeathed her estate incredible resources they could use in order to work her legacy and keep her name alive.

Vladimir Horowitz was also a compulsive recorder – but of his performances rather than his business meetings. Jeff Liebenson, the lawyer for the beneficiaries of his estate, says he was "ahead of his time with technology" and would take a recording device on the road with him. "He had a machine that would actually cut a vinyl disc as he was playing," explains Liebenson. "He would bring it to Carnegie Hall when he performed there and make his own personal copies of his performances. We had this incredible artistic treasure which he donated to Yale." Many of those recordings were eventually released by Sony.

The lessons of the past are slowly being learned in the present. There have been moves in recent years by acts and record companies to spot the recurring problems in the world of archiving and turn these into strategy plans for contemporary artists.

Tom Mullen worked at Sony Music in New York between 2012 and 2017 on numerous projects for Legacy, Sony's catalogue arm. There were projects for Bob Dylan, Johnny Cash and Miles Davis as well as the Jeff Buckley's Record Collection[139] site, which let users go through the records the singer had in his home and then, via Spotify's API, play any of them. "The sentiment around Jeff was that all Sony is doing is dredging the grave and putting out whatever they find and they don't care about him," he says. "That was the sentiment. I said, 'I need to do something that gives back and that people can go to forever.' As soon as I saw a photo of his [record] collection, this website literally popped in my head and it never left my mind."

Mullen joined Atlantic Records, part of Warner Music Group, in 2017 in a new role – VP of marketing catalogue and podcasting. He left the company, however, in summer 2020. His job title there was slightly misleading as he was not working for Rhino, Warner's catalogue division, but rather applying catalogue strategies to frontline artists (i.e. those who are currently active and making new records).

"I'm preparing them for [the future]," he says of these frontline acts. "The hitmakers of today could be tomorrow's legends. I want them to be ready so, when it is 2030, I want to make sure that there is content to share, they have photos to look at, there's an opportunity. This is their career and I think it doesn't need to be all in that first box set. It doesn't need to be all online. We can schedule these out. There will be Bob Dylan *Basement Tapes* for longer than our lives. We will be long gone and they will still be doing stuff because of how they organised it. I am helping organise the artists of today to understand how to be a legend tomorrow."

Brad Mindich is the CEO of Inveniem, a company specifically set up to help living artists – as well as estates – organise their archives and come up with strategies to release content and assets from them. The strapline of the company is "your past is your future".[140] He states that an artist can be overwhelmed by what they have collected over a career and the enormity of the job at hand can see them procrastinate here. "Typically it's rare that clients really know what they have, where things are, the state of them, what to do with them and how to think about the next steps with it," he says. "So we look at all of that holistically and figure out a plan and strategy and execute from there. We come in and we bring the resources, the technology, the perspective and business strategy to then help the artist figure out what to do with these things." He cannot, due to non-disclosure agreements, mention any of the clients that Inveniem works with, but does say one of the biggest is "a very large band with a 40-year career and currently still touring".

The company has a team of 30 archive experts who can do "as much heavy lifting" as is required, noting that living artists and estates are often too busy to be able to spare the time to make sense of a disorganised archive that may be spread over multiple locations. "The way we work with our clients is really to come in and say, 'We will take this off your hands. We will figure this out for you. We will make this not overwhelming.' Because the minute you do that then all of a sudden the kind of creative brains which these geniuses have, they can think clearly. They're not overwhelmed with this warehouse, this warehouse, this warehouse – because there's somebody dealing with it for them."

Inveniem also ensures that audio and video materials on obsolete formats are fully digitised and that they are constantly checked to ensure everything is as up to date as it can be.

The major part of making sense of what is in the archives and then how to formulate a plan for its release is the metadata used to tag each item. That is then fed into the archive database so the users know what is there, how to find it and when it has been used. This metadata can cover a variety of things – type of content, date of creation, location of creation, related content, where it is stored and so on.

"It comes down to the actual archive management and who is making those decisions," says Mindich. "We've seen bad judgement – certainly countless examples of that – of licences for things that they never should have given and probably the artist wouldn't have wanted. It's probably a little Pollyanna to be like, 'Well, you know, everything will just be fine; it'll all get worked out.' That's not realistic – but I think having the right kind of structures in place at least allows for better decision making."

As much as getting everything in order is important, so is having very clear checks and balances that govern how it should be used (or not used) long into the future in a way that benefits the artist or their estate but does not cause it long-term damage or see it become a mausoleum of wasted, misjudged or poor decisions.

One artist who completely understands how to be a legend tomorrow is Dolly Parton. The way that she is preparing for her death is a fascinating example of an artist thinking far ahead and ensuring that what comes out after they have died is fully under their control.

As part of the *Dolly Parton's America* podcast series in 2019, she spoke candidly about her career and her legacy. She said that she has "hundreds, even thousands, of songs" and that many of them have still not even been recorded. Then she revealed what her plans are. "There's enough stuff to go on for ever with my music – to do compilation albums, to do new and original stuff," she said. "And I'm purposely trying to put songs down for that very purpose – to have a click track and my vocals before any arrangement can be done. So I think ahead."

She was asked if this means these a cappella recordings she is stockpiling could be used by any producer after she passed and turned into finished songs. She said they could – that was the intention of recording them after all – and they could be moulded to fit any genre. "When I'm gone, they could take my songs, just the click track and my vocal, and build a complete arrangement around that," she explained. "Any style, anything that we do." She adds, "I mean, I'm one of those people that believe in being prepared. I don't want to ever leave my stuff in the same shape like Prince or Aretha [Franklin] or anybody that don't plan ahead."

She also revealed she had sealed an unheard track in a chestnut box to mark the opening of her DreamMore resort and spa in Tennessee in 2015, with strict instructions that it could not be opened or heard until 2045. "It would be a song that will never be heard until 30 years from the time we opened the resort," she said. "They [her marketing team] said, 'You'll be long dead.' I said, 'Well, maybe not. I'll be 99. I've seen people live to be older than that.'"[141]

There is "normal" planning ahead and then there is "Dolly Parton" planning ahead.

STREAMING LOWERS THE BAR

The impact of streaming and online content is starting to shape just what type of posthumous material gets released, especially for acts that grew up in a digital world and have seen this shape how they cut their creative cloth.

On services like Spotify and Apple Music, tracks have to be listened to for at least 30 seconds in order to count as a "play" and therefore trigger a royalty payment. That means that recordings that barely pass this running time are still deemed worthy of release. On top of this, artists who are prolific and create tracks across a variety of genres and styles can secure placements on multiple playlists, thereby increasing their total addressable audience. The streaming algorithms reward the poly-genre and the prolific.

This means that recordings that would have been deemed too short to release in the pre-digital age are viewed as wholly appropriate in the streaming environment. Sometimes this can mean quality is the first casualty in the stampede of quantity, as one source working with the estate of a young rapper reveals. "Some of [our artist's] stuff is a little bit like that [i.e. barely over 30 seconds long], quite frankly," they say. "Some of them are very short tracks. But with hip-hop there's been a trend towards shorter tracks. I will admit to having sat in various meetings and people have said, 'Make sure to have more tracks.' There are a lot of tracks on some albums, but they are not that long so it's just a high multiple on the streams. There's a commercial reasoning behind it."

The same rapper's estate, waking up to the fact that the vaults were rapidly dwindling, has moved to recalibrate its attitude to what is now considered worthy of release, just to keep the demand on streaming services ticking over. "They have taken a demo and turned it into a commercially released track," the source says of a particular track that they felt marked a scraping of the barrel from their perspective but that would, they felt, still connect with the rapper's core audience. "If you are a fan, there is a rawness to that that you desperately wanted anyway and perhaps didn't get before."

We have seen the nature of what is deemed "releasable" change significantly over the past 40 years. Until the 1980s, outtakes were regarded as such and generally treated as unworthy of release; by the 1990s, the need to fill the available space on CDs saw the tentative raiding of the vaults and The Beatles' 'Free as a Bird' offered a template for turning demos into "finished" recordings; in the 2000s, as a means of justifying high retail prices for elaborate physical box sets aimed at collectors in an age of digital, multiple discs stuffed with unheard music became the norm; and by the late 2010s, almost anything could get released provided it was at least 30 seconds long, when it could generate a streaming royalty.

The ethics of this all have been defined less by a change in public attitudes and more by both the possibilities of technology and the constraints of the latest formats. Now that pretty much anything in the vaults can (and often will) be deemed worthy of release at some point in the future, artists need to ensure their archives are not only well run while they are still alive but also tightly controlled after their death. By setting out clear rules in the present they can exert future control of their past.

CHAPTER 6

Brand of Gold

The Hereafter's Merchandising Bonanza

Scanning the menu is, in itself, an education. The Stir It Up fondue costs $9.95 as does the Kaya Mon calamari. Moving up the price range a little, the No Woman, No Cry jerk chicken salad and the Catch A Fire chicken char-grilled dish will each set you back $13.95. Should you wish to push the boat out, Sun Is Shining curry chicken is $16.95. If you have children with you, they can pick from the Lil Legends menu where Jamacaroni & Cheese, Lil Reggae crispy chicken fingers and Island Flavor burgers (beef or vegetarian) are all $6.99 each. For dessert, there is the Is This Love key lime cheesecake for $6.45.[1]

At Universal Studios Orlando, as part of the Universal CityWalk™, the Bob Marley – A Tribute To Freedom restaurant has been open for business since 1999.[2] It was created in collaboration with Rita Marley, the reggae star's widow, and the Bob Marley Foundation and is based on his home at 56 Hope Street in Kingston, Jamaica. "Artifacts, photos, and video clips from his storied career surround you in the open-air veranda and courtyard," says the website.[3] The restaurant also has an astonishing tagline: Get Up, Stand Up, Eat Up.

In 2019, the Bob Marley estate turned over $20 million and in the two decades that *Forbes* has been tracking posthumous celebrity earnings, there have only been a handful of years where the Marley estate was not in the top 13 earners. Between 2008 and 2011 it was not in the *Forbes* shortlist, but in every year since 2012 it has been in the top 8 consistently.[4]

A huge reason behind this economic renaissance is the branding and endorsement efforts the estate has undertaken. Sponsorship and trademarks have effectively brought the Bob Marley estate back to life. It is the powerhouse of posthumous branding. Merchandise is a given, with Marley's face, name and song titles on everything from T-shirts, hoodies and jackets to sweatshirts, beanie hats and baby onesies.[5] During the global pandemic in 2020, his official store started selling face masks. They cost £15 and featured Marley's face as well as the legend, "Don't worry about a thing".[6] Fans can also buy mugs, enamel pin badges, face towels, baseball caps, socks and a lion blanket (that costs £100). Within his clothing line is the Redemption sub-brand.

To mark what would have been his 75th birthday in 2020, Wrangler (a brand he often wore in his lifetime) created a limited-edition "capsule collection" around the star in collaboration with his estate. It included T-shirts, jeans and shirts.[7] The lead item was the Buffalo Soldier X Wrangler denim jacket, which cost £128. It was been, according to the Wrangler site, "remixed to riff off elements of Marley's life with bespoke patches complemented by instantly recognizable lyrics from 'Trenchtown Rock', 'Small Axe', and 'Soul Rebel'".[8]

On top of this is the House of Marley range focused around consumer audio products. It sells a wide range of headphones (in-ear and over-ear) and earbuds as well as portable Bluetooth speakers and turntables. In the accessories section on the House of Marley site, fans can also buy a Stir It Up spare tone-arm counterweight for their turntable, a spare remote control, tote bags and backpacks.[9]

In 2009, the Marley Beverage Company was founded in Southfield, Michigan to "promote relaxation and well-being [...] in a variety of great tasting flavors".[10]

The most debated and controversial move, however, by the Marley estate was the launch of the Marley Natural marijuana range in 2016, an idea that had been in development since 2013. It was created in partnership with Privateer Holdings to make use of changes in drugs laws in a number of states in the US, starting first in California. *The Verge* reported that Privateer secured a 30-year licensing deal with the Marley family for the marijuana line, with four strains initially available, including Marley Green, Marley Red and Marley Black.[11] This is a booming market, with $5.4 billion in legal cannabis sales in 2015, the year before Marley Natural launched, with forecasts saying it would quadruple to reach sales of $21.8 billion by 2020.[12]

"My dad would be so happy to see people understanding the healing power of the herb," said Cedella Marley on its launch. "Marley Natural is an authentic way to honor his legacy by adding his voice to the conversation about cannabis and helping end the social harms caused by prohibition."[13]

This was a significant swerve for the estate, which had been focused for several years before on trying to shift Marley away from an association with marijuana. "[One product] he did use and tout heavily – ganja – has been almost entirely laundered out of the estate's official merchandise," wrote the *Globe & Mail* in 2012.[14]

Notable Marley experts such as Professor Mike Alleyne from Middle Tennessee State University (co-author of 2012's *The Encyclopedia of Reggae: The Golden Age of Roots Reggae*),[15] Ian Thomson (author of *The Dead Yard: Tales of Modern Jamaica*)[16] and Chris Salewicz (author of *Bob Marley: The Untold Story*)[17] all voiced their objections to the move into legal marijuana.

In 2016, however, Salewicz revised his thinking and had a slightly more nuanced take on it. "Some assume Marley would not approve," he said of the fact that his name is consciously being tied to marijuana by his family. "Yet the reggae superstar had a well of intelligent pragmatism, and never undersold himself when it came to promoting an alliance with marijuana. And the Bob Marley estate – his family, essentially – are playing a larger game, giving his fans what many of them want." He argued it was wrong to try to brush over or ignore what was a major part of his lifestyle and belief system. "Marijuana always was part of the marketing of Marley: there are libraries full of pictures of him smoking spliffs," he argued.[18]

When asked in 2018 about the dizzying multitude of products that his father's name and image were being used on, Damian Marley chose his words diplomatically. "Yeeeaaah," he said. "I'm a fan of some of them and some of them... not so much."[19]

There are, however, limits to what the Marley estate will put his name to. In 1991, Miller Brewing Co wanted to license his hit 'Jamming' for use in a beer ad. As the Rastafarian faith discourages the consumption of alcohol, the Marley estate and Island Records turned down the request.[20]

However, during the protracted process to work out who should run the Marley estate – it ran for years after his death – J. Reid Bingham, the lawyer for the estate, told the *Washington Post* in 1991 that he was actively licensing the Marley name to a range of products to generate income for the estate until its organisational issues could be resolved. This included a Floridian company getting the rights to sell Bob Marley cologne (bringing in $10,000 for the estate) as well as licensing a souvenir company making Marley umbrellas. "I think it was a Rasta-colored umbrella," he said.[21]

The Marley family has been swift in its actions against bootleggers using his name or image without approval.[22] There was also a licensing dispute in 2007 between the estate and Universal over the sale of ringtones, particularly the use of Marley's name, image and likeness in the marketing around them.[23]

On 13 September, Verizon pulled all the mobile content from its store.[24] It swiftly, however, reinstated it all, saying it was for the Marley family and Universal to "work out their differences".[25] A spokesperson for Verizon told Reuters, "This was not a matter for us, we have done nothing wrong."[26] Reuters added, "It was not clear whether the Bob Marley family company, Fifty Six Hope Road Music, would still file suit against Universal Music Group [...] A company spokeswoman would not comment on the possibility."[27]

No statement from either side on how – or even if – this was ever resolved was made public.

Marley stands as a marketing metonym of what estates can do here. Recorded music might have built the global legacy but it only contributes a small proportion of overall estate revenues. Documentaries, like 2012's *Marley*, help enhance the legacy – but can only be done sparingly. It is licensing, branding and endorsement that brings in the lion's share of estate revenues today.

The Marley estate is not the only estate which fully realises this fundamental part of the business; it is simply the most prolific and the most efficacious.

THE HOLY TRINITY: NAME, IMAGE AND LIKENESS RIGHTS

As with so much of the estates business, a great deal of this comes back again to Elvis.

Mark Roesler is now chairman and CEO of CMG Worldwide, a business agent for multiple estates in music, sports and entertainment, including James Dean, Aaliyah, Amelia Earhart, Bettie Page, Ingrid Bergman, Lou Gehrig and Malcolm X.

Just before Graceland opened to the public in 1982, he was brought in to work with the Elvis Presley estate. "They wanted to have some high quality Elvis merchandise as they opened up Graceland," he told *Beverly Hills Lifestyle* magazine in 2010. "Being a young lawyer, I saw it was difficult to protect the intellectual property of a person like Elvis Presley. As I was working on the Elvis Presley estate, I realized that James Dean had a similar appeal and had similar issues – the difficulty of protecting his intellectual property rights, and the difficulty of the family to control the use of the image, name and likeness of James Dean."[28]

Many of the problems of the estate went back to Boxcar Enterprises (the merchandise operation that Colonel Parker had set up and controlled), which was in charge of manufacturing assorted Elvis-branded products. Roesler says one of his first tasks was to tidy up the Boxcar deal and bring in licensing partners who could handle a lot of the heavy lifting here. This was imperative as the Presley estate was in litigation with Parker and Boxcar, so there was a moratorium on products being made. Plus there were all the unlicensed shops springing up on the streets around Graceland selling products – an issue that took the estate many years to resolve.

"We turned it into a licensing operation where we went out and got quality companies, from the Hallmarks to the different collectible companies that did various collectible merchandise," Roesler says. "Our job was to get a licensing programme started that could get quality companies to do Elvis Presley products. That was our job – to up the image of Elvis and to perpetuate the legacy." He says these early products included Elvis dolls, high-end figurines, collectible guitars, plates, prints and calendars.

The Elvis estate was keen to take tighter control of Elvis merchandise and ensure it received proper recompense for its commercial exploitation. "The estate maintained at the time that one asset Elvis had left his daughter was his image and name," wrote the *Los Angeles Times* in a 1989 profile of the estate. "If Presley's name was valuable, then Lisa Marie should not only share in the rewards but also determine how the name could be used for commercial purposes."[29]

It was also suggested that the Elvis estate could not sue copyright infringers directly as Boxcar had been assigned the exclusive rights to market souvenirs around the singer (and therefore would have to be the one to initiate litigation against rogue traders).

It was in doing the background work here that Roesler became fully aware of the difficulties involved in protecting the intellectual property rights of the deceased so that estates could have greater control over the products that were being created using their name and image. "Initially, we started taking out trademarks – the same way a Ralph Lauren or a designer would do to protect their valuable intellectual property rights," he says, noting that the more they dug into this the more they realised that there was insufficient legislation to help them.

He and the Presley estate focused on lobbying to have the law changed, initially in Tennessee where Elvis had lived most of his life. The end result was the Personal Rights Protection Act of 1984 being enacted by the Tennessee legislature (and subsequently upheld by state and federal courts).

This Tennessee law change was followed in 1985 by the passing of Section 990 of the California Civil Code relating to use of a "Deceased Personality's Name, Voice, Signature, Photograph, or Likeness in Advertising or Soliciting".[30] This initially protected the rights of personalities for 50 years after their death but was later updated (to California Code, Civil Code – CIV § 3344.1) where it expanded the rights to 70 years to bring parity with copyright laws governing things like songwriting.[31]

"Then we went about to pass it in other pivotal states," says Roesler. "We passed the statute in Tennessee that protected it for 10 years after one's death and that continued until there were two consecutive years of non-use. So somebody like Elvis could theoretically last like a trademark. As long as there's use, there's protection." The law here is based on domicile – so it relates to primary residence of an individual. "That's why California is so important – because so many celebrities are domiciled there," Roesler explains.

This is of great importance for the business of estates because it all gets treated as a property right and, as such, can be transferred. In the case of a deceased artist, those rights can transfer to their heirs and give them control over the individual's name, image and likeness rights.

Not every state in the US has this change of law and the expiration period differs in each state that has implemented the changes.[32] "States like New York say you can't transfer those rights," says Roesler. "States like Tennessee, as we passed in the 1980s, say you can do it for 10 years […] California started off as 50 years and then changed to 70 years. I wrote the Indiana right of publicity legislation and that lasts for 100 years after death. So there's this mix of different laws."

The estate does not make money from Elvis's pre-1973 sound recordings because Colonel Parker sold them back to RCA for $5.4 million. It is one blow against the estate's earning potential and value; but having control over his name, image and likeness is arguably the most valuable asset in the entire Elvis portfolio, and other estates (especially those where the individual was domiciled in California) benefit enormously by default.

Roesler says this has all informed his subsequent work with estates across different entertainment and business sectors, ensuring they have as many rights as possible set in stone, including those relating to name, image and likeness. "The big picture is that we're building a portfolio of assets," he explains. "[These] assets are intangible property right assets. Typically on these celebrities, they're the most valuable assets that they possess. It is these intangible property rights that we create, maintain and exploit. All of that often can result in significant revenues for these various clients."

He says this has a significant bearing on how estates are valued, especially if an external company is looking to take a stake in it or even buy it outright. Auditing the rights in terms of what they have and how long they last is a crucial part of the due diligence here. "When you deal with a musician, an artist or an author, the value of their copyrights are often the majority of the value of their intellectual property rights," Roesler explains. "Typically with an artist, an author or a musician, they've become popular because of their copyrights. That's what's valuable."

These rights have only grown in importance and value over the years as the estates business matures and modernises. "Name and likeness – or branding – rights have become very desirable acquisition targets," says Lisa Alter of legal firm Alter, Kendrick & Baron. "It's not something that so much, historically, people even thought about to any great degree. But now with everyone looking to buy anything related to music content, the right to monetise the name and likeness of the artist – as well as artist performing rights or neighbouring rights – have become very, very hot commodities in their own right."

Ownership of the name, image and likeness rights was something that enabled the family of Jimi Hendrix to become operational and have income flowing in before they eventually took back control of his recordings. "We actually never lost the name, image and likeness rights," says Janie Hendrix. "In 1994, before we got our music rights back, we started doing merchandise and signing with various companies. Some of them don't exist any more – a lot of T-shirt companies. I call it tchotchkes." Tchotchkes (trinkets or bric-à-brac) they might have been, but that revenue effectively kept the Hendrix family afloat long enough to develop a strategy that would put them back in control of most of his assets and intellectual property.

"However," says Alter, "unlike copyright protection – which endures for the life of the author plus 70 years, or a flat term of 95 years for pre-1978 copyrights in the US – trademark protection only continues as long as the mark remains in continuous use."

What can, however, last in perpetuity if they are constantly maintained, policed and deftly used are trademarks. More than anything, they are an estate's most enduring asset.

TRADE MISSION: WHY TRADEMARKS ARE SO VALUABLE TO ESTATES

It will change depending on the country, but the copyright governing artists' property look roughly like this:

- **sound recording** rights: 70 years after the recording was issued;

- **composition** rights (i.e. music publishing): 70 years after the death of the author (or, in the case of a co-write, 70 years after the death of the last surviving writer[33]);

- **name, image and likeness** rights: up to 100 years.

The central point is this: sound recording, music publishing and name, image and likeness rights are finite; trademarks are infinite. This is why trademarks are the most valuable thing an estate can control, as they are the rights that endure.

As the majority of major music estates are based in the US, the following section will draw mainly on US trademark law. In general, however, the guiding principles of trademark law and its importance to estates are similar in most major capitalist markets.

In the US, it is USPTO (United States Patent and Trademark Office), a fee-funded agency of the US Department of Commerce, that governs the awarding of trademarks and assists in their policing. It has published a guide – *Protecting Your Trademark: Enhancing Your Rights Though Federal Registration* – for all companies seeking to take out a trademark.[34] "A trademark is generally a word, phrase, symbol, or design, or a combination thereof, that identifies and distinguishes the source of the goods of one party from those of others," it says, pointing out that trademarks typically refer to, and protect, brand names and logos on goods and services. They are distinct from copyrights (covering artistic works) and patents (covering inventions).

Trademarks also have to be kept active and regularly maintained but the onus is on the owner to police and enforce their rights for the life of the registration. "Rights in a federally registered trademark can last indefinitely if you continue to use the mark and file all necessary maintenance documents with the required fee(s) at the appropriate times."

The word "indefinitely" is critical here. When all the other rights in an estate dissolve into the public domain, it is the trademark that is the only thing estate managers and heirs several generations down the line will be left holding. It is the most enduring asset and bulwark that an estate can have, so the registering, exploiting and policing of trademarks needs to happen from

172

the earliest date possible. Ideally they should be put in place when an artist is still alive and enjoying a level of fame and success.

Normally band names will be trademarked, especially if they are unique, at the earliest stages; but other things can emerge through a career that are worthy of a trademark (such as the name of a hit album or single, providing it is not a commonly used phrase), meaning that this needs to be a rolling process.

Jeff Biederman is a partner at Los Angeles law firm Manatt, Phelps & Phillips and is an expert in trademarking. The firm represents, among others, the Miles Davis estate. He has been involved in trademarking the Miles Davis name as well as the iconic silhouette of the jazz musician playing the trumpet, which is used in multiple instances, notably on merchandise.

He explains why trademarks and copyright – the twin engines that estates can run on – are distinct:

> The goals of trademark and copyright are different. The goals of copyright are to protect limited-time monopolies for creators with the idea that you are fostering art. Because most people don't do things for nothing, so if you create this limited-time monopoly, artists can make money from their art and the general public benefits by more art being made. Trademark is the opposite. Trademark is designed to protect the public. Trademark lets you know, when you buy a particular product or service, who produced that. Food is the classic example. You want to make sure that this is a legitimate company with established testing procedures and safety procedures [...] So, theoretically, it goes on forever, because the public interest is the primary protection of the government. These are features of law. I think [a trademark is] the most important thing that any entertainer, alive or dead, can have. We're in a branding universe and trademarks, and in some ways internet addresses, are real estate. They're absolutely critical.

The fact that a trademark can theoretically last for ever is what elevates it above copyright, as the copyright owner has a window of exploitation and has to make that copyright generate as much income as possible in that time frame. With trademarks, the need for exploitation is less pell-mell.

A trademark does not cover all uses and all contexts, however, so it has to be filed in individual classes, of which there are hundreds. Biederman explains that with Miles Davis his name is trademarked with regard to music, live performance and T-shirts. "Whereas copyrights become global, trademark is very niche and you only file for the things that you're actually providing services or products in," he says. "Then you very aggressively protect that because, again, unlike copyright, a trademark that's not protected can be lost and fall into the public domain."

If a trademark lapses – and here Biederman cites the example of "aspirin"[35] as the warning from history for trademark lawyers – it can be very difficult, if not impossible, to file for a new trademark. It does not automatically fall into the public domain the day after the initial filing lapses, though; a recovery period applies if there is a mistake with dates. The technical term for this lapsed trademark is "abandoned", but if no one else has spotted it and swooped in to use it, it can be resuscitated. A trademark lawyer, however, has a professional obligation to ensure this renewal date is never missed. "If you blow that date," says Biederman, "that's malpractice!"

As per the USPTO rules, Biederman says "common terms and descriptive terms" are next to impossible to trademark. This can be an issue if an act, or their estate, seeks to trademark the name of a song or album. This is still not, however, completely impossible. "Generally titles are difficult – unless they take on secondary meaning," he says. "Years ago when I lived in Nashville, my firm represented Don McLean, who had the famous song 'American Pie'. We got a trademark in that for him. You need to be able to show to the PTO – and, if it's challenged, to a court – that the title represents the artist, not the album. That's the hurdle for the lawyer and the trademark representatives. Does a particular title have a broader reach brand-wise in the public view? For 'American Pie' it was absolutely an iconic song. 'American Pie' meant Don McLean."

Lisa Alter adds, "You can't copyright a title, but you can copyright lyrics, and the copyright protection extends to an excerpt from the lyrics – a significant enough phrase in the lyrics in a song – in certain circumstances. In certain cases you can trademark the title of a song, or even an identifiable line from the song. It is complicated, but trademark is an important piece of all of this estate management. We do have a number of clients who are trademarking in certain categories – entertainment services, T-shirts, mugs and so on – with various lines from songs. You have to pass muster in the Trademark Office to meet the standard for being covered by trademark protection. And you have to keep the mark active. You have to keep using it."

For the Miles Davis estate, it has managed to trademark *Kind of Blue* (the title of his legendary 1959 album) as well as *Bitches Brew* (his ground-breaking 1970 album). "Both *Kind of Blue* and *Bitches Brew* have reached that [same] point in the consciousness of the public," Biederman says. This has allowed the estate to license *Bitches Brew* to a beer developed by Dogfish Head and *Kind of Blue* to a Scotch whisky.[36] [37]

Things in Brazil are very different, however. Luciana Soares de Souza is the lawyer for a number of estates, notably Brazilian bossa nova icon Antônio Carlos Jobim as well as Brazilian poet Vinícius de Moraes. Together Jobim and de Moraes wrote 'Garota de Ipanema', which, in its English translation by Norman Gimbel as 'The Girl from Ipanema', was a major global hit in 1964.

"You cannot trademark a name of a famous person because the trademark law forbids that," she says. "For example, you cannot have the trademark 'Garota de Ipanema' or 'The Girl from Ipanema' because it's the title of a well-known song."

This was put to the test when Heloísa Pinheiro, who was the titular girl in the song, became a celebrity in Brazil after its release. In 2001, Pinheiro opened the Girl From Ipanema clothes shop in a shopping centre in Rio. The estates of both Jobim and de Moraes wanted to take action, but Pinheiro countered that she had not made money from the song so she saw it as only right to make money via association in the form of her boutique. "I never made a cent from 'The Girl from Ipanema', nor do I claim that I should," she said. "Yet now that I'm using a legally registered trademark, they want to prohibit me from being the girl from Ipanema. I'm sure that Antônio and Vinícius would never question the use of the name."[38]

It all turned into a protracted affair. "After many, many years of dispute – because the trademark process in Brazil [is very drawn out] – we reached an agreement saying that she could use 'Garota de Ipanema by Heloísa Pinheiro' to sell bikinis," says Soares de Souza. "The heirs and the estates for both Vinícius de Moraes and Antônio Jobim got the trademark of 'Garota de Ipanema' and 'The Girl from Ipanema' to do whatever they want with – for perfume and cosmetics."

* * *

Isaac Hayes III says the first thing he did when he eventually took over the intellectual property pertaining to his father Isaac Hayes's estate was to file a range of trademarks. "We started trademarking Isaac Hayes for things like food products, restaurants, services, clothing," he says. "We trademarked *Hot Buttered Soul* [his 1969 album] and we trademarked *Black Moses* [his 1971 album]. We just started creating a trademark portfolio."

Finding ways to exploiting a trademark is one part of an estate's business, but equally they have to be seen to be decisively policing their trademarks, even with small-time infringements. This is especially important if a major trademark infringement happens as non-policing of a trademark, no matter the size, could be used against them if it goes to court.

One estate manager recounts the unpleasantness that resulted after they had to go after a small-time business that was using the name and likeness of the deceased artist they were tasked with representing. "We reached out to the owners of that space," they say. "They were a mom-and-pop business and we did not remotely want to get into a situation where we were putting undue pressure on mom-and-pop businesses. They unfortunately got some bad legal advice that told them they could squat on it. We, through our attorney team, obviously corrected that thinking."

The Miles Davis estate, via Miles Davis Properties, had to take legal action against Manhattan jazz club Miles' Cafe in 2011, notably for its use of a silhouette of Davis playing the trumpet.[39] The club's owner, Satoru "Miles" Kobayashi, claimed to have had a dream in which Miles Davis came to him and told him to change his name and then open a club in his honour.

Biederman says it was an "easy" case to resolve. "That was a three-foot putt, if you're a golfer!" he laughs. Even so, the estate had to be seen to be taking decisive action here. "With trademarks come a responsibility," says Darryl Porter, who is in charge of the Miles Davis estate. "With trademarks, many people think that it's just about paying the fees and making the filings on time – but it's not. With a trademark, when someone violates your trademark, you have to defend it or ultimately it will dilute the mark if you don't."

The Johnny Cash estate, via the John R. Cash Revocable Trust, faced something similar in August 2019 with regard to Johnny and June's Reception Hall and Entertainment Venue in Illinois. It filed a federal lawsuit against the venue and its owners, Dustin and Kathy Smith. "[T]he Trust is charged with the responsibility of ensuring that the names, likenesses, trademarks and other indicia of Johnny Cash and June Carter Cash are not used in a manner that is likely to cause confusion or mistake in the marketplace," said the lawsuit.[40]

In the court documents in the case, it was revealed that the John R. Cash Revocable Trust had pending federal trademark applications for goods and services relating to "Bakery products", "Retail bakery shops" and "Restaurant and bar services". The central point here is that it had to insist in court that it was moving into these areas and that it had to take action against Johnny and June's Reception Hall and Entertainment Venue so as to avoid setting a bad precedent that could harm it in the future.

This was also done as a protective measure for the opening of Johnny Cash's Kitchen and Saloon, licensed to Icon Entertainment, next to the Johnny Cash Museum in Nashville, which was announced in early 2019.[41]

*   *   *

Mary Guibert is the mother of Jeff Buckley and also runs his estate. She says she does not take a sledgehammer approach to infringements of the trademarks she has registered and maintains around her son. "Those people that are making the Jeff Buckley cigarette lighters or the Jeff Buckley whatevers, they're not making millions of dollars!" she says, adding that her focus is instead on shutting down bootlegs of her son's music (more on this below).

Unquestionably the most unusual move is that of the Prince estate seeking to trademark a colour. Purple is synonymous with the star and his estate was seeking to take control of the hue. In October 2018, Paisley Park Enterprises filed a trademark application for "Love Symbol #2", which it stated was the "official colour across the brand he left behind".[42] The USPTO responded quickly to the application by refusing to register the mark. Paisley Park Enterprises countered in early May 2019 with a 430-page filing to try and push it through.[43] In February 2020, however, online legal resource Justia Trademarks records that the application was abandoned.[44]

The bigger the acts, the more trademarks they are likely to generate in their lifetime. They are increasingly developing vast trademark portfolios, but they cannot move to slap a trademark on everything without ever using it. They can file an "intent to use mark" for something they are developing but have not yet launched so as to protect it from others getting there first and using the time, but these are time-restricted.

Estates are inherently compromised, as a musician can only generate a set number of assets in their lifetime, most obviously recordings. But trademarks can be taken by the estate and applied to whole new product categories and ways for the estate to generate income beyond what the artist themselves created in the first place.

Biederman says, "It's half, if not more than half, of the property that you've been empowered to protect. It's that trademark, that goodwill, the name and likeness right. It's certainly of major importance to somebody alive; but somebody alive can make more stuff. But somebody who's already gone, all you can do is protect their legacy."

BRAND AID: THE LUCRATIVE WORLD OF BRANDING DEALS

Picasso exists as a ghostly reminder of the importance of leaving a will, but his estate has not been as tentative or hesitant when it comes to linking his name to brands and clamping down on bootleggers. There are important lessons for music estates to learn here on all counts.

The Picasso estate is faced with an ever-expanding black market that uses his name and art on everything from fishing hooks and inflatable dolls to rice and toothpaste.[45] Trademark policing helps to a point, but it becomes hugely complex when trying to work across the multiple territories where he is famous. This costs upwards of $1 million a year, according to Claudia Andrieu, head of legal affairs at the Picasso Administration.[46]

One of the most lucrative, if controversial, deals the Picasso estate signed was with automotive company Citroën in 1999 to have one of its cars named after the artist and feature his signature on the body. The idea came from Olivier Widmaier Picasso, the artist's grandson, but another grandchild was far from happy with it. "I cannot tolerate that the name of my grandfather […] be used to sell something as banal as a car," said Marina Picasso at the time.[47] The initial deal was estimated at $20 million and Citroën also pays royalties to the Picasso Administration on each vehicle sold. By 2016, it had sold 3.5 million cars bearing his signature.[48]

The importance of branding to estates has grown exponentially since the 1990s. What was once regarded as the ultimate act of "selling out", very much a hangover from the 1960s counterculture, is regarded as part and parcel of estates business today. Estates are also taking a much more proactive role here, seeking out brand partnerships rather than waiting for them to come knocking. Estates of all sizes are increasingly bringing in branding experts or working with branding agencies.

Nowhere are the twin goals of estates – of maintaining musical/cultural legacies and driving revenue – laid bare as explicitly as they are in the branding and licensing world. It is also a symptom of a dramatically changed music business where recorded music and publishing income (generally from sales and airplay) is such a minuscule part of the business. Crucially, branding and licensing rights typically exist outside of the control of record labels and music publishers, meaning this is not only the most powerful but also potentially the most lucrative card in the estate's hand.

The constant through all of this for estates has been merchandise. This is an area in which the artist, from the 1950s onwards, will have been active during their lifetime – from T-shirts sold at concerts to all manner of gewgaws that end up being licensed when the act becomes truly famous. This is an easily transferable business for an estate as it has been running before the artist's death. New recordings cannot be created out of thin air – but new merchandise ranges can. This can be the financial bedrock of an estate.

Josh Matas of Sandbox Entertainment, which looks after the Johnny Cash estate, says that income from the licensing of name and likeness makes up "a very sizeable portion of the revenue stream" for the Cash estate, but that pales in comparison to merchandising. "The reality is, and specifically on somebody like Johnny Cash, merchandising revenue can represent easily 50 per cent plus of what the overall revenue income is," he says.

One of the biggest and most experienced names in music merchandise is Norman Perry. His company, Perryscope Productions, handles the official merchandise for enormous active artists like AC/DC, legacy acts like Pink Floyd and The Police, enormous cultural brands like Woodstock and a multitude of deceased icons such as Syd Barrett, Muddy Waters, Charlie Parker, Janis Joplin, Miles Davis, Isaac Hayes and David Bowie.[49]

His thesis is that merchandise, as much as music, can keep a dead artist in the public consciousness. "There still is an enormous demand," he says of the assorted products generated around the artists and estates he works with. "But there's also an obligation and a mandate to make sure that what one does when somebody has passed on is to still try to ensure that their DNA and their ethics and their wherewithal and what they stood for is not taken advantage of in a commercial way."

This means having to tread carefully and not creating products – or licensing to existing products – that an artist would not be happy to be associated with. Tobacco is a common one, but equally many acts do not want to be associated with alcohol brands or products with a poor environmental record. The estates have to be careful not to do something the act would have disapproved of or vetoed in their lifetime.

The death of any musician will see a spike in sales of merchandise and it is then down to the merchandise companies involved to keep the public interested (and buying) with the development of new product lines. "In a perfect world, every band should have a bespoke approach," says Perry. "Yes, if you have a great idea like wrapping paper, you love to see it extend over three or four or five of your clients; but none of that wrapping paper should look the same. But at the end of the day, what's right for David Bowie and Bowie's audience and Bowie's licensing programme is probably never going to be what works for AC/DC's audiences and licensing programme because they are so diametrically different as bands."

Bowie in particular has his name and image on a plethora of products that Perryscope has helped to develop. Beyond the obvious clothing lines like T-shirts, hoodies and jackets, or the typical items one might expect to see like calendars, mugs and art prints, the official Bowie online store sells the following: wrapping paper ($20 per roll); "holiday ornaments" ($10 each); a "Bowie Logo Laser Engraved Paddle Slate Cutting Board" ($10); a "David Bowie Laptop Sleeve" ($45); a "David Bowie Serious Moonlight Throw Blanket" ($80); a "David Bowie Logo Beach Towel" ($24.99); and "David Bowie Diamond Dog Pencils" ($1.50 each).[50]

Perry had worked directly with Bowie and his team and says he has an innate understanding of what the singer would want his name and image reproduced on. "It starts with, 'What would David think?'" he says of the development of different product lines. "Do we know what David thought about corduroy? Do we know what David thought about blue? Do we know what David thought about any of these issues before we throw them into the mix? We all know that David was very, very, very much a chameleon. We know that his look evolved continually. So we know that our merchandise has to evolve."

He also argues that Bowie was "a guy that was willing to have some fun" and that is reflected in the product lines they have developed that an outsider might raise a quizzical eyebrow at. "There's no rocket science to this way [of working] and it's not [...] formulaic," he says.

Merchandise and clothing are fail-safes for most estates, but as this becomes commonplace, estates want to elevate what they do above what else is in the marketplace and move from the generic towards the more high-end.

"I designed most of the shirts that are on the site," says Isaac Hayes III of what is on his father's official store. "More than just memorabilia, I wanted to make fashion. I wanted to make things that people would wear. A concert tour T[-shirt] is different to something like the dopest pair of shoes that I got or the flyest jacket that I have. So that's what the apparel side was really about – just creating fashion, not memorabilia." This includes the *Hot Buttered Soul* collection featuring off-the-shoulder sweatshirts ($49), cropped hoodies (also $49) and slouchy tank tops ($32).[51]

Isaac Hayes III feels that clothing lines like this play a significant role in introducing his father's music to new generations, with fashion acting at the gateway. It also serves as a form of cultural reinforcement for consumers who grew up listening to his music. "Fashion is one of the things that is very transferable," he says. "I'm not slapping Isaac Hayes all over shirts, but I'm taking part of this culture, or his images [and using that]."

Bringing the artist's name outside music or their particular lifestyle (such as marijuana lines) when working with brands is a difficult act to pull off convincingly but can help to broaden the available audience. "We have done a Miles Davis Montblanc pen set, which obviously is not just designed for music lovers," says Darryl Porter. "These pens range from $600 to about $4,500.[52] That's outside of the norm, but it makes good sense because a lot of people who like Miles are affluent. I should say he has an affluent fanbase in addition to just the average Joe. When we looked at the Montblanc pen set, we decided that it made good sense for us to go that route, because it would create an opportunity for us to go back out into the marketplace and talk about Miles's relevance in pop culture."

Porter also says the *Kind of Blue* Scotch deal was done in part because "we knew that Scotch was trending younger and we wanted to get with a younger audience". He adds that estates need to move carefully here and be selective in not only the deals they sign but also the companies they work with. "We get pitched on products all the time," he says. "But what's most important is that: 1) the products are great products; and 2) the companies have to have enough resources to actually market it. Because if you don't, then it becomes a great product that no one's ever heard of."

The easiest – or certainly least controversial – brand deals for an estate are those that the artist was closely associated with when they were alive. These were brands they used or were photographed wearing, so creating a relationship with those brands after they have died feels less jarring. The brand world loves to use terms like "organic", "natural" and "affinity" – words that become incrementally drained of meaning the more they are batted around in sales presentations and pitch meetings – but in certain cases they perfectly distil what has happened.

In 2008, Converse created a limited-edition range of shoes that included Kurt Cobain's name, signature and lyrics. This was done with the full involvement of the estate. "Distressed in the way Kurt Cobain wore them, the shoes provide a rarely seen glimpse into the head of this musical and lyrical genius with sketches that display his hopes, dreams and lyrics from amazing songs such as 'Come as You Are'," said the brand on their release.[53]

Some fans responded vehemently, deriding them as "simply corporate, marketed bollocks" as well as saying the shoes were "exploitative and [it] goes against everything these artists stood for".[54]

Larry Mestel, founder and CEO of Primary Wave, was involved in that deal, having bought a stake in Nirvana's publishing in 2006. The stake was estimated at 50 per cent but that was then reported to have been divested when Primary Wave signed a $150 million deal with BMG in 2013. When I asked if he still had an interest in Nirvana's publishing, Mestel said an NDA prevented him from speaking about it. However, he responded to the criticism of the Converse deal by saying it was done with care and integrity. "If you knew anything about Kurt Cobain, you knew that he wore Converse sneakers," he says. "It was very organic to the brand. So I think that the fans loved it. And I think Courtney [Love, lead singer in Hole, and Cobain's widow] loved it as well because it was exactly what Kurt was associated with and what he wore. It's very important when we do deals like that to be organic and do what would be in the image of the artist themselves."

He also stresses that such deals for the Cobain estate were intentionally rare. "You have to remember Kurt Cobain was one of the most credible artists ever," he says. "He was not a commercial artist. So it was never the intention [...] to ever become hyper-commercialised. It was really things that were opportunistic and organic. So you don't go out and do ten types of those things a year."

For acts who understood the power of branding and merchandise in their lifetime and embraced it with open arms, it becomes difficult to argue against their estate if all they are doing is a continuation of what the artist was doing when they were alive.

The Ramones unquestionably thought of themselves as a brand as much as a band – all members adopted the Ramone surname (even new members), they all wore a uniform of torn jeans, leather jackets, scuffed sneakers and T-shirts for their entire career and even had a logo designed early in their career by Arturo Vega, who has been described as their "creative director".[55] The mythology around the band was such that a possibly apocryphal claim – that they sold significantly more T-shirts than records – eventually ossified into accepted fact.

Linda Ramone is the widow of Johnny Ramone, the guitarist in the band, and she controls 50 per cent of the Ramones estate via Ramone Productions. The other 50 per cent is controlled by late singer Joey Ramone's brother, Mickey Leigh. She is joyfully unapologetic about the brand deals she has done since her husband died. "I love doing products because Johnny and me were collectors," she says. "I love doing Bobble Heads [figurines]. I love doing everything. I love doing the packaging, the record releases. That's amazing to do. The fans love that. I think it's great to keep putting out products – and if people don't want to buy them, they just don't buy them."

When we spoke, she had just launched a Linda and Johnny Ramone range of socks with Happy Socks.[56] This was, as far as she was concerned, simply a continuation of what Johnny had done all through his time in the band. "That came out amazing," she says. "Happy Socks came to the house and they filmed me at the house. I designed four pairs of socks for them. I love Happy Socks because they did a Beatles sock. So we got in touch with them. Stuff like that, whenever it's Ramones or just Johnny, I look at everything."

Mickey Leigh is also favourably disposed to all manner of merchandise ideas related to the band. This might actually be one of the few areas where he and Linda can find common ground. (The many problems underpinning Ramone Productions are covered in Chapter 11.) Leigh says that he is happy to approve lots of different branded Ramones products simply because he and his brother were avid merchandise collectors when they were young and he sees this as part of a grand tradition stretching back to the 1960s. Much of the Ramones' merchandise has been outsourced to a third-party company but Ramone Productions help to oversee things. "We don't tell them what to make, but we can tell them not to make things," says Leigh. "If it's a cool item, why not? Me and my brother, when we were growing up, we would buy Beatles wigs and buttons and anything we could find. People say, 'They just want the money and they're making this or making that.' But we liked that kind of stuff!"

Jerry Garcia, who died in 1995, had also embraced branding in his lifetime, eventually arranging a royalty deal with Ben & Jerry's for the Cherry Garcia ice cream after it launched in 1987, initially without his approval.[57] He also launched a range of neckties in 1992.[58] The Garcia estate has subsequently licensed his name, artwork and image to other products such as Funko (large-headed collectible vinyl figurines), Street Plant skateboards, Icelantic Skis (limited-edition skis based on one of his airbrush paintings from 1986), a footwear line with Keen that also draws on his artwork (the Keen X Garcia Collection) and a line of hats with Grassroots (again using his artwork).[59 60 61 62]

In what is possibly the least surprising brand partnership ever, the Garcia estate developed the Garcia Hand Picked cannabis line with Holistic Industries, launching in California in November 2020, with other US states where cannabis has been legalised set to follow. They also created the Jerry's Picks range of edible gummies in the shape of guitar picks.[63] On the garciahand-picked.com site, merchandise (such as T-shirts, posters and caps) are also being sold.[64]

In 2014, Jimi Hendrix estate, via its Experience Hendrix arm, concluded a six-year legal action against hendrixlicensing.com and its founder Andrew Pitsicalis, who was a business partner of Jimi's younger brother Leon, for multiple trademark infringements pertaining to Hendrix. It was selling "T-shirts, posters, lights, dart boards, key chains and other items designed to capitalize on the fame of the rock legend" according to the *Hollywood Reporter* coverage of the case.[65]

Before this case was resolved, the Hendrix estate was still signing deals. In 2010, Converse developed a Hendrix-inspired line in cooperation with his estate. The three lines of Chuck Taylors were based around the artwork of two Hendrix albums (*Electric Ladyland* and *Axis: Bold as Love*) as well as one of his jackets.[66] Then in 2013 it worked with designer John Varvatos on a line of clothes replicating those the star wore in his prime, such as silk shirts, military jackets, a pouch belt, boots and a fringed shoulder bag. "He is my number one music icon, and a lot of peoples', so you know, you don't want to fuck with that the wrong way," Varvatos told *Rolling Stone*. "But we're not trying to be 1960s. Everything is about the fit."[67]

The Hendrix estate, arguably making up for lost time when the estate was out of the family's control, has been highly active in this field in recent years. In April 2018, it reached an agreement with Epic Rights and Perryscope to further develop the Authentic Hendrix retail brand. "The Authentic Hendrix brand program will include fashion apparel, headwear, footwear, tops, figures, wall art, accessories, jewelry, home décor, digital products, collectibles and never-before-licensed products from a wealth of material handed down from Authentic Hendrix and Experience Hendrix," said the press statement on the deal.[68]

In December 2019, the Hendrix estate signed a deal with Sony Music's Thread Shop division to produce a Hendrix merchandise line.[69] This builds on the deal the Hendrix estate already has with Sony covering the guitarist's music catalogue and film archive. "We placed Jimi in good hands with Sony Music, so we are more than comfortable with expanding our relationship to merchandise," said Janie Hendrix on the deal. "Jimi's persona encompassed more than music. He had a sense of style that we want to continue to present to the world [...] boldly and vividly."[70] In July 2020, a new online store selling merchandise arising from this deal opened.[71]

Janie Hendrix says that now she is in control of this part of the estate's business she wants to ensure she has as much sway over things as possible. "I would take less money from a licensee or even a record deal if it means I have more control," she says. "We've been in this business now for 25 years. At first, it was like jumping on a train that's going 90 miles an hour and trying to get inside to figure out where we're driving it to. Once we got in – and you can't be on the outside looking, you have to be immersed in it – then you realise that really Jimi is our treasure and we have to protect him and we have to protect the legacy. Everything we do is with him in mind."

Leon Hendrix found himself, along with his daughter, Tina, at the sharp end of trademark law again in January 2021, related to what *Billboard* called their "tuition-free" Hendrix Music Academy.[72] The dispute was over the academy using the Hendrix name and creating related merchandise. An updated ruling, however, by a US District Court judge in February 2021, removed both the Hendrix Music Academy and Tina Hendrix from a contempt order relating to the trademark infringement issue. This meant that the school would not have to change its name. The fresh ruling came after the school formally cut ties with Leon Hendrix.[73]

Such prolific branding activity, according to Nicole Beckett (creative director at Four Screens Management, who represent the estate of Wu-Tang Clan member Ol' Dirty Bastard) is second nature for estates today. "Over the years, we've moved more and more into licensing," she says. "We have apparel, shoes, we have some housewares coming out, posters – just running the gamut of whatever you would buy. We do have a few different figurines coming out. Collectible things like that that we think would really resonate with the fans. These are people who have full man-garages filled with Wu-Tang things! They would be happy to have a beautiful figurine. It's very authentic. It's a fun thing to do."

She says, however, that the estate wants to have enormous input and final approval over everything that comes out with ODB's name or likeness on. "It's a fun process to go through with all the creative people we work with to [take] our assets and say, 'OK, here are the assets. Go out and create something new.' We give them a lot of guidance to make sure they stay within the parameters of what we want to portray."

Estates also need to ensure that they do not work with brands that might undermine or contradict the legacy of the artist, as David Hirscland, EVP at BMG, which runs the Buddy Holly estate, explains with reference to a range of endorsement opportunities that have surfaced for the singer in recent years. "We're very, very careful about merchandising," he says. "We did a deal with Raymond Weil, the watchmaker.[74] They had a music series where they did The Beatles and Frank Sinatra – and Buddy was the third music artist that they did a special watch for. People ask why we didn't do a deal with Ray-Bans as Buddy wore Ray-Bans. No, as a matter of fact, he didn't wear Ray-Bans. His glasses were manufactured in Mexico by a rather small optometrist and Buddy found those glasses. They're not Ray-Bans [...] Buddy was a class act, and we're going to make sure that that's how it's treated."

In this world, the earliest approach was to put the act's name on as many products as possible. This had not really been done before, and the Elvis estate stood, for both good and bad, as a metonym for the whole process. As the estates market has developed, however, this scattergun approach is becoming viewed less as a licence to print money and more as a way of causing long-term damage. If the act is plastered all over trinkets and other gaudy products it can reflect badly on the estate and make it look cheap or desperate, with quality the first casualty. There is a real risk of everything starting to look like the brand promiscuity of Krusty the Clown from *The Simpsons*. His rapacious catchphrases – "I heartily endorse this event or product", "It's not just good – it's good enough" – are satirical warnings from recent history that all estates would be wise to listen to.

This is certainly behind a recalibration of what the Elvis Presley estate has been trying to do since Authentic Brands Group bought an 85 per cent stake in Elvis Presley Enterprises from Core Media Group in 2013. "The first thing that we wanted to do is really clean it all up," says Jamie Salter, chairman and CEO of Authentic Brands Group, with regard to the product promiscuity he saw as eroding the value of the Elvis estate and staining the Elvis brand. "Yes, we still make shot glasses, but we really wanted to go after better partners. If you look at the way the Elvis business was originally worked, Colonel Parker licensed anything and everything. So we pared it back very quickly, meaning that from 300 licensees, we took it down to 100 – kind of overnight."

Accusations of over-licensing and promiscuous product development have dogged the Elvis estate since its earliest days. Such deals needed to happen to bring in revenue and prevent the estate from collapsing under the weight of debt; but it has been felt that quality control, especially during the 1980s and 1990s, was severely lacking. A profile of the Elvis estate in the *Los Angeles Times* in 1989 made this clear. "Licensed Elvis souvenirs often invite employment of the word *tacky*," it said. "The Graceland shop offers everything from a clock sporting Elvis in a gold lamé suit ($19.95) to a sort of Elvis-in-ice sculpture that lights up ($49.95)." It added that while these products might not be the apotheosis of good taste, they brought in $750,000 for the estate in 1988 alone.[75]

Jack Soden, then executive director of Graceland, added that there were 2,700 different product lines around Elvis (including T-shirts and postcards) and even then admitted it might be construed as somewhat excessive. "I look at our inventory sheet and ask, 'What are we, Sears?'"[76] He said this was all part of a long tradition of sometimes over-the-top merchandise, referencing Elvis lipsticks and dog tags that were made in the 1950s ("That stuff was fun, and it should have been"). He also revealed that one of his favourite items, fuzzy slippers with Elvis's head on the toes, appeared on the *David Letterman Show* on TV where they were roundly mocked. This ridicule forced one of the estate co-executors to refuse to renew the manufacturer's licence. "Now, they are collectors' items," said Soden.[77]

Even with the Authentic Brands Group clean-up, the range of licensed Elvis products in that time sometimes tips over into the ludicrous or even laughable. In July 2019, Authentic Brands Group partnered with Bellevue Brands to create an Elvis Presley fragrance line. "The fragrances Legend and Forever are offered in variations for men and women, each capturing distinctive elements of Elvis' essence," says the press announcement on the deal.[78]

Such deals are par for the course for a major estate – with perfume brands and technology companies being important partners – but other deals might sharply raise one's eyebrow, notably the partnership with Better Choice Company in June 2019 to create "an all-new line of CBD pet products under the Elvis Presley Hound Dog brand". (CBD, or cannabidiol, is extracted from cannabis but does not cause intoxication.) Daniel W. Dienst, EVP of Authentic Brands Group, said in a statement, "Launching Elvis Presley Hound Dog chews and treats infused with CBD is a natural extension of the Elvis Presley brand as Elvis loved his dogs as much as we do."[79]

As part of the research for this book, I was given a copy of the branding guidelines document that Authentic Brands Group uses for Elvis, showing how it works and the shape its marketing of Elvis should take. The 21-page document includes sections such as "THE ORIGINAL COOL" with quotes from the likes of Bruce Springsteen, Beyoncé, Mick Jagger and Bob Dylan explaining what Elvis meant to them. It also gathers together images of contemporary artists like Lady Gaga and Miley Cyrus who explicitly reference Elvis in their clothing or performances, showing both his historic and modern impact.

Authentic Brands Group defines the brand values of Elvis as: individuality; generosity; freedom; community; and authenticity. There is also a breakdown of his demographic reach and his posthumous social media reach. "Elvis Presley has never been more relevant," the document says. "A hero for modern times, no matter how often those times are reimagined." It also refers to Elvis as "the ultimate brand". In summing up its core thrust, it says, "Elvis

Presley speaks to the rebel inside all of us, the rebel that defies convention and strives to forge a path of truth, passion, and individuality."

Branding is increasingly less the preserve of a handful of major estates, with even the estates of cult artists drawing in brands. In quick succession, in May 2020 the Daniel Johnston estate signed a deal with Supreme to create a clothing range featuring his artwork, and then in June 2020 the estate signed a deal with Vans to make a range of shoes, shirts, tote bags and hats that will also feature his artwork.[80] [81]

They can also ride trends and developments that suddenly appear in the market far outside of music, with the Frank Zappa estate licensing a colouring book company in 2019 to cash in on the wellness and mindfulness movement. "This entire project brings the biggest smile to my face," Ahmet Zappa told *Billboard*. "People who don't like coloring books, I fear, are dead inside."[82]

Related to this, in 2019 Mary Guibert worked with author Tiffanie DeBartolo to create *Grace*, a graphic novel based on the life of Jeff Buckley.[83]

Musicians, especially guitarists and drummers, frequently have sponsorship and endorsement deals in place with instrument manufacturers when they are still active and these are often carried on (or new ones sought out) by their estate and heirs when they die. In some ways, signature instruments are a form of validation from the music community and can carry on the name of a player to whole new generations of players. There is a great deal of cultural capital wrapped up in it – a guitarist or drummer can be held up as an inspiration for other players – but there can also be a lot of economic capital in it.

Daniel Gallagher is the nephew of Rory Gallagher and a driving force in his estate. He says that a limited-edition replica of Rory's famously worn Fender Stratocaster was created and it proved so popular that the run was extended. "Fender are going to keep making them," he says. "It's their second most expensive model, but they're still being bought in shops all the time. It's something that started off as a small tribute from Fender UK and now [Fender US is picking up on it]. There is a whole part of the guitar world called 'relic-ing' where people age up their guitars to make them look cool. They attribute a lot of the desire to do it on the basis of that Rory remodel."

In the world of guitarists, they need to have one brand that becomes their signature (in part as they are sponsored by them or given free instruments), so the guitar brands will often look to secure an exclusive partnership with the estate of an artist who is synonymous with their brand.

For the Jimi Hendrix estate, however, things were handled slightly differently. "We signed with Gibson and Fender, which very few artists are able to do," says Janie Hendrix. "But because Jimi didn't just play Fender and he didn't just play Gibson, they're coexisting."

THE BLAND LEADING THE BRAND: SOME OF THE
LESS-CELEBRATED ENDORSEMENTS

Not all endorsements are a success, either commercially or creatively, and some end up dragging estates into years of litigation and turmoil. And some are just utter disasters. Here are some of the most notable flops.

"Jim's ghost was in my ear, and I felt terrible": stopping ad deals on behalf of a deceased member

The very idea of working with a brand or licensing your music to it was seen as the ultimate act of selling out to a whole generation of acts who came to prominence in the 1960s and 1970s. Brands were seen as the enemy and it was taken as read that any deal with them automatically tainted art and was a truly Faustian pact. Some acts have changed their minds about this over time, whereas others have dug their heels in even more.

The case of The Doors illustrates this tension as two of the members (keyboardist Ray Manzarek and guitarist Robby Krieger) mellowed in their attitude towards endorsement deals, while drummer John Densmore held firm to his views and felt he also had to represent those of Jim Morrison, the band's singer, who died on 3 July 1971.

In 1968, Morrison found out that the other three members had agreed in theory to have 'Light My Fire' used in a commercial for Buick for a fee of $75,000. It would have involved changing the song's lyrics to "Come on, Buick, light my fire."

"Fuck you!" was Morrison's response when he found out what had been approved in his absence. "We always agreed that our music would never be used in commercials. You guys just made a pact with the devil."[84] Morrison threatened to "smash a fucking Buick to dust onstage" if it happened.[85] As the band was run on a four-way split, if one member opposed a plan or idea, it was a total veto. Morrison got his way.

Densmore said this outburst was "etched on my brain, never to be forgotten" and shaped how he approached business dealings after Morrison's death.[86] While he agreed to have the band's music used in *Apocalypse Now* in 1979, he felt that was artistically justified. Then he (and the other surviving members) did agree to let 'Riders on the Storm' be used in an ad for Pirelli tyres in the UK in the 1970s. Densmore claimed he was sick when he saw the finished ad. "I gave every cent to charity," he said. "Jim's ghost was in my ear, and I felt terrible."[87]

With the memory of that still stinging, Densmore blocked an offer of $1.5 million (which some say rose to $4 million) to have 'When the Music's Over' used in an ad for Apple Computers, believing he was also representing the wishes of Morrison.[88]

The same year, however, Cadillac wanted to use the band's music in an ad. Manzarek and Krieger were keen to do the deal; Densmore refused.

Relations between the surviving members had been curdling for years, exacerbated by an ugly and protracted court case over Manzarek and Krieger touring under the name The Doors/The Doors of the 21st Century and Densmore seeking to make them change their name. Rolled into this legal war was Densmore's refusal to agree to license the band's music for use in commercials. The scuppered Cadillac deal was at the very heart of it, especially when, after being rebuffed several times, the money on the table rose to $15 million.

In 2005, a court ruled that Manzarek and Krieger's use of the name The Doors for their touring show was false advertising and they could only use "The Doors" in any form in the title if they had the written consent of all sides of The Doors partnership. They were also not permitted to use "the name, likeness, voice, or image of Jim Morrison to promote their band or their concerts".[89]

Manzarek and Krieger were ordered to pay $5 million to Densmore as well as the parents of both Morrison and Pamela Courson (who collectively controlled the Morrison estate).[90] The Cadillac ad never happened.

"You're ruining one of the greatest songs of all time!": losing control over the rights to a deceased artist's image and publishing

It emerged in 2012 that publicity rights for Kurt Cobain had transferred from Courtney Love, his widow, to Frances Bean Cobain, his daughter. The story actually dated back to 2010 when it was claimed that Love stepped down from the company (The End of Music) that administered Cobain's publicity rights. The story came from sealed documents obtained by *The Fix*, an online magazine dealing with addiction and recovery issues.[91]

Frances Bean had turned 18 in 2010 and took over most of her trust. She was reported to be "locked in a battle" with her mother over ownership of a number of Cobain's possessions, including clothes, paintings and instruments.[92] Frances Bean had also cut out Love in 2009 when she moved to have her aunt and paternal grandmother named as her legal guardians.

In 2011, 'Smells Like Teen Spirit' was covered in a sketch in *The Muppet Movie*. In the scene, Muppet characters Sam Eagle, Rowlf the Dog, Link Hogthrob and Beaker perform the song as a barbershop quartet. "Wait a minute!" says Jack Black, who also appears in the sketch tied to a barber's chair as the assembled Muppets start shaving him. "What are you doing? Is that Nirvana? Stop it! You're ruining one of the greatest songs of all time!"

The following year, Courtney Love made her thoughts on it clear. She reportedly told *TMZ* that "the Muppets are raping Kurt Cobain's memory".[93] Her controversial use of language aside, the licensing decision was far beyond her purview and shows how those outside the decision-making process at estates can feel greatly aggrieved at deals over which they have no approval.

"This is a case that's delicious, factually and legally": when an estate gets sued over a branding deal done in the artist's lifetime

In 1987, ice cream brand Ben & Jerry's launched the Cherry Garcia flavour. There is a wistful essay on the company's website telling its story, "Back in the olden days, before cell phones and web sites and tweeting for ice cream, our fans spoke to us via hand written notes pinned to the bulletin boards in our scoop shops," it says.[94] It continues that a customer in Maine left a note in her local shop but it was not passed on. She was persistent and wrote to the company's head office in Burlington. "We're great fans of the Grateful Dead and we're great fans of your ice cream," she said. "Why don't you make a cherry flavor and call it Cherry Garcia? You know it will sell because Dead paraphernalia always sells. We are talking good business sense here, plus it will be a real hoot for the fans."

It went into development and eventually launched on 15 February 1987. "We sent the first 8 pints we made straight to Mr. Garcia himself, and Jerry's wife and publicist even called to say that he gave it the thumbs up!" says the Ben & Jerry's site.

Except that was not the full story. Missing from this whimsical history is the fact that Garcia's lawyer regarded it as an infringement on his client's name and asserted that this brand of ice cream could set a dangerous legal precedent for future protection of that name. Eventually a licensing deal was reached whereby Garcia was paid a royalty on every tub of Cherry Garcia sold. It was a hugely lucrative deal, with the *New York Times* in 1997 estimating that it generated $200,000 a year for the Garcia estate.[95]

Trouble brewing: when an oral agreement falls apart

Jazz musician Thelonious Monk died on 17 February 1982 and his son, Thelonious Monk Jr, took over as administrator of the estate. It was reported that Monk Jr entered into an oral agreement with North Coast Brewing Co to use his father's name, image and likeness in relation to a Trappist-style beer called Brother Thelonious Belgian Style Abbey Ale. As part of this oral agreement, a percentage of the profits from sales of the beer were given to the Thelonious Monk Institute of Jazz.

"In addition to the ale, North Coast produces and sells other products that feature Monk's name, image and likeness, including cups, hats, hoodies, iron-on patches, soap, T-shirts, tap handles, metal and neon signs, pins, playing cards, mouse pads, posters and food products," reported *Forbes*.[96] The issue was, according to Monk Jr, that a licence had never been granted for those ancillary products.

In January 2016, the Monk estate wrote to North Coast revoking any previous licence allowing use of Monk's name, image and likeness and saying that it must enter into a new licensing agreement with the estate if it wished to continue making and selling any of the products under dispute.

The case dragged on and in February 2019, a federal judge rejected North Coast's move to have the case dismissed. The judge argued that the public might be confused into believing that any Monk-centric merchandise created by North Coast was fully sanctioned by the estate.[97]

The case was eventually settled and by February 2019, North Coast had reintroduced the beer to its product range. "North Coast Brewing Company produces Brother Thelonious Belgian Style Abbey Ale under a licensing agreement with the Thelonious Monk Estate," says its website.[98] It was also reported that the brewer was to donate a portion of all sales to Monterey Jazz Festival's jazz education programme.[99]

POLICING BOOTLEGS AND BRAND INFRINGEMENTS

"This is something we shouldn't have been doing"

If an estate is big enough to have a successful merchandising arm, it will be big enough to attract bootleggers. Bootleggers see death as something attractive to capitalise on. But general copyright and trademark infringements (as well as violation of name, image and likeness rights) are not confined to shady backstreet and online operators who pump out poorly manufactured T-shirts and other ephemera, with little concern for those whose fame they are riding on, just as long as they can turn a profit from it. Major brands and celebrities can also cross the line here.

Policing all this is a costly and time-consuming process, but it has to be done even for small infringements to ensure that their legal case is not weakened when a major infringement happens. The fact that the Picasso estate spends upwards of $1 million a year doing this is not atypical.

There have been some significant cases in recent years relating to brands, designers and celebrities that show even legitimate operators can play fast and loose with the laws governing this area. The estate of Kurt Cobain has been one of the most affected and also one of the most proactive here. CNBC referred to the "brand of Kurt Cobain" as "clearly big business" in 2014 and estimated his estate was worth $450 million. "There is the Beatles, and then there's everybody else," Larry Mestel of Primary Wave told CNBC. "Between the Beatles and everybody else, there's Kurt Cobain."[100]

Protecting his worth but also his credibility underscored his estate's actions when several major brands looked to hijack his image and name. In 2007, an advert for Dr Martens created by Saatchi & Saatchi whipped up a storm of controversy. The print ad series featured Photoshopped images of a number of deceased artists – Kurt Cobain, Joe Strummer, Joey Ramone and Sid Vicious – in heaven, wearing Dr Martens boots.

Courtney Love was angered and upset by the campaign. "Courtney had no idea this was taking place and would never have approved such a use," her representative told *People*. "She thinks it's outrageous that a company

190

is allowed to commercially gain from such a despicable use of her husband's picture."

David Suddens, CEO of Dr Martens' parent company AirWair, was also approached by *People* and offered contrition. "We are really, really, really sorry," he said. "We do think that it is offensive. We made a mistake. My message to Courtney Love is: This is something we shouldn't have been doing."[101]

As the story erupted, AirWair fired Saatchi & Saatchi, claiming it had not commissioned the series of images of the deceased stars. Suddens added that it "runs counter to our current marketing activities".[102] Saatchi & Saatchi was, however, less apologetic. "We believe the ads are edgy but not offensive," Kate Stanners, executive creative director at Saatchi & Saatchi, told the *Guardian*. "There has been blog commentary both for and against the ads, but it is our belief that they are respectful of both the musicians and the Dr Martens brand."[103]

The lessons from the Dr Martens case in 2007 were clearly not learned by Dutch brewing company Bavaria. As part of the promotion in 2014 for Radler, a new fruit-flavoured beer, it created a TV ad based around the idea that a number of dead icons were in fact still alive and actually just hiding away together on a tropical island, presumably to escape the pressures of fame. The cast of lookalikes included Elvis, Tupac, Marilyn Monroe, Bruce Lee, John Lennon and Kurt Cobain.

Rolling Stone speculated that the ad might "see some complaints from the estates of these deceased stars".[104] In this case, however, nothing happened, perhaps because the ad did not explicitly name them all; that said, it dropped clues like the John Lennon-alike saying "Hey, Jude" and the captain of a ship passing the island saying he thought he had spotted Elvis.[105] The fact that the ad was played for comic effect also would have helped its creators to use satire as a defence.

Then in 2018, designer Marc Jacobs created the Bootleg Redux Grunge fashion range that included a doctored smiley face logo on a T-shirt. The Kurt Cobain estate and Nirvana Inc (representing both Cobain and the surviving members of the band) took legal action on copyright grounds. The logo originally used by Nirvana in merchandise in 1991 was a version of the classic smiley logo with an "X" on each eye, and a wobbly mouth with a tongue poking out in yellow, along with the Nirvana logo, all appearing on a black T-shirt. The Marc Jacobs design was also in yellow and had the same wobbly mouth and tongue, but the "X" eyes were replaced with the letters "M" and "J". It said "Heaven" across the top in a font reminiscent of the Nirvana logo, and it too was on a black T-shirt.

Litigation began at the very end of 2018. Marc Jacobs moved to have the case dismissed in March 2019, with its legal team claiming the smiley face was a "commonplace image"; then they countersued in November 2019.[106] *Billboard* noted that copyright in the "X-Eye Smiley Face" was registered to Cobain around 1991 but it was "unclear when or how the registration [...]

was transferred to Nirvana, Inc. as both the author of the work and the copyright claimant".[107] In November 2019, it was ruled that the case could move forward.[108]

An extra twist came in September 2020 when graphic designer Robert Fisher filed a motion to intervene in the case "claiming to be the rightful creator and owner of the copyright design".[109] He had been working at Geffen Records when it signed Nirvana and collaborated with them on the sleeve design for the *Nevermind* album that sent the band stratospheric. He claimed he was asked to work on merchandise ideas for the band and from that sprang the smiley design.[110]

(At the time of writing, the case had not been resolved.)

The Frank Sinatra estate, despite being relatively late to the branding and endorsement world, was also fiercely protective of the singer's image and name. Speaking in 2015 on the 100th anniversary of her father's birth, Tina Sinatra said that tawdry and unlicensed cash-in products were a concern for him when he was alive and it was the duty of the estate to ensure the market was not flooded with shabby unofficial products now he had passed away.

"The notion that people were getting [his image] on coffee mugs and T-shirts scared the crap out of Pop," she told NPR. "He didn't want that at all." She said the estate took a hard-line stance here. "People were ready to start to rip him off," she said. "And when we sort of showed up and put a sign outside the door, it sent a message. And they didn't screw with us as much as they were screwing already with other estates, living or dead."[111]

The estate said that it wanted to turn him into an upscale lifestyle brand, but that was something that was not completely possible when dealing with a mainstream figure like Sinatra. Inevitably, a move into more affordable mass-market products happened – including, with throbbing symbolism, coffee mugs. The difference, of course, being that the estate controlled this and profited from it.

"Well, he ended up on a coffee mug because when you do live theater, you've got to give something in memorabilia and merchandise," sighs Tina. "And you have to make it affordable. So we were stuck with hats, coffee mugs – it's a running gag, don't tell Tina but we've got to do coffee mugs and they sell – they're gone."[112]

Alongside brands and designers finding themselves accused of infringement, the modern phenomenon of the reality TV star and social media influencer has been mired in this debate.

In June 2017, representatives of The Doors and the Jim Morrison estate sent a cease-and-desist letter to Kendall and Kylie Jenner in relation to a line of T-shirts the sisters had developed, wherein their faces were superimposed on a number of musicians. On one item, the face of Kendall Jenner was placed on The Doors' logo.

The letter, sent by Anthony M. Keats, a partner at Beverly Hills law firm KeatsGatien, demanded that manufacturing and advertising of the products should cease and requested they file full accounting of all proceeds from sales up to that point.[113] At the same time, the sisters also got a cease-and-desist letter from the estate of Notorious BIG.

Kendall Jenner, as is so often the way with these things, issued an apology on Twitter and said the offending items had been withdrawn from sale. "The KENDALL + KYLIE brand apologizes for any insensitivity," they said in a statement to the *Hollywood Reporter*. "When deciding to work with one-of-a-kind repurposed vintage tees, it was not the brand's intent to offend anyone. These designs were randomly selected and not well thought out. The brand would like to apologize, especially to the artists that have been featured in the series. We did not mean to disrespect these icons and understand that we missed the mark completely. The designs have been removed. We sincerely apologize to the artists, their families and estates and anyone who may have been offended."[114]

In March 2019, the Notorious BIG estate also took action against Swiss snowboard company Yes Snowboards.[115] While copyright cases make headlines – in part due to the fame of the artist involved but also playing on the face-clasping idea that this is an act of desecration – a lot of this legal activity happens very quietly and, more to the point, routinely, as infringements of this type (for living artists and deceased ones) is a moving target and needs to be responded to quickly.

With the rise of online retail and new technologies like print on-demand that allow much smaller operators to come in here, how estates respond is what separates some estates from others. Platforms like eBay, Alibaba and Etsy have created a whole new world of micro-commerce where individuals, rather than corporations, can create and sell products and licensing is frequently the first casualty. Corporations, of course, can also increase what they do on these platforms, but it is the sheer volume of unlicensed operators out there that makes policing it all a Sisyphean task for estates.

Norman Perry calls the small sellers "scoundrels" and says it is an endless task to tackle the problem. "You are probably familiar with the game whack-a-mole," he says. "It feels like that some days because for every three guys you stop, there's three more that have cousins that start again the next day under a slightly different name [...] there are some legitimate companies that have become the biggest companies on the planet; you could call Facebook one of them, you could call eBay a subsidiary of another one."

In 2008, Jamie Salter was at restructuring and refinancing company Hilco (before he set up Authentic Brands Group and bought into the Elvis business) and while there he worked with the Marley estate in a management capacity for the Marley brand, seeking to clean up the bootlegging and counterfeiting around his name.[116] This was allowed to go unchecked for years due to the struggles pertaining to control of the estate, locking it into a form of legal and commercial limbo. Salter estimated that counterfeiters were making upwards of $600 million a year and the Marley estate was seeing none of that.

He said Hilco promised to spend "as much money as it takes to stop them" by driving the bootleggers out of business.[117] He suggested that identifying the rogue operators was relatively straightforward as many of the licensed operators would notify the estate if they spotted anyone operating without a licence. "You get the guy and, say, he sold 600 shirts," Salter told the *Globe & Mail* in 2012. "So he'll stop and he'll donate $600 or $6,000 to a charity."[118]

Salter later said in a BBC documentary in 2019 that this clean-up operation for the Marley estate was swift and decisive. "Within 12 months, we cut out 90 per cent of the counterfeiting [...] People are scared to go up against us. We go very hard at them. We think counterfeiting is something that people just should not do."[119]

Some of what happened here was regarded as somewhat heavy-handed. Speaking in the same BBC documentary, Roger Steffens said, "There was a guy who stood outside the headquarters of Island Records in Greenwich Village with these beautiful hand-painted shirts [of Marley], and they arrested him."

Jeff Jampol says it is a quotidian war against bootlegging and counterfeiting for a company like JAM Inc given the number of estates and living artists it represents. "Piracy is everywhere," he says. "I believe in a great [American football coach] Vince Lombardi quote from the 1960s. He said, 'The best defence is a good offence.' I also believe that nature abhors a vacuum. I always tell estates, 'If you're not doing something in this area, don't think nothing is being done. Somebody is going to be driving the bus; it just better be you.' You can't stop everybody all the time, but you can police the market. And sometimes the best defence for bootleg apparel is to come out with a really great apparel line yourself. It's a constant process."

Cease-and-desist letters and threats of legal action are one (arduous) route to take here, but the official outlets must, he feels, trumpet their inherent legitimacy. He says the message companies like his have to send out to consumers is the importance of the official online store as the place to buy licensed products. "So, when in doubt, let's go to davidbowie.com," he says. "When in doubt, let's go to milesdavis.com. Because then there is no doubt."

This is not just confined to huge stars, with Celeste Bell saying that bootleg merchandise around her mother, founder of X-Ray Spex Poly Styrene, remains an issue for her. Partnering with management firm ie:music (whose roster includes Robbie Williams and Passenger) is something she says will help as it was an issue she was unable to tackle alone. "There are tons of bootlegs out there at the moment and that is something that has been neglected," she says. "Having a bigger company's support on that side of things will be a big help."

Mary Guibert is more sanguine and says her primary concern is stemming bootlegs of Jeff Buckley's recordings from circulating online. "I was one of the first people to start shutting down bootleg auctions on eBay – literally!" she laughs. "They were doing all kinds of things in the beginning there."

Buckley himself had tried to stop this when he was alive, seeking to have only his team work on the sound desk at venues he played to prevent others recording straight from the desk. These recordings by Buckley's own team form the basis of the official live recordings that have come out posthumously. Other recordings were made, often from the crowd, and began circulating and Guibert says she is especially concerned with cauterising such recordings, because they are of such low quality.

She says, "I did have a conversation with a British gentleman once at a tribute for Jeff who said, 'I just had to congratulate you because I am a swap meet seller and I had some concert bootlegs of your son that I was selling on eBay and I was told that if you want to sell on eBay, do not bootleg Jeff Buckley as his mother will take your licence.'" Her concern, she says, is less the existence of bootlegs and more the existence of *bad* bootlegs. "My promise to his fans was that – and I like saying this – 'If you ever hear something come out that is a piece of shit, send flowers to my son because I'm dead!'"

For bootleg Jeff Buckley merchandise, however, she is less concerned about that as something to tackle head on with the same tenacity she reserves for bootleg recordings. "I do shut down the music, but anybody who's trying to get Jeff out there and make pictures or rugs – these people are making a paltry living," she says. She adds that she will only license to merchandise companies under certain conditions, one being where the items are manufactured. "If you can't guarantee me that the products are going to be made in the USA, I will not approve it," she says. "And their response to me has always been, 'Well there's going to be people who are going to bootleg it. They're just going to put it out and you're going to have no control over it.' And I say, 'Well at least I can say it's not coming from me.' I cannot control the bootleggers."

The Jimi Hendrix estate addressed the issue of bootleggers by setting up its own label, Dagger Records, to play the bootleggers at their own game by releasing high-quality audio versions of concert recordings that had been in circulation on the black market for decades. Dagger explicitly acknowledges these recordings are in the wild but positions itself as the place for fans to buy the cleaned-up versions.

"If you are a true aficionado of Hendrix, your collection has probably been augmented over the years by underground, unauthorized bootleg recordings," says the Dagger website. "No matter what form – vinyl, cassette, CD-R, and now a myriad of digital formats like MP3, WMA, APE, SHN and a host of others – these haphazard compilations of random studio outtakes, television and radio performances, interviews, and amatuer [sic] audience recordings of concerts have helped fans fill in the gaps left by Jimi's authorized albums. The underground market for Jimi Hendrix recordings is rife with expensive, poorly annotated bootlegs. These haphazard compilations are often poor quality and too frequently deliver far less than they advertise."[120]

Janie Hendrix says the idea for Dagger came from Carlos Santana, who suggested to her that she should "bootleg the bootleggers" to take control over this market and ensure that high-quality official recordings were made available to fans. "I was like, 'Wow, what a great idea!'" she says. "So I came up with the name Dagger Records, from [the Hendrix song] 'Dolly Dagger', but it's also a double-edged sword where we're going to basically pierce through the music and put it out, whether it's mono, whether it's an apartment recording, or maybe it's something that is kind of rough, but it's something the fans want to hear. Now, some may argue that Jimi may not have wanted that to come out. But for us, it was like, as my dad once said, 'Jimi never played a bad note.'"

These releases are only available through the Dagger online store and are not, in Janie Hendrix's words, "frontline release". They are there simply to meet existing collector demand. They are kept separate from the releases and reissues that go through Sony as part of the estate's licensing deal with the major label, with a Dagger release scheduled roughly every two years.

Adopting a similar philosophy, but with regard to merchandise rather than audio recordings, the estate of Ol' Dirty Bastard believes it is more advantageous to work with bootleggers and counterfeiters rather than against them. Or, to be more precise, to work with the platforms where some bootleg and counterfeit products can be found.

Redbubble positions itself as an online marketplace for creators to sell their products and designs. On-demand printing technology lets them sell things like T-shirts without having to manufacture them in advance, merely responding to orders. "Redbubble was born in 2006 in Melbourne, Australia," says the company on its website. "The dream was simple. Give independent artists a meaningful new way to sell their creations. Today, we connect over 700,000 artists and designers across the planet with millions of passionate fans. A brave (and dare we say stylish) new world of self expression."[121]

It was, however, cited by several estates as a place where unlicensed designs freely circulate and taking them down is a costly and arduous process. Breaking somewhat from the pack here, however, in March 2020 the Ol' Dirty Bastard estate partnered with Redbubble to create a fan art programme to mark the 25th anniversary of the release of his debut solo album. "As part of Redbubble's Partner Program, artists create fan art according to brand guidelines, and fans can purchase unique designs and have them printed on 120+ everyday, high-quality products on redbubble-.com," said a press statement on the deal.[122] It is being sold by the estate as a way of legitimising fan art that already exists and allowing fans to turn their creations into products for sale. The art, however, will first need to be approved by the estate, so there is an element of control – but this also gives the fans a sense of direct endorsement.

"That is a huge problem – all the bootlegging," says Nicole Beckett of Four Screens Management. "We have gone after that over the years. This strategy that's come up now is actually using Redbubble and places like this to make it legit and make a profit on what is the estate's rights to make a profit on. Now on Redbubble, you don't have any bootlegs. You only have estate-approved merchandise. So that means something – to have that stamp of approval."

As with living artists, the music might be what establishes and cements a legacy, but rarely is it providing the bulk of the income in the 21st century. Artists in the 1960s and 1970s could make their stance against brands and sponsorship a political one, but both society and the music business have changed dramatically over the last half-century.

"The past is a foreign country; they do things differently there," is how L. P. Hartley opened his 1953 novel *The Go-Between.* For some of the estates of older artists, a break from the past is something they are ideologically struggling with, even while the harsher economic realities of the modern music industry snap at their heels.

For the estates of contemporary artists, the brand world is all second nature precisely because it was second nature to the artists when they were still alive. Lil Peep (real name Gustav Elijah Åhr) died on 15 November 2017 but his estate has been incredibly proactive here, releasing a variety of clothing collections in a range of distinct tones that "pay homage to Lil Peep's signature bold hair colors". These retail for between $150 and $300 each.[123]

Launching a new collection in October 2020, Lil Peep's brother Oskar Ahr said, "I know that Peep's style and aesthetic are also very influential, and my brother told me himself that he had goals of getting more seriously involved in fashion. Taking influence from Gus' style is my favorite way of staying close to him. Cue my best effort to further the cultural impact of my younger brother in the fashion world: the Lil Peep 'Rockstar' Collection."[124]

This is the modern reality for all estates. Entering this world is not necessarily a betrayal of everything a deceased artist stood for, but ensuring quality control is critical. Pulling off a good deal here can bring in money and introduce an act to new generations of fans; but fumbling or forcing it is the quickest route to not just ignominy but something much worse – irrelevance.

CHAPTER 7

The Future of the Past

Museums and Auctions

What strikes you most when going inside is how small it is.

Occupying the top floors of 23 Brook Street in Mayfair, the flat where Jimi Hendrix lived in London between July 1968 and March 1969 is what mendacious landlords might describe as "bijou" or "cosy". The bed occupies most of the room and a portable TV squats on the floor. The feathers, drapes and rugs give it a rock-star-just-back-from-Marrakesh feel and the sparse furniture suggests it was a place to sleep rather than a place to entertain. Hendrix, however, conducted multiple interviews and photoshoots there, which is how it was able to be recreated with unnerving detail when it opened to the public in February 2016 as part of the newly expanded "Handel & Hendrix in London" house.[1]

George Frederick Handel had lived next door at number 25 between 1723 and 1759 and his home was opened to the public in November 2001, with the Handel House Trust expanding its remit to acquire and restore the flat where Hendrix lived and make it a dual attraction.[2] It is not an official visitor location, run by the estate in the same way Graceland or Paisley Park are; but it is a rare instance of the house as museum that draws in fans keen to drink in where their heroes lived and created at pivotal moments in their career.

During his brief time in the flat, Hendrix played two headline shows at the Royal Albert Hall in February 1969 and had appeared on the *Happening for Lulu* TV show on the BBC the previous month. His cover of Bob Dylan's 'All Along the Watchtower' was a number five hit in the UK charts in October 1968 and 'Crosstown Traffic' went into the Top 40 the month after he left the flat.[3] The recording of *Electric Ladyland*, the final album by the Jimi Hendrix Experience, was finished between April and August 1968 in New York, but Brook Street was his home during that time. The album was released in October 1968 and was a Top 10 hit in the UK by November that year.[4]

London was the key city for Hendrix. It was where he first made his name and where he was based during the most prolific and successful period of his life. He lived in other places in the capital, but Brook Street was where he set up home with Kathy Etchingham and was a short walk from Carnaby Street, the Marquee, the Bag O' Nails and the Scotch of St James – the very epicentre of Swinging London at the time.

This is why Brook Street resonates so much for his fans and why the opening of his flat in 2016 gave them a place to congregate and to contemplate. Hendrix never owned the flat, but that is inconsequential. He lived there at a critical period in his life and Hendrix fans are drawn there in the hope that it gives them a new insight into an artist at the white-heat peak of his creativity – a portal through time to a rich banquet of memories.

* * *

Shrines occur across all religions, these physical locations that take on incredible significance and power for believers. They are places to meet and be with others of the same faith. They are ways to connect with a religion or spirituality, to amplify what is already there or reinvigorate what is perhaps becoming dormant or questioned. They are also places for conversion. They become imbued with such potency and symbolism that they start to feel unreal – a tiny glimpse of a higher power from down here in the material world. Shrines are also a place to grieve, a location where people come for catharsis and understanding. They are either officially marked as such – like a church, a temple, a synagogue – or they are places that have a deep connection with an individual or a religion, often where a person of importance in that faith was born or where they died.

In the 20th century, celebrities took on quasi-religious meanings for their fans and so too did the physical locations and spaces where they lived, created and died. When Elvis died, fans flocked to the gates of Graceland and it has now become an annual event every August as part of Elvis Week.[5] When John Lennon was assassinated, fans held a candlelit gathering outside the Dakota building in New York as there was no public funeral for him.[6]

After Kurt Cobain took his own life, vigils took place all around Seattle, most notably at the Space Needle where up to 5,000 people attended and a recording of his widow, Courtney Love, reading out extracts from his suicide note was played to the crowd.[7]

When Michael Jackson died, his star on the Hollywood Walk of Fame became a mass congregation point, but it resulted in the bleakly comic incident where fans gathered at the wrong star – one dedicated to KABC talk show host Michael Jackson, who was very much alive – because the singer's star outside Grauman's Chinese Theatre "was covered by scaffolding in preparation for the 'Bruno' movie premiere".[8]

When David Bowie died, a mural of him on the side of Morley's department store in Brixton, a few streets from the south London house where he was born and grew up, became the epicentre of fan grief and it quickly took on such significance that Lambeth Council decided to list it in order to protect it.[9]

Fans need to come to these spots as part of the grieving process. Topography and memory are now woven so tightly together as to be iridescent. And just like religions, these places can also became commercialised. The gift shop in Lourdes is, after all, no different from the gift shop at Graceland.

KEEPING ELVIS'S HOME OPEN FOR THE AGES

"We've been able to grow it, to adapt it so that new, young generations find something that's relevant to them when they come here."

In the book's opening chapter, the story behind the opening of Graceland revealed that the decision to let in fans was done out of economic necessity because the Elvis estate was circling the plughole of insolvency. Since those shaky, uncertain days in the late 1970s and early 1980s, Graceland has become a branding and tourism powerhouse, the template for what everyone else – be it the estate itself or the owners of a building of cultural and historical significance – has tried to replicate.

Graceland, according to its official site, attracts over half a million visitors a year[10] – *Rolling Stone* stated in 2020 that it pulled in 700,000 people a year at its peak[11] – and *Forbes* claimed in 2018 that it is "the second-most visited house museum in the U.S. [...] Only the White House sees more tourists."[12]

It has evolved a lot since those early years when large parts of it were closed to the public, notably the upstairs rooms, lest Elvis's aunt Delta Presley Briggs and her dog Edmond (who both lived there) be disturbed. Key additions in that time include:

- the Elvis Presley Automobile Museum, opened in Graceland Plaza in 1989;

- the acquisition of the Graceland Crossing shopping centre in 1997, which had previously been independently owned and operated for just over a decade;

- the renovating and reopening of an existing hotel nearby, renamed Elvis Presley's Heartbreak Hotel in 1999, then closed in 2016 and replaced by The Guest House at Graceland;

- a new visitor centre announced in 2007, costing $125 million and involving a three-year refurbishment of the whole visitor experience that would "involve razing the cramped visitor centre and replacing it with an 80,000 sq ft facility – seven times the size of the house";[13]

- a new entertainment complex called Elvis Presley's Memphis at a cost of $45 million in 2017, replacing both the Graceland Plaza and the Graceland Crossing complexes and featuring "the world's largest and most comprehensive Elvis museum in the world", Elvis: The Entertainer Career Museum.

Graceland does not say how much it generates but it claims to have $150 million ("or possibly much more") in total economic impact annually on the city of Memphis from the tourists it brings in, employing 350 people part-time or full-time (rising to 450 in the summer, its busiest season).[14]

A visit to Graceland does not come cheap and there are four different tickets on sale that become a very visible test of just how big a fan each visitor is.[15]

At the bottom end is the Elvis Presley's Memphis + Planes tour, which costs between $25 (for children aged 4–10, with children under 4 getting in free) and $45.50 per visitor (those over 65 get a marginal discount and pay $41.25 for their ticket). This does not, it should be pointed out, get you access to Graceland Mansion.

The next bracket is the Elvis Experience tour, which costs up to $73 (seniors get in for $66.70 and children aged 4–10 get in for $42). This will also get you into Graceland.

For those willing to spend more, the Elvis Entourage VIP ticket costs $112.50 and there is no discount for the seniors or children aged 4–10, but thankfully those under 4 still benefit from free entry. This lets you hop to the front of the line for Graceland Mansion and you get a "backstage pass" as a keepsake.

Finally, for those who can spend like royalty, the Ultimate VIP Tour costs $184, but only children under the age of 2 get in for free. For that, you get assorted benefits such as access to the Ultimate Lounge and Exclusive VIP Exhibit, the option to buy merchandise that is only available to Ultimate guests, a meal voucher for Vernon's Smokehouse (where you can "enjoy classic southern cuisine and Elvis' favorite home cooking, including meatloaf, catfish and BBQ spaghetti"[16]), and an exclusive photo opportunity.[17]

(In February and March 2021, due to restrictions on public gatherings in light of the global pandemic, Graceland was selling virtual tours of the building and grounds. A two-hour tour cost $100, with a guide on hand to answer fan questions.[18])

It does not just draw in an audience who grew up with Elvis but who will eventually age out. In 2004, Jack Soden, president of Elvis Presley Enterprises, said that 53 per cent of visitors to Graceland were 35 or younger (so at that time, they had been, at most, 8 when Elvis died). "That's a great statistic," he said, but did not elaborate if they attended with people their own age or were simply accompanying their parents or grandparents.[19] He did add in 2019 that, "We've been able to grow it, to adapt it so that new, young generations find something that's relevant to them when they come here."[20] Again, a precise demographic breakdown was not forthcoming.

Despite the massive economic contribution it makes to the local area and its position as a major employer, Graceland's aggressive expansion plans have not always landed well with those in the city's planning and finance departments.

In 2018, Elvis Presley Enterprises was battling with the City of Memphis in the courts over plans to build a 6,200-seat arena in the city.[21] It announced the plans for the venue in August 2017, with development costs of between $40 million and $50 million, and claims it could bring 50 events there a year, the idea being to extend the stay of the tourists to Graceland late into the night after the house itself had closed for the day. It had originally approached Memphis City Council in 2014 with plans for a venue and asked for tax support. Joel Weinshanker, who manages Graceland, argued that this expansion was critical for its future survival as a business, saying it drew in 750,000 people in its peak year in 1997, but this had slipped to 550,000 a year.

By June 2018, Memphis City Council members were raising questions around Elvis Presley Enterprises and asking if it was using a Graceland redevelopment plan as a Trojan horse to smuggle through its arena plans. While laying out his case, Weinshanker rained blows on the city's politicians, in an op-ed piece for *Commercial Appeal/USA Today*. "When we first tried to secure financing for the Guest House at Graceland – the largest new hotel construction in Memphis in 90 years – we were met with resistance," he said. "No bank in the United States would consider taking the risk. They scoffed at building a large luxury hotel in Whitehaven. No one thought it was a good bet. The only way the project was able to move forward was with me personally guaranteeing the loan."[22] His core argument was that Graceland was a major tourist destination and played a key role in keeping the memory of Elvis alive. It also plays a key role in keeping the *business* of the memory of Elvis alive.

Graceland serves as a figurehead for the entire tourist attraction business within music. It was the first major example of a musician's home being turned into a tourist location and, therefore, is also the first major example of such a tourist attraction facing the challenges of ageing out and becoming a dusty architectural anachronism.

With so much of the estates business, it often comes back to Elvis. In the 1980s and 1990s, it paved the way and showed other estates how to become a commercial and cultural juggernaut. It also showed the need to evolve, adding new moving parts in order to endure. But almost half a century after he died, the Elvis estate is also the first major estate to wake up to the fact that, unless it does something, it might not be in the top-earning estates for the next half-century.

And sitting at the beating heart of all of this, through all those decades and through all the bad times as well as all the good times, is Graceland.

STEPPING INTO PRINCE'S PRIVATE WORLD

"We treat those rules as being sacred"

Elvis and Prince may have both died in their homes, but in the latter's case the estate did not wait around to get the ticket booth up and running. Prince died on 21 April 2016 and Paisley Park – his Chanhassen, Minnesota, home and studio since 1987 – welcomed its first paying guests on 28 October 2016.

In that interim period, the administrators of the estate had to issue a statement denying that Paisley Park was going to be sold, alongside a number of other properties owned by the star. The rumour originated on *TMZ* but the Bremer Trust (the bank the Minnesota courts appointed to administer his estate until the rightful heirs could be identified) said this was false.[23] The *Guardian*, however, summarised a piece from *Vice* (subsequently deleted online) that claimed Owen Husney, Prince's first manager, was saying that Prince was planning to turn Paisley Park into a Graceland-style visitor attraction before his death.[24]

This was confirmed by Ken Abdo, a partner at legal firm Fox Rothschild LLP, who represented three of the half-siblings of Prince – who were all eventually adjudicated as heirs – with regard to the singer dying intestate. "The thing there was to complete what was seen to be [started]," he says. "Prince had already commenced work on creating a museum environment for Paisley Park. [They had to] go in and take inventory of all the property and all the memorabilia and finish decorating the rooms in the building. It was a big project, but it's successful."

The museum idea, as it turns out, was to be fast-tracked by the administrators. There was a deep symbolism, a real passing of the torch, in the fact that Joel Weinshanker was to be involved in the opening of Paisley Park to the public. Soon after Prince died, Weinshanker approached the Bremer Trust to see what could be done to keep the estate active during this time of uncertainty. The heirs, whoever they were going to be, were going to face a substantial tax bill: no will means no estate tax planning and this can often sink heirs. "There [was] a tax issue because he was exposed to about 50 per cent of estate tax – federal and state tax – so there's an issue and evaluation," says Abdo.

Making Paisley Park a museum was going to be the quickest and easiest way to start making money out of an asset that – barring its sporadic use as a recording studio by acts like Madonna, REM and Stevie Wonder in the 1980s and 1990s – had barely been commercialised. Living quarters are, however, closed to visitors.

As with Graceland, there is tiered pricing. The Paisley Experience costs $45 and runs for 70 minutes; it gives visitors access to the main floor (including studios), the soundstage/concert hall where he rehearsed and NPG Music Club where he held late-night performances. For $85, the VIP Experience adds on an extra 30 minutes and includes access to "additional content, rooms, and studio areas", viewing of additional artefacts from the archives and what is described as "a unique and exclusive photo opportunity". Finally, The Ultimate Experience lasts for three hours and costs $160. For that there is access to Studios A, B, and C (including audio playback in the control room of Studio B), private screening of exclusive video footage in the building's editing suite, viewing access to even more artefacts and the serving of "light beverages" at the end of the three hours.[25] [26]

"Absent its owner, Paisley Park is a husk," concluded the *New Yorker* in June 2018 after its tour. It did add, however, that "there's something profound about how Paisley Park insists on maintaining Prince's privacy".[27] It concluded, "During parties, Prince sometimes stood in a dark corner of the balcony and watched other people dance. Visiting Paisley Park now evokes a similar sensation – of being near Prince, but never quite with him."[28]

In October 2019, the Prince estate named Alan Seiffert as executive director of Paisley Park and also appointed two entertainment development companies – MR-ProFun and Mycotoo – to "enhance the overall experience for guests touring the facility".[29] Seiffert joined from Midnight Blue Management where, as president, he was focused on a range of live events. "My role is to very much keep the idea of Paisley Park and the vision for Paisley Park alive, to build upon it and very much drive the vision that Prince had," says Seiffert. "Because I'm a member and part of the overall Prince estate, what I do here is very much aligned with and coordinated with what the overall initiatives are for the estate and, as such, for the heirs."

Seiffert says that Prince was already some way along in terms of converting Paisley Park into an operational museum – with some of the spaces and walls used in the experience having been designed by him before he died.

Beyond the actual ticket sales, there is another commercial thrust to Paisley Park in utilising the studios and the 25,000-square foot soundstage and getting in artists, ad agencies, TV companies and film studios to hire them. "There are three elements to the building," explains Seiffert. "There's what we call the museum portion with the artefacts exploring Prince's life and his music. Then there are the recording studios. And then we have the soundstage where we've done concert performances etc."

The word "authentic" is one Seiffert and the estate seem to use a great deal, continually asking themselves if what they are doing feels "authentic" to Prince and his legacy. "He would want to amplify, enrich and really work with and really give exposure to a lot of different artists," he says. "Our job here is we're never going to be Prince, obviously, but we can at least try to, to the best of our abilities and with the creative instincts that we have, really focus on how we can end up amplifying artists who are authentic and unique. I think that's what he did and I know that that's something that he had strived for."

While Paisley Park is so woven into the legacy of Prince, there is finite space to exhibit items and Seiffert says he and the estate are not discounting the idea of items being collated for a touring exhibition in the same vein as *David Bowie Is*. "Paisley Park is a destination and is part of that idea that, to understand Prince, you need to really visit and understand and see and explore and experience Paisley Park," he says. "We've, in the past, done loans to the Met in New York and to the Rock and Roll Hall of Fame. There's a slew of requests for different artefacts. We are selective about it."

Seiffert reveals that part of the running of the space is determined by how Prince conducted his own life. Prince did not allow photos in certain parts of the building and those remain photo-free spaces on the tours. But this was not, Seiffert says, something that was universally imposed on every square inch of Paisley Park so he feels that gives them, as operators of a tourist attraction, some wriggle room. "One of the myths [...] were some rules about photography," he says. "What we decided to do was to actually open up photography in very specific spaces. You can go in the front of the building and then you can go at the very end of the tour, because those were areas in which Prince did allow photography. Not all the time, but he did take pictures back there."

Family members, however, stressed that upstairs was closed to everyone when Prince was alive – so that rule remains. "There are certain ground rules that we keep to this day," he says. "Prince would allow fish and veggies – that's it. So no chicken, no beef, whatever. So we keep to that now. He did not allow photos in parts of the building and he did not allow smoking on the property. We treat those rules as being sacred."

A possible option for the future is creating a membership programme, but Seiffert would not elaborate on that. He says this is all part of trying to ensure they can "stay fresh and stay relevant" with what they offer to visitors. "Prince had a saying," he mentions by way of illustration. "People would ask, 'Why do you go to the bakery every single day?' 'Because I want fresh bread every single day.' I think with that idea, whether it's a museum or otherwise, it is important for them to maintain the relevance [...] to keep art and these stories alive."

He is, however, wary of chasing trends – something that all museums face in the shape of an exhibition arms race, where the "new" (new technologies, new ways of presenting and new approaches to curating ideas) can some-times be venerated over the "good" or the "interesting" and they can quickly start to feel like desperate novelties. "You've got to keep it relevant," he says. "It doesn't mean that you cater every two years to the next generation that is named by Madison Avenue in New York. It doesn't mean you have to be overly commercialised but it does mean, I think, that you have to just continue to be fresh every day."

SEEING HOW HENDRIX LIVED IN LONDON

"When you go into this flat it's literally as if he's just gone out for a pint of milk"

The Handel & Hendrix in London house not being an official part of the Jimi Hendrix estate comes with challenges in terms of what it can do, what it can display and how it markets itself; but it also means it does not have to tread as gingerly around the sensitivities and the politics that are part and parcel of some estates. There are absolute constraints in some regards and absolutely no constraints in other regards.

Claire Davies is deputy director of Handel & Hendrix in London and oversees all curation and displays there as well as being in charge of loans and exhibitions. She says the appeal of Brook Street, especially to Hendrix fans, is the "sense of pilgrimage" which she says "seems to be key to music fans – to literally come and touch a wall that Hendrix touched".

The haptic is critical to the space and visitors are encouraged to touch items and parts of the building. Much of Hendrix's room is based on recreations of items like furniture and bedding so there is less concern about something historic and invaluable being damaged. The oval mirror, however, hanging on the bedroom wall, is the original from his time there.

"There's that amazing exchange with the visitor where they look into the mirror that Jimi looked into and that's quite a magical thing," says Davies. "We play on the small-time intimacy that this space has." She refers to it as "tactile space" and adds that they do have valuable original items but they are only display behind glass in a different room.

A design company called Outside Studios was brought in to forensically analyse all the photos taken of Hendrix in the flat to work out what items there were and where identical items – such as heavy velvet turquoise curtains that were originally bought from department store John Lewis – could be sourced. For more one-off items, such as certain wall hangings, they were digitally recreated.[30] "We try to be precise," says Davies. "I feel like it's important."

This need for verisimilitude is critical, especially for a space where the original items are not available. What is taking place is a piece of historically accurate *trompe-l'œil* as a type of workaround – giving the impression of what was there without drawing too much attention to the fact that these items are not the exact ones fans will know from photographs of the rooms. "There's a scientist in me that just wants it to be [neatly ordered]," says Davies. "I sometimes get a bit envious about National Trust properties who are curating a space as it was left."

Fans are seeking that point of connection and a real location peppered with real objects from that individual can amplify all that for the visitor. "I think people come to understand the context in which that creativity happened," she says of opening up the rooms where Hendrix lived for a period. "You literally have a three-dimensional representation of that." It is all amplified by the fact that these were domestic spaces and the fan, half a century on, can get to look behind what would have been closed doors. "One of the things I love the most about the domestic story we have of Hendrix is that we can really delve into that private persona which is so contrary to perhaps to his legend and his public persona," says Davies. "Just the idea of him enjoying English breakfast tea or watching *Coronation Street* is actually just normalising this very unique man."

She feels the lack of official connection to the Hendrix estate is not a drawback to what they can do with the space. She also feels the way it is run – as a trust – means they can operate with relative autonomy as the estate knows they are not going to do anything that would be detrimental to his image. "There's no animosity but there's also no agreement there," she says of the Hendrix family. "To be frank we're quite small fry in the grand scheme of the Hendrix estate simply because we're not really very commercially driven [as part of a trust]. They are much more interested in the bigger picture."

The one drawback, however, is that none of his original recordings can play in the rooms because of licensing issues. Perhaps that is fitting in a way if this is to work as a time capsule as Hendrix would have been more likely to play other people's music when he was at home as opposed to his own. In that sense, then, it is a true portal into how he lived for that relatively short period of time. The visitor is eavesdropping, peeking through doors and through time.

"It is literally stepping inside someone's world – it's that whole point of empathy," says Davies. "When you go into this flat it's literally as if he's just gone out for a pint of milk."

PROPERTY MANAGEMENT: HOMES IN THE SHADOW OF GRACELAND

Other deceased artists have had their homes open to the public, but few have the deep and symbolic association that Graceland has with Elvis or Paisley Park has with Prince. Few, also, have done anything even approaching this scale. Handel & Hendrix in London sits in its own curious hinterland – not an official attraction as sanctioned by the estate, and not so immediately synonymous with the artist; but as it draws in more people and becomes known as a place of pilgrimage it retrospectively takes on a deeper connection with the artist. There are other Hendrix homes but none are open to the public in this way so, to all intents and purposes, Handel & Hendrix in London takes on an "unofficially official" resonance for fans.

The Bob Marley Museum at 56 Hope Road, Kingston, Jamaica was where the reggae star lived after 1975 and was where the Tuff Gong label was also based. It was converted into a museum in 1987 by Rita Marley, his widow.

Tickets cost $25 for a 75-minute tour. "All the original rooms have been kept as they were when Bob lived here to ensure authenticity," says the website.[31]

A 2001 feature in the *Guardian*, however, described it as relatively small: "Both gift shops would easily fit into the porch of one of Graceland's" and said that "labyrinthine legal disputes" were holding back what the estate could do with the house. "This extraordinary legal backdrop helps explain why there is no Graceland-style machine, why Marley's life and death have been of such little benefit to the Jamaican economy," it said.[32]

The costs involved in taking over a building where an artist lived and turning it into a tourist attraction are enormous and planning permission is an administrative nightmare – which puts off all but the richest estates or trusts with supportive backers. Plus the ex-owner needs to be at a certain level of fame to even have the potential to draw in regular paying visitors 12 months a year and justify the heavy initial investment costs.

Plans to turn one of Janis Joplin's childhood homes at 4048, Procter Street, Port Arthur, Texas, into a museum came to nothing and the building was demolished in 1980, although the developer did seek to sell off bricks as souvenirs to fans.[33] A local man, Michael Petry, reportedly bought all the salvage bricks he could and they were subsequently sold to Port Arthur's Museum of the Gulf Coast; by 2015 they were selling in the museum's gift shop for $35 each.[34]

The Beech Island mansion near Augusta that belonged to James Brown was also considered by the estate as being worthy of conversion into a museum, with indications in 2015 that the process was under way. The estate had reportedly spent $500,000 repairing it and keeping it maintained. "It's history," said Russell Bauknight, who manages the Brown estate. "You just can't get it any more. My job is to preserve history."[35] Nothing, however, could happen until all the issues and challenges to Brown's will had been resolved. At the time of writing, a final resolution had not been reached.

Having a museum in the home of a pop star gives it a phenomenal resonance and a sense of spectacle, but the potential audience is always going to have a natural ceiling. They are for super-fans who are prepared to travel to very specific locations almost exclusively to visit that home-cum-museum-cum-shrine. To capitalise on this fan base, the National Trust in the UK, for example, has been buying up the childhood homes of pop stars including John Lennon, David Bowie and Freddie Mercury.[36]

There are, however, a number of museums that are purpose-built to honour a musician, which are not restricted so much by location and available space. They can be both official and unofficial with a commercial remit; or they can be academic collections for research purposes that can also be seen by the public. They offer a different lens on the artist, bringing rich insights.

THE MUSEUM MAN

"People want to see something that this person wore or touched or lived in"

Bill Miller is the founder of Icon Entertainment Group and has, it is fair to say, museums in his blood. For him it derives from fandom rather than pure museology. Johnny Cash, Patsy Cline, Frank Sinatra and Roy Orbison are all artists he grew up loving and he channelled that fandom into creating museums and attractions around each of them.

The starting point for it all was Cash and his friendship with the country singer. Miller was 13 in 1973 when he first met Cash at a concert in Denver, Colorado. "He handed me a harmonica he'd just played while he was on stage," he said. "That was the first of many gifts from him."[37]

He says he created the Johnny Cash Museum in Nashville simply because no one else had even thought to open one and the County Music Hall of Fame had, in his view, "very, very little Johnny Cash in there". Nashville, he felt, should honour Cash as Cash helped put the city on the music map. "I thought it was a crime for my friend who had blessed my life and inspired me in so many ways to have nothing at all honouring him in the town that he branded," he says.

From his youth, Miller was collecting artefacts related to Cash, a situation that accelerated when they became friends. He describes that time as "a search and rescue mission" to ensure important items were not lost. He would gather items sporadically – some from eBay, some from family members – but "there was absolutely no method to my madness". Everything was stored in his house, but he says he "did not have an altar to Johnny Cash in my home".

Cash also gave him items over the years "that he wanted to be sure would be in the right hands", but the starting point for the museum was, of all people, Richard Nixon. Nixon was a Cash fan and had him play to 250 guests in the East Room of the White House on 17 April 1970.[38] The Richard Nixon Presidential Library and Museum wanted to do an exhibit to mark Cash's 70th birthday (in February 2002) and approached Miller to loan out a number of items for what was to be the first non-Nixon exhibition it had put on.

He recalls, "They sent a team of seven curators, all with white cotton gloves, which is kind of funny because I wasn't a museum guy." But the way his previously disorganised collection was expertly presented and displayed by the Nixon team planted a seed in Miller's brain. "When I saw the black suit in a case with a spotlight on it that made it look like one of the crown jewels, it really, really awoke me to how important the selection really was," he says. A subsequent loan of items to the Fender Centre for the Performing Arts served to reinforce what he was thinking of doing.

He and his wife, Shannon, decided that a Cash museum in Nashville was how they needed to present this lifetime of collecting. "There was never any plan," he says. "It opened without a business plan. I would say that it was totally out of love and emotion as opposed to business."

Miller had also been involved with Cash on an aborted plan to open a theme park (Cash Country) in Branson, Missouri, in the early 1990s. The plan was that Cash would go into semi-retirement there and perform at a purpose-built 4,000-seat venue when the urge took him. A museum was going to be one of the attractions within the theme park. Cash, however, met producer Rick Rubin in 1993 and together they embarked on a series of albums – starting with *American Recordings* in 1994 – that completely revived his career and repositioned him in the market.[39] "So he went from potential relative obscurity in Branson, Missouri, to that amazing third rebirth of his career," says Miller. "So, thank God Branson didn't happen. Thank God we didn't do *that* museum. Thank God that we did *this* museum."

Miller opened his museum in 2013, a decade after Cash passed away, and it operates on a licence from the Cash estate relating to name, image and likeness. "I won't get into business details," he says, "but we do have a licence agreement with them where they receive royalties. It's a great relationship that we have with them." By 2017, the museum had seen over a million visitors. "We had no idea," says Miller. "We would have been happy with 200 or 300 visitors a day." Josh Matas of Sandbox Entertainment Group, which helps to run the Cash estate, says, "The museum is, quite frankly, an incredible illustration of the passion and interest there is around Johnny Cash."

The estate and Miller worked together to open Johnny Cash's Kitchen and Saloon, a 15,000 sq. ft restaurant beside the museum, in July 2019.[40] "Obviously, we're intimately involved in the nuances of that space," says Matas, "but we're not operators of hospitality spaces, so it is great to have a partner who is [qualified] in that."

Miller says that the success of the museum is down in a large part to the fact that Cash's appeal is global and it passes down through generations (arguably a continuation of what the *American Recordings* series started in the 1990s). "If you walk through there during the season, you will see every demographic, every age, every ethnicity, every sexual orientation, everything you can ever imagine," says Miller. "Mohawks, pierced lips, 90-year-old women with walkers – they all come together. I have seen children aged nine years old dragging their parents to the museum – not vice versa. One day I was in the gift shop and a group overheard me talking and figured out that I was the owner. They introduced themselves and there were five generations of Johnny Cash fans there. There was a 101-year-old woman from Texas celebrating her birthday that day. I met the kids, the grandkids, great-grandkids, and the latest, great-great-grandchild who was in a stroller. They were all influenced by Johnny Cash."

He says that only 10 per cent of visitors use the senior citizen discount on tickets, which he reads as proof that Cash has a "vibrant, youthful audience", although he does not say what proportion of them are coming with older relatives. "I hear all the time about other museums and organisations that are extremely concerned because their demographic is literally dying," he says, "whereas there's a new Cash fan being born every day."

The Cash museum building expanded in 2017 to house the Patsy Cline Museum in the floor above, but each museum is run separately.[41] Cline had died on 5 March 1963 in a plane crash but Miller was in talks with Charlie Dick, Cline's husband since 1957, with a view to opening a museum dedicated to her. "He was a larger-than-life personality with whom nothing would happen if he didn't want it to happen – no matter what," says Miller. "He was very hesitant during his lifetime to exploit Patsy in any way." Dick passed away on 8 November 2015[42] and Miller continued conversations with Julie, one of Dick and Cline's two daughters. One original idea was a Cline-themed honky-tonk bar, but when the second floor of the building housing the Cash museum became free, the idea for a Cline museum gathered pace.

Cline's family had held on to furniture from her house in the early 1960s and it was this, along with the items Julie found in the safe (like handwritten lyrics for 'Walkin' After Midnight' and 'I Fall to Pieces'), that convinced Miller they had enough to work with, even though he says there are no audio or video interviews with her in existence, items that most music-centric museums regard as their bread and butter. There were, however, a multitude of letters from a number of pen pals Cline had throughout her career. "I really believe that museums should be artefact-heavy," he says. "Graphics are great, copy is great, digital footage and audio are great – but to really do a world-class museum, people want to see something that this person wore or touched or lived in." This was bulked up with the loan of costumes from an organisation in Cline's home town of Winchester, Virginia.

Miller is also in talks with the Roy Orbison estate to help it open a museum dedicated to the singer. Finding a location, however, is proving difficult. "Nashville has got at the point where all the 'beachfront' [i.e. prime real estate] properties are taken up," he says. "When something does come available, it is just ridiculous. You're almost looking at New York prices per square foot for real estate."

Chuck Fleckenstein is general manager and COO of Roy's Boys, Orbison Music and Publishing and Still Working Music and helps run the Orbison estate. He says the planned Orbison museum is "to be frank, piggybacking off the great success" of the Cash and Cline museums. "I am working with Bill to make sure that we have the best Roy Orbison museum possible," he says. "The Roy Orbison museum is [...] going to be full of Roy Orbison memorabilia that we have from all over the world."

Many of the Orbison artefacts are split between the estate's offices at the Orbison Building in Nashville and the Iron Mountain storage facility. "We have a huge – I don't know if 'archive' is the right word, 'collection' is probably a better word – of Roy memorabilia that's going to go into the museum," says Fleckenstein. "We're also pretty confident – and I know they experienced this with Cash and Cline – that once you put a museum out there, items seem to appear out of the woodwork and people bring you things."

In June 2020, Fleckenstein told the *Nashville Business Journal* that the museum was scheduled to open in 2021 and would create 20 or more full-time jobs for the city of Nashville. "People can expect a thorough immersion into everything of the great, late Roy Orbison," he said. "It'll showcase Roy's career that was a roller coaster, but also extraordinarily fruitful."[43]

Miller says that the location of a museum is important but the building itself is incidental. It is what is in the museum that is doing the heavy lifting, not the architecture. "Let's make the artefacts the star of the show," he says. "Present the artefacts and present the story accurately. Of course, my museum is beautiful. I put it against anybody's. But I think people go off the rails when they start thinking about being fancy and the structure in which it is housed rather than the meat of the matter."

*   *   *

In June 2020, the Tim Bergling Foundation announced plans to open the Avicii Experience in Stockholm city centre to celebrate the music of the Swedish dance superstar who tragically took his own life on 20 April 2018 when he was just 28.

It described the planned museum as "an intensively emotional tribute" to the musician that would follow "Tim's journey from a reclusive music nerd to a celebrated superstar".[44] It will include unseen photos and videos as well as unheard music. It added that a portion of the revenues will go to the Tim Bergling Foundation, which campaigns for better mental health awareness and helps to fund research into the causes and prevention of suicide as well as aiding the climate change, poverty and environmental organisations that Avicii supported in his lifetime.

Per Sundin is the CEO of Pophouse Entertainment Group and co-founder of the Avicii Experience. He also sits on the board of the Tim Bergling Foundation and, before that, was MD of Universal Music Sweden, helping to sign Avicii to the major. He says that Avicii had been fascinated by the ABBA Museum in Stockholm and before he died had talked about possibly doing something similar around his music. Klas Bergling, father of Tim, met with Sundin to discuss how they could take this idea and turn it into a tribute to his late son. Some of the team involved with the ABBA Museum were recruited to take it to fruition and plans started to be put in place in 2019.

"We are constantly meeting people who have been involved in Tim's career through the years and just checking with them," says Sundin. "We are trying to keep his memory valid – showing why he was a genius and how he composed music."

The development team spent a period of time travelling around the world looking at other museums and exhibitions to ensure that what they do here is as up to date as possible and based around best practice from successful exhibitions. "They have been doing all that so it doesn't feel old fashioned and traditional," says Sundin. "It must taste fresh." Talking the year before the Avicii Experience opened and while the layout was still being finalised, Sundin suggested that up to five unheard tracks could feature. "What I am 100 per cent sure of is we're going to play the music how it sounded when he passed away," he says. "Then you can compare that with what the producer did. On his computer there were more than 150 songs – sketches, short demos, clips. Tim was more of a starter than a finisher. He loved to start different songs and then work with collaborators to finish them in the end. He started new things all the time."

Sundin says that the museum will not gloss over aspects of Tim's life as he and Tim's family believe this is critical to telling the full story. "We're not hiding from it," he says. "He took his own life when he was 28. It's a sad story. It's going to be really uplifting, but it's also going to have some melancholic stories about everything that happened."

He says that the museum and exhibition can only do so much to introduce future generations to the music of Avicii and that the estate will be focused more on things like streaming to keep him relevant in the future. "The democratisation of music and the music streaming services also help the new generation to embrace the superstars from the past," says Sundin. "If I owned the brand Avicii, that is more important than the exhibition – even though the exhibition is super cool and important to have a place to go to think about Tim's legacy. I don't see it as a worldwide campaign but more a place in Stockholm where you can go."

John Branca, who runs the Michael Jackson estate, makes a similar point when discussing the role of exhibitions for the business he is in charge of. "We had a traveling exhibit called *Michael Jackson: On the Wall* at the National Portrait Gallery in London that then was exhibited in Paris, in Germany and in Scandinavia, with some of the most decorated artists of the 20th and 21st centuries paying homage to Michael," he says. "You're not going to make your money from an exhibition; they are more like advertising and promotion for the brand. But it's good to own them. It's good to have them."

THE ACADEMIC AND INSTITUTIONAL ARCHIVE

Bob Dylan chose in his lifetime to sell his personal archive of 6,000 items to the George Kaiser Family Foundation and the University of Tulsa in 2016 for a figure estimated at between \$15 million and \$20 million.[45] For certain estates, this is an option to make money or to have someone else take charge of putting a multitude of items in order and on display; or sometimes it can be both.

In the mid-1980s, Vladimir Horowitz established the Horowitz Archives at Yale University School of Music and when he died two years later his will stipulated that "his memorabilia, musical scores, correspondence, recital transcripts, photographs, awards and trophies, along with programs from concerts during his career" would also be donated to the archives there.[46] Items of note belonging to his widow Wanda Toscanini Horowitz, who died in 1998, were also added. It was built up from 12 separate donations between 1986 and 1992 from Horowitz himself and his widow.

It is all still stored at Yale and the full collection includes "correspondence, programs, photographs, clippings, scrapbooks, contracts, royalty statements, awards, certificates, jewelry, and a wide range of memorabilia".[47] There are also 218 recordings from his Carnegie Hall recitals in the 1940s and 1950s. Yale adds that all papers are available to qualified researchers and there are no restricted papers in the archive.

There is also a form of cultural and historical validation in having a university take custody of these items, elevating the musicians involved far beyond mere entertainers and anointing them as great artists for the ages.

In June 2018, the Institute of Jazz Studies at Rutgers University in New Jersey acquired an archive of close to 1,000 items belonging to jazz pianist Count Basie. It included instruments, such as organs and pianos, as well as letters, business records, concert programmes and even housewares.[48] Of even greater significance was that Rutgers also obtained rights to Basie's name, image and likeness – as well as associated trademarks – as part of the deal.

"We have home recordings, newspaper clippings, correspondence, love letters to his wife and daughter, telegrams when he was ill from Duke Ellington and Oscar Peterson and Frank Sinatra – just wonderful stuff that fans of the music would be interested in," said Wayne Winborne, the executive director of Rutgers' Institute of Jazz Studies. "But also ledgers – the amount they paid the band – things that historians and writers will be interested in. We've got his home collection of books and records, suits, his signature cap, tailor-made articles of clothing that he would wear on gigs."[49]

Bob Donnelly, from legal firm Fox Rothschild, works with the Basie estate and explains how the deal with Rutgers came about. "There are two reasons," he says. "One, Count Basie was from New Jersey. And two, Rutgers probably has the single greatest collection of jazz archives of any university in the country. They have a very active programme there and the fellow who runs it is very well respected."

Donnelly also works with the Erroll Garner estate and explains that his archive was treated in a slightly different way when it went to the University of Pittsburgh compared to how Basie's was at Rutgers. "The estate wanted to remain very active in continuing to put out his work," he says of the Garner archive. "Even though all of the original masters and the arrangements and scores and photos and so on reside at University of Pittsburgh, there is nothing in the deal [...] that prevents the estate from exploiting those masters. Which is what they've continued to do." He adds, "In the case of Count Basie, those exploitation rights were sold to a third-party publishing company that is continuing to do the same thing. They're continuing to put this stuff out – even though scholars are free to go to the archives at Rutgers and do their research on all of that material."

In November 2018, the archive of another jazz pianist, Billy Strayhorn – made up of 18,000 documents, of which 3,000 were classed as music items (such as sheet music) – was acquired by the Library of Congress in Washington, DC. Not all the items at the time were digitised, but it was all made available to the public.

This is another form of validation beyond what universities can bestow on an archive, indicating that the items contained within are of national importance and national interest. As the *New York Times* put it, "By placing Strayhorn's papers at the Library of Congress, rather than at the nearby Smithsonian Institution, which houses [Duke] Ellington's papers, the estate is making a symbolic point about Strayhorn's stand-alone genius."[50]

Outside of jazz and classical, the Lou Reed Archive was opened at the New York Public Library in March 2019. It has been donated by Reed's widow, the musician Laurie Anderson, and includes notes, photographs and up to 600 hours of recordings. It took two years to catalogue all the items and the library created 6,000 library cards featuring a 1972 shot of Reed to mark the occasion.

Anderson told the *New York Times* that it was imperative to have a major institution preserve and showcase all the items no matter how sprawling the collection was. "It's very important to be able to present raw material and let people make up their own minds," she said.[51]

THE SMALL AND THE FAN-RUN

Not all museums dedicated to musical artists are major operations and their small size can become part of their charm. And then there are ones set up by fans – without the involvement of the estate or heirs – that make up in enthusiasm for what they might lack in expert curation.

The Midland Continental Depot Transport Museum in Wimbledon, North Dakota, includes a renovated depot building where, on the top floor, Peggy Lee lived with her family when she was a child. It was opened in May 2012.[52] Holly Foster Wells, granddaughter of Lee and the person in charge of her estate, says it is "kind of in the middle of nowhere, but it is a world-class museum".

As part of the celebrations marking what would have been Lee's 100th birthday in 2020, the estate put together an exhibition at the Heritage Centre in Los Angeles and there was also a celebration in North Dakota for her. "They hired a firm out of Seattle to create the exhibit," says Foster Wells. "This executive came here to my office for a week and did nothing but scan items, photos and memorabilia; she also scanned her [Peggy's] scrapbooks.

From these images, she created these panels that are on display there. In addition, they do have some gowns of hers and other three-dimensional objects. They have a listening station."

She adds that a restricted number of valuable items went to the North Dakota museum – not because they did not want to send them but because the operators of the Midland Continental Depot Transport Museum simply did not have the infrastructure to handle it all. "They didn't want to have a lot of tangible artefacts just because of security," she says. "It is a little town and they don't have security guards. But they do have a few items. It's really beautiful."

The Ramones museum in Berlin is not official, but a blind eye is turned by the estates who look after the Ramones as it is small and clearly a fan endeavour, set up by Flo Hayler.[53] "I don't mind it," says Linda Ramone, widow of Johnny Ramone. "He's [Hayler] a real fan. It's fine, it's nice, it's a small museum. It's good for fans to go and he enjoys doing it. I don't mind it because I like him. But I'd rather have a Ramones museum that's put up by us."

Perhaps the most singular fan-run museum is the Musée Édith Piaf in Paris. It is located in the French singer's apartment on rue Crespin du Gast where she lived at the start of her career. It is free to visit but it does not have an official website, only a phone number. Tours are offered strictly by appointment, with the only slots open between 1pm and 6pm on Mondays, Tuesdays and Wednesdays. It was set up by Bernard Marchois, a fan who met Piaf in 1958 when he was 17. He also lives in the apartment but two rooms are devoted to keeping the memory of Piaf, who passed away in 1963, very much alive. He has kept the same hours since the museum opened in 1967 and tours are only conducted in French.

Visitors are greeted by a life-size (4 ft 8 in.) cardboard cut-out of the singer, and a stuffed bear, as tall as she was and gifted to her by her husband, occupies one of the chairs. There are many photos of her as well as one of her trademark black dresses and a pair of her shoes.

"The space has a sense of intimacy not often achieved in a museum, perhaps because the collection itself, with all its sad memories, is in a private home," noted the *Guardian* on its visit in 2012. "Or, maybe it's that reading her correspondence with family and friends scattered among her personal belongings, feels private and slightly voyeuristic."[54]

The *Paris Review* visited in 2017 and noted, "Paris is filled with strange museums – from the museum of absinthe to the museum of carnival equipment – but the Musée Édith Piaf is among the strangest."[55] It noted that the small space feels crowded and Marchois said this was intentional. "We did not want to make a traditional museum," he said. "We wanted to make a space that felt inhabited."[56] He is adamant that he is performing an important cultural duty to ensure that Piaf is not forgotten in her home country. "Her public will never forget her, but the media can," he warned. "Piaf must not die a second death."[57]

"A DISTILLED NARRATIVE WITHIN A FINITE SPACE": THE GENERALIST MUSEUM

The generalist music museum is a very different proposition from the one devoted to a specific artist. On the one hand, they can write their own brief and change what they cover, making space for touring exhibitions. On the other hand, they are somewhat restricted by the generality of what they do – having to pull in a diverse audience and not having the space or material to explore a subject in the way the specialist museums can.

They all, however, have a calling and a role far beyond the objects they put in glass cases for the public to look at as they shuffle past.

"Museums have been central to the institutionalization of popular music heritage," argued Lauren Istvandity, Raphaël Nowak and Sarah Baker in the introduction to their 2019 book *Curating Pop: Exhibiting Popular Music in the Museum*. "Museum curators are cultural agents, in that they 'participate in a production of cultural value' [...] and take on a great responsibility in communicating popular music's past."[58]

The generalist museum presents a unique challenge to the curator as they must "navigate how to feature star performers within exhibitions alongside lesser-known artists in the popular music canon".[59] What they are doing through their choices on what artists to feature, and what artefacts to feature around them, is an act of "cultural consecration" by selecting a handful of acts they deem worthy of veneration.[60]

In doing so, they are striking a delicate balance between venerating lesser-known acts but also featuring the kinds of acts who can draw in crowds large enough to make the whole enterprise economically viable. They also have to be keenly attuned to what they are presenting being both interesting and enjoyable for the visitor as they are "rooted within the experience economy".[61] This has implications for what they choose to focus on and how they tell the story through the objects they put on display. At the heart of this is the "signature object" – or what non-academics would call the show-stopper object – which is an "artefact imbued with the power to stand in for a wider array of ephemera and memorabilia, to capture visitors' attention and convey the essence of the story being told".[62]

Jacob McMurray is the director of curatorial, collections and exhibits at the Museum of Pop Culture in Seattle (known colloquially as MoPOP). He explains how it was originally opened in 2000 by former Microsoft executive Paul Allen as the Experience Music Project and was devoted to Jimi Hendrix. Allen grew up as a Hendrix obsessive and, when he became wealthy, started buying up items at auction that belonged to Hendrix, including the white Fender Stratocaster he played at Woodstock in 1969, eventually amassing enough material to open a museum space devoted exclusively to Hendrix. (Allen was also a key figure in helping the Hendrix family re-take control of the Hendrix estate – see Chapter 3.)

"The idea was that he [Allen] wanted to make a shrine to Jimi in Seattle, since that's where Jimi was born," says McMurray. As the museum space broadened beyond just Hendrix – although it has over 7,000 Hendrix-related artefacts, including over 100 pages of handwritten manuscripts – it changed its name to Museum of Pop Culture in 2016 to reflect its more generalist ambitions. Hendrix remains a core part of MoPOP's attraction to visitors and McMurray describes the relationship the museum has with the Hendrix estate as "pretty tight", noting it has done seven different Hendrix exhibitions over the years. "All of those have been in some way in collaboration with the Hendrix family," he says. "The challenge working with artist estates is that sometimes you have to kind of strive to keep your independence, because often the estates think, 'This is the way that we see our artists.'"

He says a major concern for museums focused on legacy acts is that "there oftentimes is this desire to steer the narrative in a certain way"; but he says within that curators need to accept that they are only telling one part of a much bigger story, although they can choose to focus in on things that perhaps get overlooked elsewhere and can play a role in amplifying the cultural worth of an act on their estate's behalf.

"An exhibition isn't a novel and it's not a documentary," he says. "It's a distilled narrative within a finite space. So by its very nature you are selecting strands of the narrative to focus on. The challenge is giving that impression of nuance and breadth when you literally do not have it."

The closeness with the Hendrix estate also means the museum can take items on loan. "They've got a significant collection," he says, adding that other lenders can be turned to in order to flesh out new Hendrix exhibitions if they need it.

Being based in Seattle, grunge plays a major part in MoPOP's exhibitions – most significantly Nirvana and, indirectly, the estate of Kurt Cobain. In 2011, a Nirvana exhibition (*Nirvana: Taking Punk to the Masses*) displayed 1,200 different objects drawn from 20 different lenders, including band members and those around them at the time.

McMurray makes the point that time as much as location are the determining factors in all of this and shapes the types of stories they can tell – and the types of mythologies they can start to create – in their exhibitions. "That's the big difference between, say, a Hendrix versus a Nirvana," he says. "Hendrix is in the mists of history, all of the sharp edges have worn off and most people are dead. There's an apotheosis that has happened and he's fully godlike at this point. With Kurt, I think that's the case for the wider world, but for Seattle, everybody is still here and they know the stories. No one's going put up with somebody trying to tell a story that isn't based in actual fact."

Verification of objects will make or break an exhibition, especially if they are not coming directly from the estate with that stamp of authority. Museums have to be incredibly careful here, especially for major acts where most of the main items are owned by an estate or rich private collectors.

With a dearth of items in the marketplace, forgeries can surface and an attempt can be made to present them as real and, as such, highly valuable. Equally, items that are too similar to other items already on display lose their significance through proximity. Sometimes, however, serendipity can turn what might have been dismissed as ordinary into something truly extraordinary.

"There was this guy in Portland and he sent me a picture of this broken Mustang guitar body," explains McMurray. "He had done all this research – 10 pages of research – showing that this was the guitar that was on the cover of [Nirvana's debut album] *Bleach*, that it was used at the show that Nirvana played in Bellingham where Kurt had a Soundgarden sticker on it and all these different configurations. I was just like, 'Wow, this is amazing research, but I've got eight other broken guitars in this exhibit. I don't know that I need another one.' Then about three weeks later another guy contacted us and he had another broken guitar half. I was like, 'Wait a second! These are the same guitar!' These were two guys that were at the Pine Street Theatre in Portland on February 9 1990 when Nirvana had played there and Kurt had smashed his guitar and threw it out in the audience – but they didn't know each other. When we put it on display it was the first time that guitar had been together [since Kurt played that show]." To verify items related to Nirvana, McMurray has developed a network of expert sources he can turn to, such as Earnie Bailey, who was Cobain's guitar tech.

An ongoing challenge for all museums is that items can and will perish, with McMurray saying that solvents used in old guitars can, over time, start to corrode other parts of the instrument and so display boxes have to be fitted with mesh vents to avoid a noxious microclimate building up inside and damaging them. Equally, items handwritten by artists can, especially if they used red ink, start to fade dramatically over time. This puts a limit on what items can be publicly displayed and for how long. The existential threat here is history physically erasing itself.

Certain star attractions will be the climax of exhibitions and what fans are really there to see. Chief among them is the white Hendrix Stratocaster. "I have seen several people cry when they see that," says McMurray. "For me it's like Christmas every day. I'm so used to being around this stuff that it's really great to see a reaction like that because it reminds me how special this shit is and how lucky I am to get to work with this stuff. That's a big one."

All items belonging to deceased artists will naturally take on a new and deeper resonance as time passes and their legend grows. Some, however, take on a darker meaning that poses ethical and moral challenges for museums. A white glove belonging to Michael Jackson is one such item at MoPOP.

"It's something that we're still struggling with and we need to come up with an institution-wide perspective on how we deal with this," admits McMurray when we speak in the summer of 2020. "With something like Michael Jackson's glove, that was a piece that we would often bring out and put in an isolated case and it would have a small caption with it. It kind of sells itself. But to me, I don't know that we could do that any more because we literally do not have the interpretive space to provide context for Michael Jackson and that glove and his celebrity versus his problematic aspects. That's how you have to do it. It's our responsibility to be able to provide that context. If we are not providing that, then we're going to be accused of ignoring the problematic aspects – which I don't think is good."

Museums can retire items that might cause controversy and where their cultural value (if not their economic value) becomes tainted, but they also need to ensure they add in new objects that keep exhibitions fresh and add new perspectives to the stories they are trying to tell.

The collector market in recent years – especially with online auctions – for objects owned by deceased pop stars has boomed. The irony here for museums dealing in music is that they have inadvertently contributed to this collector market that has sometimes driven up prices until they are out of their financial reach. The number of items that museums can now show will be compromised by the concurrent growth of the collector market.

"SCARED SHITLESS AND SHAKING": THE GROWTH AND GROWTH OF THE CELEBRITY AUCTION

With a price tag of $6,010,000 when it went under the hammer on 21 June 2020, the 1959 Martin D-18E acoustic-electric guitar that Kurt Cobain played during Nirvana's *MTV Unplugged* show in November 1993 broke all manner of world records. It was, according to Julien's Auctions, who handled the sale: the most expensive guitar sold at auction; the most expensive piece of memorabilia sold at auction; the most expensive acoustic guitar sold at auction; the most expensive Martin guitar sold at auction; and the most expensive piece of Nirvana memorabilia sold at auction.[63]

It was bought by Peter Freedman, an Australian businessman and owner of Rode Microphones, and the final bid far exceeded the original auction estimate of $1 million. He told the PA News agency he was "scared shitless and shaking" when he put in what was to be the winning bid. "It's a big deal," he said. "I didn't even buy it for me. I paid for it but I'm going to use it to highlight the plight of artists worldwide by touring it around and then I'm going to sell it and use the dough for that as well, later."[64]

Cobain's guitar was just one of 800 music-related items sold at Julien's Auctions in Beverly Hills that weekend. These included an ivory macramé belt worn by Elvis on stage, which sold for $298,000, a guitar (previously thought to have been lost) belonging to Prince that sold for $563,000 and John Lennon's handwritten and annotated lyrics to the 1963 song 'I'm in Love', which sold for $102,400.[65]

The sale came only eight months after a cardigan Kurt Cobain wore at the same *MTV Unplugged* performance sold for $334,000. That sale was also handled by Julien's Auctions, this time as part of a two-day auction of 700 items of music memorabilia at the Hard Rock Café in New York.[66]

Death literally sells.

Darren Julien is president and CEO of Julien's Auctions and works directly with living celebrities as well as the estates of dead celebrities to help them auction off particular items or a job lot. He says the items at auction, as opposed to those being sold privately, command these record-breaking prices as they come with a stamp of authority – these are the genuine items and there is a paper trail to prove it. "You never dispute the provenance of something coming from the collection [of a living individual or their estate]," he says. "When you sell something privately, you don't have that benefit – it's hearsay that this came from the collection of so-and-so. Whereas when you do an auction, it's featured in the catalogue, it has lot tags, there's images of it, there's a bill of sale. You know that it's authentic."

Gemma Sudlow is the head of private and iconic collections at Christie's in New York. She says that celebrities who keep full records of the items they buy make the verification process much easier and this, in turn, can have a beneficial impact on the sale price. She worked with David Gilmour when he sold his guitar collection for charity in June 2019, raising $21,490,750 in total.[67] Gilmour and his long-standing guitar tech Phil Taylor could verify every item as they had kept "these extraordinary records" and receipts showing where everything was originally purchased. "That inevitably added value when we were selling the collection," she says. "Obviously our team of experts also do all the research they can possibly do into an object. Some of that anecdotal information – unless it's recorded now for an artist, if they are no longer with us – is lost. So where one has a receipt or an invoice for a piece, always keep it if you can because it means something [...] Record keeping, where possible, will add value in the long term."

A problem with estates looking to sell items several years after a musician has died is that the documentation may not be as watertight as it could be and that may impact negatively on the sale price. "That becomes more complicated in terms of authenticating for our buyers," Sudlow says. "They want insurance that that material was owned by that individual."

Julien says that modern pop stars are much more diligent in tagging and storing items as they are keenly aware of the prices such items can go for. "People like Lady Gaga and Madonna, they archive their clothing, their records, their awards," he says. "Whereas you wouldn't have had that before. With The Beatles, [manager] Brian Epstein would get their awards. Paul McCartney didn't care, John Lennon didn't care. Brian Epstein just kept them all. They didn't mean anything to the guys because they were winning so many awards. And now they are worth a lot of money. I think that's a good lesson for a lot of these artists."

For less-prepared artists (or their estates) a lot of background research has to happen before items can be put up for sale. "Provenance is everything," says Julien. He says Delia Becker, widow of Walter Becker from Steely Dan, was well prepared to auction his items. "She knew everything," he says. "She worked with Walter as he was alive archiving things. She knew what was important coming to us."

Items belonging to Becker were sold in late 2019, two years after he died, and included a range of instruments, rare effects pedals and customised tube amplifiers. In total 1,100 items were lined up for sale (mostly guitars and amplifiers).[68] The auction in October 2019 brought in $3.3 million.[69]

Sudlow says that the "storytelling component" is central to an auction – not just gathering together a random selection of items and relying on a vague thread to hold them together. "It's something we pride ourselves on at Christie's [...] For us, a really great collection is something one can almost consider as being like a biography in objects. In the same way you have them in a biography, the words and chapters that you include are just as important as the things that don't make your final edit." As with an album, she says there can only be one "final auction" of their items and so the pressure is on the curation team to get it right. That then all feeds into the buzz and marketing hype around a major auction that can turn it into an event, with public viewings of items also helping to whip up excitement. These auctions can turn into enormous events that draw in the public beforehand when the items are put on display and then attract a flurry of wealthy buyers looking to buy their own personal piece of history.

"The exhibitions that they put together for the estate of Elizabeth Taylor [in 2011], the Audrey Hepburn estate [2017] and the George Michael collection [in 2019] – those were incredible experiences in and of themselves as exhibitions," she says. "We had lines out the door for the tours that went to London [George Michael] and New York [Elizabeth Taylor]." The storytelling aspect can become more important for estates than for living artists. "Inevitably when one works on these estates, it's an opportunity to tell new stories as well as the ones that everybody knows or associates with that individual's name," she says.

An auction at somewhere like Christie's helps to confer a rarefied authority onto not just the items being auctioned but also the person to whom they belonged. "If we've done our job well – and it's something we take very seriously, that responsibility – those sales should become those moments where the legacy of that individual is celebrated and it reaches an incredible audience on global sales," says Sudlow. "It can become a celebratory moment after a life well lived."

In November 2016, the first items from David Bowie's personal art collection were auctioned at Sotheby's in London and raised over £24 million. *Air Power*, a 1984 painting by Jean-Michel Basquiat, went for £7.1 million. His collection was sold over three separate auctions (Modern and Contemporary Art parts 1 and 2 as well as Design: Ettore Sottsass and the Memphis Group) on 10 and 11 November.

"David's art collection was fuelled by personal interest and compiled out of passion," said a spokesperson from the Bowie estate. "He always sought and encouraged loans from the collection and enjoyed sharing the works in his custody. Though his family are keeping certain pieces of particular personal significance, it is now time to give others the opportunity to appreciate – and acquire – the art and objects he so admired."[70]

The commission an auction house takes on sales like these can be significant, but the competition between auction houses to run the auction can be fierce as blockbuster events like the Bowie auction can raise their profile and credibility. It was claimed that Christie's was prepared to run the Bowie auction "almost for free", but Amy Cappellazzo, who had been at Sotheby's just four months in April 2016 when negotiations were under way and headed its fine art division, refused to cut their commission to get the auction. "We told them [the Bowie estate] we needed an incentive to perform," she said. "If you took that away, we would still be motivated to win the business but not to execute success."[71] Bowie's estate admired her stance and gave the auction to Sotheby's.

It turns out that some of the items sold in the Bowie auction may have more significance and some less than the buyers realised. "What was sold at Sotheby's, 95 per cent of that was in storage," says a source close to the Bowie camp, suggesting that very few of the pieces sold ever hung on the walls of Bowie's home and were merely bought on a whim or as a calculated investment by the singer. "Some of the stuff in there was actually his office furniture. They never said which bits. Somebody somewhere owns his book cabinet but doesn't realise it's his book cabinet."

The auction of George Michael's art collection on 8 March 2019 at Christie's in London attracted bidders from 52 countries and the end total – which included pieces by Tracey Emin, Sarah Lucas, Damien Hurst and Marc Quinn – was $12 million from bids in the actual room and a further $2.7 million online.[72]

Other major sales of art belonging to music stars include the 2018 auction in Sotheby's New York of Frank Sinatra's personal collection, which featured pieces by Pablo Picasso, Joan Miró and David Hockney as well as scripts from films he appeared in such as *The Man with the Golden Arm*, *Ocean's 11* and *The Manchurian Candidate*.[73]

Julien says that, as items pass down generations in families, when they finally go up for auction, the descendants of the original owner come in with over-exaggerated expectations of what they might get for them. "When you get into children of a celebrity and they have never worked – they've always been given stuff – that becomes extremely difficult because their expectations are a lot higher than what the market bears," he says.

The record-breaking Cobain guitar was sold over a quarter of a century after he died, but he is a rare example of an artist who continues to resonate through generations. This is what Julien would term an iconic item and they tend to create their own centre of gravity and rise in value rather than depreciate.

However, these are the exceptions that prove the rule that time, as far as auctions go, is of the essence. Julien says that the optimum time for an estate to sell items is as soon as possible after the artist passes away. There is a market for items being resold at auction, but it is only a select number of truly iconic items that can withstand being put back on the market. "Most collectors know they have got to hold on to it for ten years for it to really increase in huge value after it has been sold publicly," suggests Julien. "Smaller stuff, yes. We see a lot of this stuff come back around, but none of the bigger stuff." He adds, "You want to do the auction within a year. That is when they are at their prime." He then gives an example to illustrate this.

"That's why with Michael Jackson we sold everything for crazy prices – because we did some of his auctions right after he passed," he says. "Now those prices are still good, but jackets that we sell now for $60,000 or $70,000, right after he died, we sold them for $300,000 or $400,000."

In December 2010, a year and a half after he died, a studded glove worn by Jackson during his *Bad* world tour in the late 1980s sold for $300,000 at auction. A fedora he wore on stage sold for $96,000 and a jacket he performed in went for $72,000.[74] Another glove was sold for $350,000 almost a year earlier (a mere five months after the singer's death) while a jacket worn by Jackson during a 1989 tour went for $225,000 in the same auction.[75]

Julien notes that the iconic jacket worn by Jackson in the video for *Thriller* sold for $1.8 million at auction, but this was in June 2011, two years after he died.[76] "That jacket today would probably bring $200,000 or $300,000. It wouldn't bring $1.8 million."

Julien does point out that controversy around Jackson – which was revived again in early 2019 with the release of the *Leaving Neverland* documentary that levelled more accusations of child sexual abuse at the singer – has not demonstrably damaged the market for items that once belonged to him. He feels this is down to the fact that the buyers are typically Jackson fans and choose to ignore or simply disbelieve any accusations about his behaviour behind closed doors.

"I would say for the most part that Michael Jackson fans and people who love his music don't give the two [accusers in *Leaving Neverland*] a lot of credibility," he says. "It's more of the people that aren't really a Michael Jackson fan. I think that makes a lot of difference. Also outside the United States, it doesn't impact him at all. His biggest base is in Asia. So the Chinese and Japanese still spend $100,000 or $200,000 on items with us."

There is also a highly buoyant private market for Jackson items and perhaps this is down to the fact that bidders feel more comfortable buying things without the risk of public judgement and condemnation if the celebrity in question is enveloped in a miasma of scandal. Julien says he cannot give precise details but reveals one Jackson-owned outfit was sold privately for over $1 million.

He does, however, admit that Jackson is an outlier here and that other stars accused of such serious crimes would see their reputation and value seriously plummet. The market, it seems, operates with impunity and without morality.

"With Michael, his music is so vast and his fanbase is so global," says Julien. "He's one of the all-time highest collectible artists – and continues to be. The whole scandal thing did not impact his collectibility at all."

Online auctions have had a significant impact on the value of the items that get sold, allowing wealthy bidders (notably from Russia and Asia) to bid remotely and, in doing so, drive up the end sale price. Previously such bidders may have sent a representative to bid on their behalf if they were not able to travel or else they put in bids over the phone. Being able to watch online in real time means they can get more caught up in the moment and the adrenaline drives their bids ever higher.

Sudlow says it is becoming a much more global business and online is broadening the types of bidders who step forward. "Whilst most of our buyers want to remain anonymous, I think one can speak in generalities," she says. "The scope of the different countries that our buyers come from, it's often surprising. Yes, it's private collectors. Yes, it's institutions. Sometimes it's just a die-hard fan who comes with a budget and it's that individual sale or object that speaks to them. It's very much a mix."

She also says that auctions of items from those in the popular arts world are growing in importance and being treated with much greater reverence than perhaps they were two or three decades ago. This cultural validation rolls into and amplifies the prices that some items here can command. "There is this recognition now that popular culture is coming to the fore and in a different way it is being recognised by institutions for its importance," she says. "There has been increased value and thirst in the market for this material because there is now an added acknowledgement that there is a social, political and cultural importance to these objects."

Often families are the ones putting items that once belonged to a musician up for auction, but there are occasions when they were unaware that such items had been sold and react with a mixture of anger and dismay. This is best illustrated in the fallout after three of Eddie Van Halen's guitars were sold via Julien's Auctions at the start of December 2020 for a combined $422,000.[77] The auction happened less than two months after Van Halen's death on 6 October 2020.

Wolfgang Van Halen, the guitarist's son, was swift to condemn the auction as well as those individuals who were quick to sell off items his father had given them or they had otherwise acquired. Responding to a news story on the auction, Wolfgang posted on his Twitter account, "The headline should read: 'Three guitars that are striped were sold at an auction for charity.' They weren't stage guitars. I had nothing to do with this. I don't EVER plan on selling any of my father's iconic guitars. The only place they'd possibly belong in is a museum."[78] In a follow-up tweet he posted, "Also one was a gift. I don't know who'd want to give that away. Timing is a little fishy to me."[79] A third tweet spelled out his position in even clearer terms. "Oh wait, scratch that. It WASN'T for charity. They're just taking advantage of my father's passing. What a surprise. Fuck 'em."[80]

Not every auction happens in the rarefied space of Christie's or the more razzamatazz world of Julien's. Some are just terribly mundane and exude a cruel bleakness that this is what the life of an incredible creative force is reduced to – items coldly put up for sale to help pay the bills. Auctions to pay tax bills or clear debts are not uncommon and the estate generally prefers to sell off tangible items rather than intangible ones (like copyrights) that can bring in recurring income.

On 29 November 2006, items belonging to Syd Barrett, who died on 7 July that year, were auctioned by his estate at Cheffins auction house in Cambridge. In his biography of Barrett, Rob Chapman described the auction catalogue that day as having "a slightly surreal air about it", where items like silver salvers and mahogany tables that normally predominate at that auction house shared space with a ragbag of Barrett's items. These included a Billy bookcase from Ikea, an artificial Christmas tree (and decorations), a home-made bread bin and "a modern wheelbarrow" – casting a very ordinary shadow over an extraordinary life.[81]

"Items that ordinarily would have found their way into a skip after a house clearance went for hundreds, sometimes thousands of pounds," noted Chapman.[82] The Christmas tree reached £800, the wheelbarrow £400. More tragically, people pretending to be interested in buying the house where he lived had used the viewing opportunity to steal items such as hippo doorknobs.

What was presented as possibly the last painting he had done (a watercolour of lemons and bottles) sold for £9,500, a collection of reference books (some signed by Barrett) went for £4,000 and a psychedelic cushion reached £1,600. In total, the auction raised £121,000, which went towards a bursary for local arts students.[83]

Even more dispiritingly, in October 2019, the possessions of Keith Flint from Prodigy, who took his own life on 4 March 2019, were packaged up into 170 lots and sold to help pay off a reported £7.3 million he owed in debts and taxes. This auction was also handled by Cheffins and included Flint's gold discs for record sales, his clothes and furniture from his home.[84]

In 2004, a major auction at Sotheby's of items belonging to Johnny and June Cash raised $4 million, twice what the guide prices suggested it would make, and this was done in part to pay off estate taxes.[85] Items sold included a 1986 Grammy that went for $187,200 (it was initially expected to sell for $7,000), a custom-made Grammer guitar that sold for $131,200 and a black Martin guitar that also raised $131,200. Other items sold included art and furniture and collectively it was estimated they made up one-third of the Cash estate.[86]

Some auctions also attract immense controversy for being ghoulish, or for selling items that do not belong to the seller. In January 2020, the car that Tupac Shakur was travelling in on 7 September 1996 when he was fatally shot was put up for auction. It had been refurbished but the listing said one indentation, caused by a bullet, had been left. It had a listed price of $1.75 million. It had been put up for auction three years earlier for $1.5 million.[87]

Finally, auctions can also draw in governments keen to acquire items belonging to celebrated citizens that are deemed to be of national import-ance. In December 2007, the Greek government was among the bidders at Sotheby's in Milan for items belonging to opera star Maria Callas. It came 30 years after her death. "The sale of all these items interests us hugely," Panayiotis Kakoliris, a senior adviser to the Greek culture minister, told the *Guardian*. "Right now, we are looking into how we can raise the funds, to both buy and bring them here."[88] The items belonging to Callas – made up of 330 lots and with an initial guide price of £500,000 – included letters, jewellery, clothes, furniture, annotated musical scores and paintings.

An auction of Callas items in Paris in 2000, including a mink stole given to her by Aristotle Onassis, had seen representatives from Athens' town hall significantly outbid. "As a result, admirers in Athens have had to make do with a Maria Callas museum whose exhibits include little more than a wig, a set of gloves and photographs of the singer playing with her favourite pooch," noted the *Guardian*. "Augmenting the country's paltry Callas collec-tion has become a priority for a government that, this year, has also gone out of its way to celebrate the great dramatic singer with a series of recitals, concerts, exhibitions and shows."[89]

In the end, items from the Callas collection fetched €1.76 million. A metronome belonging to her sold for €17,000 while a bowl given to her by President Kennedy in 1962 went for €26,650. Reuters described the bidding as "hectic" and Sotheby's representative Iris Fabbri said of Callas, "She came back to be more popular than before."[90]

* * *

The more museums and the more auctions there are, the more items owned by estates, big and small, will be taken out of private storage to be either exhibited or sold.

In October 2020, Natalie Curtis, daughter of Joy Division singer Ian Curtis, who took his own life on 18 May 1980 when she was barely a year old, revealed she was selling his Vox Phantom VI Special guitar. Curtis used it on the band's 1980 European tour but most significantly was playing it in the video for 'Love Will Tear Us Apart' that was shot three weeks before he died. It had a pre-sale estimate of between £60,000 and £80,000 at Bonhams.[91]

"The guitar came to me at a time in my life when I was keen to learn more about my late father," she said. "I'm not at all musical, yet it is fascinating to see my father's guitar, I mean, it's such a personal thing [...] If I had any kind of aptitude, it's the sort of guitar I'd want for myself!"[92]

The reasons for selling an item like this can often only be guessed at. Perhaps the decision was financial or perhaps having the item there as a constant reminder of a lost father was simply too much to deal with. Either way, that adds a whole new layer of meaning to the object for whoever eventually buys it. These are not just items owned by a dead artist – these are items owned by the people they left behind.

In March 2021, the red Hagstrom Viking II electric guitar used by Elvis Presley in his 1968 *Comeback Special* (and which also appeared on the cover of the following year's *From Elvis in Memphis* album) was sold by GWS Auctions $625,000.[93] Its high price was driven in part by the fact that it had not been seen in public for 52 years.[94]

There is something both ghoulish and celebratory about the demand for such items. They are a physical link back to a dead artist – a means to let the fan (or the collector) imagine a kind of proximity to a person who is no longer alive. These are items that are imbued with something more, something glowingly intangible, that have become elevated to the level of religious scriptures, holy relics or the bones of saints.

CHAPTER 8

Corporation Death

The Industrialisation of Estate Management

The publication in early 2001 of the first *Forbes* list of the world's highest-earning estates (see Chapter 1) was a landmark event, although few recognised at the time just how important a landmark it was to become.

The record industry was sliding into chaos in 2000 as the impact of Napster, launched the previous year, ripped apart all the old certainties. The entire music business was forced through a long and painful period of unprecedented upheaval.

The way artists made money was changing and also the way artists broke through into the mainstream was changing. The very nature of success in the music industry – previously measured out in gold discs, ticket sales and radio plays – was becoming much more intangible, where streams and social media likes became a new type of success metric. There was also the sad reality that many major stars from the first few decades of rock'n'roll and popular music who had built up phenomenal legacies were dying – sometimes from the effects of a hedonistic lifestyle but often simply of old age.

The 20th century saw the meshing of these two defining factors: the music industry itself changing to become more multifaceted than ever before, plus legendary artists expiring of natural causes and old age.

Elvis Presley and David Bowie may have shared a birthday (8 January) but the former was 42 when he died and the latter was 69. Their deaths were 39 years apart (Elvis in 1977 and Bowie in 2016) and in that time the music industry had become a remarkably different beast. Elvis died leaving his affairs in chaos, while Bowie died with what is commonly accepted as the most carefully structured estate plan a musician has, so far, left behind.

These two acts are legendary in their own way but they also bookmark a very particular era – moving from the birth of the estates business to its industrialisation.

REAL ESTATE: BUYING AND SELLING AN ARTIST ESTATE

The Elvis Presley estate – as we have seen repeatedly in this book – is both a roadmap and a weathervane for the estates business overall. It is only fitting, then, that it was the first major estate to attract outside investment and also to see investors come and go. Much as *Father Ted* mockingly drew attention to the "Three Ages of Elvis",[1] we can talk about the "Three Ages of Investment in Elvis".

The first few years were a financial tightrope walk for the Elvis estate as it struggled with debts and taxes, but by the mid-1980s, it was turning into a financial powerhouse. By 2004, Elvis Presley Enterprises had a valuation north of $100 million[2] and was the biggest celebrity estate in the world (a position it had held every year since 2001 when *Forbes* first starting collating the data), with turnover that year of $40 million.[3] Revenue at the time was evenly split between two separate, but interconnected, streams – royalties/ licensing and Graceland. Graceland revenues tended to nosedive in the winter months, but the summer boom, especially around Elvis's anniversary in August, more than offset this.[4]

In the early 2000s, as the music industry was changing due to the impact of digital, the estate business had to change too. An estate can do this in one of two ways: either spot the demographic and market shifts themselves, anticipate change and shift around this to capitalise on it; or bring in outside experts or investors skilled in reinventing businesses and for whom disruption in a sector is their bread and butter.

The Elvis estate chose the latter path. CKX Inc[5] – set up by media entrepreneur Robert F. X. Sillerman, who would be listed by the *Forbes* 400 list in 2005 as having a net worth just shy of $1 billion[6] – bought "the rights to control Graceland's tourism, the Presley trademark rights, all intellectual property owned by the estate and control of all the music rights held by the estate" as well as his music publishing.[7] The deal, which gave CKX 85 per cent control of the Presley business, was pegged at $53 million, with half of it paid in cash and the other half split between preferred stock and debt repayment.[8] (There are conflicting reports on the details of the deal, with *Fortune* claiming it was worth $114 million, with Lisa Marie getting $50 million in cash along with $26 million in CKX common and preferred stock, and that a further $25 million went to pay off EPE debts and $6.5 million went to Priscilla Presley for use of the family name.[9])

Crucially, Lisa Marie Presley kept the deeds to Graceland and the 13.6 acres it sits on as well as family and personal items.[10] She was also retained for a minimum of 10 years to carry on the work she was already doing for the estate. Priscilla was kept on as an executive consultant. An eyebrow-raising clause in the deal suggested that CKX got a 90-year lease on Graceland but that there were strict stipulations in the deal which meant it could not be used as "a massage parlour, a mortuary, or [for] the manufacture, sale, or distribution of feminine hygiene products".[11]

Sillerman told the *Seattle Times* that investing in Elvis was simply smart business. "I don't think there's much likelihood his influence is going to wane anytime in my lifetime," he said.[12]

CKX immediately swung into action, outlining plans to turn a three-mile section of Elvis Presley Boulevard in Memphis into an "entertainment district" and buying up 125 acres of land in the area. It also planned a hotel, a theatre and a convention centre, with ambitions to open Elvis-centric attractions in Europe, Asia and the Middle East to take the brand global.

The arrival of a new investor with bold ambitions and huge financial targets saw marketing efforts accelerated considerably, including national TV ads for Graceland for the first time.[13] In 2007, the *Daily Telegraph* reported that a three-year modernisation programme for Graceland was under way, with an estimated cost of $125 million. This would see the "cramped visitor centre" replaced with a new purpose-built facility (see Chapter 7).[14]

The timing, on paper, looked excellent as the Elvis business was considerably bigger than that of any other music estate. In 2005, it made $45 million while the John Lennon estate made $22 million.[15] A feature in *Fortune* in December 2005, however, alluded to things being far from rosy inside the Elvis business, suggesting it was "stagnating", citing the collapse of a restaurant in Memphis and "little profit [available] to invest" in new ventures like hotels.[16]

Sillerman's business associates were, however, quick to defend him and his corporate strategies. "Bob is like a Clint Eastwood character in an old Western movie," claimed Dennis Arfa, founder of live entertainment agency Artist Group International, who had a line in questionable analogies. "He rides into town and leaves with all the money and the women. He made a lot of people wealthy, and he made himself even wealthier."[17] The *Fortune* piece summarised Sillerman's thinking here by describing Elvis as "an underexploited asset, like a poorly managed textile company or a baseball team without a marketing department", saying that his job was to address this.[18]

Only a few years after the CKX deal, the financial crash happened in 2008 and things started to unspool. Graceland visitor numbers tumbled and in 2009 Lisa Marie unloaded 100,000 of her shares in CKX. Two years later, a planned development at Graceland was put on ice.[19] Not everything stopped, however. A show with Cirque du Soleil – *Viva Elvis* – opened in Las Vegas in February 2010, with tickets costing between $99 and $175.[20] It did, however, close in 2012, with Daniel Lamarre, Cirque du Soleil's president and CEO, saying that "ticket sales have not met expectations".[21]

Just three months after *Viva Elvis* made its Vegas debut, CKX went through its own restructuring. Sillerman resigned as chairman and CEO (but remained as the company's biggest shareholder). Then in 2011 the company, including its Elvis investment, was sold to Apollo Global Management, a private equity firm, for $509 million.[22] Apollo initially focused on reviving the Graceland attendee numbers (and it was responsible for pulling the plug on *Viva Elvis*). Then in May 2012, CKX rebranded itself as Core Media as part of a restructuring plan by Marc Graboff, who joined as president of the company earlier that year.

Long-time watchers of company restructurings know that statements such as this can often foreshadow a volte-face and the placing of assets on the auction block. And so it was with Core where, within a year, it was rolling up its investment in Elvis Presley Enterprises along with its interests in Muhammad Ali Enterprises for a joint sale. In May 2013, the *Financial Times* was estimating this bundle could sell for $200 million.[23] Among the companies rumoured to be interested were Sony/ATV Music Publishing as well as investment firms Guggenheim Partners and G2 Investment Group.[24]

A buyer was eventually found at the end of 2013. Authentic Brands Group – which was already deep in the estates business, looking after the intellectual property rights of Marilyn Monroe since 2011[25] and with involvement in the Bob Marley estate – bought out Core's 85 per cent stake in Elvis Presley Enterprises (including an archive of photos and video footage of the singer) as well as the Muhammad Ali image rights.[26] No sale price was made public, but a month before the deal was signed, the *New York Post* claimed Authentic Brands Group was tabling an offer of $125 million, which was $15 million above what a consortium made up of G2 Investment Group, Sony/ATV Music Publishing and Highbridge Capital were collectively offering.[27]

As part of the deal, Joel Weinshanker acquired the rights to the management of Graceland, with Authentic Brands Group and the Presley family as partners in the venture. "We will usher in a new era of an enhanced Graceland experience, run for the fans, by a fan," he said.[28] Soon after the completion of the deal, work started on a new 450-room hotel to replace Heartbreak Hotel in Memphis, with costs estimated at $70 million.[29]

This changing hands is always sold as being beneficial to the estate – that here, finally, is someone who understands the legacy and value of what they have and will treat it with the utmost respect. One senior industry figure who has dealt with many major estates feels that this is mere lip service and that the more times an estate changes hands, the more ruthless the new owner has to become in order to extract the biggest return on their high-stakes investment. "The Elvis Presley estate has been bought and sold like a *major corporation*," they say, placing an emphasis on the final two words that has a distinct tang of cynicism about it.

I ask Jamie Salter why his company, Authentic Brands Group, wanted to invest so heavily in the Elvis estate less than a decade after CKX/Core had bought in and cashed out. He chooses his words carefully, but the subtext was that he felt that CKX/Core had fumbled it and failed to revitalise the Elvis brand for a new generation. "We looked at what was going on with Elvis Presley and we thought that it was very undervalued in terms of exploitation to the younger generation," he says. "We felt that it needed a facelift."

232

He suggests that CKX/Core had become detrimentally fixated on the slightly kitsch version of Elvis, sweating out his final years under the spotlights of Las Vegas – locked in a kind of corpulent cabaret. "We thought that if we could bring back the old Elvis and not necessarily the Elvis in the jumpsuit, that's the Elvis that all the young people grew up with and were so excited about," he explains. "To me, if we could bring that old Elvis back one generation down, we would definitely start to gain momentum."

He claims that this was a trick Authentic Brands Group had pulled off for Marilyn Monroe, suggesting that her core audience is now aged 15–25. "When we bought Marilyn Monroe, the age demographic was my mother, and I am 56 years old – so you know my mother's old!" he laughs. "You have to bring Elvis back to a younger demographic; and the only way you can do that is by bringing old Elvis back with his cool haircut, the '68 *[Comeback] Special*, him bopping and running around the stage and being a great performer." (See Chapter 9 for more on introducing old acts to new audiences.)

Salter says that cutting back and being much more selective in its licensing was key to this repositioning. By doing less but being more precise, he says, the estate's revenues went up significantly, claiming it had an EBITDA[30] of $14 million when his company came in but it was running at $40 million at the end of 2019. "We've almost tripled the business from a profitability standpoint," he says. He adds that having the Presley family involved is critical and becomes part of the marketing strategy. "Priscilla works with Graceland and then she also works with us on certain collaborations," he says. "Priscilla tends to fly closer to the media and entertainment stuff and Lisa Marie focuses more of her time working with my partner, Joel Weinshanker. It is unbelievable what Joel and our team have done with Graceland. So that's where she spends most of her time. But I will tell you that working with the family has been nothing but amazing. They're passionate. They care."

He adds that this all works to distil the essence of his company, where Authentic Brands Group wants a hefty (if not total) investment stake in an estate rather than just being a licensing partner. The upfront costs might be higher, but the profit potential is greater. Plus he is more in charge of the creative and the economic direction of the estate. "I came to the conclusion," says Salter, "that it's better to own the real estate than rent the real estate."

The Presleys are, it should be stressed, still involved in the Elvis estate both for financial reasons (15 per cent of the estate remains with Lisa Marie) but also for emotional reasons, ensuring that they have visibility on, and some active involvement in, every deal that is struck and every decision that is made. They are also the lure for media coverage around a new venture, with Priscilla in particular deeply involved in the promotional circuit to keep the Elvis name in the spotlight.

Others who are investing in estates also regard continuing family involvement as akin to a fixed asset when they are tabling offers.

In May 2019, Primary Wave acquired a 50 per cent stake in the estate of Whitney Houston, meaning it now takes a cut across all of its revenue streams. This includes master recordings, publishing, film royalties, merchandise and her name and likeness. The Houston estate is also able to plug into the marketing, publicity and digital teams at Primary Wave. *Billboard* said the deal valued Houston's estate at $14 million, suggesting (but not actually saying explicitly) that Primary Wave invested $7 million for its stake (although that could be a mix of cash and stock as well as certain commitments on marketing and so on).[31]

The first major project as part of the deal was the Whitney Houston hologram tour, which launched in Europe in early 2020, and *Billboard* added that plans were in place to create a Broadway-style musical as well as a reissue programme that would see unheard material surface.

When a deal like this happens, everything is dialled up and estates are able, with the benefit of new investment and a new infrastructure around them, to take on projects that would have previously been too big or too risky to shoulder themselves. Alongside cash and expertise, the estate is also spreading the risk by not betting the entire farm on a single major project.

Before the Primary Wave deal, Pat Houston, executor of the Whitney Houston estate, says it was a small operation in terms of staffing. "I don't think people really understand what it takes to handle an estate," she says. "First things first, you just have to make sure that all the assets are protected. And you have to make sure that her debts are paid out and that the beneficiaries are taken care of and that everything else is done. You are creating situations for the estate to make money, by making the proper decisions to do that. That was the connection with Primary Wave." She had worked with Primary Wave founder and CEO Larry Mestel when he was EVP and general manager at Arista Records between 2000 and 2004. He was there when the singer negotiated a new $100 million multi-album deal with Arista in 2001, reported as being the biggest in the label's history.[32] "So it was a no-brainer to come together with him and to help promote and continue building a legacy that was worthy of staying on top," she says of the Primary Wave deal. "That's why I did it."

Primary Wave helped put together the Kygo remix of "Higher Love", the singer's first major posthumous hit. "It seems like a very fresh perspective," says Pat. "We've started where she started – with the music. And it's working out."

Mestel had already worked with the Kurt Cobain estate, buying into his publishing catalogue as well as working on branding deals with Converse using his lyrics as well as his name and likeness. "It's an investment in the future of the legacy of the artist," he says of deals like the ones with the Cobain and Houston estates. "In which case, when you partner, both parties reap the benefit."

On the reasons behind the Houston estate investment, he says, "It wasn't so much about money as it was a partnership that they were looking for – somebody to help them roll out ideas creatively."

Not one to hide his light under a bushel, Mestel feels the work Primary Wave has done with the Whitney Houston estate is clear proof of concept for his business model and that other estates will be drawn to him to deliver similar results. "I think as more estates see the opportunity that people like Primary Wave have created it's going to create more excitement for estates […] to have that same level of a personal involvement and the same level of marketing and pitching," he says. "I think more estates will want that service."

Speaking on the *Bob Lefsetz Podcast* in February 2020, Mestel said that having a family member or heir still involved in the estate is a fundamental requirement of Primary Wave's deals (as is having a living songwriter also involved in any investments). Although there was one exception. "Our model is to partner with the artists, the writer, the heir," he said. "So we'll buy 50 per cent of a catalogue or 75 per cent of the catalogue. In the case of Glenn Gould, where there was no heir, the trustee was going to sell 100 per cent or nothing so, yes, we bought 100 per cent of the Glenn Gould estate.[33] But we partner because – as much as we're music fans and we love the music, because we only buy what we love – we'll never know the artist or the catalogue as well as the artists will or the heir [will]. And if you're marketing […] you really want the help and the participation of the artist. To have a little skin in the game and to be aligned."[34]

One source with knowledge of the Glenn Gould catalogue suggests that Primary Wave made a significant misstep here as it was moving into a world they believe it does not fully understand. "I think they feel they bought a lemon because they don't know what to do with any of this," they say. "They don't know anyone in the classical world and Glenn Gould is, at the end of the day, a classical pianist who plays Bach. He is not Whitney Houston. He should be treated differently; it's a different market."

In 2015, BMG bought out the US publishing rights to "virtually every song" written by Buddy Holly as well as his name and image. The deal was done with María Elena Holly, the singer's widow. "This marks the first time since the singer's death in 1959 that someone other than María Elena Holly will be custodian to Holly's song catalog and overall image," noted *Billboard*.[35]

David Hirshland, EVP at BMG, states that this is, so far, a unique deal structure for the company. "That is really the only estate that we work with where we control everything – we control the image and the legacy," he says. "I work closely with María Elena Holly and her team. She likes to be involved in everything we do, but basically has no approval rights. But we honour her wishes and do those things that she wanted to have done."

Asked if BMG was going to look to replicate this deal, Hirshland says that its starting point is always the publishing and then it considers if this can be used as leverage to create new revenue opportunities. Unlike a Primary Wave deal, it is looking for a total buyout and the ongoing involvement of the heirs is seen as less of a deal breaker. "I wouldn't call it a *big* investment opportunity target – I would call it very selective and nuanced," he says. "The reason, of course, that we were so interested in Buddy is that the publishing became available and that's a huge driver of revenue. Most of the other assets are speculative in terms of how to exploit name, image and likeness. So unless there is a component of either master recordings or publishing involved, it's not really a goal of ours to just represent an estate for possible future revenue incomes. We want to have some sort of music component attached to it."

The competition here has been increasing in recent years. There has been something of a passing of the flame from CKX to Authentic Brands Group (where non-traditional music companies invest in estates), but also from Primary Wave to BMG (where more traditional music companies want to bring new thinking and new strategies to the estates business). These are all, of course, well-funded businesses that can make major investments in estates.

As more companies see the investment potential in estates, bidding wars – just as in the record business for hot new artists – could become the new reality here and really start to define the temperature and the future shape of the estates business.

A new entrant in 2020 is Los Angeles-based Iconic Artists Group, which is seeking to buy up rights from living artists as well as from estates. It was set up by Olivier Chastan and legendary music manager Irving Azoff. Chastan says the company was inspired by what Robert Sillerman did but adds that it also has to take a different approach from some of the biggest names in the sector so as to avoid overlap and cannibalisation.

"Bob Sillerman really was a visionary," he says. "He was the first one to really see that way ahead of anyone else when they did the deal with Elvis and Marilyn Monroe as well. What Authentic Brands Group does that is a little bit different is that it's very product- and retail-driven. They're, I would say, not completely focused on really exploiting the IP. I am much more IP-driven, meaning the ability to develop opportunities that are intangible."

He says that Iconic Artists Group is not interested in buying into catalogues, as BMG or Primary Wave might do. Instead it is focused on name, image and likeness. It is looking to do deals with living artists as well as with estates. As with Primary Wave, Iconic Artists Group wants the artist (or their heirs) to have a significant stake in the rights, suggesting that 51/49 in Iconic's favour is the ideal split.

"The reason is twofold," he explains. "One is that I want partners. I don't want to buy them out. There's usually a knowledge in there and certain senses that are quite important that I want to be able to tap into. The second aspect is that we absolutely believe that their 49 per cent will be worth more in five to ten years from now than it is today. We want them to feel that when they enter into this transaction they are not being sold short."

The first major deal that Iconic Artists Group signed was with The Beach Boys, closing it at the end of summer 2020 but not making it pubic until February 2021. It includes the income on the band's recordings for Capitol Records (though the label retains ownership of the masters) and some, but not all, publishing from all the different members. The deal terms were not made public, but *Bloomberg*, based on conversations with "a person familiar with the situation", valued the total assets involved at between $100 million and $200 million.[36]

"There are some Brian Wilson compositions, but not the entire catalogue because of some rights issues," explains Chastan. "In 1969, Brian's dad, Murray [who was also manager of the band], sold the publishing company to Rondor, which was the old A&M Records' publishing company, which then became Universal. It's this huge mess. It really destroyed the relationship between the dad and the kids. It was a semi-traumatic event for Brian as he felt he lost his children. So there's really nothing we can do there in the sense that it's owned by Universal until it reverts back." (For more on the issue of copyright reversion, see Chapter 10.)

The deal also includes name, image and likeness rights that Chastan says can be used in advertising and sponsorship as well as opening up the possibility of a documentary and a biopic. "It also includes the trademarks as part of that – so 'The Beach Boys' in multiple categories," he continues. "We bought a lot of archive material. A tremendous amount of memorabilia and archive material. That can be anything from old touring T-shirts from the seventies to individual calendars – like Al Jardine's calendar from 1977."

He says that many of these assets can be used to feed the band's official social media channels and that the company will also be looking to replicate vintage merchandise lines. The goal for Chastan is to take all of these assets and rights and use them to revitalise The Beach Boys brand. "We have to close the gap between the brand recognition and what it means in terms of engagement, monetisation etc.," he says. "It is one of the most famous bands in the world and yet they're doing very little. They all recognise it themselves so I don't have any problem saying it. It was so dysfunctional because of in-fighting that they couldn't have consensus. The band members just not being able to find consensus in general meant that they were crippled in terms of their ability to really properly leverage their fame, the brand, etc."

To illustrate what he means here, Chastan sent me a copy of the five-year plan document the company put together for its pitch to The Beach Boys. It runs to 31 pages and outlines how Iconic Artists Group will build and preserve the band's legacy, what marketing and promotional plans it can put into operation, how it will monetise the wider brand and specific assets, the different business areas and digital platforms it can open up and what the targets will be for each of the first five years. Because it is a confidential document, I cannot quote directly from it, but it is incredibly detailed in terms of what is covered and how the company will look to reawaken the band for new generations of fans.

While he is talking about living artists with regard to The Beach Boys (although Dennis Wilson died in 1983), Chastan says the exact same approach can be taken for dead artists, mentioning the names of some estates that the company was in discussions to acquire, one of which was a ground-breaking and hugely influential post-war artist.

(After we spoke, Iconic Artists Group announced two further deals – although both were with living artists. In early March 2021, it announced it has acquired David Crosby's publishing and recorded music rights covering his solo career as well as his with work The Byrds, Crosby & Nash, Crosby, Stills & Nash, and Crosby, Stills, Nash & Young.[37] Later that same month, it acquired the recorded music assets of Linda Ronstadt.[38] No deals with estates had been announced as this book was going to press.)

While there can be huge sums of money involved, some estates remain resistant to being bought. In certain instances this can be for emotional reasons, where family members feel a deep personal connection to the estate and would regard selling it as a betrayal. That was the case with the Ike Turner estate, according to music lawyer Don Wilson, who represented a number of Turner's heirs. "We were approached by several companies wanting to purchase Ike's catalogue – both the sound recordings and musical compositions," he says. "But the heirs felt that that was their father's legacy, that was what he left for them in order to have income for the rest of their life. So they really didn't want to sell it. Plus the fact that it had been inactive for nearly ten years, the value would have been diminished somewhat because usually those purchases are based on prior years' earnings."

Cally Callomon says he understands why estates may want to sell – particularly at a time when major companies are offering mouth-watering sums of money as they all seek to scoop up catalogues as a means of boosting their market share and stealing a march on their competitors. Even so, the Nick Drake estate is, quite simply, not for sale and all approaches to buy it have been declined.

Callomon does reveal that he and Gabrielle Drake, Nick's sister, have clearly defined plans for the estate when they are no longer around to run it; but for now it will just be the two of them driving everything. "Gabrielle is not old and she's not tired – and neither am I," he says. "We have other plans for what could possibly happen with Nick's songs and assets after we've gone. You have to build those things in while you're alive. How does mankind benefit? How do charities benefit? How do trusts benefit from the income of something after the originators have died? Setting up a trust is quite an easy thing to do and I think it's quite a sensible thing to do. What it means is that Gabrielle and I will not be benefiting from the income Nick earns in 50 years' time because we'll be dead. But other people will."

Those making an acquisition approach do not always respond well when their offers are rebuffed. They regard rejection as somehow being a veiled criticism of their business acumen; but they can also take it very personally.

One investor in estates says they put in a bid a few years ago for the estate of an artist that has done moderate business for years but that they felt could be more active in bringing in new fans, moving with the times and generating more income. It did not go well. "I tried to buy the artist's estate," they say, "but the person in charge was a total blocker. They have no clue what they're doing, I have to be honest. I think they're the worst company."

As if trying to settle a score, their opprobrium rises the more they talk about the deal that never was. "I did a whole analysis on the artist and I sent it to the estate as I thought at that stage that I had nothing to lose," they say. "It is massively underperforming on streaming. The metrics are very simple. If you don't grow at the same pace as the rest of the industry, either you made a deliberate choice for whatever reason – but that has to be justified and they couldn't justify it – or you're doing a shitty job. It's a shame."

They say the estate was opposed to evolving – having a limited social media presence – and tended to regard any commercial idea as selling out the ideals of the artist. "It doesn't have to be selling out. Move with the times," says the thwarted acquirer. "By the way, if it's good enough for the fucking Beatles it should be good enough for everybody. That is my rule. There are two aspects here: one is marketing; two is monetisation. You don't have to do number two, but you do have to do number one. That estate is not even doing that. There are zero promotional efforts. Zero."

It was clear that this failure to buy the estate seriously wounded the investor. That is because what it revealed to them is that – in their big business world of estates at least – not everything is for sale.

PART AND PARTIAL: SMALLER INVESTMENTS IN ESTATES

The deals mentioned above that were driven by Authentic Brands Group, Primary Wave, BMG and Iconic Artists Group are about headlines and scale – showing that they are trading in blockbusters and taking a major or controlling stake, moving into the totality of an estate rather than one of its many moving parts. But there is also a more quotidian process at play here where companies are buying into a small part of the rights around an estate, and this was happening long before CKX made its bid for 85 per cent of the Elvis business.

In many ways, these smaller deals laid the groundwork for what has become the industrialisation of both estate management and estate investment. They can also be a foot in the door – or a toe in the water – for investors and estates to see if a partial coalition delivers results and, from that, if a more encompassing deal can be tabled and thrashed out.

There have been a multitude of these minor or mid-level deals to draw on in recent years, but these examples below show the process in motion and how buying and selling here can be fast and furious.

March 2006: Courtney Love sells 50 per cent of her share of Nirvana's publishing catalogue to Primary Wave for an estimated $50 million.[39] Primary Wave's interest was reported to have eventually increased to 50 per cent of the total estate[40] but it had to divest its interest in September 2013 when BMG paid $150 million for the "bulk of Primary's publishing assets".[41]

April 2007: Julian Lennon sells a share of his interest in his father's publishing to Primary Wave. This deal – relating to the songwriter's share of royalties (which is passed down to heirs under US copyright law) – covers only John Lennon's solo work and not the Lennon/McCartney catalogue.[42]

April 2009: The estates of Richard Rodgers and Oscar Hammerstein III sell the rights to their compositions to Imagem Music Group, the investment arm of a Dutch pension fund. Before that, all licensing for their music was handled by the Rodgers & Hammerstein Organization. Its long-term president and executive director, Theodore Chaplin, was retained in his role to ensure continuity. Other prospective buyers included Andrew Lloyd Webber. "Figuring out the right time to sell a family business is always tricky, but you never want to be in a situation where a family business has frayed and it's too late to fix or to sell," Chaplin told the *New York Times*. "And since Imagem is global, I hope they can help us disseminate the works we represent with a little more moxie."[43]

June 2017: The broader Imagem catalogue, covering 5,000 copyrights from not just Rodgers and Hammerstein but also others including Irving Berlin, was sold again as part of the deal when Concord Bicycle Music bought the music company.[44]

January 2018: Primary Wave pays $50 million to take 80 per cent of Island Records founder Chris Blackwell's publishing catalogue, which includes a number of Bob Marley songs. It was reported at the time that the Marley family would still control over 50 per cent of his catalogue.[45] At the time of the deal, Primary Wave suggested it had upwards of $400 million to invest in music. "Primary Wave's pitch to songwriters is that it can find new ways to market old material," wrote the *New York Times* on the deal announcement.[46]

October 2018: Primary Wave acquires the publishing catalogue of Count Basie as well as royalty streams from his master recordings.[47]

April 2019: Downtown Music Publishing signs a publishing administration and catalogue marketing deal with the George Gershwin estate.[48]

October 2019: Downtown Music Publishing signs a global publishing agreement for the entire Miles Davis catalogue. "In addition to catalog marketing, licensing, and royalty collection, Downtown will collaborate with the Miles Davis Estate on a range of events and other special projects," said Downtown in a press statement.[49]

January 2020: BMG partners with Dark Horse Records, the label set up in 1974 by George Harrison to cover his solo work, as well as HariSongs, the label imprint set up by the Harrison estate in 2018 that focused on Indian music.[50]

May 2020: Primary Wave acquires a majority stake in the pre-1964 compositions of Ray Charles. Financial details were not made public, but it was described as "a multi-million deal" that would slot the catalogue into Primary Wave's infrastructure covering licensing, synchronisation, marketing, branding, digital strategy and more.[51]

June 2020: Warner/Chappell Music signs a global co-publishing deal with the estate of Pop Smoke covering all his compositions.[52]

This offers a mere snapshot of the types of deals that increasingly happen, but it also shows how certain estates are growing in attractiveness as investment opportunities, and also the scale of the deals that are starting to define the sector.

Amid all this investment, there has been a concurrent infrastructure change at music companies, with dedicated departments and divisions being set up to specialise in estate management and the acquisition of copyrights and other assets from estates. In October 2015, Sony Music Entertainment set up a joint venture with Artist Legacy Group to offer estate brand-management services for the former's Legacy Recordings catalogue division as well as other labels dealing with estates. Artist Legacy Group was in charge of licensing, branding and merchandising for estates. Adam Block, president of Legacy Recordings, was put in charge of the new operation. "[W]e see a terrific opportunity to create even greater awareness and opportunities for the artists and estates we'll work with," Block told *Billboard*.[53]

In June 2019, Arron Saxe was appointed vice president of estate management at Universal Music Group. "Managing an estate is to protect, first and foremost, the integrity of the art," is how he described his role in an interview with *Pollstar* in 2021. "These songs and artists are really important."[54]

Then in November 2019, Craft Recordings – the reissue label division of Concord Music – named Michele Smith as VP of estate and legacy brand management, a new role created within the label. Smith said in a statement that she was looking forward to working with "the estates of the musical trailblazers who have entrusted us with their legacies".[55] A year and a half into the new role, Smith told *Billboard*, "What we consider history are these artists' lives. And that's what I love about my job: the preservation and protection of legacies. But it's also about finding creative ways to expose this music to younger generations while keeping original fans intrigued."

It is not just record companies setting up dedicated roles to deal with estates. In March 2021, the William Morris Endeavor talent agency (whose client base covers not just music but also sports, books, TV, movies, chefs, comedy and social media influencers) set up the WME Legends division to handle the estate and brand management of a wide range of dead celebrities. It appointed Phil Sandhaus – who has worked with a wide range of estates over the years – to run it.[56] In April 2021, the estate of Notorious BIG signed a deal to have WME Legends represent it and the late rapper's assets.[57]

These estates companies are expanding their skills both to address a real need in the sector as estates become more valuable, and also to try and give themselves a strategic advantage over rivals when competing to work with estates or acquire a stake in those estates.

Writing in *Billboard* in 2019, music lawyer Erin M. Jacobson laid out the case for estates to bring in such specialists to help them run their operations as effectively as they can. "Typically, heirs that inherit a catalogue are overwhelmed by the vast amounts of information and don't know where to start in getting a handle on the catalogue," she wrote. "The heirs that are more adept at navigating the music industry have typically learned over many years and from astute advisors."[58]

Bruce Lampcov, head of West Coast business development at Downtown, says his company is selective about the estates it wants to work with or invest in, suggesting other publishers are concerned more with volume and market share and will happily add new names to their already voluminous catalogues. "We don't say yes to everybody," he says. "We only bring on clients that we feel that we can partner with in a very positive and proactive way and create value for them." He does, however, state that Downtown, when it invests, does so across the bulk – or ideally the totality – of an estate's business. "The way we are preparing is the way we are growing our business – which is to be part of every service income stream," he says. "That's really how we see it. We think that being part of the entire music ecosystem is very important. So we're investing in excellent businesses that we feel fulfil that."

For these established music companies, investment is driven in part by a need for growth and increased profitability; but it is also driven by protectionism so that they are not left behind in a market that is increasingly defined by consolidation. In short, if they do not work with or buy into an estate, a rival will. And it is no longer just music companies muscling their way in here as the wider investment world is spotting the start of a posthumous gold rush.

"The catalogue acquisition market has boomed because, first of all, everybody has always wanted to be in entertainment; and, secondly, [for] a lot of these investors and venture capital funds copyrights are a more stable investment than the stock market or things like that, because there have been some volatile economic times," says Erin M. Jacobson. "The second reason, specifically for estates, is that some of these estates are much older. They're oftentimes what we call evergreen catalogues, which means they are music that keeps earning money. These are songs that continue to have a life, that continue to earn royalties. So they feel that it's a more stable investment that is going to keep producing income over time. It's not something that needs to be built up from scratch. There's already a fan base. It's already either making money or has potential to be making more money. So they see it as something that will be a good return on the investment."

Owen J. Sloane, a partner at legal firm Eisner Law, says that he advises clients running estates to bring in specialist help as without it the estate may be financially compromised and the artist's legacy could become diminished through inertia or ill-informed decisions. "If somebody is trying to run it himself or herself without professional assistance, they could run the business into the ground," he warns. "It's not only a question of whether you sell or not; it's a question of whether you continue to run the business or you bring somebody else in – not necessarily selling it – but somebody like a Jeff Jampol [of JAM Inc] who could help you."

A major label catalogue head says that the estates working with experts or skilled investors are dramatically improving the business from their perspective. "In terms of what labels can do, it's often been a function, not just of rights ownership, but also of consents and permissions," they say. "Labels haven't always been able to do just whatever they feel commercially is the right thing to do. The industrialisation or greater commercialisation of estate management has maybe unlocked opportunities that previously the label wasn't able to exploit or [...] develop."

Bringing in such expertise comes with a high cost attached to it. Only estates of a certain size can justify the expenditure – or they have to start selling a proportion of the assets and copyrights they control in order to bankroll investment in the future of the estate. A clear class system is emerging here where already big estates attract the big investment required to ensure their longevity, while the medium and smaller estates get shunted even further to the periphery.

This is exacerbated by the fact that the major investors in estates or specialists are utterly uninterested in working with smaller estates to potentially grow them, or to make artists such as Nick Drake and Eva Cassidy considerably more famous posthumously. Larry Mestel's repeated thesis about being in "the icon and legend business" was echoed by a number of other specialists I spoke to for this book.

Jeff Jampol of JAM Inc is especially resistant to working with the estates of acts that were not already superstars in their lifetime. "It's very expensive and time-consuming to move these legacies forward," he says. "I don't think that we would take a legacy that's unknown and then try and make it known."

While they share similar views on mainly wanting to work with only major estates, Jampol and Mestel represent two philosophically distinct approaches to running those estates. They symbolise the division between the specialist owner and the specialist manager.

THE RISE OF THE SPECIALIST

In parallel with the investment opportunities being spotted here by established music companies that want to grow their portfolios, market share and experience, a new breed of estate managers has stepped forward in the past few decades, working with estates but without necessarily being an investor in those estates.

This opens a wider philosophical debate within the estate business. Is it better to work as a manager, where you get a cut of the overall earnings? Or is ownership of assets and IP a more lucrative approach to take?

Jamie Salter of Authentic Brands Group says his company's strategy is to buy into estates and work with them rather than simply work for them. "We're owners," he told a BBC documentary in 2019. "We're not renters and we're not agents. And I'm not taking a shot at the agency business, but at the end of the day, we're not working for commission. So when you're not working for commission, you're working for the longevity of the brand. You want it to last for ever because you're going to own it for ever."[59] This obviously involves having an investment pool that runs into the tens of millions, something that excludes all but the rich, the ambitious or the foolhardy.

Unquestionably the leading specialist in this area is Jeff Jampol, founder of JAM Inc, whose roster includes Jim Morrison, Janis Joplin, Charlie Parker, John Lee Hooker, the Ramones and Henry Mancini. His company also works with the Michael Jackson estate. "We manage legends" is the company's strapline and its website URL is even wemanagelegends.com.

He is a formidable character and one who is abrasively forthright in his opinions, his voice rising sharply as he makes his points and machine-guns out his words. He also has a strong line in analogies and rarely holds back when discussing those who have come in his wake but who have not, as far as he is concerned, got it right.

He came from an artist management background and says this – or more specifically the limitations of this – informs how he does business today when representing deceased artists. "Successful managers in the music business, I think, come up knowing three and a half things – and really only three and a half things," he says. "And with those things, they cover probably 98 per cent of an artist's income. Those three things are touring, tour merchandise and radio. And the point five is putting songs in film and TV."

He says he became an autodidact out of necessity while managing living artists, learning about publishing, international licensing and apparel – all areas he felt were overlooked or misunderstood by his contemporaries. He met Danny Sugerman, who had known The Doors since he was a teenager (and became their manager after the death of Jim Morrison) in the late 1990s and they began working together formally on The Doors' business in 2002.

"First of all, Danny knew everything; he just didn't realise what he knew," he says. "And I knew nothing about the legacy business, but I knew about marketing and promotion and sales and deal-making and intellectual property law etc. Danny and I were able to hold up very effective mirrors for each other. And what happened was once we joined forces, The Doors' business exploded."

They targeted the Janis Joplin estate as one they wanted to work with ("the same time period, the same zeitgeist, the same kind of ethos" as The Doors) but Sugerman passed away on 5 January 2005 from lung cancer before the deal could be finalised. Jampol closed the deal and says it was soon turned around like The Doors' business had been, "albeit on a smaller scale".

He now found himself in the estate management business, but remains deeply unimpressed with much of what happens outside the purview of JAM Inc. "There's very little 'estate management' in the business," he snorts. "First of all, this business suffers from what I call Jackson Pollock Syndrome. What I mean is when you take a kid to see a Pollock drip painting in the museum and you turn to the kid and say, [dismissively] 'You could do that!' I think people approaching this business or entering this business look at it and think, [dismissively] 'I could do that!' Unfortunately, the chief symptom of Jackson Pollock Syndrome is that you don't have a clue that you don't have a clue. Right? And I know this because *I had* Jackson Pollock Syndrome."

He continues, "When I first partnered with Danny, I looked at The Doors and I thought, 'I could do this!' But I couldn't do it. But again, I didn't have a clue that I didn't have a clue. And I don't necessarily think I was that smart or that wonderful. I just think I had a secret weapon. I had Danny. And Danny became what I call the thing between my gun and my foot. Danny kept me alive and prevented me from making fatal errors several hundred times. Until the lights started to come on. Once the lights started to come on, they started to come on in droves. And then I started to really see this business for what it was. It is hyper, super specialist. Think about the education that most managers have – which is in radio, touring and touring merchandise. When an artist is no longer active, guess which three things we don't do any more?"

When talking about those estates his company is not involved with, Jampol lights up like a Christmas tree, his derision tangible and his exasperation almost overwhelming. The more he points out what he feels their flaws are, the faster he speaks, almost as if he cannot get the full extent of his critique out quickly enough. He is equally derisory about heirs, who are, to his mind, dangerously out of their depth here. "If there are virtually no experts in the business – in estate management or legacy management – imagine how many there are within the ranks of beneficiaries and heirs," he says. "It's got to be near zero. My staff and I have become somewhat of estate whisperers in a way."

He may be forthright and assured in terms of his own abilities when it comes to estate management but he is also keenly self-aware. "I was quickly branded by the industry," he told the BBC. "They used to call me Tomb Raider."[60] This is obviously an attractive sell to some estates who want to elevate what they do and who see bringing in a bullish expert as the most expedient way to do this.

Linda Ramone, widow of Johnny Ramone and the person who controls half of the Ramones' estate via Ramones Productions, said Jampol's track record and the types of acts he worked with drew her to his company to get it to work on behalf of her late husband's estate. "I always heard about Jeff Jampol as he has The Doors and The Doors happened to be one of Johnny's favourite bands," she told the same BBC documentary. "I met him, he's Jeff Jampol. He has his own ego, but he knows what he's doing."[61]

Linda Ramone tells me that part of the reason she brought in JAM Inc was because she was often at loggerheads – or even in court – with Mickey Leigh (aka Mitchel Lee Hyman), brother of Joey Ramone and the person in charge of the other 50 per cent of the Ramones estate. (See Chapter 11.) Jeff Jampol was brought on board as much for mediation as he was for management. "I had a different manager at that time and then that didn't work out," she says of why she eventually appointed Jampol. "It is always really trying to get along with the other estate. That's really my main problem. It always has been. Because you have to both agree on Ramones stuff. And, you know, it's impossible to agree with someone who is… bitter. That's how I look at it. So you try to go around everything. So getting Jeff Jampol in the picture was going to be a new, big happy family kind of thing where we all could work together."

She says it has not always been a smooth road, but having someone sitting between the two halves of a split and combative estate can help remove much of the bitter personal politics and point-scoring that can get in the way of the business. "When they go through management to try to work together, offers come in and you agree or you don't agree," she says. "I mean, it's as simple as that. It's either you're going to agree on something or you don't agree on something. And then you do it or you don't."

Leigh, when I speak to him, is quick to point out that Jampol is only Linda's manager – not his manager. Dave Frey is his manager for estates business but he also manages living artists, something Leigh feels makes his approach very different from that of Jampol. "Jeff Jampol won't work with living artists, but Dave does," says Leigh. "There is a big difference, I think. It's not as warm a feeling working with people who are in the industry of working with dead people. As opposed to Dave who actually worked with my brother when he was alive and works with living musicians. It's just a different kind of feeling."

Jampol says that bringing him and his team in to work on an estate can never be a quick-fix solution as they have to tie up a great many loose ends and try to undo a multitude of mistakes and missteps that happened before they got involved. "I'm very clear with my potential clients," he says. "Usually it's going to take us two to three years before we even pay for ourselves. So you sign with me, you're probably going to lose money for the first year and we may not even see significant gains for a couple of years. Because the first year is almost always forensics. We have to research, we have to dive deep, we have to review every single contract, we have to go through every statement, we have to look at all the royalty percentages, we have to see what the deals are, we have to see how they've been handled and where they've been mishandled, and we have to fix any problems with metadata."

Ultimately, he says, the clean-up job he does on an estate often dates all the way back to when the artist was alive but had failed to prepare properly for every eventuality in their will. The artist's affairs are often not in order, they pass on a damaged estate to their heirs and then the heirs simply make a bad situation even worse. That is a brief synopsis of his pitch explaining why a specialist like him needs to come in and recalibrate everything.

On the JAM Inc site, there is a checklist of topics for estate managers, attorneys, beneficiaries and heirs, covering things they need to think about when running an estate. "If you're not sure how to answer these questions, don't panic," says the website, reassuringly. "We can help. We're a management company, and our job is managing our extraordinary clients' legacies."[62]

Jampol says the ideal situation – and one that would save time and money in the long term for estates – would be for him to sit down with living artists and work out a legacy plan for them that they can sign off on. They may have their business issues in place, he says, but how their legacy is managed is what they need to place equal emphasis on because that will shape what heirs can (and cannot) do with their copyrights as well as their name, image and likeness.

"The odds are likely that they have really great estate plans and they have a trust set up and the trust is funded and their heirs are all in place and everybody's got that buttoned up beautifully," Jampol says. "They've anticipated tax issues, estate issues, probate issues. But nobody – nobody! – has addressed the legacy issue. I've spoken to several entertainment lawyers, entertainment business managers and estate lawyers, and I just said, 'Look, you guys have done everything in your field. But this is not your field. This is my field. Sit me down with that artist for a week and I want to write an owner's manual for their legacy so that if and when something happens to them, their heirs will have this owner's manual and will know exactly what to do.'"

He feels this manual is the key to legacy management as it anticipates all the issues an estate is likely to face. Guesses can be taken and assumptions can be made, but unless the artist themselves has outlined clear rules on what they are happy to have happen after their death, everyone is scrambling around in the dark. "Imagine there's a 150-page manual just sitting there waiting go," he proposes. "For the artist, whatever he or she wants done with their music and their legacy will be followed to the letter. And the heirs and the beneficiaries will not be frozen by fear because they will know what their father or mother wanted. It's right there in writing."

This is something Bill Zysblat concurs with. He is co-founder of RZO and represents the estate of David Bowie in business dealings. He is talking here about estates in general and not the Bowie estate in particular. "I think it's a wonderful idea," he says about Jampol's owner's manual thesis. "But it's almost never done. The only flaw is that you have to continually update it. People mellow over time. The younger idealistic artists will say, 'I never want my songs in a commercial. I never want my songs on TV.' Then of course they realise that: a) it's great publicity; and b) there's nothing wrong with it. It is a wonderful idea – if you can get an artist to sit down and focus on it. It's a very hard thing to do."

Expert estate managers, naturally, consider themselves a wise investment for an estate as they can help grow the business and also extend the legacy of an act. As Allan Steckler, who runs the Vladimir Horowitz and Arturo Toscanini estates, says, "I have made them – the estates – a fair amount of money. And I never thought there would be income coming in this far after their passing. Both of these artists' reputations are as strong as they ever were."

Cally Callomon was pivotal in dramatically elevating the profile of Nick Drake in the late 1990s and early 2000s – continuing to ensure his music is talked about and his influence passes through to new generations of musicians and music fans. He says the strategy was to treat Nick Drake as one would treat a living artist, but also to allow new fans to feel as if they discovered his music for themselves rather than having it forced upon them. "My term for Nick is that he will remain in demand, not on demand," he says.

He adds, "As the new channels of listening are settling into a pattern today we are open minded as to how Nick's songs appear on these. I see streaming as a replacement for radio, not necessarily a replacement for physical sales; the two co-exist in comfort today. Nick never got played on the radio in his day. Now it's a different story."

Nick Drake was a rare example – certainly in the 1990s – of an estate that did not have significant turnover but that understood that appointing a full-time person to run it was an important investment. Not all estates have had the prescience, or the resources, to make such a downpayment on their own future.

Music lawyer Don Wilson says that estates, regardless of their size, need to seriously consider bringing in expertise to help turn them into viable businesses with staying power. The simple equation runs that the longer they are active, the longer the artist's legacy will be. "A professional really has to get in there and turn things around and start doing things to make it profitable," he says. "You have got to have quality and competent people around you who can guide and lead you. A lot of these heirs are around the business but are not in the business. Even when they are not grieving, they still need someone to guide and direct them because they really don't know what the proper thing is to do."

Mark Roesler is the founder and chairman of CMG Worldwide and cut his teeth (after law school and an MBA) while working for the Curtis Publishing Company, which owned the copyrights to a large number of works of art by Norman Rockwell. From there, he worked with the Elvis estate in the early 1980s as it was sorting out many of its financial issues, helping to turn it into a powerhouse. He now works with the estates of a variety of individuals across the entertainment and culture sector, including Chuck Berry, Christopher Reeve, Maya Angelou and Rosa Parks.[63]

His position is that an estate slotting into a multi-personality estate business like his allows it to avail itself of his company's expertise and market scale. The bigger his collective client base becomes, runs the logic, the more powerful each estate becomes in its particular commercial negotiations because it is part of a much bigger machine. "The big picture is that we're building a portfolio of assets," he proposes. "This portfolio of assets is intangible property right assets. Typically for these celebrities, they're the most valuable assets that they possess. It is these intangible property rights that we create, maintain and exploit. All of that often can result in significant revenues for these various clients. That's the overall objective."

In wider music industry terms, these estate specialists are becoming like major labels – the bigger their client base, the greater their leverage.

Nick Rizzuto, a digital strategist who works with a range of artists, says this is all a necessary response to changes in the wider music industry. "Over the past few years, artists have increasingly brought in outside experts to supplement the resources of their label and management company," he says. "Estates have followed suit in recent years by bringing in experts in digital marketing, content production, media archive management, etc. I think we will continue to see artist estates evolving into their own quasi-media companies by either growing their team in-house or hiring third-party experts."

Seth Berg began in the record business in licensing and synchronisation – notably at Capitol Records – and turned his contacts with major estates into a major consultancy role in the early 2000s. He says he felt that there was a disconnect between labels and estates and this lack of alignment meant they often rubbed up against each other or found themselves at crosspurposes. This relationship was always delicate but, he feels, it becomes much more fraught when too many outsiders are brought in who are not in sympathy with the late artist.

"I had seen, when I was at the label, that a lot of these estates were not given the attention that the current artists were given," he says. "With a lot of them, either the estate has been passed down to a lawyer, or there's a trustee; they don't necessarily care about the archive or they didn't have the wherewithal to actually sees the estate as a 360-degree entity. And I just saw there was a real hole there. So I went to the Dean Martin estate and the Frank Sinatra estate and said, 'Would you be interested in having a guy like me work independently for you?' And they said yes. Then the Peggy Lee estate came on and the Bing Crosby estate came on."

Jim Griffin is managing director of OneHouse and focuses on digital changes in the business. He has a label background, having set up and run the technology department at Geffen Records, and has now carved out a specialist consultancy role for himself, working with a number of estates. Like Jampol, he is a commanding figure, holding forth on a number of issues relating to the estates business.

Naturally, he feels that an expert, such as he, working with estates is essential to their growth and survival. He says this all comes from the fundamental fact that heirs are prone to making mistakes from the off as they are invariably dangerously out of their depth. "The heirs of an estate don't really understand the business," he says bluntly. "I mean not always [...] but almost always."

He is, however, scathing of what he sees as unskilled individuals coming into this part of the business and selling a form of business snake oil to heirs. "I just want to observe that the activity around the space is not necessarily evidence of professional involvement," he proposes. "I think it's evidence of opportunity – that some people have come to understand that this represents opportunity. Because if you're looking for a space where others may not have fully mined the rights, then estates are a good place to go [...] obviously families and heirs are not the most knowledgeable about the rights involved. So if you're looking for a less intelligent client, certainly estates are a better place to look than, say, active musicians who might talk to other musicians and actually come to understand their rights somehow. But the families are very unlikely to. I think the idea that there is a neon sign that represents opportunity tells us something; but it does not necessarily tell us that the best and the brightest have arrived on the scene!"

This, then, is the dark side of the industrialisation of estate management, where ill-equipped individuals can swoop in and exploit a grieving family's naivety or ineptitude. This, however, is not unique to the estate business and has long characterised the music business from its earliest days in Tin Pan Alley. Except, in this case, it is the artist's family – not the artists themselves – getting a shakedown.

Griffin sells himself as someone who can help heirs get their heads around what is a complex and intentionally confusing business. "One of the reasons these estates become especially problematic is that the parties involved are not fully cognisant of their rights," he says. "It's exciting for someone like me to get involved with an estate because I figure there is going to be some great educating to do! If you can get past the psychology, that's really true. You can get enlightened new owners who have a real understanding of how their loved one got screwed throughout their life. And they can put an end to that."

What Griffin warns of is, sadly, far from rare in the estates business.

In early 2014, the estate of Ol' Dirty Bastard appointed Four Screens Production to help run the late rapper's business. Nicole Beckett is the head of content development at Four Screens and explains what the company's role is for the ODB estate and how it was brought in to turn around a number of problems created in its early years. "It's walking a tightrope between promoting his legacy and keeping it authentic while also making a profit for the estate," she says. "That is essentially our role."

Beckett says that Icelene Jones, ODB's widow, was "working in the dark" for many years as his "untimely death left the estate in a bit of a mess" and he died without leaving a complete will. "There was no one to guide Icelene through the process," Beckett says. "So things got really, really jumbled." It also left the estate open to abuse from duplicitous outsiders. "She was not part of the music industry," says Beckett. "Of course, there were people who came in who didn't do a great deal. You could say that probably some people did take advantage at the time. Because nobody of expertise was around to legitimately help her, things went by the wayside as far as the residuals or the royalties [were concerned]. When we got involved that took years to just iron out everything."

For the biggest specialists in this space, there is often a great deal of fighting and rock throwing as they compete to be the alpha estates expert, all of which makes for scurrilously combustible headlines. They may feel that dissing or dismissing a competitor is the most effective way to sell their own brilliance: I am the best because I am not *that*.

"A lot of people approach these legacies as vultures winging around this decomposing body looking for little islands of still-pink flesh they can consume," Jeff Jampol told the *New York Times* in 2016. "I take the opposite approach. I believe in reanimating the body, and then all the revenue streams will come with it [...] This business is rife with opportunists and money wolves. People just want to get hold of something and 'exploit' it. 'Content' and 'exploit' are two words that I forbid people from using. We use the word 'art'; we use the word 'utilize' or 'deploy'. It really changes your thinking."[64]

When I speak to him, Jampol does not pick on rivals by name, but the subtext is there when he chooses to speak more generally about where and why he sees everyone else as lagging behind JAM Inc. "We're one of the premier marketing companies in the world in this niche, in this field," he says. "I look at it [the estates business] completely backwards from every-body else I know. Every time we have an opportunity to create something, I look at it as a legacy exercise first, a marketing exercise second and a revenue exercise third and last. I don't always have the right answers, but I have more than anybody I know."

Authentic Brands Group bought up 80 per cent of the Marilyn Monroe estate in 2012 for a figure estimated at between $20 million and $30 million (it eventually bought up the other 20 per cent as well).[65] The Monroe estate was previously being run by CMG Worldwide, a relationship that ran for 17 years. Anna Strasberg had inherited 75 per cent of it in 1992 when her husband Lee Strasberg died. He was Monroe's mentor and acting coach and was left the bulk of the actor's estate.[66] Anna Strasberg was reportedly unhappy with CMG's work and started shopping around for someone else to take charge of it on her behalf, alighting on Jamie Salter and Authentic Brands Group. Salter bought it, but would not disclose the transaction fee, teasingly telling the *Globe & Mail* that others – not him – estimated the deal to be worth between $20 million and $50 million.[67]

There was, inevitably, bad blood between CMG's Mark Roesler and Authentic Brands Group as a result, but Salter appeared to revel in the fact that he gave a rival a serious drubbing. "You could have bought Marilyn Monroe, but you didn't write the cheque," Salter crowed to Roesler. "You had 20 years. You lost."[68]

When I speak to Salter, I mention both Primary Wave and JAM Inc as examples of the industrialisation of estate management that could be understood to run in parallel with what Authentic Brands Group does. They have, I suggest, a great deal in common. Salter is not convinced and although ostensibly praising these competitors, he cannot help but zoom in on what he sees as their limitations.

"They are very different," he says. "They [JAM Inc] are a good company and Jeff Jampol is a good guy – but you are talking night and day. We do all aspects of the business. We're advertising. There are many ways we look at the business. [Primary Wave] are amazing on the music side. Amazing. But are they going to invest in a Broadway show? Are they going to invest in a movie deal? Are they going to invest in building up the merchandising side of the businesses? Do they have those rights? I don't know."

Rather than windmill into other estate management companies, Larry Mestel of Primary Wave instead looks to land a haymaker on other publishers who he feels are operating in 2D compared to Primary Wave's 3D. "Almost every music publisher says they market and brand," he told *Billboard* in 2019. "And most of them are full of shit. There's a big distinction between synchronization – which is licensing – and real marketing. Marketing is creating a holiday [Father–Daughter Day] for Smokey Robinson. Marketing is doing a deal with a major beer company that's going to create a One Love One Heart beer for Bob Marley. It's developing a Whitney Houston Broadway musical."[69]

When we speak, he moves to puncture the importance of what would be deemed Primary Wave's closest competitor, suggesting that size is a design flaw here rather than a merit. "If you look at it, it's got to be a lot harder for a BMG to figure out how to partner with somebody because they're a big, faceless music company," he says. "The employees are employees. It is owned by Bertelsmann, so the employees aren't equity owners. On our team we have over 20 people in the company who are profit interest holders in the company. So it's a big difference when you're dealing with partners. They are people that are going to be around a very long time and who are personally invested. As opposed to when big companies do it, there's no personal involvement. It's a faceless company."

As a new entrant into this business, Iconic Artist Group is not immune from slipping into playful trash talk when discussing competitors and trying to stress what new thinking it is bringing into the market that – it feels – others cannot. "First of all, estate or live for me is no different," says Olivier Chastan on the Iconic Artists Group model that is buying into the rights of both living artists as well as deceased ones. "It's not just about estates, just to be very clear. Jeff [Jampol] only does estates and has carved out a niche because of his work with The Doors. For me it's really more figuring out how to organise and plan for a legacy that is not just post-mortem."

He also says that buying up rights rather than working as a manager is the only viable way to get involved in this business. "The difference between Jeff and us is that Jeff is a manager," says Chastan. "He works on 15 per cent or 20 per cent. So it's subject to two things: one is resource constraints. Because I'm an owner, obviously I have much more incentive to spend and do things a bit more aggressively. He's working with a thin margin on a much bigger infrastructure. The second part with Jeff is, because he's a manager, he is a hired hand and is subject to approvals from the estate; that restricts quite a lot what they are probably able to do. I imagine if he had more approval rights he would do 10 times more than what he's doing today."

Then, to drive the point home, he says that ownership will always trump management as you are in total control and answerable only to your board and investors. "The manager is a hired gun," says Chastan. "No offence to my friend Jeff, but he can be fired tomorrow."

MANAGEMENT AND LAWYERS

The specialists in this space will argue that they have the skills, the contacts and the objectivity to run estates well. They will say they treat the artist and the art with respect but they are not as caught up in the emotional web that a family member or a long-standing colleague (almost always the manager or lawyer of the artist in their lifetime) would be.

To counter this, former managers and lawyers argue they have years of knowing this artist personally and representing them professionally. These are, they feel, the magic ingredients in ensuring their estate stays true to the artist's vision. They knew what the artists wanted in life and, it follows, they know what they want in death. This is a skill that cannot be bought in from outside.

By far the most successful example of this is John Branca, who has managed the Michael Jackson estate from day one. He turned it from one laden with phenomenal debt – on his own website, Branca says the singer was "roughly $500 million in debt"[70] when he died – and made it the most profitable celebrity estate every year since 2010 (the year after Jackson died), with the exception of 2012 when Jackson's friend Elizabeth Taylor's estate, following an auction of her jewellery and other possessions, made her that year's biggest dead earner.[71]

"In just under seven years, Branca's shrewd supervision of his assets put the Michael Jackson Estate $500 million in the black," reads Branca's site, with little apparent shyness. "It was the billion-dollar turnaround heard round the world."[72] Branca also drove the sale of Jackson's share of Sony/ATV Music Publishing in 2016 for an estimated $750 million.[73] That meant the estate's earnings for that year were a phenomenal $825 million.[74]

He was Jackson's lawyer from 1980 and represented him, on and off, for over a quarter of a century. "I did not represent him for the last several years of his life," says Branca. "But he hired me back eight days before he passed away [in June 2009]. We met while he was rehearsing at the Forum [in LA] for the *This Is It* tour."

Branca was named, alongside John McClain, as co-executor of Jackson's will and the probate judge appointed the duo to manage the estate's business. He argues that having such a long personal and professional relationship with Jackson puts him and McClain in a unique position when it comes to estate and legacy management. "It is very similar to what you would do if you were with Michael and he were still alive," he says of his work. "You have to make artistic and business decisions on whether to green-light certain projects and what you would do with them [...] I knew Michael and I represented him through the *Off the Wall*, *Thriller*, *Bad*, *HIStory* and *Invincible* eras and tours, so I had the benefit of understanding how Michael would think and how Michael would approach certain things."

Branca's first job in a law firm in the 1970s was actually as an estate planner. "This was as a lawyer, not as an entertainment lawyer or as a manager," he stresses. "It was a different role, putting together an estate plan, tax advantages, etc." He did, however, work with The Doors[75] and the Jim Morrison estate from the 1980s, and has also worked with the estates of Elvis Presley, Muddy Waters, Kurt Cobain and Otis Redding during his career.

He continually stresses the importance of knowing an act in their lifetime to be able to properly represent them posthumously (for example, Jackson served as best man at Branca's first wedding[76]), but adds that an appreciation of their art can also make up for that lack of personal contact. "Let me be clear – John [McClain] and I are not Michael Jackson," he says. "There is only one Michael Jackson, so we would never pretend that we could substitute our judgement for his," he says. "I would say this, since I work with other estates, if it's an artist that I have an understanding of and a feel for, I don't need to have had a long-term relationship with that artist. I just need to understand who they are and what the assets are. On the other hand, I would not likely, as a manager, take on an estate where I was not a believer or a fan of that artist as I don't think I would do it justice."

He makes a distinction here between being a lawyer, where he can represent the estate on deals, and a manager, where he is more involved in creative decisions. "If someone hired me to be the lawyer for the Vladimir Horowitz estate [for example], I could do that as a lawyer," he explains. "If someone wanted to hire me to manage the Horowitz estate in terms of the brand and the decisions, I might find that more difficult because I don't have enough familiarity with his work and who he was. That's the difference between being a lawyer and a manager."

He explains this further with regard to the different needs of an estate and why different specialists should be brought in for different parts of the operation. "It depends on how big the artist is and how many assets they have," he says. "If it's passive income, you probably want an investment adviser. If the artist estate owns assets, you probably want a manager who is skilled in making business decisions for artists of that kind. Having observed it, I'm a big advocate that an artist appoint somebody who is skilled at managing entertainers and entertainment assets. It tends not to work too well if you pass it on to family members – because they don't necessarily have the business training to properly handle the estate. They can be the beneficiary but not necessarily the manager."

He is rewarded handsomely for his work for the Jackson estate. *Billboard* reported in 2019 that Branca and McClain receive a 10 per cent commission "on new entertainment revenues generated for the estate"[77] which, as the biggest estate in the world, is significant and, despite the scandals that rocked it in 2019, continues to turn over phenomenal sums of money. There was the blockbuster Sony/ATV deal in 2016, but others included securing a $60 million advance for the *This Is It* film, renegotiating Jackson's recording contract with Sony (pegged at $250 million), and the *Michael Jackson: The Immortal World Tour* in conjunction with Cirque du Soleil, which opened in October 2011 and had grossed $75 million in the first half of 2012, according to *Pollstar* numbers.[78] While Branca's biography on his website does not hold back when it comes to trumpeting his abilities (Michael Jackson, apparently, called him "the greatest lawyer of our time"), when one looks at the cold, hard numbers, it is difficult to wave this away this as mere puffery.

Having the incumbent manager take over the running of the estate is one route that is seen as the most beneficial – or certainly least disruptive – as there is an important continuity here. Pat Houston, for example, was not only Whitney Houston's sister-in-law, she was her manager for the last decade of the singer's life. She was named by Whitney as executor of her will before she died.

"We had a great relationship and always kept things intact," says Pat. "I never did anything without letting her know. It was just that kind of relationship – just respecting her wishes and dealing with her in a very professional way. Being a family member, I know a lot of people would say that was tough, but you have to know when to hold them and when to fold them. When she passed, we just continued to do things the way we always did – in a very respectful manner. I would never take on or do anything that I know that she would not do or that would disrespect her legacy in any way. We are still coming together to make sure things are in perspective."

She did, as noted above, sell half of the estate to Primary Wave; but that was in part to bankroll and bring to fruition a number of hefty projects – a hologram tour, a musical and a biopic, to name three – that would require heavy investment as well as expertise that sits outside of traditional music artist management.

The existing manager also has key relationships in place, especially at the record labels, so they can ensure that things do not grind to a halt when the artist dies. One label head recounts the astonishing story of how the long-term manager of an A-list star did not miss a beat when that artist passed away, ensuring that plans for a posthumous hit were not put on pause. The manager said that this was something the artist, knowing they were dying, had entrusted them to oversee. As such, they were personally and emotionally committed to making it happen.

"[The manager] had all the skills, all the longevity and continuity, and the closeness to [the deceased artist] that was needed in order to construct a situation which would mean that things would be done right," says the label head. "This was exemplified by the fact that on the afternoon after [the artist's] funeral, [the manager] had arranged for us to have a marketing meeting. [The manager] came straight from the funeral with gossipy tales of what other stars were there and what they were wearing. And then we had a two-hour marketing meeting about next steps!"

Partnering with an existing artist management firm is increasingly a bridging option for estates that perhaps do not have the funds to pay for an expert to come in full time as the management company would work similarly to how it would for a living artist, taking a cut – typically 20 per cent in the UK – of earnings brought in under their watch. Celeste Bell, daughter of Poly Styrene from X-Ray Spex, set up a management deal with ie:music in 2019 to work with her on her mother's estate. She said the deal was done for pragmatic reasons as she was limited in what she could do on her own – she was working in education full time when we spoke and effectively running the Poly Styrene estate in her spare time – and she needed a professional structure to plug into. "It can free up a bit of time for myself so I can focus on other things," she says. "I'll still be connected to the estate, but I was getting to the stage where it was just too much. I've taken it as far as I can myself and I think having a bigger company, with all the resources that they have, will just make it run better."

This is an option that is not just confined to smaller estates, but a number of significantly sized estates working with management companies to boost what they are doing and to bring in new strata of expertise.

The Johnny Cash estate has been working with management company Sandbox Entertainment since March 2016.[79] They were brought in to provide digital expertise as Lou Robin, Cash's long-term manager since the 1970s (whose work transferred over to the estate), turned 90. "It was decided that it would probably be best that Lou Robin be given an emeritus status and I would be coming on board as the full-time manager for the trust," says Josh Matas of Sandbox. "[This was in] 2014 and things like Spotify were coming online pretty aggressively [...] needing to have a really strong digital presence was not becoming something that was just a nice added value but a necessity to the growth of the landscape and certainly something a 90-year-old gentleman had not really kept up with."

Similarly, the Roy Orbison estate brought in outside management in the shape of Chuck Fleckenstein, who had over a quarter of a century's experience at CBS Records International and Sony Music, ultimately working at Legacy Recordings, Sony's catalogue arm, where he regularly dealt with the Orbison heirs. "One of the key people I met as part of that was [...] Barbara Orbison, who was the late Roy Orbison's widow," he explains. "After I left Sony and Legacy, I kept in touch with her. Sadly [in December 2011], she passed away. But before that, she had put me in touch with her sons and her sons ended up engaging me to manage all of their businesses."

He began formally working for the Orbison estate in 2012. "What I specifically brought is some professional management and some savvy in how the record business and the publishing business work, having a lot of experience with the majors in those areas," he says. "And I brought a whole set of tools that she had, but her sons didn't necessarily have yet. They've actually grown into a lot of these skills with some tutoring from me. When she left, somebody had to pick it up. And I picked it up. I'm just a lucky person."

He joined at a crucial point in the evolution of the record business where CD sales were still sharply declining, but streaming was growing quickly and would soon become the dominant format. Like all estates, the Orbison estate needed to transition neatly into this new world in order to draw in younger fans. Fleckenstein, with his label experience, was able to bring in the skills that the estate was lacking at that stage.

This is a particular problem for older estates as those running them were not necessarily au fait with the changes digital was bringing to the recorded music side of the business. They had two options: cling to the CD and box set market they knew well and watch their income slip incrementally; or make the leap into digital, even if that meant bringing in experienced individuals who could take them from a standing start and build them a viable digital-centric business.

The head of catalogue at a major label gave the example of one major estate they deal with where the lawyers running it were the same ones representing the artist when they were still alive – and that was several decades ago. The heirs of the artist in question are also elderly. "[The artist's] music is used a lot on YouTube with people filming," the catalogue head says. "The same on Facebook and on Instagram. It's great, but I'm not sure the estate is figuring out how their music is spread around the world. I'm trying to explain to them all the time. I get them on the phone just to explain the new world."

When an estate is in limbo due to the lack of a will or infighting between heirs, it can grind to a halt. This is where bringing in an industry expert – even if just in the interim – can help shake it out of its inertia and ensure that deals are still being done and that the artist's legacy is being maintained.

The most high-profile example of this in recent years is the Prince estate where inheritance issues meant that Comerica Bank was put in to oversee things until matters with the heirs were resolved. Eventually Troy Carter was brought in by Comerica as an entertainment adviser in April 2017 to ensure the business of the estate kept going in the interim.[80] His management clients have included Eve, Lady Gaga and John Legend and he served as global head of creator services at Spotify between 2016 and 2018. "Ultimately, I'm working on behalf of his family," he told the BBC in 2019. "They're the ones who are going to own this estate; and the value that we're building is value that's going to be transferred from the court system over to the heirs."[81]

Carter appointed former Warner Bros. A&R executive Michael Howe to look after Prince's vault and to develop a release strategy for the material held there. He discussed the core of his job with *Rolling Stone* in 2018. "How do you preserve Prince's legacy and protect his artistic integrity but at the same time be able to commercialize some of these things for the estate?" he asked hypothetically. "If I went by 'we have to follow it to the T of exactly how Prince would do things,' you can't really do that and run an estate at the same time."[82]

Requests in 2020 to speak to Carter for this book were rebuffed. "Unfortunately, I'm under an NDA with the estate," he said.

* * *

As with living artists, good estate management is a combination of skill, experience, serendipity and – frankly – money. These are businesses and require the same attention and constant revision that any business in music depends on. One false move is highly unlikely to derail an estate entirely; but having the expertise to avoid it happening again and again is far from innate and this is where a professional can justify their salary or percentage cut of the profits.

While family members might not be fluent in the esoterica of the music business, they can learn on the job and soon start to oversee commercially successful operations and enduring legacies. But there is a delicate balance here between the high emotional investment needed to get cultural/musical legacies right, and ensuring that making business decisions is guided by precision.

The music industry in 2020 is more complex and more involved than it was even two decades ago. Digital has dragged the entire industry through its most profound (and accelerated) changes since the arrival of recorded sound at the end of the 19th century.

The industrialisation of estate management is therefore not arising from prescience on where the industry could evolve next, but rather about catching up with where things have already moved to. Change and disruption increasingly feel like features rather than bugs in the modern music business. An estate that does not accept and work with this may end up as the walking dead.

CHAPTER 9

Restoration Artists

Introducing Dead Acts to New Audiences

Despite her rapidly ailing health, making it to the premiere in Hollywood in July 1987 and seeing her son on the big screen was the dying wish of Concepcion Valenzuela. "I'm going to go through this surgery and I'm going to be fine," she told Taylor Hackford, the producer of the biopic. "Because I am going to live to see my son's movie."[1]

Her son was Ritchie Valens, who was killed in a plane crash almost two decades earlier. Since then the family had been through a protracted and painful fight to try and take back control of his music and his legacy. It had all hit Concepcion hard but, finally, the family was getting back most of what it believed it had been robbed of by Valens's producer, Bob Keane.

Concepcion made quite the entrance at the *La Bamba* premiere. "Four guys picked up the four corners of her wheelchair, picked her up on the stage," said Connie Lemos, her daughter and Valens's sister. "You should have seen the standing ovation she got that day. It was amazing."[2]

It also gave Concepcion the opportunity to put some old animosities to rest. As her other daughter, Irma Norton, recalled, "[Bob Keane] says, 'Connie, please forgive me for what happened in these years.' My mom didn't ask any other questions or anything and she said, 'Yeah.' And he turned around, he hugged her and she kissed him on the cheek and he kissed her. And he stayed there."[3]

La Bamba had been a long time in production, with the Valenzuela family having initially been approached in the 1970s by Walter Ulloa, who was working on a screenplay about a Ritchie Valens film. The family set Ulloa a two-year deadline to write something they would be happy with. "He never was able to sell it," Concepcion told the *Los Angeles Times* in July 1987. "In fact, when Donna Ludwig (Ritchie's teenage girlfriend whom he immortal-ized in the song 'Donna') read the script, Ulloa had to change it because he had portrayed Donna's parents as bigots [...] I ultimately told him to forget about it."[4]

Danny Valdez, who ended up as producer of *La Bamba*, came to the family in the early 1980s with a similar plan to make a film about Valens. Having been through one failed attempt, they were not so keen about another attempt. He persisted and they gave him five years to come up with a script and get the project off the ground. He hit their deadline two years ahead of schedule, filming began in the summer of 1986 and it was ready to screen by the following summer.

Despite the glitz of Hollywood surrounding the opening night, Hackford had cautioned the family of Valens not to expect too much from the film's box office takings, suggesting it might be a small affair when it opened to the general public. But it was a massive global hit and Concepcion attended a number of other openings of the film as momentum around it grew. "She attended all the premieres in her little wheelchair," said Lemos. "Her last public appearance was in Watsonville at the Santa Cruz County Fair."[5]

This grieving mother got her wish – seeing her son, as played by Lou Diamond Phillips, become a star again. But a mere three months after the film opened, on 20 October 1987 Concepcion died of a heart attack at the age of 72.[6]

*   *   *

The plane crash on 3 February 1959 that killed Buddy Holly, Ritchie Valens and The Big Bopper has hung over the music business like a shroud. The careers of these three new stars, with slim but highly influential discographies between them, were snuffed out and they sat as a memento mori for generations of musicians who came in their wake, reminding them that life could be short.

By the 1980s, however, popular music in general and rock'n'roll in particular had passed through enormous changes and the teenagers who grew up with 'Chantilly Lace', 'Peggy Sue' and 'Donna' were entering middle age, many of them now parents, or even grandparents. Rock music had contorted into whole new shapes and they had carried new generations along with them. Punk in particular had – perhaps intentionally, perhaps as a contrarian pose – looked to burn down the past. Nostalgia had been seen by some as a form a weakness – of opting out of the future; but the reality was also that old records were incredibly hard to get hold of before the CD reissue boom started to happen in the late 1980s.

Rock music itself was falling out of favour in the 1980s. In the UK in 1986, for example, rock held only 14 per cent of the LP market and 9 per cent of the cassette market, trailing far behind what was quaintly termed "pop/disco" with 55 per cent of the LP market and 49 per cent of the cassette market. In 1987, rock's shared slipped again to 12 per cent of the LP market and 9 per cent of the cassette market.[7] This was mainly frontline releases anyway, but things were slowly starting to change by the end of the decade.

In its yearbook showing record sales in 1989 and 1990, British record company trade body BPI had a sub-section called "1960s/1970s Originals" listing the 25 biggest catalogue album sales of the year. It did not break out what percentage of overall albums sales they made up but it makes for fascinating reading about just how far back nostalgia purchases went. Only four of the top 25 catalogue albums listed dated from the 1960s – The Beatles' *Sgt. Pepper's Lonely Hearts Club Band* (1967), Led Zeppelin's *Led Zeppelin* and *Led Zeppelin II* (both 1969), and Phil Spector's *Christmas Album* (1965). "Mid-price vinyl and cassette re-issues and full-price compact disc releases continue to extend the commercial life of a large number of catalogue items," wrote the BPI.[8] Anything from the 1950s might as well have not existed because releases from that decade were not deemed worthy of inclusion in the BPI's tabulations.

Ahead of this shift came two separate breakthroughs that changed both the business of nostalgia and the business of estates. Between them they opened up the past in whole new ways to audiences who were either feeling nostalgic for their own youth or keen to learn about the music that shaped the contemporary music of the day. And both were based around two of the three fatalities on that doomed flight in 1959: *La Bamba*, the biopic telling the life story of Ritchie Valens, opened in US cinemas in July 1987; and theatre musical *Buddy: The Buddy Holly Story*, opened at the Victoria Palace Theatre in London in October 1989 before opening on Broadway in 1990 and then going on tour in the UK and US in the 1990s and 2000s.

There had been something of a dry run here in 1978 with the release of *The Buddy Holly Story* biopic in 1978, which grossed $14.3 million and won an Academy Award for Best Adaptation Score.[9][10] Philip Norman, in his biography of Buddy Holly, is far from complimentary about the biopic, castigating Gary Bussey (who played Holly) and his "clumpy renditions of Buddy's songs".[11]

La Bamba, however, far exceeded that, with a box office taking of $54.2 million and, crucially, a blockbuster soundtrack that was a US number one in September 1987.[12][13] *La Bamba* arguably created the template for the biopic as event marketing for estates, bringing the music of Valens to whole new generations.

Buddy was not the first jukebox musical – or even the first jukebox musical based around a deceased artist. There was the *Elvis* musical, which opened in London's West End in November 1977 (a mere three months after the singer's passing) and ran until 1996, also delivering a cast recording album in 1978.[14] *Hank Williams: Lost Highway* opened in 1987 in Denver, Colorado and played intermittent tours and residencies in the US until 2003. And Patsy Cline had two musicals – 1988's *Always... Patsy Cline*[15] and 1991's *A Closer Walk with Patsy Cline*[16] – although neither was extended beyond North America. *Buddy: The Buddy Holly Story*, meanwhile, has endured and celebrated its 30th anniversary with a tour in 1989 and 1990, referring to itself as "the world's most successful rock'n'roll musical".[17] Philip Norman was much more effusive about this version of Holly's life, calling it "a theatrical phenomenon to rival anything by Rodgers & Hammerstein or [Andrew] Lloyd Webber".[18]

The timing of *La Bamba* and *Buddy: The Buddy Holly Story* also benefited from the ascent of the CD as a new format and a means for record companies to mine their archives and re-release albums by acts from the past.

Today we might regard this as all terribly rudimentary, but together, this biopic and this musical laid the foundations for estates to think beyond just the recordings and to create vehicles that could become both profit centres in their own right and also branding exercises that drove ancillary revenues like album sales. This is an important philosophical shift where the recordings started to be treated not as the main event but as an add-on for bigger entities.

OLD AND NEW SIDE BY SIDE

At the heart of all estates is a complex balancing act between the past and the future. They have to create things that will help them hold on to existing fans while also creating entry points for potential new fans. Focus too much on the former and the shutters may come down for the latter; cater too heavily to the latter and the former will feel excluded, patronised or belittled and slowly drift away. Plus there is the added fact that original fans will eventually age out and just appealing to them is betting everything on what is, literally, a dying audience. All estates must therefore navigate the tensions between unapologetic esoterica and unbridled populism.

It is a type of "cradle to grave" marketing that all broad consumer brands have to work with, although in this case the core product has already completed the journey to the grave.

As the lawyer for the beneficiaries of the Vladimir Horowitz estate, Jeff Liebenson accepts that this is all a constant state of flux for any estate, but especially so in the classical music field. "We want him [Horowitz] to be well known by the current generation and for them to appreciate his artistry," says Liebenson. "We want to maintain his legacy and his place in the marketplace by bringing him to new listeners. We have to try and accomplish both goals simultaneously."

There is a real pressure on those left to run an estate to ensure that the artist does not fade from the public's view and become an anachronism. There are more opportunities now for estates to take the lead (see Chapter 8), but for a long time the estate was at the mercy of the whims of the record labels that controlled a deceased act's recordings.

A few individuals in the past, however, took a more proactive role, seeking to spur labels into action and refusing to watch the estate sink into irrelevance. "Alma Cogan[19] was one of the first artists to die young with a high profile," says Tony Wadsworth, former chairman and CEO of EMI Music UK & Ireland. "Her sister Sandra used to come in and see me on a regular basis in order to encourage me to put her sister's music out – and she would suggest ideas for commercial release. She wanted to preserve her sister's legend."

A proactive approach like this could give the labels an impetus to push the catalogue. "Sandra would come in and she'd tell me stories about McCartney writing 'Scrambled Eggs' – that became 'Yesterday' – at Alma's flat and stuff like that," continues Wadsworth. "So the added value that somebody like that brings in would be around the package that you would do. It wouldn't just be a 12-track compilation with no sleeve notes. And they would bring photographs. In a way they were like a creative consultant or a marketer on the project. They were certainly adding value."

An estate can lose its way and fail to bring in new generations of fans, thinking that older fans have more disposable income and propensity to spend, but forgetting that they will not be around for ever. This is what Jamie Salter accuses the former custodians of the Elvis Presley estate of slumping into – a posthumous dereliction of duty – before Authentic Brands Group bought its way into the Elvis business. Behaving like a private equity firm, he spotted what he saw as a major flaw in the operation of the estate under CKX/Core Media and one that, if turned around, could dramatically boost revenues. "We looked at what was going on with Elvis Presley and we thought that it was very undervalued in terms of exploitation to the younger generation," he says. "We felt that it needed a facelift." Part of that facelift was to use the young Elvis to appeal to young audiences, including the creation of a cartoon series (explored in more detail below).

Music writer David Browne, however, argues that this remains an existential concern for the Presley estate even after Authentic Brands Group got involved. When we spoke, he was working on a story for *Rolling Stone* about the Elvis estate and he spoke about the challenges it was facing. "It's sort of declined a bit now financially – it's not quite what it was," he says. "It makes money, but not as much. And it's 66 years since the Sun sessions [Elvis's first recordings]. That's an insanely long ago period of time."

In the *Rolling Stone* piece, published in March 2020, Browne argued that the Elvis "empire is in need of a reboot", noting that Elvis memorabilia sales slipped from $4 million in 2017 to $1.5 million in 2019.[20] He added for good measure that a poll of consumers aged 18–24 in the UK in 2017 found that almost 30 per cent of respondents had never listened to a single Elvis Presley song.[21] The piece concluded that the estate had to stop treating Elvis as a deceased rock star and put him into a much broader context so that young consumers could find their way in. "You don't present him as a rocker," John Jackson, the Sony Music executive in charge of the Presley catalogue, told Browne. "You present him as this iconic American story."[22]

David Hirshland, an executive at BMG in the US, claims this macro recontextualisation is something the Johnny Cash estate has achieved – in part by playing on ideas of him as an outsider, a maverick and a man of the people. He has become a country music icon but also, and arguably more importantly, an American iconoclast. "Johnny Cash, every year, becomes more and more a popular figure in American culture," he says.

Moving an act beyond just the genre they are most associated with comes with risks as it may dilute their appeal, but their ongoing relevance is index-linked to the continued relevance of that genre of music happening in the background. The figure quoted above, 30 per cent of respondents not knowing an Elvis song, is a clear and present danger not just for estates but also for entire genres of music.

Sam Arlen, who runs the estate of his father, the composer Harold Arlen, says this is visibly affecting the Great American Songbook writers. While artists like Rod Stewart will cover these jazz and popular music standards from the early 20th century, younger acts are more fearful of tackling them, believing it could date them. As such, the songs are starting to slip from the public consciousness.

It is too simplistic to see this in terms of fans and non-fans, as if there is a reductive and binary process in action here. Bill Zysblat, co-founder of RZO and a key figure in the business dealings of the David Bowie estate, suggests there is a typology of fandom that should guide how estates operate and the types of projects they undertake. "The most important thing you can possibly do is maintain the integrity of the estate and continue doing only what the artists would have done," he argues. "The public is very, very smart and if you do something that a fan truly knows that artist never would have done, you have hurt more than that one project: you might have lost a super-fan. You're not gaining super-fans every day of the week in an estate like you might be with a hit single on the radio. So the best advice you can give anyone is this: do what the artist would have done, do what's right for the legacy and don't worry about the money. The money will either come or it will not." Then he adds with a flourish, "Just don't screw it up."

Jeff Jampol of JAM Inc is firmly of the belief that screwing it up is the default setting of too many estates, especially those who are promiscuous in their licensing and who do not realise that short-term boosts in revenue can cause long-term damage to an estate. As he told the BBC, "I don't think that builds anything. I think what it does is it decays the body of work until there's no body left. To me, my goal is to put my hands underneath the body of work and reanimate and bring it back up and put it back to the pop culture conversation today in a way that's meaningful and resonant to an 11–30-year-old. And if I can do that, the art and the message will live on for ever. And so far, so good."[23]

Jampol has many arguments and analogies here for how bad estates are run and why good estates can learn from their many mistakes. The biggest problem, he feels, is that estates are wasting too much of their time and expenditure super-serving existing (older) fans. "As a company, we spend 85–90 per cent of our efforts focusing on 11–30-year-olds whereas all my vendors and partners are focused 100 per cent on 40–80-year-olds," he claims.

His first major lesson comes from the matchstick analogy. He argues that every estate, when they begin, has between six and eight matches, with each match representing a different project. Do too much too quickly, the argument goes, and you will soon run out of matches. "If you're a beneficiary and somebody comes to you and says, 'Hey, let's do a biopic', you might think, 'OK, great, that sounds good,'" he proposes. "And then you do it and then you strike the match and you light it and everybody looks and it glows and everybody says, 'Ohh, look! There's light.' Then after 10 or 15 seconds the match goes out and you've got a big empty dark fireplace again and you're left with one burnt match. Just do that five or six times – end of legacy!"

His other major analogy is related to escalators and the need for estates to keep moving against odds that are propelling them into irrelevance. "Having a pop culture legacy is kind of like walking up a down escalator," he says. "So if you're standing still, you're actually not standing still – you're moving backwards, you're moving downwards. So what you have to do is you have to have enough forward momentum to overcome the downward trend of the escalator; but not move so fast that you trip all over yourself and you end up at the bottom anyway. So standing still is not standing still; standing still is receding."

He regards himself as a cultural custodian and the conduit through which to take the art of deceased artists on to new generations of fans. "What we do is we figure out what the magic is and we put it in front of potential new fans in a way that is authentic and credible to them," he says. "To me, this stuff is important. Art is important. Art saves lives. Art was my road to sanity. There are messages in these songs and the way these artists lived their lives and it's fucking important and it needs to be carried to future generations. I'm here to help do that to the extent that I can."

Marc Allan of Red Light Management, who represents the Jerry Garcia family, says that the past is critical to draw in new fans and give them the correct context through which to understand an artist and their legacy. In the US in particular, there is a strong college tradition of having a period where The Grateful Dead soundtrack covers much of your social life. Allan says that the nature of fandom today around Jerry Garcia and The Grateful Dead has to replicate the nature of fandom around them in the 1960s and 1970s.

> One key thing that I would want to say is this: what we're really trying to do when we are preserving the legacy and when we're making these actions is we're trying to deliver something for the fans and we're trying to continue that relationship that was there. Fandom is a very special thing. That is the thing that we work from. We're trying to make sure that the new fans have the same relationship to this music that the older fans do – and that they understand the history and the story of this community so it can be passed on, moved on and continue to grow in this modern day.

Darryl Porter, who runs the Miles Davis estate, argues that there are ways (covered in detail below) to use remixes and samples to introduce old acts to new audiences, but the original albums – especially those regarded as the peak of the artist's work in their lifetime – should remain sacrosanct. If the art is good enough, he argues, it will carry through to each subsequent generation of listener. "Keeping the integrity of the albums is very important to us because, as we introduce those albums to new generations and to new Miles fans, this music is new to them, it's fresh to them," he says. "The Persians have a saying that the fish is always fresh when you catch it. That's how we view Miles's albums when we're introducing them to new generations of fans."

A failure to bring in new fans through whatever route works best could mean that the business of the estate will start to shrink and the act's legacy could go into terminal decline – essentially meaning a second death for the artist.

Chuck Fleckenstein from the Roy Orbison estate lays it all out in cold economic terms. "You have to continue to maintain that artist or that artist's relevance," he says. "Estates that are not actively and properly managed are seeing downward revenues."

The paradox for estates is that new audiences are most open to becoming fans of a deceased artist in the immediate aftermath of their death – a period when the heirs are grieving and the estate is often unprepared to capitalise on this, simply because all the organisational and legal issues around its establishment have yet to be resolved.

THE DATA EXPRESS: HOW REAL-TIME CAN HELP ESTATES LAST A LIFETIME

The media coverage around a major pop star from the past naturally creates a spike in interest in their music. In the physical era, LPs, cassettes and CDs would have to be manufactured and distributed to the shops, a process that could take weeks. As one catalogue executive at a major label puts it, "If somebody dies or suddenly something is used, sampled or covered or used in a big sync, you used to need a couple of months to figure out how you can get that CD single out quickly. Now it's just, 'OK, we've got that track up, let's spend money on social media to push people to that song.' You can react so much quicker."

In the digital age, firstly with downloading and then with streaming, the technology is now in place for new audiences to start to instantly explore an artist's recorded music catalogues as well as watch live performances and documentaries on free-to-access platforms like YouTube, as well as subscription platforms like Netflix and Amazon Prime Video. This gives estates breathing space to move in to capitalise on this interest, with trails of digital data coming out of services and social media that can start to be gathered together.

"With that sudden media focus on a particular artist [when they die], for some people that may be the first time they've ever come across them," says a former executive at a large music distribution company. "There's that additional new fanbase coming in and then they're off on their journey of discovery."

There are, however, limitations here. "That's certainly true for various artists, but only if that artist was quite prolific," says the same distribution executive. "If it's an artist that has really only had one album, there's not that much to dig into yet. It's limited. Whereas for an act who has decades of catalogue it's different. There is also the longevity of the conversation in the news."

Record labels in particular have become incredibly adept at dissecting data across a multitude of platforms and using that to pull together marketing campaigns and strategies, almost instantly. This cuts across all their activities equally – for frontline artists and living catalogue artists as well as deceased ones. The major labels and larger independent labels all have complex data dashboards and analytics tools that help them make sense of the billions of lines of data that they can access from Spotify, Apple Music and YouTube as well as Twitter, Facebook and Instagram, enhancing this even further with their own audience data from research they carry out on a rolling basis.

Previously consumption was something that record labels only saw long after the fact (when retailers would send back sales reports, for example) and the effectiveness of advertising and marketing spend was presumed. In the past two decades, however, this has increasingly become something they can see – and respond to – almost immediately.

This has helped the companies segment audiences and better understand how they operate – in terms of size as well as in terms of what they do online and how they can be better targeted and grown as fans.

One label executive argues that data tools are only helpful to a point and that having people working at the label who understand the artists on the roster is something that data can only complement rather than replace. "You take the personality of the artist or the band and you think about what they stand for – traits to do with them that are important as a band," they explain. "Then you marry that with the insight data that you've got on the audience and you look for connections between the two. They're the real connections that make things work."

The same executive, however, says that the window of opportunity to convert someone from a position of casual listening to an artist to becoming a potential fan is incredibly short. They are now able to monitor this in real time – and this is especially critical in the days after an artist has died. "You have to get their attention," they say, "and then you need to be able to keep their attention."

Streaming is now the dominant format for recorded music, accounting for over half (51 per cent) of the global market for the first time in 2019 according to global record company trade body IFPI's numbers. Revenue grew by 22.9 per cent from 2018 to a value of $11.4 billion in 2019.[24] As such, it is an important gateway to discovery for audiences, helping bring older or deceased artists to younger audiences at a scale and a speed that was unimaginable in the early days of the estates business. "A kid can go to a Buddy Holly playlist on Spotify and hear every song he ever wrote," says BMG's David Hirshland. "That just wasn't a possibility 10 years ago. As long as you do the right thing and get the word out and the historical perspective right, kids can rediscover this and kids can realise how cool he was."

The listener data from streaming can also be used to push similar artists to a listener. This is becoming an increasingly powerful way for label catalogue departments, working with estates, to introduce young listeners to artists who are no longer around.

That said, some estates are still struggling to make the transition into the digital age, creating problems with connecting a dead artist with modern music consumers. The Aaliyah estate is a case in point. She died in 2001 but for several years her estate has been trying to cut through the licensing red tape that would allow for all her music to finally appear on digital services.

"The disarray around her business affairs in the wake of her death was complicated by the fact that all three of her albums were on the now-defunct Blackground Records," wrote *Variety* as it dug into these issues. "Further complicating matters is the fact that each album was distributed by a different label."[25]

There have been a number of false starts to solve the problem and in January 2021 her estate posted a message on Twitter addressing mounting fan frustration.

"We hear you and we see you," it said. "While we share your sentiments and desire to have Aaliyah's music released, we must acknowledge that these matters are not within our control and, unfortunately, take time. Our inability to share Aaliyah's music and artistry with the world has been as difficult for us as it has been for all of you. Our priority has always been and will continue to be Aaliyah's music. In the meantime, however, we are working diligently to protect what is in our control—Aaliyah's brand, legacy, and intellectual property."[26]

The estate announced the launch of a Funko Pop! Rocks figurine at the end of January 2021 showing that name and image rights are not holding it back. But while an estate can do as much as it can in terms of merchandise, without music the entire enterprise is stripped of context. A music estate with no music is really no estate at all.

SOCIAL ANXIETY: FACEBOOK, TWITTER AND INSTAGRAM

Social media has created an always-on culture where estates are battling for attention alongside other active pop stars on social media, trying to cut through the general noise on social platforms. "Pre-social media and pre-streaming, it was anniversaries and reissues," says a record label executive working in catalogue on posthumous marketing. "Now there's the opportunity for the artist's message to still be heard or their presence to be felt."

Alicia Yaffe is the founder and CEO of the Spellbound Group, a digital agency that is linked with JAM Inc and works with a number of the estates it represents. One part of what the company does is run the social media accounts for a variety of deceased artists, using new platforms to present deceased artists to contemporary audiences. "Our goals fundamentally are to not only keep current fans engaged, but to reach 11–30-year-olds who may not have been exposed to our clients yet but who are likely to be fans if they have the opportunity to discover them," she explains. Yaffe says that the role is heavily based on research and sourcing quotes from – and stories about – dead artists that can be used to connect with new audiences on Twitter, Facebook and Instagram. "It's about, as much as possible, letting the artist speak in their own words," she says. These quotes have to work on social platforms that are heavily visual and require brevity. Yaffe says the quotes they pick are deemed "pithy", "easily shareable", "bite-size" and "tweetable" as they have to be able to jump out from constantly scrolling feeds on users' smartphones.

"Check out Jim Morrison's Instagram," she says by way of example. "We just started handling socials for Jim Morrison last February [2019]. What we're doing is we're pulling excerpts from his interviews, we're pulling excerpts from his poetry, we're pulling excerpts from his prose. The idea is to really give people an opportunity to connect with Jim the poet, the writer, the thinker, the philosopher, in his own words. They are direct quotes and not edited at all. They are selections that we think best mirror what Jim might have posted or the tone and tempo of social media."

(This theme of the estate communicating in Morrison's own words was cemented with the news that a 600-page book, *The Collected Works of Jim Morrison: Poetry, Journals, Transcripts and Lyrics*, was being published by HarperCollins in June 2021. It includes extracts from 28 of his notebooks that have never been made public before, most significantly the notebook he was using in Paris just before his death.[27] A special edition of the book, limited to 2,000 copies, also came with exclusive audio recoridngs.)

As part of wider social media management, Yaffe gives the example of Janis Joplin and how Spellbound was focusing on her fashion choices in posts on the official Joplin accounts, whereas with Mama Cass the emphasis was on body image issues, chiming with what young audiences today consider to be important. "With Cass Elliott for a while, we were really focusing on and tapping into the body positivity movement and sort of this Lizzo-esque [movement]," she says. "I hesitate to call it a trend but this vibe to really urge people to love themselves at any size and relating that back to Cass who was really a pioneer in that. At the time in the late 1960s, fashion [rules were that] if you were fat, you did not exist, you hid your body and you made room for the skinny people. Cass wore bright colours and huge jewellery and demanded that people look at her and engage with her and didn't apologise for being fat. We really try and tap into that with some of the messaging there."

Cally Callomon, who runs the Nick Drake estate, remains unconvinced, however, about the appropriateness and effectiveness of running social media accounts for deceased artists that act as if the artist themselves is somehow updating it from beyond the veil. "Although Universal had a Nick Drake Facebook page, we've never got involved with anything like that," he says. "We just think it looks odd, you know, that Nick Drake has a Facebook page when Nick Drake's dead."

He accepts it is useful from a marketing perspective to alert fans to new projects and products as well as to potentially see the word spread to others who might not know Drake's music. He says that in 2021 the Drake estate will be updating its BryterMusic.com website so that "Nick's web-based presence will be slightly more relevant". Speaking in late 2020, he refers to the site as "laughably lame" but says this remains the main way that the estate is approached for synchronisation and licensing deals, with almost no approaches coming via social media.

Most, however, in the estates business regard social media as giving them greater autonomy by making them less reliant on – or beholden to – partners like record companies. They also see it as critical in bringing in new generations of fans.

Digital strategist Nick Rizzuto argues that marketing to known fans does not preclude marketing to potential new fans, and that in social media targeting the former, it can fire up the platform's recommendation tools for the latter. "Paradoxically, super-serving existing fans might be one of the best ways to attract new fans," he proposes. "For example, if you post a video of the artist giving a virtuosic performance from decades earlier, this will result in existing fans commenting on the post to rave about and share their memories of the performance. That engagement will likely amplify that post via the platform's algorithm, thereby increasing the likelihood of that video reaching brand-new fans beyond the artist's existing audience. Next thing you know a teenager may see that post, learn about the artist for the first time and end up becoming a lifelong fan. In this way, by posting something likely to excite the existing fans you've also cast out a net to attract brand-new fans."

He explains that marketers working on the official social media channels for deceased artists should follow the best practices for posting on Facebook, namely making at least a post a day to keep engagement levels up which, in turn, feeds into the algorithms. "In recent years, the appetite for artist-related content on social media has become never-ending," he says. "This helps explain why there's been a rise in fan-run pages on Twitter, Instagram and TikTok that simply post an endless drip feed of videos, photos, memes and facts about the artist. Major artists might have dozens of these fan-run pages, each with thousands to hundreds of thousands of followers. These are essentially the new 'unofficial fan clubs'. For artists and their teams, these pages are a fantastic indicator of what sort of content fans are most eager for. Artist camps may also coordinate with these pages to amplify new content or important updates related to the artist."

He continues, "On TikTok, the platform's algorithm rewards any given post based on its own merit. Traditionally, social platforms have determined how many people see a post in a large part via how many people follow the page making the post. This required pages to focus on slowly accumulating followers and posting content tailored to that audience. TikTok evolves upon this dynamic by also analysing the actual visual contents of the post and the velocity of engagement on that post in the minutes and hours after it's first posted. If the post is performing well in that crucial time period, the post is then further amplified. This algorithm helps explain why we've seen so many 'overnight successes' on TikTok compared to traditional social media platforms. It also means that any given post you make could be the one that breaks out and achieves virality."

This "velocity of engagement" is the direct opposite of how estate marketing used to work – often focusing on projects tied to anniversaries, having a flurry of activity there and then going quiet for long periods of time. In social media marketing, if posts are not being created, the algorithm stops doing what it does and the posts get seen by incrementally fewer followers. It is a vicious circle where the more you feed the algorithm, the more insatiable it becomes. This, more than anything, is the biggest change in estate marketing where, ironically, artists in the digital age are not allowed to rest in peace.

"Four or five years ago, it was the conventional logic that all artists needed to post once per day because that's what Facebook's algorithm rewarded," says Rizzuto. "But now we're in the middle of a shift where there may no longer be a limit on the volume of content that fans are willing to engage with. With major artists, we could really be publishing content about these artists and their legacies 24 hours a day – almost like an ESPN [US sports channel] dedicated to this artist – and we still would never reach the end of the fanbase's appetite for that content."

Estates can also turn marketing efforts and competition into data-gathering exercises that will guide further marketing ideas. With everyone in music engaging in an arms race around data, the estate with the weakest data today is the estate most likely to dissolve into irrelevance.

Rizzuto talks of the number of ways estates can gather fan data and the techniques they can use here. "One tried and true method that artist estates can use to engage fans is to host giveaways of memorabilia or merchandise, or competitions that resonate with the fan base," he says. "For example, if an artist was known for their lyrical ability, the estate could create a platform for the artist's fans to submit lyrics of their own and then have fans vote on the best submission in a given timeframe. These sorts of campaigns are incredibly effective because they get the artist's fans talking about the artist, but also allow the estate to collect first-party data points, like email addresses, in order to market to these fans directly in the future."

This is a relatively new strategy for estates but it is slowly becoming standard practice, according to Rizzuto. "Estates are getting more savvy here in terms of understanding the correlations between their activities and the results these may have on an artist's catalogue and business. There are clear correlations between the release of projects like documentaries, films about the artist or album reissues, and outcomes like increased streams of the artist's catalogue, their e-commerce sales, visits to their Wikipedia page or searches made for that artist on Google. With modern tools, it is now much easier to quantify the results and return on investment of efforts like these."

All of this shapes the wider architecture of estates marketing in the modern era, but there are very specific categories that estates are moving into in terms of how they make money, bring in new fans, extend legacies and maintain relevance.

THE BIOPIC

Biopics put estates in much greater control of the narrative and mythology that is subsequently built up around the artist, where they often have approval over everything from the script to the casting. Within that comes not just a repositioning but also a sanitisation of the narrative. The complexities and contradictions of the artist at the centre of them are often removed, gingerly sidestepped or simply brushed over. They often become gleaming but ultimately bland corporate videos where anything that might damage the "brand" of the artist is expunged. Like official biographies, they offer up a partial and airbrushed truth of the totality of an artist.

Sometimes they can work as films if the script and, most importantly, the casting are right. But for every Jamie Foxx in *Ray* (telling the life story of Ray Charles), there are a thousand atrocities clogging up the schedules of the Hallmark Channel that poorly and clumsily tell the story of a deceased artist.

In 2014, the *Guardian* listed the 10 worst music biopics of all time – including 1991's *The Doors* and 2004's *The Man in the Mirror: The Michael Jackson Story*.[28] Finding good ones among the dreck is a harder ask, but iHeartRadio had a go and alighted on 2005's *Walk the Line* (Joaquin Phoenix as Johnny Cash), 2013's *Behind the Candelabra* (Michael Douglas's astonishing turn as Liberace) and 2014's *Get on Up* (with Chadwick Boseman as James Brown).[29] Meanwhile *Rolling Stone* also offered 2007's *La Vie en rose* (with Marion Cotillard as Édith Piaf) and the same year's *Control* (with Sam Riley playing Ian Curtis in Anton Corbijn's film about Joy Division) to the good list.[30]

With the arrival of Netflix and Amazon Prime Video, however, there has been a marked increase in the number of music films being commissioned; with that comes a commensurate rise in the number of commissions the

Hollywood studios are making here. The phenomenal success of 2019's *Bohemian Rhapsody* (ostensibly about Queen but really about Freddie Mercury) and the fact it has grossed $903 million as well as its knock-on effect on the band's streaming numbers marks the start of a new gold rush.[31] Its impact also saw Freddie Mercury return to the *Forbes* list of top-earning dead celebrities in 2020 with revenues of $9 million.[32] This was only Mercury's second appearance in the *Forbes* list since it began in 2001. He was previously listed in 2004 with annual earnings of $5 million.[33]

Taking a biopic from an idea to a finished film is a long and arduous process, with the risk of collapse being a clear and present danger every step of the way.

There is an argument that good or bad things happens in threes – and that appeared to be the case with Jeff Buckley biopics. In 2001, there were three separate films about him at various different stages of development, each hoping to be the first to open and scoop not just the glory but also the box office takings. There was *Greetings from Tim Buckley*, a second one directed by Jake Scott and starring Reeve Carney which had the support of the Jeff Buckley estate (with the working title of *Mystery White Boy*) and *A Pure Drop*, directed by Brendan Fletcher.[34] So far, only *Greetings from Tim Buckley* has made it to the screen (in 2012) and has reportedly grossed a paltry $12,155.[35]

Mary Guibert, Jeff Buckley's mother and the person in charge of his estate, has a multitude of stories about the attempts to have both official and unofficial biopics of her son completed. She had a meeting with Brad Pitt, who wanted to make a Jeff Buckley biopic through Plan B, the production company he set up in 2001 with his then-wife Jennifer Aniston and film and TV producer Brad Grey. Guibert met with Pitt at his house in Los Angeles to discuss the project. She asked Pitt who was going to play her son. Pitt said he would. It did not land the way the Hollywood A-lister perhaps intended.

Guibert takes up the story. "I said, 'Oh, Brad – let's just think about this for a minute. You would be up there on the great big screen, a huge screen. Your eyes are this big [holds hands up to indicate three feet in size] and they're blue. So we put brown contacts on those and then you open your mouth and Jeff Buckley's voice comes out.' And he goes [deflated], 'Yeah.' I said, 'What do you think your buddy Thom Yorke would think about that?' He goes [wounded], 'Oh!' [laughs]. He said, 'OK, right, I don't have the voice and I can't play guitar. I could learn. I could teach myself. I could learn to play guitar.' I said, 'Man, you know, I really see it being an unknown. I really see it being somebody who could really disappear into the role as we would always know it's you, Brad.'"

Guibert says she was previously wary of a Jeff Buckley biopic getting the Hollywood treatment (as they would "screw it up") and was resistant to doing one. "There were people who approached me for years to try and do a biopic – but they wanted to be in charge of it themselves," she says.

"They just wanted me to give them permission to have the music and then they would go and do whatever they wanted. And I was never going to do that."

She says that *Greetings from Tim Buckley* – based around Jeff's perform-ance at a 1991 tribute concert to the late father he barely knew[36] – played fast and loose with the truth, creating a love interest for Jeff who never existed in real life. "There was no such woman in his life," she says. "The only thing that's true is that he did perform at Tim's tribute."[37] She says that Penn Badgley, who played Jeff in *Greetings from Tim Buckley*, had previ-ously auditioned to play Jeff in the planned official biopic, sending in a video audition. "He didn't think he had to show up in person, because he was [supercilious voice] on TV," says Guibert. "The same video that he sent us to audition, that we turned down, was the video that got him the role [in the other film]. It was like, OK, you know, that was so sleazy. It cost them $5 million [to make it]. It made $12,000."

The Jake Scott film eventually imploded. "We were having trouble with the script," she says. "It's always been the script, the script, the script."

When we speak in the summer of 2020, Guibert says that an official biopic is in motion, but the global pandemic meant that everything had to suddenly go on hold. "Except for this [whispers] fucking virus, we are in pre-pre-production," she says. "We are ready to go, Orian Williams is going to direct. Reeve Carney is our Jeff. We have an amazing young actress to play Rebecca [Moore, his girlfriend]. And I have a script that I absolutely adore. I've finally got what I wanted out of the script!"

In March 2021, the biopic's title was confirmed as *Everybody Here Wants You*. "This will be the only official dramatization of Jeff's story which I can promise his fans will be true to him and to his legacy," said Guibert in a press statement. "Thankfully, my determination to assemble all the right participants, no matter how long it took, is about to culminate in the best way possible."[38]

In 2010, the *Sex & Drugs & Rock & Roll* film was released, telling the story of Ian Dury (played by Andy Serkis) a decade after his death. It was a moderate success, taking over $1 million at the box office.[39]

Jemima Dury is daughter of Ian and the most directly involved of his four children in the running of his estate. She had been responsible for putting his sprawling and chaotic archive in order (see Chapter 5) and was also brought in as a consultant on the film.

She says that any dramatic recreation of a musician is going to bend the truth slightly and that family members need to be prepared for an interpret-ation of their life playing out on the screen rather than a definitive version. "It's quite an odd experience," she says. "If I was to pass on any advice to anyone with that kind of project it is this: you've got to have a lot of reassurances up front about, not necessarily how well represented *you* will be in the whole picture, but just [general] reassurances. Like, 'This is going to involve a lot of artistic licence. We're not going to be 100 per cent truthful, *you* might not be in it.' So all of those kinds of things are quite hard to prepare people for in a family if they're getting involved in that sort of project."

She says the film ultimately became a father-and-son story – focusing on Ian's relationship with Baxter (himself a successful musician) – and she had to accept that this was the way the team on the film wanted to push the story. "You can't control portrayals and ideas – and you shouldn't," she says. "You should let somebody do it their way. So it was a very odd experience because it was seeing somebody else's interpretation of what you took as absolute truth."

Ultimately, however, she was happy with the film and the fact that it kept her father's name fresh in the public consciousness – regardless of the narrative framework the filmmakers used. "From some stories I've heard, the director or writer might not get on with the family by the end of the film, so when the film still comes out you all hate each other," she says. "We didn't have any of that. It was a joyful experience."

HOLLY-WOULDN'T: ESTATES BLOCKING A FILM

The estate of Nick Drake has always been resistant to the idea of anyone making a biopic about the singer. His sister, Gabrielle, is an actor and so has both personal and professional objections, rejecting a number of filmic advances over the years. "He's a wonderful romantic hero," she told the *Guardian* in 2004. "But any films about the lives of artists end up making them smaller, not bigger. It's hard to think of someone capturing those almost un-capturable nuances. Also, any film, in the end, is trying to be an explanation of the artist."[40]

According to Cally Callomon, who runs the Drake estate, there is a flat policy of rebuffing any approach to make a biopic. "We get asked once a month by producers about whether we would do a biographical feature film," he says. "The answer is always no. To see Nick Drake as an actor may portray him would be to defy all the 'Nick Drakes' that currently exist in his fans' minds. Biopics have a habit of making their subject smaller by depicting them in 90 minutes, with all the restrictions that medium carries. Nick's songs are, by far, the best biopic that could be, and most of them are about the people around Nick at the time – not Nick per se."

Callomon also feels that the narrative requirements of most contemporary biopics would sit uneasily with the story of Nick Drake. He argues that the truth of Drake's story would make most people "fall asleep" in the cinema and there would be too much pressure from film producers, screenwriters and directors to spice the story up. "You'd have to add a car chase, you'd have to add rampant sex scenes, you'd have to have a dragon!" he jokes. "Something would have to be added to make the story vivid on screen. There are very few Alan Bennetts[41] around who can pull it off by just having one person talking."

For the Jimi Hendrix estate, the challenges are even greater as he remains a powerfully iconic figure, continually being discovered by new generations. As such, filmmakers look at that posthumous fame as something they can capitalise on as opposed to amplify, as would be the case with a lesser-known artist.

In 2015, Legendary Pictures struck a deal with Experience Hendrix to make a biopic about the star, securing the rights to use original recordings, the first planned biopic to do so. Director Paul Greengrass was signed up, having failed to get a 2010 project off the ground as he could not secure the rights for Hendrix's music in the film.[42] Janie Hendrix says this project ascended quickly with a lot of promise but eventually deflated. Legendary Pictures was sold the following year to Chinese entertainment conglomerate Dalian Wanda Group for $3.5 billion and the Hendrix project fell through the cracks.[43] "They're more interested in doing Godzilla films than biopics," sighs Janie. She claims that the team working on it never produced a screenplay but even discussions with them suggested they wanted to take the film in a direction she was not happy with. "He did a lot in four years; he wrote over 200 songs and he really broke a lot of ground in that time," she says. "The screenplay writer really didn't understand. He really wanted to concentrate on the girlfriends, on the drama, all of that. We never actually saw the screenplay. It was just all ideas. We would tell them a different direction. Anyway, it didn't get off the ground."

She says the estate would like to make a biopic, at least in part to counter the "really terrible films" out there which "portrayed Jimi in a very bad way". Unwilling to name names here, she adds that if a film did not have original Hendrix music in it, that was a clear sign it was unapproved by the estate.

She did, however, comment on *Jimi: All Is by My Side*, the 2013 biopic starring André 3000 from Outkast in the title role, noting that its soundtrack was limited to covers Hendrix performed in his lifetime rather than anything he wrote, the rights to which the estate controls. "The funny thing is, though, I have a handwritten letter by André 3000 saying, before this movie was announced, that he would never be involved in anything that didn't have our blessing and that we weren't involved in," she says. "And then literally a week later, he's announcing on TV that he is involved in this movie. That was really sad, because I think that he could have been a good contender had we done a movie back then."

For many estates, the *idea* of a film circulates regularly, but often it stays frozen at the hypothetical stage due to a variety of reasons – family uncertainty, concerns about the script, funding issues, studio prevarications or worry that it might do more harm than good.

Bill Straw of Blix Street, the label that releases Eva Cassidy's records, sums up the reality for many estates. "There has been talk of a movie [about Eva] from the time she went to number one in the UK in March of 2001," he says. "There's never not been talk about a movie. There have been different people involved with different ideas. Some of them not good at all; and some of them not bad. But so far out it hasn't happened." In 2010, there were rumours that a film, provisionally titled *Songbird* (with a script by Kathryn Sheard and Amy Redford as director), was going to be made and that Kate Winslet was possibly going to play Cassidy.[44] Since then the project appears to have petered out.

Biopics can languish in what Hollywood grimly terms "development hell" for many years. Plans for an approved Roy Orbison biopic, for example, were announced in September 2016, with the estate signed up as co-producers.[45] The listing for *Only the Lonely* on IMDb in late 2020 had scant details beyond saying that the estate was involved, his music would be used and the film was still in pre-production.[46]

Equally, *All Eyez on Me*, a Tupac Shakur biopic, had been in discussion and development for over a decade before its release in 2017, with *Billboard* referring to it as "long-delayed".[47] It had a budget of $40 million and made $55.6 million at the box office.[48] It was, however, generally panned by critics, with the *Guardian* calling the script "leaden and flatly expositional" while the *New York Times* damned it as "a clumsy and often bland account of his life and work".[49] [50]

Miles Ahead, the 2015 biopic starring Don Cheadle as Miles Davis, was in development for 11 years, according to Darryl Porter, who runs the Miles Davis estate. He does, however, take issue with the term "biopic" when referring to the film. "*Miles Ahead* was not a biopic," he asserts. "*Miles Ahead* was a mostly fictitious work that had some degree of fact base to it." He says that the script went through "many iterations" before it made it to the screen. Erin Davis and Cheryl Davis, two of Davis's children, were executive producers on the film and it was made with the full cooperation of the estate.[51]

"It started as a true biopic," says Porter. "Don realised along the way that he wasn't comfortable with that because Miles didn't live his life in a conventional manner; so he didn't think it would be good to tell a conventional story. Miles never wanted to look back and a biopic just looks back. We acquiesced and went with that story."

The family having approval on the script was a deal-breaker, but the fact that *Miles Ahead* was initially pitched more than a decade after Davis's passing (in 1991) helped, as the family members could consider it without the emotional rawness of his death still present. Shortly after he died, former president of CBS Records Walter Yetnikoff was looking to get a Miles Davis movie off the ground, possibly with Wesley Snipes in the lead role. "We were all still kind of mourning the loss back then," said Erin Davis.[52] She also added that another film pitched to them was vetoed at the earliest stage because of its narrative approach, something which landed incredibly badly with the family. "I remember having a meeting – I'm not going to say who the principal was in this pitch, but the first thing he wanted to do was have

Miles crash his car and have a kilo of cocaine fly out of the car," says Erin Davis. "And I thought, *Eh, that's not gonna be too good*."[53]

Marc Allan of Red Light Management works with Jerry Garcia's family and says they have moved hesitantly here as they feel rushing into a project with a weak script and the wrong cast could cause lasting damage to his legacy. "There are a number of people that can tell the story, but the question is about who we want to tell that story with – because there's only one authorised moment," says Allan. "I would rather take the time and do it right – because the legacy is going to be the legacy forever, even when the 'hot moments' have passed."

(In March 2021, however, the Garcia estate announced it was working on the *Jerry Garcia, Artist* documentary.[54] It will be based around an interview he gave in 1987 and Garcia's family will act as co-producers.)

The David Bowie estate was much less diplomatic in its objections to what it regarded as a film project that was seriously lacking. In early 2019, it was announced that Johnny Flynn was signed up to play Bowie in *Stardust*, a film telling the story of his first trip to the US in 1971, which proved to be the catalyst for the creation of Ziggy Stardust.[55]

The Bowie estate could not block the film but it could ensure that it put huge obstacles in its way, notably with regard to licensing. Duncan Jones, Bowie's son, responded on Twitter, "I'm not saying this movie is not happening. I honestly wouldn't know. I'm saying that as it stands, this movie won't have any of dad's music in it, and I can't imagine that changing. If you want to see a biopic without his music or the [family's] blessing, that's up to the audience."[56]

The *Stardust* production went ahead – but without any of Bowie's music. It leans on the fact that Bowie's fateful US trip was actually compromised anyway as he did not have a work visa so was unable to play shows. Paul Van Carter, the film's producer, told the *Sunday Times* that the block on using his music could actually be turned into a feature, arguing that it will become "an arthouse drama, not a greatest hits album".[57] When music is used, it will be based on songs Bowie covered at the time, such as those by Jacques Brel, which the film's producers had secured the rights to.

A trailer for the film was posted online in late October 2020. The reaction was, it has to be said, not great and it quickly became the focus of barbs on social media, much of it focusing on Johnny Flynn's appearance and how unlike Bowie he was made to look. "Oh, he's Noel Fielding doing a weird Eddie Izzard impersonation after an ill-advised dye-job on his way to the world's fourth most successful Kasabian cosplay convention," mocked the *Guardian*.[58] Its reaction was far from isolated.

Of course a film about a musician without any of their music is, at best, only half a film. Licensing is the trump card and has been deployed with aplomb by not just the Bowie and Hendrix estates but many others to reduce the scope of films they are not involved with. Even so, many films do make it beyond the pitch and get to the screen (and not always with the estate's involvement). In recent years there has been a marked increase in the number of these going into production.

In June 2020, the trailer for *Respect*, telling the story of Aretha Franklin with Jennifer Hudson in the lead role, was posted online ahead of the film's premiere in January 2021. (The film's producers announced in late October 2020 that its cinematic release would be pushed back to August 2021 due to the global pandemic.[59])

However, Kecalf Franklin, one of the singer's sons, made his displeasure known. He posted on his Facebook account (in caps) that "THE FRANKLIN FAMILY (DOES NOT) SUPPORT THE MOVIE THAT IS IN PRODUC-TION!!!!!" He added, "HOW CAN YOU MAKE A MOVIE ABOUT A PERSON AND NOT TALK TO THE PERSONS [sic] SONS OR GRAND-CHILDREN ABOUT IMPORTANT INFORMATION?" Perhaps cooling down a little, he oscillated between upper and lower case to add a side note. "[T]he 'ONLY' person my mother was in favor of for the movie was JENNIFER HUDSON. Period. Everything else is being done against our wishes (please share)."[60]

In March 2021, Franklin's family also denounced another biopic about the singer, *Genius: Aretha*, which was developed by National Geographic and starred Cynthia Erivo in the title role. National Geographic asserted that it had permission from the estate to make it, calling it a "tribute to Aretha's genius – something we hope we can all celebrate", but family members disagreed and urged fans to boycott it.

"During the process of writing, directing, and filming this movie, we've reached out to Genius as a family on multiple occasions," said Grace Franklin, Aretha's granddaughter (and daughter of Kecalf Franklin). "As the immediate family – emphasis on immediate – we do not support this film and we ask that you also do not support this film, as we feel extremely disrespected, and we feel there will be many inaccuracies about my grandmother's life."[61]

Ahead of its broadcast on 21 March 2021, Kecalf told *Rolling Stone*, "What we've found out in the past is that usually when people don't want to work with you, that is a prelude to some type of unprofessional behavior or a prelude to some type of untruth or slander, so we're not quite sure where [sic] we're going to see in this series.." When asked if he had seen a preview of *Genius: Aretha* before its broadcast, he said he had not. He added he had no intention of watching it when it aired.[62]

Three of the most lucrative estates were also, in 2019 and 2020, in various different stages of production on biopics, something that will surely spur other estates into action here.

Graham King, producer of *Bohemian Rhapsody*, confirmed in late 2019 he was working with the Michael Jackson estate to make a film about the singer and that it would include his music. *Deadline* wrote that the planned film "isn't intended to be a sanitized rendering of Jackson's life" and that "the complexity of Jackson's life is well known and will not be ignored in a film that will span his entire life".[63] Beyond that, however, nothing else was confirmed and it is not known, at the time of writing, when it will come to fruition or who will play Jackson.

The Elvis Presley estate was working with director Baz Luhrmann on a film – simply called *Elvis* – about the singer and especially his relationship with his manager, Tom Parker. Austin Butler was confirmed in 2019 for the lead role, although Harry Styles was also reportedly considered for it.[64] Speaking to me across two interviews in late 2019 and early 2020, Jamie Salter of Authentic Brands Group outlined the plans for the film. "It's a $190 million motion picture being shot in Australia," he says. "It's a biopic. Baz could be, in my opinion, one of the best directors in the world. I am beyond excited to see that movie in 2021. It's going to be pretty, pretty amazing. That is for sure an important part of building a brand."

(The global pandemic, however, pulled the brakes temporarily on the film. Tom Hanks, taking the role of Tom Parker, tested positive for coronavirus in March 2020 and production was immediately halted. Filming resumed in late September 2020 and, despite the six-month shutdown, a release date of November 2021 was being worked towards.[65] In January 2021, however, Warner Bros. announced that it was moving the film's release date again to June 2022 to ensure it had a full theatrical run given it was unclear in early 2021 when cinemas could return to normal.[66])

In April 2020, a Whitney Houston biopic (*I Wanna Dance with Somebody*) was announced by the Houston estate and Primary Wave, which has a 50 per cent stake in the estate. Clive Davis, the record executive who helped make the singer a global star in the 1980s, was also announced as being involved. Stella Meghie was confirmed as director and Anthony McCarten (who wrote the script for *Bohemian Rhapsody*) was signed up as scriptwriter and producer.[67] In December 2020, Naomi Ackie was confirmed as taking the lead role.[68]

Like the cliché about waiting ages for a bus and then two turn up at once, in October 2020 it was revealed that two biopics about B. B. King were in production. King's estate had to quickly move to try to clarify things after actor Wendell Pierce posted on his Twitter account that *The Thrill Is On*, a drama about King's friendship with drummer Michael Zanetis, was happening and that he was playing the blues guitarist. After being contacted by the King estate, he posted a follow-up tweet to clarify that the film was "not a biopic in the traditional sense", calling it instead a "dramatized version of a real-life friendship story".[69]

Vassal Benford, the chairman of King's estate, then spoke to *Variety* to confirm that it was also working on its own, completely separate, film and that it was in no way involved with *The Thrill Is On*. "We want to be crystal clear that the film announced by Pierce is not a biopic, as there are several major players involved in the new B. B. King biopic and the estate does not want there to be any confusion as to the nature of each separate project," Benford said. "One is a docudrama, and the other is the official B. B. King biopic approved by corporate management of the B. B. King estate and trust as a part of B. B. King's legacy initiative."[70]

The January 2021 release of *One Night in Miami* on Amazon Prime Video – a biopic telling the story of the night of 25 February 1964 when Cassius Clay, Jim Brown, Sam Cooke and Malcolm X met to discuss their roles within the civil rights movement – coincided with what would have been Cooke's 90th birthday. "Seeing that movie for us was the climax of our pride because it showcased Sam's brand amazingly," said Nicole Cooke-Johnson, the singer's granddaughter and the person in charge of his estate.[71] Central to the film was 'A Change Is Gonna Come' – a song that had been inducted into the National Recording Registry in 2006 as a recording of cultural and historical significance[72] – and it saw a significant boost in popularity in the wake of the biopic. It was reported to have had over 20 million streams in January 2021 alone.[73]

In February 2021, Todd Haynes was announced as the director of *Fever*, a Peggy Lee biopic, and Michelle Williams was confirmed as taking the lead role. The film had been in the planning stages for several years and had a screenplay written by Norah Ephron. It was, however, put on hold after Ephron's death in 2012. Around the same time as the confirmation of Haynes and Williams on the project it was suggested that Billie Eilish (herself a Peggy Lee fan) was in talks to join the production as executive producer.[74]

Having the family involved can push these projects over the finish line as it gives their heirs a level of control and assurance that makes access to music and background information much more straightforward. But having a family member actually *in* the biopic offers something else entirely.

Nicole Beckett is head of content development at Four Screens and works with the estate of Ol' Dirty Bastard. She says that his son, the perfectly titled Young Dirty Bastard, actually played his father in holographic form in 2013 (see Chapter 12). This now opens up the possibility that Young could play ODB in a future biopic, especially given how remarkably alike they look.

"His son is always an option," says Beckett, only adding that a biopic is a possibility rather than something that is in motion. "Once you hook up with a studio system and things like that, you can't always guarantee that. They could be looking for more star power, they could be looking for this or that – so it's definitely not a guarantee. Obviously he would be a great pick as far as I'm concerned."

THE DOCUMENTARY

On the flip side of the cinematic coin is the documentary. Where biopics can bend the truth – adding in stories and quotes that never happened and characters that never existed – documentaries are tied much more explicitly to the facts. Of course there will be conflicting interpretations about events, but they cannot spiral into the fictional in the way that a biopic can.

They can set the temperature of a legacy soon after an artist's death but they can also become a hugely important source of revenue. *This Is It*, for example, helped claw the Michael Jackson estate out of serious debt – estimated at $500 million – in its earliest years and set it up to become the most lucrative celebrity estate in existence. It was released in October 2009, barely four months after the singer died, and was drawn from rehearsal footage in Los Angeles for his planned run of comeback shows at the O2 in London.

It was criticised for coming too soon after Jackson's death and for being an explicitly commercial undertaking. It was, however, a vast commercial success, with a US opening weekend of $23.2 million and eventually taking in $261.2 million at the box office globally.[75] "When we took over his estate, there were certain issues with debt that had to be addressed and we needed to generate income in order to pay off that debt," says John Branca, who runs the Jackson estate. "The first project we did was to produce the movie *This Is It*, which went on to become the biggest-grossing concert film and biggest-grossing worldwide documentary in history."

The documentary format has been a lucrative vehicle that the Jackson estate has returned to a number of times. "It started with *This Is It*, which gave an up-close-and-personal look at Michael in the creation of the tour and then people began to understand that he was the absolute, ultimate artist, completely in control of his art," says Branca. "We followed that up with a documentary by Spike Lee called *Bad 25* [in August 2012] which was an up-close-and-personal look at Michael in the recording studio, looking at how he created and produced that album and those videos. There was also another Spike Lee documentary, *Michael Jackson's Journey from Motown to Off the Wall* [in January 2012] that showed the path that Michael took from being a child star at Motown at the age of 10 to being somewhat down and out where people felt that Michael was over and that the Jackson 5 were over. Then Michael resurrected and reinvented himself and became the biggest star in the world."

Beyond the pure economics, Branca also argues that such projects help introduce acts to younger audiences and lay the foundations for the fans of tomorrow. "I think there's an education component to keep the legacy of the artist alive and introduce the artists to new generations of fans – whether that's a documentary or a biopic," he says.

Another documentary, however, was to plunge the Jackson estate into its biggest crisis to date. The impact of *Leaving Neverland* in 2019 is explored in more depth in Chapter 11.

Ron Howard's 2019 documentary about Luciano Pavarotti, simply entitled *Pavarotti*, came out 12 years after the tenor's death and helped revive interest in him. While the reviews may not have been glowing – NPR said it "lacks any dramatic arc, and fails to make us feel much for its subject"[76] and the *Guardian* called it "a 114-minute montage of obsequious syrup"[77] – it still made $7.8 million at the global box office.[78]

A more powerful and profound documentary was 2015's *Amy* about the life of Amy Winehouse. It did not skirt around any of the pain in her life, covering her addiction issues, her eating disorders, the toxic partners she found herself with, the breakdown in her family relationships, the scalding glare of fame and the creeping nightmare of tabloid intrusion in unflinching detail. Despite being a shocking and often painful watch, it was both a critical success and a commercial one, with global box office takings of $23.7 million.[79]

Winehouse's record label, Universal Music, was an investor and co-producer in the film. Ahead of its release, David Joseph, the chairman and CEO of Universal Music UK & Ireland, said, "About two years ago we decided to make a movie about her – her career and her life. It's a very complicated and tender movie. It tackles lots of things about family and media, fame, addiction, but most importantly, it captures the very heart of what she was about, which is an amazing person and a true musical genius."[80]

The record label as an investor in a documentary goes beyond the economic and into the cultural, hoping to impose its own angle on the wider narrative around a deceased star. One senior UK record industry figure was incredibly uneasy. "Who is the arbiter of good taste?" they ask hypothetically. "Who is the arbiter of what is important to this artist or not? I think Universal took it upon themselves to be the arbiters – over and above the estate."

Just as with biopics, documentaries can also find themselves starved of light and oxygen in development hell, eventually losing all impetus. This happened with a planned Martin Scorsese documentary about the Ramones. It was being discussed in the media in 2014, with Jeff Jampol of JAM Inc, who works with the Johnny Ramone estate, telling *Billboard* that "we just secured a ton of footage, much of which has never been seen before" and that the goal was to have it released in 2016 to mark the 40th anniversary of the release of the band's debut album.[81] That date came and went and no documentary was ever seen.[82]

Linda Ramone fills in the details of what happened (or, more precisely, what did not happen). "At that point, [Scorsese] was just going to be a producer on it," she says in early 2020. "It was through a friend of mine, Rick Yorn. I ain't saying it's off the table, but right now, the way things are [pauses, referring to issues with the Joey Ramone estate], it can't move forward right now. Martin Scorsese is interested and I would love to do something with him. That's always on the back burner because of Rick Yorn who is a personal friend and he manages Martin Scorsese. That's something for the future. Hopefully one day we can all get together and do that. But that would be amazing."

Nicole Beckett says that a documentary series about Wu-Tang Clan, 2019's *Wu-Tang Clan: Of Mics and Men*, and a mini documentary on Amazon to push the release of *Return to the 36 Chambers: The Dirty Version* (a reissue of Ol' Dirty Bastard's 1995 debut album) were the catalyst to make a full documentary about Ol' Dirty Bastard. That is the filmic priority for the estate, with a biopic taking second place.

"We are actually in the works of doing a documentary on his life, more based on his personal life," she says, speaking in the summer of 2020. "There's been a lot of stuff that's been Wu-Tang-related with the whole group, but this will be very much more focused on him, his family and his family life. It'll be a different viewpoint along with stories from different fans and people who have worked with him in the past. Everybody has an ODB story! Anybody that was in alive in the 1990s and was in that circle, definitely has a story. And they are all great stories. So we are working on that."

Having control of an act's catalogue – be that records, publishing or both – is something some estates want before they consider making a documentary. Having all those rights, as well as access to the archive, gives them considerable control over the finished product.

This is something Isaac Hayes III says needed to happen before he could consider making a documentary about his father. As all the rights slowly revert back to the Hayes estate, he feels he can now start putting plans together and, when the last set of rights come back, green-light it.

"Now we have the opportunity that when we do a documentary or a movie we don't really have to seek that much permission because now we control the publishing," he says.

The plan, he says, is to make three separate but themed documentaries and then consider a biopic.

"The first documentary that I want to do is a documentary just on my father's life. A classic from the beginning – from picking cotton to being an Academy Award-winning singer to a Grammy Award-winning singer and this icon," he says. "Secondly, I want to do a documentary on my father's bankruptcy [in the 1970s]. Thirdly, my father's one of the architects of hip-hop along with James Brown and other soul greats. I would like to go around and speak to all these producers and all these artists that sampled Isaac Hayes and who created this great work."

He says that the clock is ticking on this as he wants to speak to people from across his father's career, which started in the 1960s. "A lot of those people are old and we want to make sure that we get them on camera and get that information down and start to gather and hear those stories," he says. "That's really one of the most important things."

The Miles Davis estate has overseen both a biopic and a documentary about the artist. *Birth of the Cool*, directed by Stanley Nelson, was released in 2019 and had the full involvement of the estate. "The documentary was a big opportunity," says Darryl Porter. "We gave them access to everything [from the archive]. The way that they used it just had to be very respectful and balanced. And I have to say, in the end, Stanley Nelson and [producer] Nicole London did a beautiful job of balancing out who Miles is as a person."

Often having family members and collaborators involved is a prerequisite to getting the documentary made. The March 2021 Netflix documentary on the life of Notorious BIG, *Biggie: I Got a Story to Tell*, had the late rapper's mother Violetta Wallace named as an executive producer alongside Sean Combs, his friend and label head at Bad Boy Records.[83] On the one hand, having friends and family involved can give the documentary makers incredible access to sources and the archive but equally it runs the risk of becoming a sanitised and partial telling of the story.

Large estates can often pick and choose when it comes to documentaries and the more famous the artist is, the less challenging it is to raise the funding to make a documentary. Whereas previously small estates were locked out of much of this, the rise of crowdfunding platforms has at least given them the opportunity to make a documentary.

Celeste Bell says that she turned to Indiegogo to raise the initial capital to start work on a documentary about her mother, Poly Styrene of X-Ray Spex. "We raised our target of £75,000 and that was going to fund the initial part of the film process – all the filming, the crew, editing," she says. "It will be a feature-length documentary. Out of that £75,000, unfortunately a lot went already on fees for the platform. Then you've got to pay for all the rewards – the T-shirts, the mugs, tote bags, posters. You have to pay for all of that to get that sent out."

She says that she applied for Arts Council funding to cover the next stage, which involved licensing video and music footage, but was unsuccessful. Speaking in late 2019, she says she was considering seeking private investment or doing a second crowdfunding project to take it over the line. In February 2021, it was announced that the completed film – *Poly Styrene: I Am a Cliché* – would get its North American premiere at the following month's SXSW Film Festival.[84] It received its general release on 5 March 2021.[85]

"I was always determined to be really open, warts and all," said Bell when promoting the film in February 2021. "But at the same time, what's really important for me, more than anything else, is giving my mother the respect she deserves, and making a film she would be happy with."[86]

While this is an onerous process today, it would have been impossible for any estate even a decade ago. Such films will invariably be low generators of revenue – that is if they even break even – but they do give small estates another means of drawing in fans and extending legacies when estates have to be run in their spare time rather than as a full-time job.

Estates sometimes have to create documentaries themselves simply because they feel the ones already in the market are inferior. This was certainly the case with the Johnny Cash estate. Josh Matas of Sandbox Entertainment, which helps to run the Cash estate, spells it out in stark terms.

"One of the things that I came into the mix here on was this idea that this thing had not existed – that we did not have a proper documentary," he says. "There have been a number of documentaries and I'm on record with this and so I'll say this very candidly – most of them were quite frankly shit! What I set out to do very specifically was look for incredibly qualified and talented filmmakers that I felt would give the depth and richness of story that Johnny Cash deserved on screen."

Frank Marshall was brought on board as producer and *The Gift: The Journey of Johnny Cash* was eventually released in 2019. It got its online premiere on YouTube which Matas says was critical in broadening the audience for it. "When the YouTube deal came into place, for me, it was like a double-down on this notion of creating a next generation of fan," he says.

As the *Amy* documentary proved, having the record label involved can open many doors and also help with the funding. While these tend to be single-artist documentaries, Rhino, the catalogue arm of Warner Music, was deeply involved as producer on the two-part *Laurel Canyon* documentary series in 2020 which focused on the music scene there in the late 1960s and early 1970s. Warner got involved because many acts on its roster were pivotal to that scene and so the uptick for both living artists and the estates it works with was significant.

"I feel like that will be a great vehicle," says Mark Pinkus, president of Rhino Entertainment, the catalogue arm of Warner Music Group. "Documentaries are certainly one way to get the story out. We're producers on it. We had an initial conversation, just about the viability of the project. And we obviously got super excited about it. It's just snowballed. It was supposed to be a 90-minute documentary. Now it's a four-hour documentary film. We are thrilled. There are so many of our artists who are part of that."

THE MUSICAL

A musical about the life of a musician – or a jukebox musical based on the catalogue of one performer – is a kind of meta-project that makes sense to a number of estates. The theatre audience is also, because of its very nature, much broader than the audience for a hologram show, for example, and so can fulfil that remit of going beyond the core super-fans to attract a wider demographic to the music of a particular deceased artist.

Rather than pursuing the nuance of a biopic or documentary, musicals paint in broader brushstrokes in order to make their appeal as wide as possible. Perhaps nowhere else in the estates business is the disparity between "credibility" and "commercial ambitions" laid out so explicitly.

Buddy: The Buddy Holly Story was, as noted above, not the first jukebox musical put together around a deceased artist; however, it is the one that has most shaped what happened in the theatre world from the early 1990s onwards. It took some time for other estates to see the benefit here, but the eventual success of *We Will Rock You* (which opened in London in 2002 and was based around the music of Queen) came in the wake of *Mamma Mia!* (the phenomenally successful musical, as well as film and restaurant franchise, based around the songs of ABBA, which debuted in 1999) and together they opened up the possibility of modern musicals becoming international blockbusters.

The original pitch for what was to become *We Will Rock You* was that it would tell the story of Freddie Mercury and was being developed by Jim Beach, Queen's manager, from the early 1990s. Tribeca, the production company of Robert De Niro, was interested in investing, but only if the plot was broadened out. Eventually it became a dystopian tale set in the near future where rock music had been banned but an underground resistance knew this music, if it were to be found, could eventually liberate the cowed populace.

As a story, it was – frankly – gobbledygook and the production nearly closed as the reviews were almost universally terrible and attendance figures almost as bad. The team behind it persisted and it eventually became a success, running until 2014 in London as well as playing in multiple countries around the world. It played to 16 million people in 28 countries and was one of the 10 longest-running musicals in the West End.[87] It also, arguably, laid the groundwork for 2018's *Bohemian Rhapsody* film, maintaining Queen and Freddie Mercury's place in the public eye.

EMI, Queen's long-term record label, had a stake in *We Will Rock You* and it helped push sales of the band's albums and greatest hits compilations through its run. "We were co-investors in it," says Tony Wadsworth, who was chairman and CEO of EMI Music UK & Ireland at the time. "The whole structure of West End musicals in relation to who gets the money back first [is complex]. Tribeca also invested. Jim Beach, Queen's manager, knew after Freddie Mercury had died that there had to be vehicles and there had to be activity to maintain the spotlight on the catalogue; there had to be sustained activity."

Despite poor sales in the opening months, Beach refused to admit defeat. "He had a vision, he's very persuasive, extremely hard working and he wasn't going to let *We Will Rock You* not work," says Wadsworth. "It got to a point where he gained momentum and a critical mass and then it became unstoppable. And they marketed the living daylights out of it. He made it work. I think, honestly, if any other artist manager had been involved in that, it would have closed. It probably wouldn't have made it through the year."

Michael Jackson has made multiple reappearances in musicals since his death, including *Thriller Live*, which opened in the West End in London in 2008. By early 2019 it was the 13th longest-running musical in London, and has extended to Europe.[88]

The Jackson estate partnered with Cirque du Soleil on the *Michael Jackson: The Immortal World Tour* production that toured between 2011 and 2014. "It grossed close to $400 million at the box office, making it one of the biggest grossing tours of all time," says John Branca. "The *Immortal* tour ranked with U2 and The Rolling Stones as one of the biggest grossing tours in history." In 2013, the Jackson estate partnered with Cirque du Soleil again on *Michael Jackson: One* for a residency in Las Vegas. Following that, *MJ: The Musical* was originally due to open on Broadway in the summer of 2020 but the opening date was pushed to March 2021 due to the global pandemic and the shutting of theatres.[89] It was developed as a co-production between Lia Vollack Productions and the Jackson estate.

News came in November 2019 of one musical, however, that did not have the Jackson estate's involvement. It was called *For the Love of a Glove: An Unauthorised Musical Fable About the Life of Michael Jackson, as Told by His Glove* and it was claimed it was being produced by Johnny Depp (Depp later denied any involvement).[90] As the title suggested, it is told from the perspective of his sequinned glove. Julien Nitzberg wrote the script and told *Page Six* the origin story. "A major TV network wanted me to write a [Jackson] movie... but the question came up [about] how to deal with the child-abuse allegations," he said, adding that the network and he were at loggerheads about it. "I said, how's this? Everything MJ has been accused of has actually been caused by his glove, which is actually an alien from outer space [and] feeds on virgin boy blood. They laughed and said, can you do the normal version?"[91]

It opened in Los Angeles in early 2020 and, yes, the plot involved a sparkly glove from outer space called Thrihil-Lha which gave Jackson his talent but in exchange for virgin blood. "*For the Love of a Glove* isn't a play about answers," said NPR in its review. "It's about questioning legacies – and the legacies of kings are never really settled."[92] The Jackson estate has not commented publicly on the production.

Some musicals have relatively short runs despite being based around big names. *A Night with Janis Joplin*, for example, opened on Broadway in October 2013 and closed the following February after 22 preview shows and just 141 regular performances.[93] A planned off-Broadway downsizing and relocation at the Gramercy Theatre in April 2014 was pulled just two days before it was due to open. "The implosion of 'A Night With Janis Joplin' – which had a budget of $3.9 million on Broadway and about $650,000 for the Gramercy – stands as one of the messiest of the theater season," wrote the *New York Times*. "But it is also an object lesson in making rosy assumptions about ticket sales in the unpredictable world of commercial theater."[94]

Another short-lived musical was *Holler If Ya Hear Me* based around a world presented through the music and lyrics of Tupac Shakur (but it was not a biography of the rapper). It opened at the Palace Theatre on Broadway on 19 June 2014 and closed on 20 July 2014 after just 17 previews and 38 regular performances.[95] *We Will Rock You* managed to survive a run of genuinely terrible reviews, but the critical response to *Holler If Ya Hear Me* helped sink it. Even before it opened, theatre critic David Cote said it had an uphill struggle. "You have to hit the lowest common denominator if you want a show to really run," he told CBS News. "Now lowest common denominator does not mean necessarily bad quality, it just means it has broad appeal."[96] This and the many bad reviews – CBS called it "tepid", *Variety* dismissed it as "clunky", *Time Out* said it was "a shapeless mix of melodrama, music video and half-grasped musical clichés" and the *Guardian* witheringly said "strictly all eyez on the exit"[97] – did for it, making it one of the shortest-lived musicals based on the songs of a major star.

Despite the towering commercial and credibility risks here, major estates are planning musicals for 2021. In February 2020, it was announced that *Get Up, Stand Up! The Bob Marley Story* would open at the Lyric Theatre in London in February 2021. It had been in development for several years and was given the stamp of authority by having Chris Blackwell, founder of Island Records, involved as a producer as well as the blessing of the Marley estate.[98]

There have also been recurring rumours of a Whitney Houston musical being developed. Larry Mestel of Primary Wave told the *New York Times* in May 2019 that he was in discussions with Broadway producers about a Whitney musical as well as others about a Las Vegas-based show.[99] Speaking to me in early 2020, however, Pat Houston pours cold water on much of the speculation about a Whitney Houston musical. "People have always come to us about a Broadway musical," she says, refusing to comment any further about plans or rumours.

Mestel also talked about the plans for a Bob Marley show in the epicentre of global razzamatazz that one might suggest flies in the face of Marley's wariness about crass commercialisation. Primary Wave was a partner in these activities, having bought a stake in Marley's publishing in 2018 for $50 million.[100] "In conjunction with the family, we're developing a destination Marley show for the Las Vegas market," he says when we speak in early 2020. "Think of The Beatles' *Love* show – that kind of extravaganza."

Mary Guibert also says that there are plans in place to take a small production of a musical drawing on the songs of Jeff Buckley to Broadway. She says,

> We have Alex Timbers – who directed *Beetlejuice* and the Broadway production of *Moulin Rouge* – who wants to produce a version of *The Last Goodbye*, which is Shakespeare's *Romeo and Juliet* and Jeff's music together as a musical. We put it up on the boards in Williamstown in 2010[101] and it broke the box office record for the Williamstown Theatre Festival that they have every year. Then we did it again at the Old Globe in San Diego [in 2013[102]] and had a great run there. Alex directed it [...] He wants to put that up on Broadway, but we have to get Broadway back to work [it's closed due to the pandemic]. God knows we're never going to be filling theatres again.

At the opposite end of the scale – away from the glitter and high investment stakes of Las Vegas, Broadway and the West End – sits *Reasons to Be*

Cheerful, a musical based on the music of Ian Dury, which opened in 2010 and was revived again in 2017, playing in smaller regional theatres in the UK such as the Belgrade Theatre in Coventry.[103]

It opened in Stratford East in London and Jemima Dury recalled attending it. "I went to the toilets in the interval, there were all these young black kids from Newham College, they're in the toilets, *Sex & Drugs & Rock & Roll*," she said. "I just thought, God, talk about a new audience, it was amazing."[104]

Dury says the origins of the musical came from theatre company Graeae, of which her father had been a patron. It describes itself as "a force for change in world-class theatre, boldly placing D/deaf and disabled actors centre stage and challenging preconceptions".[105] Ian Dury became involved as he had contracted polio as a child which left him with a paralysed left leg and arm.[106] Graeae had originally asked Dury for permission to use the song 'Reasons to Be Cheerful' in a production it was putting on at the Riverside Studios in London and he agreed, letting them have it for free.

After Dury's death, Graeae contacted the family about the idea of an entire show built around 'Reasons to Be Cheerful'. Jemima says the family at that stage was worn out from involvement in two separate Ian Dury biographies as well the biopic, so they trusted Graeae, but without really paying much attention to the script. "They had press nights and were begging for us to go and see it but none of us were getting back to them," she says. "And eventually the run at Stratford East opened and I was feeling more and more guilty about having not replied. So I said to the family, 'I'm going to go. I'll be the rep.' I booked myself in to see one of the performances and I was so blown away! […] ever since that time I've kind of slaved for them. I've just done whatever they wanted me to do in any respect. So I'm now one of their patrons. Down the line I got more and more involved with them. So that's been a very happy outcome. That's been great."

The high risk of failure here does not, however, put off estates from trying, believing they can create something that runs as long as *Buddy: The Buddy Holly Story* or *We Will Rock You*.

While 1977's *Elvis* was in no way officially endorsed by the Presley family, the Presley estate, led by Authentic Brands Group, has had its own swing at the world of musical theatre, announcing in July 2018 that it was developing *Heartbreak Hotel*, a stage musical about the early years of Elvis, and had Sony/ATV Music Publishing involved as a co-producer and investor. Part of Sony/ATV's involvement was ensuring the licensing of a number of the hits from the opening years of his career.[107] Since then, nothing has been heard about the musical, suggesting that even Elvis is not immune from falling into production limbo, with *Heartbreak Hotel* trapped in development hell.

THE ANNIVERSARY

A failsafe through the early years of the modern estate business since the late 1960s and early 1970s, the anniversary of a late pop star's death or birth – eventually broadened out to include the release date of classic albums – was almost the default setting of estates. It has now become so routine as to be utterly unremarkable.

Never willing to do things in a restrained manner, the Elvis Presley estate does not confine its activities to a mere day. Elvis Week is a solid fixture in its calendar and its name is now a misnomer as it actually lasts much longer than a week. Ostensibly there to mark the anniversary of his death on 16 August 1977, in 2019, for example, it ran from 9 to 17 August and included an Elvis Gospel Brunch, a tribute act contest (with meet 'n' greet) and an auction "featuring artifacts authenticated by Graceland Authenticated".[108]

In 2020, due to the global pandemic, Elvis Week still took place, this time between 8 and 16 August, in a modified form, including "pre-recorded content" and "a socially distanced Candlelight Vigil" with limited numbers of tickets on sale.[109] There was also a virtual programme of events for fans to watch remotely, with tickets costing $39 each.[110]

For most other estates, however, activity is based around a major anniversary rather than treated as a sprawling annual event.

In early 2020, the Bob Marley estate had a flurry of activity to mark what would have been his 75th birthday (he was born on 6 February 1945). Under the umbrella of MARLEY75, the estate undertook a variety of activities such as creating a new video for "Redemption Song", putting out previously unreleased tracks, hosting exhibitions and tribute shows and culminating with the takeover of the 1 Hotel in West Hollywood, temporarily renaming it the One Love Hotel for a week, to coincide with the Grammys.[111]

"Bob Marley is my boss and he keeps me really busy," Cedella Marley, his daughter and a key figure in the estate, told *Billboard*. "But I love my job. I don't just sit down and say, 'Oh, that's cute.' I'm in the dirt, planting the seeds. Then we get the flowers."[112] Larry Mestel of Primary Wave says the renaming of the 1 Hotel "became the epicentre of all things Bob Marley in Los Angeles that week" and it included a pop-up Marley merchandise store as well as hosting live performances from the Stephen Marley Band. "I have to give credit to our brand team – they really did a spectacular job of putting together great events, great sponsors, and getting artists excited around the event," says Mestel. "It was an entire week of celebration of Bob's 75th birthday. It was highly successful. I think the family were absolutely blown away by the respect and the quality of the events and the work that our team did."

Sadly, 2020 was a big, but ultimately doomed, year for estates marking milestone anniversaries with the global pandemic pulling the brakes on assorted projects.

Peggy Lee was born on 6 May 1920 and her estate was planning a number of major tribute shows in the US and the UK to mark her centenary, but they all had to be cancelled.

Also temporarily affected was the *This Is Nat King Cole* exhibit at the Grammy Museum that was due to open on 17 March 2020 to mark 101 years since his birth (the actual centenary had been missed).[113] The missing of an anniversary due to a global pandemic is unfortunate but understandable. Missing it, however, in normal times is deemed unforgivable for some estate managers. Darryl Porter from the Miles Davis estate, speaking in early 2020 before details of *This Is Nat King Cole* had been announced, said the missing of his 100th birthday was a squandered opportunity. "Ella Fitzgerald had her centennial a couple years back [2017] and there were hundreds of tribute concerts to her across the United States alone," he says. "Juxtapose that to last year [2019] and Nat King Cole's centennial. What did you hear? What did you see?"

He adds, "That really broke my heart because Nat King Cole is a guy who wasn't fully celebrated in his lifetime. He experienced a lot of discrimination, but he accomplished a lot. And it was an opportunity to rebrand Nat King Cole and to put him on TV shows and movies and to do remixes or have people just do tributes. It would have been a perfect opportunity to do something at the Grammys this year. I watched it and there was not a word about Nat King Cole's centennial. It broke my heart. Not a word."

The increasing willingness to dig through the archives and finally release material that was gathering dust on the shelves has meant that classic albums can now be reissued multiple times for landmark anniversaries. Unheard material is increasingly earmarked for anniversary issues as a means of hooking in fans to make them buy an album they already own in multiple editions.

It can even go so far as to release different expanded editions of the same album at the same time, each created with a certain demographic, defined by their willingness to spend, in mind. There is a remastered edition, an expanded edition and a deluxe box set edition (where often the bulk of the material is kept off streaming services, so paying several hundred pounds for the top-end edition is the only way fans can, legally, hear it).

Warner Music France, for example, used the 100th anniversary of the birth of Édith Piaf in 2015 to release *Intégrale*, a major box set of her work across 20 CDs, spanning 350 tracks (as well as an LP edition). It was limited to 10,000 copies globally and each set came with a 30-page book as well as a bonus 10-inch vinyl single.[114] A truncated version across just two discs was also made available for more casual consumers.

The limited-edition box set sold out. "It was 10,000 box sets with 20 CDs, so we sold 200,000 CDs of Édith Piaf's back catalogue – that's not bad!" says Thierry Jacquet, head of catalogue at Warner Music France. "With the box set, we won a Grammy Award in 2017 for the Best Boxed or Special Limited Edition Package." It was awarded to Gérard Lo Monaco, the art director.[115]

In late 2020, the John Lennon estate marked what would have been his 80th birthday on 9 October with a major push. This included a two-part documentary on BBC Radio 2, hosted by his son, Sean Ono Lennon.[116] On top of this was the LENNON80 pop-up TV channel on Freeview in the UK, screening documentaries as well as classic appearances by Lennon on chat shows like *Parkinson* in 1971 and *The Dick Cavett Show* in both 1971 and 1972. BBC 6 Music also broadcast *John Lennon's 25 Greatest Songs*, counting down his standout tracks with The Beatles and as a solo artist.[117]

As the estates business has evolved and become more complex, the album reissue or the tie-in greatest hits to mark an anniversary is pushed out further and further from the epicentre of an estate's activities. It cannot be a standalone project and has to fit into something broader, one moving part in a much bigger machine.

The techniques of experiential marketing[118] are now deeply embedded in the marketing activities of a number of estates. The 50th anniversary of *Morrison Hotel*, the fifth studio album by The Doors, in February 2020 sits as a highly illustrative example of this thinking in action. The album itself was reissued in a remastered form and was expanded with an hour of previously unreleased studio outtakes, but it also came with a "biographical comic book" created by Z2 Comics.[119]

On top of this, it was tied into the fourth annual Day of The Doors event in Los Angeles in January that year. The original Morrison Hotel on Hope Street in downtown Los Angeles, where the album sleeve was shot, became the focal point of the day.[120] A duplicate of its original façade was created so that fans could book a time slot and recreate the cover shoot in the hotel window, the idea being they would share their photos and videos on the social media channels with a dedicated hashtag and give the feel – or the illusion, at least – of "organic" marketing.

Spellbound Group was in charge of the marketing on behalf of The Doors and the estate of Jim Morrison. "For us, our job on the social side and as marketers is really, at this point in this day and age, to drive people to streaming," says Alicia Yaffe, founder and CEO of Spellbound. "For social media, always-on means always putting out that content and giving people something to listen to. Yes, the big anniversaries only come every once in a while, but we've got birthdays, anniversaries, we've got other focal points that we can tie into that you need for traditional marketing."

The recreation of the original album cover was done in collaboration with Relevant Group who own the hotel and they used the parking lots around it to host the day's events. This included live performances, film screenings and a photography exhibition, with Spellbound saying that 3,000 people attended on the day.

Record companies in particular embrace the anniversary approach to marketing the catalogue of a deceased artist as this is where they make the bulk of their money via record sales and streams. Even music companies who have bought into the wider business of an estate still cling to the power of the anniversary to increase business overall.

"I think anniversaries are still important," says David Hirshland of BMG who now runs the Buddy Holly estate. "February 3 is a huge day for us because that was the day the music died [when Holly, Ritchie Valens and The Big Bopper all died in a plane crash]. You can't ignore that anniversary. You have to work with that. If you have those seriously key moments in an artist's career, you have to continue to honour them and work with them." He adds, however, that this only works as an annual event – akin to the anniversary of Elvis's death – for a select few artists.

"For the Johnny Cash estate,[121] just to contrast, nobody really remembers the day John died or, frankly, his birthday," he says. "Buddy's birthday is honoured every year in Lubbock with a concert and his death day is obviously a huge marker. It really depends on the artist. I like 50th and 60th anniversaries because, among other things, they give you a press angle. You're going to get much more press around a 60th anniversary of the plane crash than you are for any other day. We have to utilise those markets."

For some of these projects there is great serendipity in timing, but hooking something explicitly to an anniversary date can potentially garner more media attention than the project would attract if it were not tied to a significant date. "Anniversaries are just periods of time that you're marking with something," says a former executive at a major music distribution service. "All right, the dynamics change around whether or not you could maybe put something new into it, whether it's just a re-compilation or whether there's any new photography or videos that could be created or anything else that you might want as part of the product or the marketing to go along with it."

Milestone anniversaries are not just about reawakening the interest of existing fans but are also a means through which younger audiences can be introduced to a classic artist, as Mark Pinkus of Rhino explains with regard to Otis Redding.

"We have had Otis with us since 1967 and we're constantly introducing new fans," he says. "It becomes as much about introducing them to Otis as it does to getting them excited about '(Sittin' on) The Dock of the Bay', which had its 60th anniversary in 2018. You constantly need to be coming up with clever and interesting ways to keep the artist and the music in front of people."

That said, some estates are starting to question if anniversary marketing is even viable in an age when marketing an estate has to move in lockstep with how new artists are marketed – not tied to a single event but an ever-present and always-on flow of activity, primarily through digital and social media channels. One label catalogue executive says that as anniversary reissues become increasingly routine and the default setting for labels, they become incrementally more anaemic affairs, as the archives quickly get stripped of anything actually worth hearing. "As the 25th anniversary remaster comes around, how many people are actually going to be interested in it compared to the 20th or the 10th anniversary one?" they ask. "That audience is getting smaller in terms of the hardcore consumer. Now that *Abbey Road* [by The Beatles] has come out for its 50th anniversary as a hardback edition, if there's a 60th, it's not going to be particularly interesting."

In certain quarters of the estate business, the anniversary angle is starting to be regarded as a busted flush and something that has little, if any, impact. If everyone is doing them, goes the argument, it becomes increasingly difficult to stand out and have consumers – be they existing fans, lapsed fans or potentially new fans – care. Their ubiquity gelds their power.

"A few recent so-called deluxe packages have been well worth the exercise and spend required, but so many are garish rehashes of what has gone before," says Cally Callomon. "I'd hate to be a die-hard King Crimson fan today. We will venture into this territory, I know, but it won't be due to an 'anniversary', we won't be including badges or trinkets and it will be at a price people can afford."

Speaking to me in late 2020, Callomon says that July 2019 would have marked the 50th anniversary of *Five Leaves Left*, Nick Drake's debut album, with March 2021 being 50 years since *Bryter Layter* and 2022 being the half-century of *Pink Moon*, Drake's final album. Callomon admits to "getting really nervous about it" as it could have been the start of a major anniversary-centric marketing programme for the Drake catalogue. He feels that just reissuing or remastering the albums would be a creative dead end for the estate and he believes that focusing on other projects beyond his triptych of studio albums would be more satisfying for the estate as well as for the fans. "I get worried because we've only got X amount of material on Nick and it would appear that we are milking material more and more," he says. "We have put together what we think is a five-year plan of things that involve broadcast, dramas, live work and releases. Very fortunately for us, the pandemic came along and put the mockers on the whole thing. That means there is a lot more time to get our house in order."

There is arguably a very label-centric approach to marketing, as the record companies often own or control the sound recordings and this technique has become stuck in their marketing lexicon. It is a legacy of when record companies were the axis on which estates primarily turned. But music publishers, as they get more actively involved in the estates business, regard album anniversary marketing as inherently anachronistic.

"The album cycle no longer has the same meaning any more," argues Bruce Lampcov from Downtown Music Publishing. "The format is completely different. For example, with *Bitches Brew* [by Miles Davis], we talked about the anniversary – it's more of a talking point internally among the artistic community and less so for the punters out there. It doesn't really have very much meaning. Also the competition for these anniversaries is absurd. There's an anniversary every day now and no one cares about it."

He gets warmed up on the topic, and asserts:

> Doing an album cycle, you're not going to really get anywhere. It's really about putting stuff out and getting people's attention right away and it's going to fall off after that. You are talking to a publisher here. We've rarely thought in those terms anyway in the past. That's always been a difference between labels and publishers. Our business of how we manage publishing catalogues hasn't changed that much. We've always been about keeping stuff alive every day of the week. It's always been important to us. We're in a cycle of keeping a body of work relevant all of the time. So I wouldn't say that we've really changed that much [...] Labels, without a doubt, have. They've been forced to. And often our priorities have just clashed with the labels because of that.

BEYOND THE RECORD

The hit record was often the catalyst that made a pop star's name and so classic singles or albums are a hook to bring back fans and a portal into the artist for new fans. Estates, however, need to treat the recordings as an important part of a legacy as well as a way to earn money; but they cannot be seen as the totality of an estate.

For smaller estates, the options beyond the records are somewhat limited, but for bigger estates, the fame and cultural importance of an artist can be parlayed into a whole host of new areas that keep their legacy alive, or that bring in new forms of revenue, or, ideally, do both.

Below are just some examples of the different approaches estates have taken that do not have to genuflect in front of the artist's discography.

The stamp and coin

Appearing on a stamp is a form of cultural confirmation and not many estates have an opportunity like this. It is debatable if such a thing can bring in new audiences, especially as writing letters is becoming generationally irrelevant. A study by the National Literacy Trust in 2015 found that only one in six teenagers in the UK write letters outside school.[122] The ultimate point for the estate, however, is that appearing on a stamp or a coin confers a legitimacy and an authority on an artist that few other things, apart from perhaps a museum exhibition, can. It is an elevated validation that their own efforts are unlikely to ever come close to.

The United States Postal Service started its Music Icons series of stamps in 2013.[123] Deceased artists honoured this way include Marvin Gaye, Ray Charles, Lydia Mendoza, Johnny Cash, Jimi Hendrix, Janis Joplin, Elvis Presley, Sarah Vaughan and John Lennon.

"It brings me great pride and pleasure to see my father finally get a stamp," said Marvin Gaye III on the unveiling of his father's stamp in 2019 on what would have been the soul singer's 80th birthday. "Such a monumental achievement for his legacy."[124]

Freddie Mercury has been commemorated several times by the Royal Mail with a stamp, once in 1999 as part of a Famous Britons series and again in 2020 as part of a series of stamps celebrating Queen.[125] [126] Mercury also appeared on a series of commemorative coins in 2020, again as part of Queen, from the Royal Mint in the UK as the inaugural focus of its Music Legends series.[127]

David Bowie was also honoured as part of the Royal Mint's Music Legends series in December 2020. The coin featured Bowie in profile and a special edition of the coin also included the lightning bolt from the cover of the *Aladdin Sane* album that came with a glittering stardust effect. The launch of the coin, however, tipped over into gimmickry as it became, according to the Royal Mint, the first coin to be sent into space. What this actually meant was that it was attached to high-altitude balloons and launched to a height of 35,656 metres for a period of 45 minutes before returning to Earth. "In recognition of Bowie's first hit single 'Space Oddity', we felt it was fitting to send his coin into space and celebrate the Starman in his own pioneering fashion," said Clare Maclennan, divisional director of commemorative coin at the Royal Mint. "David Bowie's music has inspired and influenced generations of musicians and we hope this commemorative coin will be cherished by fans around the world."[128]

In a moment of cultural exchange in 2012, the US Postal Service and La Poste in France collectively created a Miles Davis stamp and an Édith Piaf stamp.[129] "In the US, Miles's stamp was one of the best-selling biopic stamps in recent history," says Darryl Porter from the Miles Davis estate. "We sold almost 25 million stamps. We were looking around and we knew that a lot of other greats had had stamps. We reached out to them, they loved the idea, took the ball, ran with it, made it bigger by adding Édith Piaf and then included La Poste as a tandem release."

He says La Poste went with the idea of partnering with the US Postal Service on a stamp for a non-French artist because Davis was so revered in France. "One of the things that is key is that when you have a deceased icon like a Miles, you have to take advantage of every single opportunity," says Porter. "Anniversaries are huge opportunities. A stamp release is a huge opportunity."

The kids' book

Previously estates focused heavily on teenagers as the first demographic group they could start targeting and hoping to develop into fans. In recent years, however, they have started to aim much younger, creating products for pre-schoolers.

In 2017, the Elvis Presley estate partnered with Dial Books, an imprint of Penguin Random House, and author/illustrator Stephanie Graegin to create *Love Me Tender*, a book aimed at children aged between 3 and 5 and built around the lyrics to the 1956 hit of the same name. "[T]he sweet, inclusive illustrations make it a book every family will treasure 'all through the years, till the end of time'," says the book's listing on the Penguin Random House website.[130]

Speaking to the BBC in 2019, Jamie Salter of Authentic Brands Group explained the reasoning for the book. "When we took over Elvis, the one thing that we were noticing is the brand was getting older and older," he said. "And we needed to fix that. This is *Love Me Tender* [holds up copy of the kids' book]. We're super excited about the direction that the team has been taking Elvis. So not only are we going after the millennials, but we're also going after even the younger generation. Elvis is really having a year the last few years – and I think the best is yet to come."[131]

In 2020, the Otis Redding estate created a book based around the lyrics to his song 'Respect'. "Bring the words of Otis Redding to a child in your life with this beautiful new children's lyric book based on the lyrics of 'Respect'," said the listing on the Otis Redding Foundation website. "Packed with playful vignettes as they imagine a life full of possibility, *Respect* provides families an opportunity to explore themes of mutual respect – while revisiting one of the greatest songs ever written."[132]

To invert the old marketing maxim, this is promotion from the grave to the cradle.

The animated series

The Beatles had one between 1965 and 1967[133] while the Jackson 5 had one between 1971 and 1972,[134] but these were active artists at the very height of their fame and these were cartoon shows aimed at a young Saturday morning TV audience. The notion of creating a new animated series around a pop star who died almost half a century ago would appear to be, on paper at least, an idea that redefines the ludicrous.

Yet that is exactly what the Elvis Presley estate is doing with *Agent King*, described as an "adult animated action comedy series", which was developed for Netflix. Plans for its development were announced in August 2019, with Priscilla Presley and John Eddie credited as co-creators while Authentic Brands Group, Sony Pictures Animation and Sony Pictures Television were listed as partners on the series. "Elvis Presley trades in his white jumpsuit for a jet pack when he is covertly inducted into a secret government spy program to help battle the dark forces that threaten the country he loves – all while holding down his day job as the King of Rock and Roll," said Netflix in a statement.[135]

"It's sort of like a take-off of Sherlock Holmes – and we really like it," says Jamie Salter. "It's all character-based."

The collectibles

Dolls representing artists date even further back than the early wave of Beatlemania, with a genuinely terrifying Elvis doll – with oversized head, high-waisted jeans and plaid shirt – being sold by Celebrity Products in 1956. It was described as "the only doll of its kind approved by Elvis Presley" which, when you see its oversized and disquieting features leering at you, makes you wonder what the ones he did not approve looked like.

Every major pop act since has tried to cash in with their own official dolls – including Take That, The Spice Girls, Westlife, One Direction and BTS. Acts who perhaps see themselves as slightly more "credible", such as Gorillaz, have also created official vinyl figures.

Estates, however, have not quite jumped into this synthetic world with both feet. The estates of Ol' Dirty Bastard and Notorious BIG, however, worked with action figures and collectible toys company Super 7 to create figures based on the late rappers.

The statue

Getting a statue erected to commemorate a dead pop star is a significant piece of cultural elevation, putting the pop star on the same footing as politicians and authors in terms of civic pride and cultural importance.

Some can take on a more tongue-in-cheek unofficial name, something the statues in Dublin are often subjected to. A brass statue commemorating Phil Lynott from Thin Lizzy, for example, was unveiled in 2005 and positioned on Harry Street, just off Grafton Street, in the city centre.[136] Soon, however, it earned itself a colloquial sobriquet – becoming unofficially known as the Ace with the Bass. It is certainly a step up from the local nickname for the statue, a mere 15-minute stroll away on North Earl Street, of James Joyce complete with walking cane, which is known locally as the Prick with the Stick. Most other cities treat statues to dead artists with greater reverence than Dubliners do.

Things can move quickly here. Little Richard died on 9 May 2020 and by 26 May plans were already afoot to erect a statue to him outside his childhood home in Macon, Georgia.[137] Others are timed to coincide with an important date such as the Amy Winehouse statue that was unveiled in Camden, north London – a place of huge significance for her – on what would have been her 31st birthday.[138]

They are often expensive undertakings. The Johnny Ramone statue at the Hollywood Forever Cemetery in Los Angeles was reported to have cost $100,000.[139] A statue of former AC/DC singer Bon Scott in his home town of Kirriemuir in Scotland cost £45,000 and was made possible in 2016 due to a crowdfunding drive by fans.[140] Finding the most apposite home for them can be a hugely political decision. Local residents in Kirriemuir had originally opposed the idea of a Bon Scott statue, with some annoyed at the volume of visitors to the annual Bonfest event and others saying he was "no role model".[141] As a curious side note, the small town already had a statue of Peter Pan to honour J. M. Barrie, who was also born there.

Plans for a statue to honour former INXS singer Michael Hutchence ran aground in 2019 when his family were split over where it should go – Melbourne or North Sydney.[142] One way around that is to have statues in multiple symbolic locations. Irish blues guitarist Rory Gallagher has one in Ballyshannon in County Donegal in Ireland where he was born (and where the Rory Gallagher Festival is held annually), a replica of his trademark Fender guitar is on the wall of what is termed Rory Gallagher Corner in Temple Bar in Dublin and there is a more abstract piece commemorating him in Rory Gallagher Place in Cork. On top of this, Belfast City Council was planning one in 2020 to stand outside the Ulster Hall, a place Gallagher played multiple times, in the city centre. "It is to recognise Rory for performing all the way through the Troubles and coming to Northern Ireland to play when no one else would," says Daniel Gallagher, the guitarist's nephew, who is also in charge of his estate. "It was the East Belfast fans who started the petition for it."

Cost and planning permission are two major obstacles here for many estates and statues can take many years to come to fruition. When they do, however, the commemorated artist becomes a fixture in a location of great significance for them, a daily reminder to the locals of what they achieved but also a place of pilgrimage for international fans.

Making new videos

There is some debate over what was the first promo video, with The Beatles and Bob Dylan possibly laying claim to the honour in the mid-1960s – but by the mid-1980s, spurred on by the ascent of MTV, they became as essential for promoting an act as a record sleeve or a world tour. For whole generations of acts, however, few – if any – official music videos exist. With the rise of YouTube, however, these are being made retroactively.

In 2014, the Otis Redding estate had run a competition online to make the official video for "These Arms of Mine", with Nicolas Beauchemin being the ultimate winner.[143]

In March 2021, to mark the 50th anniversary of it going to number one on the Billboard Hot 100 chart in the US, Legacy Recordings and the Janis Joplin estate created an official video for 'Me and Bobby McGee'.[144]

(Side note: 'Me and Bobby McGee' was only the second posthumous single to go to the top of the US charts after... Otis Redding's '(Sittin' on) The Dock of the Bay' in January 1968.)

Understanding just how much younger music fans consume videos on YouTube, estates and record companies are creating post-factum videos for classic tracks to try and appeal to younger consumers but also pull in existing fans again. A label catalogue executive says,

Think about the amount of consumption that takes place on YouTube now, but also the amount of music that was recorded, released and even successful in an era before music video was a thing. Really, really significant music isn't properly represented on some of the biggest digital platforms. There are some significant songs – really successful songs – that never had a music video shot before. That's an interesting area in terms of how those decisions get made around new videos. If their only representation is with later career videos, that might not be the best picture [of them or the] best experience. It is about optimising the catalogue.

Another catalogue executive clarifies further on the thinking here. "We can already see the younger audience, who are going to become the future catalogue audience, tend to be much more engaged with visual material," they say. "So if we don't have visual material for really big tracks and we just have audio, that's a problem."

The ballet

A less obvious route than the musical, the ballet is arguably more about having an artist's music considered high culture and having greater depth than "mere" pop music.

Mary Guibert said that a ballet built around the music of Jeff Buckley was in the early stages of development. "I can't mention a name yet because the name isn't signed on the bottom line," she says in the summer of 2020 when we speak. "He wants to take some of his masters and choreograph them into a ballet. That just knocks my socks off! It'd be something that would be a live performance and also be on film [that] he'd like to do."

Estates are now in a better position to seek outside funding for something like this than they were two or more decades ago. Back then, the label was regarded as something of a development fund by representatives of major estates and this sometimes became a way for these estate heads to indulge their worst excesses. One senior label executive recounts how a major estate came to them looking for significant funding to get a ballet project off the ground. The estate had already approached a ballet company and recorded rough sketches of what the ballet would be like. They then asked the label for £500,000 in investment to make it a reality.

The label executive recounts their reaction. "I watch the video and I think, 'Am I dreaming? This is the most ridiculous thing I've ever seen in my life.' It was a huge amount of money they wanted. Even if it was five grand, it was too much as far as I was concerned. I said, 'No. I don't want this.'"

Given the size of the deceased artist involved, this was likely to have been a rare instance of an estate trying to take an ill-judged ballet project to the stage. The look of utter disbelief in the executive's face recounting what could have become a bottomless money pit and an enormous credibility drain for the label suggests both it and the theatre-going audience dodged a ballet bullet.

The graphic novel

This is a relatively under-explored area for estates. There have been graphic novels about deceased musicians – notably *Johnny Cash: I See a Darkness: A Graphic Novel*[145] in 2009, *GodSpeed: The Kurt Cobain Graphic Novel*[146] in 2011, *Gabba Gabba Hey!: The Graphic Story of the Ramones*[147] in 2013, *Glenn Gould: A Life Off Tempo*[148] in 2016 and *California Dreamin': Cass Elliot Before The Mamas & the Papas* in 2017 – but having the direct involvement of the estate from the off is rare.

    Grace: The Jeff Buckley Story, published in 2019, is an exception here that may be the real start of something for estates to get involved in. Speaking on the *Consequence of Sound* podcast in 2019, Mary Guibert revealed she was initially aghast at the idea. Now, however, the copyright in the book is owned by Mary Guibert, and she collaborated with the writers and illustrators on its creation. "You don't hear [Jeff's music] on the radio as much, unless you listen to certain channels," says Guibert on why projects like the graphic novel came into being. "So his work finds his audience. There's always the effort to try and widen it, so we have now published the book with his journals and then the graphic novel that we did with Tiffanie DeBartolo."

    This is something that other estates are dipping a tentative toe into. Larry Mestel says that Primary Wave is working on one with the Bob Marley estate. "We're developing an animated comic book series around the history of Jamaican music and religion – and Bob Marley is a big part of that," he says when we speak in early 2020. "There's a lot of stuff that we're doing right now, but I don't want to get into too many specifics because we don't want to spoil the surprise. But you have got to remember, we've only been involved with the Marley music for a little less than a year. All of this is happening and it has been less than a year."

The institute and foundation

Since the Concert for Bangladesh (and its tie-in album) in 1971 as well as Live Aid, Band Aid and USA for Africa in the 1980s, charity work is something pop stars are drawn to – partly for magnanimous reasons but also, if we are being cynical, for the PR boost it can give them (not to mention the tax breaks that can come with donations).

    Many artists do, however, have a charitable organisation or cause that is genuinely close to their hearts and make preparations in their will to give a one-off donation or a rolling contribution, often through a share of royalties. Artists can establish charities or foundations in their lifetime – Michael Jackson set up Heal the World Foundation in 1982, for example, which continues today – or they can be set up after they die by their family as both a tribute and also a means of carrying on the charity work they were engaged in during their lifetime. It also helps imbue their name with a sense of enduring humanitarianism.

For those who had addiction and mental health issues, the families can set up a foundation specifically to offer help and support here, in part as a tribute but also to try and ensure that others can get the help the pop star in question was unable to. The Amy Winehouse Foundation, for example, was launched by her parents on 14 September 2011, just over three weeks after the singer's death on 23 July, on what would have been her 28th birthday. "The Amy Winehouse Foundation works to prevent the effects of drug and alcohol misuse on young people," explains the foundation's website. "We also aim to support, inform and inspire vulnerable and disadvantaged young people to help them reach their full potential. We are driven by a powerful vision for young people, a world where young people can flourish."[149] In 2013, the foundation created the Amy Winehouse Foundation Resilience Programme for Schools to go into classrooms to "explain the risks associated with substance misuse through the prism of people's real life experiences".[150]

Families and colleagues can also set up bursaries to commemorate a late artist, such as that set up in October 2019 in memory of Cranberries singer Dolores O'Riordan, who died on 15 January 2018. It was set up by her family as well as the City and County Council of Limerick, her hometown, to help support musicians in the local area.[151]

Also helping new musicians is the Luciano Pavarotti Foundation which was set up in 2007 by his widow, Nicoletta Mantovani, shortly after his passing. It describes itself as "a non-profit organization that perpetuates the human and artistic legacy of Maestro Pavarotti by supporting young, talented opera singers and organising events all over the world".[152]

There are a multitude of charitable bodies set up in honour of late artists such as the Joe Strummer Foundation,[153] the Holst Foundation (set up by the estate of Gustav Holst to support new composers[154]), the Muddy Waters Foundation (to support blues artists[155]), the Joey Ramone Foundation for Lymphoma Research,[156] the Michael Hutchence Foundation that was set up in 2005 by his half-sister Tina to mark what would have been his 45th birthday and to "provide financial assistance to talented but underprivileged artists",[157] the Tim Bergling Foundation (set up in 2018 to honour Avicii and which "advocates for the recognition of suicide as a global health emergency and actively works to remove the stigma attached to suicide and mental health issues"[158]), the Live Free 999 Fund (set up in April 2020 by Carmela Wallace, mother of Juice WRLD who died on 8 December 2019, to help young people with addiction, anxiety and depression issues[159]), the Fela Kuti scholarship for aspiring musicians (established in March 2021 by Partisan Records and the Fela Anikulapo-Kuti estate)[160] and the Bob Marley Foundation.[161] They all serve a double function: keeping the artist's name alive, and explicitly presenting them as deeply philanthropic, whereby the halo of saintliness can start to envelop their legacy.

While these are all, on paper at least, altruistic exercises, they can run out of road – something that can reflect badly on the estate and, ultimately, the legacy of the artist they were set up to honour.

For example, the Tupac Amaru Shakur Center for the Arts (coming out of the Tupac Amaru Shakur Foundation) was opened in 2005 by the late rapper's mother, Afeni Shakur, but was then closed in 2015. "[T]he facility largely sustained itself off the efforts Shakur made to uphold her son's legacy," wrote *Rolling Stone* in 2016 as it tried to piece together what happened. "The center cost $4 million to launch [...] 80 per cent of that was funded by proceeds from Amaru Entertainment, the company Afeni Shakur founded to release Tupac's posthumous work. With seven of his 11 platinum albums being posthumous releases, Tupac made money like he was still alive. In 2008, his estate made $15 million. Two years later, though, it was a quarter as much. By then, Tupac's catalog of unreleased music had dwindled."[162]

Some can fall apart spectacularly when disputes erupt around ownership and control of an estate. As mentioned in Chapter 3, the Ray Charles Foundation was at loggerheads with his children over who would control his copyrights and earn from them. Perhaps the saddest of all is the limbo the I Feel Good Trust, set up by James Brown to help impoverished children, found itself in, where none of the promised royalties have come through even after many years. The incredibly complex issues around the Michael Hutchence estate also meant that significant donations he had specified in his will that were to go to Amnesty International and Greenpeace were never honoured.

When estates are sold, one precondition (be it a legal one or a moral one) can be that the new owner carries on the charitable work started by the estate. For example, the Buddy Holly Educational Foundation was set up in 2010 by his widow, María Elena Holly.[163] When BMG bought into the Buddy Holly estate in 2015, carrying on the work of the Buddy Holly Educational Foundation was seen as paramount. "Buddy wanted to continue the legacy musical education through the schools and support young song-writers," says David Hirshland of BMG. "So we are carrying on that legacy; that's something that was important to María Elena. She established the Educational Foundation before we bought the catalogue and we were more than happy to support that. We also, in our deal, agreed to establish a scholarship at North Texas University in the music department. We paid for that. These are all things that meant a lot to María Elena and the people around her."

Sampling

The rise of hip-hop from the late 1970s to become one of the dominant genres and cultures in music globally was often about a recontextualisation of the past – lifting out breaks or musical refrains from an old song (ideally an incredibly obscure one) and using it to build something new. From the past came the future.

That used to be based on the creator's intricate knowledge of music and their voracious appetite for crate-digging to find a long-forgotten record and being the first person to sample it. The website WhoSampled was set up specifically to catalogue all of this, showing exactly where modern producers found their samples. It records, for example, that 'Amen Brother' (the source of the legendary 'Amen' break) is the most sampled track of all time, followed by 'Think (About It)' by Lyn Collins, 'Change the Beat' (Female Version) by Beside, 'Funky Drummer' by James Brown and 'La Di Da Di' by Doug E. Fresh and Slick Rick.[164]

The deft use of a sample has helped totally revitalise the life of records and artists as they are hailed as being of great cultural and musical importance by the people who sampled them. This is something estates are increasingly aware of, proactively pitching music to modern artists and producers and being prepared, if a licensing request comes in, to clear it and then build a follow-up marketing campaign for the estate around it.

Initially, it was US soul and R&B tracks (with occasional forays into rock) that hip-hop producers turned to, but this has expanded to cover everything from Turkish funk to Bollywood soundtracks as producers hunted down the perfect sample. Even the estate of Richard Rodgers & Oscar Hammerstein II has benefited here recently, taking 90 per cent of the publishing of Ariana Grande's 2019 hit '7 Rings' as it interpolated 'My Favourite Things' from *The Sound of Music*.[165] The two estates also benefited from Gwen Stefani sampling 'Lonely Goatherd' from the same musical on her 2006 track 'Wind It Up', with Rodgers & Hammerstein getting 50 per cent of the publishing royalties.[166]

This can bring in money for estates but, crucially, it can also introduce fans of contemporary artists to the music of writers or performers from several decades, or even generations, back.

The Miles Davis estate in particular is very proactive here. "We're in the process right now with Miles of taking a fresh view and it might not be recognisable stuff of his, but we are now looking for ways to get to producers to create beats or remixes around it," says Bruce Lampcov of Downtown Music Publishing, which took over global representation of his publishing in late 2019.[167] "With Miles, it's really about the beat-making and sampling and remixing side of things."

There are, however, restrictions on how his music is sampled, with the estate and heirs wanting approval on usage.

"We try not to do anything that is offensive," says Darryl Porter from the Miles Davis estate on its policy on sampling. "There was one sample that used Miles's music, and it was a phenomenal record. I won't say who the group was, but they went on to have incredible success in the hip-hop world. But the song was about a topic that was just not respectful. Let me say it differently. It was incredibly disrespectful and to most people it would have been offensive. So we decided that, as much as we liked the musicality of it, we could not support it."

Mary Guibert has a similar approach to licensing the music of Jeff Buckley for samples, although she is less concerned about profanity than about what the finished piece actually sounds like. "There have been a couple of rappers[168] who have wanted to sample some of Jeff's stuff," she says. "And I do enjoy some really good rap. It has to be somebody who knows. Rap is a really specific art. There is high art in terms of rap and there's low art in terms of rap. There is someone who keeps reaching out and they refer to him as G, so I don't even know who this person is! And I said, 'Well, let me hear it. I'm open to anything. Let me hear it.' I love Snoop Dogg [...] Jay-Z just knocks my socks off. I'm there. I could do that."

Enabling widespread sampling, and easing the licensing process, was behind the partnership in 2019 between the estate of Isaac Hayes and licensing platform Tracklib to offer 20 previously unreleased Hayes tracks that were pre-cleared and available for sampling.[169] "A lot of these legacy acts are forgotten – and quickly so," says Pär Almqvist, founder and CEO of Tracklib. "The turnover rate is faster than people realise. Sampling is one of the greatest ways to extend the music legacy and to reach new generations of fans. Tracklib is a legacy extender. And we're also a second chance machine in that a song that wasn't a hit can now become part of a new hit too."

The company has been proactively approaching estates to use the platform as a means of reawakening their catalogues. "We've heard a concern from many estates that they're not visible on the DSPs [digital service providers, like Spotify and Apple Music]," Almqvist says. "Representing an estate, you want to maximise relevance and visibility for the particular artist in a music economy where the focus is still very much on the hit and the latest release."

Isaac Hayes III says this push to have his father's music sampled more was driven in part by a refusal by Hollywood to use a number of unreleased Hayes tracks in the 2019 remake of *Shaft*. (Isaac Hayes had, of course, created the soundtrack album for the original *Shaft* film in 1971.) "I held those masters for the intention of using them on the *Shaft* film," says Hayes III. "It didn't work out with Warner Brothers as they decided to go in a totally different direction and the soundtrack to *Shaft* was terrible."

He says the closure of this soundtrack opportunity made him more open to other ideas to get the unheard music out, leading to the partnership with Tracklib.

I was like, "OK, let's do this." Because simply just putting out masters is not really the best marketing strategy. TrackLib has a great marketing strategy, they have a great team, they have a great idea. So I wanted to go with them because it's just a dope concept and it works very easily. With my dad's sampling catalogue over recent years, we've had a significant amount of success with material that's owned by the label. It doesn't necessarily mean they're hit records, but Isaac Hayes is just someone that people like to sample – because of the style and the way he made records.

Cover versions

Running parallel to sampling, of course, are cover versions of famous songs by dead artists, but these are so common and so numerous that they cannot sensibly be listed here. The estate also has less control over this than it would in the case of a sample.

The tribute concert

As soon as news breaks of a major artist dying, it can be safely assumed that someone somewhere is already planning a tribute concert. They can be one-off events that become a focal point for public grieving; equally, they can become regular, or even annual, events that help keep an artist's name alive and use contemporary acts to introduce their music to new generations of fans.

It sometimes needs the passing of time before a tribute concert can feel appropriate. Given the tragic and shocking nature of his death, it was over a year and a half later that a tribute concert to Avicii was finally organised in Stockholm in December 2019. It was streamed on his official YouTube channel and had the full involvement of his family. "We are grateful that his friends, producers, artists and colleagues are coming to Stockholm to help," said Klas Bergling, Avicii's father, in a press statement. "They have all expressed a sincere interest and desire to engage in efforts to stem the tide of mental illness and lend their support to our work with the Tim Bergling Foundation. We are very much looking forward to this evening, which will be a starting point for the foundation's work going forward."[170]

Concerts can also be created to mark a significant anniversary, such as one that was planned to mark the 10th anniversary of the death of Ronnie James Dio in May 2020 (but which had to be cancelled due to the global pandemic).[171]

The Johnny Cash Heritage Festival is an annual event but in 2019 the estate was also involved in Cash Fest in Nashville, which was created in part to promote *The Gift* documentary on YouTube.

"That was 100 per cent tied to this idea that I wanted to do, rather than a traditional premiere, a concert event that would allow people to remember the great Johnny Cash music and be a promotional vehicle effectively for *The Gift*," says Josh Matas of Sandbox Entertainment, who run the Cash estate. "Cash Fest was specifically a one-off event. I don't anticipate us doing it any further in the future, but the Johnny Cash Heritage Festival will continue to be an annual event. It's a great reminder for us of the continued passion fans have for Johnny Cash music out there – because when we do do these things, they always sell out."

A number of tribute shows to Nick Drake[172] have taken place over the years. It also important to remember that Jeff Buckley's first live performance was at a tribute concert to his own late father, Tim Buckley, in 1991.

Elvis Week is packed with numerous concerts. As well as this, in what is perhaps a first, a meta-tribute concert to Elvis took place in January 2019 and was broadcast on NBC to mark (just over) 50 years since Elvis's original *'68 Comeback Special*, as well as what would have been Elvis's 84th birthday. "A healthy mix of young stars (Post Malone, Ed Sheeran, Alessia Cara, Shawn Mendes, Adam Lambert and Kelsea Ballerini) and established names (Blake Shelton, John Fogerty, Dierks Bentley, Keith Urban, Jennifer Lopez, Josh Groban, Darius Rucker, Pistol Annies, Carrie Underwood, Little Big Town and Mac Davis) recreated the look and feel of the famed Elvis *'68 Comeback Special*," wrote *Variety*.[173]

Jamie Salter of Authentic Brands Group suggests that it could now become a regular event, using contemporary stars to introduce Elvis to their fans. "I mean it was insane," says Salter. "It was so good. I can do that now annually."

The Johnny Ramone Tribute is now an annual fixture at the Hollywood Forever Cemetery and features a mix of performances and film screenings.[174] Linda Ramone says it began when Johnny was still alive but has carried on after he died. "Johnny loved baseball and horror – and he was a movie fanatic and buff," she says by way of contextualisation. "For sure. He thought he'd be in the Ramones for four years, be the biggest band in the world, retire and become a director. That's what he really wanted to be – besides being a rock star. He wanted to be a director. So doing the tribute is all about Johnny. We show a movie – one of his top 10, something that he liked."

Proceeds from the tribute go to the Johnny and Linda Ramone Foundation for prostate cancer research, the cause of his death in 2004. "It's a lot about telling the story about who Johnny Ramone was, what he stood for, what his role was within the Ramones and the larger cultural history," says Alicia Yaffe of Spellbound Group. "I produce it every year for Linda at Hollywood Forever Cemetery. From spring to summer, it's always promoting that and getting people excited and talking about Johnny's legacy in terms of what people will be able to experience at the event, which is always built around something that Johnny loved."

Those in and around estates are convinced that tribute concerts are a proven way to introduce the music of a dead artist to younger fans. "One big way of reaching out is to create events or concerts around these brands or these artists and be able to connect somehow to millennials in that way," says Bruce Lampcov of Downtown Music, for example.

It is also something Daniel Gallagher holds to be true, talking about the Rory Gallagher International Tribute Festival that has been running since 2002 in his hometown of Ballyshannon.[175] "This tiny town in Donegal is swamped for a week," he says. "It's a bank holiday weekend [at the end of May]. It's a free festival up until the main stage. Everything else is free and there are just gigs going on in [every] pub, every street corner, every Chinese restaurant – everywhere. Young kids, mainly in Ireland, come up for it as it's a free concert and you see all these kids really getting into Rory. It's a really great experience that weekend. All the tribute bands are keeping Rory's music going. It's not just guys in their sixties doing it. There are much younger guys coming in and playing – guys in their twenties coming up and performing."

While much of this is anecdotal, it is something the organisers of other tribute concerts repeat when asked about the role of their events. The festivals and concerts are, they argue, a way to hold on to existing fans but, more importantly, they provide an entry point for young fans. On its own, what a tribute concert can achieve is limited, but when considered in the wider context of what a modern estate has to do, they are a cog which might not power the whole machine but whose absence would definitely be noticed.

The ad sync

As mentioned in Chapter 4, the use of Nick Drake's 'Pink Moon' in a Volkswagen ad in 1999 was critical in introducing his music to whole new audiences. While some estates, or former band members such as John Densmore of The Doors (see Chapter 6) regard ads as the ultimate sell-out, most estates accept them as either a necessary evil or, simply, a way to simultaneously make money and keep an artist and their music in the public consciousness.

The Johnny Cash estate found that getting relatively obscure track 'These Are My People' used in a Volkswagen ad managed to cast a new light on his catalogue by boosting the streaming numbers of a track that had previously been overlooked. It also put Cash's music in front of whole new demographics that had previously been hard to reach.

"Johnny Cash's music continues to be synced in a very, very strong way [but] oftentimes people go for the most recognisable music," says Josh Matas, who explains that the ad sync came from the proactive pitching work of Sony and BMG. "This song is a great, great example of that. When it was presented and when I saw the rough cut of the commercial and the multi-ethnic faces within that commercial, I felt that that was just so on-brand for us that I said yes to it immediately." He adds, "Johnny Cash was somebody who united people. That's a big part of what his motivation was. There was an incredible opportunity via a commercial means to share that message."

What the estate found, however, was that the message of inclusivity in the ad meant that Cash was put in front of entire new social groups for the first time. "We saw multi-ethnic faces within this commercial for Volkswagen," he says. "That was also important to me because Latin audiences, very specifically, had not been strong Johnny Cash fans."

A good sync can shake new life into a dormant estate but can also, because music supervisors are increasingly keen to go beyond the obvious hits (as was the case with Johnny Cash), mean that tracks that were buried at the time of their release can rise again.

One catalogue head at a label regards this as the ideal outcome for any sync deal. "Often ad creatives want to go beyond the usual big hits – something that's a bit more unique," they say. "So then you do get songs that aren't part of the usual Greatest Hits suspects being synced to an ad, and that reaches a whole new audience. And suddenly that track becomes a staple for the artist – possibly with a different audience as well."

Just as the Volkswagen ad massively elevated the profile of Nick Drake, other cult – or simply ignored – artists and their estates can have a second swing at things through a timely placement of their music in an ad. "I have clients that released a song 40 years ago that did nothing at the time of release and then recently got discovered for a sync project and [they] now have a whole new life," says music lawyer Erin M. Jacobson. "For the estates, there are these opportunities for this music to continue having a life and earning money long after the person that created that music has passed away. There's only going to be more of that as time goes on because people are getting creative in how to continue exploiting these assets and to earn income from them in new ways."

There is a disparity here between those who want a highly reverential ad doused in credibility and those who are simply concerned with hitting the biggest and broadest possible audience – and credibility be damned. "Look at where [major estates] find themselves now," says one catalogue executive about a particular act only interested in ads if they pay well and reach mass audiences, showing scant regard for any sort of quality control. "Decades after radio stopped playing them, young people can still hear their music. It may be an ad for [mid-range but non-aspirational brand], but you're still hearing their music. Obviously there's a commercial return from that but it's also a route to ears."

A danger exists that sync deals want to focus on an act's most popular hit as that has an instant recognisability factor for the audience; but it can lock a catalogue into ever-diminishing circles, whereby only one or two songs ever get used and that reduces the act's entire output – a life's work – to a few minutes of music. The biggest hits naturally command the highest fees, but the long-term damage can be immense, whereby the over-exposure of one or two songs dramatically decreases their value in the marketplace and also locks off other songs from being used. One song can become the distillation of an entire career and, in doing so, incrementally diminishes in value every time it is used.

The Jeff Buckley estate was quickly made aware of the risks here when it became clear that the most-requested track for synchronisation was his cover version of Leonard Cohen's "Hallelujah". "We've turned down some big licensing opportunities for Jeff's version of 'Hallelujah' because Mary [Guibert, Buckley's mother] correctly didn't want Jeff's version to become over-exposed," says Conrad Rippy, the lawyer for the Jeff Buckley estate. "There were big licensing opportunities there. If Mary was turning to someone who made 15 per cent off these big licensing requests, then you might not be getting the best advice. You might not care about overexposing Jeff's version of 'Hallelujah' because you want that cheque. Getting approval of all licensing is such a big deal, because otherwise you're going to find 'Hallelujah' over every one-hour drama in a montage [sequence] for ever."

Music lawyer Erin M. Jacobson runs through the checklist estates should have when entering into a sync deal. "Would this harm the legacy of the song? Would this create an association that might turn off other people from using it? Is it being overexposed so that other people won't want to use it because everybody else is using it?" She adds:

> There's always that balancing act. That's the power of sync licensing because there have been situations where a song is so associated with a certain scene or a certain commercial or branding campaign that it does then deter other uses. Then there's the added factor in that sometimes, when requests come in, a certain project or brand or whatnot will also ask for exclusivity regarding the song. Let's say it's a car commercial, they might ask for exclusivity in the automobile market – so you could license it for cereal, but you couldn't license it for another car commercial. In those situations you also have to think about if other people in this space would also want to license that song. Can you agree to exclusivity? Or will that harm you?

The sync departments of record companies and music publishers will be responding to multiple requests to use music in ads but equally they will be proactively pitching to music supervisors on TV shows, on films and in ad agencies. They will invariably be the ones negotiating fees and usage terms (such as the length of the campaign, the media it can be shown on, the countries it is broadcast in); but they also need to be sharply aware of the nature and message of the ad and how that could reflect on the artist whose music is being used.

"Happily we have a wonderful licensing company that we work with who knows our catalogue really well," says Portia Sabin, former president of independent label Kill Rock Stars, whose catalogue included a number of Elliott Smith albums. "Obviously, Elliott's stuff is incredibly important in that as well. His family is aware of that – and that's a good point to make. I think maybe some estates don't feel that same way, but his family really does, they see the value of it. Then, of course, they also want to review everything really carefully; so we always work with them before we do any kind of licensing of his music."

Having the family involved in approving all synchronisation is not always a legal requirement (as per the terms of the late artist's contract with them), but a good label and publisher should do it out of courtesy and to ensure that a deal does not goes through that could end up damaging the estate.

It is an extreme example, but the following story from Jemima Dury about a licensing request for an Ian Dury & the Blockheads track illustrates the risks here and why family approval is critical. "I think you can really overexpose the work and you can weaken the meaning of the work," she says about not paying attention to how music is being used in an advert. "For instance, somebody applied to the estate on behalf of a domestic abuse charity and wanted to use 'Hit Me With Your Rhythm Stick' as part of the campaign. We said, 'You are absolutely not getting that song at all. It's quite the opposite [meaning].' I fully support the charity, but we had to say no to that because obviously the meaning was completely wrong." She adds, "You can't just go for the money because you've got to be so mindful of the legacy of the work."

Dury does, however, admit that smaller estates do not always have the luxury to turn sync requests down flat, but that they have to enter these deals with an awareness of what the longer-term implications might be. She explains,

> We've let a few things go and be rewritten or reworked for Vauxhall or Shreddies or whatever it might be. It's a financial thing, partly because it's not such a big earning estate. It's useful to let a few of those things happen. If you were getting enough purely in mechanical rights [from record sales and streams], you don't need to do all that advertising and then you really keep the sanctity of your work protected. I think if you're in a position to be able to do that, then good because you just don't want to sell it out. Not for such wonderful music. Not for Nick Drake's music. Not for Ian's music. It's too precious.

The airport

Admittedly this is not a huge category for estates, but having an airport named in honour of a deceased musician is both a significant honour and also a symbol of permanence. What is says is that this artist is deemed to be of such importance and of such significance that a major transport hub should carry their name.

In 2002, John Lennon became the first individual to have a UK airport named after him when Liverpool Airport was renamed Liverpool John Lennon Airport "along with the slogan "Above us only sky" (from the lyrics to 'Imagine').[176]

He was not, however, the first dead musician anywhere in the world to have an airport renamed in their honour. Liverpool John Lennon Airport joins a select list including Louis Armstrong New Orleans International Airport,[177] Salzburg Airport W. A. Mozart,[178] Budapest Ferenc Liszt International Airport,[179] Warsaw Chopin Airport,[180] Donetsk Sergei Prokofiev International Airport in Ukraine, Rio de Janeiro/Galeão–Antonio Carlos Jobim International Airport,[181] Giuseppe Verdi Airport in Parma,[182] Ástor Piazzolla International Airport in Argentina, Cesária Évora Airport in Cape Verde, Leoš Janáček Airport in the Czech Republic[183] and Poznań–Ławica Henryk Wieniawski Airport in Poland.

* * *

Of course there are plenty of other approaches designed to put dead artists in front of new audiences. Some are covered in specific chapters elsewhere in this book. These include: the exhibition/museum (Chapter 7); the hologram (Chapter 12); and the posthumous duet (also Chapter 12).

CHAPTER 10

Move It

The Rights and Wrongs of Rights

They called it Cliff's Law, named after Cliff Richard, the artist who became the public face for the artist-led demand for an extension to the copyright period covering sound recordings in the UK.

The copyright duration for sound recordings stood at 50 years, after which point the labels who owned them lost their monopoly and they entered the public domain. Anyone could then release these recordings (although getting the original master tapes was unlikely) and sell them without having to pay royalties to the acts who recorded them. They would most likely still have to pay publishing royalties as the copyright term for them ran for 70 years after the death of the author.

In 2006, a campaign to change the law was reaching fever pitch, arguing that songs recorded in the late 1950s in the first rush of rock'n'roll were going to enter the public domain in just two years. Cliff Richard was the most famous act who was going to be immediately impacted, with his first hit, 'Move It', which got to number two in the UK charts in September 1958.[1] Campaigners wanted the term extended from 50 years to 95 years. Record labels argued that they were massively disadvantaged compared to the US, where the term was 95 years, and they wanted parity, as this would be an incentive to invest in new acts today.[2]

This question was the focus of a report by the Treasury led by Andrew Gowers, former editor of the *Financial Times*, as part of a wider review of intellectual property. In December 2006, the bad news landed, with Gowers' report concluding the copyright term should stay as it is, at 50 years. Legal experts had predicted this, saying the UK could not break ranks from the rest of the European Union (where 50 years was the standard copyright term) as intellectual property laws had to be harmonised across member states.

Gowers also argued that extending the period was anti-competitive. Copyright laws safeguarded the creators for an agreed period but to extend that was against the spirit of intellectual property's inherent finite legal shelf life, as it would negate or weaken innovation in the future that drew on those once-protected rights. "Getting the balance right is vital to driving innovation, securing investment and stimulating competition," he said.[3]

Bowed but not beaten, the campaigners regrouped and began to recalibrate their arguments. It eventually went to the Council of Ministers at the European Union and on 7 September 2011, five years after the failure in the UK, a vote was cast that approved a directive that would extend the copyright term covering sound recordings in Europe from 50 years to 70 years. It was not the 95 years that Cliff and his peers were looking for, but it was definitely an improvement.

At the time it was expected that member states would implement the changes in law by 2014.[4] There was, however, a "use it or lose it" clause whereby record labels had to make the recordings commercially available or else allow the artists to release them themselves, cutting out the label and its majority share of the royalties. With downloading and streaming this was less of an issue than it would have been two decades earlier. In 2011, 99.3 per cent of singles sales were digital in the UK although just 23.5 per cent of album sales were;[5] but things were shifting and digital – without the manufacturing and retail space considerations of digital – was sharply in the ascendant. By 2019, only 15.3 per cent of album sales in the UK were on CD, 2.8 per cent were on vinyl and 0.1 per cent were on cassettes; everything else was digital.[6]

The original copyright term was set in parity with those covering printed works in the Copyright Act of 1911 (which extended the term to 50 years from the 42 years as outlined in the Copyright Act of 1842). Updates to the Act in 1988 enshrined it for 50 years specifically for sound recordings. For music publishing, however, it used to be 50 years after the death of the author but this was extended to 70 years in January 1996.

One argument behind the copyright term extension was that artists were simply living longer and so needed to ensure that royalties would continue to roll in throughout the entirety of their lives, especially as they became too old to perform. In 1911, the average life expectancy in the UK was 51.5 for males and 55.4 for females. A full century later, this had risen to 79 for males and 82.8 for females.[7]

This all has massive repercussions for the business of music estates as it means they have monetisable assets and rights that will likely go beyond the life of the person who created them. Chances are the estate will have a number of years – and often decades (especially for recordings made at the end of someone's career) – to earn money from the sales, streams, downloads, broadcast, public performance and synchronisation of the original recordings before the trapdoor of public domain opens below their feet.

These recordings are typically the cornerstones of an act's career – the hits that made their name and made all their other revenue streams possible. It also means, most importantly, the estate (along with the label that owns them) has control over how and where those recordings are used. There is a financial value to them, but equally there is a legacy value to them that they lose as soon as they become public domain. For an estate, these rights are – for as long as they last – invaluable.

While the focus in the UK and Europe has been about extension of copyright periods, the focus in the US (where copyright terms were historically longer) has shifted to reversion of rights. This also has massive repercussions for the business of music estates.

US RIGHTS TERMINATION

The UK/European copyright term extension was specifically about recordings and they are, of course, incredibly valuable. But even more valuable are music publishing rights (i.e. the rights in the song composition). They last longer before going into the public domain as the countdown clock on their expiration only starts ticking as soon as the writer dies. The copyright term covering recordings, as far as the estate is concerned, is pot luck when it takes over depending on how long the recording artist lived for. But for publishing, the copyright term only starts to run down when the individual dies. This is like the estate being handed fresh rights.

Such rights are usually licensed to, or owned outright by, a music publishing company who administer the rights and collect the resulting revenue on behalf of the writer, taking a cut of the earnings. Specific to US law, however, is the ability to terminate those rights at a certain point and have the author (or the author's estate) claim them back *in toto*. This process has become a defining characteristic of the estates business in the US in recent decades. It is called the Termination of Transfers and Licenses Under 17 U.S.C. §203 and falls under Section 203 of the Copyright Act.

"[It] permits authors (or, if the authors are not alive, their surviving spouses, children or grandchildren, or executors, administrators, personal representatives or trustees) to terminate grants of copyright assignments and licenses that were made on or after January 1, 1978 when certain conditions have been met," the copyright documentation around this says.

It continues, "Notices of termination may be served no earlier than 25 years after the execution of the grant or, if the grant covers the right of publication, no earlier than 30 years after the execution of the grant or 25 years after publication under the grant (whichever comes first). However, termination of a grant cannot be effective until 35 years after the execution of the grant or, if the grant covers the right of publication, no earlier than 40 years after the execution of the grant or 35 years after publication under the grant (whichever comes first)."[8]

In brief it means that the earliest a writer or their estate/heirs could serve notice of termination – effectively taking back their composition rights from music publishers – was 25 years after the execution of a post-1977 grant. So from 1 January 2003 the floodgates opened and this is a major strategic option for a range of estates of US-based songwriters.

Lisa Alter of New York law firm Alter, Kendrick & Baron offers a synopsis of how it all works and how the rights, if terminated by an estate or heirs, are divided up. "For pre-1978 assignments, the author or artist can terminate the grant and reclaim rights in the United States 56 to 61 years after the date of the copyright," she says. "And for assignments made by the author from and after 1978 – regardless of when copyright was initially secured – the author or artist can recapture rights 35 to 40 years after the contract date. If the artist is dead or the songwriter is dead, then his or her 'statutory heirs' hold the termination right. Congress decides who the statutory successors are for the purposes of reclaiming rights."

She continues, "According to the US Copyright Act, the author's surviving spouse is entitled to 50 per cent of the termination right and the author's children are entitled to the remaining 50 per cent in equal shares. If there's no surviving spouse, then the kids collectively hold 100 per cent; if any of the children has died prior to exercising the termination right, his or her children – i.e. the author's grandchildren – will inherit their parent's right in equal shares."

It does, however, get head-spinningly complicated if the artist – and this is not uncommon in the world of music and entertainment – has been through multiple divorces before their death. Alter explains:

> It is important to note that, where a songwriter or artist dies prior to serving notice of termination, a majority of the statutory heirs must, together, serve notice of termination in order to recapture rights in the United States. If you have a songwriter who was married multiple times – and I see this all the time – but the wife at death is not the mother of the children or maybe the wife at death is the mother of one of the children but there's five other kids from previous relationships, that may shift the balance of power. As an example, the wife at the time of death and her child may be able to not only direct the course of what happens with the copyrights in certain circumstances, but also to take a greater share of the rights – and the income – that the songwriter might have meant to leave them. So it's complicated.

Marc Toberoff has turned this into an area of immense expertise, having cut his teeth in the world of comic books and helping creators (or their heirs) recover their rights. He runs Toberoff Associates in Los Angeles, a boutique entertainment and litigation law firm, and has worked with the families of both Ray Charles and James Brown in this regard. "Everything I do has to do with helping creators – or when the creator is no longer living – the creator's immediate family to exercise, enforce, protect and monetise their intellectual property rights," he says.

Working with the majority of Ray Charles's children, he succeeded in enforcing the termination rights that saw the return of over 100 songs, including undeniable classics such as 'I Got a Woman' and 'Fool for You', from Warner/Chappell Music Publishing. The initial termination move happened in 2010 and the publisher did not challenge the notices; but that was not to be the sticking point here.

The move, however, brought forth a protracted battle between the children and the Ray Charles Foundation which, as covered in Chapter 3, was a relationship defined by almost biblical animosity and bad blood. The Foundation was named his sole beneficiary in his will and the children received an irrevocable trust of $500,000 each but had to waive the right to any future claim against the estate. Toberoff tells me,

> Various laws in the United States have anti-SLAPP laws. Those laws are basically tied to an exercise of free speech or the right of petition. The right to petition is defined as things like filing a court action or filing a complaint with an administrative body. They don't want people retaliated against for filing complaints or being a whistleblower or anything of that nature. You have to qualify under the statute as the exercise of First Amendment rights or the right of petition. I filed an anti-SLAPP motion. I showed the court that this was an exercise of the right of petition, that you had to file termination notices with the Copyright Act. We won that anti-SLAPP motion and they dismissed their breach of contract action and other retaliatory actions.

In January 2013, the courts, presided over by US District Judge Audrey Collins, in the ongoing dispute between seven of Charles's 12 children and the Ray Charles Foundation, which had been headed up in its early years by Joe Adams (the manager of Charles since 1961), ruled in favour of the children. It permitted them to move to reclaim the rights in an initial batch of 60 compositions. The Ray Charles Foundation said it would appeal.

"The very clear and unmistakable intention of both Ray Charles and all his children was that, in exchange for a substantial payment, the children were not to raise any claims against their father's estate," said Valerie Ervin, the president of the Ray Charles Foundation. "The law is very unsettled in these matters and we intend to seek resolution through the courts."[9]

It went to the 9th Circuit (the equivalent of the Court of Appeal in the UK) in 2015, with Mark D. Passin, the attorney for the Ray Charles Foundation, arguing in February that year that Judge Collins had, in her 2013 ruling, overlooked a US Copyright Office regulation that should have protected "beneficial" owners such as the foundation.[10] "The termination provision specifically gives spouses, children and grandchildren an inalienable right after decades to recover their parents' or spouses' copyrights by simply serving notices of termination on the grantees," said Toberoff at the time.[11]

At the end of July 2015, however, 9th Circuit sided with the Ray Charles Foundation and overturned the 2013 decision. "The Foundation alleges injury to its interest in continuing to receive the royalty stream generated by Charles's works, which is the same interest that the Terminating Heirs seek to redirect to themselves," wrote Morgan Christen, the judge in the case, giving the Ray Charles Foundation the right to challenge the heirs' terminations.[12]

Toberoff says this was a significant case because these are related to rights that default to statutory heirs – surviving spouses, children or grandchildren – and are not affected by anything outlined in a will. These statutory heirs automatically inherit the author's termination right. "People don't realise that, but that's a very powerful aspect – and also relevant to estate planning – of the termination provision," he says. "It sometimes helps to reset the playing field and it opens up a whole area which has to do with people who are disinherited who actually still have rights."

Speaking in summer 2020, Toberoff says the ruling from the chief justice of the District Court in the central district in California upholding the children's right to seek termination in Charles's compositions is still in place. "I believe it's a correct ruling," he says. "What happened in that case was we also dismissed the copyright action saying that they don't have standing."

Getting these rights back allowed the Ray Charles heirs to then sell a majority share in the US publishing revenues of his pre-1964 compositions to Primary Wave in May 2020. Financial terms were not made public beyond it being described as a "multi-million [dollar] deal".[13]

Ken Abdo, a partner at legal firm Fox Rothschild, was one of the first US lawyers to represent writers in the US in a copyright termination filing. He filed on behalf of Lipps Inc (who had a global hit with 'Funky Town' in 1980) relating to post-1978 copyrights. "I did that in 2005, which was really early," he says. "I got the notoriety of being a little ahead of the curve on these legacy acts."

Publishing rights reverting back to the family of a deceased artist can sometimes go some way to offsetting the pain (and the financial losses) of other rights being taken out of their control. As noted in Chapter 3, the family of Ritchie Valens were unable to get his master recordings back from his former manager and promoter Bob Keane. However, at the end of 1987, all of his publishing rights reverted to his mother.[14]

Isaac Hayes III says that chasing down copyright termination was one of his priorities when he took over the running of his father's estate. "We started terminating his old publishing," he says. "So all of his classic songwriting hit records, they get terminated and that publishing returns to the family. The post-1978 material was terminated in the fall of last year [2018]. Everything he [wrote] after 1978 terminated and came back to us."

Taking back control of these rights gives the estate not just a bigger share of revenues from things like licensing; it also gives the estate total control over how and where they are licensed. "There's pretty good hit records in there," Hayes says of the compositions they pursued termination of. "'Déjà Vu' was a Grammy-nominated song.[15] 'A Few More Kisses to Go' had been sampled [by acts including Snoop Dogg and Redman]. And then his pre-'78 works – he started as a songwriter in 1963 – came back in February of this year [2019]. So for the next four or five years, his classic songwriting songs like 'Hold on, I'm Comin'' and 'Soul Man' [both hits for Sam & Dave], all these songs are starting to come back to us. So we'll have full control of the publishing." This was also something of a righting of wrongs for the Hayes family as Isaac Hayes had lost many of his copyrights when he was declared bankrupt in 1976 as a result of Stax Records going bust the year before.

Rondor Music ended up with the publishing rights to the Stax music catalogue.[16] Lance Freed, president of Rondor, said in 2008, just after Hayes died, that Hayes at the time of his bankruptcy was forced to sell his writer's share for $30,000 and those compositions went on to generate vast sums of money.

With Stax going under, they were unable to pay Hayes the royalties he was due. "He was the biggest star on Stax and was bringing in 70 per cent of the income on the label when they had over 30 artists," Hayes' son claims, estimating that he lost out on an eight-figure sum at the time.

Isaac Hayes III clearly understands the monetary and strategic advantage of termination, but it is a very complex and arduous process to go through for estates. The more convoluted it is, the higher the lawyer fees can be, so this is sometimes simply not an option for small estates that see a modest turnover of revenue each year.

Jim Griffin is a US-based music consultant who also advises estates on their business dealings. He says there is still a great deal of naivety or ignorance about termination rights and how they can fundamentally change the architecture and thrust of an estate. "[A l]ot of people don't even know their termination rights," he says. "These rights are in the US, but they apply to an enormous amount of the revenue from the music. Many of these parties, they read the [publishing] contract and the contract certainly doesn't mention the termination rights. And the contract makes it sound like they are owned in perpetuity by someone as if they were a piece of property. But they're not. And so often these parties have no idea they're entitled to termination or expiration. They're not sure when expiration happens or where all of this stuff occurs. They really don't know." He says he stresses to new estates that this is the issue that should be at the very top of their agenda when they are starting to put things in order and figure out how the estate should be run.

Of course, songwriters in their lifetime can start the termination process, but if they don't and then they pass away, they can leave a scramble for the heirs to get wheels in motion.

Daniel Novick from legal film SRIP Law says there is a limited time period in which termination action has to be taken otherwise the opportunity simply evaporates. "You have a 13-year window in which to give notice," he says. "Then you have a five-year period in which termination can become effective. The issue for estates is usually if the artist or the songwriter wasn't on top of things or their team wasn't on the ball enough [...] [and if] they haven't filed notice of an intention to recapture with the Copyright Office and they pass away, it makes their will [lose] control."

One estate management executive explains just how protracted it can all be. "We are working with some musicians – their estates, that is – on termination rights," they say. "We are working with one estate in particular on that – we can't say who it is – and it is a lengthy process. There's a lot of information you have to dig up to try to find out if it's possible for them to take back certain songs. It will, of course, depend upon how long their term has been." They add that this has been a major focus for their estate clients in the past decade as they all come alive to the importance of this matter to their business and future planning.

Beyond the basic rights to terminate, there are arguments from some in the publishing world that taking the rights back is essential to revitalise the earning potential of an estate, especially if those rights have not been proactively worked by the publisher in charge of them.

Bruce Lampcov, head of West Coast business development at Downtown Music Publishing, argues this represents an opportunity for estates to put themselves in the driving seat if they have been knocking on locked doors at publishers to do something – *anything* – with the publishing rights they are sitting on. "Especially right now, there are a lot of opportunities for estates in getting their rights back," he says. "And their catalogue, to be quite frank, has been languishing at the big companies. I am not an anti-majors person in any way whatsoever, but the fact is that these companies have tens of thousands of clients and they just really don't have the bandwidth, or even the desire, to really spend much time working estates and helping to create a significant value."

Marc Toberoff did a lot of work with Ray Charles's heirs, but this was a mere *amuse-bouche* for the work he was to do with the children of James Brown, another estate with a combustible structure and ever-shifting politics. The Ray Charles case related to around 100 compositions; with James Brown's heirs it was around 1,200 songs, according to Toberoff's calculations. When we spoke in summer 2020, he said, "He was extremely prolific. Many of the termination windows were only coming up recently."

The problem was that as the children that Toberoff represented made their filing for termination, so too did Brown's last wife, Tomi Rae Hynie, on behalf of herself and the son she had with Brown who was not named in his will. (Their marital status was, however, to play out in ugly detail in court and she was eventually ruled by the South Carolina Supreme Court in July 2020 to not be legally married to Brown.[17] See Chapter 3.[18])

"What lies in the balance is basically control of the termination rights," says Toberoff, before the ruling on Hynie's marital status was made. "There's another interesting aspect of a case where the estate is claiming that their right to the writer's share of royalties, as opposed to the publishing share, is left undisturbed as their contractual right. Usually when an author sells the copyrights to songs that he or she has composed, the writer still will retain under that publishing deal the writer's share of royalties – roughly 50 per cent of royalties. They claim that that is undisturbed by the termination; and we claim, no, that follows ownership of the copyright and essentially that original grant is terminated, including whatever split of the royalties."

He explained that under US law, even if Hynie was legally ruled to be Brown's wife, she still would have had to split 50 per cent of the termination interest with all of Brown's children (her own and those from his other relationships).

He adds that in instances like these – where there is a dispute over the ownership and the control of the rights – any pending licensing partners (e.g. a synchronisation request) would have to be alerted and warned that legal process was under way and they should halt their plans until everything is resolved. "It logically would [pause any pending licensing deals] because the [licensing] party wants to pay money to the correct person, otherwise they're buying air," he says. "So I put them on notice that these rights are disputed, they're in play and they are proceeding at their own risk."

Before the ruling on her marriage, Hynie had previously agreed to give 65 per cent of any proceeds from her termination rights to I Feel Good Trust, a charitable trust for the poor set up by Brown in his will but which had received no money because brutal fights over the estate had dragged on for years. "Mrs. Brown had given up her contests to the estate and charitable trust and agreed to give substantial funds from her very valuable federal rights to the charitable trust for needy students, which otherwise would not go to the charity," said Robert Rosen, one of her attorneys. "In our opinion, under her plan, many more millions of dollars would have flowed from those federal rights to the charitable trust if she had been confirmed as the surviving spouse."[19]

The *New York Times* reported that "much of the value" in Brown's legacy was linked to these termination rights, which were not part of the estate itself. According to a federal lawsuit by nine of Brown's children and grandchildren, Hynie had sold her share of termination rights in five of Brown's songs to Warner/Chappell Music Publishing in 2015 for $1.9 million.[20]

"The James Brown case is one of the craziest things I have ever seen," is how consultant Jim Griffin sums it up.

Not every song is worth the same amount of money, but if the termination rights in just five songs, out of a catalogue of over 1,000, can be sold for close to $2 million, that gives a good indication of the scale of the commercial worth of such termination rights for a prolific and successful songwriter. An artist sorting these issues out in their lifetime can help ward off a living hell for their heirs. Bob Donnelly, a transactional attorney at legal firm Fox Rothschild, tells me:

> This is a category where people have to pay close attention because you have all these triggers that are involved, these timelines when notice has to be served. If you don't do it, you can trigger the law of unintended

consequences, like in the Miles Davis situation where he had disinherited some of his children but he didn't exercise his right during his lifetime. And as a result, when he died, it became statutory – meaning that the heirs, who were the children and the wife, they then became the inheritors of the property. So, in effect, Miles Davis's songs wound up being shared in part by the children that he had specifically disinherited in his will.

It's really important that, even before folks die – particularly the older artists who are now in their sixties, seventies and eighties – pay some close attention to these rights [...] Otherwise they might find themselves in that position where something that they specifically didn't want to happen is going to happen.

SIDE NOTE: REVERSION OF RIGHTS WHEN NO CONTRACT EXISTS

The bulk of the notable rights reversions have happened in the US due to the specifics of copyright laws there. However, contractual idiosyncrasies can also see estates reclaim ownership of sound recording and publishing rights.

The estate of Nick Drake has managed to take back full ownership of all his rights (recordings and publishing) because it appears he never signed a contract in the first place that would have assigned them to a record label or publisher in perpetuity – or even for a set period of time. "When I first took over looking after Nick's estate in the late 1990s, we couldn't find any contracts at all – no recording contract, no publishing contract," says Cally Callomon. "We reckon that most things were done at will – as was often the way in the late 1960s. If you're an artist signed to Warlock or Witchseason, Joe Boyd [who signed Drake and who produced his first two albums] wasn't hot on stuffing pieces of paper under artists' noses notices saying, 'I won't do anything until you sign this.' So technically we were free of any kind of deal by the late 1990s."

He says at this stage the estate signed a renegotiated deal with Island Records (part of Universal Music Group) and Hannibal Records (Boyd's label) which allowed reversion of rights after a specified period. "It's amazing how quickly 20 years goes by," says Callomon, now that contract period has ended. When we spoke he was in the process of shopping the Nick Drake catalogue around different companies, but suggested that he wanted to do a deal with a smaller set-up than he was used to at Island/Universal Music Group.

"I have a number of options, but they all involve a team of three people," he says. "I'm one of the three and obviously I report at all times into Gabrielle [Drake, Nick's sister] who is really the keeper of the keys. But the team that actually puts the work together is three – maximum four – people across recording, publishing, everything. That's a very unfashionable cellular approach now."

In January 2021, the Nick Drake estate announced that it had signed a global deal with Blue Raincoat Music Publishing (a joint venture between Blue Raincoat Music and Reservoir Media) to represent Drake's compositions.

"Working with Nick's songs has always demanded and rewarded close attention and focus so it was a relief to find that there are still a clutch of song publishers who have the time and dedication to concentrate on the subtleties and details that these songs deserve," said Callomon on signing the deal. "Blue Raincoat is one such, along with their American partners, Reservoir. The fact that the company also owns the newly reformed Chrysalis is an added bonus. Chrysalis were once bed partners with Island Records and so this move will be like a return to the fold."[21]

Plans for a new home for Drake's recorded music catalogue were still being finalised by his estate as this book was going to print in early 2021.

CATALOGUES FALL INTO THE PUBLIC DOMAIN

"It always felt a little icky"

The extension to the copyright term for sound recordings, the Cliff's Law of legend, was a huge victory for recordings artists and record labels. But, really, all it represented was buying time and delaying the inevitable. These rights, unless there is another extension (which will be hard to argue given how recent this one was), will eventually fall into the public domain. Copyrights expire – that is simply an inherent fact of their creation. The question for all, and especially for estates, is a matter of "when" rather than "if".

During the copyright term, record companies (or the artists themselves if they paid for, bought back or earned back the rights) hold the exclusive right to recordings. When they fall into the public domain, anyone can release them. A number of labels sprang up specialising in public domain recordings, generally cobbling together compilations that sell for bargain-basement prices rather than compiling expensive box sets.

Rarely, if ever, were they pressing discs from the original masters – instead they were simply taking existing commercially released recordings and basing their new compilations on them. Studio costs were non-existent, the original recording artists did not have to be paid and only mechanical royalties for the songwriters, where applicable, had to be paid. The end result was that such cash-in labels took the bulk of the revenues.

In the CD era, there was a set-up cost involved as the discs would still have to be manufactured and distributed to the shops. In the digital era, however, manufacturing costs disappeared and distribution costs to get the releases on iTunes initially, and later the other streaming services, were marginal. This became a business where it was almost all profit.

One senior executive, then at a digital distribution company in the first decade and a half of the new millennium, says there was a gold rush among new companies to exploit public domain recordings and take full advantage of low-entry digital distribution. "As the digital era dawned, there was all of a sudden this kind of huge business around things like PD [public domain]," they say. "So you had these older bits of music that were coming out [of copyright] and you had all these companies that were suddenly just releasing this stuff."

They say distribution companies were utterly complicit in this, working with any new public domain label as they just wanted to boost the size of their catalogues, which they could then use as leverage when negotiating deal terms of download stores and streaming services. The whole thing became a volume game. "As a distribution company, masses of tracks were important at one point," says the same executive. "We had a lot of these companies because it did that for us. And also, because it wasn't frontline, there wasn't any marketing money we needed to get involved with or have to deal with marketing campaigns. It was good business, but it always felt a little icky."

As Jimmy Devlin, founder of UK independent label River Records, puts it, "If recordings are falling into the public domain in Europe you'll have 300 record companies all through Europe – particularly Holland and Germany – putting these things out as they are public domain."

The distribution executive says the change of the copyright term in 2011 means that those fly-by-night labels – all hoping to exploit early rock'n'roll records– suddenly disappeared or went into the re-compiling business where they would have to license and pay for recordings.

Estates did not earn money from public domain releases (unless they represented someone who wrote the tracks they recorded, as long as their publishing was not in the public domain). Most importantly they could not control them. This meant releases of variable quality were flooding the market and also competing with those that were more professionally produced. This all resulted in consumer confusion as releases officially sanctioned or overseen by the estate (even if they were public domain) sat cheek by jowl with unofficial releases. Anything an estate was going to do to promote a deceased artist's recordings would automatically be compromised by what public domain labels were doing with the same recordings.

The recordings that saw their copyright term extended tended to be handled with more care and attention, with labels like Ace and Beechwood Recordings hailed as shining examples of this.

The former distribution executive says one small re-compiling label they looked after was doing "hundreds of thousands of pounds" a year, so this was not an insignificant part of the business. Even so, the early rock'n'roll and other recordings that got a stay of execution in the 2011 changes to the law in Europe will still, eventually, fall into the public domain. This is already an issue for early classical recordings as well as many blues, folk, jazz and country recordings from the first half of the 20th century in Europe – and this will soon start to impact in the US.

"That's much more of a problem with European masters than with the US masters at this point," says Erin M. Jacobson, a music industry lawyer based in Los Angeles. "So those are other considerations when you're dealing with an estate. [That includes] what assets you can exploit so that you are earning the income from them rather than just letting all this stuff be out there for free because certain aspects are in public domain."

The major advantage the estate and the label who originally released the recordings have over public domain labels is they have access to the original master tapes. This means they can remix and remaster old recordings so the audio quality is as high as it can possibly be. They will also have access to outtakes and unreleased material to give any reissues they do a considerable advantage in the market.

Audio mastering expert and archivist Jessica Thompson says that low-quality audio releases entering the market will reflect badly on the estate – even if they had nothing to do with them. "For me, my biggest heartbreak is shitty bootlegs – when someone just puts out a terrible release of something," she says. "People can license something legally for a reissue but then they just do a terrible job. They source it from subpar sources and don't put a lot of thought into contextualising it. When you go on Spotify and you look up a track, there are 10 versions of it and eight of them sound like crap. Then there's the good ones and it breaks my heart that the other eight are out there. It makes the master tapes so much more valuable," says Thompson. "That's something that I feel like we need to educate consumers on. There's such value in going back to the original tapes."

The labels themselves who owned the masters for the duration of the copyright protection period also have long-standing relationships with the major DSPs[22] which means their recordings can get prioritised in playlists and in the search bar. Then there is the additional fact that the copyright period for master recordings is different in different jurisdictions, so global DSPs will tend to work with the label who owned the original recordings even if they are still in copyright in some markets but not others.

Thierry Jacquet is head of catalogue at Warner Music France and explains how this works with particular reference to Édith Piaf. The bulk of her catalogue was controlled by Warner Music while Universal Music controlled some other parts. Her recording career stretched from the 1930s to 1963, but everything except the recordings she made in the final year of her life is now in the public domain in Europe. Warner was in charge of her post-1946 recordings. The major problem is that she made very few recordings in 1963, so the bulk of her catalogue is in the public domain in European countries. Warner France has to compete against a range of public domain labels putting out Piaf recordings, a situation that has been exacerbated in the digital age. "The streaming business has given us the opportunity to make the full repertoire discoverable now," he says. "A big part of her repertoire in

Europe is in the public domain." He says, however, good relations with the likes of Spotify and Apple Music puts Warner France and the Piaf estate in a strong standing. "One thing we try to be careful about is that the streaming services, when they do playlists, try to take our tracks instead of the public domain ones," he says. "But there is no obligation, of course, to use them. But because the tracks are not public domain in the US, their playlists will have gaps if they are based on public domain tracks."

He also says that copyright laws in other media work to benefit Warner and the estate. "We also have the copyrights for the artwork, which they [the public domain labels] don't have," he says. "We are sure that the quality of our releases is better in terms of sound quality and the photos, text and everything else is better than what they are releasing."

They do have to lower the price when dealing with physical music formats, however, as that is one area where public domain labels have a strategic advantage. "They do all kinds of PPD[23] pricing and we are also trying to be on the same level," he says. "We cannot sell the CDs at full price when the public domain labels are selling them at a cheaper price. We are trying to have the same formats and a decent PPD."

Michele Monro, who runs the estate of her late father, Matt Monro, argues that there is very little a small estate can do to fight public domain releases beyond working with a major label to use their market position and muscle. "I'm very protective," she says with regard to her father's legacy. "Unfortunately we've now got public domain shit happening. With that, I can't control it; but with what I can control, I do."

She says that when she works with a label like Universal for reissues of her father's catalogue, she will help do the promotion and this gives the releases an important coating of credibility. "I don't endorse them," she says of the public domain releases that have come out. "I tell fans, 'If it's not on the website, it ain't from me.'"

Record labels, even though they got a stay of execution in 2011 of an extra 20 years, are having to operate knowing that, as each year passes, more and more of their deepest catalogue will fall into the public domain.

Talking about the earliest recordings of a late artist who was a towering figure in music from the 1960s onwards, a catalogue executive at a major label says all reissues are done with one eye firmly on the ticking public domain clock. "We've got to a stage now where there is certain repertoire that will go public domain, as it has for so many artists in Europe," they say with regard to a major reissue campaign around that artist in partnership with the estate (who actually own the bulk of their masters but license them to the major label in question). "I felt this is something that we should address as part of the plan."

As digital now allows a fresh exploitation of the long tail of catalogue, this major label executive explains the bind their company and the estates they work with now find themselves in with regard to material that is now public domain. "We can obviously still exploit them, but other people can too, depending on what masters they use," they say. "Of course, this is all a bone of contention."

The fact that Europe has a different sound recording copyright period – and especially when it was 50 years rather than the extended 70 years – has proven to be a huge political issue for record labels when dealing with estates based in another jurisdiction that has a much longer copyright term.

Steve Davis, who was director of catalogue at EMI from 2000 to 2009 and then a catalogue consultant from 2009 to 2013, when they became aware that precious parts of their catalogues were becoming public domain in Europe, tells me:

> The American estates were quite unhappy. Especially the estates of Frank Sinatra, Dean Martin and Nat King Cole as well as a couple of lesser lights. That was because, at the time, the copyright laws were different in the UK compared to America. A lot of their artists' repertoire had gone out of copyright, which meant that when the estates came over for meetings, they were going into record shops and seeing a load of their artists' stuff at £2.99 because companies who thrive on releasing out-of-copyright material just flooded the market. The day they came out of copyright, a lot of these out-of-copyright companies just jumped on it, putting it everywhere, using different sleeves and so on. I can understand their frustration.

This caused a lot of complicated politics for the UK and European arms of EMI in their dealings with the estates of major US artists from the pre-rock'n'roll era who suddenly woke up to public domain issues impacting not just on their potential revenues but also their management of the estate. "Those management companies call the shots – virtually completely on repertoire in terms of when it is released, what support it would get, every aspect," says Davis. "The prime movers were the estate managers."

The primary concern has so far been around recordings falling into the public domain in certain markets, but that is just a dry run for when publishing rights become public domain. The countdown clock on this period of copyright only starts when the composer dies or, in the case of a joint composition, when the last surviving writer dies.

In the US, for songs written after 1978, this period is life + 70 years. "For works made for hire and anonymous and pseudonymous works, the duration of copyright is 95 years from first publication or 120 years from creation, whichever is shorter (unless the author's identity is later revealed in Copyright Office records, in which case the term becomes the author's life plus 70 years)," says the US Copyright Office. For anything before 1978, "the law automatically gives federal copyright protection" to them and the "duration of copyright in these works is generally computed the same way as for works created on or after January 1, 1978."[24]

In the UK, it is life + 70 years.[25] The situation is identical in the European Union.[26]

There are bifurcated duration provisions within US copyright law meaning, as legal firm Alter, Kendrick & Baron describes it, "the duration of the
copyright differs depending on the date of creation of the work, as well as
the date the work is initially registered or published". This essentially divides
the publishing world in pre-1978 work and post-1977 works where the
earliest ones are starting to enter the public domain.[27] "Works from 1923
were set to go into the public domain in 1999, after a 75-year copyright
term," noted the Center for the Study of the Public Domain with Duke
University School of Law in the US. "But in 1998 Congress hit a two-decade
pause button and extended their copyright term for 20 years, giving works
published between 1923 and 1977 an expanded term of 95 years."[28]

This may feel like a long period of time, but culturally significant works
are now starting to reach the end of this period. Songs that became public
domain at the start of 2019 included 'Yes, We Have No Bananas' as well as
'The Charleston' and 'Who's Sorry Now?'.[29]

Then, at the start of 2020, George Gershwin's *Rhapsody in Blue*, which he
wrote in 1924, became public domain as part of a process where all
copyrights created that year expired.[30] "It's entirely understandable that the
Gershwin Family Trust would want to keep copyright over their works," said
Jennifer Jenkins from the Center for the Study of the Public Domain at
Duke. "But the problem is that only maybe 1 per cent of works is still
generating any income. And so for those 99 per cent of works, no one got
any benefit. But the rest of us – the public, all of the future creators – we lost
out on the ability, for 20 years, to freely build upon those works."[31]

The case of 'We Shall Overcome' reveals just what happens when a song
goes into the public domain and the battles that can exist between those who
want to avail themselves of its public domain status and those who would
prefer it was still under copyright protection.

The song that later became an anthem of the civil rights movement in the
1960s has its roots in an African American spiritual, but was copyrighted as
'We Shall Overcome' in the 1940s when it was adopted by the labour
movement. Folk singer Pete Seeger had, in the folk tradition, amended some
wording in the first verse and lawyers in a copyright case in 2017 tried to
argue that his changing of lyrics meant it was not in the public domain
(having only been published in that form in 1947).[32]

Two years later, a federal judge partly rejected the copyright claim, arguing
the lyric changes were not significant enough to make it a new creation and
therefore give it a new copyright term. The case stemmed from two filmmakers
wanting to use it in a documentary about the song. The Highlander Research
and Education Centre in Tennessee had been bequeathed the song in the
early 1960s and set up the We Shall Overcome Fund to distribute royalties
from its use in the form of grants and scholarships for black students. It had
been seeking upwards of $100,000 to allow it to be used in the documentary.
The two sides in the dispute did reach a settlement but, in doing so, it meant
the song was now officially in the public domain.[33]

What estates need to be constantly awake to is the fact that, eventually, the songs that built the 20th century will no longer be covered by copyright. This may be a number of generations down the line from the original heirs, but it is a harsh inevitability for them, especially for those who manage to serve notification of termination.

Death gives birth to an estate, but the eventual expiration of composition copyrights represents a second death for their business.

SALE ON BUY: ESTATES BUYING BACK RIGHTS

Some families have to sell off rights for various reasons – often to settle debts or inheritance taxes after a musician passes away in order to keep the estate from tipping over into bankruptcy.

These rights, however, can be re-acquired when the estate is more profitable. This happened with Frank Zappa's masters. He passed away in 1993 and his widow, Gail, sold the masters he owned under instruction from him before he died, when he recommended that she get out of the music business.[34] They did, however, revert back to Zappa Records and the Zappa Family Trust in 2012 and the estate eventually licensed them to Universal Music in June 2015.[35] Gail Zappa died in October of that year.

Ahmet Zappa, co-trustee of the Zappa Trust, revealed that his mother had used the sale of the masters to pay for a major life insurance policy – but it came with significant repayment clauses that could have sunk the estate. "She pre-paid for this big life insurance policy," he explained in the *Bob Lefsetz Podcast* in 2019. "And there's something that I guess she wasn't aware of [...] she was under the impression if she ever needed money she could borrow against it. There's this thing called a mech that was in there, that I guess would have had to make her pay like a crazy amount on taxes. That was never part of her understanding. So actually when she needed to make a payment to save all the music, she reached out to all of us kids. She's like, 'Hey, listen, you know, ultimately this life insurance policy is for you guys. But what's more important to you? Money or saving the family business?'"[36]

This move brought up old animosities between the siblings over how control of the estate had been carved out. "And for me, it was no question," said Ahmet. "I think the family is the most important. Whatever you need, you should do. My little sister [Diva] was the same. And my older brother [Dweezil] and older sister [Moon] just had a different opinion. It's a big disappointment because there was a lot of arguing that was going on between [us]. There was a lot of stress for me because I was the person who had to find the money to make these payments."[37] He was able to raise the capital and the insurance policy did not have to be cashed in, meaning the estate was able to eventually take the masters back.

The Roy Orbison estate was also to benefit from his widow, Barbara (who passed away in 2011), being able to take back control of a number of her husband's masters, and the estate also owns most of his publishing rights.

"A very important part of the Roy Orbison pie, if you will, took place before I was involved," says Chuck Fleckenstein, who works with the estate as general manager and COO of Roy's Boys, Orbison Music and Publishing and Still Working Music. "The very savvy Barbara Orbison was able to regain control of the majority of Roy's masters. For the ones that she didn't control she actually successfully had him re-record, which is something that modern artists threaten to do but never do. [On top of this,] the Orbison estate owns 99 per cent of Roy Orbison's publishing in his songs. So we control both the masters and the publishing. Those are very significant pieces of the pie."

Equally, David Bowie owned most of his rights in his lifetime and ownership simply transferred to his estate and gave it enviable freedom to exert even greater control over his legacy. "I think it is very important if an estate can possibly either get those rights back or – obviously – if they owned them to begin with, keep them for exploitation," says Bill Zysblat, Bowie's business manager. "David Bowie is a great example. He owned or repurchased almost all of his masters and publishing from day one, so our ability to do things exactly the way David would have wanted is unencumbered."

Another source with knowledge of the Bowie estate adds more flesh to the bones here, as it appears the estate does not quite own everything, but eventually it will – with just one exception. "The only records they currently don't own are the first record that came out on Decca[38] – that Universal has, and has released multiple times," they say. "They don't own *The Next Day* [from 2013] and *Blackstar* [from 2016]. But those two do revert, I believe, in 2021. Sony owns them at the moment." They then repeat and stress that last sentence. "*At the moment.*"

Perhaps the most famous estate that does not own important rights is the Elvis Presley one. This was because Presley's manager, Tom Parker, sold the singer's recorded music income up to that point to RCA for $5.4 million in exchange for waiving the right to any future sound recording royalties. It remains a sore point with the estate, particularly for Authentic Brands Group, which bought 85 per cent of Elvis Presley Enterprises in 2013. That said, it has been taking back control of much of Presley's publishing so that should salve some of the pain. "Would I like to own the masters of Elvis Presley?" asks Jamie Salter, the founder, chairman and CEO of Authentic Brands Group. "The answer's yes. Is that happening anytime soon? I don't think it is – but you never know. There may be an opportunity one day to buy the masters and, if there was an opportunity, we would do it. When we bought Elvis, we only had 50 per cent of the publishing and now we have 75 per cent."

For the estates of older artists who had their heyday in the pre-digital and even pre-CD age, there can be issues related to their historic recording contracts that were signed in an earlier age and perhaps never renegotiated to cover new means of exploitation. It does not always follow, however, that labels modernise the contracts as new forms of exploitation come along.

They may only do so as the result of an audit demanded on behalf of the estate – sometimes just hoping it never arises as an issue.

"It's a sensitive issue, because a lot of the contracts done in the 1960s and 1970s didn't anticipate every possible technological development," says Costa Pilavachi, who has held senior positions at a number of classical labels over the years, including Philips Classics, Decca Music Group, EMI Classics and Deutsche Grammophon. "For the ones I did, when I started, I always put those clauses in to cover any and all technological developments, which would include digital and other forms of distribution."

He notes that digital is the major issue for classical music artists and the estates of classical recording acts. "Perhaps there's a little wariness and suspicion about whether they're getting fairly compensated in the digital era," he continues. "I would probably put that as the number one concern. Nobody has tried to stop anything, but there have been people who had read stories about how little money people get from Spotify."

Certainly the biggest estates have full teams of lawyers and business managers keeping abreast of all this and rigorously interrogating contract terms. It would have been extremely reckless of a label to start exploiting rights they did not have. When dealing with smaller estates, however, the label might only have stopped or changed things when asked or – unfortunately – when they got caught red-handed. Often it was only when the contracts had a clause where permission for certain exploitations was required that the label would go back to the estate to get clearance of a proposed release or licensing plan. Things are much more by the book today, but several decades ago, it was felt it was easier and quicker to bend rules and not even mention when they eventually contorted into whole new and highly improbable shapes.

"For pretty much everyone from the 1960s onwards, except those few who became superstars, record labels had contracts which enabled them to do anything really without having to constantly go back for permissions," says one senior record label executive. "The contracts effectively said the labels could do anything on any format that might exist in the future. You can argue that it was good or bad, but that was the way it was pre-1970s."

They did, however, admit they were sometimes guilty of rule bending in the earlier years of their career with regard to the oldest and most lucrative catalogues on the label's books. "I was reissuing stuff by dead people," they say. "However, the contracts were such in the olden days that there was no legal obligation with almost all of these artists to actually talk to anybody before you did anything. So a record label could just simply dive in there, repackaging it in the way that you wanted to and make it as good as you can – or as shoddy as you could, if you were of that mind […]"

A wider change in the industry and contract law, hastened by the arrival of the CD in the 1980s, changed all that. "As the rights of artists have developed over the years, so the rights of dead artists have changed," the same executive says. "That's quite a significant thing, I think. I was freely banging stuff out by people on [our different labels] from the 1950s or even stuff from the 1940s and 1930s."

This is something that specialist managers of big estates seek to address and cauterise as soon as they take over a new estate. "We go back to some of the vendors," says Jeff Jampol of JAM Inc when helping to clean up the business of an existing estate his company has just taken on as a client. "Some of these artists were signed to deals that were normal for their time but are egregious by today's standards. We go back to the vendors and say, 'Look, I get it. You're not evil. You gave this artist a deal back in 1965 that was equivalent to deals of the period. But guess what? You made millions of dollars, the artists made millions of dollars. They're all recouped. Every-body's happy. Now let's re-carve this deal for the next generation and you give them what they really deserve.' And if they know we're on board, and because they enjoy a close working relationship with us, they know that there's going to be a lot of work done on behalf of the estate and they're good partners. In many cases we've been able to improve those deals and get those deals moved up to 21st-century standards, which can revolutionise the income of an artist."

In some instances, certain things can be used as negotiating leverage for better terms from a label. The US lawyer for a major figure in their particular genre reveals how it can work. "They had an ongoing audit with [a major label]," they say. "There were a lot of issues with the contracts they had signed as they didn't always deal with digital rights. They had antiquated royalty rates. I addressed that with [the major label]. I am sure they loved me for that!"

The same lawyer says that the estate had a number of high-quality recordings in its archive and this was used as leverage as the renegotiation talks progressed. This is how negotiations can start to exist in a continuum. "We found these great recordings that have never been put out before," they say. "So we dangled them in front of the record label. Of course, all the contracts had to be revised. It gave us the opportunity, even though [the artist] had passed, to rejig all the deals. Since then, we just kept coming back every couple of years for further renegotiations."

Blockbuster estates, however, are in a position of even great power, especially when contracts are up for renewal with record labels. They have phenomenal proven worth in the market and past success strengthens their hand significantly in renegotiation talks.

In March 2010, less than a year after he died, the Michael Jackson estate signed what was called "the biggest recording contract in history", which came out of its renegotiations with Sony Music, Jackson's long-term label. It was estimated at up to $250 million in advances and covered up to 10 releases by 2017, including previously unreleased tracks. It was, said the *Guardian*, "a huge bet on the singer's continued popularity" and covered exploitation of his recordings in the standard places (like CD, vinyl, downloads and streaming) as well as in video games, amusement parks, TV ads, DVD compilations and memorabilia.[39]

John Branca, co-executor of the estate, said in a media statement, "Michael's contracts set the standard for the industry. By all objective criteria, this agreement with Sony Music demonstrates the lasting power of Michael's music by exceeding all previous industry benchmarks."[40]

Rob Stringer, chairman of Sony Music's Columbia Epic Label Group, told the *New York Times*, "It's not just a record deal. We're not basing this on how many CDs we sell or how many downloads. There are also audio rights for theatre, movies, computer games. I don't know how an audio soundtrack will be used in 2018 but you've got to bet on Michael Jackson in any new platform."[41]

While not made public, it was understood that Branca had negotiated "an especially high royalty rate for sales both inside and outside the United States".[42] Looking back on that deal in 2016, when I interviewed him, Branca said, "We renewed the distribution deal with Sony Records for Michael's catalogue and were fortunate to be able to secure the biggest guarantee on a recording contract in the history of the record business. That contemplated new releases and re-releases of various albums – which we have done."

Renegotiating contracts in the artists' favour was something Branca excelled at throughout his career, as he revealed when we spoke again in April 2020. "One of the main things I've done as a lawyer in most estates and artists is make sure they have contracts that are fair," he says. "For example, with The Beach Boys, I had to renegotiate their contracts over the years to bring them into today's standards. And the same with The Doors. I had to continually figure out ways to offer new projects to the label in return for increased royalties."

There was, however, one mega-deal that pushed the Jackson estate out of the driving seat – when Sony/ATV Music Publishing bought out Jackson's 50 per cent stake in the company in March 2016 for an estimated $750 million.[43] This was made up of a lump sum payment of $733 million along with up to $17 million in a final dividend.[44]

The publishing giant came out of a partnership between Jackson and Sony in 1995, but the origins of it date back to 1985 when Jackson bought ATV Music Publishing for $47.5 million. The company contained over 4,000 compositions including, most significantly, almost all the songs John Lennon and Paul McCartney wrote together, but also songs by Bruce Springsteen, Hank Williams, Little Richard and The Rolling Stones.[45]

"In recent years, Sony/ATV has been paying an annual dividend of approximately $23 million to the estate, according to Sony's filings with the SEC [Securities and Exchange Commission]," wrote *Billboard* when news of the deal broke. "Over the life of his ATV and Sony/ATV stake, those annual dividends averaged about $15 million, according to a source which, if accurate, means Jackson and his estate have collected $560 million from

Sony/ATV ($110 million in the initial deal, and $450 million through the years) before this week's deal, which will deliver another $750 million to the estate."[46]

Five years earlier, on 3 October 2011,[47] Branca had appeared on *Piers Morgan Live* on CNN. He downplayed the debt the estate was in and said he was not going to be selling assets. "Those are cornerstone assets that we plan on keeping for Michael's children and keeping those in the family," he said."[48]

Cornerstone assets or not, the sale happened because Sony triggered a buy/sell clause in the deal in late 2015 that meant one side could buy out the other. *Billboard* claimed the Jackson estate "was caught by surprise" but soon "warmed to the deal" and was hoping to be the buyer. That was not to be – in part because, according to sources *Billboard* had spoken to, the estate wanted to use the windfall to clear $250 million in debts that would, in a single movement, leave it debt-free.[49] The deal still left the Jackson estate with its 10 per cent stake in EMI Music Publishing, although Sony eventually bought that out in July 2018.[50]

"This transaction further allows us to continue our efforts of maximizing the value of Michael's Estate for the benefit of his children," said Branca and John McClain, his co-executor in the estate, putting a brave face on it all in their joint statement on the deal. "It also further validates Michael's foresight and genius in investing in music publishing."[51]

Looking back on that deal four years later, Branca confirms that the estate had its hand forced by Sony. "We didn't have a choice as they [Sony] exercised the buy/sell," he says. "We had no choice. It was not our election to want to sell."

Could the estate, however, have bought out Sony if it had raised the funding? "If it made sense to buy out Sony on Sony/ATV, yes, we tried," he says. "We investigated that possibility. Based on the contracts that Michael had signed when I was not involved, the leverage was on Sony's side and they exercised the buy/sell and we had no choice but to either buy or sell. The price we got for selling was more attractive than the price we would have had to pay for buying."

(Branca did, however, say in January 2021 that Mijac – the publishing company that handles all Jackson's compositions as well as songs by Sly and the Family Stone, Kenneth Gamble/Leon Huff and others – was not going to be shopped around. "We will never sell Mijac in a manner to give up control – it will be passed down to Michael's children," he said.[52])

It was to prove a landmark deal for not just the Jackson estate but the estates business overall. *Forbes* estimated that the Jackson estate generated $825 million that year, with the lion's share coming from the Sony deal. To put the scale of the deal in context, the next 12 largest estates that year brought in $243 million *collectively*.[53]

As Branca says of the staggering scale of the deal, "I doubt you'll see that happen for anybody again."

FIGHT FOR YOUR RIGHTS: WHEN LICENSING DISPUTES GRIP ESTATES

A certainty in the music business is that when considerable sums of money are being generated, legal action is rarely far behind. As explored in detail in Chapter 3, battles over the control of estates are far from uncommon; but neither are legal actions over the carving-up of earnings from dead musicians.

Blix Street Records, which releases the recordings of Eva Cassidy, has been on different ends of different legal actions over the years over issues relating to both royalties and rights. In March 2004, Blix Street sued Eva Cassidy's parents, Hugh and Barbara Cassidy, and Allen Gelbard over a proposed film about the late singer. The dispute was over who had the right to negotiate sync licences for her recordings.[54]

The case went to trial in March 2006. During a break in proceedings the following month, both parties met with mediator Anthony Piazza. The Cassidys stated they would enter into a settlement "so long as they did not have to pay money and received full general releases".[55] An armistice was arrived at. "The settlement agreement extended the licensing agreement and provided for, inter alia, minimum royalties over a period of years, a means to determine the amount of royalties, a business plan, cooperation concerning the motion picture, and releases."[56]

Bill Straw from Blix Street voiced reservations about the settlement. Much wrangling followed and the trial court eventually ordered Blix Street to comply with the orders of the eventual settlement agreement. Speaking in late 2019, Bill Straw was diplomatic about the case, not wishing to discuss it in any great detail. "We [myself and her family] have had our ups and downs," he says, "but we're certainly on the same page now."

I ask him if litigation is a common – or even inevitable – aspect of working with estates having success with the recordings of deceased artists. "Sometimes you have to do it as a matter of principle," he says of taking legal action. "Anybody who thinks they are going to come out financially [better off] is in for big disappointment. You have to decide how you are going to be able to look in the mirror going forward having done it and spent the money – or just letting it go. Everybody has got a different answer at a different time for those kinds of things."

Royalty disputes appear with clockwork regularity in the record and publishing business for living artists – and disputes led by estates are no less common. Sometimes they relate specifically to recording royalties from new forms of exploitation, such as the estate of 1950s teen idol Ricky Nelson launching a class action against Sony Music in September 2018 over how international streaming royalties were paid through to the estate.[57]

That case was settled in September 2020 when Sony agreed to pay $12.7 million to a number of artists (and artist estates, including that of Ricky Nelson) who had brought a class action lawsuit against it. It was to be shared among all claimants on a pro rata basis.[58] "In addition to that one-off $12.7m payment, Sony has agreed to increase the future royalty payments calculated on ex-US streaming revenues by 36 per cent for the 'qualifying recordings' of all affected artists who opt-in to the class action," reported *Music Business Worldwide*.

At other times, suits can arise from the transfer of ownership of recordings from one company to another and how royalty accounting is thereafter conducted, as was the case with Afeni Shakur, mother of Tupac and co-administrator of his estate, and Entertainment One in 2013. Earlier that year, Entertainment One had purchased the catalogue of Death Row Records, including a number of Tupac recordings. Afeni Shakur was seeking $1.1 million in royalties as well as the return of unreleased masters made by the rapper.

"According to the latest lawsuit, Tupac's estate entered into a settlement agreement in 1997 with Death Row and its then-distributor Interscope Records that confirmed that the estate had exclusive ownership over unre-leased master recordings and audiovisual work, that Death Row would be provided with one 'album's worth' of material, and that the estate would receive royalties from future exploitation of released and unreleased Tupac material,"[59] reported *Billboard,* noting that the suit claimed Death Row had no ownership rights in the unreleased material.

Former band members suing estates is another regular and recurring issue. One of the biggest cases here was brought in front of the high court in London in 2006 when Aston "Family Man" Barrett, former bassist in The Wailers, took legal action against the Bob Marley estate relating to royalty payments.

It was the third time round for the case, having gone through the courts in both Jamaica and New York in the 1980s. Barrett claimed Marley had promised members of The Wailers an equal cut of royalties from a number of albums.

The case in London, however, was thrown out by the judge, who sided with the Marley family and Island Records, stating that, following a 1994 settlement, Barrett had surrendered his rights to any further royalties.[60] "I conclude that all the claims that Mr Aston Barrett brings in his personal capacity have been compromised by the settlement agreement," said high court judge Mr Justice Lewison.[61]

Plagiarism is proving to be a new legal route for estates, both to pursue and to be pursued on. The most controversial plagiarism case of recent years related to the song 'Blurred Lines' – written and performed by Pharrell Williams, Robin Thicke and TI (real name Clifford Joseph Harris Jr) – and was initiated by the family of Marvin Gaye.

The song was released in March 2013 and was a massive global hit. In August that same year, however, Thicke took pre-emptive legal action and filed a claim for declaratory relief that 'Blurred Lines' did not copy 'Got to Give It Up', a single by Gaye from March 1977.

In what became a very ugly and very public battle, the case went through numerous twists and turns. There were appeals over the ruling in favour of Gaye's children and the damages due (going from $7.3 million in March 2015 to $5.3 million in August 2016).[62] Eventually, however, in March 2018, the 9th Circuit Court of Appeals sided with Gaye's children and ruled the Gaye estate was entitled to half of the publishing royalties in the song for ever.[63] Damages were set at just under $5 million in December 2018 in a final judgment on the case.[64]

Richard Busch, who represented Gaye's heirs in the case, told *Rolling Stone* in July 2020 it was a very straightforward decision to take legal action here. "Older [people] like the Gaye family, for example, rely on Marvin's royalties to live," he said.[65]

Howard King from Los Angeles-based law firm King, Holmes, Paterno & Soriano represented Thicke and Williams in the plagiarism case. Unsurprisingly, he was not happy with the eventual ruling, the way the case played out or the legal precedents it set. He calls it "a shitty result".

He does, however, raise an important point about the damage that such a case can cause an estate and the reputation of the deceased artist in question. Victory in court can bring in significant settlement in the short term, but such an aggressive approach to perceived plagiarism can cause long-term erosion to an estate.

"The bigger issue is that Marvin Gaye never would have brought a lawsuit like this," says King. "He had such respect for other artists. He built his songs on the songs of other artists and he would have been delighted, even if it were true that Pharrell had built 'Blurred Lines' on the Marvin Gaye song, which is not true other than Pharrell certainly appreciated Marvin Gaye and wanted to do something in the same genre. But it's pretty clear from the people I talked to, who knew Marvin Gaye, [and they] said he would have never done it." Looking at the money versus the tainting of Gaye's legacy, this could prove to be a posthumous Pyrrhic victory.

On the other side of the plagiarism debate is the estate of rapper Juice WRLD (who died on 8 December 2019). Before he passed away, pop-punk band Yellowcard filed a lawsuit against him in October 2019, claiming his track 'Lucid Dreams' contained an uncleared sample from their 2006 track 'Holly Wood Died'. Following Juice WRLD's death, the suit temporarily stalled and then in February 2020 it was put on pause because the rapper's estate had still not gone through probate, meaning there was no legal representative who could respond to the plagiarism suit.[66] The coronavirus outbreak in April delayed things further.[67]

After the rapper's mother, Carmela Wallace, was put in charge of his estate, the Yellowcard suit was revived in July 2020, with $15 million in damages being sought, covering past and future royalties.[68] By late July 2020, however, the suit was quietly dropped against the estate.

Yellowcard were represented by Richard Busch, on something of a roll after the 'Blurred Lines' case, and he had described the case – and the sensitivities of pursuing a mother mere months after her young son had died – as having awkward "optics".[69] It was Busch who signed the one-page form on behalf of Yellowcard voluntarily withdrawing the legal action. "My clients are very sympathetic not only of Juice WRLD's death but also needed time to decide whether they really wanted to pursue the case against his grieving mother as the personal representative of the estate," he said.[70]

That did not, however, ward off a separate lawsuit against Juice WRLD's estate that arose in August 2020. The writers of a track called 'Ice' – an unnamed minor and his father, Thomas Willisch – claimed it had been infringed in Juice WRLD's 2018 track 'Lean Wit Me'.[71]

(At the time of writing, the case had not been resolved.)

Bootlegging is a perennial problem for record companies and estates, especially if material that has never been released before leaks, because that can dilute its impact if and when it eventually appears in a box set or expanded edition of an album. This used to be a black market economy and was limited to those who had access to pressing plants, but the age of the MP3 and user-upload streaming sites like SoundCloud and YouTube made this even faster – if not always monetisable – than in the days when bootleg and counterfeit CDs and LPs were being sold under the counter.

Sales through official channels, however, are another matter entirely, where ownership is claimed (or presumed) by others and they simply sell online and take all the profits. The estates of Harold Arlen, Ray Henderson and Harry Warren were spurred into action in April 2020 to sue Apple's iTunes download store and UK company Adasam Limited in a dispute over the rights to sell over 80 different recordings. The estates put forward a 148-page filing outlining their objections to the sale of the recordings in question.[72]

When I spoke to Sam Arlen, son of Harold Arlen and in charge of his estate, in the summer of 2020, the case was still ongoing and there was only so much he felt he could say about it as it was still an active case. "There is always going to be, unfortunately, people in any walk of life and in any business that are going to want to do things or try to do things that are not appropriate," he says. "You try your best to keep track of what's going on and how the licences come in. But obviously it's a giant industry. So you do your best to keep track. By having your hands on the copyrights and seeing what's going on out there, it gives you that closer connection to how things are used."

(The case had not been resolved before this book went to press.)

An authorship case from 2018 could have momentous implications for estates and how ownership of composition rights can subsequently change after songs are written.

'Cathy's Clown' was a major hit for The Everly Brothers in 1960 and was originally credited to Don and Phil Everly as the writers. In an agreement signed in 1980, Phil Everly reportedly relinquished "all of his rights, titles, interests and claim[s]" in the composition and, as such, his name was removed from both public credits for the song and royalty statements on its earnings. In 2011, Don Everly filed to recapture ownership from Sony/ATV, which had acquired the catalogue of Acuff/Rose, the original publisher of the song.[73] However, Phil Everly died on 2 January 2014 and his estate moved to recapture the rights in the song later that year, arguing that although he might have relinquished his credit and earnings, the agreement he signed in 1980 never disputed his authorship. It went to court in Nashville and in November 2018, the judge ruled that Don Everly was the sole author of the song and barred the estate of Phil Everly from claiming a stake in it. "If your name's been left off a song by accident and liner notes come out, you've got an obligation to speak up or forever hold your peace," said Linda Edell Howard from legal firm Adams & Reese, who was acting as Don Everly's attorney.[74]

Another relatively modern conundrum facing estates is the use of music from deceased artists being associated with political events and causes. This is not entirely new, but a number of flashpoint moments around rallies and public events hosted by President Trump in the US, especially in the run-up to the 2020 presidential election, has made this a very contemporary problem for estates.

What is critical here is that a living artist can do interviews or use their social media to distance themselves from a politician or party using their music at public events, making it clear they are not endorsing them by association. For deceased artists, it is down to their estate to voice objections on their behalf.

In October 2018, the estate of Prince objected to President Trump's use of 'Purple Rain' at his pre-midterm rallies around the US. "The Prince Estate has never given permission to President Trump or the White House to use Prince's songs and have requested that they cease all use immediately," tweeted Omarr Baker, Prince's half-brother, on 12 October.[75] But the message had clearly not got through to the White House. In October 2019, the official Prince account on Twitter posted a copy of a letter it received from Megan Newton, a lawyer at legal firm Jones Day, with regard to the complaint a year earlier (dated 15 October 2018). "Without admitting liability and to avoid any future dispute," she wrote, "we write to confirm that the Campaign will not use Prince's music in connection with its activities going forward."[76]

The reason the official Prince account on Twitter posted a year-old letter was because Trump had used 'Purple Rain' again at an event in Minneapolis, the hometown of Prince – an act that was surely petulantly intentional. The tweet added, "The Prince Estate will never give permission to President Trump to use Prince's songs."

The Prince estate was far from the only one to object to Trump politicising its music. In late June 2020, the estate of Tom Petty issued a cease-and-desist letter to the Trump campaign after it used 'I Won't Back Down', a hit for Tom Petty and The Heartbreakers in 1989, at a rally in Tulsa on 20 June. A statement was also posted by Petty's official Twitter account on 21 June, signed by his daughters Adria, Annakim and Dana as well as his ex-wife Jane. "Trump was in no way authorised to use this song to further a campaign that leaves too many Americans and common sense left behind," they said. "Both the late Tom Petty and his family stand against racism and discrimination of any kind. Tom Petty would not want a song of his used for a campaign of hate. He liked to bring people together."[77]

Just two months later, the estate of Leonard Cohen was dragged into the same debate and dealt with it both assertively and with a certain wry humour. The Cohen estate said it was considering legal action for the use of two different cover versions of his song 'Hallelujah' at the Republican National Convention between 24 and 27 August. In a posting on Cohen's Facebook page on 29 August, Michelle Rice, the Cohen estate's lawyer, posted a statement.

> We are surprised and dismayed that the RNC would proceed knowing that the Cohen Estate had specifically declined the RNC's use request, and their rather brazen attempt to politicize and exploit in such an egregious manner 'Hallelujah', one of the most important songs in the Cohen song catalogue. We are exploring our legal options. Had the RNC requested another song, 'You Want It Darker', for which Leonard won a posthumous Grammy in 2017, we might have considered approval of that song.[78]

*   *   *

The issues surrounding rights (ownership and control of them as well as where any resulting revenues should flow) are as much a regular fixture in estate management as they are for living artists; but very different battles can grip estates that call into question the very character and past behaviour of the artist at the centre of them.

These go far beyond the somewhat commonplace music industry battles outlined in this chapter. These battles are particular to the individual – an individual who is no longer around to respond to them or try to defend themselves. They can present estates with the biggest challenge they will ever encounter and risk significantly damaging not just an estate's reputation but also its earning potential.

And, at their most extreme, they can threaten to destroy an estate completely.

CHAPTER 11

From Deification to Demonisation

When Music Estates are Embroiled in Scandals

He told me that if they ever found out what we were doing, he and I would go to jail for the rest of our lives […] I want to be able to speak the truth as loud as I had to speak the lie for so long.

Wade Robson, *Leaving Neverland* documentary

Secrets will eat you up. You feel so alone.

James Safechuck, *Leaving Neverland* documentary

They should be ashamed of themselves.

John Branca, co-executor of the Michael Jackson estate, on the makers of *Leaving Neverland*[1]

When it aired in early March 2019, the *Leaving Neverland* documentary had an immediate and far-reaching impact. In it, Wade Robson and James Safechuck went on the record, alleging that when they were both young boys Michael Jackson groomed them and repeatedly sexually abused them.

The Jackson estate immediately and categorically disputed the claims, and suggested it would take legal action against Dan Reed, the director of the documentary, as well as broadcaster HBO.

Leaving Neverland had shone a new spotlight on extremely serious and upsetting allegations that had been made against Jackson in his lifetime and hung like a dark cloud over his legacy as well as the business of his estate after he died on 25 June 2009. The story stretches back decades. Following growing media speculation, the LAPD opened investigations into Jackson's alleged sexual abuse crimes in August 1993. In September that year, the family of one alleged victim, Jordan Chandler, took legal action against Jackson. To avoid a March 1994 court date, the singer settled the civil suit in January 1994, with suggestions that payment ran to over $20 million. In September 1994, prosecutors said they would not take action against Jackson.

The *Living with Michael Jackson* documentary aired in February 2003, in which Jackson spoke about his friendship with a number of young boys but vigorously denied that anything improper happened during sleepovers. On 18 November 2003, 60 law-enforcement officials raided Neverland Ranch, Jackson's home in Santa Barbara County, California. The following day, a warrant was issued for Jackson's arrest. He was then booked and released on bond, but on 18 December 2003 he was charged with seven counts of child molestation as well as two counts of administering an intoxicating agent for the purpose of committing a felony. Between March and April 2004, a 19-member grand jury heard evidence and indicted him on further charges, notably the new charge of conspiracy involving child abduction, false imprisonment and extortion as well as "four counts of lewd and lascivious behavior with a minor under 14, another charge of attempting to commit a lewd act with a minor, and four counts of providing an intoxicant to a minor in order to seduce him".[2]

The criminal trial against Jackson opened on 28 February 2005 and it quickly became a media event, at times collapsing into a circus. Distressingly graphic details contained in the allegations against him were made public, coming from witnesses as well as those who said they were victims of abuse perpetrated by Jackson.

All through this, Jackson protested his innocence.

The case stretched over several months but by 14 June 2005 the jury, after 32 hours of deliberation, produced their unanimous decision: Jackson was ruled as not guilty on all charges.

One of the defining images of the case was of fans outside the courtroom releasing a white dove for each acquittal.[3] His fans would continue to play a role any time allegations resurfaced, were repeated in the media or new allegations were made. Like an ad hoc militia in fedoras and bejewelled gloves, they would target anyone – accusers, the media, Sony Music, even the estate itself[4] – who they felt had slighted their hero, wronged him, cast aspersions on his innocence, exploited him or somehow sold him short. They would make their biggest reappearance when *Leaving Neverland* was screened.

While these allegations had dogged Jackson during his life, they were not getting in the way of the business of Michael Jackson, with his planned run of an initial 50 shows at the O2 in London selling out in a flash and breaking all manner of live music records.[5] His comeback was going to be the biggest the world had ever seen. But these shows were not to be.

Jackson's funeral was turned into a TV spectacular and, while the allegations were still circulating, there was a concurrent deification process happening around the singer. His estate, largely out of necessity to clear debts of $500 million, swung into immediate action. Business, if anything, increased.

From 2010 onwards, with the exception of 2012, Jackson topped the *Forbes* rich list of dead celebrities. The business of Michael Jackson after his death was as phenomenal as it was unprecedented. His estate massively out-earned other estates. A large chunk came from his investments, most notably his stake in the cash juggernaut that was Sony/ATV Music Publishing, but record sales, streams, merchandise, shows, theatre productions and more also did staggering business.

The posthumous Michael Jackson business, however, was not going to be allowed to run smoothly. In May 2013, almost four years after Jackson's death, Wade Robson looked to sue the Jackson estate, claiming he was abused by the singer when he was a young boy. Almost exactly a year later, James Safechuck filed a sexual assault complaint against Jackson's estate. Robson's suit was dismissed in May 2015 but in 2016 he filed an amended complaint. In July 2017, Safechuck's amended allegations were dismissed and in December 2017 Robson's second lawsuit was dismissed. Then in January 2019, *Leaving Neverland* got its first screening at the Sundance Film Festival, featuring Safechuck and Robson making their allegations against Jackson public.[6]

Estates fundamentally have two jobs: to maintain/build the reputation and cultural significance of a dead star; and make money around that. *Leaving Neverland* threatened to plant bombs under both of these functions for the Michael Jackson estate.

Jackson's was not the first estate to face a mounting scandal, but the nature of the allegations, how the public responded and the staggering sums of money from future earnings for the estate that hung in the balance made this a controversy without precedent. The Jackson estate continues – and continues to earn vast amounts of money – but it will never fully escape this scandal. This is not, as the Jackson estate must be keenly aware, going to completely disappear.

* * *

The business of estates comes with many potential disruptions. Chief among them is that disputes over ownership and control, often stemming from a badly written will or the total absence of one, can and do erupt. But equally a scandal – created internally or due to external factors – can also blow up. I have already described some of the fights and scandals that are specific to a will or trust left by a dead artist, in Chapter 2. This chapter focuses on scandals and problems that arise when the estate as a business is up and running. Below are some of the biggest and most illustrative scandals to have hit music estates.

THE FAMILY FIGHTS

Abby North of North Music Group represents the estate of her father-in-law, Alex North, and also works with the families of a number of other composers. She says that, even when "a will or trust is tight" there can be family in-fighting over certain issues or the direction an estate is going. "If somebody is left out or if somebody *feels* they are left out, then it turns into battles," she says. This is, she argues, the unnaturally natural state of inter-family politics where old animosities, as they existed in the past, are never far from the surface in the present and future. "I don't actually know very many families where it's all copacetic [i.e. in good order]," she suggests.

The more rights there are involved in an estate, however, the more chance there is of conflict arising. Add composition rights to recorded music rights and then layer name, image and likeness rights on top of that – and understanding just how complex and fraught the management of all of these separate things are – and it is like adding gallons of petrol to a naked flame. There will be a fire, but whether the family can control it or not is never clear.

"The one benefit, I would think, of the composer situation is, because almost all of the works are work for hire, they don't control the copyrights," North says. "They just receive money. And it's the money that creates conflict, I think. It's not so much the management of the rights."

While that might be true of estates where there is one composer involved, it is more difficult where two very successful composers whose work is indelibly linked pass away. When their respective families take over the running of their estates, old politics can arise, as can a power struggle between them as to who is going to have the most decision-making power and sway in negotiations.

A senior music lawyer at one of the major music companies, working across both recorded music and publishing, explains just how delicate these relationships can be and how they can potentially get in the way of deals being signed and projects being entered into. The longer the estates were at war with each other, the worse things would be for the music company trying to act as mediator.

"At [our company] the big one that was always difficult to deal with was the estates [of two hugely successful and celebrated composers]. There was [Composer A] and [Composer B] and their two estates could not agree with each other on anything. They were constantly at loggerheads. So to get anything done, you would have to try to get both the estates in the same room and on the same page to get anything agreed. That was a major trial."

Another industry executive who worked with these same two enmeshed estates confirms the agony of having to deal with them. "Dealing with the [two estates] was a nightmare," they say. "There were some of the descendants who were difficult and measly. We were dealing with [both estates] at the same time." They then sigh in such an exasperated way as to hint at the painful professional memories the mere mention of their names causes to rush to the surface.

In this case, the in-fighting was merely in meeting rooms and boardrooms, so it did not spill over into the public domain. The animosity between both sides was a political minefield for their licensing and business partners; but they did manage to keep enough of a lid on it that the public believed the two estates ran perfectly in sympathy. What appeared to the outside world as consonance was actually barely concealed dissonance. Both sides, however, understood that if their ongoing battles were played out in public, no one would win and the reputations of two highly popular composers could be irredeemably stained.

As described in Chapter 2, setting up a trust as part of an estate plan is the best way to prevent family in-fighting in the aftermath of an artist's death – or even decades down the line when new generations of heirs start to get involved. "I don't care how much you think your children get along and won't fight or whatever," says music lawyer Don Wilson on the long-term importance of trusts. "When you're gone, all is fair. And a lot of times, they'll fight over things and they'll change because their circumstances are different. It's a real problem. I know more and more lawyers are using those examples to say, 'This is why you have to do it. You want to preserve your legacy. You want to preserve as much money for your heirs as possible. There's no sense in letting it get tied up in the court system for a decade and have the lawyers make the most money.'"

Costa Pilavachi has worked closely with the biggest frontline artists in classical as well as the biggest estates in classical. Unlike in other genres, he argues that classical estates, for the most part, tend to be devoid of controversy. "In general," he says, "you're not going to find that many scandals on the classical music side." However, rock music is packed to bursting point with stories of family members fighting between themselves after an artist has passed away.

In Chapter 2, I described how the combustible politics between Frank Zappa's four children, due to an unequal splitting of the estate – Moon and Dweezil each getting a 20 per cent stake with Ahmet and Diva each getting 30 per cent – went public multiple times. There were a number of public disagreements between Dweezil and Ahmet over how the Zappa family name could be used in certain business and professional contexts,[7] leading to Dweezil changing the name of one of his tours to *50 Years of Frank: Dweezil Zappa Plays Whatever the F@%k He Wants – The Cease and Desist Tour.* Ahmet responded in a 2016 interview with *Rolling Stone*, denying any involvement in trying to derail his brother's touring activities.[8] The siblings eventually reached an armistice in 2018, with Dweezil issuing a statement on the matter on his website. "It may be a bumpy road at times – we are a passionate Italian family – but we have decided to work toward privately discussing issues rather than using public forums and lawyers," he wrote.[9]

Ahmet responded with his own statement. "What I think should be happening is Dweezil should be out kicking ass playing Frank's music on the road, while we are kicking ass here creating different outlets of our father's work, both new and unseen for generations current and those to come," he said.[10]

Their very public in-fighting is, however, likely to follow them – and the estate – around for years to come. Talking about it on the *Bob Lefsetz Podcast* in September 2019, Ahmet was asked what the inter-family politics were like now. He described them as "better" but added that things were still highly charged and that the relationships were ones of begrudging cooperation rather than joyful unity.[11]

Equally public but no closer to ending in even an unsteady truce is the fighting between Janie Hendrix, who runs the Jimi Hendrix estate, and Leon Hendrix, the guitarist's brother. As covered in Chapter 3, it took until 1995 before the Hendrix family, via Experience Hendrix, was able to regain control of his music. Leon Hendrix was, however, cut out by Jimi's father Al Hendrix in his own will and the running of the estate was taken up by Janie (who was Al's adopted daughter).

A number of court cases followed whereby Leon tried to take control, but they were in vain. "I won't say much about it, but what I will say is in my dad's will, he did not include Leon," says Janie Hendrix when I ask her about the disputes with Leon. "When my dad put together Experience Hendrix and Authentic Hendrix, he did not include Leon. That was my father's choice. He was the chairman of both companies. Unfortunately, my brother [Leon] is an addict. People wonder why my dad didn't leave him anything. Honestly, to tell you the truth, I was shocked as well. But my dad was approached by some of Leon's [pauses and chooses her words diplomatically] 'partners', many of which we have fought because they are bootleggers, and Leon has sold all his rights to his partners. So even if my dad had left him anything, Leon wouldn't have received anything because he has sold his rights." A number of attempts to reach Leon Hendrix to speak to him about these issues were ignored.

Fighting between heirs – or fighting between heirs and those who feel they should also be heirs – can cause serious damage to the reputation of an estate; but equally it can utterly derail it as a business. If heirs cannot agree on things, it stops being a functioning business and will start to atrophy.

Often the estate's lawyer is caught in the middle, having to placate two opposing sides and trying to negotiate some sort of compromise to ensure that projects can keep happening and that the estate can remain a viable commercial operation.

Music consultant Jim Griffin works with a number of estates and says that disputes among heirs need to be understood within the wider psychological toll of running an estate if you are a family member. You are grieving but you also have to think with the precision and presence of a sharp business person. Balancing these two things is not always possible. "Heirs can even love each other and have disputes in this particular area over how they should go forward," he says. If someone is not sitting in the middle as a mediator, these animosities can make the entire estate inoperable, and court cases to try and somehow fix things just make everything infinitely worse.

"That is the issue – the entropy that will set in at some point," says Griffin. "Essentially the horizon diminishes."

A senior record company executive who deals with a number of high-profile estates on a daily basis tries to downplay the damage that internal fighting can have on an estate. Even when litigation is happening, they say their own projects – such as reissues, digging through the vaults or synchronisation deals – generally carry on as normal. That is possible because the label invariably owns the rights in the sound recordings and seeking approval from estates is often a courtesy rather than a requirement. Heirs may be at each other's throats but the reissues can keep pouring out. "There's typically a judge somewhere telling us who to speak to today," they say. "That may change tomorrow and that may change again in three months, but we get that direction. We go with whoever we're told we should speak to. All of these situations ultimately do get ironed out."

Truculence has been a constant in the estates of Joey Ramone and Johnny Ramone, with the entire business of the Ramones, via Ramone Productions, also being controlled by two estates that are often locking horns. Singer Joey Ramone and guitarist Johnny Ramone had a very difficult relationship for most of the band's existence, being barely on speaking terms for much of their career.[12] They did, however, manage to keep the band active during that time by touring and making albums.

As in life, so it is in death, with the two estates effectively carrying on the animosity that had Joey and Johnny lashed together – needing each other but frequently at loggerheads.

Joey's estate initially transferred to his mother, Charlotte Hyman, when he passed away in 2001, but when she died in 2007 the estate transferred to Joey's brother, Mitchel Hyman (a musician who goes by his stage name Mickey Leigh). Johnny's estate was immediately taken over by his widow, Linda, when he died in 2004. A tremendous amount of bad blood existed between Linda and Mickey and it took several years – following a number of very ugly court cases – before, through gritted teeth, they called a truce of sorts.

Key to this was the use of the Ramone name with regard to what Linda called her home – Ramones Ranch – and the perceived damage to the business of the Ramones.[13]

He also wanted her to stop using "Ramone" as her surname (deeming it "improper and unauthorized"), deactivate the lindaramone.com website and cease using the #Ramone hashtag (or any variation thereof) on her social media posts. He also accused her of positioning herself as company president of Ramone Productions when she was actually co-president. He was seeking $275,000 in damages from her.[14] Linda counterclaimed, drawing on the use of the Ramones name in certain commercial contexts.[15]

A year-long arbitration process ensued before a compromise could be agreed in late 2019. Arbitrator Bob Donnelly, referring to a legendary and brutal inter-family war in the late 1800s in West Virginia/Kentucky, termed it all "a feud worthy of the Hatfields and McCoys, but unworthy of the highly esteemed Ramones brand".

Donnelly stated that their "destructive behavior is likely to have resulted in lost opportunities and casting a pall on the Ramones' brand in a manner that might discourage third parties from wanting to be become involved with similar commercial or promotional activities". For good measure he added that "the internecine fighting has probably created a toxic environment that would discourage many promoters and presenters from wanting to invest their time and money in developing a Ramones exhibit".[16]

The settlement stated that Linda could not use the name "Ramones Ranch" for her home without the express approval of Mickey but that "Johnny Ramone Ranch" or "Linda Ramone Ranch" were acceptable alternatives. Both sides would now have to inform the other in writing about any business plans or opportunities they had around the Ramones while Linda could obtain, if she wished, the "Johnny Ramone" and "Linda Ramone" trademarks.

Apart from what was published as part of his arbitration, Donnelly says he is not able to discuss the case further. "I can't talk to you about the Ramones estate, but if you do some research in terms of things that have been printed very recently in relation to the Ramones estate, you'll see my name," he says, referring to the quotes (published in *Billboard*) above. "It involves a court case, for which I'm bound by a confidentiality obligation – meaning that I can't talk to you about [it] because one side took the initiative to publish a lot of material related to my decision in the case."

Linda Ramone, however, is not so gagged when we speak in early 2020 just two months after the case was settled. Neither is Mickey Leigh when I speak to him in late 2020. "It was fine when the mother [of Joey] was alive, but now she's not, it's almost impossible to deal with him [Mickey]," says Linda. "I think it's because he wasn't left the legacy. That's really how I look at it. He just acquired it. People acquiring it look at the legacy differently."

Leigh disputes this. He says that Joey left everything to their mother, Charlotte Hyman, but it was on the full understanding that it would eventually go to him, as Joey's only sibling, when she passed away. "When my brother was in the hospital for those last three months as he was battling to survive the lymphoma, he wanted to change his will," he says. "He wanted to make things different. He wanted to put me in it. I do actually have that in writing from my mom."

He continues, "I said to him [Joey], 'Listen, let's not bring in any lawyers.' I was just wanting my brother to survive, really. I wasn't concerned about the will. I never thought people would be talking about, 'He didn't leave it to you – he left it to your mother.' That is the truth [...] He left everything to my mom and we all understood that obviously she was going to be leaving it to me and that she would be relying more on me to be running the business [of the estate]. She was an artist but she didn't know anything about the music business. I have been doing this since I was 10 years old." (Mickey was in bands with both John Cummings, aka Johnny Ramone, and Thomas Erdelyi, aka Tommy Ramone, long before the Ramones were even formed.)

Leigh also says that relations between Charlotte, while she was still alive, and Linda were not as harmonious as Linda suggests. Following our interview, he sends me select transcripts from an unpublished conversation with his mother in which she makes her feelings about Linda clear. It is fair to say they are far from complimentary.

Linda claims Mickey had retrospectively tried to be credited as a performer on the first Ramones albums for providing handclaps and backing vocals. This, she says, is at the heart of the animosity between them, especially as she believes his own musical endeavours will always be overshadowed by what the Ramones did. She says,

> The problem is he's very angry and it's hard to run an estate with someone who isn't happy in who they are. I guess he always wanted to be famous and he isn't. Unfortunately, you know what, the Ramones are the famous ones and you've got to put the Ramones first. With me, I always feel like I can put the Ramones first. Of course! I put Johnny first. It's Johnny Ramone from the Ramones. So I think whenever egos are involved, egos are a big problem. Charlotte, his mom, didn't have an ego. She loved Joey and she loved the Ramones. I mean the brother [Mitchel] always wants his name on things. He always wants to say he was this, he did that. And it's like it was never said before. I think that's one of the major problems with him. He wants credit on 'Blitzkrieg Bop'. And that's a fact. That you can look up. He was constantly wanting to add his name on the records.
>
> He wants a backing vocal and handclaps. It's really an ego thing. That's the problem. And with me, I love the Ramones. Johnny would, at the end, be like, "It always annoyed me how you were a big Ramones fan. But now I'm dying, I guess I'd rather have you as a Ramones fan than not!"

Mickey says this is not quite the full story. "They asked me to do those background vocals," he says of the recording sessions for the Ramones' debut album. "And when I did them, when I got back into the control room they said it was great. I did help them make that album so quickly and cheaply because there I was and they were having a little trouble with some of the background vocals."

He says that rather than insisting that just he get a credit on the album sleeve notes, he says that he wanted all the others who played or sang on the record to be credited.

> I wanted not only me to get a credit but also Craig Leon, the producer, who played the organ on 'Let's Dance'. Arturo Vega [who designed the band's logo], Danny Fields [their co-manager] and me did the handclaps on several songs. I wanted everyone [credited] – on a secondary list […] They were the ones who told me they were going to put my name on the album. I didn't ask to sing, I didn't ask to have my name on there. But

351

when they told me they would put my name on there, I thought they would. Bands do that all the time. They have additional performers. What's the big deal? Is everybody who was credited trying to be a band member? It's a ridiculous argument. I never wanted to be in the Ramones; I never wanted to be a Ramone.

Linda says her relationship with Mickey was one defined by dragging each other through the courts. Rather than working in collaboration, they were locked in litigation. She says,

> He has sued me three times. I counter-sued him the last time. He is constantly trying to sue me and after a while you've just got to sue back. I mean, he sued me over my name. I've been Linda Ramone since I don't know when. Joey called me Linda Ramone. His mother called me Linda Ramone. I hang out with Marky Ramone and he calls me Linda Ramone. I did interviews with Tommy Ramone. He calls me Linda Ramone. It's like you can't tell someone who they are. So that was an initial part of it. And he'll say things like, "Oh, [only] the band should use the name." There are a billion other Ramones in the world. What are you going to do? Tell everyone they can't be Ramones? [Laughs]

On the issue of the Ramone surname battle with Linda, Leigh says that it all boiled down to a simple trademark dispute. He argues,

> It was a name that was associated with the band and its members. When Linda decided to change her name to Ramone, it made it harder for me to promote the Ramones. When you see things like a "celebrating 40 years of the Ramones" panel "featuring Linda Ramone", it's a distraction. It confuses people. It distracts from the actual band members. That's what my complaint was.

His approach was that, as far as the business of the band is concerned, the surname "Ramone" should be sacrosanct. "If it's kept out of the band's business, products, merchandise and all that and promotional things, she can do it," he says. "I never cared if she wanted to make a reservation in a restaurant as Linda Ramone if that's what she gets her kicks from."

Leigh says when we speak that relations between him and Linda are at an all-time low and that this is negatively impinging on what the estate management of the Ramones could be doing. "There's really nothing happening at the moment," he says when I ask about future projects for the band. "There's no communication. You could call it a cold war or something. The situation has become almost unendurable, really. It's not good for the band in my opinion."

Leigh follows up after our phone interview with a series of messages about an issue he was initially hesitant to go on the record about. It all relates to the profit splits on Ramones merchandise but now he feels that he is, after some contemplation, prepared to discuss the inner workings.

He says that in 2001, following Joey's death, he (along with their mother, Charlotte) looked into the late singer's business dealings and learned that after founding members Tommy Ramone and Dee Dee Ramone had left the band (Tommy in 1978, Dee Dee in 1989) they surrendered their shares in Ramone Productions. This, says Leigh, "included merchandise revenue, and whatever rights of approval they had when in the band".

Following Dee Dee's departure, revenue from Ramone Productions was split equally three ways – between Joey, Johnny and Arturo Vega (as the band's artistic director). Leigh says that no other band members who later joined the band – meaning drummers Marky Ramone, Richie Ramone and Elvis Ramone (Clem Burke from Blondie under a pseudonym) and bassist C. J. Ramone – ever had a share in Ramone Productions.

"I had several issues with that, fairness being one of them," says Leigh. "So, in 2003 I approached John about restructuring the merch income to include the other band members." Leigh's plan was that Joey's estate and Johnny would each take a smaller percentage and Vega's share would drop to 10 per cent in order to allow the other members to share in the collective spoils. Leigh says the revised splits were "an amount that John and I agreed was fair". Agreements were drawn up, but before a final deal could be signed, however, Johnny passed away. "His widow [Linda] then reneged on the agreement she inherited from her husband and was refusing to sign the contracts with the other Ramones band members," says Leigh. "This compelled [...] my mother to bring legal action."

Leigh says this deadlock was eventually broken and Linda finally agreed to the revenue splits that Johnny had approved before his death.[17] "It's the truth," he says, "and I stand by it. I'm willing to share the wealth – and maybe that message will plant a seed in anyone else who finds themselves in this position. Don't be greedy. That's the message."

I approached Linda to ask her about this. Her manager stated that she does not comment on internal business matters or the specifics of deal structures.

It was not just Joey's family that Linda had legal issues with – it was also Johnny's mother, Estelle Cummings. Estelle had a public dispute with Linda over what share of Johnny's estate she was due.[18] Linda argues that none of Estelle's accusations against her were true. "She was never in the will," claims Linda. "She tried to sue me for money, but she wasn't in the will and she wasn't in the estate and he [Johnny] didn't leave her anything. He told his mother while she was alive, 'If you're nice to Linda, she'll give you what you need.' Instead, she decides to sue me and tell me I have to give her this. She went around saying, you know, crazy stuff. 'Can't you give me some money to survive on?' And she talked to the [*New York Post*]."

Estelle Cummings died on 4 June 2012.[19]

Of course the public and the media are drawn to drama and will zone in on families fighting over fortunes as it appeals to the gossip in many of us. There is some rubbernecking going on as well as gorging on *Schadenfreude*, delighting in the fact that these heirs of the rich and famous spend most of their time badmouthing each other or hacking chunks out of each other in very ugly and very public battles for control.

"If you're not in harmony, whenever an heir comes to the press and says something, it's the artist that pays," argues music lawyer Luciana Soares de Souza, who works with the estates of Vinícius de Moraes and Antônio Carlos Jobim. "People love to see heirs fighting over the legacy. But this is something that really weakens the artist's value."

The reality is, however, that these are the exceptions and most estates very quickly get on with things. There will be disagreements as this is the nature of any business where two or more people are involved; but like most businesses, they work through their differences quickly and quietly.

"I think there have been points as a family when we've struggled a bit and not always agreed," says Jemima Dury of how the estate of her father, Ian Dury, is run. "But actually in terms of business, we're always in 100 per cent agreement. We are really lucky there because things could go so horribly wrong – as it can with any family, even without all of [the] estate [stuff]. I know people in a far worse situation without the type of estate we are dealing with."

HISTORIC SEXUAL ABUSE CLAIMS

Between the first screening of *Leaving Neverland* on 25 January 2019 at the Sundance Film Festival and its US TV broadcast in two parts on HBO on 3 and 4 March 2019, the full machinery of the Michael Jackson estate had swung into action. On 21 February 2019 it was reported that Optimum Productions[20] and the co-executors of Michael Jackson's estate were taking legal action against Time Warner, the parent company of HBO, in a $100 million lawsuit.[21]

The opening salvo in this legal action was not specifically about the content of the documentary – in a large part it could not sue for defamation on behalf of Jackson as he was deceased – but rather it hinged on a contractual issue. It was claimed the documentary was a breach of a non-disparagement clause related to a contract from the 1990s. In 1992, HBO beat off competition to air a concert (*Michael Jackson in Concert in Bucharest: The Dangerous Tour*) following the release of Jackson's album *Dangerous*, and the estate argued this new documentary violated these prior deal terms. It said, "HBO profited off the *Dangerous World Tour* by airing a concert from the tour and promoting Michael Jackson's talents. Now, HBO is profiting off the *Dangerous World Tour* by airing a 'documentary' that falsely claims Michael Jackson was abusing children on the same tour. It is hard to imagine a more direct violation of the non-disparagement clause."[22]

His estate reiterated that Jackson had been cleared of all charges during his trial in 2005. "Ten years after his passing, there are still those out to profit from his enormous worldwide success and take advantage of his eccentricities," it said. "Michael is an easy target because he is not here to defend himself, and the law does not protect the deceased from defamation, no matter how extreme the lies are."[23]

This legal action was foreshadowed on 8 February 2019 with the Jackson estate sending a 10-page letter to HBO requesting a meeting to discuss a "solution" to what it regarded as serious problems with the documentary. The estate publicly questioned the veracity and credibility of the documentary, adding that no one from the estate was spoken to for it, and therefore did not appear on camera giving right of reply, and criticised what they saw as sensationalist tactics.[24]

HBO refused to blink and stated that its plans to air the documentary at the start of March were not being altered. "Dan Reed is an award-winning filmmaker who has carefully documented these survivors' accounts," it said. "People should reserve judgment until they see the film."[25]

When it was broadcast, the wider media pick-up was phenomenal, with multiple reviews, think pieces and discussions combing through the accusations and asking if this would completely destroy both Jackson's reputation and the enormous business around him.

The immediate response of the Michael Jackson estate was to file litigation. Running parallel with that, however, was a programme of damage limitation and crisis management to ensure that an estate that had generated almost $2.5 billion between 2009 and 2019 did not go under.

John Branca, as co-executor of the estate, had to handle the media requests for comment alone. (When I approached the estate to also speak to John McClain, its other co-executor, I was told that "John McClain is not available for any interviews ever".)

On 16 March, just under a fortnight after the screening in the US, *Billboard* spoke to Branca after his appearance on the appositely named "Trial By Media: Guilty Until Proven Innocent" panel at the Institute of Politics at Harvard, alongside Howard Weitzman and Bryan Freedman, a fellow lawyer for the estate. They indicated that Dan Reed, the director of *Leaving Neverland*, could also be targeted with litigation.

Branca argued that this was a flashpoint that should, to his mind, necessitate a change in the law relating to defamation. "Because the laws of defamation are what they are, there is nothing we can do or say," he told *Billboard*. "The man can be damaged, his kids can be hurt and theoretically nothing can be done. I'm going to suggest the law should be changed to protect the deceased at least for a period of time. Because it's about the truth, it's about fairness, and it's about balance."[26]

(He elaborated on this "trial by media" point in an interview with *Music Business Worldwide* in January 2021. "In this era, sometimes very unfair conclusions and opinions can be drawn, based not on fact or evidence, but instead based on a media phenomenon," he said. "Unfortunately, the legacy press are not in a position to do their homework or their research anymore. And tragically, deceased artists have no protection under the libel laws, which is completely unfair and must change. Media and information travels so rapidly now without verification. In the modern era, especially in the United States, it's become popular to take a position or opinion without examining the facts."[27])

Branca questioned the integrity of the documentary, adding that he had already noticed a hit in the estate's earnings because of it. This was, however, waved away as a blip and things would, he felt, return to how they were and the estate would remain a powerhouse. "Michael," he said defiantly, "is too big to fail."[28]

From there things moved as quickly as the courts would permit. In May 2019, HBO countersued the Jackson estate. Lawyers for HBO argued that the 1992 contract had expired as both sides had fulfilled their obligations when the concert (*Michael Jackson in Concert in Bucharest: The Dangerous Tour*) was aired in October that year and it had not been screened again.

"HBO also contends that the estate's interpretation of the [non-disparagement] clause as conferring perpetual immunity from disparagement – even beyond the grave – is excessively broad," wrote *Variety*.[29]

The estate was pushing for an arbitration to make the whole thing public. "If HBO thinks the contract does not apply or is expired then why are they opposing adjudicating it?" asked Bryan Freedman on behalf of the estate. At the end of May, however, the court rejected the Jackson estate's motion to take the case to an arbitrator.[30]

As all this was happening, the story was returned to again and again by the media – sometimes being stoked by outside forces.

In July, three Michael Jackson fan groups – The Michel Jackson Community, the MJ Street and On the Line – tried to sue Robson and Safechuck in a court in Orléans, northern France. They were seeking symbolic damages of €1 and chose France for the action as its defamation laws extend libel protection of an individual after death (unlike in the UK or US). This was more a publicity stunt than anything, but ultimately it swung attention back to the documentary.[31]

Following this, a Netflix stand-up special by comedian Dave Chappelle ignited a controversy in August. In his show, he discussed *Leaving Neverland* – including the allegations against Jackson – in detail and said he did not believe any of the accusers. "I know it seems harsh, but somebody's gotta teach these kids – no such thing as a free trip to Hawaii," he said. "He's going to want to look at your butthole or something."[32]

It was intentionally designed to stoke controversy. It got its desired effect. Vince Finaldi, the lawyer for Robson, said, "It's unfortunate that he has chosen to use his platform to shame sexual abuse victims, and spread his ignorance of sexual abuse and the way it is perpetrated upon children, in an attempt to resurrect his career."[33]

TMZ spoke to Branca to get his response to the Netflix show. Branca made it clear he agreed with Chappelle.[34]

On 19 September 2019, things moved forward with the HBO case when George Wu, a federal judge in the case, issued a tentative ruling that rejected the broadcaster's move to have the case dismissed, and it was suggested he was leaning towards the estate's desire to take it to arbitration. "You're a big company, they're a wealthy estate," said Wu to HBO's lawyers. "It's a clash of the titans."[35] On 28 September, Wu confirmed his tentative ruling to dismiss HBO's anti-SLAPP motion.[36]

A further twist came in January 2020 when a court ruled that Wade Robson and James Safechuck could pursue legal claims against two of Jackson's companies. Lawsuits by both individuals in 2014 had been rejected because California's statute of limitations stated that claims of childhood sexual abuse had to be filed before the accuser turned 26; however, a new law that came into force on 1 January 2020 extended this timeframe to the accuser's 40th birthday.[37]

The following month, HBO moved to request the 9th Circuit Court of Appeals dismiss the litigation against it from the Jackson estate.[38]

On 21 October 2020, Judge Mark Young dismissed a lawsuit from Safechuck against MJJ Productions and MJJ Ventures. Vince Finaldi, lawyer for Safechuck, told the BBC, "He was an employee that was working on behalf of them as a dancer and entertainer on the stage with Michael. Because he was a minor, and he was an employee working for them, they had a duty to protect him. That's our argument."[39]

Judge Young disagreed. The BBC reported, "Corporations cannot be direct perpetrators, he said". Jonathan Steinsapir and Howard Weitzman, lawyers for MJJ Productions and MJJ Ventures, told the BBC, "We are pleased that the court agreed that Mr Safechuck had no grounds to pursue his lawsuit." Safechuck said he would appeal the decision.[40]

With poignant timing, on the exact same day as the judge's dismissal of Safechuck's case, *Deadline* reported that Dan Reed was running into new problems with the Jackson estate over a planned follow-up film to *Leaving Neverland*, this time following the legal actions against the estate by Wade Robson and James Safechuck:

> In producing the second documentary, however, MJJ Productions and MJJ Ventures have sought to entangle Reed in the court proceedings. Jackson's companies served Reed and his production outfit, Amos Pictures, with subpoenas demanding that he personally appear for deposition and hand over documents and materials related to *Leaving Neverland* and the sequel. They are also attempting to ban him from filming in the courtroom.[41]

Reed moved to quash the subpoenas. He also revealed that Howard Weitzman had met with him in June with a view to appearing in the second documentary but then emailed him to say he would not be taking part. "I have resolved that neither myself nor anyone in my offices will participate in the documentary we all discussed for several reasons," said Weitzman in the email. "Among them is the fact that you are already clearly on the record saying that you believe both accusers' stories without hesitation." Reed added that John Branca was also refusing to take part.[42]

A hearing on Reed's move to quash the subpoenas was scheduled for April 2021.

Ahead of that, however, in December 2020, a three-judge panel of the 9th Circuit Court of Appeal (made up of Circuit Judges Richard Paez and Lawrence VanDyke and District Judge Karin Immergut) upheld a lower court ruling from 2019 to grant the Jackson estate's motion to take the HBO dispute to arbitration, something the broadcaster has tried to appeal against. The judges did, however, caution that the suit could prove "frivolous"; but now it was to be put in the hands of an arbitrator to make that call. "HBO had sought to avoid arbitration, saying that the network had never intended to grant Jackson and his heirs a veto over anything the network might ever want to say about him," wrote *Variety*.[43]

Howard Weitzman and Jonathan Steinsapir, on behalf of the Jackson estate, issued a statement on the ruling. "The trial judge and now the Ninth Circuit Court of Appeals have unanimously rejected HBO's arguments," they said. "In the court's own words, HBO 'agreed that it would not make any disparaging remarks concerning Jackson.' It's time for HBO to answer for its violation of its obligations to Michael Jackson."[44]

On 26 April 2021, LA County Superior Court Judge Mark A. Young ruled that Wade Robson could not sue MJJ Productions and MJJ Ventures as the companies had no legal duty to protect minors and that they had "no legal ability" to control Jackson's behaviour due to the fact, as the sole owner, Jackson could "remove any and all of the board members without cause or notice".[45]

Young also dismissed Robson's long-running lawsuit against the companies. *Variety* reported that Young's ruling "held that the companies had no ability to control Jackson because Jackson wholly owned both of them throughout his life". Vince Finaldi, the attorney for Robson, said his client planned to appeal the ruling.[46]

"If allowed to stand, the decision would set a dangerous precedent that would leave thousands of children working in the entertainment industry vulnerable to sexual abuse by persons in places of power," said Finaldi in a statement. "The children of our state deserve protection, and we will not stop fighting until we [ensure] that every child is safe."

Finaldi stated that Young's ruling contained "fatal flaws" and that he would escalate the appeal "to the Supreme Court if necessary".[47]

At the time this book was going to print, both the Robson and the Safechuck cases were still on appeal.

I spoke to John Branca in April 2020 about the documentary, the legal action and the impact of all this on the Michael Jackson estate. He did not hold back. He says of *Leaving Neverland*:

HBO should be ashamed of themselves, Dan Reed [director] should be ashamed of himself. And the media should be ashamed of itself for not properly investigating and fact checking

I ask him, beyond the legal action against HBO, what the estate can do when a scandal like this erupts. "It's already in the rear-view mirror," he says. "I've done a seminar at Harvard and I've done a seminar at USC and UCLA about the need for fact checking and truth in documentaries. I think some parts of the media have accepted the fact that that thing was not truthful."

He says that the estate intentionally requested that the arbitration in the case be public – a move he felt would rebalance much of the discussion. "We demanded that it be public and everybody could see Tom Mesereau[48] and Howard Weitzman cross-examine these two gentlemen."

(Howard Weitzman died on 7 April 2021 after a brief illness. He was 81.[49])

I then turn to the wider media coverage – something the estate is less able to litigate against – of the documentary and the historic allegations against Jackson. Branca says it becomes an information war where the estate uses what opportunities it can to issue a counter-narrative. "Well, you start with the media," he says. "But when the media has an agenda – and they're not interested in the other side – you have to take whatever steps you can to get the truth out."

Part of that was putting a social media programme in place as part of what can be seen as a very modern propaganda war. The Jackson estate worked with strategic digital marketing company Spellbound Group to, in modern parlance, "change the narrative" around Jackson in the aftermath of the documentary. More used to running the social media accounts and digital activities of deceased acts like Jim Morrison, Janis Joplin, John Lee Hooker, Peter Tosh, Otis Redding and Henry Mancini, this was a very different and elevated undertaking for the company. "We handle socials for Michael Jackson," says Alicia Yaffe, the founder and CEO of Spellbound. "Not to pat ourselves on the back, but I think we've done a really excellent job throughout the various controversies keeping people focused on his work and expanding awareness of his work as a humanitarian – in a very specific way."

I ask her what she and her team did when *Leaving Neverland* aired.

Rather than just [saying] he was a great humanitarian and philanthropist, [it's] talking about exactly and specifically what he did and when and how he contributed to areas including environmental causes, health causes, societal causes for endangered children of all sorts to animal welfare to support education, particularly for black and minority students – that sort of thing. And really keeping people focused and keeping the larger fanbase and potential fanbase – particularly the potential fanbase – focused on who he was and what his art represented, rather than the narrative that is dedicated to tearing him down.

Yaffe regards the damage limitation and the reputation rehabilitation it did as a major success. "His streams were up 50 per cent in 2019," she says. "That certainly wasn't the intended effect of the people behind certain documentaries and media narratives." She says that because the accusations in *Leaving Neverland* were not made against Jackson in his lifetime, Spellbound, on behalf of the estate, had to find ways to counter them on his behalf – but it cannot outright deny them. "We can't issue denials on behalf of Michael because Michael never denied it, because these accusations didn't exist during his life," she says. "It would be inauthentic."

She explains what the company did to try and lessen the negative impact of the documentary. "We obviously believe that Michael is innocent," she says by way of set-up. "I'm saying that on my behalf – I cannot speak in Michael's terms. But we have been pointing out all the inconsistencies in their stories and the estate managers are fighting them in court. That's where the direct responses have to happen. There's no benefit to Michael to fight in the public sphere because we're not Michael – we weren't there."

She continues, "Social media, all it does is give fire to the haters. So we have to focus on reminding people of who Michael was and what he did – and let them interpret that. And the fact that he was acquitted of all charges. We keep people focused on who Michael Jackson was."

Jeff Jampol of JAM Inc was forthright in his views on the *Leaving Neverland* documentary and how the estate responded. "I don't manage the Michael Jackson estate – I consult them on social media and fan management [...] I'm merely a consultant," he says by way of contextualising what follows. "I think the Michael Jackson example is really one on one. It's very unique. In that particular instance, by the way, I hesitate to call that film a documentary. In that case, I don't believe it. I don't believe those guys. I don't believe it to be true. So in which case you have to vigorously defend it."

A senior partner at a major international law firm who specialises in music law argues that estates are somewhat legally constrained in how they can respond to accusations about the dead artists they represent. "In an estate environment, you can't answer back [to defamation charges and accusations]," they say. "Not only do you not have the right to reply, you can't make valid statements or anything that represents the views of the artist."

The head of the estate of another major artist says that *Leaving Neverland* was, in many ways, a re-run of what Jackson's team faced when he was still alive, pointing to the 2005 court case and everything that led up to it. As such, there was something of a muscle-memory reaction – the estate knew exactly what to do because it was aware of what had been done when Jackson was still alive and facing multiple child molestation charges. "The Michael Jackson estate clearly went out and they hired PR crisis managers and they did everything that you would have done [with a live artist]," they say. "In fact, they did everything that was done when Michael was alive. And it worked when he was alive. He wasn't here to say anything – I'm not sure what he could have said! – but he wasn't here to help mitigate the problem."

Jeff Jampol argues that *Leaving Neverland* was, ultimately, a storm in a tea cup and its damage to Jackson and the Jackson estate was short-lived and minimal.

I say to him that there were serious public calls to pull his music from radio stations and to cancel shows bearing his name.

"Some radio stations pulled his music and then started again," he says. "New ones added his music that never had it there before. No stage shows were pulled."

Jampol suggests the public outcry here amounted to little more than hot air. "Sure, there were calls for it," he argues. "I mean look at the orange clown we have in office in my country! There are calls to do all kinds of things. We are in a cancel culture, but I think we're in a blip. If something truly negative truly did happen, you have to deal with it. You have to acknowledge it and you have to move forward. If it didn't happen, then you have to vigorously defend it and move forward. Depending upon the power of legacy, it will either survive or it won't."

An industry source with good knowledge of the Jackson estate says that *Leaving Neverland* was unquestionably a flashpoint but that other incidents had threatened to break in public before that. In a way, they argue, the estate was already prepared for something of this magnitude. "There had been moments with Jackson in the past – but none quite as big as that one," they say with regard to *Leaving Neverland*. "You say 'no comment' and you don't withdraw product or stop projects."

They say this "business as usual" approach in the streaming age is one that can – in their minds at least – scrub estates and record companies of any sense of guilt by association. Those who work in and around an estate caught in a scandal like this can absolve themselves of responsibility by saying that today the listener is the one who is in control and if they want to keep listening to a pop star who is accused of terrible crimes then that is a matter for them and their own conscience. "It's down to the consumer about whether they want to buy something or whether they want to stream something," they say. "I think there are people who refuse to listen to Michael Jackson because of all of these things and there are people where he just seems to be completely Teflon."

It is all a convenient deflection technique for those who ultimately benefit from the success of an estate. It means that business can continue as it was and that no moral stain can land on them as part of the machine that makes that happen. They regard themselves as Teflon too.

The head of another estate (in no way connected to the Jackson estate) argues that something like *Leaving Neverland* is a huge media issue for a matter of weeks and then just dissolves into the background. "The public reads about it and they go on to something else," they say matter-of-factly. "I don't think they really give it much thought."

Yet another estate head says that a scandal like this can and will cause damage, but it is mostly in the short term and that the estate just has to front it out. "I think we're back to where Michael was at the time after the original trials where people are reluctant to give the estate money," they say. "There are still radio stations that won't play his music. It's tough. On the other hand, there's still half the world – maybe more than half the world – that couldn't care less. He passed away, he's an amazing musician, they're willing to celebrate his life and ignore the rest."

Ultimately *Leaving Neverland* did not kill or even severely dent the Jackson estate. In the *Forbes* list of highest-earning dead celebrities in 2020, the Michael Jackson estate was in its usual position at number one with earnings of $48 million, far ahead of Dr. Seuss in second place with earnings of $33 million. The next biggest musician on the *Forbes* list was Elvis Presley at number five with earnings of $23 million, less than half of what Jackson made that year. As *Forbes* itself put it, "The 2019 release of the damning documentary *Leaving Neverland* didn't cost the King of Pop his crown."[50]

Branca spoke to *Music Business Worldwide* in January 2021 and stated that Jackson's songs were streamed 7.3 billion times in 2020 and that he was the top streaming catalogue artist globally that year, the implication being that *Leaving Neverland* did not cause the damage some expected (or hoped) it would.[51] In the same interview, when asked why he remained so certain of Jackson's innocence despite multiple accusations, he said, "Nobody else [since *Leaving Neverland* was broadcast] have made these allegations – doesn't that tell you something? It does to me."

Streaming services have not banned a number of major artists accused of serious crimes from their platforms, but a move by Spotify in May 2018 to take the music of artists such as R. Kelly and XXXTentacion off playlists (a powerful discovery tool for users) as part of its Hate Content and Hateful Conduct policy was praised by some but faced a backlash that it was disproportionately targeting black artists.[52] By the following month, Spotify had reversed its decision. "We don't aim to play judge and jury," it said in a statement. "Across all genres, our role is not to regulate artists."[53] Against this, the moral conundrum of listening to certain artists who are either accused of or found guilty of certain crimes was left to the listeners themselves to resolve.

One record company executive says that a scandal like this ripping through an estate is rare but that it is an occupational hazard that companies are now learning from and basing damage limitation strategies around. What happened with *Leaving Neverland* did not go unnoticed by major estates. "A lot of the time, that's out of your control," the label executive says. "A group of people have to sit down and work out what the hell they're going to do and understand that there are outside influences and that whatever you say is not going to change their minds. You have to try and grab back the narrative

– if you can – and focus on just the music. You have to disassociate the person almost from the artist and the music."

The Michael Jackson case went public in the most dramatic fashion possible, but other scandals – with deceased pop stars being retroactively accused of the most shocking and serious crimes – have threatened to erupt and have been quashed before they became public. "There was an artist I heard of who had been accused of something and there's potential that there was no smoke without fire," says one lawyer at a major legal firm. "But the general consensus was: a) the estate had good lawyers; and b) people were distancing the person from the music."

While social media can fan the flames of a scandal, estates can also use digital technology to bury bad stories about an artist, bringing in specialists to down-rank certain articles in internet search results by gaming the search engine. While technically not illegal, this is highly dubious in moral terms. It might not be actively expunging stories from the internet, but if they can be shunted to the fourth or fifth page of a Google search result then they have been as good as erased.

"There are lots of cover-ups," says one senior music lawyer at a private practice. "There is one law firm whose whole job is to cover stuff up. That's all they do and they are paid huge amounts of money to do it. It's a combination of legal and tech. It's reputation management – and one way to manage someone's reputation is to shut things up. You pay [the specialist law firm] £50,000 and make [bad stories] drop below the first page of search rankings. It's the right to be forgotten."

There are huge ethical considerations for estates and those who work with them – be they lawyers, record companies or publishers – when they are proactively and unapologetically attempting to bury stories and accusations that could damage an act's legacy and their posthumous earning potential. All of these people and companies have a financial stake in that business not being damaged and so have to navigate a tricky moral pathway here. The artist may not be alive to defend themselves, but if legal threats are issued against accusers to force their silence and industry professionals are complicit in this, the whole thing becomes toxic and repugnant.

Horrific stories about the behaviour and actions of some artists – living and dead – are widely known in the music industry and batted away as being "unfounded" or from "a different time", as if that exonerates them. Estates absolutely have the right to defend a dead artist against accusations, but it does not follow that it is morally fine to threaten accusers or buy their silence. This is an ongoing issue for estates and it is quite possible that a *Leaving Neverland*-style scandal for another artist will surface at some point in the near future.

LITERALLY CASHING IN

It was all over the matter of £3.00, but the repercussions cost those involved dearly.

Mere hours after the news broke of the death of Whitney Houston on 11 February 2012, something happened on iTunes in the UK that was to see Sony Music, the singer's long-standing label, sucked up into a cyclone of controversy.

The day before her death, the 18-track *Ultimate Collection* of her biggest hits – which was originally released in 2007 – was quietly sitting on iTunes for the very attractive discounted rate of £4.99, working out at just over 27p a track. It was, frankly, a bargain.

Soon after her death was made public, the price on iTunes flipped from £4.99 to £7.99. The *Guardian* initially reported that Sony had increased the wholesale price of the album, which automatically triggered an increase in the retail price on iTunes (Apple sets its retail price based on the wholesale price that goes to suppliers, in this case Sony, plus its retailer margin on top of that).[54] In the days afterwards, as controversy raged, conflicting stories about what actually happened played out in the media.

Sony sprang into damage-limitation mode. "Whitney Houston product was mistakenly mispriced on the UK iTunes store on Sunday," it told *Billboard* in a statement. "When discovered, the mistake was immediately corrected. We apologise for any offence caused."[55] It blamed an "internal mistake due to an employee error" for the price rise and said that it had only stayed at the higher price for a matter of hours before it was spotted and corrected.

The Next Web[56] and *Wired*[57] both came out in favour of the tech company, saying fans should blame Sony and not Apple for the price increase. Apple also said the fault lay with Sony.[58] Sony stuck to the "employee error" excuse, apologised profusely and hoped everyone would move on.

It is also understood that Sony swiftly instigated a new policy in the wake of this whereby the retail price of digital albums should never be changed after an artist dies. Much of this is academic now as the emphasis is on streaming, but in 2012 just over 30 per cent of album sales were digital in the UK, so the revenues were not insignificant.[59]

This policy of price hiking was far from an accidental one-off when downloads were still a significant part of the business. A source at the UK arm of a large artist services company recounts what happened when news broke of the untimely death of one of the artists they worked with. "When we found out that they had passed away," they say, "there was one particular email internally that came from America and it was, 'OK, so we need to change prices.' And it was weird because they were one of our biggest artists. So for us, as music fans, certainly in the UK, we were sitting there going, 'Oh my God, we're devastated!' And there was this internal email that was saying, 'Right, let's just commercialise the shit out of it.'"

Estate managers, heirs and record companies often run the risk of being accused, especially by fans, of cashing in on a dead artist, and running the estate in a ragingly commercial manner that sacrifices legacy for cash, tainting the artist's work and reducing everything to dollars and cents.

Crassly cashing in is not just confined to increasing the price of an album the day an artist dies; it can become a philosophy that slowly eviscerates an estate. This can come years, or even decades, later when revenues are not what they were. The worse an estate is doing financially, the more incrementally likely it is that those involved in an estate will make a run of bad commercial decisions.

"I think the biggest mistake people make is making the money grab," says BMG executive David Hirshland. "There are opportunities that come with a pretty big payday that heirs will jump at because they need the money. In some cases it's their only form of income and they'll go for it because it's a bigger dollar than what should be a more modest and, let's say, reasoned approach."

He argues that short-termism is the enemy of the estate. "You have to take the long view," he says. "Even if it's going to get the heir a bigger payday, in the long run it is going to diminish the legacy. You have to have a three-to-five-year plan. You have to know that some of these things are going to take time and you have to develop them properly. That's the biggest mistake I see out there."

A senior lawyer who works with a number of superstar artists as well as major estates argues that some heirs find it impossible to resist the impulse to cash in and undertake projects that bring in huge sums of money but that are ultimately damaging for the estate. "You can't ignore the human tendency towards greed and avariciousness," they sigh.

A label executive adds that a desire for money can lead to heirs making some very questionable decisions. "It depends on how desperate they are for money," they say. "If they don't have anything to live on or they are not rich, or they have been ripped off all their lives, then they'll do stuff which would make the creator turn in their grave."

Mickey Leigh says that he experienced a great deal of fan blowback when he took over the running of the estate of his brother, Joey Ramone. "I don't know what it is or where they get this feeling from or this empowerment," he says of the fans who would congregate online to criticise his running of the estate on the official Joey Ramone Facebook page as well as the message board on the official Joey Ramone website. "I had to reply to these people sometimes. You never met [Joey]. How have you appointed yourself as his protector when you never met the guy? It really gets strange and you wonder if you should even [reply]. You kind of know that you shouldn't be getting into those kind of exchanges with these people. After a while, where they keep pushing and pushing and pushing, sometimes you just find yourself pushing back."

He says, over time, the personal attacks began to fade away, but some of them can sting. "Eventually they did stop the attacks – or there were certainly less of them," he says. "It's not like I won them over but something changed where they stopped saying things every day like, 'You would dig up your brother's grave and sell his bones!'"

While these personal attacks can really wound – especially when directed at a family member who is still grieving – Leigh says that subconsciously they can guide his decisions and ensure he does not rush into things without first carefully thinking them through and ensuring they are not going to damage the public perception of either Joey or the Ramones. "My main goal is to just perpetuate his legacy and keep his cool – be respectful to his fans and the band," he says. "The main job is to not screw up what they had going. Just don't screw it up. Keep it really simple. Don't fuck with it – excuse my Queens. Don't fuck with it. Be respectful of it and be respectful of their fans, even though they're attacking you and saying, 'Everything you do – it's another cash grab!'"

Sam Arlen, who runs the estate of his father, Harold Arlen, says that commercial decisions have to be made that do not taint the legacy of an act. He says estates have a duty of care to the music they work with so as not to create damaging associations from the way they exploit it. "It's not just about dollar signs," he cautions. "If somebody's coming up or a young person hears the music used in a way that could be questionable or not appropriate, let's say, for their age group, they may never listen to that song again. To me that's a tragedy. There are so many beautiful, wonderful songs out there of the different eras of music that you want to see them live and you want to see them enjoyed."

A major label executive, unsurprisingly, argues that being unashamedly commercial in some instances is not necessarily a bad thing. An estate, they argue, has an obligation to get the music of a dead artist to as broad an audience as they possibly can. If that involves explicit commercialisation, then so be it. But they refuse to see that in pejorative terms. "What might appear as, or could be called, 'cashing in' is also celebrating," they propose. "Would the artist not want their music to be heard by as many people as possible? Would they not want their heirs, successors or estate to benefit and to continue to benefit from that? I think generally they would."

Therefore, it becomes a matter of how this is done.

On the one hand, showing the commercial power of an artist in the days and weeks after their death is regarded as a form of validation – that records shooting to the top of the charts following their death is proof that they were important and cherished, with all of this setting the foundations for the work the estate will do over the following decades.

A catalogue executive at the offices of a major label in the UK recounts how in the pre-digital days the stakes were high, but the returns could be enormous for record companies. This was especially true if they set record-breaking targets for albums where anything other than a chart topper was deemed a washout for the label in economic terms; but also they felt that they were somehow failing the artist by not sending them to number one in the charts as a last act.

The executive recounts what happened when a megastar who had been with their label for decades died. News broke of their death in the morning in the UK when the global heads in the US office were still in bed. They made the decision to order an unprecedented run of albums at the pressing plant.

"I immediately phoned the guy who ran our factory in Germany," they say. "Off the top of my head I said, 'OK. I want you to make half a million [of their biggest album], half a million of this greatest hits album, 300,000 [of their next biggest album] and so on. Stop making anything else. Everything in the factory has to be [records by the deceased artist]. I'll give you more numbers when I get to the office.' He started pumping away. I got to the office, got in touch with him again. 'These are the priority things.'"

It was all done on the understanding that time was of the essence and the records would have to be distributed to record shops around Europe, meaning that every day of delay was a day of lost sales.

When executives in the US office woke up and learned the news of the artist's death, they had a call with the UK office. They told the UK office to cancel the order at the pressing plant in Germany because the company's global head, who was still not in the office and would not arrive until the afternoon US time, would have to have the final say on how many records were pressed. The UK executive says they knew that this would halt the German pressing plant until at least the next day and chose to overrule what their superiors in the US were saying.

They pick up the story. "I said, 'Well let's pretend we never had this conversation because we're fucking making this and we're making more tomorrow. We're doing it. I've put in a three-and-a-half-million-unit order. We're making it.' Then the next day they go, 'Oh, yeah, it's a pretty good idea that you did, just go ahead.' And I fucking got my best bonus ever at the label because of the quick action I took over [the death of this major artist]."

On the other hand, however, some express a deep uneasiness about this emphasis on sales and number one albums, feeling that commercial concerns always overshadow artistic and cultural ones.

Music PR Jane Savidge in her 2019 memoirs *Lunch with the Wild Frontiers: A History of Britpop and Excess in 13½ Chapters* recounts what happened when she was working at Virgin Records in December 1988 when Roy Orbison died.[60] Virgin was about to release Orbison's *Mystery Girl* album early in 1989 and Savidge was doing the press for it.

She heard the news of Orbison's death on her drive into Virgin's London offices and was called into an emergency meeting when she got to her desk. "Everyone who'd been assigned to work on Roy's record was in the meeting, and a good deal of them appeared to have been crying," she wrote. "However, it didn't take long before someone suggested that it might not be such a bad thing that Roy had died, since it meant that he was now headline news and everyone would surely want to buy his new record. Several other people in the meeting nodded their heads in agreement, and a decision was reached to bring the release forward in order to capitalise on the attendant publicity generated by Roy's death. I couldn't believe what I was hearing, and I resolved to get out of the meeting as quickly as possible." *Mystery Girl* was rush-released in early February 1989 and went to number two in the UK charts.

This is a narrative about a rapacious record company that would be familiar to anyone who has heard 'Paint a Vulgar Picture' by The Smiths, in which singer Morrissey castigates the "sycophantic slags" at the record company and their "sickening greed" as they rub their hands in anticipation at the vast profits they will make from repackaging and reissuing a late star's records. Morrissey holds that the crass commercialism of the record company will not soil the love the true fans have for their dead idol.

It is a very rudimentary reading of what actually happens here. In Morrissey's mind the fans are pure and everyone at the record company is a carrion crow. At their very best, record companies can be important custodians of a legacy and while they do still want to make money here, to reduce everything they do to the fiscal is so oversimplified as to be laughable.

"That is the line the record company must walk," says Steve Davis, a former director of catalogue at EMI between 2000 and 2009. "Anything that smells of cashing in is not desirable and won't be appreciated by fans. Keeping the legacy alive is exactly it."

Anything relating to shamelessly mining the archives (see Chapter 5) or working with brands that are deemed inappropriate (see Chapter 6) comes with huge risks and accusations of cashing in can start to fly like bullets. This is part and parcel of every estate and they do not get everything right every time. None of this, of course, is unique to estates; the same can be said for living artists. As it is in life so it is in death.

LITIGATION: PLAGIARISM, ROYALTY PAYMENTS AND IMAGE RIGHTS

As we saw in Chapter 10, estates can get hit with plagiarism lawsuits – some that date back to before the artist passed away or in the months following their death, as the case of Juice WRLD reveals.

This is, of course, a two-way street as estates themselves can also take action against living acts for alleged plagiarism. The most famous example in recent years was the heirs of Marvin Gaye suing over 'Blurred Lines', also covered in Chapter 10, and eventually being awarded half of the publishing royalties in the song as well as $5 million in damages.

Around the same time that the 'Blurred Lines' case was ping-ponging around the courts was the 'Stairway to Heaven'/'Taurus' case where the estate of Randy Wolfe, formerly of US rock band Spirit, who died in 1997, took legal action against Robert Plant and Jimmy Page of Led Zeppelin in 2016.

A suit was filed in 2015 and the case went to court in Los Angeles in June 2016. The Randy Wolfe estate was suing Page and Plant to have Wolfe recognised as a co-writer of the song, saying the Led Zeppelin song lifted part of its intro from 'Taurus', an instrumental track that appeared on Spirit's 1968 debut album, three years before 'Stairway to Heaven' was written and recorded. The estate also wanted a share of the revenue 'Stairway to Heaven' had generated to that point, which was estimated at $500 million.[61]

A jury cleared Page and Plant after a six-day trial. "Musicologists summoned for the defence said the descending chromatic minor line progression shared by both songs had been a common musical device for centuries," reported the *Guardian*. "One example cited was 'Chim Chim Cher-ee', from the 1964 Disney musical *Mary Poppins*. [Peter] Anderson [attorney for Page and Plant] said Wolfe's estate was overreaching. 'He didn't create the key of A-minor.'"[62]

As with 'Blurred Lines', the case subsequently ricocheted around the legal system, with the 2016 ruling being overturned in 2018 by a three-judge appeal court in San Francisco.[63] A later ruling by the federal appeal court in March 2020 upheld the 2016 jury decision and rejected the moves by the Wolfe estate to get a songwriting credit and between $3.4 million and $13.5 million in damages.[64] In August 2020, a new petition by the estate requested that the US Supreme Court review the earlier court decisions.[65] By October 2020, however, it was all over as the Supreme Court declined to hear the case.[66]

The heirs of Marvin Gaye eventually triumphed in their case, but it was regarded by Robin Thicke and Pharrell Williams as setting "a horrible precedent for music and creativity going forward", a view that was echoed by many songwriters and others in the music publishing business.[67] That opprobrium did not, however, totally define the Marvin Gaye estate, in large part because he left behind an enormous and celebrated body of hits.

For the Wolfe estate, not only did it lose the case, the doomed litigation will likely be the event that defines his legacy for many years to come. That is the enormous risk in these matters for the estates of acts whose work has not endured in the public consciousness in the way that Gaye's has. Even if they do win the case, the litigation becomes the thing the estate (and, by default, the artist) becomes best known for – and that is a very difficult thing to move on from. The stench of failure is hard to scrub off.

Perhaps the most common legal issue that estates are likely to encounter is allegations of non-payment or under-payment of royalties or commissions, especially if the act dies before things can be resolved in their lifetime. Examples, as covered in Chapter 10, include the estate of Ricky Nelson taking action against Sony Music over royalty deductions and Aston "Family Man" Barrett losing his case against the Bob Marley estate.

These are not uncommon issues and for most estates they are dealt with reasonably quietly. When it is the estate of a megastar, however, the media attention is greatly amplified and the lines between litigation and scandal start to become blurred in the way the progress of the case is reported and discussed in newspapers, online and on TV shows.

Several years after his death, the Michael Jackson estate faced two separate legal actions from the producer so synonymous with the singer's most successful records as well as from a former manager of the star. Both cases could have caused severe reputational damage to the singer's legacy – a legacy that one cannot forget had already found its reputation badly tarnished and tattered by much more serious accusations and court actions. It equally risked damaging the estate and its co-executors because of their involvement.

Tohme R. Tohme, a former manager of Jackson with a great name, sued his estate in a dispute over his commission.

Tohme was a curious and unknowable figure, his very role resulting in enormous speculation about Jackson towards the end of his life. Tohme was reported to have been a Lebanese financier and medical doctor as well as an "ambassador at large" for Senegal.[68] He stated that his work involved negotiating the run of shows at the O2 in London that were supposed to kick-start Jackson's career again, but which never happened as he died before they started. He also said he was involved in a musical based around *Thriller* as well as a clothing line that would include "moonwalk shoes". The bizarreness of all this was compounded by the fact that Tohme claimed that he was a "stranger to the music business".

He stated in an interview that his role with Jackson was to "maximise his profits and minimise spending" and that he dropped all his work to focus on Jackson and his career. "I saw how kind he was and what a wonderful human being. I saw him with his children and I had never seen a better father... I decided to do what I could to help him," he said.[69]

In September 2010, just 15 months after the singer died, Tohme sued the Jackson estate over commissions. He also asked that the courts unseal the estate's financial records.[70] Doing so would expose what the estate's co-executors, John Branca and John McClain, were paid.[71] The estate countersued on fiduciary grounds.[72]

With all of these stories about Jackson and his business dealings towards the end of his life being played out so publicly, the estate was keen to clear his name and also clear its name in regard to the case (as well as keep private what Branca and McClain earned from their running of the estate). In May 2019, after five days in court in Los Angeles, a settlement was reached, putting the brake on the case. Terms of the settlement were confidential.[73]

By October 2019, however, that settlement collapsed. "The Michael Jackson Estate refused to pay Tohme Tohme his settlement money unless he agreed to a non-disparagement clause," wrote the *Hollywood Reporter*.[74] It added that the judge in the case said Tohme was free to "file a new lawsuit aiming to enforce the settlement agreement". In November, Tohme sued

Branca and McClain for breach of contract. "He claims the draft of the agreement the estate sent him included terms he hadn't agreed to and it was never signed, but that doesn't matter because they made an oral agreement," said the *Hollywood Reporter*.[75]

A final resolution was reached in July 2020 when it was reported Tohme would receive $3 million as part of the settlement. "The estate hasn't paid, but it argued that's because they never executed their agreement in writing and the deal required a mutual release," wrote the *Hollywood Reporter* at the time. "Through that release both the estate and Tohme would 'irrevocably, unconditionally, release, acquit and forever discharge' any and all claims against each other. The estate in its response filing argued such an agreement was necessary because the 'intent of the settlement was to finally put to rest all of Tohme's claims, so that the Estate is not burdened by future litigation of old claims'."[76] The $3 million settlement was contingent on Tohme promising not to take any further legal action against the estate. It also cut off the possibility that any more details of the inner workings of the Jackson estate could be made public.

As the Tohme case was protractedly playing out another – arguably more high-profile and potentially deleterious – case was happening.

Legendary musician, songwriter, arranger and producer Quincy Jones had worked closely with Jackson since late 1978 on what was to become the following year's *Off the Wall* album. He was also deeply involved in both *Thriller* (1982) and *Bad* (1987), the albums that made Jackson the biggest pop star in the world and that cemented his legacy. He sued MJJ Productions (which is controlled by the estate) in 2013 over royalties relating to the *This Is It* film, the 25th anniversary edition of the *Bad* album and two separate Cirque du Soleil shows using Jackson's music.[77] [78]

The estate countered that the shortfall, due to what it classed as minor accounting errors, was actually $392,000. Howard Weitzman, representing the Jackson estate, said, "Any amount above and beyond what is called for in his contracts is too much and unfair to Michael's heirs." The Jackson estate said Jones had earned $8 million in the two years since Jackson's death (it was estimated by 2017 that he had made $18 million).[79] "You don't deserve a raise," added Weitzman. "You can't have any more of Michael Jackson's money."[80]

The jury in the case in Los Angeles awarded Jones $9.4 million in damages, agreeing he had been underpaid in his cut of royalties. "While the jury denied Quincy Jones $21 million – or more than two-thirds of what he demanded – from the estate of Michael Jackson, we still believe that giving him millions of dollars that he has no right to receive under his contracts is wrong," said Weitzman in a statement. "Any amount above and beyond what is called for in his contracts is too much and unfair to Michael's heirs. Although Mr. Jones is portraying this as a victory for artists' rights, the real artist is Michael Jackson and it is his money Mr. Jones is seeking."[81]

That was not the end of the case, however. The Second District Court of Appeal in Los Angeles ruled in May 2002 that Jones was not entitled to most of the $9.4 million settlement from 2017, adding that the original judge had "erred in allowing jurors to interpret producer agreements and then issue awards in two specific categories", according to the *New York Times*.[82]

"These two awards must be reversed," the appeals court wrote. "Interpretation of the producer agreements was solely a judicial function, yet the trial court allowed the jury to perform that function and ultimately misinterpret the relevant terms."[83]

It reversed an award of $5,315,787 on record sales and licences from Jackson's production company's joint venture with Sony Music as well as $1,574,128 in fees Jones said he would have received if MJJ Productions had given him first refusal to remix Jackson's recordings. The court did, however, allow damages of $2.5 million to stand.

"Quincy Jones was the last person we thought would try to take advantage of Michael Jackson by filing a lawsuit three years after he died asking for tens of millions of dollars he wasn't entitled to," said Weitzman in a statement. "We knew the verdict was wrong when we heard it, and the court of appeal has completely vindicated us."[84]

Jones disagreed with that. "I'm not suing Michael," he said. "I'm suing you all."[85]

While the Jackson estate did not have to pay out as much as Jones was originally seeking, it still had to pay a considerable sum, and also to face yet more indignity as its internal workings were made public, and Jackson's name was, once again, in the media for negative reasons. None of this, of course, is as damaging as *Leaving Neverland* and the accusations made in the film, but cumulatively it all chips away and undermines pop music's most lucrative estate. The business continues but will operate beneath the shadow of all these scandals and court cases for many years to come.

CATALOGUE JAM: THE ALBUM LICENSING DEAL THAT WASN'T TO BE

The Prince estate found itself in the middle of an unfortunate deal with regard to the licensing of his extensive and highly prized catalogue of released albums as well as his legendary vault of unreleased recordings.

In February 2017, it was announced that Universal Music Group had acquired the exclusive licensing rights to 25 albums that Prince had released via his own NPG Records label. It was also stated at the time of the deal that this gave Universal first refusal on unreleased material from the vault. The deal was rumoured to have been worth $35 million.

By April 2017, however, the wheels were starting to come off. The *Wall Street Journal* reported on a dispute between Universal and Warner over which label owned which rights, and what could or could not be sold.[86]

The *Independent* added, "The 2014 deal with Warner had different terms for certain albums, making it incredibly complex: Warner retained the rights to soundtrack albums to Warner Bros. films – including Prince's biggest-selling albums *Purple Rain, Parade*, and *Batman* – in perpetuity. Other albums were subject to varying terms, territories, formats (digital vs. physical), and term lengths."[87]

Then in July 2017, a court order stated that Universal should get its money back, with the *Hollywood Reporter* claiming that $31 million was at stake.[88] None of this affected Universal's existing agreement with the estate to administer Prince's publishing globally; this case just related to his sound recordings. "The estate can now shop the recorded-music rights to another buyer, though they will likely fetch less than $31 million," added the *Hollywood Reporter*.[89]

Another buyer was indeed found and the whole sorry issue was ultimately resolved in June 2018 when Sony Music signed "an exclusive distribution agreement" with the Prince estate for 35 previously released album titles. The deal would extend in 2021 to cover a further 12 non-soundtrack albums.[90]

While it was ultimately settled, the negative impact on the estate – given its multitude of other problems (see Chapters 2 and 3) – was unfortunate in the extreme. It once again reduced the estate of one of the greatest artists of all time to unbecoming and, frankly, grubby squabbles over money and control.

THE BLOOD OATH REVOKED

The most unusual example of a posthumous controversy around an estate arose first in July 2017 when Judith Van Zant, the widow of Ronnie Van Zant of Lynyrd Skynyrd, moved to shut down a biopic about the band in 2017 that she claimed violated a "blood oath" between members of the band.

Street Survivors: The True Story of the Lynyrd Skynyrd Plane Crash was a film that aimed to tell the story of the October 1977 accident which killed the band's lead vocalist and founding member Ronnie Van Zant and guitarist/vocalist Steve Gaines, as well as backing vocalist Cassie Gaines, assistant road manager Dean Kilpatrick, pilot Walter McCreary and co-pilot William Gray.

In 1988, surviving members of the band and representatives of deceased members reached an agreement on how they should collectively govern the band's name and legacy. This included the "name, likeness, portrait, picture, performances or biographical material" of Ronnie Van Zant and Steve Gaines.[91]

The following month, August 2017, US District Judge Robert Sweet sided with Judith Van Zant and surviving member of the band Allen Collins, agreeing the film violated the 1988 "blood oath" whereby surviving members and the estates of deceased members agreed that no one could ever again perform as Lynyrd Skynyrd. Sweet blocked the distribution of the film.

Artimus Pyle, the band's drummer, was pushing the film, having signed a deal in 2016 with Cleopatra Records and Cleopatra Films whereby he got a co-producer credit and 5 per cent of the film's profits.[92]

In October 2018, a federal appeals court overturned the ruling blocking the film and ruled instead that Pyle had a right to sell his life story despite objections from surviving members and the estates of deceased members. "The crash is part of the 'history' of the band, but it is also an 'experience' of Pyle with the band, likely his most important experience," ruled the court.[93] It also overturned the previous ruling that Cleopatra and Pyle would have to pay the plaintiffs $632,110.91 in legal fees.

Street Survivors: The True Story of the Lynyrd Skynyrd Plane Crash received its premiere at the Hollywood Reel Independent Film Festival in February 2020 and had a full US release in June 2020.

THE FAMILY SUES OVER THE DEATH OF A MUSICIAN

Lil Peep passed away on 15 November 2017 at the age of 21. The cause of the rapper's death was ruled to be an accidental overdose of fentanyl (a synthetic opiate used as a painkiller and tranquilliser) and Xanax (the brand name of a short-acting tranquilliser).[94]

In October 2019, however, Liza Womack – mother of Lil Peep and the executor of his estate – filed a claim in the Los Angeles County Superior Court against First Access Entertainment, the management company that represented the artist in his lifetime, over its duty of care to the artists on its books.[95]

First Access Entertainment denied all the claims raised in the case,[96] and in October 2020, they countersued over the sale of Lil Peep-related merchandise.

According to legal experts that *Rolling Stone* spoke to, this case could be years, possibly even a decade, away from any resolution.[97]

(The case had not been resolved before this book went to press.)

THE TAINTED AND UNWANTED ESTATE

So far, every estate – despite its economic problems or reputation issues – has had one thing in common: they have all been wanted by their heirs or their executors. They have all been deemed valuable – in both cultural and economic terms – and therefore seen as worth nurturing and developing.

Some estates, however, can be left to wither on the vine due to an inherent laziness or lack of interest of those in charge, especially if they generate so little money as to be deemed a burden and are seen to be more hassle than they are worth. Or they can be left to atrophy, as no one can find the rightful heirs.

"It can be frustrating sometimes when you see rights that are in limbo, or see that no one seems to be exploiting them," says one label catalogue head. "Meanwhile you're trying to find out who is their successor or inheritor [to no avail]."

There are, however, estates that are unwanted by heirs or come with so many problems that mean they might be considered impossible to work with. "There is the issue of the unwanted estate," says a partner at a major legal firm who has had to deal with precisely this issue. "It's not always the case that whoever inherits it wants it. You may have fallen out with your spouse or whoever and you just end up with it on your hands."

And then there are estates of individuals who are convicted murderers and notorious cult leaders whose reputation is going to be impossible to rehabilitate outside of a very small group of people wilfully drawn to venerate the truly transgressive. Such as, for example, Charles Manson.

Manson, who died in prison on 19 November 2017, had been convicted in 1971 of first-degree murder and conspiracy to commit murder in relation to the brutal deaths of seven people, most notably the actor Sharon Tate. Manson also believed himself to be a promising songwriter, although those who heard his songs begged to differ. The Beach Boys, through Manson's association with Dennis Wilson, did an altered cover of Manson's song 'Cease to Exist', retitling it as 'Never Learn Not to Love', in 1968.

While he was in prison awaiting trial, the 14-track album *LIE: The Love and Terror Cult* was released in March 1970, based on recordings Manson had made in 1967 and 1968. It was released by music producer Phil Kaufman, who had met Manson in prison, through the Awareness Records label. It had an initial run of 2,000 and Kaufman tried to get local record shops in Los Angeles to stock it but was rebuffed. "Kaufman did his best but soon realized that there was no market, underground or otherwise, for a Charles Manson album," wrote Jeff Guinn in his biography of the cult leader.[98] A *Rolling Stone* feature on Manson from June 1970 put a sales number on his budding music career a few months in. "Of the 2,000 albums of his music that were pressed, less than 300 have sold," it said.[99]

Even so, the fame of the cult leader grew following his incarceration, reaching its apotheosis (or its nadir) in 1993 when Guns N' Roses included a cover of Manson's 'Look at Your Game, Girl' on their *The Spaghetti Incident?* album.

The *Los Angeles Times* reported the controversy in the wake of the album that Bartek Frykowski – the son of Wojciech Frykowski, one of the victims of the Manson Family – would get publishing royalties for the song under a 1971 court order against Manson. "When we heard Manson might get the money, we were ready to pull the song off the record," said Slash, lead guitarist in Guns N' Roses. "But then we found out that all the money would go to this guy in Poland who lost his dad (in the murders)."[100] The royalties were estimated at $62,000 for every one million copies of the album sold. Axl Rose, the band's lead singer, added that his performance royalties for the song would be donated to a non-profit environmental organisation. The track was also uncredited on the sleeve of the album.

When Manson died in late 2017 it raised complications about who would take over his estate and, more importantly, what they would do with it. In January 2018, it was reported that three competing claims were being made for the estate. The Los Angeles Superior Court was tasked with trying to resolve those three claims – from a purported son, a grandson and a pen pal of Manson (as well as a collector of Manson-related memorabilia). This situation was exacerbated by the presence of "at least two conflicting wills".[101] Another individual claiming to be a second biological son also came forward.[102] Yet another son, Charles Manson Jr, had committed suicide in 1993.[103]

Included in the Manson estate were his copyrights, commercial rights to his name and image as well as personal possessions. "We think Manson's worth more than anyone realizes," stated Mike Smith, a music agent for an unnamed claimant who stated that he was fathered by Manson during an orgy. "There's a lot of money there."[104]

In March 2018, a court ruled that Jason Freeman, who claimed to be Manson's grandson, should take possession of his body. "Kern County Superior Court Commissioner Alisa Knight chose among three competing claims – by Freeman, Michael Brunner, who says he's the cult leader's son, and Michael Channels, a Manson friend and memorabilia collector who says he has the only valid will," wrote CNN. "A fourth – Matthew Lentz – who says he is also Manson's son and has a will that only addresses Manson's estate, sided with Brunner."[105]

Freeman told CNN, "This is unreal – this is something I actually played out in my mind ever since I was a kid." He added that he would cremate Manson's remains at a small family gathering and extended an invitation to Brunner and Channels. "I wouldn't want them to miss out," he said, somewhat chillingly.[106] At that stage it was still undecided which of the four competing claims would be awarded the estate.

The use of 'Look at Your Game, Girl' in Quentin Tarantino's 2019 film *Once Upon A Time... In Hollywood* (which was in part based around the Manson Family) saw the controversy around the estate blow up again. The *Daily Mail* was claiming that Freeman was "poised to profit" from the use of the song in the film despite the fact that Tarantino had been led to believe that the "cash would go to victims' relatives".[107]

The issue over inheritance of the estate dragged on. Attorney Dale Kiken had been appointed by the courts as special administrator for the Manson estate in August 2018 and this was extended to August 2019.[108]

Michael Channels was pushing Los Angeles Superior Court Judge Clifford Klein to get Jason Freeman to submit to a DNA test (something he had said he would not do voluntarily). Judge Klein, however, wanted to see court orders from Kern County that supported Channels' claims that Manson's 2002 will (which he claimed named him as executor of the estate) had been filed there in 2017 before he would order a DNA test.[109]

Klein eventually signed an order for Freeman to provide a DNA sample in November 2019, issuing it on 5 December and stipulating that it had to be done by 10 January 2020. Freeman, however, filed an appeal a day before that date.[110]

Around the same time – December 2019 – Michael Brunner filed papers to drop his claim as an alleged heir of Manson. The non-appearance of Matthew Lentz at a hearing in the probate case on 14 December 2019 weakened his claim on the estate. Lentz had no lawyer but had hoped to forge an alliance with Brunner, who did have a lawyer. "I blew it," Lentz said outside the court. "I wasted how many years of my life for this dumb crap? For what?"[111] He said he was not looking to take the whole estate, but rather just the rights to a song he claimed Manson had written for him.

By March 2020, both Lentz and Brunner were eliminated from the inheritance claim by Judge Klein as they had insufficient proof they were the rightful heirs. That left Freeman and Channels tussling for the estate.

At the time of writing, the heir to Manson's estate had not been agreed on by the courts. Despite the fact that it was referred to in the media as "Satan's estate",[112] it was still viewed as valuable by those fighting over it – either in commercial terms or, more likely, in ghoulish terms – but it is utterly unlike any other estate out there. "[I]f there is money to be had, how could someone claim profits generated by a man who became famous for committing profound acts of evil, and still sleep comfortably at night?" asked estates lawyers Danielle and Andy Mayoras in a feature for *Forbes*.[113]

Many would regard it as a cursed estate, but the dark draw of Manson over half a century on from the murder spree that made him one of the most notorious figures of the 20th century does not adhere to normal rules. Hybristophilia comes with its own malevolent logic.

(The case had not been resolved before this book went to press.)

CHAPTER 12

Virtual Signalling

Holograms and New Technologies

"Yeah! Do you know what the fuck this is?"

Those were the first words Tupac Shakur said on stage at the Coachella Valley Music and Arts Festival in Indio, California on 15 April 2012.

Bare-chested, wearing white trousers and a gold chain with a crucifix swinging around his neck, he paced the stage and whipped up the crowd as he duetted with Snoop Dogg as part of the latter's headline show with Dr Dre. "Yo, Pac, let these motherfuckers know what kind of party they are at right now," said Snoop Dogg.

"Ain't nuthin' but a gangsta party," sang Shakur.

After racing through two songs ('Hail Mary' and '2 of Amerikaz Most Wanted') in barely four minutes on stage, he flashed the peace sign and stood with his head down as the crowd cheered. Then, with a blinding flash of light, he was gone.

The only issue here, of course, was that Tupac Shakur had been dead for over 15 years, having been shot four times on 7 September 1996 in Las Vegas, eventually dying of internal bleeding on 13 September 1996.

He appeared on stage in the form of what was described as a "hologram" but was actually a visual illusion whereby a moving image of the late rapper was projected onto an angled sheet of glass that would be invisible to the audience. (The same trick was repeated on 22 April 2012, as the festival is hosted over consecutive weekends with an identical line-up.[1])

If there was a single moment that drew a line between the music estates business of the past and the music estates business of the future, it was this.

The core illusion itself was actually based on a technique that dated back to Christmas Eve 1862 when John Henry Pepper demonstrated it at the Royal Polytechnic Institution in London in a stage production of *The Haunted Man and the Ghost's Bargain*, an 1848 novella by Charles Dickens.[2] It was initially used to make it seem as if a ghost was on stage with the actors in a play. Its immediate impact was such that a number of plays in 1863 were specifically written to incorporate the illusion. Its novelty, however, soon fizzled out in theatres due to the fact that the ghost could not speak.[3]

The technique, subsequently known as Pepper's Ghost, lived on in theme parks before becoming a way that dead musicians could perform "live" and "tour" once again in the 21st century. It is commonly referred to as a hologram but, as will be explained below, is incredibly far removed from actual holographic technology. The nomenclature, however, has stuck. Unless specified, the term "hologram" in the rest of this chapter will be used to refer to Pepper's Ghost-style optical illusions.

Tupac was the first act to rise from the dead on stage, but subsequently a whole new subset of the estates industry (and a whole new division of the touring business) was created. The Tupac hologram was developed by AV Concepts and Digital Domain Media Group using CGI – based on the movements of a live actor made to look like the rapper – as well as the fundamentals of the Pepper's Ghost *trompe-l'œil*.[4] Digital Domain Media Group had previously created virtual versions of Brad Pitt in *The Curious Case of Benjamin Button* in 2008. Similar technology had already been used on stage by Gorillaz at the MTV Europe Music Awards 2005 in Lisbon[5] and again at the 2006 Grammys.[6]

"The team [at AV Concepts] pulled together Tupac's performance by looking at old footage and creating an animation that incorporated characteristics of the late singer's movements," wrote the *Washington Post*.[7]

Ed Ulbrich, the chief creative officer at Digital Domain, spoke to the *Wall Street Journal* after the show about how it was all pulled together. "To create a completely synthetic human being is the most complicated thing that can be done," he said.[8] The image was computer-generated based on Tupac's physical characteristics and his movements from recorded performances, but Ulbrich stressed that it was not old performances by Tupac that had been digitally repurposed. "This is not found footage," he asserted. "This is not archival footage. This is an illusion. This is just the beginning. Dre has a massive vision for this."[9]

Rather than project the image onto glass or Perspex, the 20-strong production team behind it used Mylar foil. "There were rotoscoping and paint teams to warp and pull the design to make it look like Tupac's body," explained *The Undefeated* in a piece marking the fifth anniversary of the performance. "There was someone in charge of lighting. There was a technician who figured out ways to automate certain tasks in composite work."[10]

Dr Dre and his production team began speaking to Digital Domain a year earlier and work on the hologram began in earnest four months before the show.

"The effect itself is difficult to do," Nick Smith, president of AV Concepts, told *The Undefeated*. "People think the hologram can just appear in thin air.

It's a very elaborate staging apparatus that has to be built to do this, and it has to be in the right conditions."

He added, "One of the challenges of doing this effect out at Coachella was you had everything working against you. You had heat, you had cold, you had rain, you had wind. It had to be dark. You had to control all of the lighting, including the moon, which is difficult to do. It's a perfect effect for a theater, but it's not the perfect effect for uncontrolled environments."[11]

The cost of creating the Tupac hologram has never been made public, but Randy Phillips, who was head of promoter AEG at the time, suggested that Dre had been paid a fee "into the multiple millions" for his double Coachella set but that he barely broke even after all production costs, including those related to the hologram, were deducted. His profitability was seriously compromised as he spent both time and money "tweaking the ersatz Shakur" with its developers.[12] "Dre's such a perfectionist," said Phillips. "He really wanted it to be something that no one's ever done before."[13]

Reports in the wake of the Coachella show claimed that tentative plans were being made to take the hologram on tour. "It was strictly for Coachella – get it right," Dre said in a video message backstage after the final performance at the second weekend of the festival. "I want to get rid of all the rumours out there. This was not done for a tour." Then somewhat undermining himself, he said, "If a tour happens, we'll see."[14]

The lawyer for the Tupac estate says touring the Tupac show was never a serious consideration. "Dre was certainly aware that it was going to be a spectacular and unprecedented event – but I'm not sure he or we were looking to the future of getting involved with hologram tours," says Howard King of Los Angeles-based law firm King, Holmes, Paterno & Soriano.

Then he corrects himself. "That's not true, we did discuss that [a Tupac tour] and actually he had a concept for doing a hologram tour – but with a new artist," says King. "He [Dre] was going to create an artist from thin air and operate as a hologram. That has not yet happened. But the people who provided the technology were certainly thinking that they could go forward and create a business of doing hologram tours."

King also states that the estate of Tupac always regarded it as a one-off (well, a two-off given it was at both Coachella weekends). The resurrection of Tupac on stage was always going to be temporary. "It wasn't even their event – it was really a Dr Dre event," says King. "The estate has never considered going that route. I'm not speaking for the estate because I don't know what their feelings are, but I know other people in the business think that it's kind of a cheap stunt – a hologram tour. Because you're not getting the movement of the artists; you're getting the movements of some guy who thinks this is what the artist would do."

He concludes by saying the rapper's estate is choosing to focus on other projects rather than have the hologram reappear at other shows or go on the road. "It is far more focused on releasing new music in the right way and doing other exploitations of the name and likeness of Tupac," says King.

Jeff Jampol of JAM Inc was working with the Tupac estate at the time of the hologram show. He says everything was driven by Dr Dre for one very simple reason – it was his headline show and the Tupac appearance was just one component of it rather than the epicentre.

"You have to look at the way that Dre applied it," says Jampol of the Coachella show. "Here you have two guys – Snoop and Dre – and they're headlining Coachella. They've got, I don't know, 20 songs. They come on, they do a bunch of songs and all of a sudden on song eight – oh, here comes this Coachella quote hologram unquote who says, 'What's up, Coachella?' And people are freaking out and Snoop and Tupac do two songs together. And then it's gone. By the way, never to reappear. That was a beautiful use of an effect."

This "effect", however, was the catalyst for a whole new business category and a whole new way for estates to make money as well as to try and introduce the music of a deceased artist to new audiences.

Digital Domain was, for a brief moment, the hottest technology company in the world and won the Titanium Award at Cannes Lions International Festival of Creativity that June.[15] It did not last. In September the same year, it filed for bankruptcy, just 10 months after its IPO. At its peak it was valued at $400 million but had to sell its production arm, which was the majority of the company, to private equity firm Searchlight Capital Partners for $15 million, showing just how boom-and-bust this new business area could be.[16]

New companies like Base Hologram and Eyellusion were launched in the wake of Coachella 2012, soon filling the vacuum left by Digital Domain, with the precise intention of picking up the Tupac idea and running with it, taking it to its logical conclusion and putting dead acts on tour again. The estates of a range of acts from different eras and across different genres – including Maria Callas, Frank Zappa, Glenn Gould, Ronnie James Dio, Roy Orbison, Buddy Holly and Whitney Houston – all got on board and the holographic touring business got moving in earnest.

All of this has not been without problems or controversy – and that will be explored in much greater detail below. But the 'Lazarusisation' of dead pop stars through technological manipulation pre-dates Coachella in 2012. In fact, it stretches back to the early 1990s when the modern estates business was still finding its feet.

THE DEAR DEPARTED DUET

Nat King Cole died on 15 February 1965. His eldest biological child, Natalie, had only just turned 15 when he died, going on to have her own successful music career and releasing her debut album in 1975.[17] Father and daughter were, however, reunited in the summer of 1991 on a reworking of a song that was first a hit for Nat in 1951. In what was described as a "virtual duet", the two sang together on a recorded version of 'Unforgettable' and Natalie also performed it live with footage of her father on a screen behind her.

It appeared on the album *Unforgettable... with Love*, released the same year as the single, in which she paid tribute to her father by reworking a number of his hits.

"Her voice was spliced with her father's in the title track, offering a delicate duet more than 25 years after his death," wrote the *Guardian*. "The album sold about 14m copies and won six Grammys, including album of the year, and record and song of the year for the title track."[18]

As a single, 'Unforgettable' was a medium-sized hit – going to number 14 in the US[19] and number 19 in the UK[20] – but it marked a whole new way that estates could start to work. Where 'Unforgettable' got to in the charts was less important than what it represented. "Nothing had been attempted like that," said Natalie Cole of the duet. "To lift Dad's voice, literally, off of that track and put it on a brand new one, and then line it up, match it up, get the phrasing right. I remember listening – everyone listening at the end, and we were just enthralled. It was really wonderful."[21]

While not joining a cadaver gold rush, other estates have used the same strategy, believing that if it worked for Nat King Cole's estate – who took the brunt of the initial criticism about the squeamishness or inappropriateness of such a venture – then they could slipstream it.

These tracks are distinct from albums that were unfinished by an artist before their death (which is covered in Chapter 5), as they are creating duets that would otherwise be impossible. As such, and because the voice is seen as more sacrosanct, imbuing something of the essence of the performer in a way that instruments do not, these duets require their own special attention.

Elvis, it appears, has become something of a repeat offender here. In 2007, Celine Dion performed a duet of 'I Can Dream' with him on the *American Idol* show. "Now, prepare to be startled," said host Ryan Seacrest, the show's host, before the performance. "Prepare for magnificence. Prepare for a duet you thought was impossible. Celine Dion is travelling back to the year she was born, 1968, to sing with the man who is and always will be the world's greatest idol. Ready – here we go."

While it happened in the studio, it was not using hologram-like technology, but rather was the result of judicious camerawork and editing. "We're told Dion sang with a Las Vegas Elvis tribute artist whose body was shown in wide shots," wrote WMC Action News 5, the Memphis-based TV station, on its website after the show. "That's what gave it the realistic look. At times, his face was replaced with the real Elvis taken from the *1968 Elvis Comeback* special. They even used some full body shots from that special. Web chatter says Celine Dion sang the song five times and that it was all edited together to create the performance you saw."[22]

Echoing what the Coles did more than a quarter of a century earlier, Lisa Marie Presley duetted with her father from beyond the grave in 2018 on the title track from *Where No One Stands Alone*, a compilation of Elvis's gospel tracks. The rest of the album was based on archival Elvis vocal performances embellished with new instrumentations and backing vocals. "It was a very powerful and moving experience to sing with my father," wrote Lisa Marie in the liner notes for the album.[23]

Perhaps the oddest sepulchral singing project was Barry Manilow's 2014 album, *My Dream Duets*, wherein the 'Mandy' hitmaker exhumed all manner of artists – including Mama Cass, Frankie Lymon, Whitney Houston, Judy Garland, Dusty Springfield, Sammy Davis Jr, Louis Armstrong and even Marilyn Monroe – for a graveside cantillation. David Byrne published an essay on the album. "[H]e and his partners sound unanimously chummy and affirmative and defect-free," he wrote. "If you just listen, the illusion is totally believable."[24] The public agreed, with the album entering the Billboard chart in the US in November 2014 at number four.[25]

Critics, however, tend to take the opposite view, regarding these reanimations as grotesque creations that are morally and ethically suspect – especially as more of them are released, and seeing how normalised the whole thing is becoming.

Two separate features in the *Guardian* and a further one on the BBC's website in 2017 castigated the trend. One referred to *The King and I* – a duets album by Notorious BIG and his widow, Faith Evans – as "creepy". It added that the album was "unable to decide if it's a wanton cash-grab or a private form of grief gone horribly public". It also highlighted other examples ploughing a similar posthumous furrow, like Scarlett Johansson and Dean Martin's 'I'll Be Home for Christmas', as well as Susan Boyle and Elvis's 'O Come, All Ye Faithful' (yes, the Elvis estate cannot seem to help itself here) for particular opprobrium.[26]

The second *Guardian* piece also used *The King and I* as its launch pad, adding that the Notorious BIG vaults had been raided more than enough at this stage. It called this trend "uniquely creepy", adding that "[a] duet where only one person knows what's going on isn't worthy of the name".[27]

The BBC piece again deployed the c-word ("creepy"), making it an adjective that makes as many appearances here as Elvis.[28]

THE LONG HISTORY OF THE HOLOGRAPHIC RESURRECTION

Coachella in 2012 was seen as the spur that brought holographic-style performances into, if not the mainstream, then at least the public consciousness.

It had a very long gestation period, with its origins stretching back to the 1990s and German inventor and electronic engineer Uwe Maass, who made his first hologram projector in 1992.

Maass took the core idea of Pepper's Ghost but expanded it so that it switched the use of glass for a stretched translucent foil that sits at a 45-degree angle, and patented the idea.[29] He then founded Musion to commercialise his creation. "The Pepper's Ghost system is a relatively simple system, but not big enough for a proper stage, so I was just thinking,

'What can you use to enlarge the Pepper's Ghost system?'" he told CNN in 2014. "The result was a special polymer foil."[30]

Due in large part to the high entry costs, the long development times and the fact that the number of specialist companies working in this area were limited, the first wave of estates that followed the lead of Tupac's estate here were focused on a hologram-style performance as a one-off event. Building an entire show around a hologram was, firstly, prohibitively expensive and, secondly, utterly unproven in its viability.

In swift order, however, they started to appear. On 8 September 2013, the Rock The Bells festival in San Bernardino, California saw former NWA star Eazy-E appear in holographic form during the set by Bone Thugs-N-Harmony.[31]

The following night, a hologram of Ol' Dirty Bastard joined members of Wu-Tang Clan at the same festival. He also appeared with his son, Young Dirty Bastard. The Wu-Tang Clan's set had been marred by technical difficulties but the Ol' Dirty Bastard performance went off without a hitch.[32] Nicole Beckett, head of content development at Four Screens Production, worked with the Ol' Dirty Bastard estate on the Rock The Bells show, helping to broker the deal to make it happen. "That was a pretty major thing because that was a relatively exciting technology at the time," she says. "It was our first time doing something like that – testing that out with an audience. It went over very well. Of course, there were kinks along the way and technical situations; but at the end of the day the fans really enjoyed it."

On 18 May 2014, a Michael Jackson hologram appeared at the Billboard Music Awards at the MGM Grand Garden Arena in Las Vegas. It had reportedly been in development for six months ahead of the show and the award show's producers had not actually seen it in operational form until eight days before the event.[33]

The Jackson hologram appeared halfway through the show on a specially built stage at the rear of the arena to perform 'Slave to the Rhythm', accompanied by 16 dancers and a five-piece band. "It's so important to experience Michael Jackson in a live setting," said John Branca, co-executor of the Jackson estate. "This is something where we wanted a live performance in front of a live audience and nothing speaks to that more than an awards show."[34]

Things, however, did not always go according to plan in these early days of the hologram performance. On 23 May 2016, Christina Aguilera was supposed to perform two songs – 'I Have Nothing' and 'I'm Every Woman' – with a hologram of Whitney Houston on US talent show *The Voice* on NBC. The hologram was developed by Hologram USA but when footage was leaked online ahead of the planned TV performance, the Whitney Houston estate pulled the plug. "After closely viewing the performance, we decided the hologram was not ready to air," said Pat Houston, executor of Whitney Houston's estate. "Holograms are new technology that takes time to perfect, and we believe with artists of this iconic caliber, it must be perfect. Whitney's legacy and her devoted fans deserve perfection."[35]

Hologram USA founder Alki David was, inevitably, keen to absolve himself and his company of any wrongdoing or unprofessionalism. "We hadn't digitally composited the face yet and NBC freaked out," he told *Wired* in 2018.[36]

I spoke to Pat Houston in early 2020, just as the UK tour of the Whitney Houston hologram was about to begin. Looking back at the false start in 2016, she says, "We were working on the hologram – it was almost there, but it wasn't. If you're going to do it, you have to do it right. She wasn't ready. And we just moved on. After the deal [with Hologram USA] was over, we moved on."

She says the idea for a hologram actually had its genesis when Whitney was still alive and it was something she and Pat Houston, who was then her manager, discussed in early 2011, just before her death, around a proposed *Whitney Unplugged* tour in small venues. "That's where the idea came from," says Pat. "I'm just making the dream happen with her music. It just happens to be by way of a hologram, which is new technology that's being introduced to industries like the music industry. But it's a way for people to have that Whitney experience. We all know that she's gone, but it's that Whitney experience if you've never had it. To come into a small theatre and be able to hear that music. It's really something that she wanted to do. I'm just carrying it out. It just happens to be a hologram."

The Whitney Houston hologram tour was eventually developed and launched by Base Hologram, but the relationship with Hologram USA was to come back to cause issues for the Houston estate (see later in this chapter).

HOLOGRAPHIC CONTENT: LICENSING COMPLEXITIES AND LEGAL PROBLEMS

As a relatively new technology that is still finding its way, it is inevitable that there will be legal pitfalls along the route. After all, the rights and licensing side of the music business has been playing catch-up with the technological side since the 1990s, exposed most brutally with the arrival of Napster in 1999.

At the heart of all holograms are licensing issues relating to name, image and likeness. As covered in Chapters 2 and 6, it is not automatic that an estate inherits or controls all of these rights, especially as only certain states in the US recognise them as being transferable after death. "You have to license the rights," says entertainment lawyer Jeff Liebenson of New York-based firm Liebenson Law. "You could say most people don't really understand how to do it. Like anything else that's come along over the last few decades, anything that is new has to be thought through. When there is no precedent, the first thing you do is think about it and what intellectual property rights are involved. Here, it is name and likeness rights and they are a little tricky, because they really differ from one jurisdiction to another. In America, it's not a federal law – it's state laws."

These rights are, however, the building blocks of a hologram business, and then there are the rights in a composition as well as any recorded music rights used that have to be cleared to make a holographic performance possible. This is probably the most complex undertaking – in pure legal terms – that an estate will face as there are so many different sets of rights involved. Just as with a complex buyers' chain in the property market, if one part fails, it all fails.

Marty Tudor, CEO of Base Hologram, says that working in collaboration with the estates – both in terms of licensing and creative direction – is "imperative to us". He states, "We do this as a celebration and an honouring – not as a way to take advantage of the artist."

For the most part, Base pitches the idea to the estates, rather than the other way around, having identified artists around whom it believes it can build commercially viable shows. "We consciously went to the estate of [Roy] Orbison and we consciously went to the [Maria] Callas estate," he says. "For Buddy Holly, actually it was mutual. As we were thinking about approaching them, they were coming to us and so that was relatively easy. And [as for] Whitney Houston, I had been talking with them for years, actually. It wasn't until [Pat Houston] saw our Maria Callas hologram and Roy Orbison holograms that she said, 'OK, let's do this.'"

Pat Houston says that the Whitney Houston estate only agreed to work with Base if the estate was deeply involved in her hologram's production. She brought in a team of people who had worked with the singer in her lifetime to ensure levels of verisimilitude were as high as they could be. "People that have worked with her for nearly 30 years are involved in this project," she says. "For the hair that is on her head, we used one of her hair stylists, Kim Kimble. She did a phenomenal job creating the hair for the hologram. You have Timothy Snell that worked with her for 15 years as her stylist. He came on board and he helped with the wardrobe as it relates to the hologram using one of the premier designers that Whitney used, Marc Bouwer."

The Buddy Holly hologram – which really should have been called Buddy Hologram, but no matter – was developed by Base Hologram and was part of a co-headline tour with the Roy Orbison hologram (another Base production). The first show of a US tour was at the Saban Theater in Beverly Hills on 27 September 2019 and it moved to Europe in October that year.[37]

It came after BMG took over the Holly estate, making its development relatively straightforward from a rights perspective. "We control the image and the legacy so it's been interesting," David Hirshland, EVP of BMG. "We did this hologram tour with Base where we exercise all the approvals, who the actor was, how we shot the hologram, the content, which songs [were used] etc."

However, BMG, as the new operator of the estate, had to first extricate itself from a deal that Holly's widow, María Elena Holly, had signed with Hologram USA. This proved more complex than one might have expected.

Hologram USA originally announced the deal with María Elena Holly on behalf of the Holly estate in early 2015. The original plan was to host a show in Texas, Holly's home state, in 2016 and then take it on the road. "I am so excited that my partnership with Hologram USA on the Buddy Holly concert project will allow a new generation of fans to experience the thrill of seeing Buddy 'live' and in concert for the first time in many decades," said María Elena.[38]

The relationship with Hologram USA was to crash spectacularly. "We actually inherited an agreement that María Elena had entered into with Hologram USA," says Hirshland. "We tried at the beginning of 2013 to work with them. So we finally had to take them to arbitration to get out of the contract, which we were successful in doing, and then immediately entered into our own agreement with Base who had already got the Roy Orbison show and wanted to enhance the Roy Orbison tour with Buddy."

In relation to that original contract, he adds, "The founder [Alkiviades 'Alki' David] was hit in 2019 with a $50 million[39] sexual harassment judgment."

David, the billionaire heir to a Coca-Cola bottling fortune, originally got into the hologram business when he bought Musion's patents in September 2013, creating a new company and calling it Hologram USA. "[I] saw the Tupac that they had done and walked over the heads of the other executives to make a deal," he told *Wired* in 2018, saying he invested $25 million in his new company.[40] He specifically targeted estates, looking to create hologram shows for deceased artists such as Amy Winehouse, Liberace and Buddy Holly as well as comedian Richard Pryor.

Hologram USA fought with Pulse Evolution – a rival hologram company – over who owned key technologies in the sector, specifically regarding patents brought up around the time of the Michael Jackson/Billboard show.[41]

David also faced legal action from the heirs of Roy Orbison in 2017 over termination clauses in their contract and their right to go to another hologram company, Base Hologram.[42]

The Orbison estate and Base toured the Orbison hologram in 2018 and again in 2019 in a co-headline tour with a Buddy Holly hologram. "It wasn't a breach of contract – it was just how the contract worked," explains Chuck Fleckenstein of the Orbison estate on the Hologram USA legal case. "The contract had a timeframe in it and, if you didn't meet the timeframe, the contract ended. So we ended our contract with Hologram USA and we found the newly formed Base Hologram. A hologram performance is a show and Base delivered."

WE HAVE THE TECHNOLOGY: THE COMPANIES COMPETING TO CORNER THE HOLOGRAM MARKET

Each different hologram company – and there are, it is important to remember, only a handful of them – has a characteristically different approach to developing their products. They will all boast about how they are distinct but, due to competition concerns, they are less willing to boast specifically about why they are different in terms of the underlying technologies they use.

With Hologram USA effectively derailed in ignominy, the market for holograms of deceased artists has become a duopoly, with Base and Eyellusion competing to have their technology accepted as the industry standard. They have many similarities but also many differences – so we will look at each in turn.

Eyellusion

Founded by Jeff Pezzuti (who is also the company's CEO), Eyellusion first made a splash with a Ronnie James Dio hologram, but has garnered more attention with its Frank Zappa hologram.

Having previously worked in finance for almost two decades in New York, Pezzuti heard about the Tupac/Coachella hologram in 2012 and wanted in. "That really inspired me," he says. It was, however, something of a delayed reaction as it took until 2014 before he "started to really spend time on research", setting Eyellusion up in 2015 and launching publicly the following year.

"I did think there was something we can do there that hadn't been done," he says. He was, by his own admission, untutored in the bewildering and often illogical world of the music industry but had noticed that touring was becoming the earnings catalyst for heritage acts. "With every instance of an announcement or a performance, a spike in the catalogue goes up, a spike in interest goes up and it truly is a way to get legacies passed to the younger generation," he says.

This, stating the obvious, was what estates lacked – the tour as a cultural focal point as much as a driver of income. He went to Los Angeles to meet some industry managers in the rock market about his hologram idea, among them Sharon Osbourne and Wendy Dio, widow of Ronnie James Dio (who had passed away in 2010).

"When I met with Wendy – it was a long meeting, like two hours – she said, 'You know, if we do do something, can you promise that Ronnie would be first?'" he says. "I am a huge, huge Ronnie James Dio fan and Dio fan. As a matter of fact, in my sixth-grade class picture I am wearing a Dio T-shirt. So it was a true dream to put that together."

Through LinkedIn, he got in contact with Scott Ross, who had founded visual effects and digital production company Digital Domain in 1993 alongside film director James Cameron and make-up effects creator Stan Wilson, with *Titanic* in 1997 serving as a blockbusting showcase for its work. Digital Domain had created the computer-generated likeness of Tupac for Coachella. Ross introduced Pezzuti to Chad Finnerty and they became business partners, with Finnerty serving as director of creative development.

The first project was a hologram of Ronnie James Dio that was created to perform one song at the Wacken Festival in Germany on 7 August 2016 with Dio Disciples, a band made up of former members of Dio (who are also managed by Wendy Dio). "When I first experienced the full production of Ronnie performing with his band as a hologram, I couldn't believe my eyes and ears," said Wendy. "We have been able to get Ronnie back up on stage where he belongs, ensuring that his music and memory live on."[43]

From that, Eyellusion raised $500,000. "That was proving the model and showing what we were capable of," says Pezzuti. A further funding round of $400,000 was used to work on a Dio show that could be toured. The hologram appeared at the Pollstar Awards[44] on 2 February 2017 in Los Angeles, with a world tour, under the title of *Dio Returns*,[45] starting in Helsinki, Finland on 30 November 2017.

"Ronnie was always wanting to experiment with new stage ideas and was a big Disney fan," Wendy Dio told *Rolling Stone*. "I am sure he is giving us his blessing with this hologram project. It gives the fans that saw Ronnie perform an opportunity to see him again and new fans that never got to see him a chance to see him for the first time."[46]

Chad Finnerty, speaking to *Revolver* in June 2019, termed it all "an illusion – a magic trick", saying that Eyellusion "is not really centered around technology" but rather is "focused on the content".[47] He said it was an arduous and involved process and it took "probably about two months per song" to create.[48]

Off the back of the *Dio Returns* tour, in May 2018 Eyellusion secured $2 million in seed funding from Thomas Dolan, board member of the Madison Square Garden Company, who also took on an advisory role at the company.[49]

Pezzuti says that money was used to update the Dio hologram and also to launch the *Bizarre World of Frank Zappa* tour. Pezzuti had met Ahmet Zappa, the co-trustee of the Frank Zappa estate, through a music lawyer acquaintance. "Ahmet and I hit it off and we became best buds," says Pezzuti. "He's my number two."

Speaking on the *Bob Lefsetz Podcast* in September 2019, Ahmet Zappa called the Frank Zappa show "a smorgasbord of awesome" and added that the source vocals they used were from a soundstage rehearsal his father had recorded in the 1970s.[50] "The benefit, actually, of the fact that we have Frank's vocals and his guitars to a click track meant that all the visuals can be done in time," he said.[51]

Ty Roberts was chief technical officer at Universal Music Group between 2016 and 2017 and then worked with Eyellusion as a technical consultant.

He says that having the soundstage audio was the critical ingredient in the Zappa hologram. "Because it is a live recording, it is his guitar with the right effects, so we have the proper wah-wah he used to play," he says. "His shows at that time were sometimes three or four hours. We didn't have the opportunity to get that but we got around two hours of music and a selection of songs that we thought were relevant today."

The fact that Zappa himself had spoken about holograms and even wrote about the possibilities of 3D technology in his 1989 autobiography, *The Real Frank Zappa Book*, was taken as pre-emptive approval by the estate. "As a kid, I was like 'what are you even talking about', but he walked me through what he was thinking," Ahmet Zappa told *Pollstar*.[52]

In a BBC documentary, Ahmet says his father was toying with the idea of a hologram as a proxy for his own touring activities. "Growing up, Frank was always sharing his big ideas with all of us kids," he said. "And one of the things that really stuck with me was the fact that he wanted to start his own hologram company in the sense that he could actually stay home and work on new compositions while a tour existed of himself out there in the world."[53]

He also told live industry trade title *IQ* that this hologram tour was merely bringing everything he talked about in his lifetime to its logical conclusion. "My father was an early adopter – of state-of-the-art recording equipment, digital, all kinds of technology," he said. "I feel, as his son, I'm completing something he started and didn't get a chance to finish. That was a big part of my motivation here."[54]

The emotional impact here for families grieving the loss of a parent, a partner or a sibling cannot be discounted when a person who has passed away is suddenly regenerated on stage. There is much discussion (covered in detail below) about the appropriateness or otherwise of this new strand of the estates business, but it is always important to remember these are real families approving these holograms and such decisions are not made lightly. "The first time I saw Frank [as a hologram] I burst into tears," Ahmet told a BBC documentary in 2019. "It's Frank with his band. It's him playing guitar. What son wouldn't want the opportunity to suspend disbelief for a moment, to feel like you could have your father back?"[55]

Pezzuti suggests that the hologram is the focal point of Eyellusion shows, but it is used sparingly, especially in the case of the Frank Zappa one, rather than being on stage for the duration of the show. This, he feels, is an important point of differentiation for the company and its productions. "We have a certain set up we call the Eyellusion Stage," he says. "We don't like the sole focus to be just on the centre of the stage. We like to surround what's going on with content. It keeps the fans engaged. There is a thing called 'hologram fatigue'. What that means is that if you just have the artist standing there with no action, the audience will get somewhat bored after they have debuted one or two songs. What we do is we actually find ways to keep it interesting for the 90-minute performance."

Roberts estimates that the Zappa hologram was only on stage for a quarter of the show's run time. "During the other 75 per cent of the show there are other visuals and he may appear in those visuals but in other forms – so as a hologram, as animation, as another character, different kinds of things," he says. "He is in the show but we are talking about animation. The lyrics of each song were interpreted visually by Ahmet Zappa and his video production crew. There was a 3D graphics company that was working with Eyellusion. Ahmet was interpreting his dad's stories and coming up with a visual creative brief for each song and then the 3D company would illustrate that song visually. In some cases, with the guitar solos in particular, Frank will appear as a hologram in the middle of all of this inside a special area of the stage."

Pezzuti says that, rather than take vocal stems from a deceased act's studio work, in the case of both Frank Zappa and Ronnie James Dio, they are drawing on isolated vocal tracks from live performances. "It just keeps that 'electricity' of a live performance there," he says. "I think once you get that studio track aspect you do lose some of why people go to see live shows."

Eyellusion announced in September 2018 that it had signed a deal with Primary Wave to create a hologram show for classical pianist Glenn Gould.[56] Gould does seem a curious choice for a hologram show especially given that he said "the concert is dead" and quit live performance in 1964 at the age of 32. The reason? "I detest audiences," he said. "Not in their individual components, but en masse. I think they are a force of evil… I find it a very chilling fact. It seems to me a rule of mob law."[57] At the time of publication, however, no tour dates for Gould had been announced.

Base Hologram

The spark for Base Hologram was exactly the same as it was for Eyellusion – Tupac at Coachella. They both wanted to take the same idea and make it bigger. "They did two songs and that's it?" said Marty Tudor, CEO of Base Hologram. "You teased me, but now I want to see a show."[58]

Base Hologram is a division of Base Entertainment, a live entertainment company with offices in Los Angeles, New York, Las Vegas, Houston and Singapore. It has put on shows such as *The Lion King* in Singapore, *The Million Dollar Quartet* (a musical about Johnny Cash, Elvis Presley, Jerry Lee Lewis and Carl Perkins), *Jersey Boys* and *Magic Mike Live*.[59]

Tudor previously ran a management company looking after actors, writers, directors and Hollywood executives and was involved in the sale of Madonna's label Maverick Records to Warner Bros.[60] In 2017, Tudor and Brian Becker, the chairman and CEO of Base Entertainment, set up Base Hologram.[61]

"It's not just going to see, if you will, a hologram just singing a bunch of songs, but to get a true feeling of the artist from the evening overall," Tudor tells me. "We do this with – and I'm hoping this is what you heard from the

391

estates you spoke with! – the utmost care and in extreme collaboration with the estates. Because we believe that: a) they are the guardians of the artist's legacy; and b) as much as I might think I know Roy Orbison or Whitney Houston or whomever it may be, I don't know them as well as the estates."

The technological approach that Base takes is something it regards as giving it a competitive advantage over a rival company like Eyellusion. It projects the dead artists onto a translucent screen in front of the other musicians on stage whereas Eyellusion projects its moving images onto Plexiglas.

Robert Ringe, the CEO of distribution and touring at Base, told *Rolling Stone*, "Our technology gives us an enormous amount of freedom. It gives us the ability to have the hologram walk onto the stage from the wings and interact with either the band, the orchestra, the musical director, the audience, etc."[62]

Base's first major production was *Callas in Concert*, putting the Greek opera star back on stage for a 105-minute show. The opening show of a world tour was on 23 September 2018 at the Jackson Hall at the University of California, Davis.[63] It involved a 55-piece orchestra and was based on original recordings of Callas, provided by Warner Classics, that had been digitally remastered.[64]

Ahead of the first Callas show, Tudor was keen to impress that this was both a creative and a technological barnstormer. "This is brand new proprietary technology and if we didn't have this type of groundbreaking technique at our disposal we wouldn't be doing this," Tudor told *Opera Wire*. "If we can't honor the spirit and legacy of these performers we would be doing everyone a disservice."[65]

Music, the company said, was just its way into the market, but at that stage it was already working on other categories, notably a dinosaur show with Jack Horner, the lead scientific consultant for the *Jurassic Park* movies, as well as plans to build shows around scientists, politicians, chefs and athletes.[66]

From there came the Roy Orbison show, followed by the joint-headliner with Buddy Holly, and then the Whitney Houston show, putting Base ahead in the market in terms of the number of dead musicians it has managed to digitally regenerate and tour around the world.

THE COST OF CREATING A HOLOGRAM AND GETTING IT ON THE ROAD

There remains a tremendous amount of secrecy around how much this all costs. It was speculated that the Tupac hologram at Coachella cost "somewhere between $100,000 and $400,000", a figure that is unhelpfully nebulous.[67]

The Tupac hologram was only for two songs, but building a full show – where every single song has to be shot, modelled and manipulated separately – is an enormously expensive undertaking.

Marty Tudor will not reveal the development and production costs for the shows Base Hologram puts on other than to say "it is in the millions of dollars". He does say, however, that from first signing a contract with an estate to having a show ready to go, it takes a full year, a period that has been reduced somewhat now that it has a number of hologram shows under its belt. "We spend an inordinate amount of time getting the tiniest detail of their movement down," he says of the holograms.

Ty Roberts of Eyellusion is, however, a lot more forthcoming on the level of upfront investment here. "Building that digital stage [for Frank Zappa] and figuring out what to do with it costs about $1 million or $1.5 million," he says.

A major drain on budget is often working and reworking the holograms to be as lifelike as possible in order to meet the estate's approval, each tweak ratcheting the pre-production costs up significantly. The Roy Orbison one, for example, had to have its sunglasses changed before the estate was completely happy. "Could it have been better?" says Chuck Fleckenstein of the Orbison hologram. "Oh, everything can be better. But in my opinion, it was wonderful."

He says the development time was actually two years until everyone was happy. "I personally was convinced, even in the rehearsal at the first show that I was at in London, that it was going to suck – for lack of a better word," he says. "And it wasn't until it went live that I just said, 'Oh my God! We pulled it off!' It was that kind of knife-edge with me."

The Buddy Holly hologram also caused problems in its development. Tudor says that only a handful of colour photographs of Holly are in circulation (which he claims were all colourised anyway), making the creation of a colour hologram very difficult. He says the fact that the hologram had brown hair shocked people initially because they presumed, from having seen black and white photos of Holly, that his hair was black. "It's those kinds of things that really make a difference and give authenticity to it all," says Tudor. "And authenticity is key for us. We do spend a lot of money and a lot of time on this because you'd be surprised how one little thing could make the difference between it working and not working."

Base operates by recording a lookalike actor performing each song to be used in the show. Getting the right body double takes time as they do not have to just look like the artist; they also have to move like the artist and lip-sync perfectly with the backing track.

Fleckenstein says getting the right person to double for Roy Orbison was no easy task. "We went through a couple of those," he says. "We worked on every aspect of the hologram and the recording of the holographic image and spent a ton of time on making sure that the sound was perfect. We handled that ourselves. That's how we delivered what you saw."

Pat Houston compares finding the right body double for a hologram to finding the right actor to play another famous individual in a film. She says this was the thought process she had to go through when the Whitney Houston hologram was being developed, especially given how close to the wire it went before she pulled the proposed hologram appearance on *The Voice*. "The music is there because it's Whitney Houston, but you have to find that person to embody her," she says.

Stephen Wadsworth is director of opera studies at the Juilliard School, the private performing arts conservatory in New York, and has a phenomenal CV in the classical world. He has directed operas at the Met, La Scala, the Royal Opera House in Covent Garden, the Vienna State Opera, the Netherlands Opera, the Edinburgh Festival and the San Francisco Opera.[68] Crucially, he also directed *Master Class*, Terrence McNally's play about Maria Callas, at the Kennedy Center in 2010 as well as its move to Broadway. Wadsworth was brought in by Base Hologram as creative director for *Callas in Concert*, both scripting and directing it. He says that it was a gruelling process to get the Callas hologram right. The Callas estate was, in his words, "extremely wary" of the idea anyway and it took several attempts to convince them to go ahead.

Base had put a call out for actors to play Callas. One of the people to show up was an Italian-born police officer from Connecticut who had grown up with people often remarking on how similar to Callas she looked. After her audition, Base was convinced it had lucked upon its Callas. Wadsworth was not involved in the first photoshoot and had put forward some other suggestions of singers they might consider, but Base was keen to push forward with its discovery.

Wadsworth calls the first photoshoot of the Connecticut cop "a disaster" and says he warned Base against sending the photos to the Callas estate. Base ignored his advice and sent the photos. The Callas estate said no. Wadsworth says he and Tudor spent 45 minutes on a call to the estate and its lawyers, convincing them that a reshoot using a different look would solve the problems. The estate eventually agreed.

The same body double was used for the second shoot, which Wadsworth oversaw. "She was remarkable – quite a brilliant person," he says. "She turned out not only to be someone who looked exactly like [Callas], but she was a singer [...] who is also a linguist. She speaks fluent English, French and Italian – the only languages that Callas ever recorded in. She was astonishing."

He says they worked for several weeks to get the shoot right, notably giving her a different hairstyle to the first shoot. "I talked to her throughout this shoot and we looked at angles," he explains. "It was clear that from the side – the jawline in particular was so alarmingly like Callas – that these side shots were going to be more valuable. I also figured if she had her head down and she looked up a little bit that these would work better."

Wadsworth says he showed photos from the new shoot to people from the opera world who knew Callas when she was alive. They were flabbergasted by how similar to Callas the double looked. He shows me two photos from the shoot, both in black in white. In one, the double is looking down with her eyes closed; in the other, her eyes are open and she is looking just off camera. The similarity to Callas is genuinely arresting. "We just wanted to get her into a position where literally it would shock the Callas people that it was Maria."

It worked. "They [the Callas estate] wrote back and they said, 'Absolutely – go ahead.'"

In August 2017, Wadsworth flew to Hollywood to direct a 10-day video shoot of the body double that would become the hologram. "It's a single-camera shoot and you have a fixed position that has to be at a certain distance from [the actor]," he explains. "So all of the camera work, such as it is, had to be [around] the way she moved. We had to choose, based on the way she was moving, how the cameras moved."

It all had to be shot in single-take chunks, usually 14–18 minutes in length. If there was a single mistake, it would all have to be shot again. "So she had to do a number, bow, receive applause, next number, receive applause, next number – some of them quite long – receive applause, walk offstage, walk back," he says. "All of that had to be in one take."

He says the double was as much of a perfectionist as he was, insisting on re-takes if she felt she had made even the most minor of mistakes. "She would do three takes in a row," he says. "She was a star. A brilliant, brilliant person."

The video was not the only part of the Callas production that proved laborious. Getting the sound right was equally challenging. They drew on her studio recordings going as far back as 1963; but making them fit a live context was far from straightforward. "To marry that in a live space with a symphony orchestra that's playing [is hard]," he says. "They had some idea that the orchestra was going to be able to play and accompany in a normal acoustic [setting alongside] this piped-in thing."

Base, he claims, was starting to get anxious about the costs involved and were not open to his calls to invest more money to get the sound as perfect as he felt the visuals were. This would, Wadsworth says, be a decision that would soon come back to bite them.

Because everything had to be scripted tightly to marry the visuals and the audio together, the technology would not allow for any improvisation or deviation from the performance. There was, however, some pseudo-spontaneity baked into the script in a knowing way, to fleetingly give the audience the impression that this was a real person on stage.

"There were a number of places in the script that I made where she interacted with live people," says Wadsworth. "She looked at the first violinist and pulled her dress back at a certain point and the first violinist had to say, 'Oh, no, don't worry about it.' And then she turned around and looked at the people and bowed to them. At the back of the scrim [the gauze used as a backcloth in a theatre] they saw the same thing that we saw up front, but they could tell when she was turning around and then they would tap their bows. There was a moment where she reached out her hand to the conductor and the conductor came and they would bow like this, not touching each other, and then at the end the conductor took Callas's hand and the image of Callas faded out."

Relishing talking about these little touches, he continues, "There were some beautiful things. There was a moment where she tore up a letter and she threw it up in the air and then we [finger snap] stopped the motion. She kept moving but the paper stopped falling. And then we started the next number and in the introductory bars of the next number, the paper came down in slow motion around her as she was looking around. There were some beautiful things that we got."

He says the audiences reacted well to these moments, gasping or laughing at the sheer audacity of it all. "She had great looks at the audience, where she would look at them and say, 'Stop!' and she put her hand [to indicate they should] stop talking," he says. "There was one number where the conductor began before she was ready. She put up her hand and the whole orchestra came to a stop. The audience would go, 'Wow!' It was a little bit meta. But it was also her, right? We were playing with it, but not a lot, not too many times. It all had, I think, a really appropriate subtlety. But it was just a question of teching it. They didn't have the money or they had allocated the money in such a way it wasn't budgeted for the tech end of things. And that became, I think something which compromised their ultimate product. But I think they learned. They were learning."

On the issue of faux-improvisation, even those who are working on the same hologram show do not always agree on just how this can be worked into a show and precisely how difficult or otherwise it can be to convincingly achieve this.

"It makes it easier to do a show with Frank Zappa as the artist because he did open it up to different possibilities," said Jeff Pezzuti on the artist's history of experimental and avant-garde music.[69]

"I don't think so," countered Ahmet Zappa. "I call bullshit on that! I think it's actually harder to do a show with Frank. There's so many real factors that go into doing a show and, unless you have someone who knows what the fuck they're doing, you can't actually have a Frank Zappa show!"[70]

When the hologram has been through the development and approval process, the costs involved in putting it on the road can be greatly lowered. Or it can be in some cases. The Maria Callas show involved a 55-piece orchestra and the Whitney Houston one had a full band as well as backing vocalists and dancers. This exposes a harsh economic reality for touring hologram shows. The genres of music that typically involve the most people on stage – classical with its orchestra and pop with dancers and a larger number of musicians – are less economically viable than a show based around rock'n'roll artists.

The Roy Orbison/Buddy Holly show, for example, used the same small live band for both acts and so touring overheads were significantly lower than they would be for the Houston or Callas shows. There are different economies of scale impacting here, but it is a fact that more shows can be packed into a tour because the "singer" does not need rest days to preserve their voice. Then there is the added fact that shows are unlikely to be cancelled due to the star falling ill, injuring themselves on stage or – and one cannot shy away from this reality of touring – pulling shows due to stress or excess.

"There is a cost element to it because you're not having to pay a diva," is the blunt summation of one record label executive who has worked with a number of hologram productions. "You've got the technology, you've got a band that is going to be paid whatever a backing band gets. So you've got that technology and that initial investment, but it's got to be relatively cheaper to run when it's on the road."

The fact they are now touring endeavours is the most significant development for estates as, finally, dead acts can go on the road where the lion's share of money is made today for heritage acts. Plus they can do something that normal live tours cannot – they can be replicated so multiple versions can, potentially, tour different parts of the world simultaneously. "You could have one permanently in Vegas and you could have it permanently somewhere else," says the same executive. "And could have one version touring Europe and another touring America and yet another touring Asia."

As the technology improves and companies like Base and Eyellusion become more experienced in what they do, the development costs of a hologram show should fall exponentially. Costs may rise again as shows become more ambitious and start to use artificial intelligence and deepfake technologies (which are both considered later in this chapter), thereby raising the entry costs again. This, however, will ebb and flow as new technologies are developed and normalised. The fact remains, however, that getting a straightforward hologram on the road in 2030 will be significantly cheaper and quicker to do than it was in 2018.

"Over the course of years, developers and artists are going to get better and better – and hardware/software is going to get better and better," says Travis Cloyd, the CEO and co-founder of Worldwide XR, an immersive media company focusing on augmented reality, virtual reality and mixed reality. "The quality of those assets is only going to increase and therefore get better. It's like this with many things – cellphones, TV. It could be any form of software and hardware – it evolves. I think holograms, digital humans and virtual beings are at the early, early stages and will evolve."

There is, however, a bigger existential issue for the business to consider here. Scarcity was always the blessing and curse of live music. A blessing in that ticket prices can be set to capitalise on the fact that the act is only in town for that one show; and a curse because the artist has to be in that one town for that one show. It is more than a philosophical conceit to say that hologram tours can negate scarcity and create a new type of ubiquity. Whether or not there is an inexhaustible audience for something like this – where hologram tours become franchised like burger bars and they do not fizzle out as a gimmick – is a whole different matter; but the important point to note, especially at this early stage in its development, is that it is *entirely possible*.

NEW INCOME, NEW AUDIENCES?

Hologram tours themselves, just like tours by living artists, make money in two ways – from ticket sales and from in-venue merchandise sales. The sums involved are not insignificant and this is the explicit pitch to estates.

John Simson is counsel at US legal firm Fox Rothschild and represents, among others, the estate of Muddy Waters. He says the estate was approached by an agent with a view towards putting together a Legends of Blues-style hologram tour that would also include B. B. King. "Obviously I was being directed to look at the numbers that Roy Orbison was doing – which were really quite surprising," he says. The estate at the time was, in his words, "still exploring" the idea.

Rolling Stone reported that the Huntington, New York date of the Frank Zappa hologram tour in the US in April 2019 had sold out and the rest of the tour had "sold well", with tickets at the top end selling for $125 each. The same feature added that the 2018 Roy Orbison hologram show was selling on average 1,800 seats per show.[71]

The companies behind holograms, and the estates involved with them, also argue that they do much more than make money at each venue they play. They can also push record sales and streams in the short-term as a slipstream effect of being on tour. Their evangelists also argue they will keep a dead artist's name in the public consciousness and potentially introduce the acts to new audiences. In doing so, they can ensure the longevity of the estate for future generations.

"I think that's a good argument to make," suggests Simson. "I think anything that's driving essentially mailbox money for the heirs of these estates is something to be interested in."

Ty Roberts refers back to his time at Universal Music and suggests that when he looked at its catalogue business he noticed that for a significant number of acts, their annual earnings, much of it from streaming, were declining each year. "What I was seeing was that, other than an artist passing away – which was not a great business model! – generally speaking the catalogue had a tendency to head downstream," he says. "Every year it was generating a little lower than the previous year."

There were occasional peaks for some catalogues, he accepts, around such things as a milestone anniversary or when a sync deal happened, but after a brief upswing, it would return to a natural state of slow decline. "What I realised was that the reason that was happening was because these people were not touring," he suggests. "They were not alive or they were not able to tour any more. There was nothing keeping them in the mindset of people except these anniversary dates."

He also says that Universal had historically not been deeply involved in the live side of an artist's income and so there was a mismatch between these parts of the business and how it thought about working and reviving catalogue. "There was," says Roberts, "this gap of knowledge and experience." This, he says, was the sell to estates and to labels – that a hologram would spike streaming interest in the catalogue and, more importantly, those could be recurring spikes every time the hologram toured.

Marty Tudor says that the first Roy Orbison hologram tour was timed specifically to come off the back of promotion for the *A Love So Beautiful* album in 2017 where Orbison's vocals were accompanied by the Royal Philharmonic Orchestra. In that regard, it was slipstreaming existing marketing activity, but Tudor claims that the tour revived interest in the album, especially globally. "When we first aligned with the Orbison estate, we went with them together to Sony and pitched them on the idea of doing that Roy Orbison album with the RPO," he says. "When do you ever get a posthumous release being supported by a tour? And consequently, that sold a ridiculous amount of units. I heard something like 300,000 units in the UK alone. That's extraordinary for a posthumous release."

A senior label executive concurs that holograms can help catalogue acts. "In some cases, we are a partner in those things," they say of hologram shows. "In other cases we might not be a partner at all, but we'll still work with the estate in amplifying that opportunity around our marketing."

One person utterly sold on the idea of the hologram tour is music lawyer Ken Abdo, a partner at the Minneapolis offices of Fox Rothschild. "My thesis is it's the next billion-dollar music business," he says. "So I'm very bullish on holograms."

He wrote a piece for *Variety* in July 2019 arguing this very point. "While it's still in a relatively early phase, holograms can protect (and perhaps immortalize) artists' legacies, keep audiences in venues, introduce younger generations to the artists, provide continued protection of artists' intellectual property and create revenue for artists' estates," he proposed.[72]

Roberts says that hologram shows can end up playing larger venues than the act did in the final years of their career. Part of that could, of course, be the novelty factor, but he suggests there is something more profound happening. He offers the Dio hologram tour as an example. "Eyellusion took it on tour and it did OK," he says. "It wasn't massively successful, but the reality is he was playing larger rooms as a hologram than he was at the time of his death!"

David Hirshland of BMG says the Buddy Holly hologram was a key component of a wider push by the estate to revive interest in his music and image. The visual side of Holly was, he says, as important as the audio side. "We felt that Buddy was the least recognisable of the big early rock stars and that the way to reintroduce him to the culture was not just through the music – which was an obvious way to do it – but also through getting his image out there," he says. "We're trying – not just through the music, but through who he was – to try to get people to recognise his dynamism as a performer."

Pezzuti, as one might expect of the head of a hologram company working with estates, is utterly convinced this is a sure-fire way to get the next generation of fans into the music of a deceased artist. "There's the lack of radio airplay, the lack of any way of really hearing music unless people are touring," he says. "And, at the same time, the artist doesn't make any real money unless you're touring. It becomes a twofold way to convince the estate. 'Hey, listen, this is a great way for your mom, dad, whoever, to get back out in the public eye, to get people inspired to hear the music, to get people to understand what the legacy is about. We can celebrate the legacy together.' We can get a new generation of fans to support it."

Those behind the hologram shows will often anecdotally say that they see a range of ages at their shows. Jeff Pezzuti, for example, spoke to *Rolling Stone* about the Dio tour and made a guesstimate about the audience's age. "We finished our 18th show last night, and maybe 15 per cent of the audience has been made up of kids 15 or younger," he claimed. "To me, it's amazing."[73]

While no granular data exists for precise audience demographic breakdown at such performances, I can only put forward my own anecdotal evidence from going to some of these shows.

On 24 October 2019, I went with my girlfriend Sonja to the *Roy Orbison and Buddy Holly: The Rock 'N' Roll Dream Tour* show at the Apollo in London. "We are easily the youngest people here!" exclaimed Sonja. From where we sat, the audience was almost exclusively people old enough to have seen Buddy Holly play in the flesh. Some couples had brought their children, but even they were in their fifties and already familiar with the catalogues of both acts. Sonja and I were still the youngest people in the stalls.

I subsequently saw *An Evening with Whitney* at the same venue on 10 March 2020. The audience this time was younger but they were around the same age as me, people who became fans of Whitney Houston in the 1980s. These shows appeared to appeal to existing fans and from my own experience of them they were not gateway concerts for new fans. These were very much exercises in nostalgia for those who grew up with these artists.

Jeff Jampol of JAM Inc puts it in even harsher terms. "It's another effect," he says when I ask him about hologram tours. "A lot of really smart people are putting a lot of money behind these tours and these companies. So what do I know? I do think it's going to be really interesting for a very limited time."

Can they, I ask, introduce old artists to young audiences? No, he says. Absolutely not. "I've gone to a couple of these shows," he insists, "and the median age of the attendees is dead. I think I skewed it down just by walking in the room."

Also in the camp of naysayers is Bill Zysblat, co-founder of RZO, who works with some of the biggest names in music and also represents the estate of David Bowie in business dealings. When I speak to him, I paraphrase the sales pitch of Ty Roberts, Jeff Pezzuti and others and ask him if he thinks hologram tours can shake other parts of an estate's business into new commercial life.

"I'm not so sure – and I'll tell you why," he says. "I have represented The Rolling Stones for over 40 years now and when The Rolling Stones come to town, the circus is coming to town. The news media talks about it and everybody's talking about it because they are going to make it a spectacle. I feel like if the day ever comes when The Rolling Stones hologram comes to town, it may sell tickets, but it won't necessarily be newsworthy. I think it's the newsworthiness that gets people to start streaming and playing their old records. I feel like the people who go to the hologram shows, they're self-selected; they are already fans who want to reminisce about the experience. Never say never, but I don't know if hologram tours will stimulate sales or streams."

He does, however, concede a little ground as he starts to think it through. "If you've got the Frank Sinatras of the world and you have a generation who's just never seen them, they may want to experience it through a hologram and that may be the impetus for them to start streaming," he says, but then caveats that by suggesting that any impact will probably be marginal. "I don't know if that moves the needle. I'd love to think it does because I'm on that side of the business, but I don't know."

The real unreal: the difference between a "hologram" and a hologram

The touring shows based around deceased artists like Maria Callas, Frank Zappa and Roy Orbison are commonly referred to as "hologram" shows, even though they are 21st-century updates on the Pepper's Ghost ruse. At best, these shows are hologram-like, but the nomenclature has stuck. They are more *allusion* than *illusion*.

The world of holography, however, has direct links to the music business stretching back several decades.

Professor Martin Richardson is head of the Imaging and Displays Research Group at De Montfort University in Leicester, UK. He has been working and researching in the field of holography since the 1980s, publishing the paper 'Mixed Media: Holography Within Art' in 1987.[74]

In 1994, he met and befriended David Bowie, who was greatly interested in his research. They worked together on a 30-minute experimental short in 1998

401

that was shot on 35mm film to show the potential of holographic film techniques. Richardson then helped create a 3D version of the cover photo of Bowie's *'hours…'* album in 1999, which appeared as an insert in 500,000 CD copies of the album.

"I think Bowie was fascinated because the big difference between AI [artificial intelligence] digital media and holography is the point of inter-action," said Richardson. "When you wear an augmented reality headset you have to enter that world. You are aware of the pixels, the limitations of the headgear and you end up having a limited experience. A hologram does not have to be turned on. There is an instant connection with your primal senses that goes beyond anything digital can offer. When you look at a hologram you are experiencing something there and then."[75]

The film they produced together sat unseen until January 2020, when it was finally shown at the National Space Centre in Leicester.[76] Short clips from the 1998 film, where Bowie pulled assorted poses, were also made available online on the De Montfort University YouTube channel.[77]

Richardson says that he is often approached by companies wanting him to create a hologram akin to what they might have seen in films but he has to patiently explain the science of what is and is not possible today. "There are physical limitations in physics and science which we cannot get around," he says. "We cannot focus a beam of light into thin air. You always need a point of focus. Part of my job is this: education is about disillusionment. So people come to me and after half an hour chatting with me about what a real hologram is and what it isn't, they go away more informed than perhaps they were."

Even though they are not creating holograms in the truest sense, he says he is not so concerned about the semantics used here by estates and companies like Base and Eyellusion. "For the average person in the street, they don't really care about the word 'holographic' – but it meets their fantasy halfway and produces its high-tech Pepper's Ghost gee-whiz factor," he says. "But it couldn't be further from the truth."

Richardson says that Bowie, when they worked together in the 1990s, had done plenty of research into the subject and was sharply attuned to the difference between true holograms and the illusions used on stage today. "I think he [Bowie] would have been horrified of the idea of using the Pepper's Ghost, given its current state and where it is the moment," he says.

Richardson is certain that, the more productions that the likes of Base and Eyellusion do, the more shows will become normalised and the more audi-ences will want the next level up from that which he says will come from light field technology.

He explains how the Bowie film was shot using a 35mm Mitchell film camera ("one of these big Hollywood movie cameras with Mickey Mouse ears") for which they created a new lens system. The camera was set on a track and moved 15 metres over the space of three seconds.

"As the camera moved, the lens moved," he says. "This enabled us to take in real 3D film of David doing his motions. We then had to transfer, frame by frame, that film onto a digital format, which we did using something like 200 CD-ROMs. We had to compact all of that into a coded programme for a machine, which is only just now online, that can produce a digital hologram. And instead of using pixels, we use hoggles – the holographic optical elements – which work in the same as lenses but on a microscopic level."

He stresses the end result was stereoscopic, meaning that unlike virtual reality technology, the viewer does not need to wear a special headset. "The actual 3D image of Bowie is standing in front and, as you move left to right, you activate the film," he says. "So in the hologram of him, he's moving his arm very slowly down and welcoming you to the scene on the hologram. And as you move the other way, he pulls you into the hologram."

This was all very time-consuming and costly, meaning they only produced short bursts of animation of around five or six seconds each.

The technology has moved on significantly since 1998, but the shooting and development process is still going to take a great deal of time and would be prohibitively expensive for a commercial company looking to resurrect a dead artist and have them perform a 90-minute show. Hence the visual techniques Base and Eyellusion draw on that give a suggestion of a hologram but without the lengthy and costly production process.

For now, cost and convenience will trump what the technology at its upper tier can achieve.

THE ONE-OFF SPECTACULAR OR THE AVA-TOUR?

Until late November 2017, holograms had been single-performance events – from Tupac at Coachella through Michael Jackson at the Billboard Music Awards and Ol' Dirty Bastard as well as Eazy-E at Rock The Bells. The *Dio Returns* tour changed all that, meaning a hologram for an entire show, rather than one or two songs, had to be created and a touring production put in place.[78]

Following Dio came what we might term ava-tours from Frank Zappa, Maria Callas, Roy Orbison, Buddy Holly (co-headlining with Roy Orbison) and Whitney Houston. These acts were all playing multi-date national tours in mid-sized venues that had mostly or completely sold out. Both the shows I attended in London were at the Hammersmith Apollo, which has a capacity (when in a full-seating configuration) of 3,632[79] and there were barely any empty seats at either show.

In his review of the Roy Orbison and Buddy Holly show at the Saban Theater in Los Angeles in September, industry writer Bob Lefsetz dialled down his normal opprobrium. With the average ticket price for the show being $55, he called it "not exorbitant" and said that it felt "like a regular concert". He did admit that in the first half of the show he could only watch the hologram for two songs after which his mind would drift off. However, as the evening progressed he became more effusive – something that one might not ordinarily expect from a writer whose calling card is his excoriating takedowns.[80]

Part of the first-time draw may have been morbid curiosity and it is unproven if these tours could sell out the same size of venues a second time round. The Roy Orbison hologram toured the UK once solo but the second tour was packaged up with a Buddy Holly hologram. There were certainly signs that these could be on tour as frequently as living heritage artists.

Marty Tudor says that Base cannot discuss the business terms it has with the estates of Roy Orbison, Buddy Holly, Maria Callas or Whitney Houston, claiming they all have non-disclosure agreements with the company. "We approach it as if they are our partner," is as much as he will reveal. "There is obviously a monetary split, but I cannot give you the details."

Jeff Pezzuti is slightly more open about how Eyellusion does things here, but still only makes the general terms of the deal structure public. "It's always a profit split – that is one of the big components of the deal," he says. "We basically fund it financially. So we build the entire show and that's basically our good faith investment. We don't ask for capital from the artists. We actually say, 'Hey, listen, we're going to take this thing on the road, we'll figure out the split.' There's always different revenue components. There are obviously [things] they're going to see that we won't see. They are going to see a spike in catalogue sales, streams will probably go up once the announcement is made."

He does, however, reveal that Eyellusion takes more than a cut of the ticket sales. "We put the merchandise together," he says. "There is a big merch component. It's really a success all the way around."

Howard King, lawyer for the Tupac estate, is sceptical that this is the great holographic cash bonanza that the companies here are presenting it as. "Has anyone actually put on a successful hologram tour?" he asks. While he accepts these shows can play to audiences in their thousands, he remains unconvinced that they can be profitable, given how expensive they are to develop. "I don't know if the cost has come down, but the cost was a big factor," he says, referring back to the time when the Tupac hologram was created. "So I'm not sure they make any money."

Of course the economic modelling and risk assessment for a one-off show will be different for a tour that can, theoretically at least, be on the road for ever. That said, none of the hologram companies would say if shows were profitable after going on tour. With any production that has enormous upfront costs, tours have to run for a long period of time before they can break even; although the fact remains that hologram tours do not have the same set-build time as a Rolling Stones or U2 tour, where a stadium will have to be booked for several days before and after the show to build and then dismantle the stage.

Equally, they can play more nights in any given week than a living band so there are not a multitude of dates on the tour that are written off as travel or rest days. This is industrialised touring, but recouping the initial investment is something that one tour of major cities in a couple of continents is unlikely to achieve.

Some estates are simply uninterested in making this gamble or seeing hologram tours as a recurring source of revenue. John Branca says the Michael Jackson hologram that appeared at the Billboard Music Awards in

2014 was never considered as a touring possibility. He is assured in his belief that the spectacle diminishes exponentially the longer the hologram is on the stage, holding firmly to the idea that it should not overstay its welcome. "I'm not a fan of hologram tours," he says. "They're fairly static. No hologram can create the same level of intensity and excitement over a long period of time that a live performance can. I think as a 5- or 10- or even 15-minute piece of entertainment, it can work – like it did for Michael Jackson on the American Music Awards. But for a 90-minute show? I don't think it would have the dynamism and excitement of a live show."

As far as the Ol' Dirty Bastard estate is concerned, the idea of taking the Rock The Bells performance and turning it into a tour is not a priority, but equally it is not being discounted entirely. Nicole Beckett of Four Screens Production says that the ideal option would be using Young Dirty Bastard again to play his father in the filming of the performance footage for a touring show just as he did for the Rock The Bells show. "The estate is lucky in that respect, because we don't have to find a person [who looks like ODB]," she says. "He's right there! It's just incredible how much he looks like ODB. It's just natural; it's not something that he's trying to do. He just is. We did that hologram and that was great. That was a one-off."

She does say, however, that they would have to start again from scratch as the technology has improved significantly from 2013. "We are interested in maybe pursuing something like a tour," she says. "We're looking at different companies and just seeing what those options are – and if there really is a market for that. It is a very expensive process – even if you have a doppelgänger."

An executive working in catalogue at a record label is less convinced that, even if these tours can turn a profit, there will be audience demand to go to large venues to watch the show as it tours the world. "Hologram companies definitely see that there's a niche there that they're going for," they say. "I think it's one of those things where you have to ask how long it will last. Will people want to do that for ever? Will they be as keen in 10 years' time to see Rod Stewart as much as they would be to see Whitney now? Or will they think that's a bit passé?"

YES, NO, MAYBE... THE ESTATES STILL TO BE SOLD ON THE IDEA OF THE HOLOGRAM TOUR

The major hologram companies regard the existing tours as proof of concept to take to other estates to sell them the idea. This, they will say while pointing at the ticket sales and spikes in streaming data, is what we can do for you.

Some estates will be wary for ethical issues, others will be hesitant as they think the technology is too reliant on gimmickry, while more still will be waiting things out until the next iteration – or the iteration after that – of the technology. Ultimately they will all want to see if this business is sustainable and if it raises the stock of the artists involved; or if there is a short-term lift that does nothing beyond its moment in the spotlight. There is a tension here between wanting to leave it long enough to catch the wave at its peak or leaving it too long and belly-flopping into shallow water.

Bill Zysblat of RZO is not discounting the idea entirely, but is also not hailing it as a runaway success or the shape of the future just yet. "From my conversations with Brian Becker at Base, he'd like to think it's cross-generational," says Zysblat. "From what I could tell, there are definitely older people who are bringing their kids to experience it. But I have not seen throngs of kids saying, 'I have to see the Roy Orbison hologram.' I think that's just because if you were born from 1980 on, you're the MTV generation. You've seen visuals of almost all of these artists. And while you might be impressed with the technology, by the third or fourth song, you're kind of like, 'Yeah, I get it.' But that doesn't mean it won't evolve into something a little more exciting."

Jamie Salter of Authentic Brands Group is coming from a similar position with regard to the development of an Elvis hologram tour. He has seen the technology, he says, but he does not feel it is at an advanced enough stage for the Elvis estate to get involved with yet. But, he suggests, it is getting close enough for him and his company to start to take it seriously. "We looked at it a couple of times [but did not do anything]," he says, but does not say which hologram shows he saw. "The technology is getting way better and I think that at some point we will see Elvis Presley back on stage. [When that happens] the answer is probably yes."

The chances of a Jimi Hendrix hologram tour getting estate approval is, however, slim. Janie Hendrix, CEO and president of Experience Hendrix, has seen hologram shows and been told how they work but remains unconvinced. "A recent one I saw in New York, it seemed very [pause] odd," she says. "There were a lot of glitches in the performance. So I don't know. I really don't. Maybe in a certain arena. But a lot of people want to use it on everything, like on commercials or on our tour. I just think it becomes gimmicky. Jimi used to talk about that. He didn't want to be a gimmick. And so to me, I think that's kind of gimmicky."

Josh Matas of management company Sandbox Entertainment makes light of the situation, saying the Johnny Cash estate has been approached about a hologram, but he chooses his words in a manner that does not commit the estate for or against the idea. "I've said to the lovely folks at Base Hologram that as soon as they can tell me how they project The Man In Black in black I'm interested in the conversation!" he laughs.

The Jerry Garcia estate, however, is outright opposed to the idea of creating a hologram for the former Grateful Dead leader. The fact that the shows have to be carefully scripted goes against Garcia's improvisational spirit, despite the fact that Frank Zappa was equally improvisational in his career and his estate was happy to create a touring Zappa hologram. Marc Allan of Red Light Management, who works with the Garcia family, says,

The family and I have been approached, we've done demos, we've seen it a number of times. Yes, the technology is there. But to me, Jerry Garcia and the hologram model are very odd bedfellows because you've got an artist where the core of him was as an improviser, as a creator, creating something new every night, something different every night. The core model of the hologram business is presenting this thing in front of you that's, in essence, lifelike and that's performing and that feels like they're performing what's in front of you.

The amount of money that would have to go into modifying the behaviours of the artists to match the music that would have to be different every night to capture the core [would be enormous [...] I could pop a hologram out there and he could play the same show every night. The hologram could go through the same [routine] with live musicians around and that could be that. But that's, in essence, the antithesis of who he was as an artist. The model doesn't work for everybody. In my opinion, the core elements of what made Garcia special aren't highlighted in a presentation like that.

It is no surprise to learn that the estate of Nick Drake is not even vaguely entertaining the idea of a hologram of the singer who, like Glenn Gould, had a difficult relationship with live performance. "To go to a virtual reality Nick Drake event is just mind-bogglingly hilarious," says Cally Callomon, who runs Drake's estate. "He was meant to play at the Troubadour in Los Angeles [in the early 1970s] and didn't go. I think it was Joe Boyd's [Drake's producer and the person who signed him] idea to put a cardboard cut-out of him on stage to try and make a virtue out of the fact that with Nick Drake you can't see him so here is a life-size cardboard cut-out of him with a guitar on stage and then play back the album. That would be a good virtual tour! A cardboard cut-out on stage and you listen to the entire album."

For floating voters, actually seeing a hologram in action will almost certainly do one of two things: it will convince them it is phenomenal and should be embraced; or it will convince them it is truly awful and should be avoided at all costs.

Classical music executive Costa Pilavachi works alongside both the Athens and Epidaurus Festival as well as the Greek National Opera, and was considering bringing the Maria Callas hologram show to her – and his – homeland of Greece. But, he says, he needed to see the full show for himself before he could make a decision either way. "I haven't seen it, but I was going to bring it to Athens," he says when we speak in summer 2019. "We decided in the end not to. I didn't have a chance to see it and I got cold feet. If I brought it and it was embarrassing, it would just look really bad."

Holly Foster Wells of the Peggy Lee estate was still in two minds about the idea when I ask her if it is something she had considered. Her answer captures the mix of intrigue and dubiety that many estates feel about the idea. "It's not something I have looked into yet, but it's absolutely something I will consider if it's tasteful," she says. "There's some things where you have to think, 'Does this feel creepy? Does this feel strange?' I've seen it done both ways, actually, where I'm like, 'Wow, this is amazing!' And then other times like, 'Oh!' It just leaves you wanting the real thing that much more. But I'm absolutely open to it."

Linda Ramone says that, were she to be approached about doing one for Johnny Ramone, she would be fully on board. Whether the estates of the rest of the Ramones would be interested is something she chooses not to even speculate on, making her interest purely academic. For the moment, at least.

"Oh, I love holograms!" she says, audibly excited about the idea when I ask her about it as a possibility. "I think they look great. Ahmet Zappa just did Frank Zappa and he said it was amazing. I still haven't seen it yet, but I'm looking forward to seeing it. I think it's great. Listen, it's the same thing. Whoever doesn't like it doesn't have to go see it. But it's open to people who want to go see a hologram. I think it's a really cool idea. And if you can get it looking amazing and sounding amazing, it's definitely something I would be interested in."

This is arguably something she sees as a logical extension of the cartoon image of the Ramones that they themselves created in their lifetime – a next-generation form of trashy pop culture that the band both wallowed in and regurgitated throughout their career. They were caricatured on their record sleeves, notably *Acid Eaters* in 1994 and *Road to Ruin* in 1978, and it is not too big a leap from there to a hologram, complete with digitally scuffed sneakers and a "GABBA GABBA HEY" placard. Within the gonzo world of cartoon delinquency and the B-movie references that fuelled the Ramones, one does wonder what would be rejected for being too much in bad taste.

SONIC BOOM AND STAGE FRIGHT: GETTING HOLOGRAMS TO SOUND RIGHT AND WORK WELL ON STAGE

The idea of a hologram and its performing reality are, it has to be stressed, two very different things.

Getting it looking right is contingent on the quality of the body double – and of course not every estate has a child who is, excuse the pun, a dead ringer for their father, like the Ol' Dirty Bastard estate, or has the serendipity in casting of the Maria Callas estate – as well as the technological capabilities of the hologram company creating it. That, however, is only half the battle.

Getting it sounding right is the crucial other part of the equation and this is the element that gathers the most criticism or teeth-grinding from its critics.

Jessica Thompson, coming from the perspective of a mastering and restoration engineer as well as an audio preservationist, has few positive things to say about hologram shows as a sonic experience. When we speak, she says that she had been to see the Roy Orbison and Buddy Holly show in the US ("just out of morbid curiosity") and then gives it both barrels. "I was horrified," she says. "I could not stop laughing. But it was horrible. I could not stop thinking about what a train wreck it was."

She slowly works through everything she had a problem with or found to be severely lacking. The first was the backing band that played for both sets. "You don't put a shabby backing band [out there]," she sighs. "I wanted them to be in costume, I wanted this transporting feel. But whatever. What would Buddy Holly think of that? Give them another 10 or 20 years and maybe the technology will provide something different. But they have to figure out what they're doing with it too. Are you meant to be transported? Or is this like Chuck E. Cheese[81] but with a hologram?"

She reserves the bulk of her disdain, however, for how it all sounded to the audience. Working as an audio professional, she will be more attuned to the flaws than the average audience member, but was aghast at how poor she considered the sound to be. "The thing you miss is the room," she says of where she felt the major problem lay. "You can fake the sound of the physical space. People do it all the time with fake reverbs. But for someone with my listening skills, I'm really sensitive to if the music feels like it's meant to be in that space. You can tell when a recording of Buddy Holly isn't quite matching the acoustic space that I'm in."

For her, the psychological cost of this audio shortfall was that it shattered the illusion that the visuals had worked so hard to create, reminding her again and again that this was all a digital creation, not even allowing her to suspend disbelief for a second. Because the visuals and the audio were so mismatched, she says, each pulled the other down. "The thing with the Buddy Holly hologram is I kept trying to make eye contact – especially when you're seeing someone who's a heartthrob-type artist," she says. "I want to make eye contact and feel like he sees me and he's singing to me. He was just singing through me – and that's a weird thing."

She adds by way of conclusion, "It really comes down to the physics of a live performance versus a recorded performance. We can throw reverb to emulate different spaces and you can play around with EQ [equalisation] to mimic distance or closeness; but I think, ultimately, there's just something about air moving in space that has not yet been able to be replicated in that holograms-plus-live-performance format."

This was for a rock'n'roll show that was only dealing with a limited number of sound sources – the studio vocal stems for both Roy Orbison and Buddy Holly, and the live band comprised of drums, guitar, bass, keyboards and backing singers.

In sharp contrast to this, Stephen Wadsworth, who worked on the Maria Callas hologram, lays bare just how difficult it was to get right for a classical performance that includes a 55-piece orchestra. For him, it fell apart for two main reasons: cutting corners at the rehearsal/development stage; and the show production not being adaptable to the unique specs of the different venues it was booked into on its tour. These opera houses are designed

acoustically for unamplified instruments and voices. Taking a digital recording of a soprano voice into ornate venues where amplified voices are
generally frowned on was the nail that punctured the whole production.

Wadsworth claims he was constantly telling Base to invest more in
research and development before the production went on tour but he was
overruled. "We went into a couple of auditoriums where we put it up in front
of an audience but it was still problematic," he says. "The sound was too
tinny and too electronic."

He feels the only way the sound could have worked was if it was mixed to
the acoustic requirements of each venue the show went to, but this could
have taken days to get right, meaning a block booking of venues for long
periods of time that would have been economically unviable for the show
given its development costs and touring overheads. One option could have
been running the shows as long residencies in a particular city, but this is still
untested in the hologram touring world, where typically it plays one city and
moves on the next day. No one, it seems, is prepared to test the market to see
if lengthy residencies would work.

"You could play two weeks of the Met [in New York] or two weeks in La
Scala [in Milan] in a summer festival situation," he proposes. "Those are
the kinds of ways that you would be able to guarantee the best integrity in
the sound."

The fundamental issue, as far as Wadsworth is concerned, was that Base
was skilled in rock productions and Las Vegas-style spectaculars but was not
attuned to the specific requirements of a classical show. "I think the audio is
so much more of an issue with classical music because it is meant to exist in
an acoustic [environment] and not be piped in," he argues. "And then
suddenly you've got a big orchestra and you have to pipe them in and you
have to seat them in a way behind the receptor scrim of the hologram. We
see through the scrim naturally if the figure isn't in front of black and then
see what's behind it. Which actually I came to sort of love – being able to
see through her."

Because it was a large production with many musicians on stage, it did not
fit into different venues in a consistent manner, which Wadsworth feels
compromised the look of the show. At points, the orchestra had to be split
into two parts (something that is typically verboten in classical music) to fit
everything on stage, and the lighting then became a recurring issue.

At one production he attended in Los Angeles, the appearance of the
Callas hologram – because of the way the production was slotted into the
venue – was a damp squib. "I walk into the theatre and the stage right curtain
is a third drawn over the orchestra," says Wadsworth. "And then she just
appeared here instead of doing the whole walk out. So you missed all of the
footage of what she did in this part, where she turned to the audience and
waved or when she nodded."

He suggested an artistic director go on the road with the show to be able
to rework the production for the stage layout in the different venues – but his

advice was not followed. Ultimately, he feels, there was a misunderstanding within Base of the genre they were working with here.

"Because the people who are producing these events are essentially people who [pauses, choosing his words carefully]... the teams are pop music teams," he says. "I think they're amazing that they took this on. They invested heavily in it – for them, for what they thought was a lot. But what they found is that, because of the live orchestra and the relative niche marketing of a classical musician relative to someone like Roy Orbison – not to mention Roy Orbison doubling up with Buddy Holly – that this was going to be something where the financial return can't begin to match the investment for a very long time. And that was only if they did very smart booking."

Base wanted the validation that came with booking into celebrated classical music venues – but this was the very thing that undermined the show night after night. Wadsworth says,

> They went to the BOZAR in Brussels. They went to Salle Pleyel in Paris and they played a couple of times. I mean, the Coliseum [in London] is like a barn, right? It's a crazy place. And it's a place from the majority of seats where you are going to get a distorted view of [the stage]. You can't go up too high, you can't go out too wide, all this kind of thing. So there was a lot of R&D that needs to be perfected. And there's a lot of sound technology that may indeed not exist yet that will be necessary to the shoo-in success of a classical music event.

NPR reviewed the Callas show on November 2018 at the Moss Arts Center in Blacksburg, Virginia and picked up on these audio issues. "One overall problem is that the voice doesn't sound like it's coming from a human body; it's somehow all over the place, radiating out of loudspeakers," it said.[82]

For rock music, the audio issues are much more straightforward and the shows are booked into venues well used to dealing with similar productions. Ty Roberts says the production issues with the Frank Zappa hologram tour were all ironed out during several weeks of rehearsals with the live band. Getting the interaction between the band and the visuals was the real challenge and having the acoustics fit the venue was incidental and not the huge stumbling block it was for the Callas tour.

"The band play live to a click track that was taken from the original recordings," explains Roberts of the Zappa production. "The click track is fed to the drummer so they can be on beat with the click track and the other guys played to the click track to be on time and to pick up the changes in the song. Each one of those timing instances is a major visual change on the digital stage – so essentially they have to synchronise their performance. The music must sync to the video. But it is hard to do that when you have improvisational band members!"

Even if a production works perfectly in technical terms – where the sound and the visuals run seamlessly together in whatever venue the show comes to – there is still the public's reaction to contend with. There are huge ethical and moral issues for hologram shows to confront, with accusations of insensitivity and crassness being thrown at them. For shows that trade in digital humans, the human response of the public can be formidable.

THE CRITICAL BRICKBATS: NAVIGATING THE ETHICS OF DIGITAL NECROMANCY

All of the holograms of deceased artists to date have been created with the total approval of the estates involved and often with their full input. The message this sends out is that the family and heirs are happy for this digital reawakening and that they do not regard it as an abomination.

However, the critics and the fans may react very differently, showing two different sets of moral compasses giving out wildly contradictory readings.

Of all the different component parts of the estates business – from releasing unfinished recordings to putting music in washing powder ads – the hologram is, by some considerable distance, the most controversial.

Terms like "sacrilege",[83] "bad taste"[84] and "a creep factor"[85] have been used to describe them. Perhaps the most damning term comes from music critic Simon Reynolds. "On an ethical and economic level, I would liken it to a form of 'ghost slavery'," he told the *Guardian* in 2019. "That applies certainly when done without the consent of the star, [but rather] by the artist's estate in collusion with the record company or tour promoter. It's a form of unfair competition: established stars continuing their market domination after death and stifling the opportunities for new artists."[86]

The phrase "ghost slavery" is partly a semantic back reference to Pepper's Ghost, but it is the deployment of the word "slavery" that really makes the reader gasp. It is unquestionably a provocative word – and some will certainly see the casual use of "slavery" here as inherently problematic and insensitive – but it seemed to strike a chord in 2019 as a multitude of hologram tours were happening at the time. There was a feeling among certain critics and members of the public that these shows were happening in increasing numbers and no one was trying to unpick the ethical and moral problems bound up in them.

The reviews of some of the major hologram tours were mixed to say the least, some offering tentative praise and others focusing on how weird and wrong they found it all.

NPR in 2018 referred to the Maria Callas hologram as "surprisingly life-like, and literally electric", adding there were moments in the show "that felt unsettlingly real".[87] The *Chicago Sun-Times* in its review of the Callas hologram ahead of its appearance at the Lyric Opera House in September 2019 called it "lovingly crafted".[88]

The reviews of the Whitney Houston hologram show when it opened in the UK in February 2020 were considerably less hesitant in their assessments. Jan Moir of the *Daily Mail* saw the opening night of the UK tour at

2,721-capacity Sheffield City Hall on 25 February 2020. She laid her criticism on with a trowel – calling it a "ghoulish spectacle of this spectre", saying Houston in digital form looked like "a plasticised dolly" and bemoaning "this farrago of a show".[89]

In part reviewing the audience as much as she was reviewing the show, Moir continued, "There's a big dude in the front row who films nearly the whole show on his phone; capturing an image of an image, a palimpsest of fakery, a hollow trophy of something that never was. Whitney doesn't care. She sings 'I Have Nothing' and some fans start dancing in the aisles, lost in the moment, as if they have caught Whitney-fever. Has everyone gone mad?"[90]

The *NME* gave the Manchester date of the tour on 28 February three out of five stars and, again, reviewed the audience as much as it reviewed the show. "While Houston's stunning, soulful vocal pyrotechnics cut through the artifice, it's often more interesting to watch how the crowd reacts to the hologram than what's onstage," it said. "They clap after each song (which initially feels akin to saying 'Thank you' to a self-service checkout)."[91]

Meanwhile, the *Spectator* called the London date, on 10 March, "grimly compelling". It added for good measure, "In death, as in life, she continues to be an object for others to make money from."[92]

The biggest backlash faced by any hologram show, however, came even before it had been created. Such was the ire it provoked that it was quickly cancelled and apologies issued.

In October 2018, it was announced that an Amy Winehouse hologram tour was being planned for the following year. Her family was directly involved with Base Hologram, who were creating it. "To see her perform again is something special that really can't be put into words," said her father, Mitch, in a statement. "Our daughter's music touched the lives of millions of people and it means everything that her legacy will continue in this innovative and groundbreaking way."[93] On top of that was the news that the tour would raise money and awareness for the Amy Winehouse Foundation, the charity set up in her name to help young people with addiction issues.

Winehouse had passed away in 2011 and it was repeatedly stated by critics that this all felt too soon. "For some this is a celebration of a great and much-missed musician," wrote Laura Barton in the *Guardian* following the tour's announcement. "Others argue that an artist who loathed touring and hated fame should be allowed to rest."[94]

Vanity Fair let its headline do most of the heavy lifting here. "Please Don't Let This Amy Winehouse Hologram Tour Be Real," it said.[95] The *NME*, meanwhile, collected fan outrage from Twitter. "This Amy Winehouse hologram tour is a terrible idea," tweeted one. "Didn't y'all exploit that woman enough when she was alive?" Another tweeted, "Like she hasn't been exploited enough??! Let her rest in peace and stop tarnishing her legacy." A third added, "Amy Winehouse's estate is literally doing everything they can to disrespect her legacy postmortem."[96]

More stories about the creation of the hologram leaked out as the story's media and social media coverage increased. In early 2019, *GQ* revealed that an LA actor, speaking anonymously, was auditioned for what she believed was a planned biopic about Amy Winehouse. It turned out to be a casting for the hologram show by Base. The different rounds of her auditions included having her photo taken, being weighed and measured and being given YouTube links to performances by Winehouse of 'Valerie' and 'Rehab' and being asked to replicate them and "really hone in on Amy's nuances".[97]

The actor did some digging and found that some of the team she met at the different audition stages were employed by Base, including CEO Marty Tudor and Gary Shoefield, the company's EVP of content development. She asked if she was being auditioned for the hologram tour but the person she spoke to "just shut it down and didn't want to talk about it".[98]

She told *GQ*, "I don't think I would have auditioned had I known that it was for the hologram tour. I almost feel like, had Amy known about this when she was alive, she would have never wanted something like this to be done. There are other ways that you can celebrate Amy's music and life, instead of getting a body double to recreate her."[99]

It took until late February 2019, after the *GQ* piece ran, for the public and media uproar to force the hands of both the Winehouse estate and Base Hologram. In a statement issued to the press, it was confirmed that the Winehouse hologram was now "on hold". The statement referred to "some unique challenges and sensitivities" in how it was seeking to remember the singer "in the most celebratory and respectful way possible".[100] Base, however, said in a Twitter posting on 20 February 2019 that it was not cancelled completely and that it was merely pausing the project until it could "determine the best path to a creatively spectacular production that would properly honor Amy's legacy at its highest caliber".[101]

One senior executive at a record company argues that it is all down to timing and how far removed the hologram tour is from when the artist actually died. The further we are in time from their death, the more acceptable a hologram becomes. The Amy Winehouse hologram tour was, they believe, simply too soon and emotions were still raw, especially given the manner of her death and how young she was. The release of the *Amy* documentary in 2015 also served as a stark reminder of the extreme psychological toll on her as her private life as well as her addictions and other problems were all played out in the public eye.

"Time is a major factor in this," they say. "Nobody seems to be complaining about Elvis Presley's posthumous life. The Whitney Houston hologram tour to me is marginal. It's a strange thing, isn't it? Artists are two things – they are people and they are products."

When we speak in April 2020, I ask Marty Tudor about the Amy Winehouse hologram, the outcry around it and its eventual postponement. "What they don't get is that we're trying to celebrate that artist," he says by way of defending Base's original intent with the show. "So bad on me if I present Amy Winehouse as she was in the end. Frankly, I wouldn't do that. I have no interest in doing that. I could probably say 80 per cent of artists have had some sort of problem, whether it's alcohol, drugs, whatever; but that's not what their genius is about. Their genius is about their art. And that's what we want to celebrate with Amy."

He then says that the real problem in trying to put the show together was not an ethical one, but rather a licensing one. Base, it turns out, was having problems clearing the music for the show. "When you do these things, you have to get the rights to a lot of different areas of their life: you need their name and likeness rights; you need music publishing rights; you need master rights," says Tudor. "That can be very, very complicated. So it became pretty daunting pretty quickly to us and we thought, all right, between the backlash that we're getting and the difficulties we're having, we'll just put it on hold for the moment and let it sit and we'll work through it."

I also ask him about the public criticism and ethical uneasiness about holograms of dead pop stars in general. He is, as one might imagine of the head of one of the biggest hologram companies in the market, defensive on what Base does and why it does it. He responds,

> Here's what I say. I respect everybody's opinion. Everybody's entitled to their own opinion and their own likes and dislikes. I don't agree with them, obviously. Social media has given literally everyone a voice. And it's the naysayers, they are the ones that jump out and make the noise. If you look at them, if you count them, while they may have the loudest voice, they are far from the majority typically. If I'm wrong about that, then you wouldn't have been in a full theatre [to see the Buddy Holly, Roy Orbison and Whitney Houston shows].

I mention that the shows I saw appeared to have all sold out, which – beyond the moral debates – shows there is an audience for it. "And we're experiencing that pretty much everywhere," says Tudor. "I respect somebody's voice, just like I expect someone to respect mine – but there's always somebody that doesn't like something."

Jeff Pezzuti from Eyellusion is, unsurprisingly, equally defensive of what his company does here. He says he treads sensitively when speaking to estates about creating a hologram of a particular musician. "What you're doing is you're talking about bringing back somebody from the quote unquote dead," he says. "What we like to say is that it's a celebration of the person's legacy."

As far as Jeff Jampol of JAM Inc is concerned, the moral and ethical conundrums about creating a hologram show are immaterial. He just believes that the technology is not yet at a stage to do justice to the artist that the show is supposed to be celebrating and whose legacy it is supposed to be extending. His reservations are technological rather than ideological.

"The issues [with holograms] are several-fold," he says. "One is that the effect is not that special yet. It's not that good. To me one of the secrets of rock'n'roll – and I use that term broadly, whatever genre there is – is the proximity and the spontaneity. You're undergoing a shared moment. It's like, 'Oh my God! There's Mick Jagger! He's looking right at me! He's looking at me, he's looking at me. What's he gonna do?' With a quote hologram unquote, there's no proximity and there's no spontaneity. What it really is, is an expensive ticket to an uncomfortable seat to watch a movie. And the movie is technically limited."

WHERE THERE'S A WILL THERE'S NO WAY: THE CLAUSES THAT CAN APPROVE OR PREVENT THE HOLOGRAMS OF TOMORROW

The holograms created so far have had to navigate all manner of rights issues – covering the songs as well as the artist's own name, image and likeness – and were given approval by the estate and the heirs who serve as the posthumous voice for the artist. The Frank Zappa estate, for example, can point to his interest in hologram technology in his lifetime and take this as proof that he would have enjoyed being turned into a hologram.

Having the family approval is also key in assuring fans that a hologram is fitting and respectful, although Mitch Winehouse saying he approved the hologram of his daughter was not enough to quell the public opposition to it.

There is proxy consent underpinning this as the technological possibilities of today were not completely known to the artists reborn as holograms in their lifetime. They could not possibly have anticipated such a digital renaissance and voiced approval or disapproval.

Now, however, living artists know what is possible and therefore will be making their thoughts on it known – both informally (in conversations with family members) and formally (in legally binding documentation). Prescient artists will be making wills not just carefully outlining who gets what, but also what can or cannot be done using their name, their image and their copyrights after they die.

At a press event announcing his *Farewell Yellow Brick Road* tour in January 2018, Elton John was asked if he would consider an eternally touring afterlife in holographic form. "We were laughing about that," he said. "I said to my eldest son, 'When Daddy dies, promise me there won't be a hologram of me going around the world doing concerts.' That's the last thing I want. It's like doing a duet album with someone who's dead. I think Barry Manilow did one! It's so spooky. [...] Who knows. They may go broke and they'll put me back on the fucking stage! I think that's a bit freaky."[102]

Even though he died without leaving a will, the fact that Prince had repeatedly and publicly expressed his opposition to holographic technology was used to derail plans to have him appear on stage posthumously as a hologram. In February 2018, it was being reported by *TMZ* that Justin Timberlake's performance at the Super Bowl halftime show would feature a hologram of Prince, in part because it was happening in his hometown of Minneapolis.[103] The story was widely re-reported by other media outlets as a done deal.

Sheila E., who had played with Prince for many years, tweeted, "Prince told me don't ever let anyone do a hologram of me. Not cool if this happens!" This was followed up by another tweet that said she had spoken to Timberlake and was assured that a Prince hologram would not appear at the show. "Family, I spoke w/Justin 2nite and he shared heartfelt words of respect for Prince & the Purple fans," she tweeted. "I look 4wrd 2 seeing what I'm sure is going 2 be a spectacular halftime show. There is no hologram."[104] Prince did make it into a cameo of sorts at the Timberlake show, with an image of him being projected onto what *Forbes* described as looking like "a giant bedsheet".[105]

The year before, Prince's sister, Tyka Nelson, hinted that the estate was considering a hologram of him. "A hologram could be done as long as it is of excellent quality," she said. "It would have to allow the fans to experience Prince in the way he allowed us to experience his music."[106]

In both instances an old interview with Prince was dug up to show that he was opposed to the very idea of holograms and that the creation of one would have gone against his deeply held beliefs and opposition to the technology.

In a 1998 interview with *Guitar World*, Prince made it clear he would not want a virtual reality incarnation made of himself, nor would he want to have other musicians rework recordings from his vault. "That's the most demonic thing imaginable," he said. "Everything is as it is, and it should be. If I was meant to jam with Duke Ellington, we would have lived in the same age. That whole virtual reality thing... it really is demonic. And I am not a demon. Also, what they did with that Beatles song ['Free as a Bird'], manipulating John Lennon's voice to have him singing from across the grave... that'll never happen to me. To prevent that kind of thing from happening is another reason why I want artistic control."[107]

Prince did not explicitly mention holograms in the *Guitar World* interview, but the testimony of Sheila E. has been taken as clear evidence that a Prince hologram would go against his deepest wishes, and this testimony will be used again and again if rumours of a Prince hologram do the rounds in the future.

This was all anecdotal evidence, but artists today are having clauses put in their will either approving or expressly forbidding their rebirth as a hologram after they die. "If the artist cares about these things, their wishes should be respected after they pass," says US music lawyer Jeff Liebenson. "But how do you write it? No one would have written a clause about holograms 15 years ago. Now they know to put in a clause about holograms. But guess what, they don't know to include this other stuff that still hasn't been developed but that will come about in another five years. Maybe you could write something that's more along the lines of guidelines or principles to be interpreted by a committee in the future. But, of course, that also means it'll be a little fuzzier and a little bit more subject to interpretation. You can't be black and white about the future. We don't even know if there will be one!"

Ty Roberts offers a general template for what this "virtual reality artificial intelligence will" could look like. "You write up, essentially, the rules about how you wish your future [self will behave]," he proposes. "You could say that you don't want anything and that's fine. But if you wish to participate in the future, here's some ground rules about what you'd like to see [your heirs] do. That could be very sophisticated like, 'Please do not engage in activities that are not consistent with my behaviour in my mortal life.' One could sit down and think about that and it would be very interesting to create such a thing."

An executive in the catalogue department of a record label who deals with many legacy artists and estates says they have not seen a specific "no hologram" clause in a will, but suggests it is only a matter of time before it becomes a thing some artists insist on in legal documents. The executive says some are already speaking to their team about what they will and will not agree to.

"Several years ago I went to a demonstration of a hologram with a particular artist and they said, 'In no way, shape or form are you going to make a hologram out of me,'" says the executive. "I do know of artists who have specifically said, 'I do not want to be involved in that whatsoever.' Specifically holograms. It's interesting. With AI, there was a specific artist who said, 'That would actually interest me. Hologram, no. But AI, yes.'"

Jessica Thompson also feels that such clauses are an inevitability. "I can imagine that artists today are going to have to outline in their wills or their legal documents saying, 'I don't want to be deepfaked into a TV show,'" she says.

When I speak to those working in the world of holograms, they all accept that this is coming and it could have a significant impact on the types of projects they work on – or, more specifically, do not work on – in the near future.

Jeff Pezzuti argues that these clauses will be a knee-jerk reaction in the short term, but as the technology develops and what hologram tours can do expands significantly, the dissenters will gradually start to acquiesce. "I think at this point, probably yes," he says of artists putting such clauses in their wills. "But what ends up happening is it becomes a very accepted form of media. We've done this throughout our entire history of music." He adds, "I think that at this point, because it's very new and we're trailblazing and pioneering this whole aspect of touring something like this, you do have initial pushback; but at the same time, you can see the acceptance."

Ty Roberts argues that, quite simply, the onus is on living artists to adequately prepare for this technology – and all variations on it – and set out terms and conditions in their will before they die. "The creative planning for what happens to your works after you have passed should really be worked out by the person while they are still alive," he says.

Travis Cloyd of Worldwide XR regards this all less as a speed bump for technology companies and more as a necessity for anyone working with an estate. "A hundred per cent it needs to be included within their will," he says. "They need to be aware. I think we're at this stage right now where people are still unfamiliar with how far this hologram or digital asset can go. I think over the coming years, it'll be more recognised in our life that this is occurring, that these technologies are evolving and that some of the biggest companies in the world are spending money on developing tools and techniques to allow for this. If they don't include it in their will today, then they are making a mistake, and they eventually should because it's already here."

He argues that this is not just necessary for holograms but is equally necessary for what follows after. A "future use" clause in a will should, he believes, be a basic requirement.

> [The hologram] is one small piece of the pie. Putting those assets in gaming, putting those assets in movies, putting those assets in virtual reality, in mixed reality, in augmented reality, in spatial computing, in a projection-mapping type of immersive experience... I think there's a lot of that upon us and families and celebrities 100 per cent should include their digital likeness and their immersive assets within their wills and within their estates so those techniques can protect them from these environments in the future.

And from here we turn to that future.

BEYOND HOLOGRAMS

There is a famous quote that is commonly attributed to speculative science-fiction writer William Gibson, but its origins are the subject of some dispute.[108] "The future is already here," it runs. "It's just not evenly distributed yet." There are, however, enough details of what new technology is currently being tested and developed being openly discussed as to give us much more than a feel for what is coming down the line.

Holograms today could, even a few years from now, be retrospectively regarded in a similar way to how we look back at Auguste and Louis Lumière's short films, such as *La Sortie de l'usine Lumière à Lyon* or *L'Arrivée d'un train en gare de La Ciotat*, both from 1895. The holograms we know now could be seen as charmingly naive and rudimentary uses of technology that give only the briefest taste of what could be achieved.

What is already out there in the market hints at what the coming years have in store and so they are things that estates (and living artists for that matter) need to be following closely and preparing for.

At the moment, holograms are carefully scripted undertakings, with body doubles being used to duplicate the movements and performance style of a deceased artist as closely as possible. In a way, it is a form of visual ventriloquism – mimicking the movements of an artist from existing footage of them in their lifetime and lip syncing so that the audio track fits perfectly with what the audience eventually sees on stage. Each and every show will be virtually identical, with the live band performing to a click track to ensure everything stays tight. This tightness is also regarded as a weakness as the show does not have the spontaneity and interaction of an actual show with a living artist, where they make mistakes but also speak to and interact with the audience.

This, however, is the technological goal of the next generation of holograms – using artificial intelligence (AI) so that shows start to feel slightly more extemporised, and things start to bend away from the obviously scripted to give at least the illusion of the instinctive.

Marty Tudor of Base Hologram pointed to an unexpected source as a sign of where his company's productions could move next – the Shoah Foundation at the University of Southern California. It was set up in 1994 by Hollywood director Steven Spielberg to record and preserve the testimonies of Holocaust survivors and first-hand witnesses. It has so far compiled over 55,000 audio-visual testimonies that were conducted in 65 countries and in 43 languages. In total it has over 115,000 hours of video testimony that has been carefully indexed.[109]

In 2016, the prototype of Heather Maio's work with the University of Southern California's Institute for Creative Technologies (ICT) and the Shoah Foundation was being shown to select audiences. The project, called New Dimensions in Testimony, delivered a responsive hologram of Pinchas Gutter, who was seven when the Second World War started and who survived six different Nazi concentration camps. He was recorded talking about his experiences and giving answers to a wide range of questions so that audiences could start to interact with the holographic version as if they were talking to the real Pinchas Gutter. He was one of an initial 12 survivors who were interviewed and recorded in this way for the project.

"The prototype involved filming extensive interviews with Gutter using an array of cameras and a specialised light stage," wrote the *Guardian*. "The team at ICT then used natural language processing software to help create an interactive version of the video footage, with vocal cues triggering responses from the pool of recorded speech."[110]

Based on linguistic technologies similar to those used in voice assistants like Apple's Siri and Amazon's Alexa, the underlying algorithms can respond to trigger words and phrases from audience members and deliver back an apposite answer from the hologram. It is important to note that nothing was faked and words are not put in the hologram's mouth – these are the exact words of the survivors that are merely indexed and then pulled out when a certain question is asked.

"As time goes by and many more users use the content, machine learning will enhance its intelligence – it will understand a wider range of questions as each interaction helps train the system," said David Traum, the director for natural language research at ICT. "We still don't consider it an AI, though, because AI assumes the machine is thinking independently. I think of it more like a smart search engine which gives you a conversation-like experience."[111]

The project expanded, and by 2018, 16 survivors of the Holocaust were recorded and could give answers to over 2,000 different questions.[112] By 2020, it was up to 20 interviews and each respondent had been interviewed for five full days in front of more than 20 different cameras to create the holographic effect, and all their answers were logged.[113]

Nile Rodgers – the enormously successful songwriter/producer and co-founder of Chic – has also experimented with similar technology, following a collaboration with the School of Digital Arts at Manchester Metropolitan University in the UK. He pre-recorded answers to 350 questions and was filmed doing so by two 8k 3D film cameras. This means that a digital version of him can now respond to unique human interaction. The results of what was termed "the world's first voice-interactive portrait" were made public in late March 2021.[114]

It is always going to be a bumpy segue from talking about New Dimensions in Testimony – a powerful and important project to ensure that Holocaust survivors' testimonies are carried through to future generations and that their stories are never forgotten – to something like a holographic pop star, which, in relative terms, is much more frivolous. But on a purely technological level, New Dimensions in Testimony is showing precisely how AI can make holographic recordings much more responsive in real time, helping to humanise the electronic.

Professor Martin Richardson says that AI will be the key to unlock all the potential here. It is, he believes, what will shift all uses of this technology to a whole new tier of possibilities. "We are working towards the ultimate vision of reality, but we're still a few years away yet," he says. "I do predict that AI will be incredibly useful. AI will be able to answer a lot of the mathematical questions that we currently find problematic."

He points to *The Irishman*, Martin Scorsese's 2019 film, as an example of AI-powered image manipulation already in the mainstream, where a flash-back scene involved Frank Sheeran (the character played by Robert De Niro) being aged down to look like a young man. "That was a kind of eerie illusion," says Richardson, who had worked with Scorsese on hologram ideas in the 1990s.

Olivier Chastan is CEO and co-founder of Iconic Artists Group. His company has started buying into the rights of legendary musicians, most notably The Beach Boys, with a view to growing their business and expanding into whole new areas. The company is also planning to buy up estates.

He is utterly convinced that hologram-style technology and AI are the future and says this is a large part of his pitch to the living artists and estates he wants to acquire – helping prepare them for the music business of tomorrow. "We're looking at doing a wide range of things," he says. "This includes facial scanning of [living] band members so that we have a digital imprint of who they are for the future, such as a VR experience."

Estates have been keenly observing what has been happening with holographic technologies, but they are not ready to commit just yet. They do, however, have ideas – some hypothetical and some more concrete – for what they would like to do when the technology reaches a developmental stage where such things are possible and commercially viable.

Jamie Salter of Authentic Brands Group, as noted above, is not ruling out an Elvis hologram, but he also had broader ideas about what the estate could do with AI. "Artificial intelligence," he says, "you think about it one way but I think of it in another way. I believe that when you take a guitar lesson, Elvis Presley will teach you how to play guitar. So for $5 a month, if you could just jump on anytime you want and get Elvis to teach you how to play the guitar, that would be pretty cool, wouldn't it? That's the kind of stuff that we work on. If you and I talked about that two years ago, you would say, 'Jamie, you're crazy.' Now, you're not going to say I am so crazy."

Equally Jeff Jampol at JAM Inc has some clear ideas about what he would like to do with new technologies here, going beyond what current concert holograms offer. "I'm interested in a true hologram," he says. "A hologram is a laser light that exists in a three-dimensional space that you can actually walk around. I would be interested to have some kind of live event where Jim Morrison walked right up to me, looked me in the eye and sang at me – and everybody around could see it – and then he turned around and walked away."

He then says that he is sketching out the concept for a show that could be a stepping-stone production between what hologram shows currently do and what they could do in the future, effectively combining technology and immersive theatre. "We're working on a really interesting live event for The Doors, which is an interesting hybrid," he reveals. "It will have some technology, it will have actors and dancers, it will have zero dialogue. It'll be like an hour-and-a-half acid trip where you get some kind of talisman at the end signifying that you took the trip and survived it."

Jeff Pezzuti says there is limited interaction in the hologram shows currently out there, but it all has to be carefully scripted. He points to a call-and-response section in the *Dio Returns* show as an example of that. It is choreographed improvisation but he suggests that full and true audience interaction, were it to become a central feature of hologram tours, would have to be handled carefully.

"I think AI would be cool and any audience interaction would be really cool," he argues. "But you've got to be careful a little bit. People get a little freaked out if it's too [real]. There's a line and you want to keep it entertainment; that, to me, has always been the key. But there is a cool aspect that could be fun."

Marty Tudor says that Base has explored the technological options but says there is a development lag between the visual side of things and the audio side of things and that both would have to be running exactly in parallel to make it work convincingly in a show. "All the words you hear from an artist on our stage and in our shows are their actual words, said by them," he explains. "To do this [and to have them interact] without a living artist means we have to recreate their voice as well. I mean, it's doable. But I haven't heard it in a way that's really convincing, where it's really natural. It still feels a little machine-like. It's like you listen to Siri or Alexa – they don't sound quite real to me. Once that all catches up, I think that will take this to a whole other level."

Interestingly, people from both estates and hologram companies talk about the next technological wave in terms of extravaganzas, where productions will become bigger and brasher, pushing the spectacle to the extreme. Professor Martin Richardson, however, predicts that the opposite will happen. "I think the key is going to be miniaturisation," he says. "I don't think it's going to be spectacular stage shows. I think once people have seen it and they understand how it works, they get bored. People move on. As our mobile phones go into ever-greater resolution and the size of the screen increases, there will be gimmicks on the market which you could attach to the phone or the iPad which will give you a very similar effect. They're already available, albeit in very substandard materials. They're incredibly expensive for the average consumer, but they are there."

He cites the work of the Looking Glass Factory[115] and the use of its patented light field technology as a foreshadowing of what is to come here. "That will lead to real-time holographic conferences taking place," he says, suggesting that the focus will turn to smaller gatherings, such as in the home, rather than in large halls, where the technology comes to the audience rather than the other way around. This could change the very fundamentals of touring. "My predictions for the future will be more intimate, smaller gatherings where the technology becomes ever-increasingly realistic through light field camera capture and the new Looking Glass devices coming through," he says.

Something along these lines has already happened in live music, in part as a response to venues being closed or deemed inoperable during the global pandemic. In mid-October 2020, Musion 3D (one of the early pioneers here) created what it called "ground-breaking interactive holographic technology" for a performance by Dan Olsen, a singer-songwriter from the Faroe Islands. In front of a small audience at London venue 8 Northumberland Avenue, Olsen and his guitarist played three songs from a recording studio elsewhere in London and the whole performance was beamed into the room in real time. "Now the technology has developed to this interactive level, the possibilities are endless," said Olsen in a press statement. "I could be in my living room interacting in real time with fans in Australia, or anywhere in the world!"[116]

Currently hologram shows based around deceased artists are created using body doubles and each performance is filmed in advance, a painstaking process to get right in terms of synchronising audio and visuals. The body double, crucially, is not the voice double (as the singing is taken from studio or live performance by the act in their lifetime), but layering in AI on the actor's voice could, theoretically, give them the scope to ad lib. The actor would have to be on tour with the production (possibly performing off-stage and the holographic image projected onto the stage), which goes against the pre-packaged model of these tours currently. The fact, however, remains that this is now a real possibility and could start to be incorporated into hologram shows by dead artists.

Travis Cloyd of Worldwide XR, however, believes that the venue-based approach to touring for hologram shows will soon become anachronistic. He says,

> The intention of the audience is to go to a physical event to view that hologram [but] I feel like that's broken. That will evolve and change in the future when we get into this XR ecosystem. It's the fourth wave of consumer technology. It goes from PC to web to mobile, and then we're going into this next phase called XR. The delivery system and the distribution is entirely different from a physical location.
>
> You're still creating a hologram that's portrayed on a glass and is being projected on that glass for an audience that's there in a physical presence. Whereas what we think is a bigger market and the future is really having those holograms or those virtual beings live inside this next wave of consumer technology.

Hologram technology went unexpectedly mainstream in late October 2020 when Kanye West gave his wife, Kim Kardashian West, an unusual birthday present when she turned 40. She called it "a special surprise from heaven". It was a holographic reincarnation of her father, Robert Kardashian (who died in 2003), wishing her happy birthday.[117] "I can't even describe what this meant to me and my sisters, my brother, my mom and closest friends to experience together," said Kim in a tweet, adding the full video (with a run time of 2' 20") so that her 67.4 million Twitter followers could see it.[118] As a crossover moment for hologram technology, this was one no one had anticipated.

This technology also became the foundation for a number of major TV shows in South Korea at the end of 2020 and start of 2021. Music channel Mnet created the programme *One More Time* in which AI voice technology is used to resurrect deceased artists as holograms in order to perform contemporary songs.

The first dead artist to appear in the show was Turtleman (real name Lim Sung-hoon) of South Korean hip-hop group Turtles where he performed 'Start Over' by Gaho, a track originally released in 2018, a decade after his death. Singer Kim Hyun-sik, who died in 1990, was also holographically brought back to life on the show. "In a music industry filled with K-pop idols, I wanted to show to the younger generation the type of music and artists their parents listened to," is how show producer Yoo Seung-yeul put it to the *Korea Herald*. "Also, everyone in Korea is weary from the lengthy COVID-19 situation. For me, the fun and upbeat songs of Turtles gave me strength. I wanted to offer consolation to everyone with Turtles' energetic songs and Kim Hyun-sik's touching songs."[119]

He also stressed that the broadcaster had the approval of the families of all deceased artists featuring in the show. "We put the opinions of family members as our utmost priority when making the program," he said. "We met with not only family members, but also teammates and close friends. If we had any trouble with copyright or obtaining permission from family members, we didn't proceed."[120]

This show was not operating in isolation in the country. Around the same time, broadcaster SBS announced a series for January 2021 called *Battle of the Century: AI vs. Human*. In it, living experts in six different fields (including music) compete against AI entities to see which is best. In this show, folk rock singer Kim Kwang-seok (who died in 1996) rematerialised to perform "I Miss You", a song originally recorded by Kim Bum-soo in 2002.[121]

Proving the "rule of three", Big Hit Entertainment (the powerhouse behind numerous K-pop acts) also announced in late 2020 that the K-pop boy bands BTS and TXT would perform with a hologram of Shin Hae-chul. This segment, presented as a tribute to the experimental rock singer who died in 2014, was part of their joint New Year's Eve show.[122]

Running in parallel with these developments is an area where ethical debates are much more complex and combustible. Deepfake technology allows existing video and audio footage to be manipulated through deep learning[123] so that an individual can seem to do or say absolutely anything. It has been described as the "21st century's answer to Photoshopping". Deepfakes are often described in dystopian terms: for example, people could be made to "appear" in pornographic movies or say things that are utterly beyond the pale, with the idea being that deepfakes could be created and seeded online to discredit political opponents or even entire governments.[124]

As they gleefully blur the lines between truth and lies, they can be used for nefarious ends, such as manipulating old footage of a deceased individual to have them express opinions and viewpoints they would have found abhorrent were they still alive. The technology is improving at such a speed that spotting deepfakes is becoming increasingly more difficult.

The technology can, of course, also be used for good, for entertainment purposes or even for commercial purposes. Hypothetically an ad could run featuring Elvis scrolling through his iPad and then turning to the camera to say that he only ever uses Apple products.

There already have been dead celebrities digitally manipulated into new films – notably actor Peter Cushing, who died in 1994, appearing in 2016's *Rogue One: A Star Wars Story*[125] and Carrie Fisher, who died in 2016, appearing in *Star Wars: Episode IX – The Rise of Skywalker* in 2019.[126] Deceased actors have also shown up in adverts, such as Audrey Hepburn, who died in 1993, appearing in a TV commercial for Galaxy chocolate in 2014.[127]

When I speak to him in late 2019, Travis Cloyd of Worldwide XR reveals that his company is working on a "digital human" version of James Dean that will appear in the Vietnam War-era movie *Finding Jack* and go beyond the existing archive footage of the actor. The *Hollywood Reporter* wrote that "Dean's performance will be constructed via 'full body' CGI using actual footage and photos" and another actor will provide his voice.[128]

Cloyd tells me,

> James Dean has been deceased for over 60 years. Those assets that existed when he was alive are kind of archaic assets – videos and images that are basically regurgitated, recycled and relicensed from then until now. We haven't officially launched a digital human product on James Dean because we're in the midst of that right now.
>
> Our first pass of distribution is through this movie, but our intention is to have a virtual being of James Dean that will live beyond that one movie and will live in this ecosystem of XR, that we could then use for different campaigns using virtual reality as the media or create different digital assets that could be used in gaming environments. Our goal is to spend the next year on putting together what we look at as the perfect or ultimate representation of a virtual being for the likeness of James Dean.

It really feels like a dead pop star doing something similar is a matter of when rather than if. Some estates are already looking at AI manipulation of the voice and considering how that could change the way that the archives of an artist could be re-explored and re-contextualised.

Dolly Parton, as we saw in Chapter 5, is already stockpiling a cappella recordings that could be pulled into whole new musical shapes and slotted into new songs after she dies,[129] but doing this retrospectively is something already on the radar of the Isaac Hayes estates.

"There have been discussions and there are technologies that are in development to actually bring back people's voices," says Isaac Hayes III, who runs his father's estate. "This technology is available; so not only a hologram, but being able to recreate a voice that hasn't been heard before. This is AI technology that can take the stems and gather all the a cappella information that you possibly could have on a particular person and then synthesise their voice. They're a few years away from really perfecting it, but that's something we've been in talks about doing. Imagine being able to bring back artists and create new records with their voice. That would be incredible."

He also suggests that it could be used outside of music, potentially being used in voice-assisted devices. "Imagine how cool that would be, where Isaac Hayes is your voice on Alexa," he proposes.

Ty Roberts picks up on this point and argues it is important to make a distinction between musical AI and vocal AI. He says,

> So Alexa doesn't sing today. But [...] this is a big area of research in colleges around the world. The first thing you have to do is create a voice that can actually sing effectively. The vocal characteristics of what's artistically successful are highly varied. Actual singing ability is not actually the most important thing for many vocalists – originality in their performance is. Not to pick on any specific artists, but artists like Tom Waits have a very distinctive voice and he knows how to perform that super well. That's really different to Maria Callas. The reality is that voices are just like people's personalities – which also is an important part of performance.

Roberts suggests that this hypothetical use of AI will be possible but it might be decades rather than years away in terms of fulfilling its true potential. He forecasts that voice assistants will become "fully conversational" in the next decade. "In 20 years, there's no reason that Alexa couldn't do interpretations [or impersonations]," he says.

He says this technology will have to move in increments, where the audience gets used to one stage of development before things can move on to the next stage. The technology will shock in its initial introduction, then become normalised, and then set things up for the next stage. He suggests,

> If you think about how people think about music artists, they think about them in time periods. So David Bowie in his glam era or David Bowie in his *Let's Dance* era. Certain artists transformed their musical style as well as their look [...] to update their image and to give a fresh new look to [their art]. This will be what will happen with these AI-driven holograms or AI-driven technologies. You'll be like, "Oh, I like the David Bowie AI 2.0. Have you seen the David Bowie 3.0?" "What does 3.0 do?" "Oh, now, he can do duets! He can dance." So in other words, the consumers are going to start thinking about and understanding the actual new capabilities as they are added to these virtual [beings] – just like they think of the new version of software.

For hologram and AI companies – as well as the estates that work with them – the first ethical hurdle has been cleared. Acts have been raised from the dead in holographic form and put on tour. The more this happens, the more the accusations of cultural necrophilia or "ghost slavery" will start to subside. The complex moral and ethical issues around this very idea of a beyond-the-grave performance mean that the first to experiment here will catch most of the heat. They will be accused of tastelessness and of ruining legacies in the shameless pursuit of profit.

Similar arguments were raised when recording vaults started to be raided and unheard material added on to box sets and anniversary reissues of classic albums. It was argued that the artist would not want this made public, but now it is so much part and parcel of the activities of record company catalogue departments as to have become not just accepted by consumers, but actually expected.

As an indication of just how rapidly technology is evolving here, in early April 2021, "new" songs by Kurt Cobain, Jimi Hendrix, Amy Winehouse and Jim Morrison were released as part of the Lost Tapes of the 27 Club project. There was a broader point to it, however, than mere digital necromancy. The project title is, of course, a reference to the numerous musicians who died at the age of 27 and it used artificial intelligence to suggest the kind of music each of these artists could have made had their lives not been cut short.

"As long as there's been popular music, musicians and crews have struggled with mental health at a rate far exceeding the general adult population," explained the project. "And this issue hasn't just been ignored. It's been romanticized, by things like the 27 Club—a group of musicians whose lives were all lost at just 27 years old."

It added, "To show the world what's been lost to this mental health crisis, we've used artificial intelligence to create the album the 27 Club never had the chance to. Through this album, we're encouraging more music industry insiders to get the mental health support they need, so they can continue making the music we all love for years to come. Because even AI will never replace the real thing."[130]

In the case of Cobain, the track 'Drowned in the Sun' was created by AI software which analysed a variety of Nirvana tracks, mimicking their writing, recording and lyrical styles. It also used vocals recorded by Eric Hogan, lead singer in Nirvana tribute act Nevermind.[131]

It does not follow that every estate needs to create a hologram of a dead artist or use AI to expand their discography, but the more that do, the more "normal" it will start to feel. As they stand, these shows are basically a simulacrum – digitally mimicking how the artist performed on stage.

The really questionable issue is when estates start to literally put words in their mouth beyond the innocuous, like having them shout, "Hello, Cleveland!" when the hologram tour hits Ohio. Having digital avatars of dead pop stars endorse a product they could never have used in their lifetime or support a politician they would have found morally reprehensible is really where the ethical shutters should come down.

Digital duplication is, after all, very different from digital duplicity.

Dramatis Personae

List of all primary interviews for the book. All job titles are correct at the time of interview

Abdo, Ken – partner at legal firm Fox Rothschild

Allan, Marc – Red Light Management who work with the Jerry Garcia family

Almqvist, Pär – founder and CEO of licensing platform Tracklib

Alter, Lisa – founding partner at legal firm Alter, Kendrick & Baron

Arlen, Sam – son of Harold Arlen and person in charge of his estate

Beckett, Nicole – head of content development at Four Screens Production (who work with the estate of Ol' Dirty Bastard)

Bell, Celeste – daughter of Poly Styrene and person in charge of her estate

Berg, Seth – consultant to estates including those of Peggy Lee, Dean Martin estate and Frank Sinatra

Biederman, Jeff – partner at law firm Manatt, Phelps & Phillips

Bligh, Laura – cousin of Eva Cassidy and person who runs evacassidy.org site

Branca, John – partner and head of the music department at law firm Ziffren Brittenham as well as co-executor of the Michael Jackson estate

Browne, David – music journalist and co-editor (along with Mary Guibert) of *Jeff Buckley: His Own Voice*

Callomon, Cally – manager of Nick Drake estate

Chacksfield, Tim – record label catalogue expert and consultant

Chastan, Olivier – founder and CEO of Iconic Artists Group

Cloyd, Travis – CEO & co-founder of Worldwide XR

Copsidas, Frank (aka SuperFrank) – final manager of James Brown

Crane, Larry – founder of Jackpot! Recording Studio and archivist for Elliott Smith estate

Davies, Claire – deputy director of Handel & Hendrix in London

Davis, Steve – former director of catalogue at EMI

Devlin, Jimmy – founder of independent label River Records

Donnelly, Bob – transactional attorney at legal firm Fox Rothschild

Dury, Jemima – daughter of Ian Dury and main person in charge of his estate

Ferguson, Tom – music industry specialist, PPL

Fleckenstein, Chuck – general manager and COO of Roy's Boys, Orbison Music and Publishing and Still Working Music on behalf of Roy Orbison estate

Foster Wells, Holly – granddaughter of Peggy Lee and person in charge of her estate

Gallagher, Daniel – nephew of Rory Gallagher and in charge of his estate

Gallagher, Dónal – brother (and former manager) of Rory Gallagher who works with Daniel Gallagher running Rory's estate

Griffin, Jim – music business and estates consultant

Guibert, Mary – mother of Jeff Buckley and person in charge of his estate

Hayes III, Isaac – son of Isaac Hayes and person in charge of his estate

Hendrix, Janie – CEO of Experience Hendrix and person in charge of the Jimi Hendrix estate

Hirshland, David – EVP at BMG

Houston, Pat – executor of the Whitney Houston estate

Jacobson, Erin M. – music industry lawyer

Jacquet, Thierry – head of catalogue, Warner Music France

Jampol, Jeff – founder of JAM Inc (whose roster includes Jim Morrison, Janis Joplin, Charlie Parker, John Lee Hooker, Johnny Ramone and Henry Mancini)

Julien, Darren – founder and president/CEO of Julien's Auctions

King, Howard E. – managing partner of law firm King, Holmes, Paterno & Soriano

Lampcov, Bruce – head of West Coast business development at Downtown Music Publishing

Leigh, Mickey – brother of Joey Ramone and 50 per cent owner of Ramone Productions

Liebenson, Jeff – founder of Liebenson Law and president of International Association of Entertainment Lawyers

McMurray, Jacob – director of curatorial, collections and exhibits at the Museum of Pop Culture in Seattle

Matas, Josh – from Sandbox Entertainment Group who run the Johnny Cash estate

Mestel, Larry – founder and CEO of Primary Wave

Miller, Bill – founder of Icon Entertainment Group in charge of the Johnny Cash Museum and the Patsy Cline Museum

Mindich, Brad – CEO of archiving specialist company Inveniem

Monro, Michele – daughter of Matt Monro and person in charge of his estate

Mullen, Tom – former Sony Music and Atlantic Records executive

North, Abby – founder of music rights management company North Music Group

Novick, Daniel – lawyer at SRIP Law

Perry, Norman – president of merchandise company Perryscope Productions

Pezzuti, Jeff – CEO and founder of hologram company Eyellusion

Pilavachi, Costa – former classical music executive at Philips Classics, Decca Music Group, EMI Classics and Deutsche Grammophon

Pinkus, Mark – president of Rhino Entertainment, the catalogue arm of Warner Music Group

Porter, Darryl – Miles Davis estate

Ramone, Linda – widow of Johnny Ramone and 50 per cent owner of Ramone
    Productions
Richardson, Professor Martin – head of the Imaging and Displays Research
    Group at De Montfort University in Leicester
Rippy, Conrad – lawyer for Jeff Buckley and Elliott Smith estates
Rizzuto, Nick – digital strategist
Roberts, Ty – technical consultant at Eyellusion and former chief technical
    officer at Universal Music Group
Roesler, Mark – founder and chairman of CMG Worldwide and previously
    worked for the Elvis Presley estate
Sabin, Portia – former president of independent label Kill Rock Stars
Salter, Jamie – chairman and CEO of Authentic Brands Group (who own 85 per
    cent of the Elvis Presley estate)
Seiffert, Alan – executive director of Paisley Park
Simson, John – counsel at legal firm Fox Rothschild
Sloane, Owen J. – partner at legal firm Eisner Law
Soares de Souza, Luciana – music lawyer who represents the estates of (among
    others) Vinícius de Moraes and Antônio Carlos Jobim
Steckler, Allan – in charge of estate of Vladimir Horowitz
Stielper, Mark – music historian who works with the Johnny Cash estate
Straw, Bill – president and owner of Blix Street Records, the label which releases
    Eva Cassidy's records
Sudlow, Gemma – head of private and iconic collections at Christie's
Sundin, Per – CEO of Pophouse Entertainment Group, co-founder of the Avicii
    Experience, board member of the Tim Bergling Foundation and former MD
    of Universal Music Sweden
Thompson, Jessica – audio mastering expert and archivist
Toberoff, Marc – founder of boutique law firm Toberoff Associates
Tudor, Marty – CEO of Base Hologram
Wadsworth, Stephen – director of opera studies at the Juilliard School and
    creative director for Maria Callas hologram (at Base Hologram)
Wadsworth, Tony – former chairman and CEO of EMI Music UK & Ireland
Wilson, Don – music lawyer
Yaffe, Alicia – founder and CEO of the Spellbound Group
Zysblat, Bill – co-founder of RZO and represents the estate of David Bowie in
    business dealings
(A number of others from different parts of the music industry were interviewed
    for this book but chose to speak anonymously.)

Epilogue

The memento mori recurs across cultures, religions and art forms – a grounding reminder of the inevitability of death. The human body may be mortal but it lives on among those who choose to remember those who have passed. Anniversaries are marked, stories are shared and a life is raised anew in the collective mind.

Estates of all kinds – not just music ones – are unavoidably in the business of death. The dark irony is that they can only come into life when someone dies: their primary obligation is to ensure the subject of all their activities remains, for as long as possible, in the collective mind. They have the tools at hand to reach a lot of people and success is measured by how broad they can go in the collective mind as well as how deep they can go in the collective wallet.

The fact that the *Forbes* list of celebrity dead earners is dominated each year by music stars speaks volumes about just how profoundly musicians connect with the public. It is also highly illustrative of the multitude of ways in which the business of pop stars operates today. There are many more moving parts and a greater set of rights linked to a successful musician than there are for any other type of creator. These include audio and video recordings, song compositions, name, image and likeness rights, trademarks and more.

The arrival of hologram technologies and AI are helping to create whole new sets of rights and assets here – and they are making the debate around how these rights and assets are monetised yet more convoluted and fraught with controversy. Even in death, musicians are leading the way here.

Hence it follows that the estates business for a pop star is more complex and more involved than it is for any other kind of celebrity. The music estate is, arguably, the apotheosis of the estates business. It has to do more, it has to protect more rights and it has to find new ways to keep going (and to keep going faster) than anyone else. Where the music estate leads, other estates follow.

This book had one chief goal – to reveal how innovative, how interesting and how difficult the business of music estate management is. This is a financial business, of course, but this is also (and equally) a legacy business. There is a complex responsibility for the estate manager who has to make money from a legacy without tarnishing, cheapening or dooming that same legacy.

People are sometimes squeamish when art and money are discussed in the same breath, especially when death is added as a third component. Money, for some, is the sworn enemy of art; but, they will argue, at least in their lifetime the artist walked that line between the two entirely on their own terms and if they ruined their legacy with a misstep it was, at the very least, their misstep. Having someone walk that line for them after they have died is trickier still as what these custodians do – or what they do not do – feeds their posthumous reputation.

There are enormously complex emotions and responsibilities tied up in running an estate. Do nothing out of fear or uncertainty and the artist dies all over again. Do too much out of greed or recklessness and the artist also dies all over again, but this time with their reputation buckled and rusted beyond repair. These tensions make music estate management one of the most parlous but also one of the most invigorating businesses out there. It is resolving all this – as it navigates this endless tightrope as it whips, sways and snaps in the crosswinds of luck, risk, good planning and ill – that makes music estate management one of the most engrossing and highest grossing businesses today.

F. Scott Fitzgerald proposed that there are no second acts in life. Music estates have a single and clear purpose – to ensure that there are second lives in death.

Acknowledgements

The "difficult second book" was made somewhat less difficult with a team around me to help ease it into the world – and to tell me what bits did and did not work.

So endless praise, thanks, hurrahs, fireworks and so forth to the team at Omnibus Press for letting me write another book and, crucially, for not letting me mess it up. That means the people I have come to think of as The A-Team of music book publishing – David Barraclough, Imogen Gordon Clark, Catherine Best (for patiently catching all my clumsy typos), David Stock, Dave Holley and Debs Geddes (putting the "PR" in POWER, or something). (Yes, I know there are more people here than were in The A-Team, but The A-Team know nothing about book publishing and how many hands are needed here so, frankly, those so-called soldiers of fortune can pipe down.)

The origins of the book can be dated back to a feature I wrote for the *Guardian* in September 2016. It was commissioned by Michael Hann so endless gratitude to him for allowing me to write it as it was where I started to formulate the ideas on these pages.

Enormous thanks to everyone who spoke to me for the book and to the assorted PRs and assistants who helped make the interviews happen. Huge gratitude to everyone who opened doors for me and put me in touch with people (most notably Zoë Howe for helping me access some truly #engaging #content).

Even though most of this book was written during lockdown when socialising was a mere whisper of a memory, friends were on hand to ease the pain and also force me to talk about things beyond how dead pop stars make money. So "shout outs" to: Alex Papasimakopoulou and Skye (even though Skye probably would have eaten my laptop or chucked it into the Aegean; to Louise Haywood-Schiefer and V-Unit, despite the fact that Cultural Friday was put on hold (p.s. Vaughan – books are printed on the same stuff sticks are made from so hopefully this will appeal); Andrew Harrison and Lili Harges, N16's true "power couple"; Ciara, Mel and Brodie (but absolutely NOT Malky).

Obviously I wouldn't be here without my parents so a special round of applause for Big Annie and Big Eddie (definitely my best parents). And lots of other family members need "props" here too – such as Declan, Kathleen, Rosie and more (please add your own name here).

Carrying on with: Mark, Jelly and John (hopefully we can return to Duckie soon); Brian David Stevens (even though he's horrible – really, he's vile); everyone on Shtum (even Cheggers); Laura Snapes; Lars Brandle (I suppose); Marty Robb (even though we prefer Charlie); Anna Derbyshire Woolgar (for the endless SAY); Stuart Dredge; and anyone else who listened to my yapping.

Thank you to all the publications I write for – not only for giving me work but also for understanding why I would need to disappear from time to time.

Special, colossal, boundless thanks to Sonja who endured (not enjoyed) my constant flapping and occasionally having to pull down the shutters to get on with writing the thing (the office chair helped enormously, thanks). It can't have been nice having to deal with someone writing all the time (or at least I am sure it felt like I was writing all the time) when all you wanted to do was go on holidays and eat in nice restaurants. But you did get this book dedicated to you so, when you look at the evidence, I'd say that was a fair trade.

You have all – every single one of you – been marvellous.

Notes

1. The Cornerstones of the Modern Estates Business

1. 'Top 1977 Movies at the Domestic Box Office': https://www.the-numbers.com/box-office-records/domestic/all-movies/cumulative/released-in-1977
2. *Close Encounters of the Third Kind, Saturday Night Fever* and *Smokey and the Bandit.*
3. Alanna Nash, *The Colonel: The Extraordinary Story of Colonel Tom Parker and Elvis Presley*, 2003 (e-book edition).
4. https://www.forbes.com/sites/maddieberg/2020/11/13/the-highest-paid-dead-celebrities-of-2020/
5. Annye C. Anderson, *Brother Robert: Growing Up with Robert Johnson*, 2020 (e-book edition).
6. https://www.guitarworld.com/news/a-new-photo-of-robert-johnson-the-third-in-existence-has-been-uncovered
7. Annye C. Anderson, *Brother Robert: Growing Up with Robert Johnson*, 2020 (e-book edition).
8. https://www.courthousenews.com/family-of-bluesman-loses-bid-for-photo-royalties/
9. Annye C. Anderson, *Brother Robert: Growing Up with Robert Johnson*, 2020 (e-book edition).
10. Ibid.
11. Ibid.
12. https://www.nytimes.com/2015/07/02/arts/music/claud-johnson-83-son-of-blues-singer.html
13. https://www.latimes.com/local/obituaries/la-me-claud-johnson-dies-son-of-legendary-bluesman-20150701-story.html
14. Annye C. Anderson, *Brother Robert: Growing Up with Robert Johnson*, 2020 (e-book edition).
15. http://performingsongwriter.com/otis-redding-sittin-dock-bay/
16. https://www.npr.org/2018/01/08/576413464/the-story-of-how-otis-reddings-dock-of-the-bay-got-released
17. Jonathan Gould, *Otis Redding: An Unfinished Life*, 2017, p. 443.
18. https://www.npr.org/2018/01/08/576413464/the-story-of-how-otis-reddings-dock-of-the-bay-got-released
19. Jonathan Gould, *Otis Redding: An Unfinished Life*, 2017, p. 443.
20. Ibid., p. 444.
21. https://www.udiscovermusic.com/stories/otis-redding-dock-of-the-bay-song/
22. Jonathan Gould, *Otis Redding: An Unfinished Life*, 2017, p. 445.
23. Ibid.
24. http://performingsongwriter.com/otis-redding-sittin-dock-bay/

25. Dave Laing, *Buddy Holly*, 1971, p. 20.
26. Ibid., p. 85.
27. Ibid., p. 89.
28. Philip Norman, *Buddy: The Biography*, 1996, p. 375.
29. Dave Laing, *Buddy Holly*, 1971, pp. 38–9.
30. Philip Norman, *Buddy: The Biography*, 1996, p. 368.
31. Ibid., p. 369.
32. Ibid.
33. Dave Laing, *Buddy Holly*, 1971, p. 39.
34. https://www.ft.com/content/d77d5e74-69e5-11e6-ae5b-a7cc5dd5a28c
35. Ibid.
36. Ibid.
37. Ibid.
38. https://www.bbc.co.uk/news/entertainment-arts-30033747
39. Priscilla Beaulieu Presley, *Elvis and Me*, 1985, p. 161.
40. Ibid.
41. Ibid.
42. Ibid., p. 226.
43. Ibid., pp. 228–9.
44. Ibid., p. 228.
45. Sean O'Neal, *Elvis Inc.: The Fall and Rise of the Presley Empire*, 1996, p. 8.
46. Ibid., p. 10.
47. Alanna Nash, *The Colonel: The Extraordinary Story of Colonel Tom Parker and Elvis Presley*, 2003 (e-book edition).
48. Sean O'Neal, *Elvis Inc.: The Fall and Rise of the Presley Empire*, 1996, p. 48.
49. Priscilla Beaulieu Presley, *Elvis and Me*, 1985, p. 161.
50. Quoted in Sean O'Neal, *Elvis Inc.: The Fall and Rise of the Presley Empire*, 1996, p. 27.
51. Ibid., p. 48.
52. Ibid.
53. Alanna Nash, *The Colonel: The Extraordinary Story of Colonel Tom Parker and Elvis Presley*, 2003 (e-book edition).
54. Sean O'Neal, *Elvis Inc.: The Fall and Rise of the Presley Empire*, 1996, p. 431.
55. Ted Harrison, *The Death and Resurrection of Elvis Presley*, 2016, p. 48.
56. Sean O'Neal, *Elvis Inc.: The Fall and Rise of the Presley Empire*, 1996, p. 31.
57. Ted Harrison, *The Death and Resurrection of Elvis Presley*, 2016, p. 49.
58. Alanna Nash, *The Colonel: The Extraordinary Story of Colonel Tom Parker and Elvis Presley*, 2003 (e-book edition).
59. https://www.latimes.com/archives/la-xpm-1989-06-11-tm-2866-story.html
60. Ibid.
61. Sean O'Neal, *Elvis Inc.: The Fall and Rise of the Presley Empire*, 1996, p. 60.
62. Alanna Nash, *The Colonel: The Extraordinary Story of Colonel Tom Parker and Elvis Presley*, 2003 (e-book edition).
63. Ibid.
64. Ibid.
65. Ibid.
66. Ted Harrison, *The Death and Resurrection of Elvis Presley*, 2016, p. 49.
67. Sean O'Neal, *Elvis Inc.: The Fall and Rise of the Presley Empire*, 1996, p. 13.
68. Ted Harrison, *The Death and Resurrection of Elvis Presley*, 2016, p. 50.

69. Ibid.
70. Ibid., p. 51.
71. https://www.billboard.com/articles/news/483328/graceland-the-tourist-attraction-turns-30
72. https://www.latimes.com/archives/la-xpm-1989-06-11-tm-2866-story.html
73. Ibid.
74. Ted Harrison, *The Death and Resurrection of Elvis Presley*, 2016, p. 43.
75. https://www.graceland.com/about-graceland
76. https://www.graceland.com/blog/posts/33-years-of-elvis-presleys-graceland
77. https://www.latimes.com/archives/la-xpm-1989-06-11-tm-2866-story.html
78. Sean O'Neal, *Elvis Inc.: The Fall and Rise of the Presley Empire*, 1996, p. 110.
79. https://money.cnn.com/2013/11/20/news/elvis-property/index.html
80. https://insidememphisbusiness.com/ceo-of-the-year/jack-soden-elvis-presley-enterprises/
81. https://www.rollingstone.com/music/music-features/elvis-presley-business-revenue-953324/
82. https://www.latimes.com/archives/la-xpm-1989-06-11-tm-2866-story.html
83. https://www.graceland.com/blog/posts/33-years-of-elvis-presleys-graceland
84. https://www.latimes.com/archives/la-xpm-1989-06-11-tm-2866-story.html
85. Ibid.
86. Quoted in Ted Harrison, *The Death and Resurrection of Elvis Presley*, 2016, p. 60.
87. https://www.elvis.com.au/presley/elvis-a-family-franchise.shtml
88. https://www.forbes.com/sites/anthonydemarco/2011/12/14/elizabeth-taylor-auction-shatters-records-fetches-nearly-116-million/#8a7e2764b830

2   The Inescapable Importance of the Will

1. https://www.nytimes.com/1973/04/09/archives/picasso-is-dead-in-france-at-91-picasso-dies-at-his-villa-in.html
2. https://www.newyorker.com/magazine/2018/06/25/paisley-park-princes-lonely-palace
3. https://www.nytimes.com/1973/04/12/archives/picasso-superstitious-of-death-left-no-will-his-lawyer-says.html
4. https://www.ranker.com/list/celebrities-who-died-without-a-will/celebrity-lists
5. Loretta Würtenberger, *The Artist's Estate: A Handbook for Artists, Executors, and Heirs,* 2016, pp. 30–1.
6. https://www.probatelawyerblog.com
7. Andrew W. Mayoras and Danielle B. Mayoras, *Trial and Heirs: Famous Fortune Fights!*, 2012.
8. https://www.caring.com/caregivers/estate-planning/wills-survey
9. Michael Hackard, *Alzheimer's, Widowed Stepmothers and Estate Crimes: Cause, Action, and Response in Cases of Fractured Inheritance, Lost Inheritance, and Disinheritance*, 2019, p. 41.
10. https://www.rollingstone.com/music/music-features/inside-the-zappa-family-feud-104088/
11. https://www.loudersound.com/news/ahmet-zappa-responds-to-brother-dweezil-in-bid-to-resolve-dispute

12. The *Bob Lefsetz Podcast*, 19 September 2019.
13. https://www.tmz.com/2018/08/21/aretha-franklin-no-will-death/
14. https://www.thetimes.co.uk/article/court-handwriting-expert-could-examine-aretha-franklin-wills-qhttv77mf
15. https://apnews.com/224a1d9a8e761de1b334209aec026a55
16. https://www.nytimes.com/2019/05/21/arts/did-aretha-franklin-leave-her-will-under-the-couch-cushion.html
17. https://www.nytimes.com/2019/08/21/arts/music/aretha-franklin-estate-wills-fight.html
18. https://www.nytimes.com/2020/03/03/arts/music/new-executor-aretha-franklin-estate.html
19. https://www.billboard.com/articles/business/8527996/aretha-franklin-uncashed-checks
20. https://www.nytimes.com/2021/03/11/arts/music/another-will-aretha-franklin-dispute.html
21. Ibid.
22. https://www.americanbar.org/groups/real_property_trust_estate/publications/probate-property-magazine/2018/july-august-2018/celebrity-estate-planning/
23. Ibid.
24. Ibid.
25. https://www.nytimes.com/2016/01/30/nyregion/david-bowies-will-splits-estate-said-to-be-worth-100-million.html?_r=0
26. https://danielleandandy.com/celebrity-legacies-jim-morrisons-will-leads-to-estate-battle/
27. https://www.dailytelegraph.com.au/news/today-in-history/sex-drugs-and-probate-when-rock-stars-leave-behind-a-legal-mess/news-story/c57482bdebe23174a1aaaf31842d1bb0
28. https://frankkraft.com/estate-plan-jim-morrison/
29. John Densmore, *The Doors Unhinged: Jim Morrison's Legacy Goes on Trial*, 2013, p. 23.
30. https://danielleandandy.com/celebrity-legacies-jim-morrisons-will-leads-to-estate-battle/
31. https://people.com/archive/a-decade-later-the-heirs-of-jim-jimi-and-janis-reap-the-troubled-legacies-of-rock-vol-14-no-25/
32. J. Randy Taraborrelli, *Sinatra: Behind the Legend*, 2016, p. 534.
33. http://news.bbc.co.uk/1/hi/special_report/1998/05/98/sinatra/98473.stm
34. J. Randy Taraborrelli, *Sinatra: Behind the Legend*, 2016, p. 534.
35. Andrew W. Mayoras and Danielle B. Mayoras, *Trial and Heirs: Famous Fortune Fights!*, 2012, p. 22.
36. http://news.bbc.co.uk/1/hi/special_report/1998/05/98/sinatra/94239.stm
37. Ibid.
38. https://www.smh.com.au/entertainment/celebrity/hutchence-millions-kiss-dirt-leaving-family-with-zilch-20050820-gdlwrx.html
39. Ibid.
40. Quoted in *The Paradise Papers* documentary. Posted on the ABC website on 7 November 2017. https://www.abc.net.au/4corners/the-paradise-papers/9124930
41. Tina Hutchence and Patricia Glassop, *Just a Man: The Real Michael Hutchence*, 2000, p. 125.
42. Ibid., p. 132.
43. Ibid., p. 142.

44. Ibid., p. 162.

45. Tina Hutchence, *Michael: My Brother, Lost Boy of INXS*, 2018 (e-book edition).

46. https://www.smh.com.au/entertainment/movies/torn-apart-the-troubled-legacy-of-michael-hutchence-20190625-p520zx.html

47. https://www.dailymail.co.uk/news/article-7643077/INXS-rock-star-Michael-Hutchence-died-16m-daughter-did-not-penny.html

48. Tina Hutchence and Patricia Glassop, *Just a Man: The Real Michael Hutchence*, 2000, p. 201.

49. https://www.dailymail.co.uk/tvshowbiz/article-7173257/What-happened-Michael-Hutchences-missing-millions.html

50. https://www.newyorker.com/magazine/2017/07/24/manufacturing-bob-marley

51. https://www.washingtonpost.com/archive/lifestyle/style/1991/08/25/dread-reckoning-the-marley-mess/94894ac0-248f-4a9f-b5b0-7429704a29d8/

52. Quoted in *Get Rich or Try Dying: Music's Mega Legacies*, first broadcast on BBC Four on 1 November 2019.

53. https://www.rollingstone.com/music/music-features/bob-marley-children-ziggy-rohan-cedella-stephen-karen-938379/

54. Maureen Sheridan, 'Talkin' Over: Marley Estate Case Ends: Island Logic, Family Can Purchase Assets'. Originally published in *Billboard* on 21 December 1991. Reprinted in Hank Bordowitz (ed.), *Every Little Thing Gonna Be Alright: The Bob Marley Reader*, 2004, p. 186.

55. https://www.forbes.com/sites/trialandheirs/2011/12/05/are-bob-marley-heirs-destroying-his-legacy/#1f56f30e52a5

56. https://www.washingtonpost.com/archive/lifestyle/style/1991/08/25/dread-reckoning-the-marley-mess/94894ac0-248f-4a9f-b5b0-7429704a29d8/

57. https://www.newsweek.com/marleys-ghost-babylon-202230

58. Ibid.

59. https://www.washingtonpost.com/archive/lifestyle/style/1991/08/25/dread-reckoning-the-marley-mess/94894ac0-248f-4a9f-b5b0-7429704a29d8/

60. Ibid.

61. Ibid.

62. https://www.theguardian.com/music/2008/mar/02/news.italy

63. Quoted in https://www.telegraph.co.uk/news/worldnews/1566997/Luciano-Pavarotti-died-in-12million-debt.html

64. Ibid.

65. https://www.theguardian.com/music/2008/mar/02/news.italy

66. https://www.nytimes.com/2007/09/19/arts/music/19arts-PAVAROTTISBE_BRF.html

67. https://www.independent.co.uk/news/world/europe/widow-settles-dispute-with-pavarottis-daughters-over-will-857662.html

68. https://theraycharlesfoundation.org/grants/

69. https://www.latimes.com/business/la-fi-raycharles20apr20-story.html

70. Ibid.

71. Ray Charles Jr, *You Don't Know Me: Reflections of My Father, Ray Charles*, 2010, p. 239.

72. Ibid., p. 240.

73. Ibid.

74. Ibid.

75. https://lasentinel.net/joe-adams-longtime-manager-of-ray-charles-dies-at-94.htm

3   Controlling Interests

1. https://people.com/archive/town-without-twitty-vol-42-no-18/
2. Quoted in *The Estate of Conway Twitty | The Will: Family Secrets Revealed*, first broadcast on Investigation Discovery on 2 November 2011.
3. https://people.com/archive/town-without-twitty-vol-42-no-18/
4. Ibid.
5. Quoted in *The Estate of Conway Twitty | The Will: Family Secrets Revealed*, first broadcast on Investigation Discovery on 2 November 2011.
6. https://people.com/archive/town-without-twitty-vol-42-no-18/
7. Quoted in *The Estate of Conway Twitty | The Will: Family Secrets Revealed*, first broadcast on Investigation Discovery on 2 November 2011.
8. Ibid.
9. https://www.theguardian.com/music/2008/mar/02/news.italy
10. https://www.independent.co.uk/news/world/europe/widow-settles-dispute-with-pavarottis-daughters-over-will-857662.html
11. https://variety.com/2019/biz/news/tom-petty-daughter-widow-estate-battle-1203180081/
12. These included Lawrence Jenkins (Petty Unlimited's designated estate manager), Anthony Dimitriades (Petty's long-term manager) and Alan Arora (Petty's social media and merchandise manager). https://www.billboard.com/biz/articles/news/legal-and-management/8513842/tom-pettys-widow-files-new-appeals-against-daughters
13. https://www.latimes.com/entertainment-arts/music/story/2019-12-18/tom-petty-estate-settlement
14. Ibid.
15. https://uk.reuters.com/article/uk-france-hallyday/rocker-hallydays-estate-to-be-shared-under-french-not-u-s-law-idUKKCN1SY1LT
16. https://www.musicbusinessworldwide.com/confirmed-johnny-hallyday-album-shatters-records-selling-more-week-one-units-in-france-than-drakes-scorpion-did-in-the-usa/
17. https://www.lemonde.fr/culture/article/2019/03/14/musique-johnny-champion-des-ventes-en-2018_5435912_3246.html
18. https://www.theguardian.com/music/2018/mar/15/johnny-hallydays-children-seek-to-freeze-estate-in-row-over-will
19. https://www.bbc.co.uk/news/world-europe-43757713
20. Quoted in https://www.theguardian.com/music/2018/apr/13/johnny-hallyday-court-freezes-assets-in-inheritance-dispute
21. https://www.nytimes.com/2019/05/29/world/europe/johnny-hallyday-instagram-will.html
22. https://uk.reuters.com/article/uk-france-hallyday/rocker-hallydays-estate-to-be-shared-under-french-not-u-s-law-idUKKCN1SY1LT
23. https://www.dailymail.co.uk/femail/article-8494395/French-rock-singer-Johnny-Hallidays-widow-wins-row-pockets-30-7million.html
24. Michael Jackson, *Moon Walk*, 1988, p. 29.
25. J. Randy Taraborrelli, *Michael Jackson: The Magic, the Madness, the Whole Story*, 2010, p. 20.
26. Ibid., p. 21.
27. https://www.cbsnews.com/news/joe-jackson-to-inherit-nothing-from-son/
28. Ibid.

29. https://uk.reuters.com/article/centertainment-us-jackson-idCATRE60L5EI20100122

30. https://nypost.com/2014/08/31/joe-jackson-is-cut-out-from-the-rest-of-his-family-insider/

31. Ibid.

32. Ibid.

33. https://www.bbc.co.uk/news/world-us-canada-44633980

34. https://www.theguardian.com/music/2016/jul/30/prince-judge-rules-out-30-potential-heirs-to-singers-estate

35. https://www.bbc.co.uk/news/uk-england-merseyside-15606017

36. https://www.theguardian.com/music/2013/aug/22/john-lennon-tooth-clone-dna

37. https://www.thesun.co.uk/news/6403562/dentist-john-lennon-beatles-tooth-love-children-estate/

38. Ibid.

39. Quoted in *The Estate of Johnnie Taylor | The Will: Family Secrets Revealed*, first broadcast on Investigation Discovery on 16 November 2011.

40. Ibid.

41. Ibid.

42. Ibid.

43. https://www.officialcharts.com/artist/2746/t-rex/

44. Quoted in *Who Got Marc Bolan's Millions?* first broadcast on Granada TV on 20 September 2003.

45. Mark Paytress, *Bolan: The Rise and Fall of a 20th Century Superstar*, 2006, p. 244.

46. https://www.telegraph.co.uk/culture/4728611/Behind-the-glitter.html

47. Mark Paytress, *Bolan: The Rise and Fall of a 20th Century Superstar*, 2006, p. 196.

48. Lesley-Ann Jones, *Ride a White Swan: The Lives and Death of Marc Bolan*, 2012, p. 346.

49. Mark Paytress, *Bolan: The Rise and Fall of a 20th Century Superstar*, 2006, p. 245.

50. Quoted in *Who Got Marc Bolan's Millions?* first broadcast on Granada TV on 20 September 2003.

51. https://ultimateclassicrock.com/rock-bands-taxes/

52. Mark Paytress, *Bolan: The Rise and Fall of a 20th Century Superstar*, 2006, p. 244.

53. Ibid., p. 245.

54. Quoted in *Who Got Marc Bolan's Millions?* first broadcast on Granada TV on 20 September 2003.

55. Lesley-Ann Jones, *Ride a White Swan: The Lives and Death of Marc Bolan*, 2012, p. 348.

56. Mark Paytress, *Bolan: The Rise and Fall of a 20th Century Superstar*, 2006, pp. 245–6.

57. Quoted in *Who Got Marc Bolan's Millions?* first broadcast on Granada TV on 20 September 2003.

58. Ibid.

59. Lesley-Ann Jones, *Ride a White Swan: The Lives and Death of Marc Bolan*, 2012, p. 348.

60. Mark Paytress, *Bolan: The Rise and Fall of a 20th Century Superstar*, 2006, p. 318.

61. Quoted in *Who Got Marc Bolan's Millions?* first broadcast on Granada TV on 20 September 2003.
62. Ibid.
63. Ibid.
64. Ibid.
65. Mark Paytress, *Bolan: The Rise and Fall of a 20th Century Superstar*, 2006, p. 246.
66. https://www.telegraph.co.uk/culture/4728611/Behind-the-glitter.html
67. https://www.standard.co.uk/showbiz/my-daddy-of-britpop-by-marc-bolans-son-6665946.html
68. Lesley-Ann Jones, *Ride a White Swan: The Lives and Death of Marc Bolan*, 2012, pp. 286.
69. https://www.standard.co.uk/showbiz/my-daddy-of-britpop-by-marc-bolans-son-6665946.html
70. https://www.bbc.co.uk/news/entertainment-arts-23373608
71. https://www.hollywoodreporter.com/thr-esq/hollywood-docket-don-henley-sues-739836
72. https://www.hollywoodreporter.com/thr-esq/sony-sued-lacking-license-use-trex-song-baby-driver-1026612
73. https://www.hollywoodreporter.com/thr-esq/hollywood-docket-baby-driver-settlement-inside-ruling-tmnt-trademark-fight-1081921
74. Ray Charles Jr, *You Don't Know Me: Reflections of My Father, Ray Charles*, 2010, p. 240.
75. https://www.latimes.com/business/la-fi-raycharles20apr20-story.html
76. Ibid.
77. Ibid.
78. https://www.cnn.com/2012/04/01/showbiz/ray-charles-lawsuit/index.html
79. https://www.billboard.com/articles/business/1535910/court-rules-for-ray-charles-children-in-copyright
80. https://lasentinel.net/joe-adams-longtime-manager-of-ray-charles-dies-at-94.html
81. https://theraycharlesfoundation.org
82. https://www.wealthmanagement.com/people/lack-will-makes-prince-enigma-death-too
83. https://www.theguardian.com/music/2017/may/19/prince-siblings-inherit-estate-minnesota
84. Ibid.
85. https://www.businessinsider.com/ap-comerica-bank-appointed-to-run-princes-estate-2017-1?r=US&IR=T
86. https://variety.com/2017/biz/news/prince-heirs-petition-to-remove-comerica-bank-vault-was-moved-without-permission-1202602468/
87. Ibid.
88. https://variety.com/2017/music/news/prince-estate-troy-carter-spotify-1202027998/
89. https://theblast.com/c/prince-estate-comerica
90. Ibid.
91. https://www.billboard.com/articles/news/8508202/prince-sister-sharon-nelson-comerica-bank-accusations-estate-mismanaged
92. Ibid.
93. Ibid.

94. Ibid.
95. http://www.mncourts.gov/mncourtsgov/media/High-Profile-Cases/10-PR-16-46/(Redacted)-Declaration-of-Angela-Aycock-Re-Comerica-s-Fees-and-Costs-from-Feb-2019-through-May-2019.pdf
96. Ibid.
97. https://theblast.com/c/singer-prince-sister-tyka-nelson-sells-estate-interest-financial-problems-lawyers-music-video-heirs
98. https://theblast.com/c/singer-prince-estate-sister-tyka-sells-off-interest-comerica-bank-objects-music-deals-court-lawsuit-power
99. https://www.startribune.com/one-of-prince-s-heirs-alfred-jackson-dies-in-kansas-city/558728862/?refresh=true
100. https://theblast.com/c/singer-prince-estate-siblings-heirs-half-brother-alfred-jackson-dead-sister-tyka-one-million-owed-legal-bill-lien-music-profits
101. https://www.startribune.com/untimely-death-of-prince-heir-complicates-estate-settlement-even-more/568089142/
102. Ibid.
103. Ibid.
104. https://theblast.com/c/singer-prince-estate-fires-back-at-his-family-over-money-irs-issues
105. https://www.musicbusinessworldwide.com/john-branca-artists-need-to-pay-attention-to-their-legacy-and-be-very-specific-about-it/
106. https://www.latimes.com/archives/la-xpm-1993-04-08-ca-20656-story.html
107. https://www.independent.co.uk/arts-entertainment/scuse-me-while-i-kiss-this-pile-1595277.html
108. https://www.latimes.com/archives/la-xpm-1993-04-08-ca-20656-story.html
109. Ibid.
110. https://www.latimes.com/archives/la-xpm-1993-04-20-ca-25108-story.html
111. Ibid.
112. https://www.latimes.com/archives/la-xpm-1993-04-08-ca-20656-story.html
113. Ibid.
114. https://www.independent.co.uk/arts-entertainment/scuse-me-while-i-kiss-this-pile-1595277.html
115. https://www.latimes.com/archives/la-xpm-1993-04-08-ca-20656-story.html
116. https://www.independent.co.uk/arts-entertainment/scuse-me-while-i-kiss-this-pile-1595277.html
117. https://www.latimes.com/archives/la-xpm-1993-04-08-ca-20656-story.html
118. https://www.independent.co.uk/arts-entertainment/scuse-me-while-i-kiss-this-pile-1595277.html
119. Ibid.
120. https://www.rollingstone.com/music/music-news/hendrixs-father-wins-music-rights-247656/
121. Ibid.
122. Paul Allen was the co-founder of Microsoft and a major Hendrix collector. He opened the Experience Music Project in Seattle in 2000 initially as a Hendrix museum but it evolved into the more generalist Museum of Pop Culture. He died in October 2018.
123. https://www.chicagotribune.com/news/ct-xpm-2002-04-21-0204210020-story.html
124. https://www.telegraph.co.uk/news/uknews/1465555/Family-go-to-court-in-fight-for-Hendrixs-millions.html

125. https://www.express.co.uk/celebrity-news/884185/Jimi-Hendrix-guitar-songs-death-family-feud-130-million-estate-fortune
126. https://www.seattletimes.com/seattle-news/ruling-freezes-brother-out-of-jimi-hendrixs-estate/
127. Ibid.
128. https://www.rollingstone.com/music/music-news/jimi-hendrixs-estate-settles-licensing-legal-battle-190748/
129. https://www.theguardian.com/music/2016/sep/25/jimi-went-inside-with-his-music-when-he-got-on-stage-that-was-his-time
130. https://www.latimes.com/california/story/2019-09-17/britney-spears-conservatorship-free-britney
131. https://www.washingtonpost.com/lifestyle/style/the-battle-of-britney-spears/2019/05/17/edcc826c-7681-11e9-bd25-c989555e7766_story.html
132. https://www.theguardian.com/world/2008/feb/02/musicnews.usa
133. https://www.freebritney.net
134. https://www.bbc.co.uk/news/av/entertainment-arts-18071160
135. https://www.rollingstone.com/movies/movie-news/britney-spears-confirms-departure-from-the-x-factor-203627/
136. https://www.latimes.com/california/story/2019-09-17/britney-spears-conservatorship-free-britney
137. https://www.dailymail.co.uk/news/article-8798383/Britney-Spears-ex-estate-manager-says-conservatorship-rest-life.html
138. https://www.etonline.com/britney-spears-father-wants-to-extend-conservatorship-to-louisiana-hawaii-and-florida-125725
139. https://www.bbc.co.uk/news/entertainment-arts-56911822
140. https://people.com/music/britney-spears-father-jamie-steps-down-as-her-conservator/
141. https://hollywoodlife.com/feature/who-is-jodi-montgomery-conservator-britney-spears-3722938/
142. https://www.latimes.com/california/story/2019-09-17/britney-spears-conservatorship-free-britney
143. https://eu.usatoday.com/story/entertainment/music/2020/08/18/britney-spears-seeks-nix-jamie-spears-sole-conservator-estate/5603710002/
144. https://www.latimes.com/california/story/2020-08-25/britney-spears-sister-makes-move-to-control-assets-as-trustee-of-her-pop-star-sisters-fortune
145. https://www.latimes.com/entertainment-arts/music/story/2020-09-02/britney-spears-conservatorship-voluntary
146. https://www.bessemertrust.com
147. https://www.bbc.co.uk/news/entertainment-arts-54010661
148. https://www.independent.co.uk/arts-entertainment/music/news/britney-spears-conservatorship-andrew-wallet-jamie-free-b830686.html
149. https://www.nme.com/news/music/britney-spears-addresses-conservatorship-concerns-in-new-video-im-the-happiest-ive-ever-been-2808068
150. https://www.billboard.com/articles/news/9481872/britney-spears-quit-music-father-controls-career/
151. https://www.bbc.co.uk/news/entertainment-arts-54897918
152. https://www.rollingstone.com/music/music-news/britney-spears-previously-unreleased-track-swimming-in-the-stars-1097763/
153. https://edition.cnn.com/2020/12/15/entertainment/britney-spears-father-jamie-spears-conservatorship/index.html

154. https://redarrowstudios.com/left-rights-the-new-york-times-presents-framing-britney-spears-set-for-fx-hulu-premiere/
155. https://www.bbc.co.uk/news/entertainment-arts-55978659
156. https://www.theguardian.com/music/2021/feb/08/framing-britney-spears-documentary-conservatorship-media
157. https://www.etonline.com/britney-spears-lawyer-says-it-would-be-detrimental-to-give-her-father-more-power-in-conservatorship
158. https://www.theguardian.com/music/2021/feb/10/britney-spears-conservatorship-court-hearing-los-angeles
159. https://www.billboard.com/articles/business/legal-and-management/9525225/britney-spears-hearing-conservatorship/
160. https://www.billboard.com/articles/columns/pop/9525115/framing-britney-spears-director-interview/
161. https://www.latimes.com/entertainment-arts/music/story/2021-02-11/britney-spears-conservatorship-status-hearing
162. https://edition.cnn.com/2021/03/02/entertainment/britney-spears-conservatorship/index.html
163. https://www.billboard.com/articles/news/9537515/britney-spears-conservatorships-matt-gaetz-jim-jordan-congressional-hearings/
164. https://www.theguardian.com/music/2021/mar/25/britney-spears-father-personal-affairs
165. https://variety.com/2021/music/news/britney-spears-attorney-jodi-montgomery-conservatorship-1234937791/
166. https://www.instagram.com/tv/CND5B1RArtK/?igshid=t1o1ervr6enq
167. https://www.theguardian.com/music/2021/apr/27/britney-spears-court-conservatorship
168. https://www.smh.com.au/entertainment/celebrity/hutchence-millions-kiss-dirt-leaving-family-with-zilch-20050820-gdlwrx.html
169. Ibid.
170. https://www.independent.co.uk/news/hutchence-family-claims-share-of-pounds-10m-1186646.html
171. Ibid.
172. https://www.theguardian.com/news/2017/nov/05/revealed-michael-hutchence-adviser-used-tax-haven-to-exploit-unheard-songs
173. http://news.bbc.co.uk/1/hi/entertainment/279844.stm
174. https://www.telegraph.co.uk/music/artists/michael-hutchence-mystery-did-money-go/
175. https://www.smh.com.au/entertainment/celebrity/hutchence-millions-kiss-dirt-leaving-family-with-zilch-20050820-gdlwrx.html
176. Quoted in *Michael Hutchence: The Last Rockstar*, first broadcast on Channel Seven (Australia) on 16 October 2017.
177. Ibid.
178. https://www.rollingstone.com/music/music-news/hutchences-estate-settled-235174/
179. https://www.smh.com.au/entertainment/movies/torn-apart-the-troubled-legacy-of-michael-hutchence-20190625-p520zx.html
180. https://www.dailymail.co.uk/news/article-7643077/INXS-rock-star-Michael-Hutchence-died-16m-daughter-did-not-penny.html
181. Ibid.
182. Ibid.

183. Rob Chapman, *Syd Barrett: A Very Irregular Head*, 2010, p. xv.
184. https://www.theguardian.com/books/2002/oct/06/biography.music
185. https://www.theguardian.com/music/2016/jan/06/nick-kent-pink-floyd-syd-barrett-classic-profile-creem-1973
186. Ibid.
187. https://www.mirror.co.uk/news/uk-news/12m-will-of-floyd-star-syd-704798
188. http://www.cambridge-news.co.uk/Barrett-leaves125m/story-22479127-detail/story.html#RElvSBbU9ibrh7Qx.99
189. https://www.dailymail.co.uk/tvshowbiz/article-455376/Poverty-stricken-Syd-Barrett-1-7m-inheritance.html
190. https://www.theguardian.com/music/2016/sep/29/get-rich-or-try-dying-how-musicians-estates-are-the-biggest-earners-in-pop
191. https://www.wrdw.com/home/headlines/9959901.html
192. James McBride, *Kill 'Em and Leave: Searching for the Real James Brown*, 2016, p. 153.
193. https://www.investmentnews.com/james-browns-estate-is-a-real-mess-11144
194. https://www.atlantamagazine.com/great-reads/darren-lumar/
195. https://www.gq-magazine.co.uk/article/james-brown-fortune-lawsuits-death-drugs
196. https://www.atlantamagazine.com/great-reads/darren-lumar/
197. https://www.gq-magazine.co.uk/article/james-brown-fortune-lawsuits-death-drugs
198. Ibid.
199. "An Alford Plea is a guilty plea of a defendant who proclaims he is innocent of the crime and admits that the prosecution has enough evidence to prove that he is guilty beyond a reasonable doubt." https://www.legalzoom.com/articles/the-alford-plea-guilty-but-innocent
200. https://www.gq-magazine.co.uk/article/james-brown-fortune-lawsuits-death-drugs
201. https://www.gq-magazine.co.uk/article/james-brown-fortune-lawsuits-death-drugs
202. https://www.hollywoodreporter.com/thr-esq/fate-james-browns-fortune-turns-thanks-a-unusual-court-decision-1299368
203. https://www.theguardian.com/music/2009/may/28/james-brown-estate-battle-settled
204. https://www.gq-magazine.co.uk/article/james-brown-fortune-lawsuits-death-drugs
205. https://www.atlantamagazine.com/great-reads/darren-lumar/
206. https://www.gq-magazine.co.uk/article/james-brown-fortune-lawsuits-death-drugs
207. Ibid.
208. Ibid.
209. https://www.billboard.com/articles/news/1550123/court-overturns-james-brown-estate-settlement
210. https://www.nytimes.com/2014/12/14/us/downbeat-legacy-for-james-brown-godfather-of-soul-a-will-in-deep-dispute.html
211. Ibid.
212. Ibid.
213. https://www.gq-magazine.co.uk/article/james-brown-fortune-lawsuits-death-drugs

214. https://www.billboard.com/articles/columns/pop/8478151/james-brown-family-feud-inside-12-year-fight-over-bigamy-dna-tests
215. https://www.nytimes.com/2015/02/04/arts/music/battle-over-james-browns-estate-focuses-on-a-diary.html
216. https://www.billboard.com/articles/business/legal-and-management/9405707/james-brown-south-carolina-supreme-court-ruling-wife
217. Ibid.
218. James McBride, *Kill 'Em and Leave: Searching for the Real James Brown*, 2016, p. xvi.
219. Ibid.. p. 20.
220. Quoted in James McBride, *Kill 'Em and Leave: Searching for the Real James Brown*, 2016, p. 171.
221. https://www.chicagotribune.com/news/ct-muddy-waters-estate-suit-met-0417-20150416-story.html
222. https://www.latimes.com/local/obituaries/la-me-scott-cameron-20150312-story.html
223. https://www.chicagotribune.com/news/ct-muddy-waters-estate-suit-met-0417-20150416-story.html
224. https://www.nbcchicago.com/news/local/heirs-of-chicago-blues-musician-muddy-waters-copyright/54846/
225. https://www.latimes.com/local/obituaries/la-me-scott-cameron-20150312-story.html
226. https://www.nbcchicago.com/news/local/heirs-of-chicago-blues-musician-muddy-waters-copyright/54846/
227. https://www.chicagotribune.com/suburbs/ct-met-muddy-waters-estate-battle-continues-20180418-story.html
228. https://apnews.com/article/224a1d9a8e761de1b334209aec026a55
229. https://www.nytimes.com/2019/08/21/arts/music/aretha-franklin-estate-wills-fight.html
230. Ibid.
231. https://www.nytimes.com/2020/03/03/arts/music/new-executor-aretha-franklin-estate.html
232. https://www.billboard.com/articles/columns/country/8467147/glen-campbell-children-can-contest-validity-of-will
233. https://eu.tennessean.com/story/news/2018/07/16/glen-campbell-death-family-fight-estate/788429002/
234. Ibid.
235. https://eu.usatoday.com/story/life/people/2018/11/30/glen-campbell-estate-doubled-value-now-worth-1-2-million/2160800002/
236. https://eu.usatoday.com/story/entertainment/celebrities/2020/05/22/glen-campbell-estate-financial-details-likely-remain-private/5248486002/
237. https://www.rollingstone.com/music/music-news/courtney-love-sells-nirvana-rights-share-101726/
238. https://www.nme.com/news/music/courtney-love-93-1302291
239. Ibid.
240. https://www.cnbc.com/2014/04/04/kurt-cobain-and-the-big-business-of-dead-celebs.html

241. https://www.billboard.com/articles/business/legal-and-management/8545814/chris-cornell-widow-soundgarden-lawsuit-royalties
242. https://www.billboard.com/articles/news/9420014/soundgarden-drops-benefit-concert-claims-against-chris-cornell-widow
243. https://pitchfork.com/news/chris-cornells-wife-vicky-cornell-sues-soundgarden-over-proposed-buyout-offer/
244. https://www.nytimes.com/1997/01/16/us/jerry-garcia-s-second-wife-wins-ruling-in-fight-over-money.html
245. https://www.sfgate.com/news/article/Jerry-Garcia-Estate-Worth-9-9-Million-Probate-3505876.php
246. https://www.nytimes.com/2018/03/06/obituaries/alan-gershwin-who-claimed-a-famous-father-is-dead-at-91.html
247. https://www.thetimes.co.uk/article/alan-gershwin-obituary-rxzlhn0nc
248. https://www.nytimes.com/2018/03/06/obituaries/alan-gershwin-who-claimed-a-famous-father-is-dead-at-91.html
249. https://www.thetimes.co.uk/article/alan-gershwin-obituary-rxzlhn0nc
250. https://www.nytimes.com/2018/03/06/obituaries/alan-gershwin-who-claimed-a-famous-father-is-dead-at-91.html
251. https://www.thetimes.co.uk/article/alan-gershwin-obituary-rxzlhn0nc
252. https://www.nytimes.com/2018/03/06/obituaries/alan-gershwin-who-claimed-a-famous-father-is-dead-at-91.html
253. https://syncopatedtimes.com/alan-gershwin-who-claimed-to-be-george-gershwins-son-has-died/
254. https://www.telegraph.co.uk/news/uknews/law-and-order/12073617/Death-of-Motorhead-frontman-Lemmy-could-trigger-legal-battle-over-fortune.html
255. Ibid.
256. https://www.mirror.co.uk/3am/celebrity-news/mystery-over-lemmy-kilmisters-millions-9951670
257. https://www.irishtimes.com/news/two-sides-of-lennon-reflected-in-his-sons-1.158149
258. https://www.telegraph.co.uk/culture/4713954/Dad-was-a-hypocrite.-He-could-talk-about-peace-and-love-to-the-world-but-he-could-never-show-it-to-his-wife-and-son.html
259. Ibid.
260. https://www.irishtimes.com/news/two-sides-of-lennon-reflected-in-his-sons-1.158149
261. https://www.dailymail.co.uk/femail/article-2057764/John-Lennons-son-Julian-fears-Yoko-Ono-Paul-McCartney-trying-obliterate-history.html
262. https://www.telegraph.co.uk/culture/4713954/Dad-was-a-hypocrite.-He-could-talk-about-peace-and-love-to-the-world-but-he-could-never-show-it-to-his-wife-and-son.html
263. https://www.nytimes.com/1979/09/02/archives/glenn-millers-executor-ordered-to-return-800000-to-2-children-set.html
264. Ibid.
265. https://www.theguardian.com/music/2018/feb/23/lisa-marie-presley-sues-former-manager-14000-elvis-cash-barry-siegel-mismanagement
266. Ibid.
267. https://uk.news.yahoo.com/lisa-marie-presley-scores-victory-142406093.html

268. Kirk Semple, 'Let's Get Together and Deal All Right'. Originally published in *Miami New Times* on 18 March 1992. Reprinted in Hank Bordowitz (ed.), *Every Little Thing Gonna Be Alright: The Bob Marley Reader*, 2004, p. 189.

269. Maureen Sheridan, 'Talkin' Over: Marley Estate Case Ends: Island Logic, Family Can Purchase Assets'. Originally published in *Billboard* on 21 December 1991. Reprinted in Hank Bordowitz (ed.) *Every Little Thing Gonna Be Alright: The Bob Marley Reader*, 2004, p. 185.

270. Kirk Semple, 'Let's Get Together and Deal All Right'. Originally published in *Miami New Times* on 18 March 1992. Reprinted in Hank Bordowitz (ed.) *Every Little Thing Gonna Be Alright: The Bob Marley Reader*, 2004, p. 190.

271. https://www.washingtonpost.com/archive/lifestyle/style/1991/08/25/dread-reckoning-the-marley-mess/94894ac0-248f-4a9f-b5b0-7429704a29d8/

272. Ibid.

273. https://www.newsweek.com/marleys-ghost-babylon-202230

274. Maureen Sheridan, 'Talkin' Over: Marley Estate Case Ends: Island Logic, Family Can Purchase Assets'. Originally published in *Billboard* on 21 December 1991. Reprinted in Hank Bordowitz (ed.) *Every Little Thing Gonna Be Alright: The Bob Marley Reader*, 2004, p. 184.

275. Ibid., p. 185.

276. Ibid., p. 187.

277. Quoted in *Get Rich or Try Dying: Music's Mega Legacies*, first broadcast on BBC Four on 1 November 2019.

278. Ibid., p. 185.

279. Maureen Sheridan, 'Talkin' Over: Marley Estate Case Ends: Island Logic, Family Can Purchase Assets'. Originally published in *Billboard* on 21 December 1991. Reprinted in Hank Bordowitz (ed.) *Every Little Thing Gonna Be Alright: The Bob Marley Reader*, 2004, p. 184.

280. https://www.theguardian.com/music/2004/mar/19/popandrock.elliottsmith

281. http://www.thesmokinggun.com/documents/crime/rockers-autopsy-doesnt-rule-out-homicide

282. https://www.hollywoodreporter.com/news/smiths-girlfriend-wont-collect-152763

283. https://www.sandiegouniontribune.com/sdut-region-another-ike-turner-ex-wants-cut-of-estate-2008apr04-story.html

284. Ibid.

285. Ibid.

286. https://www.sandiegouniontribune.com/sdut-exclusive-judge-leans-toward-finding-ike-turners-2009oct30-story.html

287. https://www.factmag.com/2016/03/29/j-dilla-the-diary-feature/

288. The *Vibe* article was republished on the Stones Throw site. https://www.stonesthrow.com/news/the-battle-for-j-dilla-s-legacy/

289. Ibid.

290. https://www.factmag.com/2016/03/29/j-dilla-the-diary-feature/

291. https://www.stonesthrow.com/news/the-battle-for-j-dilla-s-legacy/

292. Ibid.

293. https://www.npr.org/2016/07/30/485700850/j-dilla-s-diary-is-now-in-the-hands-of-fans

294. https://www.stonesthrow.com/news/the-battle-for-j-dilla-s-legacy/

295. https://www.boxofficemojo.com/title/tt0120094/?ref_=bo_se_r_1

296. https://www.billboard.com/articles/columns/latin/6576089/selena-quintanilla-umg-settle-lawsuit-digital-royalties
297. https://www.forbes.com/sites/veronicavillafane/2018/12/01/chris-perez-loses-appeal-to-dismiss-lawsuit-by-selenas-father-on-the-hook-to-pay-all-legal-fees/?sh=5cc1aefe7380
298. https://celebritydollmuseum.com/237/selena-quintanilla/
299. https://www.click2houston.com/news/2012/05/11/visa-unveils-new-selena-prepaid-card/
300. https://www.billboard.com/articles/columns/latin/9491686/selena-estate-legal-battle-netflix-series/
301. https://www.npr.org/2012/07/17/156686608/looking-for-lady-days-resting-place-detour-ahead
302. https://www.billboard.com/articles/business/9561520/billie-holiday-estate-legacy-husband-ownership/
303. https://law.justia.com/cases/new-jersey/appellate-division-published/1982/184-n-j-super-217-0.html
304. https://www.dailynews.com/2008/05/30/estate-of-billie-hollidays-husband-sues-record-company/
305. https://hitsdailydouble.com/news&id=289455&title=Bicycle-gets-Billie-Holiday-catalog-(Steve-Sessa-hype)
306. https://www.musicbusinessworldwide.com/concord-music-group-merges-with-bicycle-raises-100m/
307. https://www.billboard.com/articles/business/9561520/billie-holiday-estate-legacy-husband-ownership/
308. https://theblast.com/stone-temple-pilots-scott-weiland-memorabilia-framed-albums-probate/
309. https://www.dailymail.co.uk/news/article-3386329/Mary-Forsberg-claims-executor-Scott-Weiland-s-will.html
310. https://theblast.com/c/scott-weiland-estate-irs-tax-lien
311. https://www.yahoo.com/entertainment/scott-weiland-estate-made-million-154239266.html
312. https://theblast.com/c/scott-weiland-widow-creditors-claim-denied
313. https://theblast.com/c/scott-weiland-estate-child-support
314. https://theblast.com/c/scott-weiland-ex-wife-child-support-estate
315. https://www.tmz.com/2020/06/19/xxxtentacion-mother-cleopatra-bernard-sued-half-brother-corey-pack-estate/
316. https://www.miaminewtimes.com/news/xxxtentacion-last-will-rappers-mother-cleopatra-bernard-named-beneficiary-10480437
317. https://www.theguardian.com/music/2009/jan/13/amy-winehouse-blake-fielder-civil-divorce
318. Ibid.
319. Ibid.
320. https://www.billboard.com/music/ritchie-valens/chart-history
321. Quoted in *The Estate of Ritchie Valens | The Will: Family Secrets Revealed*, first broadcast on Investigation Discovery on 26 October 2012.
322. Ibid.
323. https://latimesblogs.latimes.com/thedailymirror/page/408/
324. Ibid.
325. Ibid.

326. Quoted in *The Estate of Tammy Wynette | The Will: Family Secrets Revealed*, first broadcast on Investigation Discovery on 19 October 2012.
327. Ibid.
328. Ibid.

4   Creating Posthumous Fame

1. Home videos of him as a child exist and his estate claims he recorded a TV show in Manchester at some point during his career but, so far, a copy of this has never surfaced. http://www.rebeatmag.com/cally-callomon-remembers-nick-drake-for-a-while/
2. https://www.latimes.com/archives/la-xpm-1989-03-13-vw-419-story.html
3. https://www.washingtonpost.com/archive/lifestyle/1989/03/16/the-literary-folk-legend/ba79664d-e35a-40db-aeb6-9d3320b3acee/
4. Ibid.
5. These include: *Butterfly in the Typewriter: The Tragic Life of John Kennedy Toole and the Remarkable Story of* A Confederacy of Dunces by Cory MacLauchlin (2012); *Ken and Thelma: The Story of* A Confederacy of Dunces by Joel Fletcher (2005); *I, John Kennedy Toole* by Kent Carroll and Jodee Blanco (2020); *Ignatius Rising: The Life of John Kennedy Toole* by René Pol Nevils and Deborah George Hardy (2005); and even (astonishingly) *A Confederacy of Dunces Cookbook: Recipes from Ignatius J. Reilly's New Orleans* (named after the book's central character) by Cynthia LeJeune Nobles (2015).
6. https://folkways.si.edu/the-country-blues/music/album/smithsonian
7. https://blues.org/blues_hof_inductee/king-of-the-delta-blues-singers-robert-johnson-columbia-1961/
8. https://www.npr.org/2011/05/07/136063911/robert-johnson-at-100-still-dispelling-myths
9. https://www.udiscovermusic.com/stories/devils-music-myth-robert-johnson/
10. The 16-track *King of the Delta Blues Singers*, Vol. II followed in 1970 and the 41-track *The Complete Recordings* was released in 1990.
11. https://www.npr.org/2011/05/07/136063911/robert-johnson-at-100-still-dispelling-myths
12. https://www.theguardian.com/music/2015/may/23/robert-johnson-photo-does-not-show-blues-legend-music-experts-say
13. Only one Drake album – the 2004 compilation *Magic* – made it into the Top 40. It peaked at number 32. Its entire chart run was two weeks. https://www.officialcharts.com/artist/9339/nick-drake/
14. Quoted in https://www.theguardian.com/music/2004/apr/25/popandrock4
15. Republished in https://www.theguardian.com/music/2014/nov/05/nick-drake-requiem-for-a-solitary-man
16. Trevor Dann, *Darker than the Deepest Sea: The Search for Nick Drake* (2007), p. 195.
17. Ibid., p. 196.
18. Patrick Humphries, *Nick Drake: The Biography* (1997), p. 238.
19. Ibid.
20. Ibid., p. 240.

21. Trevor Dann, *Darker than the Deepest Sea: The Search for Nick Drake* (2007), p. 197.
22. Ibid., pp. 198–9.
23. http://www.nickdrake.com/Cally_Q_and_A.html
24. https://www.boston.com/culture/music/2016/07/21/four-boston-ad-professionals-volkswagen-shed-light-almost-forgotten-music-career
25. Ibid.
26. John and Beverley Martyn were among Drake's closest friends and cared deeply for him. John Martyn wrote 'Solid Air' about Drake.
27. Book extract published in https://www.theguardian.com/music/2020/jul/15/nick-drake-john-martyn-complex-friendship-small-hours-extract
28. https://qz.com/327763/he-died-in-1974-but-nick-drakes-legend-continues-to-grow/
29. Trevor Dann, *Darker than the Deepest Sea: The Search for Nick Drake* (2007), p. 204.
30. https://www.rollingstone.com/movies/movie-news/nick-drake-comes-to-life-in-film-197316/
31. https://qz.com/327763/he-died-in-1974-but-nick-drakes-legend-continues-to-grow/
32. *Fruit Tree – The Nick Drake Story* was broadcast on Radio 2 on 20 June 1998. Trevor Dann, *Darker than the Deepest Sea: The Search for Nick Drake* (2007), p. 206.
33. http://www.bbc.co.uk/pressoffice/pressreleases/stories/2004/04_april/06/radio2_bradpitt.shtml
34. https://www.telegraph.co.uk/culture/3618642/Wretched-boy...-if-only-he-were-here.html
35. https://www.thetimes.co.uk/article/the-missing-link-in-the-nick-drake-story-his-mum-bw5whvslr
36. https://www.telegraph.co.uk/culture/3618642/Wretched-boy...-if-only-he-were-here.html
37. Rob Burley and Jonathan Maitland, *Eva Cassidy: Songbird*, 2001, p. 114.
38. http://evacassidy.org/live-at-blues-alley/
39. Ibid.
40. http://evacassidy.org/eva-cassidy-albums/
41. Quoted in Rob Burley and Jonathan Maitland, *Eva Cassidy: Songbird*, 2001, p. 108.
42. https://www.irishtimes.com/news/who-is-eva-cassidy-1.296849
43. https://www.nytimes.com/2002/08/12/arts/death-shy-singer-finally-grabs-spotlight-cd-s-carry-eva-cassidy-s-voice-wider.html
44. https://uk.movies.yahoo.com/how-terry-wogan-launched-the-career-of-tragic-singer-eva-cassidy-154619086.html
45. Quoted in Rob Burley and Jonathan Maitland, *Eva Cassidy: Songbird*, 2001, p. 150.
46. Quoted in https://uk.movies.yahoo.com/how-terry-wogan-launched-the-career-of-tragic-singer-eva-cassidy-154619086.html
47. Quoted in Rob Burley and Jonathan Maitland, *Eva Cassidy: Songbird*, 2001, p. 151.
48. https://www.officialcharts.com/artist/5140/eva-cassidy/
49. Ibid.
50. From press release sent to media on 17 March 2021.

51. https://www.nytimes.com/2002/08/12/arts/death-shy-singer-finally-grabs-spotlight-cd-s-carry-eva-cassidy-s-voice-wider.html
52. http://evacassidy.org/videos/
53. Ibid.
54. Quoted in Rob Burley and Jonathan Maitland, *Eva Cassidy: Songbird*, 2001, p. 152.
55. Ibid., p. 153.
56. Ibid., p. 154.
57. The evacassidy.com site is dedicated to the singer's drawings and other artwork and is run by Margret and Anette, her sisters.
58. https://www.theguardian.com/technology/2002/apr/04/internetnews.onlinesupplement2
59. https://www.linkedin.com/company/the-spellbound-group/about/
60. https://www.musicbusinessworldwide.com/primary-wave-music-publishing-partners-with-whitney-houston-estate/
61. https://www.billboard.com/articles/news/9555467/dmx-music-streams-rise-after-death/
62. https://www.musicbusinessworldwide.com/buddy-holly-widow-entrusts-bmg-with-artists-rights/
63. In late April 2021, Downtown Music Holdings announced that it was selling its catalogue of 145,000 songs to Concord Music. Some sources valued the deal at $400 million. Downtown stated it would now focus its business on the music services sector rather than music copyrights. https://www.musicbusinessworldwide.com/concord-buys-downtowns-owned-music-publishing-catalog-for-around-400m/
64. https://www.dmpgroup.com/news/2017/06/downtown-x-estate-of-anthony-newley
65. https://www.adweek.com/tv-video/adobes-oscars-ad-is-a-colorful-trippy-ode-to-creativity/

5 Annals Mirabilis

1. https://edition.cnn.com/2008/US/06/01/studio.fire/index.html
2. Ibid.
3. https://www.nytimes.com/2019/06/11/magazine/universal-fire-master-recordings.html
4. Ibid. Rosen called these "the irreplaceable primary source of a piece of recorded music".
5. Ibid.
6. Ibid.
7. Ibid.
8. Ibid.
9. https://www.ironmountain.com
10. Grainge, it should be noted, did not become CEO of UMG until January 2011. The chairman and CEO of UMG at the time of the fire was Doug Morris, who Grainge succeeded.
11. https://www.billboard.com/articles/business/8516565/universal-music-group-lucian-grainge-vault-fire-owe-artists-transparency

12. https://www.nytimes.com/2019/06/21/business/media/universal-music-fire-lawsuit.html
13. Ibid.
14. https://www.latimes.com/entertainment-arts/music/story/2019-07-17/universal-music-fire-damage-memo
15. https://www.billboard.com/articles/news/8520467/umg-archivist-statement-downplaying-losses-2008-fire
16. https://www.hollywoodreporter.com/thr-esq/universal-music-asks-court-extinguish-fire-class-action-1225139
17. https://www.thewrap.com/universal-confirms-nirvana-elton-john-and-sonic-youth-masters-lost-or-damaged-in-2008-vault-fire/
18. https://www.courthousenews.com/universal-says-it-owes-artists-nothing-for-fire-that-destroyed-masters/
19. https://variety.com/2020/music/news/steve-earle-pulls-out-of-universal-music-fire-lawsuit-1203543490/
20. https://www.billboard.com/articles/business/legal-and-management/9352623/universal-music-backlot-fire-class-action-lawsuit-dismissed-tom-petty
21. https://www.billboard.com/articles/business/legal-and-management/9352623/universal-music-backlot-fire-class-action-lawsuit-dismissed-tom-petty
22. https://www.hollywoodreporter.com/thr-esq/tupac-shakur-estate-soundgarden-leave-universal-fire-class-action-1284515
23. https://www.emiarchivetrust.org
24. http://www.billholland.net/words/Labels%20Strive%20to%20Rectify%20Past%20Archival%20Problems.pdf
25. Ibid.
26. Ibid.
27. Chris Anderson, *The Long Tail: Why the Future of Business is Selling Less of More*, 2006.
28. https://www.officialcharts.com/artist/10363/beatles/
29. https://ultimateclassicrock.com/beatles-free-as-a-bird/
30. https://www.rockcellmagazine.com/interview-beatles-producer-george-martin-looks-back/
31. https://www.washingtonpost.com/news/arts-and-entertainment/wp/2016/03/09/george-martin-kept-his-hands-off-the-beatles-worst-song-it-was-one-of-his-best-decisions/
32. Ian MacDonald, *The People's Music*, 2003, p. 111.
33. https://www.theguardian.com/music/2017/feb/17/biggie-smalls-creepy-duets-from-beyond-the-grave
34. The release of *Let It Be… Naked* in 2003 does not count because, if anything, it is an unmixing of the album to remove chunks of Phil Spector's orchestration that had so annoyed Paul McCartney in 1970 on its original release because it was added without his permission.
35. The guitarist's father who was to adopt Janie after he married Ayako "June" Fujita in 1966.
36. https://www.latimes.com/archives/la-xpm-1993-04-20-ca-25108-story.html
37. https://www.rollingstone.com/music/music-news/hendrixs-father-wins-music-rights-247656/
38. https://www.latimes.com/local/obituaries/la-me-alan-douglas-20140613-story.html
39. Ibid.

40. https://www.theguardian.com/music/2014/jun/18/alan-douglas
41. https://www.independent.co.uk/news/obituaries/alan-douglas-record-producer-whose-20-year-tenure-as-curator-of-the-hendrix-back-catalogue-proved-9698010.html
42. https://www.theguardian.com/world/2018/dec/28/how-monkey-christ-brought-new-life-to-a-quiet-spanish-town
43. https://www.independent.co.uk/news/obituaries/alan-douglas-record-producer-whose-20-year-tenure-as-curator-of-the-hendrix-back-catalogue-proved-9698010.html
44. *Sandbox* (issue 234), 7 August 2019. (This is a subscribers-only industry publication.)
45. https://www.newyorker.com/magazine/2016/10/17/leonard-cohen-makes-it-darker
46. https://www.theguardian.com/music/2019/nov/24/leonard-cohen-adam-thanks-for-the-dance-interview
47. https://www.irishtimes.com/culture/music/adam-cohen-dad-i-know-you-re-not-happy-with-this-1.4079061
48. Ibid.
49. https://www.latimes.com/archives/la-xpm-2004-jun-22-et-cromelin22-story.html
50. Ibid.
51. https://www.washingtonpost.com/entertainment/books/the-beautiful-ones-isnt-the-memoir-prince-envisioned-but-its-a-moving-look-at-the-singers-life/2019/10/30/b4868632-fb16-11e9-8906-ab6b60de9124_story.html
52. https://www.nme.com/news/music/ronnie-james-dios-autobiography-secures-posthumous-release-later-this-year-2882385
53. https://www.whitneyhouston.com/track/higher-love-2/
54. https://www.forbes.com/sites/zackomalleygreenburg/2019/10/30/how-whitney-houston-found-higher-love-in-the-afterlife/#1e7435785a9d
55. https://www.nytimes.com/2019/05/20/business/media/whitney-houston-hologram-album.html
56. https://www.forbes.com/sites/zackomalleygreenburg/2019/10/30/how-whitney-houston-found-higher-love-in-the-afterlife/#1e7435785a9d
57. https://www.officialcharts.com/chart-news/higher-love-is-now-whitney-houstons-longest-running-single-ever-on-the-top-100-official-uk-singles-chart__28910/
58. https://www.officialcharts.com/artist/22775/whitney-houston/
59. Ibid.
60. *Sandbox* (issue 169), 30 November 2016. (This is a subscribers-only industry publication.)
61. He had released two mixtapes before this – *Meet The Woo* in July 2019 and *Meet The Woo 2* in February 2020.
62. https://www.billboard.com/articles/columns/hip-hop/9417336/50-cent-interview-pop-smoke-album
63. https://www.instagram.com/p/CCCQtCPnwjN/?utm_source=ig_embed
64. https://www.vulture.com/2020/06/manager-to-change-pop-smoke-album-art-after-virgil-backlash.html
64. https://www.vulture.com/2020/06/manager-to-change-pop-smoke-album-art-after-virgil-backlash.html

65. https://www.nme.com/news/music/pop-smoke-fans-are-still-unhappy-with-his-posthumous-albums-artwork-2700888

66. https://www.billboard.com/articles/business/chart-beat/9417157/pop-smoke-shoot-for-the-stars-aim-for-the-moon-number-1-billboard-200/

67. https://www.billboard.com/articles/business/chart-beat/9544881/pop-smoke-shoot-for-the-stars-aim-for-the-moon-number-breaks-record-top-rap-albums/

68. https://www.bbc.co.uk/news/entertainment-arts-54296858

69. https://www.bbc.co.uk/news/entertainment-arts-36987966

70. https://www.xxlmag.com/juice-wrld-interview-legends-never-die-album/

71. https://www.rollingstone.com/music/music-features/lil-peep-everybodys-everything-posthumous-album-912726/

72. https://www.thenational.ae/arts-culture/music/as-a-new-avicii-album-drops-we-explore-the-ethics-of-posthumous-releases-1.871130

73. https://thevinylfactory.com/features/jeff-buckley-grace-posthumous-releases/

74. https://www.nme.com/news/music/sony-music-fake-michael-jackson-songs-2370522

75. https://variety.com/2018/biz/news/michael-jackson-estate-sony-music-cleared-in-fake-vocal-lawsuit-1202919443/

76. https://www.billboard.com/articles/news/6612646/amy-winehouse-documentary-sam-smith-mark-ronson-salaam-remi-addiction

77. *My Beautiful Mistakes* podcast. Originally made available on 15 December 2020. https://podcasts.apple.com/gb/podcast/my-beautiful-mistakes/id1529869086

78. Ibid.

79. https://www.independent.co.uk/arts-entertainment/music/features/posthumous-albums-singers-death-leonard-cohen-harry-nilsson-lil-peep-prince-a9210961.html

80. https://www.theguardian.com/music/2003/oct/17/2

81. https://music.allaccess.com/erin-davis-son-of-jazz-legend-miles-davis-opens-about-his-fathers-career-and-gives-insight-into-managing-his-estate/

82. https://www.lakeshorepublicradio.org/post/celebrating-anniversary-eva-cassidys-night-bird-blues-alley-concert-recordings#stream/0

83. https://umusic.ie/news/dermot-kennedy-at-dublins-olympia-theatre

84. Warhol is officially credited as the album's producer but Tom Wilson is generally accepted as its actual producer.

85. https://variety.com/2019/music/news/lost-lou-reed-songs-for-andy-warhol-discovered-1203388986/

86. Meek was a legendary and pioneering record producer but also a highly controversial figure, not just because of his unconventional working practices but also because of the fact that on 3 February 1967 he murdered Violet Shenton, his landlady, and then took his own life.

87. https://www.cherryred.co.uk/cherry-red-records-have-acquired-legendary-producer-joe-meeks-tea-chest-tapes/

88. Podcast first posted on 29 August 2019. https://consequenceofsound.net/2019/08/the-opus-episode-3/

89. https://www.businessinsider.com/troy-carter-prince-music-industry-today-investing-ignition-2018-12?r=US&IR=T

90. Ibid.

91. https://www.rollingstone.com/music/music-features/prince-estate-big-plans-upcoming-purple-reign-698529/

92. Ibid.
93. Ibid.
94. https://www.theguardian.com/music/2015/mar/19/i-would-hide-4-u-whats-in-princes-secret-vault
95. https://www.vulture.com/2018/09/prince-vault-archivist-michael-howe-interview.html
96. https://www.theguardian.com/music/2021/apr/08/lost-prince-album-welcome-2-america-to-be-released-in-july
97. https://www.cbsnews.com/news/prince-welcome-2-america-60-minutes-2021-04-11/
98. Ibid.
99. Baking is a technique used by audio engineers when dealing with older tapes that are suffering from deterioration. The tapes are, as the name of the technique suggests, baked at a low temperature to remove any moisture that may have accumulated in the tape's binder. The beneficial effects of baking only last a few weeks or months but can allow a copy to be made of the master tape.
100. "The tapes for *The Lost New York Sessions* were housed in the Capitol vaults in Los Angeles and were impromptu arrangements that Monro originally intended for release. However, Monro's musical director took the tapes, changed the arrangements and added brass and strings for a more produced version. These revised versions appear on his 1967 Capitol album, *Invitation to Broadway* and his original versions were never released." https://www.udiscovermusic.com/news/matt-monro-lost-new-york-sessions/
101. https://www.officialcharts.com/artist/27904/john-lennon/
102. https://www.bbc.co.uk/news/entertainment-arts-37907055
103. https://www.somersethouse.org.uk/whats-on/the-jam-about-the-young-idea
104. https://www.saatchigallery.com/art/rolling_stones.php
105. https://www.vam.ac.uk/exhibitions/pink-floyd
106. https://www.latimes.com/archives/la-xpm-1988-09-06-mn-1788-story.html.
107. https://www.nytimes.com/1985/12/11/arts/the-pop-life-an-erroll-garner-trove.html
108. https://variety.com/2019/music/news/the-true-story-of-erroll-garner-the-first-artist-to-sue-a-major-label-and-win-1203413083/
109. https://jazztimes.com/features/profiles/christian-sands-the-legacy-of-erroll-garner/
110. This interview was uploaded to the Corus Radio YouTube channel on 29 November 2010 in two parts: 1) https://www.youtube.com/watch?v=xBtlZODR9D0 2) https://www.youtube.com/watch?v=hRkx-HyMz6w
111. https://www.cbsnews.com/news/michael-jacksons-lucrative-legacy-19-05-2013/2/
112. https://www.smithsonianmag.com/smart-news/johnny-cashs-tennessee-ranch-now-museum-180960189/
113. 'Miss Misery' appeared on the soundtrack of *Good Will Hunting* and was nominated as Best Original Song at the 1998 Academy Awards.
114. https://www.superdeluxeedition.com/interview/princes-archivist-michael-howe-talks-to-sde/
115. Ibid.

116. https://www.vulture.com/2018/09/prince-vault-archivist-michael-howe-interview.html

117. https://www.superdeluxeedition.com/interview/princes-archivist-michael-howe-talks-to-sde/

119. https://hastingsonlinetimes.co.uk/hastings-life/hastings-people/hallo-sausages-the-lyrics-of-ian-dury

119. https://www.theguardian.com/books/2018/oct/30/the-flame-by-leonard-cohen-poetry-lyrics

120. https://www.sfgate.com/books/article/Nick-Drake-Remembered-for-a-While-review-5990361.php

121. https://www.genesis-publications.com/comingsoon/janis-joplin-scrapbook-1966-68/0806

122. http://www.brytermusic.com/the-tides-magnificence/

123. https://pitchfork.com/features/article/8937-this-little-conspiracy-the-great-white-wonder-and-the-dawn-of-the-album-leak/

124. http://www.bobdylan.com/thecuttingedge_completetracklisting/

125. https://www.legacyrecordings.co.uk/news/bob-dylan-1966-live-recordings

126. https://www.nytimes.com/2016/03/06/arts/music/bob-dylans-secret-archive.html

127. https://www.rollingstone.com/music/music-news/bob-dylan-sells-6000-item-private-collection-for-15-million-237958/

128. https://www.nytimes.com/2016/03/06/arts/music/bob-dylans-secret-archive.html

129. https://www.billboard.com/articles/news/9487975/bob-dylan-unpublished-lyrics-auction/

130. www.neilyoungarchives.com

131. https://www.rollingstone.com/music/music-country/johnny-cash-website-music-tour-862905/

132. https://radiohead.com/library/

133. https://www.wired.co.uk/article/radiohead-public-library

134. Ibid.

135. https://www.leppardvault.com

136. https://americansongwriter.com/def-leppards-joe-elliott-shares-personal-collection-in-the-def-leppard-vault/

137. https://courtneybarnett.live

138. https://www.billboard.com/articles/news/9537585/courtney-barnett-online-archive/

139. www.jeffbuckleycollection.com

140. http://inveniem.com

141. https://www.nme.com/news/music/dolly-parton-has-a-secret-song-locked-away-in-time-capsule-at-dollywood-2852118

6 Brand of Gold

1. https://www.universalorlando.com/web/en/us/things-to-do/dining/bob-marley-a-tribute-to-freedom/dinner-menu.html

2. Its opening was not without issues, however. In June 1997, movie producer Andrew Gaty filed a $1 million lawsuit against Universal Studios Florida and several members of the Marley family claiming they had taken his idea for

the Marley-themed complex without his permission, denying him the profit participation he claims the assorted parties had agreed to in 1995 when the initial idea was developed and pitched. "In the lawsuit, Gaty says he approached the Marley heirs in early 1995 to discuss 'ways in which the Bob Marley name and legacy could be exploited for profit'," wrote *Billboard*. "Among the ideas discussed, according to the lawsuit, were a movie and a replica of Marley's home in Jamaica that would be the model for a restaurant, club, and retail venue. The Marley house venue would have been opened in different locations around the world." Eileen Fitzpatrick, 'Marley Deal Prompts Lawsuit; Producer Sues Family, Universal'. Originally published in *Billboard* on 28 June 1997. Reprinted in Hank Bordowitz (ed.) *Every Little Thing Gonna Be Alright: The Bob Marley Reader*, 2004, p. 198.

3. https://www.universalorlando.com/web/en/us/things-to-do/dining/bob-marley-a-tribute-to-freedom
4. https://www.forbes.com/sites/zackomalleygreenburg/2019/10/30/the-top-earning-dead-celebrities-of–2019/#447bab0b4e5e
5. https://shopuk.bobmarley.com
6. https://shopuk.bobmarley.com/*/*/Bob-Marley-Don-t-Worry-Face-Mask/6GN40000000
7. https://www.wrangler.com/shop/men-featured-bob-marley-x-wrangler
8. Ibid.
9. https://www.thehouseofmarley.co.uk
10. https://www.linkedin.com/company/viva-beverages-inc-/about/
11. https://www.theverge.com/2016/2/5/10921432/marley-natural-marijuana-launch-price
12. Ibid.
13. http://www.bobmarley.com/company-news/marley-natural/
14. https://www.theglobeandmail.com/report-on-business/rob-magazine/toronto-native-jamie-salter-rebrands-marilyn-monroe/article4102829/
15. https://www.theverge.com/2016/2/5/10921432/marley-natural-marijuana-launch-price
16. https://www.theguardian.com/commentisfree/2014/nov/22/marley-natural-legacy-marley-debate
17. Ibid.
18. https://www.theguardian.com/commentisfree/2016/apr/22/bob-marley-stoner-god-snapchat-filter-weed-smoker
19. https://www.theguardian.com/music/2018/jul/11/damian-marley-on-weed-politics-and-bob
20. https://www.washingtonpost.com/archive/lifestyle/style/1991/08/25/dread-reckoning-the-marley-mess/94894ac0-248f-4a9f-b5b0-7429704a29d8/
21. Ibid.
22. https://www.theguardian.com/music/2015/feb/23/bob-marley-estate-wins-court-battle-against-t-shirt-merchandisers
23. https://www.reuters.com/article/us-bobmarley-verizon-idUSN3045298520070830
24. https://www.nbcnews.com/id/wbna20763684
25. https://www.reuters.com/article/bobmarley-verizon/update-1-verizon-says-to-reinstate-bob-marley-ringtones-idUSN1340930520070913
26. Ibid.
27. Ibid.

28. https://www.bhlmagazine.com/iconic-hollywood/
29. https://www.latimes.com/archives/la-xpm-1989-06-11-tm-2866-story.html
301. https://corporate.findlaw.com/litigation-disputes/practitioner-s-guide-to-california-right-of-publicity-law.html
31. https://codes.findlaw.com/ca/civil-code/civ-sect-3344-1.html
32. A feature in *Vox* in 2018 rounded up the main state-by-state developments. "There are 23 states in which a right to publicity lives on postmortem, and the time frames vary widely, from 10 years in Washington to 100 in Oklahoma," it said. "In California, the right to publicity is held by the person's family or estate for 70 years. In New York, it doesn't currently exist at all, with the right to publicity halting at the moment of death. Nearly every year, a bill is proposed that would extend the right to publicity in New York to 40 years after a person's death – primarily to guarantee that a celebrity's family or estate would be able to profit off of it." https://www.vox.com/the-goods/2018/10/23/18010274/amy-winehouse-hologram-tour-controversy-technology
33. This is the typical length of copyright in the UK: https://www.gov.uk/copyright/how-long-copyright-lasts. In the US, there are different rules around copyright reclamation, which is covered in Chapter 10. This is, however, specific to a creator reclaiming rights from a music publisher and does not affect the overall duration of the copyright period: https://www.royaltyexchange.com/length-of-ownership-music
34. The edition drawn on and quoted from here was published in February 2020: https://www.uspto.gov/sites/default/files/documents/BasicFacts.pdf
35. Aspirin was developed by German company Bayer in 1900 and it registered the trademark, but it expired in 1917 and was struck down in a court ruling in 1921. The judge in the case ruled that it was now in the public domain and any company could use the name "aspirin" for headache and pain relief tablets sold in packets of 50 or less. https://americanhistory.si.edu/collections/search/object/nmah_730633
36. https://www.dogfish.com/brewery/beer/bitches-brew
37. https://kindofbluewhisky.com
38. https://performingsongwriter.com/girl-from-ipanema/
39. http://www.bloomberg.com/news/2011-08-19/miles-davis-trademark-owners-sue-new-york-s-miles-cafe-for-infringement.html
40. https://www.courthousenews.com/wp-content/uploads/2019/08/Johnny-Cash.pdf
41. https://popculture.com/country-music/2019/02/06/johnny-cash-kitchen-saloon-open-downtown-nashville/
42. https://www.independent.co.uk/news/prince-purple-one-love-symbol-2-trademark-copyright-songs-estate-death-a8609426.html
43. https://www.thefashionlaw.com/princes-estate-responds-to-trademark-offices-refusal-to-register-purple-trademark-with-a-430-page-filing/
44. https://trademarks.justia.com/880/09/purple-88009988.html
45. https://www.vanityfair.com/culture/2016/03/picasso-multi-billion-dollar-empire-battle
46. Ibid.
47. Ibid.
48. Ibid.
49. https://perryscope.us
50. https://store.davidbowie.com/dept/accessories?cp=99486_99538

51. https://isaachayes.com/collections/apparel
52. "The surface of the cap and barrel is engraved with symbolic motifs in reference to the five major jazz periods he helped to create," runs the product description. "Also decorating the cap is a spiral representing the tornado he witnessed as a child and spoke of as the spiritual source of the powerful wind he needed to play the trumpet." The pens were limited to 1,926 (to symbolise the year of Miles Davis's birth). https://www.wondersmall.com/world/montblanc-great-characters-miles-davis-limited-edition-1926-fountain-pen.html
53. https://hypebeast.com/2008/3/kurt-cobain-converse-collection
54. https://www.nme.com/news/music/kurt-cobain-53-1329886
55. https://www.theguardian.com/music/musicblog/2013/jun/10/arturo-vega-ramones-logo-seal
56. https://www.billboard.com/articles/news/lifestyle/8548104/linda-johnny-ramone-happy-socks-collection-photos
57. https://www.sfgate.com/bayarea/article/Jerry-Garcia-s-Estate-Sued-Ex-employee-says-2993495.php
58. https://www.latimes.com/archives/la-xpm-1992-07-10-vw-1792-story.html
59. https://liveforlivemusic.com/news/jerry-garcia-tiger-skateboard/
60. https://jerrygarcia.com/introducing-icelantic-x-jerry-garcia-limited-edition-skis/
61. https://www.rollingstone.com/product-recommendations/lifestyle/jerry-garcia-shoes-keen-sandals-1034808/
62. https://www.grassrootscalifornia.com/collections/jerry-garcia
63. https://variety.com/2020/music/news/grateful-dead-jerry-garcia-cannabis-weed-line-1234815869/
64. https://garciahandpicked.com
65. https://www.hollywoodreporter.com/thr-esq/jimi-hendrix-estate-wins-appeal-675297
66. http://www.spark-me.com/portfolio_page/jimi-hendrix-shoes-launched-by-converse/
67. https://www.rollingstone.com/culture/culture-news/voodoo-style-jimi-hendrix-clothing-line-comes-to-varvatos-54663/
68. https://markets.businessinsider.com/news/stocks/authentic-hendrix-announces-exclusive-teaming-with-epic-rights-and-perryscope-to-expand-and-enhance-the-authentic-hendrix-retail-brand-1020576532
69. https://www.billboard.com/articles/business/8546395/sony-music-thread-shop-worldwide-deal-jimi-hendrix-merch
70. https://www.musicbusinessworldwide.com/sony-musics-the-thread-shop-inks-global-jimi-hendrix-merch-deal/
71. https://www.prnewswire.com/news-releases/sony-music-entertainments-the-thread-shop-launches-new-jimi-hendrix-e-commerce-store-301097818.html
72. https://www.billboard.com/articles/business/legal-and-management/9510260/jimi-hendrix-brother-niece-trademark-infringement-court-ruling
73. https://www.seattletimes.com/entertainment/music/renton-music-school-founded-by-jimi-hendrixs-niece-can-continue-to-use-the-hendrix-name-court-says/
74. The limited-edition Maestro watch sells for £995; it was developed in collaboration with María Elena Holly, the singer's widow, to mark what would have been his 80th birthday in 2016. A contribution from each watch

sale goes to the Buddy Holly Educational Foundation. https://raymond-weil.co.uk/product/steel-on-steel-silver-dial-pale-blue-highlights/

75. https://www.latimes.com/archives/la-xpm-1989-06-11-tm-2866-story.html
76. Ibid.
77. Ibid.
78. https://www.authenticbrandsgroup.com/news/2019/7/12/wwd-abg-and-bellevue-brands-to-launch-elvis-fragrances
79. https://www.globenewswire.com/news-release/2019/06/27/1875088/0/en/Better-Choice-Company-and-Authentic-Brands-Group-to-Launch-Elvis-Presley-Hound-Dog-Pet-Wellness-Products.html
80. https://www.nme.com/news/music/supreme-to-release-daniel-johnston-clothing-line-2666060
81. https://www.nme.com/news/music/vans-announce-new-daniel-johnston-collection-2685130
82. https://www.billboard.com/articles/news/8517490/frank-zappa-coloring-book-november-fantoons
83. https://www.rollingstone.com/music/music-news/jeff-buckley-graphic-novel-grace-817223/
84. Quoted in John Densmore, *The Doors Unhinged: Jim Morrison's Legacy Goes on Trial*, 2013, p. xiii.
85. Ibid., p. xiv.
86. Ibid., p. 2.
87. https://www.latimes.com/archives/la-xpm-2005-oct-05-et-doors5-story.html
88. Ibid.
89. Quoted in John Densmore, *The Doors Unhinged: Jim Morrison's Legacy Goes on Trial*, 2013, p. 240.
90. https://www.rollingstone.com/music/music-news/the-doors-owe-5-million-to-densmore-morrison-estate-180270/
91. https://www.thefix.com/content/courtney-love-frances-cobain-publicity-rights91000
92. https://www.theguardian.com/music/2012/may/03/courtney-love-kurt-cobain
93. The original piece on *TMZ* has been removed from its website but it was repeated in multiple online news reports based on the original piece. https://www.nme.com/news/music/courtney-love-75-1272618
94. https://www.benjerry.com/whats-new/2015/cherry-garcia-story
95. https://www.nytimes.com/1997/02/02/weekinreview/it-is-money-battles-like-these-that-make-the-dead-truly-grateful.html
9. 6https://www.forbes.com/sites/oliverherzfeld/2017/10/19/thelonious-monk-and-the-perils-of-oral-agreements/#3209c189305e
97. https://www.reuters.com/article/us-northcoast-monk-idUSKBN1FL5QW
98. https://northcoastbrewing.com/north-coast-brewing-company-reintroduces-famed-belgian-style-abbey-ale-brother-thelonious-with-new-label/
99. https://jazztimes.com/blog/north-coast-brother-thelonious-returns/
100. https://www.cnbc.com/2014/04/04/kurt-cobain-and-the-big-business-of-dead-celebs.html
101. https://people.com/celebrity/dr-martens-shoes-apologizes-for-kurt-cobain-ad/
102. https://www.theguardian.com/media/2007/may/25/mcsaatchi.advertising
10. 3Ibid.
104. https://www.rollingstone.com/music/music-news/kurt-cobain-john-lennon-and-tupac-shakur-star-in-dutch-beer-ad-188488/

105. 'Hey Jude' is, of course, a Paul McCartney song so it seems odd the makers of the ad would try and link it to John Lennon.
106. https://www.theguardian.com/music/2019/mar/12/marc-jacobs-dismiss-copyright-lawsuit-nirvana-smiley-face
107. https://www.billboard.com/articles/columns/rock/8502042/marc-jacobs-nirvana-smiley-face-logo-lawsuit-response
108. https://www.hollywoodreporter.com/thr-esq/marc-jacobs-cant-evade-nirvanas-lawsuit-heaven-t-shirt-1254762?utm_source=twitter&utm_medium=social&utm_source=t.co&utm_medium=referral
109. https://www.billboard.com/articles/business/9454294/california-graphic-artist-claims-he-not-kurt-cobain-created-nirvana-smiley-face-logo
11. 0Ibid.
111. https://www.npr.org/2015/12/11/459313019/hypothetical-coffee-mug-jolts-sinatra-into-action-to-protect-his-image
112. Ibid.
113. Ibid.
114. Ibid.
115. https://www.billboard.com/articles/business/8503395/notorious-big-lawsuit-yes-snowboards-photograph
116. https://www.theglobeandmail.com/report-on-business/rob-magazine/toronto-native-jamie-salter-rebrands-marilyn-monroe/article4102829/
117. Ibid.
118. Ibid.
119. Quoted in *Get Rich or Try Dying: Music's Mega Legacies*, first broadcast on BBC Four on 1 November 2019.
120. https://daggerrecords.com/story/
121. https://www.redbubble.com/about
122. https://www.prweb.com/releases/redbubble_and_estate_of_ol_dirty_bastard_launch_official_fan_art_program_celebrating_25th_anniversary_of_hip_hop_icons_debut_album/prweb16965848.htm
123. https://hypebeast.com/2020/10/lil-peep-rockstar-collection-release-firme-atelier
124. Ibid.

7   The Future of the Past

1. https://handelhendrix.org/learn/about-hendrix/
2. https://handelhendrix.org/about-us/our-story/
3. https://www.officialcharts.com/artist/12774/jimi-hendrix/
4. Ibid.
5. https://www.graceland.com/elvis-week
6. https://www.theguardian.com/theguardian/1980/dec/10/fromthearchive
7. https://www.latimes.com/archives/la-xpm-1994-04-11-mn-44717-story.html
8. https://latimesblogs.latimes.com/lanow/2009/06/michael-jackson-7.html
9. https://www.bbc.co.uk/news/uk-england-london-35875379
10. https://www.graceland.com/about-graceland
11. https://www.rollingstone.com/music/music-features/elvis-presley-business-revenue-953324/
12. https://www.forbes.com/sites/reginacole/2018/08/09/for-elvis-week-visit-graceland-americas-true-house-museum/#fe3c20e725b8

13. https://www.telegraph.co.uk/news/worldnews/1559512/Elvis-Presley-in-return-of-The-King.html
14. https://www.graceland.com/about-graceland
15. https://www.graceland.com/ticket-information
16. https://www.graceland.com/dining
17. All prices were correct as of late 2020.
18. https://www.dailymail.co.uk/news/tennessee/article-9150731/Elvis-Presleys-Graceland-starting-virtual-tours.html
19. https://www.elvis.com.au/presley/elvis-a-family-franchise.shtml
20. https://insidememphisbusiness.com/ceo-of-the-year/jack-soden-elvis-presley-enterprises/
21. https://www.bizjournals.com/memphis/news/2018/12/18/lets-stop-fighting-epe-offers-the-city-of-memphis.html
22. https://eu.commercialappeal.com/story/opinion/2019/04/13/graceland-memphis-whitehaven-elvis-presley/3451835002/
23. https://www.theguardian.com/music/2016/aug/08/princes-estate-deny-plans-to-sell-paisley-park-tmz
24. Ibid.
25. https://www.paisleypark.com/tickets
26. All prices were correct as of August 2020.
27. https://www.newyorker.com/magazine/2018/06/25/paisley-park-princes-lonely-palace
28. Ibid.
29. https://variety.com/2019/music/news/prince-estate-paisley-park-names-new-director-1203354747/
30. http://www.designcurial.com/news/hendrix-flat-london-by-outside-studios-and-haines-phillips-architects-4860644
31. https://www.bobmarleymuseum.com
32. https://www.theguardian.com/culture/2001/jun/01/artsfeatures.bobmarley
33. https://people.com/archive/a-decade-later-the-heirs-of-jim-jimi-and-janis-reap-the-troubled-legacies-of-rock-vol-14-no-25/
34. https://www.chron.com/news/article/Relic-from-Janis-Joplin-s-home-sold-on-Pawn-6089573.php
35. https://www.islandpacket.com/news/state/south-carolina/article33596343.html
36. https://www.dailystar.co.uk/news/latest-news/national-trust-bosses-buy-childhood-21267527
37. http://www.digitaljournal.com/entertainment/music/catching-up-with-bill-miller-icon-entertainment-founder/article/570616
38. https://www.nixonfoundation.org/2011/04/rn-welcomes-the-man-in-black-to-the-white-house/
39. https://recordcollectormag.com/articles/back-in-black
40. https://www.cashkitchenandsaloon.com
41. https://www.patsymuseum.com
42. https://www.billboard.com/articles/columns/country/6754076/charlie-dick-widower-of-patsy-cline-dies-at-81
43. https://www.bizjournals.com/nashville/news/2020/06/01/exclusive-downtown-museum-to-honor-music-icon.html
44. Quoted from press release sent to media on 9 June 2020.
45. https://www.nytimes.com/2016/03/06/arts/music/bob-dylans-secret-archive.html

46. https://www.upi.com/Archives/1989/11/09/Horowitz-leaves-8-million-estate-to-wife/1497626590800/
47. https://archives.yale.edu/repositories/6/resources/10762
48. https://jazztimes.com/blog/rutgers-acquires-count-basie-collection/
49. https://ucmweb.rutgers.edu/magazine/1419archive/the-arts/count-basie-comes-home.html
50. https://www.nytimes.com/2018/11/29/arts/music/billy-strayhorn-archive-library-of-congress.html
51. https://www.nytimes.com/2019/03/15/arts/music/lou-reed-archive-new-york-public-library.html
52. the https://peggylee.com/museum/
53. https://www.ramonesmuseum.com
54. https://www.theguardian.com/travel/2012/jun/01/edith-piaf-museum-paris
55. https://www.theparisreview.org/blog/2017/09/05/visit-musee-edith-piaf/
56. Ibid.
57. Ibid.
58. Lauren Istvandity, Raphaël Nowak and Sarah Baker, *Curating Pop: Exhibiting Popular Music in the Museum*, 2019, p. 3.
59. Ibid., p. 17.
60. Ibid., p. 20.
61. Ibid., p. 38.
62. Ibid., p. 84.
63. From Julien's Auctions press release sent to media on 21 June 2020.
64. https://www.aap.com.au/cobain-guitar-sells-for-a9m-to-aussie/
65. https://www.liveauctioneers.com/news/auctions/auction-results/kurt-cobains-guitar-tops-6m-at-juliens-auctions/
66. https://www.theguardian.com/music/2019/oct/26/kurt-cobains-green-cardigan-raises-record-334000-at-auction
67. https://www.christies.com/auctions/the-david-gilmour-collection#overview_Nav
68. https://www.latimes.com/entertainment-arts/music/story/2019-10-17/walter-becker-steely-dan-estate-sale-guitars
69. https://www.rollingstone.com/music/music-news/walter-beckers-guitars-amplifiers-fetch-3-3-million-at-auction-901963/
70. https://www.theguardian.com/music/2016/nov/11/david-bowies-art-fetches-24m-in-first-round-of-sale
71. Quoted in Michael Shnayerson, *Boom: Mad Money, Mega Dealers and the Rise of Contemporary Art*, 2019, p. 341.
72. https://www.billboard.com/articles/columns/pop/8502726/george-michael-personal-art-collection-sale-15-million
73. https://www.theguardian.com/music/2018/nov/30/frank-sinatra-art-sale-sothebys-auction
74. https://www.bbc.co.uk/news/entertainment-arts-11927570
75. https://www.reuters.com/article/us-jackson-glove/michael-jacksons-glove-sells-for-350000-at-auction-idUSTRE5AL02A20091123
76. https://www.bbc.co.uk/news/av/entertainment-arts-13936013
77. https://www.nme.com/news/music/three-of-eddie-van-halens-guitars-sell-for-422000-at-auction-2830816
78. https://twitter.com/WolfVanHalen/status/1334292776159076354?s=20
79. https://twitter.com/WolfVanHalen/status/1334293551174144000?s=20
80. https://twitter.com/WolfVanHalen/status/1334294216730583040?s=20

81. Rob Chapman, *Syd Barrett: A Very Irregular Head*, 2010, pp. 397–9.
82. Ibid., p. 398.
83. https://www.independent.co.uk/news/uk/this-britain/syd-barretts-last-remnants-sold-in-frenzy-of-bidding-426398.html
84. https://www.mirror.co.uk/3am/celebrity-news/prodigy-star-keith-flints-possessions-20525251
85. https://www.reuters.com/article/us-johnnycash/johnny-cash-memorabilia-up-for-auction-in-l-a-idUSTRE69P07620101026
86. https://www.billboard.com/articles/news/66446/cash-auction-yields-nearly-4-million
87. https://www.xxlmag.com/tupac-shakur-car-shot-sale-1-75-million-dollars/
88. https://www.theguardian.com/world/2007/oct/24/italy.classicalmusic
89. Ibid.
90. https://www.reuters.com/article/us-italy-callas-auction/buyers-snap-up-treasures-from-maria-callass-life-idUSL1223375120071213
91. https://www.bonhams.com/press_release/30753/
92. Ibid.
93. https://www.guitarplayer.com/news/elvis-presleys-comeback-special-hagstrom-viking-ii-sells-for-dollar625000-at-auction
94. https://www.dailymail.co.uk/tvshowbiz/article-9417957/Elvis-Presleys-electric-guitar-used-iconic-comeback-sells-450-000-auction.html

8 Corporation Death

1. The 1990s sitcom was about three priests marooned on a remote island off the west coast of Ireland. The fourth episode of the first series – broadcast in May 1995 – was called "Competition Time" and was based around an "All Priests Stars in their Eyes Lookalike Competition". Father Dougal (young, mesmerisingly stupid) entered as Sun Records-era Elvis, Father Ted (frustrated, duplicitous) entered as *'68 Comeback Special* Elvis and Father Jack (cantankerous, dipsomaniac) entered as Vegas Elvis. They won.
2. Ted Harrison, *The Death and Resurrection of Elvis Presley*, 2016, p. 68.
3. http://www.chinadaily.com.cn/english/doc/2004-10/27/content_386176.htm
4. Ted Harrison, *The Death and Resurrection of Elvis Presley*, 2016, p. 68.
5. CKX (sometimes stylised as CKx) stands for "Content Is King" (with the "X" working as a proxy signature based on Xavier, one of Sillerman's middle names). https://www.latimes.com/archives/la-xpm-2005-aug-11-fi-graceland11-story.html
6. https://www.forbes.com/sites/ryanmac/2015/08/24/the-fall-of-an-edm-empire-sfx/#5e960ad0621d
7. Ted Harrison, *The Death and Resurrection of Elvis Presley*, 2016, p. 69.
8. https://www.independent.co.uk/arts-entertainment/music/news/presleys-daughter-sells-rights-to-the-elvis-estate-for-acircpound52m-691782.html
9. https://fortune.com/2005/12/12/robert-sillerman-elvis/
10. Ibid.
11. Ibid.
12. https://www.seattletimes.com/entertainment/elvis-estate-minus-graceland-sells-for-100-million/

13. https://www.hollywoodreporter.com/news/new-elvis-campaign-graceland-134328
14. https://www.telegraph.co.uk/news/worldnews/1559512/Elvis-Presley-in-return-of-The-King.html
15. https://www.forbes.com/2005/10/26/dead-celebrities-earnings_cx_pk_lh_deadceleb05_1027list.html#5d8c32087112
16. https://fortune.com/2005/12/12/robert-sillerman-elvis/
17. Ibid.
18. Ibid.
19. Ted Harrison, *The Death and Resurrection of Elvis Presley*, 2016, p. 73.
20. https://latimesblogs.latimes.com/culturemonster/2010/02/viva-elvis-cirque-du-soleil-brings-the-king-back-to-vegas.html
21. https://www.reviewjournal.com/entertainment/shows/viva-elvis-likely-to-close-in-2012/
22. https://www.theguardian.com/media/2011/may/10/apollo-global-management-buys-ckx
23. https://deadline.com/2013/05/ft-core-media-group-seeking-buyers-for-elvis-presley-muhammad-ali-rights-505064/
24. Ted Harrison, *The Death and Resurrection of Elvis Presley*, 2016, p. 79.
25. https://www.prnewswire.com/news-releases/authentic-brands-group-llc-and-neca-inc-acquire-the-intellectual-property-of-marilyn-monroe-llc-113448394.html
26. https://completemusicupdate.com/article/authentic-acquires-elvis-presley-brand-rights/
27. https://nypost.com/2013/10/07/authentic-brands-emerges-as-lead-bidder-for-elvis-rights/
28. https://www.prnewswire.com/news-releases/authentic-brands-group-llc-and-joel-weinshanker-complete-the-purchase-of-elvis-presley-intellectual-property-and-graceland-operations-232486551.html
29. Ted Harrison, *The Death and Resurrection of Elvis Presley*, 2016, p. 82.
30. Earnings before interest, taxes, depreciation and amortisation – a metric deployed in the financial sector to evaluate the operating performance of a company.
31. https://www.billboard.com/articles/business/8512129/whitney-houston-estate-hologram-tour-musical-album-primary-wave
32. https://www.billboard.com/articles/news/78888/whitney-houston-inks-100-million-arista-deal
33. Primary Wave bought up the music rights of Canadian classical pianist Glenn Gould in 2017. The deal covered his publishing, certain master recordings, certain audiovisual recordings and his name and likeness. https://www.billboard.com/articles/business/8476224/glenn-gould-classical-pianist-hologram-tour
34. The *Bob Lefsetz Podcast*, 6 February 2020.
35. https://www.billboard.com/articles/business/6619970/buddy-holly-bmg-song-catalog
36. https://www.bloomberg.com/news/articles/2021-02-18/music-mogul-buys-beach-boys-songs-calling-band-underappreciated
37. https://www.musicbusinessworldwide.com/david-crosby-sells-catalog-to-irving-azoffs-iconic-artists-group-including-recorded-music-and-publishing-rights/

38. https://www.musicbusinessworldwide.com/irving-azoff-buys-again-as-iconic-snaps-up-linda-ronstadt-recorded-music-rights/
39. https://primarywave.com/julian-lennon-sells-stake-in-beatles-songs-2/
40. https://www.cnbc.com/2014/04/04/kurt-cobain-and-the-big-business-of-dead-celebs.html
41. https://www.hollywoodreporter.com/news/bmg-150-million-deal-music-619632
42. https://primarywave.com/julian-lennon-sells-stake-in-beatles-songs-2/
43. https://www.nytimes.com/2009/04/22/theater/22rodg.html
44. https://concord.com/concord-news/concord-bicycle-music-acquires-imagem-music-group/
45. https://www.musicbusinessworldwide.com/primary-wave-buys-chunk-bob-marleys-catalogue-50m-deal/
46. https://www.nytimes.com/2018/01/13/business/media/bob-marley-primary-wave.html
47. https://primarywave.com/primary-wave-music-publishing-announces-three-new-partnerships-and-acquisitions-count-basie-pete-waterman-kenny-loggins/
48. https://variety.com/2019/music/news/george-gershwin-estate-signs-deal-with-downtown-music-publishing-1203201009/
49. From press release sent to media on 28 October 2019.
50. https://www.musicweek.com/labels/read/bmg-partners-with-george-harrison-s-dark-horse-records/078681
51. https://www.musicbusinessworldwide.com/primary-wave-agrees-multi-million-deal-to-acquire-majority-stake-in-ray-charles-pre-1964-publishing-catalog/
52. From press release sent to media on 16 June 2020.
53. https://www.billboard.com/articles/business/6745955/sony-music-artist-legacy-group-recordings-joint-venture
54. https://www.pollstar.com/article/qs-with-umgs-arron-saxe-on-preserving-legacies-and-creating-value-for-estates-147423
55. https://www.musicbusinessworldwide.com/concord-musics-craft-recordings-promotes-michele-smith-to-vp-estate-and-legacy-brand-management/
56. https://www.hollywoodreporter.com/news/wme-launches-legends-group-to-manage-celebrity-estates
57. https://variety.com/2021/film/news/notorious-big-biggie-estate-signs-with-wme-1234955119/
58. https://www.billboard.com/articles/business/8502636/myths-music-publishing-legacy-catalogues-faq-recapture-rights
59. Quoted in *Get Rich or Try Dying: Music's Mega Legacies*, first broadcast on BBC Four on 1 November 2019.
60. Ibid.
61. Ibid.
62. https://wemanagelegends.com/for-estate-managers/
63. https://www.cmgworldwide.com/clients/
64. https://www.nytimes.com/2016/06/19/arts/music/dead-musician-estate-manager-joplin-doors.html
65. https://www.forbes.com/sites/zackomalleygreenburg/2018/10/31/lazarus-inc-this-entrepreneur-has-turned-dead-celebritiesand-dead-brandsinto-a-400m-business/#43263661242b
66. https://www.liveabout.com/marilyn-monroe-will-testament-3505094
67. https://www.theglobeandmail.com/report-on-business/rob-magazine/toronto-native-jamie-salter-rebrands-marilyn-monroe/article4102829/

68. Ibid.
69. https://www.billboard.com/articles/business/8529887/primary-wave-larry-mestel-interview-photos-boston-catalog
70. https://www.johnbranca.com
71. https://www.forbes.com/sites/dorothypomerantz/2012/10/24/elizabeth-taylor-is-the-new-queen-of-dead-celebrities/#2a5dfced1597
72. https://www.johnbranca.com
73. https://www.forbes.com/sites/zackomalleygreenburg/2016/03/14/sony-to-buy-michael-jacksons-half-of-sonyatv-for-750-million/#7d000c091a40
74. https://www.forbes.com/sites/zackomalleygreenburg/2016/10/12/the-highest-paid-dead-celebrities-of-2016/#732cb48711b1
75. As a side note, Branca's teenage band opened for The Doors at the Whisky a Go Go in Los Angeles in the 1960s. https://www.johnbranca.com
76. https://www.billboard.com/articles/business/8503368/john-branca-save-michael-jackson-legacy-leaving-neverland
77. https://www.johnbranca.com
78. https://www.forbes.com/sites/zackomalleygreenburg/2012/08/17/the-scandalously-boring-truth-about-michael-jacksons-will/
79. https://musicrow.com/2016/03/sandbox-entertainment-adds-john-r-cash-revocable-trust-to-roster/
80. https://variety.com/2017/music/news/prince-estate-troy-carter-spotify-1202027998/
81. Quoted in *Get Rich or Try Dying: Music's Mega Legacies*, first broadcast on BBC Four on 1 November 2019.
82. https://www.rollingstone.com/music/music-features/prince-estate-big-plans-upcoming-purple-reign-698529/

9   Restoration Artists

1. Quoted in *The Estate of Ritchie Valens | The Will: Family Secrets Revealed*, first broadcast on Investigation Discovery on 26 October 2012.
2. Ibid.
3. Ibid.
4. https://www.latimes.com/archives/la-xpm-1987-07-19-ca-4551-story.html
5. Quoted in *The Estate of Ritchie Valens | The Will: Family Secrets Revealed*, first broadcast on Investigation Discovery on 26 October 2012.
6. https://apnews.com/article/3e42d6eed05433dcd026c8b71cc39647
7. *BPI Yearbook 1989/1990*, p. 88.
8. Ibid., p. 92.
9. https://www.boxofficemojo.com/release/rl2722727425/
10. https://variety.com/1977/film/reviews/the-buddy-holly-story-1200424152/
11. Philip Norman, *Buddy: The Biography*, 1996, p. 18.
12. https://www.boxofficemojo.com/title/tt0093378/?ref_=bo_se_r_1
13. https://www.billboard.com/charts/billboard-200/1987-09-19
14. As with the *Father Ted* episode about Elvis, three different actors played different ages of Elvis in the production, with Shakin' Stevens playing him in the middle period and P. J. Proby as the Vegas-era Elvis.
15. http://alwayspatsycline.net
16. https://www.walkwithpatsycline.com/about.html

17. https://www.buddythemusical.com
18. Philip Norman, *Buddy: The Biography*, 1996, p. 20.
19. Alma Cogan died on 26 October 1966. She was 34.
20. https://www.rollingstone.com/feature/elvis-presley-business-revenue-953324/
21. The precise number was 29 per cent and came from a YouGov poll of 2,034 British adults. It also found that only 12 per cent of respondents said they liked Elvis compared to 23 per cent who said the liked The Beatles and 25 per cent who said they liked David Bowie. https://www.theguardian.com/music/2017/may/16/millennials-elvis-presley-legacy
22. https://www.rollingstone.com/feature/elvis-presley-business-revenue-953324/
23. Quoted in *Get Rich or Try Dying: Music's Mega Legacies*, first broadcast on BBC Four on 1 November 2019.
24. https://www.ifpi.org/ifpi-issues-annual-global-music-report/
25. https://variety.com/2021/music/news/aaliyah-estate-update-streaming-services-1234887124/
26. https://twitter.com/AaliyahHaughton/status/1350171021391900673
27. https://variety.com/2021/music/news/jim-morrison-book-collected-works-1234913576/
28. https://www.theguardian.com/film/2014/oct/02/10-worst-music-biopics-ever-made
29. https://power1051.iheart.com/content/2019-07-31-the-23-best-worst-music-biopics-of-all-time/
30. https://www.rollingstone.com/movies/movie-lists/30-best-music-biopics-of-all-time-78623/
31. https://www.boxofficemojo.com/release/rl3439363585/
32. https://www.forbes.com/sites/maddieberg/2020/11/13/the-highest-paid-dead-celebrities-of-2020/?sh=6474b9e73b4b
33. http://www.chinadaily.com.cn/english/doc/2004-10/27/content_386176.htm
34. https://gothamist.com/arts-entertainment/everything-you-wanted-to-know-about-the-three-jeff-buckley-movies-being-made
35. https://www.boxofficemojo.com/title/tt1823125/?ref_=bo_se_r_1
36. Tim Buckley died on 29 June 1975 when Jeff was just 8.
37. The show was at St Ann's Church in New York on 26 April 1991, Jeff Buckley's first public performance. Jeff performed a cover of 'I Never Asked to Be Your Mountain', a song Tim wrote for his 1967 album *Goodbye & Hello* that was "rather explicitly about Jeff and his estranged mother" according to *Pitchfork*. https://pitchfork.com/thepitch/1052-watching-jeff-buckley-before-he-became-a-myth/
38. https://variety.com/2021/film/markets-festivals/jeff-buckley-reeve-carney-1234917252/
39. https://www.boxofficemojo.com/title/tt1393020/?ref_=bo_se_r_1
40. https://www.theguardian.com/music/2004/apr/25/popandrock4
41. Alan Bennett, the lugubrious and extremely dry British writer, is perhaps best known for his one-person radio and television plays under the title of *Talking Heads*.
42. https://www.theguardian.com/film/2015/may/08/paul-greengrass-tunes-up-for-jimi-hendrix-biopic
43. https://www.forbes.com/sites/natalierobehmed/2016/01/12/dalian-wanda-group-acquires-thomas-tulls-legendary-entertainment-for-3-5-billion/#3e91ecda1883

44. https://www.express.co.uk/entertainment/films/165710/Will-Kate-Winslet-play-songbird-Eva-Cassidy
45. https://www.theguardian.com/film/2016/sep/29/roy-orbison-biopic-in-the-works-the-big-o
46. https://www.imdb.com/title/tt5599198/
47. https://www.billboard.com/articles/news/6874787/tupac-shakur-biopic-director-benny-boom-revelations
48. https://www.boxofficemojo.com/title/tt1666185/?ref_=bo_se_r_1
49. https://www.theguardian.com/film/2017/jul/02/all-eyez-on-me-review-tupac-shakur-biopic-demetrius-shipp-jr
50. https://www.nytimes.com/2017/06/15/movies/all-eyez-on-me-review.html
51. https://www.hollywoodreporter.com/news/don-cheadles-miles-davis-film-813379
52. https://www.scpr.org/programs/the-frame/2016/03/31/47621/meet-the-miles-davis-heirs-who-keep-his-work-alive/
53. Ibid.
54. https://www.prnewswire.com/news-releases/new-jerry-garcia-artist-documentary-offers-rare-glimpse-of-the-man-behind-the-legend-301255980.html
55. https://deadline.com/2019/01/david-bowie-stardust-johnny-flynn-beast-biopic-1202546446/
56. Quoted in https://www.theguardian.com/film/2019/feb/01/david-bowie-biopic-stardust-wont-have-any-of-dads-music-says-son-neil-gaiman
57. Quoted in https://inews.co.uk/culture/music/david-bowie-biopic-go-ahead-despite-ban-music-393147
58. https://www.theguardian.com/film/2020/oct/29/david-bowie-biopic-trailer-stardust
59. https://www.billboard.com/articles/news/9474164/aretha-franklin-biopic-respect-delay-summer-2021/
60. https://www.facebook.com/eradesent.views/posts/860562911057532
61. https://www.bbc.co.uk/news/entertainment-arts-56482684
62. https://www.rollingstone.com/music/music-news/aretha-franklin-genius-biopic-family-1144692/
63. https://deadline.com/2019/11/michael-jackson-movie-bohemian-rhapsody-producer-john-logan-graham-king-1202792922/
64. https://www.independent.co.uk/arts-entertainment/films/news/elvis-presley-film-release-date-austin-butler-baz-luhrmann-tom-hanks-king-rock-a9037716.html
65. https://deadline.com/2020/09/elvis-tom-hanks-baz-luhrmann-movie-returns-to-production-australia-1234574267/
66. https://www.hollywoodreporter.com/news/baz-luhrmanns-elvis-presley-biopic-pushed-to-2022-release
67. https://deadline.com/2020/04/whitney-houston-movie-stella-meghie-directing-anthony-mccarten-writing-houston-estate-clive-davis-primary-wave-bohemian-rhapsody-1202914991/
68. https://www.hollywoodreporter.com/news/whitney-houston-biopic-finds-its-star-in-naomi-ackie-exclusive
69. https://twitter.com/WendellPierce/status/1319331498386915328
70. https://variety.com/2020/film/news/bb-king-estate-official-biopic-wendell-pierce-confusion-1234815283/

71. https://people.com/music/sam-cooke-granddaughter-nicole-steward-of-his-legacy/
72. https://www.loc.gov/item/prn-07-039/2006-national-recording-registry/2007-03-06/
73. https://www.showbiz411.com/2021/01/22/sam-cooke-dead-since-1964-has-had-20-million-streams-of-songs-since-new-years-thanks-to-movie
74. https://pitchfork.com/news/michelle-williams-cast-as-peggy-lee-in-todd-haynes-directed-biopic/
75. https://www.boxofficemojo.com/title/tt1477715/?ref_=bo_se_r_1
76. https://www.npr.org/sections/deceptivecadence/2019/06/07/730363989/pavarotti-documentary-misses-all-the-right-notes
77. https://www.theguardian.com/film/2019/jul/12/pavarotti-review-ron-howard-documentary
78. https://www.boxofficemojo.com/title/tt6964076/?ref_=bo_se_r_1
79. https://www.boxofficemojo.com/title/tt2870648/?ref_=bo_se_r_1
80. https://www.mirror.co.uk/3am/celebrity-news/amy-winehouse-documentary-trailer-upcoming-5125655
81. https://www.billboard.com/articles/news/6229437/reunited-ramones-estates-plan-big-comeback-including-martin-scorsese-film
82. A prior documentary on the band – *End of the Century: The Story of the Ramones* – had been released in 2003.
83. https://pitchfork.com/news/new-notorious-big-documentary-coming-to-netflix-watch-the-trailer/
84. https://www.brooklynvegan.com/2021-sxsw-film-fest-lineup-tom-petty-charli-xcx-poly-styrene-more/
85. https://www.standard.co.uk/culture/film/poly-styrene-bipolar-disorder-i-am-a-cliche-documentary-film-b921241.html
86. Ibid.
87. https://www.bbc.co.uk/news/entertainment-arts-26530182
88. https://thrillerlive.com/record-breaking-thriller-live-opens-a-new-west-end-booking-period/
89. Its original title was to be 'Don't Stop 'Til You Get Enough'.
90. https://www.nme.com/news/film/johnny-depp-not-involved-michael-jackson-musical-glove-2584508
91. https://pagesix.com/2019/11/28/johnny-depp-producing-musical-about-michael-jackson/
92. https://www.npr.org/2020/03/01/810036738/new-musical-imagines-michael-jacksons-story-as-told-by-his-famous-glove
93. https://www.playbill.com/news/article/a-night-with-janis-joplin-sets-closing-date-on-broadway-214290
94. https://www.nytimes.com/2014/04/26/theater/how-a-night-with-janis-joplin-was-suddenly-canceled.html?_r=0
95. https://www.theatermania.com/new-york-city-theater/news/holler-if-ya-hear-me-closing_68962.html
96. https://www.cbsnews.com/news/new-tupac-shakur-musical-debuts-on-broadway/
97. Quoted in https://www.theguardian.com/stage/shortcuts/2014/jun/23/holler-if-ya-hear-me-tupac-shakur-broadway-musical
98. https://www.nytimes.com/2020/02/16/theater/london-bob-marley-musical.html

99. https://www.nytimes.com/2019/05/20/business/media/whitney-houston-hologram-album.html

100. https://www.nytimes.com/2018/01/13/business/media/bob-marley-primary-wave.html

101. https://wtfestival.org/main-events/last-goodbye-the/

102. https://www.nytimes.com/2013/10/31/theater/reviews/the-last-goodbye-with-the-music-of-jeff-buckley.html

103. https://dluxe-magazine.co.uk/interviews/interview-jemima-dury-daughter-ian-dury-reasons-cheerful/

104. Ibid.

105. https://graeae.org/about/our-artistic-vision/

106. https://www.theguardian.com/culture/2009/nov/29/ian-dury-popandrock

107. https://www.billboard.com/articles/business/8465319/sonyatv-music-elvis-presley-musical

108. https://www.graceland.com/elvis-news/posts/elvis-week-2019-preliminary-schedule-of-events-announced

109. https://www.graceland.com/modified-elvis-week-schedule

110. https://www.graceland.com/elvisweekvirtual

111. https://www.billboard.com/articles/news/8550184/bob-marley-75th-birthday-redemption-song-new-video

112. Ibid.

113. https://www.billboard.com/articles/news/8551837/nat-king-cole-centennial-exhibit-grammy-museum-march-17

114. https://www.superdeluxeedition.com/news/edith-piaf-integrale-2015-massive-100th-anniversary-box-set/

115. https://www.nme.com/news/music/grammy-awards-2017-full-winners-list-1973626

116. https://www.bbc.co.uk/mediacentre/latestnews/2020/lennon-at-80

117. https://www.nme.com/news/tv/john-lennon-80th-birthday-to-be-marked-by-pop-up-tv-channel-launch-2771115

118. "Experiential marketing is a marketing technique that creates experiences between brands and consumers," is how Sense, a brand experience agency, defines it. "Experiential campaigns use an activation (for example product sampling, immersive experiences, stunts, events, etc.) to bring brands to life and interact directly with the target audience." https://sensemktg.com/experiential-marketing/

119. https://www.nme.com/news/music/the-doors-morrison-hotel-to-be-reissued-for-50th-anniversary-2735058

120. https://www.rhino.com/article/day-of-the-doors-2020-to-feature-original-morrison-hotel-restored-in-los-angeles-on-january

121. BMG acquired the publishing for a number of Cash compositions when it bought Bug Music in 2011 for an estimated $300 million. https://www.theguardian.com/business/2011/sep/12/bmg-buys-bug-music

122. http://www.academicis.co.uk/ac/is-letter-writing-dead-among-youngsters/

123. https://www.voanews.com/arts-culture/us-postal-service-unveils-music-icon-stamp-series

124. https://about.usps.com/newsroom/national-releases/2019/0402-usps-salutes-prince-of-soul-marvin-gaye.htm

125. http://www.mtv.com/news/1433429/freddie-mercury-stamp-creates-controversy-in-the-uk/

126. https://www.queenonline.com/news/royal-mail-issued-queen-stamps-now-on-general-sale

127. https://www.royalmint.com/our-coins/events/music-legends/queen/?

128. https://www.coinworld.com/news/precious-metals/royal-mint-sends-david-bowie-coin-on-a-balloon-ride

129. https://www.hollywoodreporter.com/news/miles-davis-edith-piaf-postage-stamps-285383

130. https://www.penguinrandomhouse.com/books/562823/elvis-presleys-love-me-tender-by-elvis-presley-illustrated-by-stephanie-graegin/

131. Quoted in *Get Rich or Try Dying: Music's Mega Legacies*, first broadcast on BBC Four on 1 November 2019.

132. https://otisreddingfoundationstore.square.site/product/preorder-respect-a-children-s-lyric-book/143

133. https://ultimateclassicrock.com/the-beatles-animated-series-premieres/

134. https://www.thejacksons.com/jackson-five-cartoon/

135. https://variety.com/2019/tv/news/netflix-elvis-animated-series-agent-king-1203304695/

136. https://www.hotpress.com/music/day-2005-phil-lynott-statue-unveiled-dublin-22785196

137. https://www.billboard.com/articles/news/9390042/little-richard-statue-erected-childhood-home

138. https://www.theguardian.com/music/2014/sep/14/amy-winehouse-statue-unveiled-camden-london

139. http://news.bbc.co.uk/1/hi/entertainment/4181485.stm

140. https://www.bbc.co.uk/news/uk-scotland-tayside-central-36162037

141. https://www.heraldscotland.com/news/13165269.rock-off-kirriemuir-residents-reject-a-statue-of-acdcs-bon-scott-in-town-square/

142. https://www.theage.com.au/national/victoria/never-tear-us-apart-michael-hutchence-statue-in-richmond-shelved-after-family-dispute-20190624-p520s9.html

143. https://www.facebook.com/otisredding/posts/watch-the-winning-video-for-these-arms-of-mine-from-our-contest-with-generotv-we/10101358425750716/

144. https://americansongwriter.com/janis-joplin-50-years-of-me-and-bobby-mcgee-video-news/

145. https://www.theguardian.com/books/2009/oct/24/johnny-cash-kleist-faber-review

146. https://omnibuspress.com/products/godspeed-the-kurt-cobain-graphic-novel

147. https://www.nytimes.com/2013/08/11/arts/music/part-ramones-biography-part-dreamscape.html

148. https://www.comicsreview.co.uk/nowreadthis/2016/11/18/glenn-gould-a-life-off-tempo/

149. https://amywinehousefoundation.org/home/

150. https://amywinehousefoundation.org/category/resilience-programme/

151. https://www.irishtimes.com/news/ireland/irish-news/music-bursary-established-in-memory-of-dolores-o-riordan-1.4046649

152. https://www.lucianopavarottifoundation.com/en/

153. https://joestrummerfoundation.org

154. http://www.holstfoundation.org

155. https://muddywatersfoundation.com

156. https://www.joeyramone.com/pages/foundation

157. http://www.michaelhutchenceinfo.com/world%20exclusive.htm
158. https://www.timberglingfoundation.org/about
159. https://www.billboard.com/articles/columns/hip-hop/9363849/juice-wrld-mom-live-free-999-fund
160. https://www.recordoftheday.com/on-the-move/news-press/fela-kutis-legacy-celebrated-with-new-scholarship-at-londons-trinity-laban
161. https://www.bobmarleyfoundation.org
162. https://www.rollingstone.com/culture/culture-news/what-happened-to-the-tupac-amaru-shakur-center-for-the-arts-227233/amp/
163. https://www.tbhef.org
164. https://www.whosampled.com/most-sampled-tracks/
165. https://pitchfork.com/news/90-of-ariana-grandes-7-rings-royalties-go-to-rodgers-and-hammerstein/
166. Ibid.
167. https://www.billboard.com/articles/business/publishing/8540704/miles-davis-downtown-music
168. WhoSampled records that samples of the music of Jeff Buckley are somewhat limited, listing only four examples. These include a sample of Buckley's cover of 'Lilac Wine' in the 2012 track '8xHundred by DropxLife' and a sample of 'You and I' in the track 'Deep Summer (Burial Remix)' by Mønic in 2017. https://www.whosampled.com/Jeff-Buckley/sampled/
169. https://www.musictech.net/news/tracklib-release-unheard-isaac-hayes/
170. https://www.billboard.com/articles/news/dance/8545187/avicii-tribute-concert-rita-ora-adam-lambert-live-stream
171. https://loudwire.com/ronnie-james-dio-death-anniversary-show/?utm_source=tsmclip&utm_medium=referral
172. https://www.newyorker.com/culture/culture-desk/a-nick-drake-tribute
173. https://variety.com/2019/music/news/elvis-tribute-68-comeback-special-post-malone-ed-sheeran-shawn-mendes-performing-1203100223/
174. https://hollywoodforever.com/event/johnny-ramone-tribute/
175. https://www.rorygallagherfestival.com/latest-festival-news/category/all
176. http://news.bbc.co.uk/1/hi/entertainment/1417595.stm
177. https://flymsy.com
178. https://www.salzburg-airport.com/en/
179. https://www.budapest-airport.com
180. https://www.lotnisko-chopina.pl/en/index.html
181. https://www.rio-janeiro-airport.com/galeao/
182. https://www.parmawelcome.it/en/place/organize-your-travel/getting-here/how-to-reach-parma/giuseppe-verdi-airport/
183. http://www.airport-ostrava.cz/en/

10 Move It

1. https://www.officialcharts.com/artist/19899/cliff-richard/
2. https://www.telegraph.co.uk/finance/migrationtemp/2951329/Music-industry-loses-copyright-fight.html
3. https://www.theguardian.com/business/2006/dec/06/musicnews.prebudget-report2006

4. https://www.theguardian.com/media/2011/sep/12/musicians-copyright-extension
5. *BPI Yearbook 2012*, pp. 10–11.
6. The BPI's *All About the Music 2020*, p. 13.
7. https://www.ons.gov.uk/peoplepopulationandcommunity/
birthsdeathsandmarriages/lifeexpectancies/articles/
howhaslifeexpectancychangedovertime/2015-09-09
8. https://www.copyright.gov/docs/203.html
9. https://www.billboard.com/articles/business/1535910/court-rules-for-ray-charles-children-in-copyright
10. https://www.courthousenews.com/9th-circuit-hears-ray-charles-royalty-fight/
11. Ibid.
12. https://www.hollywoodreporter.com/thr-esq/hollywood-docket-appeals-court-overturns-812533
13. https://www.musicbusinessworldwide.com/primary-wave-agrees-multi-million-deal-to-acquire-majority-stake-in-ray-charles-pre-1964-publishing-catalog/
14. https://latimesblogs.latimes.com/thedailymirror/page/408/
15. Dionne Warwick actually won a Grammy in 1979 for Best R&B Vocal Performance, Female, for her recording of 'Déjà Vu'. https://www.grammy.com/grammys/artists/dionne-warwick/14250
16. https://www.hollywoodreporter.com/thr-esq/lawsuit-explores-who-owns-rights-724691
17. Toberoff was speaking before this ruling and referred to her as "the putative spouse of James Brown".
18. https://eu.usatoday.com/story/entertainment/celebrities/2020/06/18/james-brown-partner-not-wife-court-rules-oks-dying-wish/3216240001/
19. https://www.nytimes.com/2020/06/25/arts/music/james-brown-will.html
20. Ibid.
21. https://www.musicbusinessworldwide.com/blue-raincoat-music-in-conjunction-with-reservoir-ink-global-publishing-deal-with-estate-of-nick-drake/
22. Digital service providers (i.e. consumer-facing download services and streaming services like iTunes, Spotify, Apple Music, Amazon Music, YouTube, Deezer and Tidal).
23. Published price to dealer (i.e. the per-unit price a label will sell stock to a retailer of physical product, be they on the high street or online).
24. https://www.copyright.gov/circs/circ15a.pdf
25. https://www.gov.uk/copyright/how-long-copyright-lasts
26. https://europa.eu/youreurope/business/running-business/intellectual-property/copyright/index_en.htm
27. https://akbllp.com/introduction-and-copyright-overview/copyright-duration/
28. https://web.law.duke.edu/cspd/publicdomainday/2019/
29. Ibid.
30. https://today.duke.edu/2020/01/welcome-rhapsody-blue-public-domain
31. https://www.npr.org/2019/12/30/792302139/1924-copyrighted-works-to-become-part-of-the-public-domain
32. https://www.theguardian.com/music/2017/sep/11/we-shall-overcome-civil-rights-anthem-copyright-lawsuit
33. https://www.nytimes.com/2018/01/26/business/media/we-shall-overcome-copyright.html

34. https://www.nytimes.com/2015/10/09/arts/music/gail-zappa-keeper-of-her-husbands-legacy-dies-at-70.html
35. https://www.bizjournals.com/losangeles/news/2015/07/30/frank-zappa-estate-signs-licensing-deal-with.html
36. The *Bob Lefsetz Podcast*, 19 September 2019.
37. Ibid.
38. Bowie's self-titled debut album from 1967 that was released on Deram, a subsidiary of Decca.
39. https://www.theguardian.com/music/2010/mar/16/michael-jackson-sony-250m-deal
40. Ibid.
41. https://www.nytimes.com/2010/03/16/arts/music/16jackson.html
42. Ibid.
43. https://www.theguardian.com/business/2016/mar/15/sony-michael-jackson-atv-music-publishing-750m
44. https://www.billboard.com/articles/news/7262961/inside-sony-atvs-buyout-michael-jackson-estate
45. Ibid.
46. Ibid.
47. https://cnnpressroom.blogs.cnn.com/2011/10/03/piers-morgan-tonight-the-business-side-of-michael-jackson/
48. A rip of the interview was uploaded to YouTube the day after broadcast. https://www.youtube.com/watch?v=t532dlt-6u4
49. https://www.billboard.com/articles/news/7262961/inside-sony-atvs-buyout-michael-jackson-estate
50. https://www.musicbusinessworldwide.com/sony-corp-snaps-up-remaining-10-stake-in-emi-music-publishing-from-jackson-estate/
51. https://www.theguardian.com/business/2016/mar/15/sony-michael-jackson-atv-music-publishing-750m
52. https://www.musicbusinessworldwide.com/john-branca-artists-need-to-pay-attention-to-their-legacy-and-be-very-specific-about-it/
53. https://www.forbes.com/sites/zackomalleygreenburg/2016/10/12/the-highest-paid-dead-celebrities-of-2016/#732cb48711b1
54. https://www.billboard.com/articles//1442053/blix-street-sues-eva-cassidy-parents
55. https://caselaw.findlaw.com/ca-court-of-appeal/1549388.html
56. Ibid.
57. https://www.billboard.com/articles/business/8477056/ricky-nelson-estate-class-action-sony-music-international-streaming
58. https://www.musicbusinessworldwide.com/sony-music-reaches-12-7m-settlement-in-rick-nelson-royalties-suit/
59. https://www.billboard.com/articles/columns/the-juice/5740495/tupac-shakurs-mom-files-lawsuit-over-royalties
60. "An earlier US action was concluded by a settlement in which Island agreed to pay £264,000 and legal costs on the understanding that the Wailers would cease any further legal action," noted the *Guardian*. "Members of the Wailers claim they were coerced into signing the deal, a claim Mr Justice Lewison rejected." https://www.theguardian.com/uk/2006/may/16/topstories3.arts
61. Ibid.
62. https://www.rollingstone.com/music/music-news/robin-thicke-pharrell-williams-blurred-lines-copyright-suit-final-5-million-dollar-judgment-768508/

63. https://www.forbes.com/sites/adriennegibbs/2018/03/21/marvin-gaye-wins-blurred-lines-lawsuit-pharrell-robin-thicke-t-i-off-hook/#5fbf983b689b
64. https://www.rollingstone.com/music/music-news/robin-thicke-pharrell-williams-blurred-lines-copyright-suit-final-5-million-dollar-judgment-768508/
65. https://www.rollingstone.com/pro/features/richard-busch-music-blurred-lines-lawyer-1031126/
66. https://uproxx.com/music/juice-wrld-estate-yellowcard/
67. https://www.nme.com/news/music/yellowcard-to-resume-multi-million-dollar-lawsuit-against-juice-wrld-2703469
68. https://www.xxlmag.com/yellowcard-juice-wrld-lawsuit-15-million-dollars-continues/
69. https://www.nytimes.com/2020/07/27/arts/music/yellowcard-juice-wrld-lawsuit.html
70. Ibid.
71. https://www.digitalmusicnews.com/2020/08/19/juice-wrld-new-lawsuit/
72. https://www.musicbusinessworldwide.com/apple-hit-with-lawsuit-by-songwriter-heirs-for-allegedly-running-a-massive-music-piracy-operation/
73. https://www.billboard.com/articles/business/8486916/everly-brothers-cathys-clown-songwriting-credit-royalties
74. Ibid.
75. https://twitter.com/PRNFamily/status/1050559774050406400
76. https://twitter.com/prince/status/1182484599781416960
77. https://twitter.com/tompetty/status/1274527971513004033/photo/1
78. https://www.facebook.com/leonardcohen/posts/10159202117194644

11   From Deification to Demonisation

1. https://www.hollywoodreporter.com/news/michael-jackson-executor-john-branca-says-hes-considering-suing-leaving-neverland-director-dan-reed-1202578
2. https://www.latimes.com/archives/la-xpm-2004-may-01-me-jackson1-story.html
3. https://www.latimes.com/archives/la-xpm-2005-jun-14-me-scene14-story.html
4. Some fans were incensed that the *This Is It* documentary was released in late 2009. "The fans blame AEG, the promoter of the singer's abandoned London residency, Sony Pictures and Jackson's own entourage for exploiting him for their own financial gain," wrote the *Guardian*. https://www.theguardian.com/film/2009/oct/27/michael-jackson-this-is-it
5. https://www.theguardian.com/music/2009/mar/13/michael-jackson-o2-arena-residency-sells-out
6. The timeline of Jackson's sexual abuse allegations was drawn from three sources: 1) https://www.vulture.com/article/michael-jackson-abuse-allegations-timeline.html; 2) https://www.npr.org/2019/03/05/699995484/michael-jackson-a-quarter-century-of-sexual-abuse-allegations; 3) https://www.rollingstone.com/culture/culture-features/michael-jackson-child-sexual-abuse-allegations-timeline-785746/
7. https://www.rollingstone.com/music/music-features/inside-the-zappa-family-feud-104088/
8. Ibid.

9. Quoted in https://liveforlivemusic.com/news/zappa-family-trust-dweezil-reconcile/
10. Ibid.
11. The *Bob Lefsetz Podcast*, 19 September 2019.
12. https://www.rollingstone.com/feature/the-curse-of-the-ramones-165741/
13. https://www.billboard.com/articles/business/legal-and-management/8545417/ramones-heirs-truce-name-use-trademark
14. Ibid.
15. Ibid.
16. Ibid.
17. Dee Dee Ramone (real name Douglas Colvin) died on 5 June 2002 so his share would have immediately defaulted to his estate. Tommy Ramone (real name Thomas Erdelyi) passed away on 11 July 2014.
18. https://www.contactmusic.com/johnny-ramone/news/wife-and-mother-battle-over-johnny-ramone-estate
19. https://www.facebook.com/joeyramone/posts/with-much-sadness-i-regretfully-convey-that-a-woman-ive-known-since-i-was-14-yea/10151056026298804/
20. Optimum Productions had made the videos for Michael Jackson's *Thriller* (and *The Making of Thriller*) in 1983 and *Bad* in 1987 as well as *Michael Jackson…The Magic Returns* (a TV special on his return with *Bad*). https://www2.bfi.org.uk/films-tv-people/4ce2b96884391
21. https://www.vanityfair.com/hollywood/2019/02/michael-jackson-estate-sues-hbo-leaving-neverland
22. Quoted in https://www.hollywoodreporter.com/thr-esq/michael-jackson-estate-sues-hbo-violating-disparagement-deal-1188759
23. Ibid.
24. https://www.hollywoodreporter.com/thr-esq/michael-jackson-estate-wants-hbo-meeting-leaving-neverland-will-become-hbos-greatest-shame-10-page-l-1184415
25. Ibid.
26. Ibid.
27. https://www.musicbusinessworldwide.com/john-branca-artists-need-to-pay-attention-to-their-legacy-and-be-very-specific-about-it/
28. https://www.hollywoodreporter.com/thr-esq/michael-jackson-estate-wants-hbo-meeting-leaving-neverland-will-become-hbos-greatest-shame-10-page-l-1184415
29. https://variety.com/2019/biz/news/michael-jackson-estate-lawsuit-leaving-neverland-hbo-counters-1203204141/
30. https://www.billboard.com/articles/business/8513548/hbo-wins-first-round-michael-jackson-estate-leaving-neverland-lawsuit/
31. https://eu.usatoday.com/story/entertainment/music/2019/07/05/michael-jackson-fans-sue-leaving-neverland-accusers-robson-safechuck/1655785001/
32. Quoted in https://www.tmz.com/2019/08/27/dave-chappelle-michael-jackson-accusers-new-stand-up-special-netflix/
33. Ibid.
34. Ibid.
35. https://variety.com/2019/biz/news/judge-michael-jackson-estate-leaving-neverland-1203342191/
36. https://deadline.com/2019/09/michael-jackson-lawsuit-leaving-neverland-dismissal-rejected-hbo-sexual-abuse-emmys-1202738895/

37. https://www.bbc.co.uk/news/world-us-canada-50990766
38. https://variety.com/2020/film/news/hbo-finding-neverland-appeals-brief-1203519726/
39. https://www.bbc.co.uk/news/entertainment-arts-54636636
40. Ibid.
41. https://deadline.com/2020/10/leaving-neverland-director-dan-reed-shooting-follow-up-film-1234599714/
42. Ibid.
43. https://variety.com/2020/tv/news/michael-jackson-leaving-neverland-lawsuit-appeal-1234853036/
44. Ibid.
45. https://www.bbc.co.uk/news/entertainment-arts-56899871
46. https://variety.com/2021/music/news/michael-jackson-wade-robson-sexual-abuse-dismissed-1234960929/
47. https://www.bbc.co.uk/news/entertainment-arts-56899871
48. Tom Mesereau successfully defended Jackson in the 2005 case.
49. https://www.billboard.com/articles/news/9553159/howard-weitzman-obit/
50. https://www.forbes.com/sites/maddieberg/2020/11/13/the-highest-paid-dead-celebrities-of-2020/?sh=6474b9e73b4b
51. https://www.musicbusinessworldwide.com/john-branca-artists-need-to-pay-attention-to-their-legacy-and-be-very-specific-about-it/
52. https://www.bbc.co.uk/news/newsbeat-44073801
53. https://www.theguardian.com/music/2018/jun/01/spotify-hate-conduct-policy-removed-r-kelly-xxxtentacion
54. https://www.theguardian.com/music/2012/feb/13/whitney-houston-album-price
55. Quoted in https://www.theguardian.com/music/2012/feb/15/whitney-houston-itunes-price-hike-sony
56. https://thenextweb.com/apple/2012/02/13/whitney-houstons-post-death-album-price-rise-blame-sony-not-apple/
57. https://www.wired.com/2012/02/itunes-whitney-houston-price/
58. https://metro.co.uk/2012/02/13/apple-claims-whitney-houston-album-price-increase-on-itunes-due-to-sony-316498/
59. *BPI Yearbook 2013*, p. 10.
60. Phill Savidge, *Lunch with the Wild Frontiers: A History of Britpop and Excess in 13½ Chapters*, 2019 (e-book edition). The book is credited to Phill Savidge as Jane transitioned after its publication.
61. https://www.theguardian.com/music/2016/jun/14/led-zeppelin-stairway-to-heaven-plagiarism-trial-spirit
62. https://www.theguardian.com/music/2016/jun/23/led-zeppelin-cleared-stairway-to-heaven-lawsuit-spirit
63. https://www.theguardian.com/music/2018/sep/28/led-zeppelin-plagiarism-taurus-spirit-stairway-to-heaven-new-trial
64. https://www.cbsnews.com/news/led-zeppelin-court-rules-band-did-not-plagiarize-riff-for-stairway-to-heaven-2020-03-09/
65. https://www.nme.com/news/music/led-zeppelin-stairway-to-heaven-copyright-case-may-go-back-to-court-2728304
66. https://variety.com/2020/music/news/led-zeppelin-win-stairway-to-heaven-copyright-1234792866/
67. https://abcnews.go.com/Business/pharrell-williams-robin-thicke-verdict-blurred-lines-case/story?id=29556110

68. https://www.theguardian.com/music/2009/jul/06/michael-jackson-mysterious-adviser
69. Ibid.
70. https://www.theguardian.com/music/2010/sep/30/michael-jackson-manager-sues-estate
71. https://completemusicupdate.com/article/former-michael-jackson-manager-wins-court-case-over-unpaid-legal-settlement/
72. https://uk.reuters.com/article/us-michaeljackson-lawsuit/michael-jackson-estate-sues-former-mj-manager-idUSTRE81H02C20120218
73. https://www.hollywoodreporter.com/thr-esq/michael-jacksons-estate-tohme-tohme-settle-dispute-mid-trial-1213311
74. https://www.hollywoodreporter.com/thr-esq/settlement-between-michael-jacksons-manager-estate-falls-apart-1248586
75. https://www.hollywoodreporter.com/thr-esq/michael-jacksons-manager-get-3m-settlement-king-pops-estate-1303432
76. Ibid.
77. https://www.hollywoodreporter.com/thr-esq/quincy-jones-files-10m-lawsuit-651045
78. https://www.billboard.com/articles/news/7881180/quincy-jones-wins-royalties-michael-jackson-estate-9-million
79. Ibid.
80. https://www.nytimes.com/2017/07/26/business/media/quincy-jones-wins-suit-against-michael-jacksons-estate.html?searchResultPosition=3
81. https://www.bizjournals.com/newyork/news/2017/07/27/quincy-jones-wins-cash-from-michael-jackson-estate.html
82. https://www.nytimes.com/2020/05/05/arts/quincy-jones-lawsuit-michael-jackson-this-is-it.html
83. Ibid.
84. https://abcnews.go.com/Entertainment/wireStory/court-overturns-quincy-jones-win-michael-jackson-lawsuit-70523594
85. Ibid.
86. https://www.wsj.com/articles/winner-of-rights-to-princes-music-fears-it-was-shortchanged-1492171203
87. https://www.independent.co.uk/arts-entertainment/music/news/prince-universal-music-deal-estate-vault-comerica-bank-spotify-a7684876.html
88. https://www.hollywoodreporter.com/news/court-voids-universal-music-groups-31-million-deal-prince-estate-1021066
89. Ibid.
90. https://www.cnbc.com/2018/06/28/sony-inks-deal-with-prince-estate-to-distribute-massive-music-catalog.html
91. https://www.courthousenews.com/widow-fights-film-fatal-lynyrd-skynyrd-crash/
92. https://financialpost.com/legal-post/judge-lynyrd-skynyrd-film-violates-3-decade-old-agreement
93. https://www.nytimes.com/2018/10/10/business/lynyrd-skynyrd-crash-movie.html
94. https://www.spin.com/2017/12/lil-peep-fentanyl-xanax/
95. https://www.nytimes.com/2019/10/08/arts/music/lil-peep-overdose-lawsuit.html
96. https://pitchfork.com/news/lil-peep-mother-sues-his-management-over-death/
97. Ibid.

98. Jeff Guinn, *Manson: The Life and Times of Charles Manson*, 2013, p. 348.
99. https://www.rollingstone.com/culture/culture-news/charles-manson-the-incredible-story-of-the-most-dangerous-man-alive-85235/
100. https://www.latimes.com/archives/la-xpm-1993-12-08-ca-65317-story.html
101. https://losangeles.cbslocal.com/2018/01/09/charles-manson-estate-song-royalties-beach-boys-guns-n-roses/
102. https://www.dailymail.co.uk/news/article-7333667/Charles-Mansons-grandson-profit-Time-Hollywood.html
103. https://www.newsweek.com/charles-manson-sons-death-suicide-kids-717025
104. Ibid.
105. https://edition.cnn.com/2018/03/12/us/charles-manson-body-decision/index.html
106. Ibid.
107. https://www.dailymail.co.uk/news/article-7333667/Charles-Mansons-grandson-profit-Time-Hollywood.html
108. https://eu.desertsun.com/story/news/crime_courts/2019/07/17/fight-control-charles-mansons-estate-returns-los-angeles-court/1759016001/
109. Ibid.
110. https://www.nbclosangeles.com/news/local/man-who-claims-hes-infamous-criminals-grandson-appeals-dna-order/2306001/
111. https://uk.news.yahoo.com/purported-son-charles-manson-drops-234743163.html
112. http://archive.jacksonville.com/news/20181213/charles-mansons-grandson-in-fight-for-satans-estate/
113. https://www.forbes.com/sites/trialandheirs/2018/01/16/the-charles-manson-estate-battle-is-the-fight-worth-it/

12 Virtual Signalling

1. https://www.nme.com/news/music/dr-dre-61-1276382
2. https://www.fastcompany.com/90365452/hologram-concert-revolution-like-it-or-not-meet-company-touring-whitney-houston-buddy-holly
3. http://www.theatrecrafts.com/pages/home/glossary-of-technical-theatre-terms/more-about-peppers-ghost/
4. https://www.wsj.com/articles/SB10001424052702304818404577348243109842490
5. https://www.mtv.com/news/1512983/coldplay-green-day-win-big-at-mtv-europe-music-awards/
6. https://www.mtv.com/news/1522950/madonnas-oddest-collab-yet-singer-to-perform-at-grammys-with-gorillaz/
7. https://www.washingtonpost.com/business/technology/how-the-tupac-hologram-works/2012/04/18/gIQA1ZVyQT_story.html
8. https://www.wsj.com/articles/SB10001424052702304818404577348243109842490
9. Ibid.
10. https://theundefeated.com/features/the-strange-legacy-of-tupacs-hologram-after-coachella/
11. Ibid.

12. Zack O'Malley Greenburg, *3 Kings: Diddy, Dr. Dre, Jay-Z and Hip-Hop's Multibillion-Dollar Rise*, 2018, p. 214.
13. Ibid.
14. https://www.youtube.com/watch?v=nwjkaMJVwus
15. https://www.latimes.com/entertainment/envelope/la-xpm-2012-jun-25-la-et-ct-digital-domain-tupac-20120625-story.html
16. https://uk.reuters.com/article/net-us-digitaldomain-bankruptcy/titanic-effects-creator-digital-domain-bankrupt-sale-agreed-idUSBRE88A0CH20120911
17. He had two older children who he had adopted. He also fathered twin girls the year after Natalie was born.
18. https://www.theguardian.com/us-news/2016/jan/01/natalie-cole-singer-and-daughter-of-nat-king-cole-dies-at-65
19. https://www.billboard.com/charts/hot-100/1991-08-24?rank=14
20. https://www.officialcharts.com/search/singles/unforgettable/
21. Quoted in https://www.independent.co.uk/news/obituaries/natalie-cole-singer-who-performed-first-virtual-duets-her-late-father-nat-king-cole-a6794906.html
22. https://www.wmcactionnews5.com/story/6434024/how-did-they-do-it-elvis-and-celine-duet-on-idol/
23. https://eu.usatoday.com/story/life/music/2018/08/10/elvis-and-lisa-marie-presley-gospel-duet-where-no-one-stands-alone/955252002/
24. https://pitchfork.com/news/57324-david-byrne-reviews-barry-manilows-album-of-duets-with-dead-singers/
25. https://www.billboard.com/charts/billboard-200/2014-11-15
26. https://www.theguardian.com/music/2017/mar/24/dead-singers-duets-faith-evans-notorious-big
27. https://www.theguardian.com/music/2017/feb/17/biggie-smalls-creepy-duets-from-beyond-the-grave
28. https://www.bbc.co.uk/programmes/articles/1gtn6WZBVZ1cPDg8y9GFgWB/seven-music-legends-we-brought-back-from-the-dead
29. https://www.wired.co.uk/article/tupac-michael-jackson-billie-holiday-dead-celebrity-holograms
30. A rip of the CNN report was uploaded to the Hologram USA YouTube channel on 22 May 2014. https://www.youtube.com/watch?v=hY_-mAtCRlk
31. https://www.fuse.tv/2013/09/bone-thugs-n-harmony-eazy-e-hologram-rock-the-bells-2013
32. https://www.billboard.com/articles/columns/the-juice/5687249/rock-the-bells-2013-ol-dirty-bastards-hologram-performs-with-son
33. https://www.billboard.com/articles/events/bbma-2014/6092040/michael-jackson-hologram-billboard-music-awards
34. Ibid.
35. https://www.theguardian.com/music/2016/may/20/whitney-houston-hologram-performance-axed-the-voice-christina-aguilera
36. https://www.wired.co.uk/article/tupac-michael-jackson-billie-holiday-dead-celebrity-holograms
37. https://basehologram.com/productions/roy-orbison-buddy-holly-the-rock-n-roll-dream-tour
38. https://www.billboard.com/articles/news/6451128/buddy-holly-hologram-virtual-maria-elena-holly
39. On 2 December 2019, the *Los Angeles Times* wrote: "A Los Angeles jury ordered British-Greek hologram entrepreneur Alki David to pay $50 million

in punitive damages on Monday after finding him liable for battery, sexual battery and sexual harassment against a former employee." https://www.latimes.com/entertainment-arts/business/story/2019-12-02/billionaire-alki-david-pay-50-million-punitive-damages-sexual-battery-suit

40. https://www.wired.co.uk/article/tupac-michael-jackson-billie-holiday-dead-celebrity-holograms
41. Ibid.
42. https://nypost.com/2017/11/22/roy-orbisons-sons-sue-over-hologram-debacle/
43. https://www.billboard.com/articles/news/7461829/ronnie-james-dio-hologram-wacken-open-air-germany-festival-2016
44. https://loudwire.com/ronnie-james-dio-hologram-u-s-debut-2017-pollstar-awards/
45. https://consequenceofsound.net/2017/07/ronnie-james-dios-hologram-is-going-on-tour/
46. https://www.rollingstone.com/music/music-news/ronnie-james-dio-hologram-plots-world-tour-202860/
47. https://www.revolvermag.com/culture/secrets-behind-ronnie-james-dio-hologram-motion-capture-peppers-ghost
48. Ibid.
49. https://www.iq-mag.net/2018/05/msg-thomas-dolan-invests-eyellusion/#.X4h2US2ZOso
50. The *Bob Lefsetz Podcast*, 19th September 2019.
51. Ibid.
52. https://www.pollstar.com/article/what-the-f-is-happening-right-now-a-look-at-the-bizarre-world-of-frank-zappa-137615
53. Quoted in *Get Rich or Try Dying: Music's Mega Legacies*, first broadcast on BBC Four on 1 November 2019.
54. https://www.iq-mag.net/2019/03/finishing-started-ahmet-zappa-frank-vision-life/#.XSTHOC2ZN-U
55. Quoted in *Get Rich or Try Dying: Music's Mega Legacies*, first broadcast on BBC Four on 1 November 2019.
56. https://www.billboard.com/articles/business/8476224/glenn-gould-classical-pianist-hologram-tour
57. https://www.cbc.ca/archives/entry/glenn-gould-quits-the-concert-stage
58. https://www.fastcompany.com/90365452/hologram-concert-revolution-like-it-or-not-meet-company-touring-whitney-houston-buddy-holly
59. https://baseentertainment.com/projects/
60. https://basehologram.com/about
61. Ibid.
62. https://www.rollingstone.com/music/music-features/hologram-tours-roy-orbison-frank-zappa-whitney-houston-873399/
63. https://basehologram.com/productions/maria-callas
64. https://basehologram.com/news/base-hologram-debuts-callas-in-concert
65. https://operawire.com/bringing-maria-callas-back-to-life-the-team-behind-callas-in-concert-on-creating-a-hologram-of-la-divina/
66. Ibid.
67. James Medd, "We Are the Holo Men", *Q*, July 2012, p. 15.
68. https://www.juilliard.edu/music/faculty/wadsworth-stephen
69. Quoted in *Get Rich or Try Dying: Music's Mega Legacies*, first broadcast on BBC Four on 1 November 2019.

70. Ibid.
71. https://www.rollingstone.com/music/music-features/hologram-tours-roy-orbison-frank-zappa-whitney-houston-873399/
72. https://variety.com/2019/music/news/rock-and-roll-dead-by-2060-holograms-1203282550/
73. https://www.rollingstone.com/music/music-features/hologram-tours-roy-orbison-frank-zappa-whitney-houston-873399/
74. http://martin-richardson.com/documents/holography-within-art.pdf
75. https://www.dmu.ac.uk/about-dmu/news/2020/january/lost-footage-of-bowie-found.aspx
76. https://www.bbc.co.uk/news/uk-england-leicestershire-51040616
77. https://www.youtube.com/watch?v=bXVMoUmA5aQ
78. https://www.revolvermag.com/culture/secrets-behind-ronnie-james-dio-hologram-motion-capture-peppers-ghost
79. https://www.eventimapollo.com/venueinfo/venue-history
80. https://lefsetz.com/wordpress/2019/09/28/roy-orbison-buddy-holly-at-the-saban/
81. Chuck E. Cheese is a chain of family restaurants in the US which, alongside fast food, offers different forms of in-restaurant entertainment, notably animatronic displays as well as arcade games and amusement rides.
82. https://www.npr.org/sections/deceptivecadence/2018/11/06/664653353/raising-the-dead-and-a-few-questions-with-maria-callas-hologram
83. https://www.cbc.ca/news/entertainment/musicians-holograms-ethics-1.4961748
84. https://www.theguardian.com/music/2019/may/25/virtual-reality-music-stars-stage-holograms-whitney-houston-jeff-wayne
85. https://www.wired.co.uk/article/tupac-michael-jackson-billie-holiday-dead-celebrity-holograms
86. https://www.theguardian.com/tv-and-radio/2019/jun/01/pop-holograms-miley-cyrus-black-mirror-identity-crisis
87. https://www.npr.org/sections/deceptivecadence/2018/11/06/664653353/raising-the-dead-and-a-few-questions-with-maria-callas-hologram
88. https://chicago.suntimes.com/2019/9/5/20850105/maria-callas-hologram-concert-lyric-opera-chicago
89. https://www.dailymail.co.uk/tvshowbiz/article-8044975/She-doesnt-deserve-holo-farrago-JAN-MOIR-reviews-Evening-Whitney-Houston.html
90. Ibid.
91. https://www.nme.com/reviews/live/the-whitney-houston-hologram-tour-review-2619187
92. https://www.spectator.co.uk/article/waking-the-dead
93. https://www.independent.co.uk/arts-entertainment/music/news/amy-winehouse-hologram-tour-2019-tickets-how-buy-setlist-a8583391.html
94. https://www.theguardian.com/music/2018/oct/19/amy-winehouse-stars-turned-into-hologram-virtual-reality
95. https://www.vanityfair.com/culture/2018/10/please-dont-let-this-amy-winehouse-hologram-tour-be-real
96. https://www.nme.com/news/music/amy-winehouse-fans-hit-plans-hologram-tour-announced-2389329
97. https://www.gq-magazine.co.uk/article/amy-winehouse-hologram-tour
98. Ibid.
99. Ibid.

100. https://www.theguardian.com/music/2019/feb/22/amy-winehouse-hologram-tour-postponed
101. https://twitter.com/BASEHologram/status/1098039574746456064
102. https://musically.com/2018/01/25/elton-john-downloaded-vr/
103. https://www.tmz.com/2018/02/03/justin-timberlake-super-bowl-halftime-performance-secrets/
104. https://www.nme.com/news/music/justin-timberlakes-prince-hologram-scrapped-super-bowl-performance-following-backlash-sheila-e-2236405
105. https://www.forbes.com/sites/zackomalleygreenburg/2018/02/05/how-justin-timberlakes-super-bowl-prince-differed-from-a-hologram/#6599cfa74afd
106. https://inews.co.uk/essentials/prince-return-stage-hologram-music-legends-sister-says-521298
107. Quoted in https://www.thefader.com/2018/02/03/prince-hated-holograms
108. https://www.nytimes.com/2012/01/15/books/review/distrust-that-particular-flavor-by-william-gibson-book-review.html
109. https://sfi.usc.edu/about
110. https://www.theguardian.com/technology/2016/jun/18/holocaust-survivor-hologram-pinchas-gutter-new-dimensions-history
111. Ibid.
112. https://www.nytimes.com/2018/12/18/arts/design/steven-spielberg-shoah-foundation-schindlers-list.html
113. https://www.cbsnews.com/news/artificial-intelligence-holocaust-remembrance-60-minutes-2020-04-03/
114. https://www.mmu.ac.uk/news-and-events/news/story/13825/
115. "Today, the company serves the holographic needs of both developers and enterprises and is committed to building the headset-free hologram-powered future we were all promised in science fiction growing up," is how the company describes itself. https://lookingglassfactory.com
116. From press release sent to media on 20 October 2020.
117. https://www.theguardian.com/lifeandstyle/2020/oct/30/robert-kardashian-resurrected-as-a-hologram-for-kim-kardashian-wests-birthday
118. https://twitter.com/KimKardashian/status/1321955928522944513?s=20
119. http://www.koreaherald.com/view.php?ud=20201207000891
120. Ibid.
121. Ibid.
122. http://www.ajudaily.com/view/20201202170821563
123. "Deep learning is a subset of machine learning where artificial neural networks, algorithms inspired by the human brain, learn from large amounts of data," explains *Forbes*. https://www.forbes.com/sites/bernardmarr/2018/10/01/what-is-deep-learning-ai-a-simple-guide-with-8-practical-examples/#77e9ef748d4b
124. https://www.theguardian.com/technology/2020/jan/13/what-are-deepfakes-and-how-can-you-spot-them
125. https://www.theguardian.com/film/filmblog/2016/dec/16/rogue-one-star-wars-cgi-resurrection-peter-cushing
126. https://www.cnet.com/news/star-wars-rise-of-skywalkers-cgi-free-carrie-fisher-is-shockingly-successful/
127. https://www.theguardian.com/media-network/media-network-blog/2014/oct/08/how-we-made-audrey-hepburn-galaxy-ad
128. https://variety.com/2019/digital/news/james-dean-worldwide-xr-1203401302/

129. *Dolly Parton's America* podcast – episode 9 ("She's Alive!"). Originally made available on 31 December 2019. https://www.wnycstudios.org/podcasts/dolly-partons-america/episodes/shes-alive
130. https://losttapesofthe27club.com
131. https://www.rollingstone.com/music/music-features/nirvana-kurt-cobain-ai-song-1146444/

Index